Environmental Economics

Fourth Canadian Edition

Barry C. Field

University of Massachusetts

Nancy D. Olewiler

Simon Fraser University

McGraw-Hill
Ryerson

 McGraw-Hill
Ryerson

Environmental Economics
Fourth Canadian Edition

ISBN-13: 978-0-07-089310-8
ISBN-10: 0-07-089310-1

7 8 9   WEB   22 21 20 19 18

Printed and bound in Canada.

Director of Product Management: Rhondda McNabb
Senior Product Manager: James Booty
Marketing Manager: Jeremy Guimond
Product Developer: Kamilah Reid-Burrell
Senior Product Team Associate: Stephanie Giles
Supervising Editor: Jessica Barnoski
Photo/Permissions Editor: Tracy Leonard
Copy Editor: Erin Moore
Plant Production Coordinator: Sheryl MacAdam
Manufacturing Production Coordinator: Lena Keating
Cover Design: Liz Harasymczuk
Cover Image: Michael Duva/Getty Images
Interior Design: Laserwords Private Limited
Page Layout: Laserwords Private Limited
Printer: Webcom

About the Authors

Barry C. Field is Professor of Resource Economics at the University of Massachusetts in Amherst. Previously, he taught at the University of Miami and The George Washington University. He received his B.S. and M.S. degrees from Cornell University, and his Ph.D. from the University of California at Berkeley.

At the University of Massachusetts, he has devoted many years to teaching natural resource economics to students at all levels, and has worked to develop an undergraduate major in environmental and resource economics.

Professor Field is the author of numerous articles on resource and environmental economics.

Nancy D. Olewiler is Professor in the School of Public Policy at Simon Fraser University. She was a Professor of Economics at Simon Fraser University as well as Queen's University. Her B.A. is from Barnard College, Columbia University; M.A. from Simon Fraser University; and Ph.D. from the University of British Columbia. She was Chair of the Department of Economics at Simon Fraser University from 1995 to 2000 and Director of the School of Public Policy from 2003 to 2014.

At Simon Fraser University, Professor Olewiler developed undergraduate and graduate courses in environmental economics. At Queen's University, she initiated undergraduate courses in environmental economics and natural resource economics, as well as a graduate course in natural resource economics.

Professor Olewiler has written a number of articles and book chapters on environmental and natural resource economics theory and policy.

Brief Contents

Table of Contents

Preface

This book is an introduction to environmental economics. It is about the way human decisions affect the quality of the environment; about how human values and institutions shape our demands for improvement in the quality; and, most especially, about how to design effective public policies to bring about these improvements.

Problems of environmental quality are not something new; in fact, history is filled with bleak examples of environmental degradation, from deforestation by ancient peoples to raw sewage in the streets, and mountains of horse manure in urban areas in the days before automobiles. But today's world is different. Many people are beginning to ask what good is material wealth if it comes at the cost of large-scale disruptions of the ecosystem by which we are nourished? More fundamentally, with contemporary economic, demographic, and technological developments around the world, the associated environmental repercussions are becoming more widespread. What once were localized environmental impacts have now become global and potentially more severe. It is no wonder that the quality of the natural environment has become a major focus of worldwide concern encompassing the public, elected officials, and private-sector decision makers in every country.

Environmental economics focuses on all the different facets of the connection between environmental quality and the economic behaviour of individuals and groups of people. The economic system creates environmental degradation, but can also be harnessed to provide incentives that improve environmental quality. There are major problems in measuring the benefits and costs of environmental quality changes, especially intangible ones. Complicated macroeconomic questions, for example, the connection between economic growth and environmental impacts and the feedback effects of environmental regulations on growth, are also prevalent. There are also the critical issues of designing environmental policies that are both effective and equitable.

The strength of environmental economics lies in the fact that it is analytical and deals with concepts like efficiency, trade-offs, costs, and benefits. It is also a valuable means of inquiring why people behave as they do toward the natural environment, and how we might restructure the current system to rectify harmful practices. As an introduction to the principles of environmental economics, the examples discussed represent a sample of the full range of issues that exist. When you confront the real world of environmental politics and policy, you will find it necessary to adapt these principles to all the details and nuances of reality. There is not enough space in one book to look at all the ways environmental economists have found to make the basic concepts and models more specific and relevant to concrete environmental issues. We stick to the basic ideas and hope that they excite your interest and make you want to pursue further study of environmental economics.

WHAT'S NEW IN THE FOURTH CANADIAN EDITION

This fourth edition of *Environmental Economics* retains the organization, content, and writing style of the third edition. Those who have used the third edition will find the same thorough and systematic treatment of environmental economics that offers readers a Canadian text highlighting Canadian issues, data, and policies. Updates of Canadian environmental data and policies can be found in the introductory chapters, as examples in Section 4, and throughout Section 5. Notable changes from the third edition include greater emphasis in Section 1 on greenhouse gas emissions, air pollution from transportation, and Canada's environmental performance compared to other countries.

The key elements of the book are outlined below.

- *New material* is added to update environmental policy, especially policies to mitigate the emissions of greenhouse gases and the use of economic instruments such as carbon taxes and emission trading.

- *Environmental policy* chapters have updated data and environmental policies that focus on Canada, and illustrate how Canada's policies compare to policies in other countries, comparisons such as controlling sulphur dioxide in the United States and greenhouse gases in Europe. The emphasis is on links between theory and policy, with more Canadian examples.

- *Improved linking between chapters* via in-text references from one chapter to another allow students and instructors to move between theoretical concepts and application. More examples of policy in action occur in the theory chapters of Section 4.

- *Example boxes* are used throughout the book to highlight key theoretical and policy issues such as how benefit–cost analysis helped change policy and remove lead from gasoline.

- *Canadian case studies* bring the real world into the text. These provide illustrations of how economic principles can be applied to environmental issues, and contain thought-provoking questions for discussion, assignments, and research papers.

- *Worked examples* are provided in most chapters to improve understanding of theoretical concepts and to show how to solve problems.

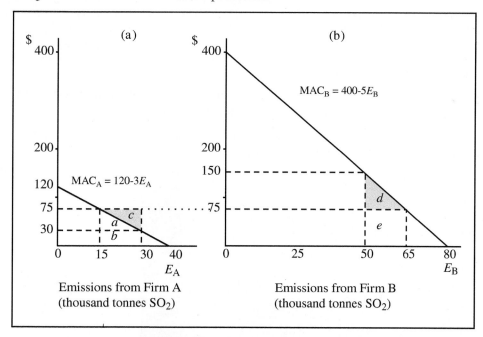

- *All theoretical models* have verbal, graphical, and algebraic solutions to show the different ways to analyze environmental problems. Specific functional forms are used so that calculations are transparent and easy to follow.

- *Graphs* are enhanced with detailed captions.

- *Data* on environmental indicators is provided to not only provide a snapshot of the state of the environment, but also to facilitate research and discussion.

FIGURE 1-4   Decomposition of the Change in Total Global CO_2 Emissions from Fossil Fuel Combustion

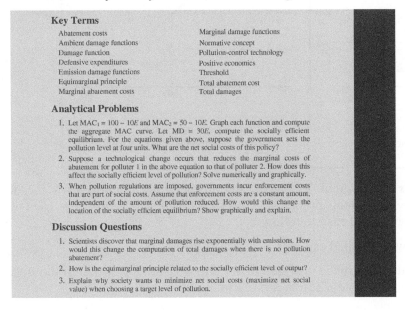

The absolute changes in total CO_2 emissions per decade can be decomposed into those arising from population growth (dotted box), GDP per capita (black), the energy intensity of GDP (gray), and carbon intensity of energy (crosshatch box). Total decadal changes in CO_2 emissions are indicated by a white triangle. Changes are measured in gigatonnes of CO_2 emissions per year (Gt/yr).

Source: IPCC, 2014: Climate Change 2014: Mitigation of Climate Change. Contribution of Working Group III to the Fifth Assessment Report of the Intergovernmental Panel on Climate Change, Figure TS.1; Figure TS.6. [Edenhofer, O., R. Pichs-Madruga, Y. Sokona, E. Farahani, S. Kadner, K. Seyboth, A. Adler, I. Baum, S. Brunner, P. Eickemeier, B. Kriemann, J. Savolainen, S. Schloemer, C. von Stechow, T. Zwickel, and J.C. Minx (eds.)]. Cambridge University Press, Cambridge, United Kingdom and New York, NY, USA.

- ***Key points*** are bulleted and bolded.

- ***Key terms*** are bolded within the text, listed at the end of each chapter, and defined in the pop-up box displayed when the cursor passes over the term in the eBook.

- ***End-of-chapter questions*** are split into discussion questions and analytical problems to give students a variety of ways to test their knowledge.

Key Terms

Abatement costs	Marginal damage functions
Ambient damage functions	Normative concept
Damage function	Pollution-control technology
Defensive expenditures	Positive economics
Emission damage functions	Threshold
Equimarginal principle	Total abatement cost
Marginal abatement costs	Total damages

Analytical Problems

1. Let $MAC_1 = 100 - 10E$ and $MAC_2 = 50 - 10E$. Graph each function and compute the aggregate MAC curve. Let $MD = 30E$, compute the socially efficient equilibrium. For the equations given above, suppose the government sets the pollution level at four units. What are the net social costs of this policy?

2. Suppose a technological change occurs that reduces the marginal costs of abatement for polluter 1 in the above equation to that of polluter 2. How does this affect the socially efficient level of pollution? Solve numerically and graphically.

3. When pollution regulations are imposed, governments incur enforcement costs that are part of social costs. Assume that enforcement costs are a constant amount, independent of the amount of pollution reduced. How would this change the location of the socially efficient equilibrium? Show graphically and explain.

Discussion Questions

1. Scientists discover that marginal damages rise exponentially with emissions. How would this change the computation of total damages when there is no pollution abatement?

2. How is the equimarginal principle related to the socially efficient level of output?

3. Explain why society wants to minimize net social costs (maximize net social value) when choosing a target level of pollution.

A GUIDE TO THE FOURTH CANADIAN EDITION

This book is an introduction to the basic principles of environmental economics as they have been developed in the past and continue to evolve. It is designed for a one-semester course. Each section is self-contained; users can rearrange the sequence of topics to suit their specific course.

Section 1 is designed not only to provide an overview of environmental economics, but also to introduce right away how economics can be used to analyze important real-world problems. This section is revised not only to update data on environmental impacts, but to provide a clearer introduction to a number of the key issues addressed in environmental economics. Chapter 1 notes why problems emerge and why they are so difficult for market economies to deal with. It defines key terms—efficiency and equity—and how they will be used to assess policies to help improve environmental quality. The role of incentives in economic systems is highlighted in the context of two major environmental problems—urban smog and motor vehicles and global climate change due to greenhouse gas emissions. The second major theme of Chapter 1 is sustainability and economic growth. The concept of trade-offs, illustrated by the production possibility frontier, is highlighted to show the choices society faces between economic growth and environmental quality, and the role of technological change. Chapter 2 introduces the notion of natural capital and ecosystem goods and services—the stock of our environmental resources and the goods and services it provides to sustain life on the planet and our economy. It highlights how the economy and natural environment are linked, using the concepts of a circular flow and how wastes can be reduced to sustain natural capital. Important terminology that is used throughout the book is defined. Canada's emissions of greenhouse gases is compared to other countries. Recent Canadian progress on reducing other pollutants is also highlighted.

Section 2 is devoted to the tools of economic analysis. Chapter 3 covers the economic principles of demand and supply. The concepts of willingness to pay and opportunity cost are the underpinnings of understanding all the benefits and costs of economic decisions. Supply and demand curves under conditions where markets work to allocate resources are derived. Chapter 4 examines markets and shows how market failure occurs because external costs and benefits arise when environmental resources are used in the economy. The important role of property rights is addressed. Causes of market failure are examined and economic efficiency is contrasted with social efficiency—the inclusion of all external benefits and costs into decision making. Chapter 5 develops a simple model of pollution control that is based on the notion of a trade-off between environmental damages and pollution abatement costs. Marginal damage and marginal abatement cost functions are derived and used to determine socially efficient levels of pollution. An important concept that will be used to assess the efficiency of environmental policies—the equimarginal principle—is derived.

Section 3 focuses on benefit–cost analysis. Chapter 6 introduces the main concepts and steps for doing a benefit–cost study, addressing the decision rule, and how to discount future benefits and costs, distributional issues, and uncertainty. Chapter 7 is devoted to the examination of techniques for measuring the benefits of improving environmental quality when market prices exist or when values have to be imputed. These include direct approaches that use market prices and indirect approaches such as preventive expenditures, hedonic estimation, travel cost, and contingent valuation techniques. A new example illustrates how contingent valuation methods can be used to estimate Canadians' willingness to pay to protect endangered marine mammals. Chapter 8 examines the cost side using the concept of social opportunity cost. Costs are viewed at different levels of economic activity from the level of the firm to the nation as a whole.

Section 4 provides the backbone for environmental policy analysis—the theoretical examination of different policy options. Chapter 9 covers criteria for evaluating environmental policies—efficiency, cost effectiveness, equity, incentives created, enforceability, and moral issues. Each of the next four chapters examines specific public policy instruments and initiatives, using graphical and algebraic analysis. A number of worked examples appear in each chapter. Chapter 10 examines decentralized approaches—liability rules, private property rights and bargaining, moral suasion, and the introduction of green goods into the market economy. Chapter 11 covers standards, a type of command-and-control policy. Different types of standards (performance and technology-based) are examined using the criteria of Chapter 9. Chapter 12 examines market-based incentive policies—taxes, subsidies, deposit–refund systems. The cost-effectiveness of taxes is contrasted with standards. The Porter hypothesis linking environmental regulation to innovation is presented. Chapter 13 presents another market-based incentive, the transferable emission permit. This is a method of assigning property rights to the environment and using market forces to achieve efficiency. Using the sulphur trading market in the United States as an example, issues in setting up and operating an emission market are covered. Chapter 14 pulls together and extends the theoretical analysis using the simple algebraic model developed in Section 4 to contrast costs of controlling pollution, incentives created to develop new cost-saving technology for pollution control, and information required. The model is also extended to cover uncertainty about the marginal damage and abatement cost curves.

Section 5 examines environmental policy in practice and is thoroughly updated to reflect current Canadian policies. The analytical tools developed earlier are applied to policies being used and contemplated in Canada are highlighted, with examples provided as well from the United States and other countries. Chapter 15 introduces key characteristics of Canadian environmental policy—the Constitution and the features of parliamentary government in our federal system. Conflict between federal and provincial powers over the environment is highlighted and illustrated with examples of regulation of Alberta's bitumen (oil sands) extraction and the proposed Northern Gateway pipeline from Alberta to the B.C. coast. Recent changes in federal legislation that affect assessment of projects with environmental impacts and environmental protection are highlighted. The next five chapters illustrate federal and provincial policies for water and air pollution, toxic compounds, recycling and solid waste disposal, and global environmental issues. Water pollution-control policies at the federal and provincial level are illustrated in Chapter 16, with emphasis on federal drinking water guidelines, national standards, and interjurisdictional policies. An example is provided of the use of an offset system similar to emission trading for water pollutants in an eastern Ontario watershed. Chapter 17 provides examples of federal and provincial regulation of air pollutants, covering the key urban air pollutants and acid rain. Featured are the significant changes underway that moves Canada's regulation from non-binding air quality objectives to air quality regulation. Progress toward air quality targets is illustrated with recent data. Chapter 18 focuses on the cornerstone of federal policy, the *Canadian Environmental Protection Act* and recent significant changes in toxic waste policy. Examples of toxic waste management policies at the provincial level are examined. A case study of pollutants from the pulp and paper industry illustrates the extensive use of command-and-control regulation in Canada. Chapter 19 begins with an analysis of technical options for reducing solid waste, and then focuses on the economics of recycling. A significant update covers recycling and solid waste disposal as well as the emerging topic of food waste and recovery. Chapter 20 rounds out the policy section by addressing global environmental pollutants and has undergone a major reorganization and update to better integrate the theory with policy chapters. A thorough update exists for Canadian greenhouse gas policy and the use of carbon pricing worldwide is a focus of the chapter. This allows for direct connection with Chapters 12 and 13 to show where international leadership and best practices are occurring. Canada's policies are contrasted with those of other countries. The successful

Montreal Protocol to eliminate ozone depleting compounds is contrasting with the less successful efforts to reach international agreement on greenhouse gas emissions. We also touch on the important issue of protecting biodiversity of the earth's ecosystems.

VERSATILITY OF THE TEXT

The book can be used by a variety of different environmental economics courses. Section 1 sets the stage for any type of course and covers core concepts while introducing important policy issues. Section 2 can be covered more or less intensively depending on the strength of students' backgrounds in microeconomic theory. Students who have had an introductory course in microeconomic principles can skim Chapters 3 and 4. Chapter 5 introduces the core model of the text that every course should cover in detail. Section 3 on benefit–cost analysis can be covered either before or after Section 4. For courses with limited time, Chapter 6 is the most important chapter in this section. For those who want to spend more time on benefit–cost analysis, Chapters 7 and 8 provide considerable detail on the methods of measuring benefits and costs. Section 4 is essential for all courses as it provides an in-depth theoretical analysis of the suite of policies that address pollution problems beginning with the criteria one needs to assess policy effectiveness. The order is important—beginning with a thorough examination of the role of property rights and voluntary agreements to reduce pollution (Chapter 10) to command-and-control policies (Chapter 11) to environmental pricing methods (Chapters 12 and 13). Chapter 14 pulls together the theoretical material to compare and contrast the types of policies using the criteria in Chapter 9. Extensions to a world of uncertainty in Chapter 14 can be skipped if time is short. Section 5 covers a broad spectrum of Canadian environmental policies and can be the focus of courses where public policy concerns are emphasized. Individual chapters can also be selected for coverage or the material in these chapters used as examples for the policy analysis in Section 4. Each chapter in Section 5 can stand alone; specific topics can be picked out and integrated with the theoretical discussion of policy instruments in Section 4. Cues are given in Section 4 to guide the reader to specific policy examples in Section 5.

- A short course for those with an economics background and focusing on theory could cover: Chapters 1, 2, 5, 6, 9–14 (first part) with examples taken from Chapters 15–20.
- A course focusing on environmental policy for those without an economics background could cover: Chapters 1, 2, 3, 4, 5, 15–20.

SUPPLEMENTARY MATERIAL

McGraw-Hill Connect™ is a web-based assignment and assessment platform that gives students the means to better connect with their coursework, with their instructors, and with the important concepts that they will need to know for success now and in the future. With Connect, instructors can deliver assignments, quizzes, and tests easily online. Students can practise important skills at their own pace and on their own schedule. With Connect, students also get 24/7 online access to an eBook—an online edition of the text—to aid them in successfully completing their work, wherever and whenever they choose.

SUPERIOR LEARNING SOLUTIONS AND SUPPORT

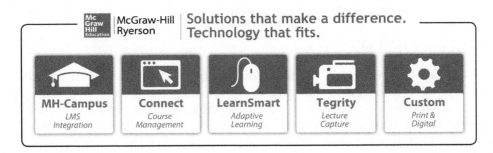

The McGraw-Hill Ryerson team is ready to help you assess and integrate any of our products, technology, and services into your course for optimal teaching and learning performance. Whether it's helping your students improve their grades, or putting your entire course online, the McGraw-Hill Ryerson team is here to help you do it. Contact your Learning Solutions Consultant today to learn how to maximize all of McGraw-Hill Ryerson's resources!

For more information on the latest technology and Learning Solutions offered by McGraw-Hill Ryerson and its partners, please visit us online: **www.mheducation.ca/he/solutions.**

ACKNOWLEDGMENTS FOR THE FOURTH CANADIAN EDITION

The Canadian material has come from my teaching experiences at Simon Fraser University, conversations with a number of my colleagues in academia and the government, and many hours of Internet research of government documents and journal articles. So much is being written daily on environmental economic issues that it is a challenge to determine what must be left out. Many thanks to Jonathan Arnold, Masters in Public Policy 2014 graduate, for his excellent research help on this fourth edition. I am most grateful to the following reviewers for their valuable comments and input:

Doug Auld
University of Guelph

Ramesh Bhardwaj
Georgian College

Brian Copeland
University of British Columbia

Rashid Khan
McMaster University

Gordon Lee
University of Alberta

Elizabeth Troutt
University of Manitoba

Nancy D. Olewiler
Simon Fraser University

Section **One**

Introductory

This first section contains two introductory chapters. Environmental economics builds on the foundations of microeconomic analysis, but introduces a number of key features that make it an important field of study in its own right. The first chapter provides an overview of environmental economics and illustrates key concepts by looking at both the global level—greenhouse gas emissions and climate change, and the local level—vehicle emissions. The second chapter explores a basic environment–economy framework and asks how can we sustain both, then defines a number of environmental terms used throughout the book, and provides a picture of the state of Canada's environment.

Chapter 1

What Is Environmental Economics?

After reading this chapter you will be able to:

LO 1 Distinguish between efficiency and equity concepts and why they are central to environmental economics.

LO 2 Describe the incentives that contribute to pollution arising from people and firms.

LO 3 Define and distinguish between open access, private, and common property rights and explain why the assignment of property rights can help reduce pollution.

LO 4 Explain why people do not take into account the air pollution their vehicle emits when they drive.

LO 5 Describe the anthropogenic sources of greenhouse gas emissions and what changes are needed in the economy to reduce these emissions.

LO 6 Explain the tradeoffs between economic growth and the environment.

LO 1

Environmental economics is the study of environmental problems with the perspective and analytical ideas of economics. Economics is the study of how and why people—whether they are consumers, firms, non-profit organizations, or government agencies—make decisions about the use of valuable resources. Economics is about making choices. It is divided into *microeconomics,* the study of the behaviour of individuals or small groups, and *macroeconomics,* the study of the economic performance of economies as a whole. Environmental economics draws from both sides, but primarily from microeconomics. The study of environmental economics, like all economics courses, is concerned with the fundamental issue of allocating scarce resources among competing uses. The concepts of **scarcity, opportunity cost, trade-offs, marginal benefits, marginal costs, efficiency,** and **equity** are key ingredients to understanding environmental problems and what can be done about them.

Environmental economics makes use of many familiar concepts in economics. What is different about environmental economics compared to other economic subjects is the focus on how economic activities affect our natural environment—the atmosphere, water, land, and an enormous variety of living species. Economic decisions made by people, firms, and governments can have many deleterious effects on the natural environment. For example, the dumping of waste products into the natural environment creates pollution that harms humans and other living things, production, and degrades ecosystems—the planet's air, water, and land. It leads to wasteful use of resources and threatens the sustainability of both our environment and economy. We ask:

- Why don't people take into account the effects of their economic activity on the natural environment?
- What inhibits economic systems from using its resources wisely and efficiently to protect the sustainability of our planet and people's livelihoods over time?

Environmental economics examines these questions by focusing on ways society can reduce its degradation of the natural environment. Equally as important, environmental economics investigates and assesses different methods of reaching an efficient and equitable use of all resources (including environmental ones) from the viewpoint of society, not just individual decision makers as is the typical focus in economic analysis.

ECONOMIC EFFICIENCY

Economic efficiency is all about using resources wisely. An outcome is said to be economically efficient if all resources are put to their highest value use, or equivalently, the economy reaches a desired outcome using the fewest resources. Chapter 4 develops efficiency concepts fully, but for now, consider this illustration.

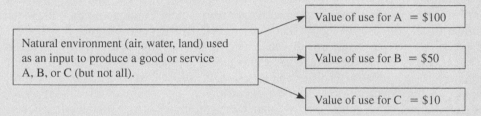

Should we pick A, B, or C? An economically efficient choice would be to pick A. Good or service A maximizes the value of the end use for which resources are being put. In using economic efficiency as an objective, economists are making a value judgment as well as empirical observation. The value judgment (known as a 'normative' approach—see Chapter 5) is that something has value if someone wants it. That 'something' can be a computer or the ability to always take a walk in a forest—it need not be a good that is produced and sold in the marketplace. Both the computer and the walk in the forest use inputs from the natural environment—minerals for the computer components, the ecosystem supporting the forest environment for the walk. Environmental economics emphatically asserts that if individuals value the forest for taking walks more than the computer, than it is the highest value use, even if there is no explicit market for walks in the forest. The empirical observation behind efficiency is hundreds of years of observing people make decisions that indicate they are looking for maximum value such as profit maximization by the owners of firms, or utility maximization by individuals. Environmental economists may have a broader definition of what constitutes utility—walks in the forest count, not just buying goods, but the notion of maximizing or making the best use of what resources are available is still fundamental to how outcomes are assessed.

To accomplish these tasks, a simple but powerful analytical model is developed that builds on, but modifies and extends standard economic principles, in particular, the marginal valuations that involve trade-offs between marginal costs and marginal benefits. While **economic efficiency** remains the central criterion for evaluating outcomes and policies, environmental economists also examine other criteria for choosing among alternative policies that attempt to improve the environment—for example, **equity** or fairness. If economic efficiency cannot be obtained, and environmental targets are established using other criteria, an economic approach can still greatly assist decision makers in reaching whatever target is set. This book focuses on how individual actions give rise to environmental degradation and what can be done about these actions. Another branch of economics—*natural resource economics*—examines ways to achieve efficient use of our natural environment over time—energy, forests, land, and harvested species such as fish stocks. We look more closely at the distinction between environmental and natural resource economics in Chapter 2.

The objective of this chapter is to acquaint you with some of the basic ideas and analytical tools of microeconomics that are used in environmental economics. We will illustrate how environmental economics helps answer important questions about our environment and economy with real-world examples. We first consider briefly what we mean by the "economic approach," then turn to two pressing environmental problems; starting first with a local and regional concern—motor vehicle pollution, then turning to a global threat—greenhouse gas emissions. In Chapter 2 we will take a look at the broad linkages existing between economy and environment and define a number of important pollution terms. After that we will be ready to study the economic principles we will need.

EQUITY

Equity is about how the economic 'pie' is divided up. Who gets how much income or wealth? Dictionary definitions of equity talk about ideals of being "just, impartial, and fair," but who decides what is fair or just? We are in normative/subjective territory again. Think about the following: suppose our government decided that every adult should earn exactly the same income; it will take the total earnings of everyone in the economy and divide them by the total number of workers. Is this equitable? In one sense it is. Every adult receives the same income as another adult regardless of circumstances. But what if a person's circumstances differ and as a society we want to take that into account. We may want to divide up the country's total income according to age, number of children people have, whether they are able to work or not due to factors beyond their control such as illness or accidents. The dilemma is that there are many possible ways to divide things up and people may have very different notions of what is or is not equitable. Economists, philosophers, and many other disciplines wrestle with the notions of fairness going back hundreds of years to the early writings in moral philosophy and economics. Environmental economics uses a number of different definitions of equity to help evaluate economic outcomes (efficient or not). These include:

- *Horizontal equity* treats similarly situated people the same way. For example, an environmental program that has the same impact on an urban dweller with $20,000 of income as on a rural dweller with the same income is horizontally equitable.

- *Vertical equity* refers to how a policy impinges on people who are in different circumstances, in particular on people who have different income levels.

- *Intergenerational equity* looks at whether future generations have the same opportunities as current ones. How does society trade off using its resources today when their loss may affect the ability of future generations to enjoy the same quality of life?

Subsequent chapters return to equity as one of the vital criteria in assessing how well the economy is doing.

LO 2

THE ECONOMIC APPROACH

Why do people behave in ways that cause environmental destruction? There are several types of answers to this question. One goes like this: Environmental degradation comes about from human behaviour that is unethical or immoral. Thus, for example, the reason people pollute is because they lack the moral and ethical strength to refrain from the type of behaviour that causes environmental degradation. If this is true, then the way to get people to stop polluting is somehow to increase the general level of environmental morality in the society. In fact, the environmental movement has led a great many people to focus on questions of environmental ethics, exploring the moral dimensions of human impacts on the natural environment. These moral questions are obviously of fundamental concern to any civilized society. Certainly one of the main reasons environmental issues have been put on the front burner of social concern is the sense of moral responsibility that has led people to take their concerns into the political arena.

But there are problems with relying on moral reawakening as our main approach to combating pollution. People don't necessarily have readily available moral buttons to push, and environmental problems are too important to wait for a long process of moral rebuilding. Nor does a sense of moral outrage by itself help us make decisions about all the other social issues that also have ethical dimensions: poverty, housing, health care, education, crime, and so on. In a world of competing objectives we have to worry about very practical questions: are we targeting the right environmental objectives; can we really enforce certain policies; are we getting the most impact for our money; and so on. But the biggest problem with basing our approach to pollution control strictly on the moral argument is the basic assumption that people pollute because they are somehow morally underdeveloped. It is not moral underdevelopment that leads to environmental destruction; rather, it is the way we have arranged the economic system within which people go about the job of making their livings.

So, a second way of approaching the question of why people pollute is to look at the way the economy and its institutions are set up, and how they lead people to make decisions that result in environmental destruction. Economists argue that

people pollute because it is the cheapest way they have of solving a certain very practical problem: how to dispose of the waste products remaining after production and consumption of a good.

People make these decisions on production, consumption, and disposal within a certain set of economic and social institutions;[1] these institutions structure the incentives that lead people to make decisions in one direction and not in another. An **incentive** is something that attracts or repels people and leads them to modify their behaviour in some way. An "economic incentive" is something in the economic world that leads people to channel their efforts at production and consumption in certain directions. Economic incentives are often viewed as consisting of payoffs in terms of material wealth; people have an incentive to behave in ways that provide them with increased wealth. But there are also many non-material incentives that lead people to modify their economic behaviour; for example, wanting your children to have the same opportunities as you have, self-esteem, the desire to preserve a beautiful visual environment, or the desire to set a good example for others. Happiness is a function of many things, not solely material wealth. What we will study is

- how incentive processes work, and

- how to restructure them so that people will be led to make decisions and develop lifestyles that have more benign environmental implications.

---

[1] By "institutions," we mean the fundamental set of public and private organizations, customs, laws, and practices that a society uses to structure its economic activity. Markets are an economic institution, for example, as are corporations, a body of commercial law, public agencies, and so on.

One simplistic incentive-type statement that you often hear is that pollution is a result of the profit motive. According to this view, in private-enterprise economies of industrialized nations people are rewarded for maximizing profits, the difference between the value of what is produced and the value of what is used up in the production process. Furthermore, the thinking goes, the profits that entrepreneurs try to maximize are strictly monetary profits. In this headlong pursuit of monetary profits, entrepreneurs give no thought to the environmental impacts of their actions because it "doesn't pay." Thus, in this uncontrolled striving for monetary profits, the only way to reduce environmental pollution is to weaken the strength of the profit motive.

But this proposition doesn't stand up to analysis. It is not only "profit-motivated" corporations that cause pollution and threaten the environment with their activities; individual consumers are also guilty when they do things like pour paint thinner down the drain, use anti-bacterial soap, or leave all the chargers for their electronic gadgets plugged in. Since individuals don't keep profit-and-loss statements, it can't be profits per se that lead people to environmentally damaging activities. The same can be said of governments that have sometimes been serious polluters and subsidize industries that degrade the environment even though they are not profit-motivated. But the most persuasive argument against the view that the search for profits causes pollution comes from political events in Eastern Europe, the former USSR, and the rapid development in China. We have become aware of the enormous environmental destruction that has occurred in some of these regions—heavily polluted air and water resources in many areas, with major impacts on human health and ecological systems. China, a country with communist leadership, has areas of the country contaminated by toxic compounds and regions where air and water pollution are at levels dangerous to human health. Many of these problems exceed some of the worst cases of environmental pollution experienced in market-driven countries. But they have happened in an economic system where the profit motive has been entirely lacking. Which means, quite simply, that the profit motive in itself is not the main cause of environmental destruction.

In the sections and chapters that follow, incentives will play a major role in the analysis of how economic systems operate. *Any system will produce destructive environmental impacts if the incentives within the system are not structured to avoid them.* We have to look more deeply into any economic system to understand how its incentive systems work and how they may be changed so that we can have a reasonably progressive economy without disastrous environmental side effects. Two concepts that are important to an understanding of the incentives that exist regarding the environment are **externalities/external effects** and **property rights.** These concepts are illustrated in the following two examples and explained in detail in later chapters. Essentially, they involve the question of a lack of ownership of environmental resources. A fundamental point is that

> *lack of ownership rights to environmental resources means that there are few incentives to take the environmental consequences of our actions into account.*

LO 3

EXTERNALITIES AND PROPERTY RIGHTS

In Section 4, we will examine the role of property rights in reaching a **socially efficient level of pollution.** Property rights—or the lack thereof—are crucial in understanding why we have today's environmental problems. The basic point is that environmental resources generally do not have well-defined property rights. No one owns the atmosphere, our oceans, or large underground aquifers. A term used by economists to describe the lack of ownership of the natural environment is **open access**.

An open access resource is one that anyone can use without paying for it. Oceans and the atmosphere are examples. See the classic article by Hardin (1968). **Private property rights** give the owner the right to exclude others from using or consuming their resource. Think of owning a private forest woodlot. No one can cut the trees or trespass without permission of the owner. **Common property rights** give the community the power to govern the resource within its borders. Outsiders to the community are excluded. A small fishing community is an example. Two examples illustrate how externalities are connected to property rights.

Auto emissions. When an SUV releases carbon monoxide and carbon dioxide into the atmosphere, you cannot jump out in front of the vehicle and shout "Stop! You are polluting my air and releasing greenhouse gases that contribute to global climate change!" We all breathe the same air in our communities and GHGs travel to our global atmosphere. For externalities that involve many different sources of pollution, perhaps spread over large areas, there is no effective way to reach any sort of private agreement to limit the emissions. Designing environmental policy is more challenging the more pervasive the externality is across regions or countries and for different sources.

Dog waste. You detect your neighbour's dog leaving its waste products on your lawn. This too is an externality. The dog and its owner do not take into account the impact dog waste is having on your lawn when they go about their activities. Contrary to the case of automobile air contaminants and GHG emissions, you and your neighbour would find it relatively easy to negotiate a mutually agreeable resolution to this problem. The neighbour might agree to keep the dog on a leash or to pick up its waste. You may build a fence, or get the neighbour to pay for it. The dog externality is internalized through discussion and negotiation. A solution that is mutually agreeable to both parties can be worked out; the only difference in possible outcomes is who pays for them. That is a function of our bargaining strengths and other factors.

Why is the dog case different from the auto emissions case? You own your property and the dog is essentially trespassing. Laws say you can keep others off your property. There is also just one other person to bargain with—the dog owner. This case could be more like urban air pollution if you don't know whose dog is dumping on your lawn. Then you must incur search costs, set up dog surveillance, and so on to detect the perpetrator.

Our most serious environmental problems are closer to the vehicle smog case than the case of the wandering dog. They involve lots of possible polluters, with perhaps very little knowledge about even the source of emissions or the link between emissions and environmental impact. Society members may not recognize that an activity they have been doing for years has a deleterious impact on the environment. For example, manufacturers of leather products in eastern Canada used to use mercury in the tanning process. They would simply dump their wastes in streams or on the ground. Over the years, the mercury percolated into groundwater and contaminated people's drinking water. But people didn't know at the time how toxic mercury is. The tanners themselves suffered from mercury poisoning. This is where the term "mad as a hatter" emerged—mercury poisoning affects brain function. The leather manufacturers are now gone, but mercury still remains a dangerous pollutant in our ecosystem. How can today's population engage in any sort of negotiation with the leather producers of 100 years ago to reach a mutually agreeable level of waste disposal and compensation for disease, shorter lifespans, and contaminated water and soils? This example illustrates the difficulties inherent in depending on individuals who act in their own self-interest to reach a socially efficient outcome. Information about potential problems may be imperfect or non-existent. People today cannot be counted on to make decisions that maximize the well-being of generations who follow. When these conditions exist, some form of government intervention is necessary.

PRACTICAL ILLUSTRATION #1: SMOG AND MOTOR VEHICLES

Canada's transportation sector produced 24.2 percent of total national greenhouse gas (GHG) emissions in 2011, with cars, trucks, and motorcycles accounting for almost half this total. The transportation sector discharges approximately 40 percent of carbon monoxide, 21 percent of nitrogen oxides, 11 percent of volatile organic compounds, 8 percent of sulphur dioxide, and 4 percent of fine particulate matter (PM-2.5).[2] These compounds, known as air contaminants contribute to urban smog, acid precipitation, and global climate change. In turn, these environmental conditions adversely affect the health of people and our ecosystem, the survival of many species, the cost of producing goods and services, and our overall enjoyment of our surroundings. Estimates are that 21,000 Canadians die prematurely each year due to air pollution, while tens of thousands more suffer from bronchitis exacerbated by pollution.[3] Exposure to urban smog may increase the likelihood of cancers in children by up to 25 percent and raise the chance of getting childhood asthma by 400 percent. Acid precipitation changes aquatic and land-based ecosystems, killing fish, amphibians, and other aquatic species and affecting forest growth. Global warming could lead to massive ecosystem changes with catastrophic worldwide impact. Motor vehicle use contributes to congestion on our roads. Congestion increases driving times, promotes accidents, costs people lost time, and generally makes people very crabby, contributing to "road rage."

Driving one's car or truck thus affects all sorts of other people (whether they too drive a motor vehicle or not) and our environment. This is an *external effect*. When you drive to school or work or to the beach, you get the direct benefit of transportation services. Others—bystanders—receive the negative impacts of your driving: air pollution, congestion, and associated impacts. The bystanders don't control your driving. And the price you pay for driving your car, your direct costs in the form of gasoline, maintenance, and monthly car payments, do not reflect the negative impacts you impose on others—hence the words *externality* or *external effects* to describe this situation. An externality occurs when the actions of one or more individuals affects the well-being of other individuals without any compensation taking place. While externalities can be positive as well as negative (think enjoying viewing your neighbour's flower garden), pollutants such as air contaminants are negative externalities. We will examine in detail in Section 4 what sorts of initiatives, both individual and with the help of government, can be used to address externalities. For now, let's think a bit more about motor vehicle externalities and what can be done about them. To do so, we look at the concept of incentives.

Incentives: Households and Vehicle Use

When you drive your car, sport-utility vehicle (SUV), or truck, the price you pay per kilometre travelled reflects your **private costs**—gasoline, oil, insurance, and maintenance. These prices do not

---

[2.] See Government of Canada, Environment Canada Emission Trends and the National Pollutant Release Inventory, Air Pollutant Emissions Data for the most recent year data on GHGs and criteria air contaminants respectively at www.ec.gc.ca.

[3.] www.fvrd.bc.ca/Services/AirQuality/Documents/2013TRAPandHealthCanada-Brauer.pdf.

take into account the damage the emissions from your car imposes on others and the environment; rather, they reflect costs of producing gasoline, retailer markups, and so on. You will respond to changes in these private costs, for example, by driving more when gasoline prices fall and less when they rise. What sort of positive incentive could we contemplate that would induce drivers to reduce the number of emissions they release? A simple relationship may help us see where incentives could enter.

Total quantity of emissions = Number of vehicles × Average kilometres travelled × Emissions per kilometre

Incentives can target the number of vehicles on the road, the average number of kilometres travelled, and emissions per kilometre. In addition, we might want to consider where people drive their vehicles. A car driven in downtown Toronto, Montreal, or Vancouver will have a larger impact on urban smog than that same vehicle being driven in Moose Jaw, Saskatchewan. The release of carbon dioxide will, however, contribute to global warming regardless of where the vehicle is driven.

What are some possible incentives to alter people's behaviour? We provide examples for each of the three parts of the word equation above that will help reduce emissions.

Number of vehicles: some jurisdictions levy a charge per year for owning a vehicle in addition to one's licence fee. If this charge is substantial, as it is in places such as Singapore, people will be less inclined to own and operate a motor vehicle. This is especially likely in urban areas that have good public transportation; people will ride the bus or train instead of driving a vehicle. Improving public transit will reinforce the incentive not to own or operate a vehicle because people will have an option for their mobility needs. They can then weigh the relative costs of operating a vehicle versus taking public transit.

Average kilometres travelled: Increasing the cost of driving per kilometre should reduce the average number of kilometres travelled. Higher costs per kilometre provide an incentive for people every time they drive their vehicle to minimize the number of trips, thereby reducing their direct costs. An example of a direct incentive to increase costs of driving is to tax people on the number of kilometres travelled. This could be done using a tax that is payable annually as people renew their vehicle licence. An indirect incentive is to tax gasoline, thereby increasing the costs of driving.

Emissions per kilometre: A tax on emissions would also increase the cost of driving per kilometre. An example is the carbon tax in British Columbia. The carbon tax of $30 per tonne carbon adds 7.8 cents per litre to the cost of gasoline, thus making it more expensive to drive. A buyback program that pays people to retire their older vehicles can also reduce emissions per kilometre. Old vehicles contribute far more per kilometre travelled to air emissions than do newer, more fuel-efficient and less pollution-intensive vehicles. Other policies to reduce emissions could include advertising and education programs that inform people about how their driving decisions affect air quality and, hence, their well-being.

Incentives for Businesses

Incentives can also apply to businesses. Think about the producers of motor vehicles and vehicle parts. All industrial firms work within a given set of incentives: to increase profits if they are firms in market economies. Firms have an incentive to take advantage of whatever factors are available to better their performance in terms of these criteria. One way they have been able to do this historically is to use the services of the environment for waste disposal. The motivation for this practice is that these services have essentially been free, and by using free inputs as much as possible a firm obviously can increase its profits. The challenge is to find incentives to alter firms' behaviour so they treat environmental services as a costly activity rather than a free good.

One policy approach is to introduce and then try to enforce laws or regulations that direct the amount of pollution a firm can emit, thus reducing emissions per kilometre. Canada has company average fuel consumption (CAFC) guidelines for all new cars and light trucks produced in Canada. Vehicle manufacturers have agreed to design their cars and light trucks to meet a voluntary target level of gasoline consumption averaged over their entire fleet of vehicles produced each year. Guidelines were introduced for cars in 1978 at 13.1 litres per 100 kilometres, and then were tightened to 8.6 litres per 100 kilometres in 1986, where they remain today. Guidelines for light trucks were not introduced until 1990 (at 11.8 litres per 100 kilometres) and were gradually tightened to 10.0 litres per 100 kilometres in 2010. In December 2012, the federal government announced that Canada will adopt the same fuel efficiency standards as the United States as its target for 2025. The U.S. standards require a combined corporate average (for all makes and models of vehicles sold each year) of 54.5 miles per gallon (4.4 litres per 100 kilometres). Fuel efficiency of all cars on the road has increased from approximately 15 litres per 100 kilometres in 1965 to 6.7 litres per 100 kilometres in 2010.[4] Light duty trucks were estimated to average 8.6 litres per 100 kilometres in 2010.

The CAFC guidelines have been voluntary, not compulsory. Vehicle manufacturers meet the standards because the United States has the same type of policy and it is compulsory in that country. The North American automobile industry is completely integrated—cars and light trucks produced in Canada are exported to the United States and vice versa. Canadian cars that do not meet the U.S. fuel efficiency standards cannot be sold there. There is a clear profit incentive for Canadian manufacturers to comply with the voluntary standard. Note that CAFC standards require the auto manufacturer to meet the standard *on average* across all its cars or trucks produced each year. If automakers produce a lot of low-polluting cars, they will more readily meet the target than if they produce high-polluting vehicles such as SUVs. The regulations thus provide an incentive for manufacturers to alter the mix of vehicles produced to reduce the emissions that will ultimately come when drivers purchase and use the vehicles. Canadian governments also regulate the sulphur content of gasoline. The regulations specify that oil refiners must produce gasoline containing on average no more than 30 mg/kg of sulphur (and never to exceed 80 mg/kg).[5] Sulphur in gasoline, when combusted, produces sulphur dioxide, a contributor to smog and acid precipitation. The incentive effect here is this: abide by the regulation or you will be fined by the government.

A more effective policy might be to design a system that takes advantage of firms' normal monetary incentives in such a way as to lead them to pollute less. For example, oil refiners could be taxed on the basis of the sulphur content of their gasoline produced. This may induce them to switch their production to lower-sulphur fuels so as to avoid the tax. They might increase the proportion of methanol derived from grains in their fuels. Methanol does not contain any sulphur. Gasoline prices are likely to rise, then providing an additional incentive to drivers to reduce their consumption of gasoline. The Canadian government decided not to tax sulphur, but to subsidize the production of ethanol at the farm level. This lowered the price of ethanol relative to petroleum, but had a number of negative consequences such as raising the cost of corn products worldwide and diverting corn from feeding people to producing vehicle fuels. Corn production is also very fertilizer and pesticide

---

[4.] For the history of the development of CAFC guidelines see www.tc.gc.ca/eng/programs/environment-fcp-history-630.htm, accessed September 26, 2010. Information on fuel efficiency of vehicles can be found at www.tc.gc.ca/eng/programs/environment-fcp-cafctargets-385.htm, accessed September 26, 2010.

[5.] See Chapter 6 for a detailed discussion of the sulphur in gasoline regulations.

intensive, and can lead to undesirable environmental impacts. Section 5 looks at different ways government can design policies that are effective in meeting environmental and equity goals while minimizing adverse impacts to the economy. The essence of the economic incentives approach is to restructure the incentives facing firms and consumers in such a way that it mobilizes their own energy and ingenuity to find ways of reducing their impacts on the environment.

Incentives in the Pollution-Control Industry

The pollution-control industry develops waste recycling techniques, pollution-control equipment, and pollution-monitoring technology. It sometimes handles and treats waste products, and is often involved in managing waste-disposal sites. It also includes firms that develop new environmentally friendly products like low-sulphur gasoline, low-phosphate detergents, and recyclable paper products. A lively and progressive pollution-control industry is obviously needed if we are to come to grips effectively with all of our present and prospective environmental problems. Thus, one of the major things environmental economists must study is the incentives facing this industry—what causes it to grow or decline, how quickly or slowly it responds to new needs, and so on. In our example of air pollution from motor vehicles, the pollution-control industry could include manufacturers of zero-emission vehicles. These vehicles might run on fuel cells, on electricity, or use other technologies. Are policies needed to encourage these industries? One might argue that the existence of policies that provide incentives to reduce air emissions will be enough to stimulate the development of alternative fuels or engines. However, various governments have also subsidized the research and development costs for these manufacturers either through tax incentives or outright grants of funds. The rationale is that the development of the new technologies will have broad-reaching social benefits.

LO 5

PRACTICAL ILLUSTRATION #2: GREENHOUSE GAS EMISSIONS AND CLIMATE CHANGE

The carbon dioxide (CO_2) content of the earth's atmosphere has increased by over 2.2 percent per year from 2000 to 2010. This compares to 1.3 percent per year from 1970 to 2000.[6] Figure 1-1 shows the rising trend of emissions by gas since 1970. Carbon dioxide emissions (CO_2) from fossil fuel combustion and industrial process make up the majority of emissions. The key question is what effect these emissions have on the earth's climate now and into the future. The science of climate change is complex, with many uncertainties due to the difficulty of measurement as well as interpretation of the data and attempts to determine cause and effect.[7] It is estimated that the average surface temperature of earth has risen approximately 0.6°C over the 20th century (with a confidence interval of ± 0.2°C).[8]

[6.] See the Fifth Assessment Reports of the Intergovernmental Panel on Climate Change, *Climate Change,* for recent data on climate change and a discussion of the state of climate-change science and policy. Unless otherwise noted, all the numerical estimates presented in this paragraph are from the report of Working Group III. The reports are available at www.ipcc.ch/.

[7.] Many hundreds of books and articles have been written on the science and economics of global climate change. This section will just scratch the surface and hopefully stimulate more reading. New information is continually released that may help to resolve the uncertainties in climate-change predictions. See Chapter 20 for more detail on Canadian policy and the references at the end of the text.

[8.] See Goddard Institute of Space Studies (NASA) at http://data.giss.nasa.gov/gistemp/graphs/ for data on world temperatures.

Figure 1-2 shows the amount of carbon dioxide in the atmosphere from the 1950s to 2010, an increase of approximately 25 percent. About half the cumulative increase in CO_2 from 1750 to 2010 attributed to human activity (**anthropogenic** sources) occurred in the last 40 years. Climate change models forecast a rise in the earth's temperature over the 21st century by anywhere from 1.5 to 6°C. Models also predict an increase in climate variability and extreme weather events due to the increase in emissions of greenhouse gases (GHGs)—carbon dioxide (CO_2) and other gases in the atmosphere. However, human and natural factors can affect models' results. Natural processes such as volcanic activity send bursts of gases and particulate matter into the atmosphere, causing changes in rainfall patterns and temporary cooling. Pollution, in the form of accumulated SO_2 in the lower atmosphere, reflects sunlight and works against the greenhouse phenomenon. Carbon dioxide is also absorbed by **carbon sinks** in the form of trees, wetlands, and oceans. Just exactly how much the sinks can absorb and under what conditions is an important area of study.

FIGURE 1-1   **Total Annual Anthropogenic GHG Emissions by Groups of Gases, 1970–2010**

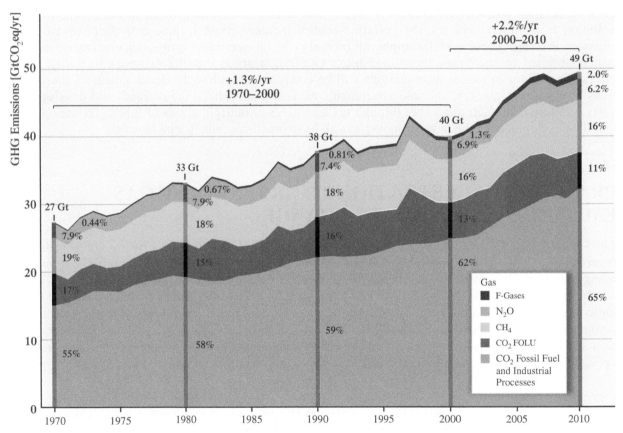

The time trend of CO_2 emissions for the past 40 years is positively sloped and has gotten steeper with emissions rising at 2.2 percent per year since 2000. Anthropogenic sources are those created by human activity.

Note: Total annual anthropogenic GHG emissions (GtCO$_2$eq/yr) by groups of gases 1970–2010: CO_2 from fossil fuel combustion and industrial processes; CO_2 from Forestry and Other Land Use (FOLU); methane (CH_4); nitrous oxide (N_2O); and fluorinated gases.

Source: *IPCC, 2014: Climate Change 2014: Mitigation of Climate Change. Contribution of Working Group III to the Fifth Assessment Report of the Intergovernmental Panel on Climate Change, Figure TS.1; Figure TS.6. [Edenhofer, O., R. Pichs-Madruga, Y. Sokona, E. Farahani, S. Kadner, K. Seyboth, A. Adler, I. Baum, S. Brunner, P. Eickemeier, B. Kriemann, J. Savolainen, S. Schloemer, C. von Stechow, T. Zwickel, and J.C. Minx (eds.)]. Cambridge University Press, Cambridge, United Kingdom and New York, NY, USA.*

FIGURE 1-2   Atmospheric Carbon Dioxide Levels Since 1950s

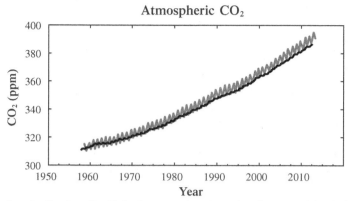

Atmospheric CO$_2$

Levels of carbon dioxide in the atmosphere have risen by approximately 25 percent from the 1950s to 2010.

Source: *IPCC, 2013: Climate Change 2013: The Physical Science Basis. Working Group I Contribution to the Fifth Assessment Report of the Intergovernmental Panel on Climate Change, Figure SPM.4(a). [Stocker, T.F., D. Qin, G.K.* Plattner, M. Tignor, S.K. Allen, J. Boschung, A. Nauels, Y. Xia, V. Bex, and P.M. Midgley (eds.).] Cambridge University Press, Cambridge, UK and New York, NY, USA.

Climate change, global warming, or the *greenhouse effect* are the common names used to describe the potentially major changes in the world's climate. The principle of a greenhouse is that the enclosing glass allows the passage of incoming sunlight but traps a portion of the reflected infrared radiation, which warms the interior of the greenhouse above the outside temperature. Greenhouse gases in the earth's atmosphere play a similar role; they serve to raise the temperature of the earth's surface and make it habitable. with no greenhouse gases at all, the surface of the earth would be about 30°C cooler than it is today, making human life impossible. Figure 1-3 shows the sources of GHGs by sector.

If global climate changes result in global warming, the earth may become very different from its current state. The rate of heating is estimated to be at least 0.2°C per decade based on current levels of GHGs in the atmosphere.[9] This may not sound like a very rapid change, but historical studies have shown that in past episodes of warming and cooling, during which agricultural societies of the time suffered major dislocations, climate change occurred at a rate of only about 0.05°C per decade. The forecast rate of change for the 21st century is six times faster than the rates faced by humans in the past. If countries do nothing to offset the increase in greenhouse gas emissions, **adaptation** to climate change by future generations may be very costly, especially for some parts of the world. Adaptation refers to actions taken to offset or reduce the adverse impacts of climate change. Adaptation costs arise from extreme weather events, higher temperatures, droughts, crop losses, impacts on health, loss of ecosystems, and sea level rise. Estimates of the costs of adaptation are highly variable across countries. A study by the World Bank puts the range at between $70 and $100 billion per year from 2010 to 2050 with a 2°C warming by 2050.[10] The Intergovernmental Panel on Climate Change (IPCC) puts an estimate at 0.2 to 2 percent of income, but note that there is a strong consensus that the estimate could exceed 2 percent.[11] Rising sea levels may inundate entire nations, such as some islands

---

[9] Fourth Assessment Report of the Intergovernmental Panel on Climate Change, *Climate Change 2007: Synthesis Report.*

[10] World Bank (2010) "Economics of Adaptation to Climate Change, Synthesis Report." Washington, DC: The World Bank.

[11] IPCC: Intergovernmental Panel on Climate Change (2014) "IPCC WGII Summary for Policy Makers."

FIGURE 1-3   Global Anthropogenic Sources of GHG Emissions

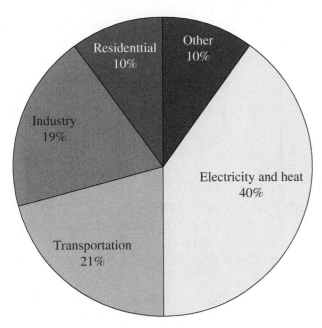

The largest source worldwide is electricity generation and heat. Coal-fired plants are a major source of emissions from the electricity sector.

Note: Others include commercial/public service, agriculture, forestry, fisheries, industry other than electricity and heat generation, and sources not identified elsewhere.

Source: *Based on IEA data from CO2 Emissions From Fuel Combustion Highlights © OECD/IEA [2012], IEA Publishing, fig. [1] p. [7]; modified by McGraw-Hill Ryerson Limited. License: http://www.iea.org/t&c.*

in the Caribbean and South Pacific, and require relocation of large populations that now live in low-lying coastal regions (e.g., those living along river deltas in Southeast Asia and the Nile). The Arctic polar ice caps are melting at a very high rate, threatening that fragile ecosystem and its inhabitants. Countries differ also in terms of agricultural adaptability—the ability to shift crops, varieties, cultivation methods, and so on—to maintain production in the face of climate changes and are likely to have very different perceptions about how they will be affected by global warming.

Responses to Climate Change: Scientific Uncertainties, the Precautionary Principle and Mitigation Strategies

Given the uncertainties in climate and natural science, there is an argument that until we "know for sure" that climate change is happening and is due to human activity no policies for reduction or **mitigation** of greenhouse-gas emissions should be introduced. There are several problems with this viewpoint. What if society does nothing today to mitigate GHG emissions, but there is a chance that global warming could lead to extremely high adaptation costs in the future? Then, some years from now, the costs of adjusting to climate change could comprise a much larger share of GDP than would be realized if society initiates mitigation policies today. People today would be imposing huge costs on future generations—violating our notions of intergenerational equity. The **precautionary principle** says that society should weigh the trade-off between the cost of measures taken today versus benefits in terms of reduced future risk. Expected net benefits are calculated as the benefits minus the costs of each scenario weighted by the probability of the event occurring, taking into account that these benefits and costs will occur into the future. Chapters 6, 7, and 8 illustrate how these benefits and costs are measured and net benefits computed over time. If the probability that global warming raises average temperatures by 3°C in 50 years is low (e.g., .0005 or .005), society minimizes its costs by doing nothing today because net benefits are higher (a smaller negative number) with no current policies adopted. But if society estimates the probability at a 5- or 10-percent chance, action now to reduce GHG emissions becomes the preferred choice.

GHG mitigation policies could include taxes on carbon emissions, introducing standards to improve energy efficiency of vehicles, appliances, and buildings, and a host of other actions. By waiting to see what happens, society may incur much higher costs than if actions were taken today to put it on a more sustainable path that reduces carbon emissions. As well, if society does nothing and turns out to be wrong, climate change impacts could be devastating. The cost to the global economy would be enormous and inequitably felt across countries and regions. Another uncertainty that is difficult to quantify is the role of technological change in helping to mitigate global warming. It may be in society's interest to delay introducing specific mitigation policies in the present in the hope that technological improvements will allow it to reach a GHG target at much lower costs in the future. However, this does not suggest that no GHG policies should be introduced in the present. For example, a GHG tax at a low rate could be introduced now with the rate rising over time. This tax will signal that it will be increasingly costly over time to release GHGs into the atmosphere. Putting a price on GHG emissions will help incent technological activity.

Recall how total emissions of vehicle pollutants were identified. A similar identity exists for GHGs and illustrates how they can be reduced.

Total GHGs = Population × GDP/population × Energy/GDP × GHGs/energy

Figure 1-4 shows the breakdown for recent decades of the factors that give rise to GHG emissions, looking at each part of the word equation above. While gains in energy efficiency help reduce emissions, they are offset by population and GDP growth as well as a reversal in the trend for carbon intensity of energy in the most recent decade.

The focus in the equation above is on energy because as Figure 1-1 illustrates, combustion of fossil fuels contributes the majority of GHGs to the atmosphere. One can read in for "energy" any other primary source of GHGs. The first term in the word equation is population. Other things remaining equal, larger populations will use more energy and therefore emit larger amounts of GHGs. The second term is GDP per capita, a measure of the domestic output of goods and services per capita. Increases in GDP are normally associated with economic growth. Neither of these first two factors can be considered likely candidates for reducing GHG emissions in the short run. Deliberate population control measures are a complex policy area that many countries do not want to pursue. Countries will be reluctant to reduce their rates of economic growth. In the long run, however, the interaction of these two factors will be important, as history seems to show that increases in income per capita are associated with lower population growth rates over time. This means that significant near-term GHG reductions will have to come from the last two terms in the expression. The third is what can be called **energy efficiency,** the amount of energy used per dollar (or per franc or rupee or peso) of output. The key here is to move toward technologies of production, distribution, and consumption that require relatively smaller quantities of energy. The objective is to **decouple** fossil fuel energy use from economic growth. The last term is GHGs produced per unit of energy used. Since different energy forms have markedly different GHG outputs per unit, reductions in GHG can be achieved by switching to less GHG-intensive fuells.

FIGURE 1-4   Decomposition of the Change in Total Global CO_2 Emissions from Fossil Fuel Combustion

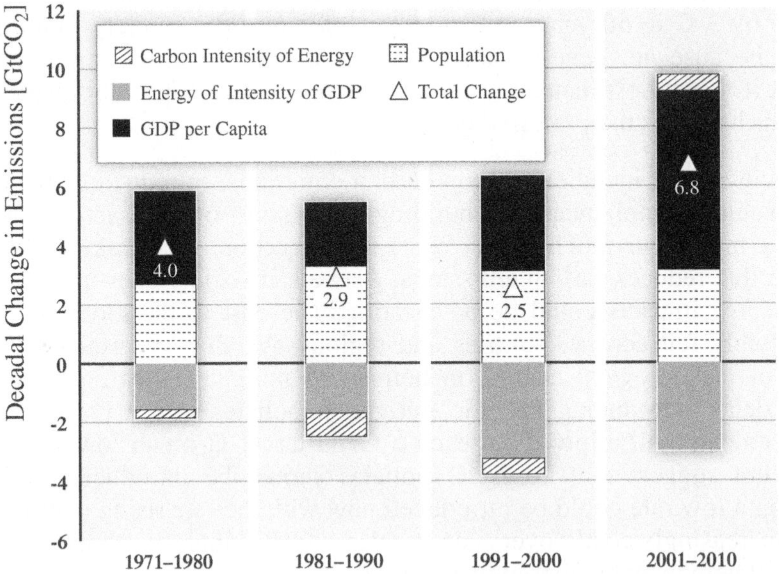

The absolute changes in total CO_2 emissions per decade can be decomposed into those arising from population growth (dotted box), GDP per capita (black), the energy intensity of GDP (gray), and carbon intensity of energy (crosshatch box). Total decadal changes in CO_2 emissions are indicated by a white triangle. Changes are measured in gigatonnes of CO_2 emissions per year (Gt/yr).

Source: IPCC, 2014: Climate Change 2014: Mitigation of Climate Change. Contribution of Working Group III to the Fifth Assessment Report of the Intergovernmental Panel on Climate Change, Figure TS.1; Figure TS.6. [Edenhofer, O., R. Pichs-Madruga, Y. Sokona, E. Farahani, S. Kadner, K. Seyboth, A. Adler, I. Baum, S. Brunner, P. Eickemeier, B. Kriemann, J. Savolainen, S. Schloemer, C. von Stechow, T. Zwickel, and J.C. Minx (eds.)]. Cambridge University Press, Cambridge, United Kingdom and New York, NY, USA.

Table 1-1 lists the major types of changes that could be made in different economic sectors to reduce GHG emissions. There is no single source that society could call on to get drastic reductions in CO_2 production. Instead, significant changes could be made in hundreds of different places—transportation, industry, households, and agriculture. These changes are both technical (as, for example, the switch to more energy-efficient equipment and low-CO_2 fuels) and behavioural (for example, changing driving habits and adopting less energy-intensive lifestyles). In Section 4, we develop economic models that show how regulation, taxes, markets, and other policies can be developed to mitigate GHGs and pollutants of air, water, and lands. Section 5 looks at what is being done in Canada to reduce emissions and improve environmental quality.

LO 6

SUSTAINABILITY OF OUR ENVIRONMENT AND ECONOMY

Basic Issues

The previous examples of smog and motor vehicle pollution and climate change resulting from GHG emissions illustrate the enormous impact human activity has on the natural environment. Environmental economists argue that it is vital to link closely the economy with the natural environment. While the natural environment has always been treated as an essential input into

TABLE 1-1   Means of Reducing Greenhouse Gases

Energy production
    Reduce demand for electricity (see Households),
    Switch to nonfossil fuels (solar, biomass, nuclear, hydroelectric),
    Switch from high-carbon (coal) to low-carbon (gas) fossil fuels,
    Reduce energy transmission losses,
    Remove carbon from fuel and emissions.

Households
    Reduce demand for energy (less heating air conditioning, etc.),
    Switch to less energy-intensive products,
    Switch to more energy-efficient technologies (solar heaters, insulation, etc.),
    Switch out of CFCs in car air conditioners.

Industry
    Increase energy efficiency of production processes,
    Switch to low- or no-carbon fuels,
    Increase energy efficiency in buildings, lighting, etc.,
    Switch out of CFCs and other greenhouse gases.

Transportation
    Reduce kilometres driven and travel speeds,
    Increase fuel efficiency of vehicles,
    Switch to mass transit systems.

Agriculture and food system
    Reduce methane production from livestock production and rice paddies,
    Improve energy efficiency in farming,
    Reduce CFC use in refrigeration,
    Reduce energy use in transportation,
    Increase land uses that lead to greater carbon storage.

Forestry
    Reduce rates of deforestation,
    Increase rates of reforestation.

Source: *U.S. Office of Technology Assessment*, Changing by Degrees, Steps to Reduce Greenhouse Gases (*Washington, D.C. 1991*).

production, few models looked explicitly at the interaction between ecological systems and the economy. The field of **ecological economics** examines these interactions more fully. An important objective of this field is to search for sustainable paths of economic development—actions that do not destroy ecological systems, but allow for increases in the well-being of people.[12] The essential idea is that a sustainable economy is one that has the ability to allow people's well-being to either rise over time or at least remain constant (i.e., not fall). To accomplish this, a number of economists argue that current generations cannot "use up" so much of the existing stocks of natural and environmental resources that future generations will be impoverished or non-existent. We must examine our economic activities with regard to the carrying capacity of our ecosystem.

[12.] See, for example, Peter Victor (2008), Herman Daly and Joshua Farley (2010), and Robert Costanza et al. (2011) in the selected references to this chapter.

All economies use natural and environmental resources to sustain life. Rising world population puts increasing pressure on our natural endowments all the time. Many fear that our current path of production and population growth is not sustainable. What can be done? One possible approach is to argue that each generation in a sustainable economy has the obligation to replace what it uses with investment in **social capital.** This is a very broad definition of "capital." It includes everything the economy can invest in—physical capital to produce goods and services, education, infrastructure, renewable and non-renewable natural resources, and, of course, the environment itself as a stock of capital. When we use up some of our existing capital, the only way the economy can be sustainable over time is to reinvest to keep the social capital stock at least constant. Pollution control and treatment is a means of keeping the environmental capital stock constant. So is recycling to some degree. Whether **sustainability** is achievable depends on the actions of people, industries, and governments. Some questions to contemplate: Will private markets keep the stock of social capital constant? Is government intervention necessary? If so, in what form?

Sustainability also depends on the degree of substitutability among natural capital (the environment and natural resources), produced capital, and labour. Technology and technological change is another vital element in the search for sustainable paths. Technology will influence the degree of substitution among factor inputs and affect the amount of inputs needed to produce a unit of output. Some technologies may promote sustainability, others not. Economists play important roles in helping to find answers to all these questions, by building models that explicitly incorporate the role of the natural environment and by examining these issues empirically. To recap,

a sustainable economy is one in which investment in social capital allows the economy to grow so that people are at least as well off in the future as they are in the present, while sustaining the health of ecological systems.

Trade-offs and Sustainability

Economists illustrate the trade-offs between output of goods and services and environmental quality by using a **production possibility frontier (PPF).** A PPF is a way of diagrammatically depicting the choice faced by a group of people between two desirable outcomes—output of goods and services and environmental quality. The basic relationship is shown in Figure 1-5. Suppose we are exploring the trade-offs that arise from our use of fossil fuels: the goods and services they produce in our current fossil fuel intensive economy versus the degradation to our ecosystem and economy from climate change. The vertical axis has an index of the *aggregate economic output* of our *high-carbon economy,* the total market value of conventional economic goods sold in the economy in a year. The horizontal axis has an index of *environmental quality,* derived from data on different dimensions of the ambient environment; for example, what the economy would look like if, for example, we had fewer GHG emissions and airborne pollutants. The curved relationship shows the different combinations of these two outcomes—a carbon-intensive economy or one with higher levels of environmental quality and fewer GHG and air contaminant emissions—that are available to a country given its endowment of resources with which to work. The PPF is shown with a dashed line from an environmental quality below *e*. Below *e*, the economy cannot produce any additional goods and services because there are too few environmental resources to sustain production. E_{MAX} shows the maximum amount of environmental quality if there is no goods production at all (presumably meaning no human population).

FIGURE 1-5   A Production Possibility Frontier (PPF) between a High-Carbon Economy and Environmental Quality

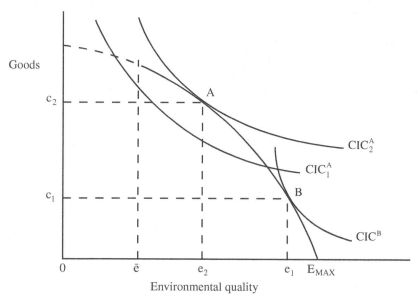

The PPF illustrates possible trade-offs between goods produced in a high-carbon economy and environmental quality. As society consumes more carbon-intensive goods, it gives up environmental quality. Below $\bar{e}$, no goods can be produced because environmental quality is too low to sustain production. Community indifference curves (CICs) indicate a country's choice of the mix of carbon-intensive goods and environmental quality. Country A chooses more goods/less environmental quality than country B.

The production possibility frontier is determined by the technical capacities in the economy together with the ecological facts—meteorology, hydrology, and so on—of the natural system in which the country is situated. It says, for example, that if the current level of economic output is c_1, we can obtain an increase to c_2 only at the cost of a decrease in environmental quality from e_1 to e_2. But while the PPF itself is a technical constraint, where a society chooses to locate itself on its PPF is a matter of *social choice.* And this depends on the relative values that people in that society place on conventional economic output and environmental quality. Economists illustrate social choices with a relationship called a social or **community indifference curve (CIC).** Community indifference curves are shown for country A on Figure 1-5. Each point on a CIC shows combinations of environmental quality and goods perceived by society to provide a given level of well-being. CICs that lie farther from the origin yield higher levels of well-being than those closer to the origin. Societies will seek the highest level of well-being that they can attain. This will be where the CIC is tangent to the PPF. For country A, this is CIC_2^A, tangent at point A, with e_2 environmental quality and c_2 goods. Another country might have a different set of social preferences that lead to choosing different bundles of environmental quality and goods; for example, at point B, with c_1 and e_1 being chosen. The choices made by society will affect the sustainability of the economy and environment.

The Environment and Growth: Sustainability over Time

Sustainability isn't just about choice in a given year, but what happens to the economy and environment over time. The PPF will not remain in the same place, as conditions such as production technology and environmental degradation change over time. We illustrate two possibilities. Figure 1-6

FIGURE 1-6   Possible PPFs in 50 Years: Two Scenarios

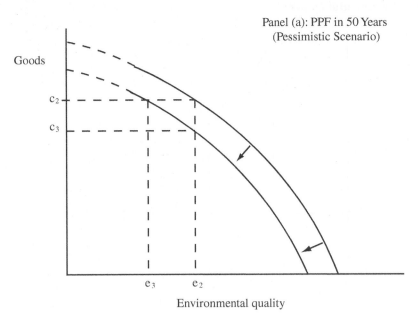

The PPF in panel (a) presents a pessimistic scenario, in which the PPF shifts inward due to environmental degradation. This means that the country can no longer consume at both c_2 and e_2; one must decline. Panel (b) is more optimistic. The PPF may shift out due to technological developments. Now consumption of goods and environmental quality can both rise over time.

shows the possible trade-offs facing society in 50 years. Panel (a) presents a pessimistic scenario. Suppose we continue on our current path of consuming large amounts of carbon-intensive fossil fuels to produce energy for our economy and we thereby deplete our natural capital in the form of a degraded air quality and climate change that reduces agricultural output, displaces human settlement, and requires other forms of adaptation to climate change. These outcomes may be the result of having chosen to be at point A on the PPF in Figure 1-5 in preceding years. As a result, the PPF for the year 2050 lies inside of the PPF today. Society, no matter where it chooses to locate, now must consume either fewer goods or have lower environmental quality than is possible today. If we try to keep production of goods at c_2, environmental quality falls to e_3. Alternatively, if environmental quality is to stay at e_2, it is possible to produce and consume only c_3 goods.

Panel (b) is more optimistic. Suppose we develop and adopt new technologies to produce substantial amounts of energy from sources that neither release GHGs nor damage other components of our natural environment. Our PPF for the present now shifts out to reflect the ability of society to produce more goods with a higher level of environmental quality. Notice that we have skewed the shape of the PPF to show that at c_2—the same level of goods society chose in the base year—we have e_4 environmental quality rather than e_2, because a non-polluting energy source was developed. Alternatively, at e_2, production at c_4 is possible. These cases illustrate that the future is not independent of the choices we make today.

Summary

The purpose of this chapter was to whet your appetite for the subject of environmental economics by indicating some of the main topics that the field encompasses, showing very briefly the approach that economists take in studying them. Our focus will be on microeconomic aspects of environmental economics—to see why externalities exist and persist and how to design and analyze economic policy instruments that can help improve the quality of our environment.

When we get involved in some of the conceptual and theoretical issues that underlie environmental economics, it is easy to lose sight of what we are trying to accomplish. We are trying to develop basic principles so that we can actually use them to address real-world problems such as air and water pollution. Although the principles may appear abstract and odd at first, remember the objective: to achieve a cleaner, healthier, and more beautiful natural environment that can be sustained over time.

Key Terms

Adaptation
Anthropogenic
Carbon sinks
Common property rights
Community indifference curve (CIC)
Decouple
Ecological economics
Economic efficiency
Efficiency
Energy efficiency
Equity

Externalities/external effects
Incentive
Marginal benefits
Marginal costs
Mitigation
Open access
Opportunity cost
Precautionary principle
Private costs
Private property rights

Production possibility frontier (PPF)

Property rights

Scarcity

Social capital

Socially efficient level of pollution

Sustainability

Trade-offs

Discussion Questions

1. "Annual testing of all motor vehicle emissions on the road is not a cost-effective policy." Do you agree with this statement? Explain why or why not.

2. Why would a tax on gasoline provide a larger incentive to reduce air emissions from motor vehicles than an annual tax on owning a vehicle?

3. The Canadian CAFC standards apply to new vehicles as they come off the assembly line. Provide two reasons why this might have a perverse effect on total emissions from motor vehicles. Explain your arguments.

4. Does Canada need a CAFC standard when the United States has a mandatory one? Discuss.

5. What factors influence the trade-offs illustrated in the production possibility frontier? How can environmental policy affect these trade-offs?

6. Suppose there is a technological change that allows firms to produce goods and services with less energy and hence fewer GHG emissions. Show graphically and explain how this will alter the PPF and a society's potential choice of where to locate on the PPF.

7. If produced capital is not readily substitutable for environmental capital (natural resources, air and water quality), how will this affect the trade-offs between economic growth and the environment?

For more information on the resources available from McGraw-Hill Ryerson, go to www.mheducation.ca/he/solutions.

Chapter 2

Natural Capital, Linkages between the Economy and the Environment, and Pollution

After reading this chapter you will be able to:

LO 1 ⟩ Describe the three components of natural capital and give specific examples of each type.

LO 2 ⟩ Explain the intertemporal tradeoffs with natural capital use.

LO 3 ⟩ Describe ways to reduce residuals from the economy.

LO 4 ⟩ Describe the different categories of pollution and contrast the degree of complexity in reducing emissions.

This chapter delves more deeply into the role of environmental economics in assessing how society can sustain its economy and environment. We introduce the concept of *natural capital* to help link the environment with the economy and to differentiate between environmental and natural resource economics. The chapter extends the concept of sustainability presented in Chapter 1 and defines terms used throughout the book. We conclude with observations about the state of Canada's natural capital.

LO 1 ⟩

NATURAL CAPITAL

Canada's **natural capital** is the stock of natural and environmental resources that sustain our ecosystems, economy, and well-being of our residents. Three components comprise natural capital:

1. Natural resource capital—stocks of renewable and nonrenewable resources (e.g., minerals and energy, forests, water, fisheries);
2. Ecosystems or environmental capital—systems that provide essential environmental goods and services such as our atmosphere and waste assimilation provided by forests, grass, and wetlands; and
3. Land.

The phrase *natural capital* has come be used by economists and environmentalists alike because it merges key elements from the economy and natural environment—'natural' to denote ecosystems and all their component parts and 'capital' to represent that nature also is:

- A store of value, like other forms of capital—human and physical—natural capital has huge intrinsic value. It sustains life, economic activity, and well-being.

- Capable of producing goods and services (food, motor vehicles, electricity, and more intangible goods such as well-being or quality of life) over time. While this is especially true of our sustainable resources—water, the atmosphere, land fertility, even resources that are depletable (minerals, fossil fuels) typically can be extracted over long periods of time. Natural capital provides inputs into everything we consume and enjoy on the planet.

- Depletable if there is not enough reinvestment in sustaining the capital stock. When human activity (or natural forces such as extreme weather events, earthquakes) run down the stock of natural capital and we don't invest in sustaining it, natural capital will decline and no longer be able to produce goods and services over time.

Sustaining our natural capital at a healthy level is essential to sustain our population and any economic system. Using natural capital to produce goods and services for people has three effects: (1) using natural capital inputs draws down the stock, producing valuable goods and services but for many forms of natural capital, leaving less to use tomorrow; (2) **residuals** or waste occur as by-products of use; and (3) these waste products may further degrade the quality and quantity of the remaining natural capital stocks. Figure 2-1 illustrates the connectedness of the environment and economy and will help highlight the focus of environmental economics versus that of natural resource economics.

FIGURE 2-1   A Circular Flow Relationship for the Environment and the Economy

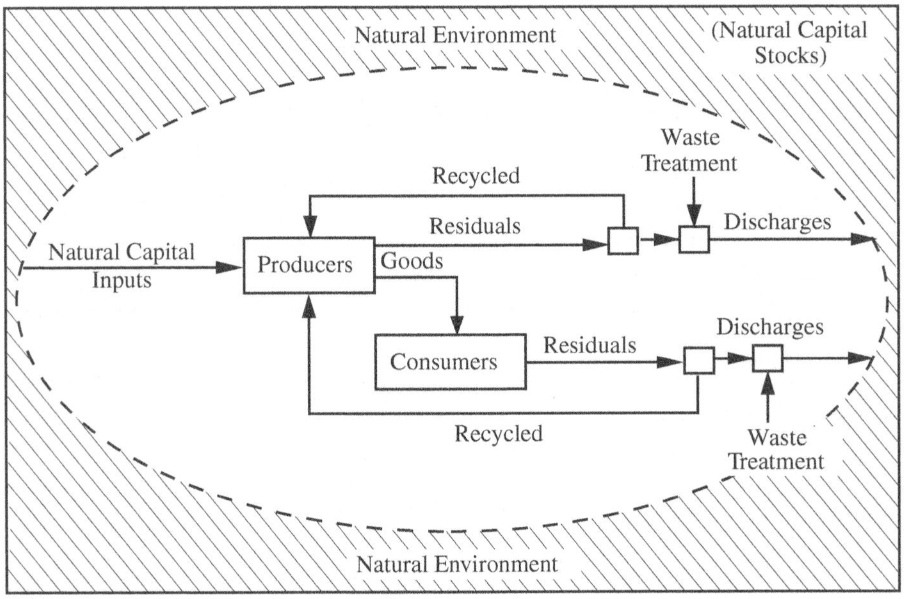

The natural environment provides natural capital inputs to the economic system. Production and consumption generate residuals that can be treated and recycled, but ultimately are discharged back to the natural environment. The residuals degrade the natural capital stock and without means of reinvestment or rejuvenation, will degrade and deplete the natural environment.

LO 2

NATURAL RESOURCE AND ENVIRONMENTAL ECONOMICS

Figure 2-1 shows the flow of natural capital inputs into the production of goods and services that are 'consumed' by people. The study of how to efficiently extract or harvest or use natural capital inputs over time is the primary subject of **natural resource economics.** The natural capital inputs come from stocks of **renewable** and **non-renewable resources.** The living resources, like fisheries and timber, are renewable; they grow over time according to biological processes. Harvesting from these resources can be sustainable over time. Some non-living resources are also renewable, the classic example being the sun's energy that reaches the earth and hydrological cycles. Non-renewable resources are those for which there are no processes of replenishment—once used, they are gone forever. Extraction is thus non-sustainable. Classic examples are fossil fuels such as petroleum and natural gas reservoirs and non-energy mineral deposits. Certain resources, such as many groundwater aquifers, have replenishment rates that are so low they are in effect non-renewable. Living resources such as fish and forests can also become non-renewable if harvests continually exceed the growth of the resource stock.

A resource that is vitally important to the survival of all species resides not in any one substance but in a collection of elements: **biological diversity** (or biodiversity). Biologists estimate that there may be as many as 30 million different species of living organisms in the world today. These represent a vast and important source of genetic information, useful for the development of medicines, natural pesticides, resistant varieties of plants and animals, and so on. Human activities have substantially increased the rate of species extinctions, so habitat conservation and species preservation have become important contemporary resource problems.

One of the distinguishing features of most natural resource issues is that they are heavily "time dependent." This means that their use is normally spread out over time, so rates of use in one period affect the amounts available for use in later periods. In the case of non-renewable resources this is relatively easy to see. How much petroleum should be pumped from a deposit this year, realizing that the more we pump now the less there will be available in future years? But these trade-offs between present and future also exist for many renewable resources. What should today's salmon harvesting rate be, considering that the size of the remaining stock will affect its availability in later years? Should we cut the timber this year, or is its growth rate high enough to justify waiting until some future year? These are issues with a strong **intertemporal** dimension; they involve trade-offs between today and the future. Certain environmental problems are also like this, especially when dealing with pollutants that accumulate, or pollutants that require a long time to dissipate. What is in fact being depleted here is the earth's **assimilative capacity,** the ability of the natural system to accept certain pollutants and render them benign or inoffensive. Some of the theoretical ideas about the depletion of natural resources are also useful in understanding environmental pollution. In this sense assimilative capacity is a natural resource akin to traditional resources such as oil deposits and forests.

Environmental economics examines the waste products or residuals from production and consumption and how to reduce or mitigate the flow of residuals so they have less damage on the natural environment and depletion of natural capital. In Figure 2-1, the arrows emanating from consumers and producers show possible pathways of residual flows. Production and consumption create all types of materials residuals that may be emitted into the air or water or disposed of on land. The list is incredibly long: sulphur dioxide, volatile organic compounds, toxic solvents, animal manure, pesticides, particulate matter of all types, waste building materials, heavy metals, and so on. Waste energy, in the form of heat and noise, and radioactivity, which has characteristics of both material and energy, are also important production residuals. Consumers are also responsible for enormous quantities of residuals, chief among which are domestic sewage and automobile emissions. All materials in consumer goods must eventually end up as residuals, even though some may be recycled along the way. These are the source of large quantities of solid waste, as well as hazardous materials like toxic chemicals found in items such as pesticides, batteries, paint, and used oil.

Environmental economics focuses on measures to reduce the flow of residuals and their impact on society and the natural environment, but it is not the only one. Humans have an impact on the environment in many ways that are not pollution-related in the traditional sense. Habitat disruption from housing developments or roads and pipelines, scenic degradation, and drainage of wetlands for agricultural production are examples of environmental impacts that are not related to the discharge of specific pollutants. Environmental economics looks for ways to change the way economic activity is done to reduce these damages to the environment and protect natural capital. Some courses combine the study of environmental and natural resource economics. Indeed, the two are part of the same big picture as illustrated in Figure 2-1. To go more deeply into the study of how society can reduce waste and help sustain the environment, this text focuses on models and analysis devoted to reducing pollution and environmental degradation.

LO 3

Reducing the Flow of Residual Wastes into the Environment

Recycling can obviously delay the disposal of residuals. But recycling can never be perfect; each cycle must lose some proportion of the recycled material. This shows us something very fundamental:

> *To reduce the mass of residuals disposed of in the natural environment, the quantity of natural capital inputs taken into the economic system must be reduced.*

There are essentially three ways of reducing the use of natural capital inputs and, therefore, residuals discharged into the natural environment:

- *Reduce the quantity of goods and services produced.* Some people argue that this is the best long-run answer to environmental degradation: reducing output, or at least stopping its rate of growth, would allow a similar change in the quantity of residuals discharged. Some have sought to reach this goal by advocating "zero population growth" (ZPG). A slowly growing or stationary population can make it easier to control environmental impacts, but does not in any way ensure this control, for two reasons. First, a stationary population can grow economically, thus increasing its demand for inputs from nature. Second, environmental impacts can be long run and cumulative, so that even a stationary population can gradually degrade the environment in which it finds itself. But it is certainly true that population growth will often exacerbate the environmental impacts of a particular economy. In the Canadian economy, for example, the emission of pollutants per car has dramatically decreased over the last few decades through better emissions-control technology. But the sheer growth in the number of cars on the highways has led to an increase in the total quantity of certain automobile emissions in many regions, most particularly large cities such as Toronto, Montreal, and Vancouver.

- *Reduce the residuals from production.* This means reducing residuals per unit of output produced. There are basically just two ways of doing this. We can invent and adopt new production technologies and practices that produce smaller amounts of residuals per unit of output produced. We can call this reducing the **residuals intensity of production.** When we discuss Canadian policy responses to GHG emissions and atmospheric warming, for example, we will see that there is much that could be done to reduce the CO_2 intensity of energy production, especially by shifting to different fuels but also by reducing energy inputs required to produce a dollar's worth of final output. This approach is also called **pollution prevention.**

The other way of reducing residuals from production is to shift the **composition of output.** Output consists of a large number of different goods and services, producing different amounts and types of residuals. So another way to reduce the total quantity of residuals is to shift the composition of production away from high-residuals items and toward low-residuals items, while leaving the total intact. The concept of a low-carbon economy is one where fewer fossil fuels are used as energy sources and consumers and producers increase the energy efficiency of their activities. Another example is to shift from primarily a manufacturing economy toward services. Most economies have experienced relatively fast rates of growth in their service sectors, especially in recent years. The rise of the information technology sectors is another example. It is not that these new sectors produce no significant residuals; indeed, some of them may produce harsher leftovers than we have known before. The computer industry, for example, uses a variety of chemical solvents for cleaning purposes. But on the whole these sectors probably have a smaller waste-disposal problem than the traditional industries they have replaced.

Consumers can influence these production decisions by demanding goods that are more environmentally friendly than others. An **environmentally friendly good** releases fewer or less harmful residuals into the environment than more **pollution-intensive goods.** Examples are liquid soaps without antibiotics added, thermometers that do not contain mercury, laundry detergents without phosphates, and energy-efficient appliances and vehicles.

• *Increase recycling.* Instead of discharging production and consumption residuals into the environment, we can recycle them back into the production process. The central role of recycling is to replace a portion of the original flow of inputs from nature. This can reduce the quantity of residuals discharged while maintaining the rate of output of goods and services. Recycling may offer opportunities to reduce waste flows for economies all over the world. But we have to remember that recycling can never be perfect, even if we were to devote enormous resources to the task. Production processes usually transform the physical structure of materials inputs, making them difficult to use again. The conversion of energy materials makes materials recovery impossible, and recycling processes themselves can create residuals. But materials research will continue to progress and discover new ways of recycling. For a long time, automobile tires could not be recycled because the original production process changed the physical structure of the rubber. Used tires are now being used as roadbed material for road construction, as garbage bins, and even to produce footwear. We no longer see vast stockpiles of used tires that used to blight Canadian landscapes and occasionally caused major environmental problems when they have ignited, such as several tire fires in Ontario in the late 1990s that spewed toxic compounds into the air for days.

These fundamental relationships are very important. Our ultimate goal is to

reduce the damages caused by the discharge of production and consumption residuals.

Reducing the total quantity of these residuals is one major way of doing this, and the relationships discussed indicate the basic ways that it may be done. But we can also reduce damages by working directly on the stream of residuals.

TERMINOLOGY

While all key terms are defined in the Glossary, the following are some of the common terms that will be used throughout the text.

- **Ambient quality:** "Ambient" refers to the surrounding environment, so ambient quality refers to the quantity of pollutants in the environment; for example, the concentration of SO_2 in the air over a city or the concentration of a particular chemical in the waters of a lake.

- **Environmental quality:** A term used to refer broadly to the state of the natural environment. This includes the notion of ambient quality, and also such things as the visual and aesthetic quality of the environment.

- **Residuals:** Material that is left over after something has been produced. A plant takes in a variety of raw materials and converts these into some product; materials and energy left after the product has been produced are *production residuals*. *Consumption residuals* are what is left over after consumers have finished using the products that contained or otherwise used these materials.

- **Emissions:** The portion of production or consumption residuals that are placed in the environment, sometimes directly, sometimes after treatment.

- **Recycling:** The process of returning some or all of the production or consumption residuals to be used again in production or consumption.

- **Pollutant:** A substance, energy form, or action that, when introduced into the natural environment, results in a lowering of the ambient quality level. We want to think of pollutants as including not only the traditional things, like oil spilled into oceans or chemicals placed in the air, but also activities, like certain building developments, that result in "visual pollution."

- **Effluent:** Sometimes the term "effluent" is used to describe water pollutants, and "emissions" to refer to air pollutants, but in this book these two words will be used interchangeably.

- **Pollution:** "Pollution" is actually a tricky word to define. Some people might say that pollution results when any amount, no matter how small, of a residual has been introduced into the environment. Others hold that pollution is something that happens only when the ambient quality of the environment has been degraded enough or its absorptive capacity exceeded enough to cause some damage. The word pollutant will be used to define a residual that degrades the natural environmental and can affect human health and the economy.

- **Damages:** The negative impacts produced by environmental pollution—on people in the form of health effects, visual degradation, and so on, and on elements of the ecosystem through things like the disruption of ecological linkages or species extinctions.

- **Environmental medium:** Broad dimensions of the natural world that collectively constitute the environment, usually classified as land, water, and air.

- **Source:** The location at which emissions occur, such as a factory, an automobile, or a leaking landfill.

LO 4

TYPES OF POLLUTANTS

Characteristics of residuals that become pollutants are important to acknowledge in the design of policies to reduce their generation and impact on the environment. A number of distinctions are made below that we use throughout the text.

Accumulative vs. Non-accumulative Pollutants

One simple and important dimension of environmental pollutants is whether they accumulate over time or tend to dissipate soon after being emitted. The classic case of **non-accumulative pollutants** is noise; as long as the source operates, noise is emitted into the surrounding air, but as soon as the source is shut down, the noise stops. At the other end of the spectrum we have **accumulative pollutants** that stay in the environment in nearly the same amounts as they are emitted. Their total stock thus builds up over time as these pollutants are released into the environment each year. Radioactive waste, for example, decays over time but at such a slow rate in relation to human lifespans that for all intents and purposes it will be with us permanently. Another accumulative pollutant is plastics. The search for a degradable plastic has been going on for decades and, while gains have been made, most plastics decay very slowly by human standards; thus, what we dispose of will be in the environment permanently. Many chemicals are cumulative pollutants: once emitted they are basically with us forever.

Between these two ends of the spectrum there are many types of effluent that are to some extent but not completely cumulative. The classic case is organic matter emitted into water bodies; for example, the wastes, treated or not, emitted from municipal waste treatment plants. Once emitted the wastes are subject to natural chemical processes that tend to break down the organic materials into their constituent elements, thus rendering them much more benign. The water, in other words, has a natural assimilative capacity that allows it to accept organic substances and render them less harmful. If the assimilative capacity is exceeded, organisms will start to perish, but once the flow of the effluent is reduced to non-toxic levels the water quality will improve again. Of course, the fact that nature has some assimilative capacity doesn't automatically mean that we have a strictly non-accumulative pollutant. Once our emissions exceed the assimilative capacity we would move into an accumulative process. For example, the atmosphere of the earth has a given capacity to absorb CO_2 emitted by human and non-human activity, as long as this capacity is not exceeded. CO_2 is a non-accumulative pollutant. But if the earth's assimilative capacity for CO_2 is exceeded, as it seems to be at the present time, we are in a situation where emissions are in fact accumulating over time.

Whether a pollutant is accumulative or non-accumulative, we still have essentially the same basic problem: trying to figure out the environmental damages and relating these back to the costs of reducing emissions. But this job is much more difficult for accumulative than for non-accumulative pollutants. Consider the graphs in Figure 2-2. Panel (a) represents a non-accumulative pollutant, while panel (b) depicts one that is accumulative. In panel (a) the graph begins at the origin, implying that current ambient concentrations are proportional to current emissions. Ambient concentrations are strictly a function of current emissions—reducing these emissions to zero would lead to zero ambient concentrations. But with accumulative pollutants the relationship is more complex. Today's emissions, since they accumulate and add to the stock of pollutants already existing, will cause damages both today and into the future, perhaps into the distant future. It also means that the current ambient quantity of an accumulating pollutant may be only weakly related to current emissions. The graph in panel (b) begins well up the vertical axis from the origin and has a flatter slope than the other. Thus, a cutback in today's emissions has only a modest effect on current ambient concentrations. Even if today's emissions were cut to zero, ambient quality would still be impaired because of the cumulative effect of past emissions. The fact that a pollutant accumulates over time in the environment has the effect of breaking the direct connection between current emissions and current damages. This has a number of implications. For one thing, it makes the science more difficult. The cause-and-effect relationships become harder to isolate when there is a lot of time intervening between them. It also may make it more difficult to get people to focus on damages from today's emissions, again because there may be only a weak connection between today's emissions and today's ambient quality levels. Furthermore, accumulative pollutants by definition lead to future damages, and human beings have shown a depressing readiness to discount future events and avoid coming to grips with them in the present.

FIGURE 2-2   Possible Relationships between Current Emissions and Ambient Pollution Concentration

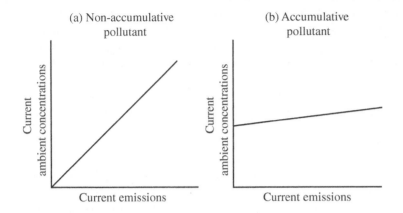

Panel (a) shows a non-accumulative pollutant where damages are proportional to current emissions. Panel (b) illustrates an accumulative pollutant where damages are dependent on the total stock of pollutant that has been released over time. The positive intercept of the curve shows that there will always be some damage even if emissions are reduced to zero.

Local vs. Regional and Global Pollutants

Some emissions have an impact only in restricted, localized regions, while others have an impact over wider regions, perhaps on the global environment. Noise pollution and the degradation of the visual environment are local in their impacts; the damages from any particular source are usually limited to relatively small groups of people in a circumscribed region. Note that this is a statement about how widespread the effects are from any particular pollution source, not about how important the overall problem is throughout a country or the world. Some pollutants, on the other hand, have widespread impacts, over a large region or perhaps over the global environment. Acid rain is a regional problem; emissions in one region of the United States affect people in Canada and other regions of the United States. The ozone-depleting effects of chlorofluorocarbon emissions from various countries work through chemical changes in the earth's stratosphere, which means that the impacts are truly global.

Other things being equal, local environmental problems ought to be easier to deal with than regional or national problems, which in turn ought to be easier to manage than global problems. If a person smokes out the neighbours with a wood stove, we may be able to arrange a solution among ourselves, or we can call on local political institutions to do it. But if that person's behaviour causes more distant pollution, solutions may be more difficult. If we are within the same political system, we can call on these institutions to arrange solutions. In recent years, however, we have been encountering a growing number of international and global environmental issues. Here we are far from having effective means of responding, both because the exact nature of the physical impacts is difficult to describe and because the requisite international political institutions are only beginning to appear and the number of players can be quite large, making agreement very difficult.

Point Source vs. Nonpoint-Source Pollutants

Pollution sources differ in terms of the ease with which actual points of discharge may be identified. The points at which sulphur dioxide emissions leave a large power plant are easy to identify; they come out the tops of the smokestacks associated with each plant. Municipal waste treatment plants normally have a single outfall from which all of the wastewater is emitted. These are called **point-source pollutants.** On the other hand, there are many pollutants for which there are no well-defined points of discharge. Agricultural chemicals, for example, usually run off the land in a dispersed or diffused pattern, and even though they may pollute specific streams or underground aquifers, there is no single pipe or stack from which these chemicals are emitted. This is an example of **nonpoint-source pollutants.** Urban stormwater runoff is an important nonpoint-source problem.

As one would expect, point-source pollutants are likely to be easier to come to grips with than nonpoint-source pollutants. They will probably be easier to measure and monitor and easier to study in terms of the connections between emissions and impacts. This means that it will ordinarily be easier to develop and administer control policies for point-source pollutants. As we will see, not all pollutants fit neatly into one or another of these categories.

Continuous vs. Episodic Emissions

Emissions from coal-fired electric power plants or municipal waste treatment plants are more or less continuous. The plants are designed to be in operation continuously, though the operating rate may vary somewhat over the day, week, or season. Thus the emissions from these operations are more or less continuous, and the policy problem is to manage the rate of these discharges. We can make immediate comparisons between control programs and rates of emissions. The fact that emissions are continuous does not mean that damages are also continuous, however. Meteorological and hydrological events can turn continuous emissions into uncertain damages. But control programs are often easier to carry out when emissions are not subject to large-scale fluctuations.

Many pollutants are emitted on an episodic basis. The classic example is accidental oil or chemical spills. The policy problem here is to design and manage a system so that the *probability* of accidental discharges is reduced. But with an episodic effluent there may be nothing to measure, at least in the short run. Even though there have been no large-scale radiation releases from Canadian nuclear power plants, for example, we could still have a "pollution" problem if they are being managed in such a way as to increase the probability of an accidental release in the future. To measure the probabilities of episodic emissions we have to have data on actual occurrences over a long time period, or we have to estimate them from engineering data and similar information. We then have to determine how much insurance we wish to have against these episodic events and how to design policies that minimize the risks of an accidental spill.

Table 2-1 provides a list of the major pollutants in Canada, whether they are **spatially differentiated** or **uniformly mixed**, the major sources of emissions, and probable environmental impacts. Section 5 of the text looks at these pollutants in more detail and examines the types of policies being used in Canada to address these environmental problems.

Environmental Damages Not Related to Emissions

So far the discussion has focused on the characteristics of different types of environmental pollutants as they relate to the discharge of residual materials or energy. But there are many important instances of deteriorating environmental quality that are not traceable to residuals discharges. The conversion of land to housing and commercial areas destroys the environmental value of that land, whether this is its ecosystem value, such as habitat or wetland, or its scenic value. Other land uses, such as logging or strip mining, can also have important impacts. In cases like these, our job is still to understand the incentives of people whose decisions create these impacts, and to change these incentives when appropriate. Although there are no physical emissions to monitor and control, there are nevertheless outcomes that can be described, evaluated, and managed with appropriate policies.

TABLE 2-1   Major Pollutants in Canada

Pollutant	Type	Major Sources	Probable Environmental Impacts
Suspended particulate matter (PM)	SD, N	FF combustion Burning organic material (e.g., garbage, wood waste)	Cardiopulmonary conditions Materials damages/soilling
Sulphur dioxide (SO_2)	SD, N	FF combustion	Cardiopulmonary conditions Eye irritations Contributes to acid rain Agricultural/forest damage Acidification of water/soils Materials damage
Nitrogen oxides (NOx)	SD, N	FF combustion Production processes	Cardiopulmonary conditions Agricultural/forest damage Contributes to smog
Hydrocarbons including VOCs (volatile organic compounds), benzene	SD, N	FF combustion Natural sources (forests) Production processes (e.g., paint, dry cleaning)	Contributes to smog Cardiopulmonary conditions Agricultural/forest damage Carcinogens, neurotoxins Corresive agents materials damage
Ground-level ozone (O_3)	SD, N	Formed from NOx + VOC in sunlight	Smog Cardiopulmonary conditions Eye irritations Suppresses immune functions Agricultural/forest damage
Carbon monoxide (CO)	SD, N	FF combustion	Cardiopulmonary conditions Lethal at high doses Contributes to smog Contributes to stratospheric ozone depletion
Carbon dioxide (CO_2)	UM, N	FF combustion Organic decomposition Respiration	Global climate change
Phosphates, nitrates	SD, A	Detergents, fertilizers	Eutrophication of lakes Damage to aquatic life Contamination of water supplies
Toxic compounds: examples include metals such as mercury, lead, cadmium, PCBs, dioxins/furans, pesticides, herbicides, and many more	SD, A	Industrial processes Mining and smelting Consumer products (e.g., mercury in dental use) Agriculture Pulp & paper production	Carcinogens Neurotoxins Reproductive failure, mutations Suppresses immune functions Eye irritants Widespread ecosystem impacts Agricultural/forest damage Contamination of water supplies
Chlorofluorocarbons (CFCs)	UM, A	Refrigerants, aeroscles (use banned in Canada)	Destruction of the stratospheric ozone layer protecting earth from ultraviolet radiation
Pathogens (bacteria, viruses, parasites)	SD, N	Human and animal waste	Contamination of water supplies and food, gastrointestinal diseases (and death), other diseases of humans, animals

Notes:

SD stands for a spatially differentiated pollutant   *UM* stands for a uniformly mixed pollutant   *N* stands for a non-accumulative pollutant

A stands for an accumulative pollutant   *FF* stands for fossil fuels

AN INTERNATIONAL COMPARISION OF AIR POLLUTION EMISSIONS

We conclude this chapter first with a brief look at Canada's **emissions** of air pollutants compared to other countries and turn next to several time trends of indicators of **ambient environmental quality** for Canada. To enable comparisons across countries with very different levels of population and economic activity as measured by gross domestic product (GDP), we show the comparisons per unit GDP and per capita. **Emissions intensity of pollution** is the term often given to emissions per unit GDP. Figures 2-3 and 2-4 provide data for greenhouse gas (GHG) emissions in a number of countries

FIGURE 2-3   Greenhouse Gas Emissions per Unit GDP for Years: 1990, 2000, 2012

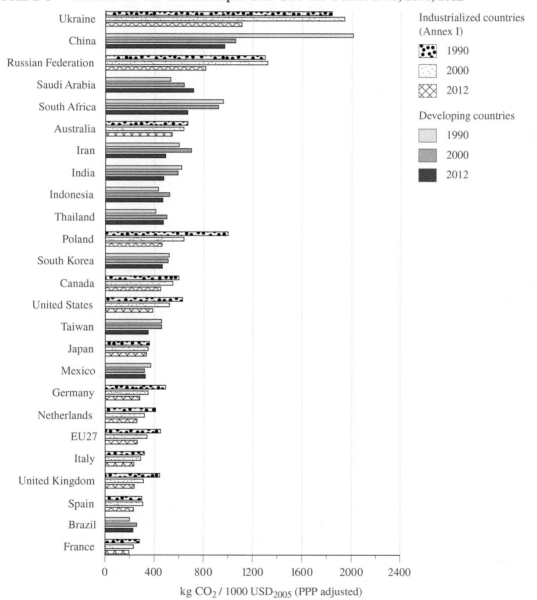

Source: *Figure 2.5 from PBL Netherlands Environmental Assessment Agency, Trends in Global CO$_2$ Emissions: 2013 Report,* The Hague (2013).

FIGURE 2-4 CO_2 **Emissions from Fossil-Fuel Combustion and Cement per Person, 1990, 2000, 2012**

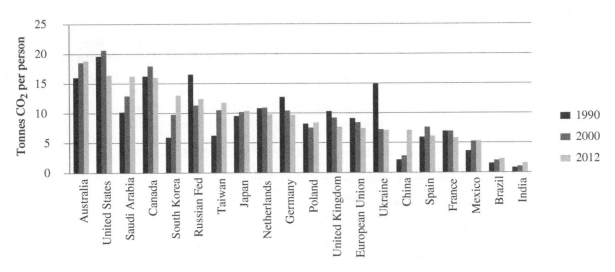

Source: *Data from PBL Netherlands Environmental Assessment Agency. Trends in Global CO_2 Emissions: 2013 Report,* The Hague (2013).

in 1990, 2000, and 2012, while Figures 2-5 and 2-6 illustrate 2010 levels of sulphur dioxide (SO_2) and nitrogen oxides (NO_x) in Canada, the U.S., Europe, and parts of Asia.These pollutants come from both point and nonpoint sources. Key point sources are industries that burn fossil fuels, especially oil and coal. Data for GHGs are from fossil fuel combustion and cement production. The major nonpoint source is motor vehicles. Canada is a major producer of GHG and air contaminants because of the fossil fuel intensity of our economy. Extraction of bitumen from Canada's oil sands has grown substantially in recent years and is one of the factors responsible for our high emissions levels relative to other developed economies. Alberta, Saskatchewan, some parts of the Atlantic provinces, and until recently, Ontario, generate much of their electricity by burning coal. Refer back to Figures 1-3 and 1-4 for the sources of GHGs and the shares attributed to population growth, output, and energy intensity. Figure 2-3 shows that Canada's emissions intensity is lower than in many countries. This is because the most emission intensive economies are the rapidly developing nations who have seen significant industrial growth and burn coal for heating and to produce electricity. Canada is second only to Australia in 2012 emissions intensity among the developed economies. Canada's emissions per capita are among the highest of the countries shown as illustrated in Figure 2-4. Chapter 20 provides the policy context for our GHG emissions.

Figures 2-5 and 2-6 show that Canada's emission intensity and per capita levels for SO_2 and NO_x are more than twice the OECD average, and it ranks in the top three worst performers among the countries illustrated.

Particulate matter, as noted in Table 2-1 is capable of penetrating deep into one's respiratory tract and causing severe health problems. The smaller the particles, the more damaging are the emissions. International comparisons are difficult to obtain, but Figure 2-7 shows data for particulate matter at the 10 micron level (PM10) for a sample of countries. The data are a weighted aggregate for cities with 100,000 people or more and represent the average annual exposure level of an urban resident to outdoor particulate matter. The state of a country's technology and pollution controls is an important determinant of particulate matter concentrations as we will explore in later chapters. Canada's emissions are among those at the lower end for this group of countries. That reflects factors such as

FIGURE 2-5   Sulphur Dioxide and Nitrogen Oxide Emissions per unit GDP, 2010

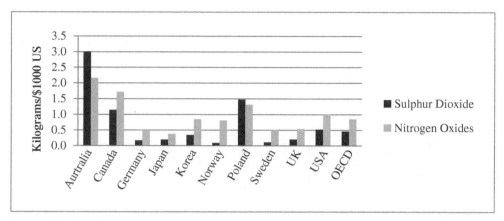

Source: *OECD (2013), Environment at a Glance 2013: OECD Indicators, OECD Publishing.*
http://dx.doi.org/10.1787/9789264185715-en.

FIGURE 2-6   Sulphur Dioxide and Nitrogen Oxide Emissions per Capita, 2010

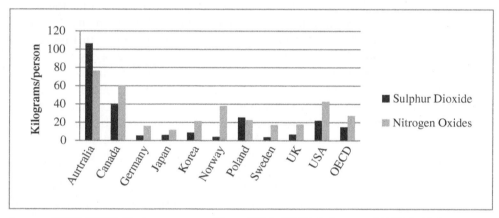

Source: *OECD (2013), Environment at a Glance 2013: OECD Indicators, OECD Publishing.*
http://dx.doi.org/10.1787/9789264185715-en.

the use of hydroelectricity, a relatively modern fleet of motor vehicles, and emissions controls on industrial sources. While comparable data for countries such as India and China are not available, given their rate of coal combustion and rapid industrialization, we expect them to have very high emission levels of particulate matter, as evidenced by their poor air quality at many times of the year.

ENVIRONMENTAL QUALITY INDICATORS IN CANADA

Emission data tell us the total amount of a pollutant released into the environment, but as defined above, ambient levels give the concentration of the pollutant at a point in time and location. Air quality monitoring stations exist across Canada and Environment Canada reports air quality in Canada's major urban areas (see www.ec.gc.ca/mspa-naps and follow the links). Average ambient levels across the country are also reported. While these can show a trend over time, they don't tell the whole story. Some regions may experience significantly improved air quality while others see a

FIGURE 2-7 2010 National Levels of Fine Particulate Matter

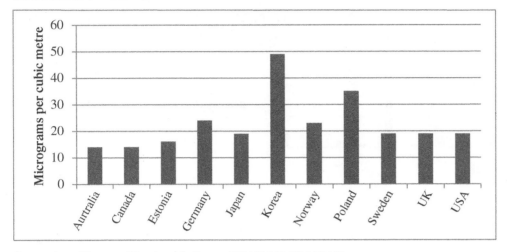

Source: *http://data.worldbank.org/indicator/EN.ATM.PM10.MC.M3.*

decline. The picture for sulphur dioxide is thus a bit of a puzzle. Figure 2-8 shows that there is a general decrease in the average annual concentration of SO_2 in Canada. Why then are Canada's emissions per GDP and per capita among the highest in the comparison group shown in Figures 2-5 and 2-6? Because a large share of Canada's SO_2 emissions comes from industrial activity and energy production, they are not necessarily affecting the air quality where large populations live. As well, averaging will blend areas of very good air quality with areas that are not so good. If people live near a petroleum refinery or where natural gas is flared, the ambient concentration of SO_2 will be much higher than if they live in an urban setting with very little industry (e.g., Vancouver). A big improvement in average ambient air quality occurred in Eastern Canada when the U.S. and Canada introduced policies to control emissions from coal-fired electric power stations, a topic we return to in Chapter 17.

A different story emerges for ambient concentrations of particulate matter over the period 2000–2011, as shown in Figure 2-9. Two measures are provided: average annual concentration and the peak concentrations. The current guidelines are also shown: annually and the 24-hour maximum. The data show that there has been very little change over the 12 years in average annual concentrations and volatility in the 24-hour peak levels. Two points emerge. First, the time periods chosen to track ambient quality can be important. Data from Environment Canada's surveillance network shows over a 50 percent decline in total particulate matter from 1970 to 2008, but as Figure 2-9 illustrates, the more recent data does not indicate a continuing downward trend. Second, it is important to measure not just an annual average concentration but what happens throughout the day (or other period of time that is pertinent to environmental quality). Very high levels of emissions can occur and may impact the health of ecosystems and their inhabitants. Chapter 17 examines federal and provincial air quality policies in detail.

There is no national indicator of water quality in Canada. Water quality is sampled in specific rivers, groundwater, and lakes and streams across the country. Water is monitored for fecal coliform (bacteria responsible for gastronomic illnesses), various parasites and viruses, toxic compounds, and compounds that contribute to excessive growth of algae (e.g., nitrogen and phosphorus). Excessive algae growth in surface waters is called *eutrophication*. Large concentrations of algae will use up the oxygen supply, making it difficult for aquatic animals to survive.

FIGURE 2-8   Sulphur Dioxide Concentrations, Canada, 1997 to 2011

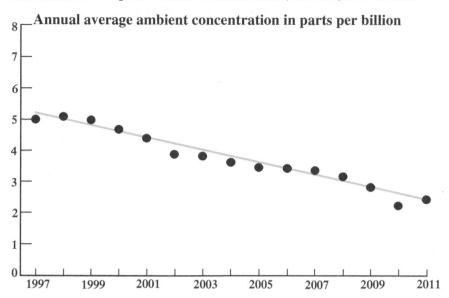

Source: © *Her Majesty The Queen in Right of Canada, Environment Canada, 2014. Reproduced with the permission of the Minister of Public Works and Government Services Canada.*

FIGURE 2-9   Fine Particulate Matter Concentrations, Canada, 2000 to 2011

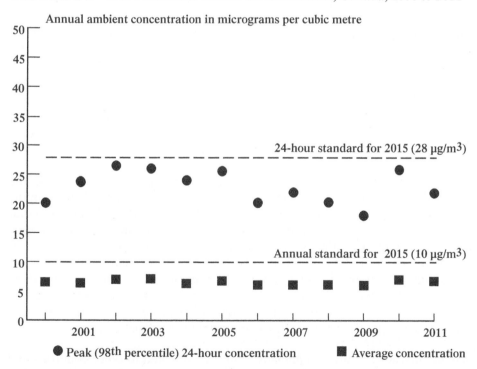

Source: © *Her Majesty The Queen in Right of Canada, Environment Canada, 2014. Reproduced with the permission of the Minister of Public Works and Government Services Canada.*

Figure 2-10 shows the percentage of sites across Canada that had poor to excellent water quality over two time periods: 2005 to 2007 and 2008 to 2010. There is good and bad news illustrated by the data. The good news is there was a drop in the percentage (and number) of sites with poor water quality and increase in those with good. The not-so-good news is there has been no significant change in the number of sites deemed marginal or fair. We would want to see a decline in the number of sites deemed marginal and more sites deemed fair to good. The number of excellent sites also declined in both percentage and number, a trend that warrants investigation. Chapter 16 provides an overview of water quality policies in Canada.

FIGURE 2-10   **National Freshwater Quality Indicator for 2005–2007 and 2008–2010**

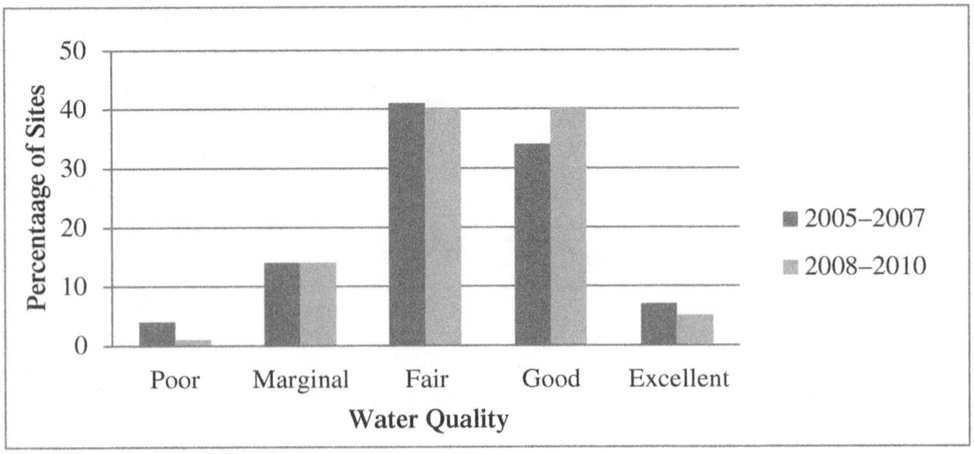

Water quality was assessed using the Canadian Council of Ministers of the Environment's Water Quality Index. The chart uses the data on number of sites for each category and converts them to a percentage of the total sites reported. The chart is based on data from 153 sites in 2005 to 2007 and 195 sites in 2008 to 2010.

Source: © *Her Majesty The Queen in Right of Canada, Environment Canada, 2014. Reproduced with the permission of the Minister of Public Works and Government Services Canada.*

Summary

The purpose of this chapter was to explore some basic linkages between the economy and the environment. We explained the role of the natural environment's natural capital that provides inputs that sustain life on the planet and economic production of goods and services and provided a circular flow framework to help illustrate the focus of environmental economics versus natural resource economics. Production and consumption activities produce residuals or wastes that if not recycled or treated to make them more benign will degrade or destroy the stocks of natural capital. The environment and economy will not be sustainable unless efforts are made to increase recycling, reduce the usage of natural capital inputs by making production and consumption more efficient (use less material throughput), or by reducing output. We provided a brief catalogue of the different types of emissions and pollutants, as well as non-pollution types of environmental impacts such as aesthetic effects.

Finally, we had a brief look at emissions of air pollutants in Canada compared to other countries and several of Canada's ambient quality indicators. We see that there are many areas for concern that we explore more fully in Section 5.

Key Terms

Accumulative pollutants	Non-accumulative pollutants
Ambient quality	Nonpoint-source pollutants
Assimilative capacity	Non-renewable resource
Biological diversity	Point-source pollutants
Composition of output	Pollutant
Damages	Pollution
Effluent	Pollution-intensive goods
Emissions	Pollution prevention
Emissions intensity of pollution	Recycling
Environmental economics	Renewable resource
Environmental medium	Residuals
Environmental quality	Residuals intensity of production
Environmentally friendly good	Source (of pollution)
Intertemporal	Spatially differentiated
Natural capital	Uniformly mixed
Natural resource economics	

Discussion Questions

1. How does population growth affect the balance of flows shown in Figure 2-1?

2. If all goods could be changed overnight so that they lasted twice as long as before, how would this change the flows shown in Figure 2-1 in the short and long runs?

3. A given quantity of a residual discharged at one time and place can be a pollutant; if it is discharged at another time or place it may not constitute a pollutant. Why is this true?

4. Why are long-lived, cumulative pollutants so much harder to manage than short-lived, non-accumulative pollutants?

5. Suppose we observe that emissions of a pollutant have decreased, but that environmental quality has not increased. What might be the explanation?

6. Consider all the items you discard each week in your household garbage. How many that are currently being thrown out could be recycled or reused? How many are toxic compounds that might have more environmentally benign substitutes? What would it take to make you change your consumption habits to reduce the disposal of these products?

7. Canada "imports" some of its air pollution from the United States. For example, sulphur dioxide emissions from coal-burning electricity generating plants in the eastern U.S. flow into eastern Canada. What has been happening to U.S. emissions of SO_2 over time? You can find out by using the website of the U.S. Environmental Protection Agency: www.epa.gov.

8. Consult the Web pages of the ministry responsible for the environment in your province. See what sort of environmental indicators they report and see how environmental quality has been changing over time.

For more information on the resources available from McGraw-Hill Ryerson, go to www.mheducation.ca/he/solutions.

Section **Two**

Analytical Tools

This section covers some of the basic ideas of economics and their application to environmental matters. Those of you who have already been introduced to microeconomics can treat the next few chapters as a review. For those who are seeing this material for the first time, the purpose is to develop a set of analytical tools that can be used to focus on issues of environmental quality.

Chapter 3

Benefits and Costs, Supply and Demand

After reading this chapter you will be able to:

LO 1 Derive the demand curve for an individual from their willingness to pay and show how to aggregate to a market demand curve.

LO 2 Derive the supply curve for a firm and show how to aggregate to the market supply curve.

LO 3 Illustrate the impact of technological progress on marginal cost curves.

This and the next chapter contain discussions of the basic tools of **microeconomics** that we use in analyzing environmental impacts and policies. A key aspect of an economic approach to decision making is the evaluation of the benefits and costs of any action. Economic actions, including environmental actions, have two sides or trade-offs: on the one side they create value, and on the other side they encounter costs. We have to measure these costs and benefits and then evaluate the trade-offs that occur from every action. We look first at the question of value, later at costs. This chapter examines private goods sold in markets that do not exhibit externalities. Starting with this simple framework introduces key concepts that will be used in subsequent chapters.

LO 1

WILLINGNESS TO PAY

A fundamental notion in economics is that individuals have preferences for goods and services; given a choice they can express preferences for one good over another, or one bundle of goods over another bundle. In a modern economy there are thousands of different goods and services available, so let us focus on just one of them—let's say, organic apples. The value of this good to a person is what they are willing and able to sacrifice for it. Sacrifice what? It could be anything they have to give up to get the good, but it makes sense to talk about sacrificing generalized purchasing power. Thus, the value of a good to somebody is what they are willing to pay for it.

What determines how much a person is willing to pay to obtain some good or service, or some environmental asset? It's partly a question of individual values. Some people are willing to sacrifice a lot to visit the Canadian Rockies, others are not. Some people are willing to pay a lot for a quiet living environment, others are not. Some people place a high value on trying to preserve the habitats of unique animal and plant species, others do not. It is obvious also that a person's wealth affects their willingness to sacrifice; the more wealthy a person is, the better they can afford to pay for various goods and services. **Willingness to pay (WTP),** in other words, also reflects ability to pay.

EXAMPLE

Willingness to pay for organic apples—a practical experiment

Economists can infer WTP from people's behaviour when buying goods and services. Suppose you could sit in a grocery store and interview people in the fruit and vegetable section. You select a customer who is buying some organic apples and ask the person a series of questions:

1. Do you have any apples with you or at home? (Assume their answer is none.)

2. How much are you willing to pay for a kilogram of apples rather than go without? (Suppose the customer answers $4.50.[1])

3. You've now bought the first kilogram; how much are you willing to pay for a second unit?

4. How much are you willing to pay for additional kilograms of apples? (Continue asking the question until the answer is zero.)

Figure 3-1 tabulates and graphs the data.

FIGURE 3-1   Tabulation of Data on Willingness to Pay for Organic Apples

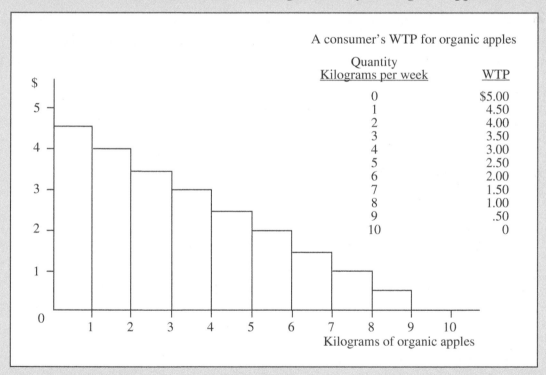

A consumer's WTP for organic apples

Quantity Kilograms per week	WTP
0	$5.00
1	4.50
2	4.00
3	3.50
4	3.00
5	2.50
6	2.00
7	1.50
8	1.00
9	.50
10	0

WTP data from $0 to $5 are shown on the left-hand side of the figure. WTP data are graphed as the height of the rectangles for each additional kilogram purchased. WTP declines as the number of units consumed increases.

---

[1] Each item has, of course, a posted price per unit. The consumer knows this price. What the interviewer is asking the person is to contemplate paying different prices per unit purchased. This sort of exchange occurs in markets where the buyer and seller bargain over a price and quantity.

The numbers in the example depict a fundamental relationship of economics: the notion of diminishing WTP.

> *As the number of units consumed increases, the WTP for additional units of that good normally declines.*

It is not very convenient to work with diagrams that are stepped-shaped, as in Figure 3-1. If we now assume that people can consume fractions of items in addition to integer values, a smoothly shaped willingness-to-pay curve, like the one pictured in Figure 3-2, is obtained. On this smooth function we have singled out one quantity for illustrative purposes. It shows that at a quantity of four units, the willingness to pay for one more unit (the fourth) is $3 per kilogram. How much is the person's WTP for eight units? Answer: $1 per kilogram.

A very important distinction is between **total willingness to pay** and **marginal willingness to pay,** since this is something we will be running into constantly in later chapters. Suppose a person is already consuming two kilograms of apples; according to the WTP curve, he would be willing to pay $3.50 for a third kilogram. This is the marginal willingness to pay, in this case, for the third kilogram.

> *Marginal WTP describes the additional willingness to pay of a person for one more unit of a good or service.*

The marginal willingness to pay for apples is shown as the height of the rectangles in Figure 3-1, or the height of the curve in Figure 3-2 for any quantity of apples chosen.

FIGURE 3-2   Willingness to Pay as a Smooth Function

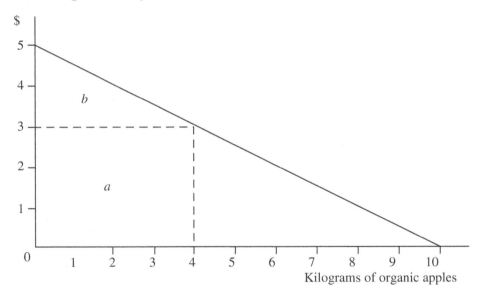

WTP data from Figure 3-1 are converted to a smooth linear function by allowing the consumer to buy fractions of units. Total WTP is also shown for 4 kilograms of apples. It is the sum of areas *a* plus *b*.

> *Total WTP for a given consumption level refers to the total amount a person would be willing to pay to attain that consumption level rather than go without the good entirely.*

Total WTP is measured as the area under the WTP schedule from zero to the amount to be consumed. The example shows how total WTP is calculated.

EXAMPLE
Computing total WTP for organic apples

Assume the person is consuming four kilograms of apples per week (that's a lot of apples!).

Calculate total WTP from the bar graph in Figure 3-1. Total WTP is the sum of the heights of the rectangles between the origin and 4 kilograms.

> The sum is $4.50 + $4.00 + $3.50 + $3.00 = $15.00.

Calculate total WTP in the smooth version of the willingness-to-pay function of Figure 3-2. Total WTP is the whole area under the willingness-to-pay curve from the origin up to 4 kilograms.

Use simple geometry for the calculation. Total WTP for 4 kilograms is area *a* plus area *b*.

> Area *a* is a rectangle with height equal to $3 and length equal to 4: $3 times 4 = $12.

> Area *b* is a triangle with height equal to $2 ($5 – $3) and base equal to 4 (4 – 0). The value of area *b* is [½ ($2 times $4)] = $4.

> Area *a* + *b* = $16 = total WTP.

A question: Why are areas *a* plus *b* in Figure 3-2 a bit larger than the total WTP calculated under the bar graph in Figure 3-1? The answer is that the bar graph is an approximation of the smooth curve. Using integers and not the entire curve underestimates the total WTP. We will therefore proceed using a smooth curve.

Demand

There is another way of looking at these marginal WTP relationships. They are more familiarly known as **demand curves.** An individual demand curve shows the quantity of a good or service that the individual in question would demand (i.e., purchase and consume) at any particular price. The data from the figure can help provide an algebraic relationship for the demand curve. Quantity demanded declines as the price of apples rises. Let Q^D be the quantity demanded, α be the intercept, and β the slope of the equation. Then, the general functional relationship for a linear demand curve is:

$$Q^D = \alpha - \beta P$$

The intercept can be found from Figure 3-1 or 3-2 by finding the price at which quantity demanded goes to zero. Let $Q^D = 0$ *and rearrange to solve for P.* The price is $5, which thus equals α/β. The slope of this equation is the change in quantity demanded divided by the change in price. Looking at the data in Figure 3-1, we see that for each unit increase in quantity the price drops by 50 cents. Our slope (β) is therefore –2. The apple demand function is therefore $Q^D = 10 - 2P$. However, the apple demand curve as conventionally graphed in economics (the smooth curve in Figure 3-2) has price on the vertical axis and quantity demanded on the horizontal. This means that we solve $Q^D = \alpha - \beta P$ in terms of P rather than Q^D. This is called an **inverse demand curve** and the general functional relationship is

$$P = \alpha/\beta - (1/\beta)Q^D$$

Substituting in the values for α and β into the apple equation yields $P = 5 - .5Q^D$. This is the equation that is graphed in Figure 3-2.

The apple demand curve is linear, but in practice it could be non-linear. A linear (straight-line) demand relationship implies a uniform change in the quantity demanded as the price of the good changes. For many goods, however, this is unlikely to be true. Consider water, for example. At low prices and high rates of consumption, studies have shown that relatively small increases in price will lead to substantial reductions in quantity demanded. At high prices and low quantity demanded, price increases have a much smaller effect; they produce much smaller reductions in quantity demanded. What this yields is a demand relationship that is convex to the origin; one that is relatively flat at low prices and steep at higher prices. Figure 3-3 illustrates a demand curve for water.

FIGURE 3-3 **The Demand Curve for Water**

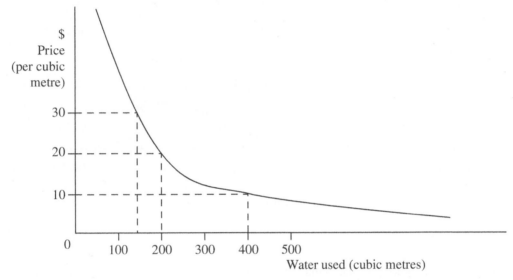

A non-linear demand curve shows how small increases in price can lead to large reductions in water used when prices start at low levels. An increase in price from $10 to $20 per cubic metre will lower water used from 400 to 200 cubic metres. But a further increase of $10, from $20 to $30, will reduce consumption by only 50 cubic metres, from 200 to 150.

AGGREGATE DEMAND/WILLINGNESS TO PAY

An individual's demand/marginal WTP curve for a good or service is a way of summarizing their personal consumption attitudes and capabilities for that good. Relationships should differ somewhat among individuals, because individual tastes and preferences vary. Some individuals are willing to pay more for a given item than are other people. People with high incomes have more to spend on goods and services. When examining real-world issues of environmental quality and pollution-control policy, economists normally focus their attention on the behaviour of groups of people rather than single individuals. It is the total, or aggregate, demand/marginal willingness to pay of defined groups of people that is of major interest.

An aggregate demand curve for a market good is the horizontal summation of the demand curves of all the people typically grouped by geographical region (e.g., a city, province, or country).

Figure 3-4 illustrates how the aggregate demand curve is derived for organic apples. Suppose there are only two consumers, Alice and Bruce. These two people are representative of different types of consumers in Vancouver. Alice really likes organic apples, while Bruce is not so keen on them; he might be just as happy with non-organic apples. Alice has a demand curve identical to that in Figure 3-2. Bruce's demand curve has a steeper slope than Alice's, indicating his different tastes.

FIGURE 3-4   Aggregating Demand Curves for Organic Apples

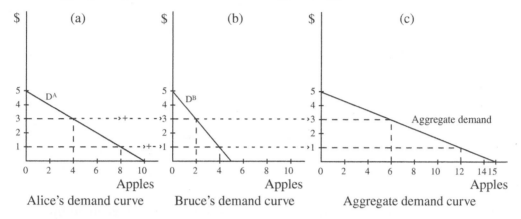

Alice's demand curve   Bruce's demand curve   Aggregate demand curve

Demand curves for two different consumers are shown. Alice's demand curve in panel (a) indicates that she is fond of organic apples; Bruce, shown in panel (b), is less so. Bruce's demand curve has a steeper slope, indicating that he is willing to buy fewer apples than Alice for each price below $5 per kilogram. An aggregate demand curve for apples is derived by summing the quantities of apples Alice and Bruce would like to purchase for each price per unit of apples. At a price of $3 per kilogram, Alice will buy four kilograms and Bruce will buy two, for a total of six kilograms. If the price is $1 per kilogram, the sum of their demand is 12 kilograms.

The principle of aggregating the demand curves of individuals is to pick a price, then add up the quantities demanded. This process is shown in Figure 3-4. When the price of apples is $3, market demand is 6 kilograms of apples. We can do the same type of calculation for other prices. Let the price be $1. Alice would buy 8 kilograms and Bruce would buy 4, for a total of 12 kilograms. Repeating this for all possible prices yields the aggregate demand curve shown in panel (c). Table 3-1 presents the demand data for Alice, Bruce, and their aggregate demand. In a real market, we could of course have many more individual demand curves to aggregate. The principle remains the same: for each price, add up the quantities each consumer wishes to purchase.

AGGREGATING INDIVIDUAL DEMAND CURVES
Algebraic solution

As Table 3-1 indicates, the aggregate demand curve can be derived by "adding up" Alice's and Bruce's individual demand curves.

Alice's demand for organic apples: $Q^D = 10 - 2P$
Bruce's demand for organic apples: $Q^D = 5 - P$
Aggregate demand: $Q^D = 15 - 3P$

The inverse-demand aggregate demand curve is $P = 5 - Q^D/3$. This equation is what is graphed in panel (c) of Figure 3-4.

TABLE 3-1 Derivation of the Aggregate Demand for Organic Apples

Price per Kilogram	Alice's Quantity Demanded (kilograms per week)	Bruce's Quantity Demanded (kilograms per week)	Aggregate Demand (kilograms per week)
$0	10	5	15
1	8	4	12
2	6	3	9
3	4	2	6
4	2	1	3
5	0	0	0
Demand curves:	$Q^D = 10 - 2P$	$Q^D = 5 - P$	$Q^D = 15 - 3P$

Aggregate demand is the horizontal sum of representative consumers' individual demand curves.

BENEFITS

The word **benefits** clearly implies being made better off; if someone is benefited by something, their position is improved. Conversely, if they are made worse off, it must be because benefits were somehow taken away from them. How do we confer benefits on somebody? By giving them something they value. How do we know that they value something? By the fact that they are willing to sacrifice, or are willing to pay, for that something. According to this logic, then, the benefits that people get from something are equal to the amount they are willing to pay for that thing.

The logic behind this definition of benefits is quite strong. It means we can use ordinary demand curves to determine the benefits of making various things available to people. For example, in Figure 3-5 there are two demand curves shown, and on the horizontal axis two quantity levels are also indicated. Suppose we wish to estimate the total benefits to the two groups of people whose aggregate demand curves these are, by increasing the availability of this item from quantity q_1 to quantity q_2. According to our previous thinking, benefits are measured by willingness to pay, and we know that total WTP is measured by areas under the demand curve—in this case the area under the demand curves between quantity q_1 and quantity q_2. So, for the lower demand curve (D_2) the benefits of such an increase in availability are equal to an amount shown by area *b*, while benefits in the case of the higher demand curve (D_1) are equal to the total area *a* + *b*.

The logic of this seems reasonable. The people with demand curve D_1 must place a greater value on this item; they are willing to pay more for it than are the people with demand curve D_2. This is the fundamental logic underlying much of environmental economics. It underlies, for example, questions of how we place a value on the damage done to people when the natural environment surrounding them is degraded. It underlies the question of how we evaluate the impacts of environmental programs and policies undertaken by local, provincial, and federal governments. This is its strength: the fact that it is based on a clear notion of the value that people place on different things.

But the idea has shortcomings. For one thing, demand (and therefore benefit) is often very hard to measure when it concerns environmental questions, as Chapter 7 demonstrates. Demand curves are also critically affected by the **ability to pay** for something, as well as preferences. In Figure 3-5, for example, the lower demand curve could represent a group of people with lower incomes than those with the higher demand curve. The logic of our argument would lead us to conclude that the increase in quantity of $q_2 - q_1$ would produce benefits that the lower-income people value less than do the higher-income people. This is not necessarily the case. The poorer people may have a very high marginal utility from the good, perhaps even higher than that of the richer people, but they cannot translate those values into WTP because of their lower ability to pay. Remember that income is a determinant of the location of a demand curve. Thus, while the logic of the concept is clear we have to be careful in using it, especially when we are dealing with groups of people with varying income levels.

FIGURE 3-5   Total Benefits and Total WTP

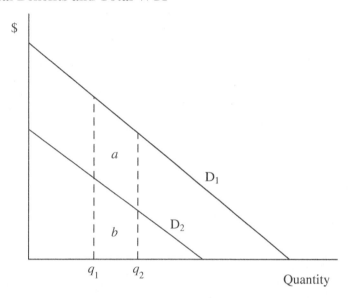

Total benefits are measured by total willingness to pay. Total WTP is the area under a demand curve. To measure the total benefit of increasing quantity from q_1 to q_2, the area under D_1 is area a plus area b; under D_2, it is area b. Those who value the good are willing to pay more for it and receive greater benefit from the increase in quantity.

One other possible problem exists in using conventional demand curves to measure benefits. An individual's demand for something is clearly affected by how much they know about it; a person would not be willing to pay for a good if, for example, they were ignorant of its very existence. We don't fully understand many of the impacts that environmental degradation is having; furthermore, people's views about the importance of many of these impacts vary due to influences by the media, the scientific press, and so on. In some of these cases, we may want to be cautious about taking people's demand curves of the moment, influenced as they are by all kinds of real and imagined factors, as true expressions of the benefits of environmental actions.

COST

The other side of the picture is cost. Any production process requires a variety of productive inputs—labour, machinery of various descriptions, energy, raw materials, waste handling equipment, and so on. Valuation of these inputs is straightforward for a private firm operating in a market economy: they are valued according to what they cost to procure in the markets for these items. However, a broader concept of cost is required. The costs of production are what could have been produced with productive inputs had they not been used to produce the good in question. The name for this condition is **opportunity cost.**

Opportunity Cost

Opportunity cost is a fundamental concept in economics.

> *The opportunity cost of producing something consists of the maximum value of other outputs we could and would have produced had we not used the resources to produce the item in question.*

The word "maximum" is in there for a reason. Productive inputs used to produce a particular good could have been used to produce a variety of other goods and services. Opportunity costs include out-of-pocket costs, but are wider than this. Some inputs that are actually used in production may not be registered as cash costs. For example, people who volunteer their time to clean up trash in parks or on roadsides have an opportunity cost: they could have been working somewhere else at that time for wages. Even more importantly, manufacturing processes may produce waste products that are pumped into the environment. These production residuals produce environmental damage, which are real opportunity costs of producing goods and services even though they do not show up as costs in a company's profit-and-loss statement.

Opportunity costs are relevant in any situation where a decision must be made about using productive resources for one purpose rather than another. For a public agency with a given budget, the opportunity costs of a particular policy are the value of alternative policies they may have pursued. For a consumer, the opportunity cost of spending time searching for a particular item is the value of the next most valuable thing to which they may have devoted their time.

How do we measure opportunity cost? It's not very useful to measure it in terms of the number of other physical items that could have been produced. Nor do we have enough information in most cases to be able to measure the value of the next best output that was forgone. In practice, therefore, we measure opportunity costs by the value of inputs used up in production. For this to work, we have to take care that the inputs have been correctly valued. If there are any distortions in markets, shadow prices will have to be used to measure opportunity costs. **Shadow prices** measure what the costs would be if markets operated perfectly. For example, volunteer labour must be valued at the going wage rate even though it is not paid in practice. If there are no markets, which may well be the case for many environmental goods, a price must be imputed. Some techniques for imputing prices are discussed in Section 2. Once all inputs have been accounted for and priced correctly, their total value may be taken as the true opportunity costs of production. This is an extremely important task for environmental economists.

Cost Curves

Cost information can be summarized with cost curves, which are geometric representations of production costs. And, just as in the case of willingness to pay, we will differentiate between **marginal costs** (MC) and **total costs** (TC) of production:

- Marginal costs measure the amount by which total costs increase as output is increased by one unit.

- Total costs are the costs of producing the total amount of output.

Consider the cost curves in Figure 3-6, for an apple orchard supplying organic apples to the market. The graph is laid out the same as we had earlier, with quantity on the horizontal axis and a monetary index on the vertical axis. The top panel shows marginal costs in terms of a stepped-shaped relationship. It shows that it costs $1.67 to produce the first unit of output. If the firm wants to increase output to two units it must spend an additional $2 for that second unit. The addition of a third unit would add $2.33 to total costs, and so on. Marginal cost is a symmetrical measure; it is the added costs, the amount by which total costs increase, when output is increased by one unit. It is also the cost savings if production were to decrease by one unit. Thus, the reduction in output from five to four units would reduce total costs by $3, the marginal cost of the fifth unit.

It is inconvenient to work with stepped-shaped curves, so we make the assumption that the firm can produce intermediate quantities as well as integer values. This gives us a smooth marginal cost curve, as shown in panel (b) of Figure 3-6. To facilitate calculations, our marginal cost curve is again linear.

FIGURE 3-6   Marginal and Total Costs of Producing Apples

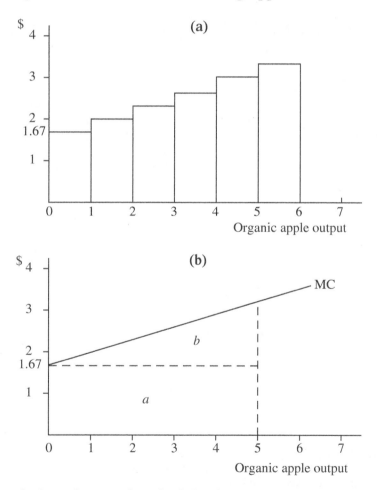

A marginal cost curve is shown for an apple orchard. Panel (a) depicts marginal costs by the height of each bar. Panel (b) is a smooth linear function for the same data. Total costs are the area under the marginal cost curve. If five units are produced, total costs can be found by summing the bars up to the fifth unit in panel (a) or by adding areas *a* plus *b* in panel (b). Total costs for five units equal $11.67.

We can use marginal cost curves to determine total costs of production. Total costs are the area under the MC curve. The example from Figure 3-6 illustrates how total costs are computed.

EXAMPLE

Computing total costs from the marginal cost curve for apples

What are the total costs of producing five units of output?

1. Using the stepped marginal cost curve, add up the area of the boxes from 0 to 5 units. First unit = $1.67, second unit = $2.00, third unit = $2.33, fourth unit = $2.67, fifth unit = $3.00. Total costs = $11.67.

2. Using the smooth MC curve, compute the area under the curve from 0 to 5 units. This is a rectangle (area *a*) plus a triangle (area *b*). Area *a* has height = $1.67 and length = 5, for a total cost of $8.35. Area *b* has a base of 5 and height of $1.33 (3 − 1.67). The area of *b* is fi (5 times $1.33) = $3.32. Total cost is $11.67.

LO 2

MARGINAL COST AND SUPPLY, AGGREGATE SUPPLY

The marginal cost of production is a key factor in determining the supply behaviour of firms in competitive circumstances. In fact, the marginal cost curve of a firm is its supply curve, showing the quantity of the good the firm would supply at different prices, assuming it can stay in business. Consider panel (a) of Figure 3-7. This is the apple orchard. Assume that the orchard is able to sell its output at a price of $2. The firm will maximize its profits by producing the quantity of output where marginal cost is equal to $2; that quantity is 2 kilograms. At any output level less than this, MC < $2, so a firm could increase its profits by increasing output. At any output level above this, $2 < MC, so a firm is actually producing items the marginal cost of which is higher than price; in this case, the firm should reduce output if it wishes to maximize its profits.

FIGURE 3-7   Deriving the Aggregate Supply Curve from Firm's Marginal Cost Curves

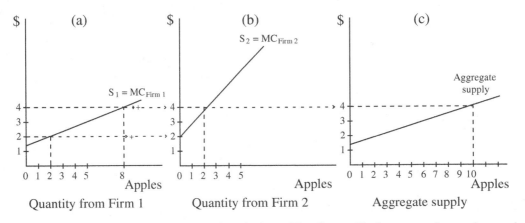

Marginal cost curves are the supply curves of each firm. The firm will always produce where price equals marginal cost to maximize profits. Panels (a) and (b) show the supply curve for two firms. Panel (c) illustrates the aggregate supply curve that is derived by summing the quantities supplied by each firm for a given price. For a price of $4 per kilogram, Firm 1 will supply 8 kilograms and Firm 2 will supply 2 kilograms, for an aggregate supply of 10 kilograms.

Economists typically work with supply curves of industries, as well as with those of individual firms. The marginal cost/supply curve of an industry refers to a collection of firms all producing the same output. This is the concept of **aggregate supply,** analogous to the concept of market or **aggregate demand** we discussed previously.

The aggregate supply curve for firms producing the same output is the horizontal summation of the individual supply curves of all the firms in the group.

Let's assume there are two orchards. Panel (b) presents the marginal cost curve for the second orchard. Market supply is the aggregation of the marginal cost curves for each orchard. The principle is the same as with aggregation of demand curves for a private good. Choose a price, and then add up the quantities supplied at that price. This is a "horizontal" summation. Panel (c) of Figure 3-7 represents the aggregate supply curve. For example, at a common price of $2, the first orchard supplies 2 units, the second supplies no units (because the price is less than the minimum it needs to produce one unit), for an aggregate supply at that price of 2 units. Complete the derivation by choosing different prices, and then add up the quantity supplied by each orchard to get the aggregate supply. For example, at a price of $4, Firm 1 supplies 8 units and Firm 2 supplies 2 units, for an aggregate supply of 10 units.

The marginal cost curves can also be expressed algebraically. Table 3-2 shows the data for each orchard and aggregate supply.

TABLE 3-2 Derivation of the Aggregate Supply Curve for Organic Apples

Price per Kilogram	Firm 1 Quantity Supplied (kilograms per week)	Firm 2 Quantity Supplied (kilograms per week)	Aggregate Supply (kilograms per week)
$1	0	0	0
2	2	0	2
3	5	1	6
4	8	2	10
5	11	3	14
Supply curves:	$Q^S_1 = 3P - 4$	$Q^S_2 = P - 2$	$Q^S = 4P - 6$

Marginal cost curves for two apple orchards are summed to produce the aggregate supply curve. A profit-maximizing producer will set market price equal to its marginal costs. For each price, the next columns show the quantity supplied by each producer and aggregate supply.

ALGEBRAIC DERIVATION OF MARGINAL COST CURVES

From the data in Table 3-2 and the graphs presented in Figure 3-7, we can derive each firm's marginal cost curve. The MC curve is found by expressing the supply curves in terms of price and assuming that each producer maximizes profits by setting price equal to marginal cost (as noted in the table).[2]

MC for orchard 1: $MC = 4/3 + 1/3Q^S$

MC for orchard 2: $MC = 2 + Q^S$

Aggregate MC: $MC = 3/2 + 1/4Q^S$

[2.] The supply curves in the table are inverted by solving in terms of price rather than quantity. Let the general functions for the supply curve be $Q^S = \phi P - \theta$. The inverse function would be: $P = \theta/\phi + 1/\phi Q^S$. Each firm is assumed to set its price equal to marginal cost, so $P = MC = \theta/\phi + 1/\phi Q^S$. The aggregate supply curve comes from the horizontal summation of the individual supply curves. The aggregate MC curve is the inverse of the aggregate supply curve: $Q^S = 4P - 6$ yields aggregate MC = $3/2 + 1/4Q^S$.

Aggregate supply is generally written in terms of Q^S, as shown in the table: $Q^S = 4P - 6$. These equations will help set the stage for determination of market equilibrium in the next chapter.

LO 3

TECHNOLOGY

The most important factor affecting the shapes of marginal cost functions is the technology of the production process. By technology we mean the inherent productive capabilities of the methods and machines being employed. Any modern production requires capital goods (machinery and equipment) of various types and capacities, labour inputs, operating procedures, raw materials, and so on. The quantity of output a firm can get from a given set of inputs depends on the technical and human capabilities inherent in these inputs. Even within the same industry, marginal cost curves can differ among firms. Some firms will be older than others, meaning that they will perhaps be working with older equipment that has different cost characteristics. Even for firms of the same age, different production techniques may be available; past managerial decisions may have put them in different positions in terms of marginal production costs today.

This concept of technology is vitally important in environmental economics because we rely heavily on technological change to find ways to produce goods and services with fewer environmental side effects and also to handle better the quantities of production residuals that remain. In our simple cost model, technical advancement has the effect of shifting marginal cost curves downward. Technological progress makes it possible to produce a given increase in output at a lower marginal cost. It also reduces total production cost. Consider Figure 3-8. MC_1 is the firm's marginal cost curve before a technical improvement; MC_2 is the marginal cost curve after some technical improvement has been put into effect.[3] The technical change, in other words, shifts the marginal cost curve downward. We can determine how much total production costs are reduced as a result of technological change. Consider output level q^*. With MC_1 the total cost of producing an output of q^* is represented by the area $a + b$, while after the reduction in the marginal cost curve to MC_2, the total cost of producing q^* is equal to area b. Technological change reduces total cost by an amount equal to area a.

Technological change does not normally happen without effort; it normally requires research and development (R&D). R&D in environmental industries is obviously an important activity to promote, and one of the criteria we will need to use to evaluate environmental policies is whether they create incentives for individuals, firms, and industries to engage in vigorous R&D programs. In very simple terms, the incentive to do R&D is the cost savings that result from the new techniques, materials, and procedures that are discovered in the effort. The cost savings shown in Figure 3-8 (area a) shows part of this incentive. These are the cost savings that would result each year, and it is the accumulation of these annual cost savings that represents the full R&D incentive.

[3.] We have drawn the marginal cost curves as non-linear in this section and the next. This shape is representative of many real-world curves where the slope initially declines then rises again. This shape will be observed when, at low levels of output, the capacity of the plant is not fully used. Increases in output in this range will lower marginal costs as more and more of the capacity is used. Eventually marginal costs begin to rise as capacity utilization rises. More inputs have to be used to produce the additional output. The key point is that eventually the marginal cost curve must be upward sloping and may indeed become vertical to show that no more output is possible.

FIGURE 3-8 The Impact of Technological Progress on Marginal Cost Curves

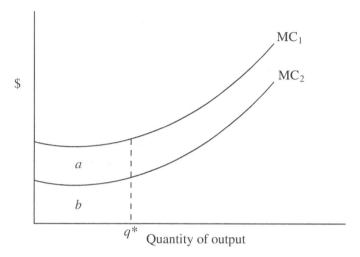

Technological progress is shown with a downward shift of the marginal cost curve. Producing q^* units with the new technology reduces total cost by an amount equal to area a.

Summary

In this chapter we have covered briefly some of the basic tools of microeconomics. Later chapters will rely heavily on these ideas, using graphs and algebra to expand understanding of the factors that give rise to environmental problems and what can be done to address these problems. When we begin to look at real-world problems of environmental analysis and policy design, it is easy to get swept so far into the countless details that basic economic ideas get lost. It is the fundamental economic building blocks, such as those in this chapter, that allow us to identify the primary economic characteristics of these problems and proceed to develop solutions to them.

Key Terms

Ability to pay
Aggregate demand
Aggregate supply
Benefits
Demand curves
Inverse demand curve
Marginal costs
Marginal willingness to pay
Microeconomics
Opportunity cost
Shadow prices
Total costs
Total willingness to pay
Willingness to pay (WTP)

Analytical Problems

1. Alvin's demand for bottled water is given by the equation $Q^d_A = 8 - .5P$. Betty's demand function is $Q^d_B = 6 - P$. Calculate Alvin and Betty's marginal and total willingness to pay for four bottles of water and illustrate graphically.

2. With the same equations as given in question 1, compute the aggregate demand for bottled water, assuming Alvin and Betty are the only consumers. Derive the aggregate demand curve if there were five people with Alvin's demand curve and 10 people like Betty.

3. Derive and graph the aggregate supply curve for tennis balls, where there are three different producers whose MC curves are

   A: $MC = 3 + .3Q^S$, where Q for each producer is measured in terms of 1,000 units.

   B: $MC = 4 + .6Q^S$

   C: $MC = 1 + .1Q^S$

4. If the price of tennis balls is $4 per container, can each of these producers stay in business? Explain why or why not. How much will each want to produce at this price?

5. Marginal cost curves are often not linear, as we have assumed in this chapter for simplicity. Why might this be the case? Draw a marginal cost curve for a firm that cannot increase its output beyond 500 units per month.

6. Refer again to question 3. If a technological change shifts producer B's marginal cost curve to that of producer C, compute B's cost saving at an output level of two units (of 1,000).

Discussion Questions

1. What happens to aggregate demand curves when consumers expect the price of the good to rise (or fall) in the future? Would this situation undermine the theory developed in the chapter?

2. The logic of equating benefits with willingness to pay could lead us to the conclusion that cleaning the air to which low-income people are exposed would probably create fewer benefits than if it were done for high-income people. Does this undermine the idea of defining benefits as equal to willingness to pay? How should economists deal with this potential dilemma?

3. What sorts of factors will influence the shape of marginal cost curves? Will they differ substantially within industries?

4. Explain to a non-economist why marginal values are so important in economic analysis. How would you counter the argument of a non-economist that he or she never makes decisions based on a marginal valuation?

connect   For more information on the resources available from McGraw-Hill Ryerson, go to www.mheducation.ca/he/solutions.

Chapter 4

Economic Efficiency and Markets

After reading this chapter you will be able to:

LO 1 Define social efficiency and graphically illustrate when it is achieved.

LO 2 Explain why a competitive market may fail to reach a socially efficient equilibrium.

LO 3 List and explain the causes of market failure.

LO 4 Contrast the equilibrium outcomes in markets where externalities are accounted for versus when they are not.

LO 5 Explain the distinguishing characteristics of public goods and why they give rise to free riding.

In Chapter 1 we introduced some concepts fundamental to environmental economics. This chapter and the next develop these concepts more fully in an economic model that we use throughout the book.

This chapter has several objectives. First is to develop more fully the notion of **economic efficiency** as an index for examining how an economy functions and as a criterion for judging whether it is performing as well as it might. Economic efficiency is a simple idea but one that has much to recommend it as a criterion for evaluating the performance of an economic system or a part of that system. But it has to be used with care. Does a market system, left to itself, produce results that are economically efficient? A single firm or group of firms may be judged efficient when examining private costs and benefits from operations. Yet, to evaluate the *social* performance of these firms, we must use the idea of economic efficiency in a wider sense. It must include all of the *social* values and consequences of economic decisions, in particular environmental consequences. It is also important to discuss the relationship between economic efficiency and **equity.**

The second task is to address the question of whether a market system, left to itself, can produce results that are at a **socially efficient level of production.** Social efficiency means that all markets operate without any distortions, including the kind that generate pollution. We examine the sources of environmental **market failures** that can prevent markets from achieving social efficiency. This leads into the next chapter, where we examine the policy question; that is, if the economy is not socially efficient, and environmental problems emerge, what kinds of public policy might we use to correct the situation?

Economic efficiency is a criterion that can be applied at several levels: to input usage and to the determination of output levels. We concentrate on the second of these because ultimately we want to apply the concept to the "output" of environmental quality. There are two questions of interest:

- What is the quantity that ought to be produced?
- What is the quantity that is produced in fact?

The first question deals with the notion of efficiency, the second with the way markets normally function.

LO 1

ECONOMIC EFFICIENCY

In the preceding chapter, we looked at two relationships: that between the quantity of output and willingness to pay, and that between output and marginal production costs. Neither of these two relationships alone can tell us what is the most desirable level of output from society's standpoint. To identify this output level, we must bring these two elements together.

> *The central idea of economic efficiency in production is that the marginal benefits from production should equal the marginal costs of production.*

Efficiency must also have a reference point. What is "efficient" for one person, in the sense of balancing his or her own costs and benefits, may not be "efficient" for somebody else. We want to have a concept of efficiency that is applicable to the economy as a whole. This means that when we refer to marginal costs we must include *all* the costs of producing the particular item in question, no matter to whom they accrue and whether or not these costs have a market-determined price. When we talk about marginal willingness to pay, we must insist that this represents accurately *all* of the values that people in the society place on the item, including any **non-market values.** This does not necessarily mean that all people will place a value on all goods, it means only that there are no missing sources of value.

> *Social efficiency requires that all market and non-market values be incorporated into the marginal benefits and marginal costs of production. If this is the case, social efficiency is obtained when marginal benefits equal marginal costs of production.*

How do we identify the rate of output that is socially efficient? We can analyze this graphically and algebraically by bringing together the two relationships discussed in the last chapter. In Figure 4-1, for the good in question we picture the aggregate demand/marginal willingness-to-pay curve (MWTP) and the aggregate supply/marginal cost curve (MC). Chapter 3 covered the derivation of these curves. A socially efficient equilibrium occurs at the output level where the MWTP = MC. The figure shows that the equilibrium output is 40 units with an equilibrium MWTP (price) of $20.

The socially efficient equilibrium can also be found algebraically as the example illustrates.

The equality of marginal willingness to pay and marginal production cost is the test for determining if output is at the socially efficient level. There is another way of looking at this notion of efficiency. When a rate of output is at the socially efficient level, the **net social value,** defined as total willingness to pay minus total costs, is as large as possible. In fact, we can measure this net value on Figure 4-1. At Q^E of 40, the total willingness to pay is equal to an amount corresponding to the area under the marginal willingness-to-pay curve, from the origin up to Q^E. This area consists of the sum of the three sub-areas: $a + b + c$. Total cost, on the other hand, consists of the area under the marginal cost curve, or area c. The net social value is $(a + b + c)$ minus area c, which equals area $(a + b)$.

FIGURE 4-1   Determining the Socially Efficient Level of Output

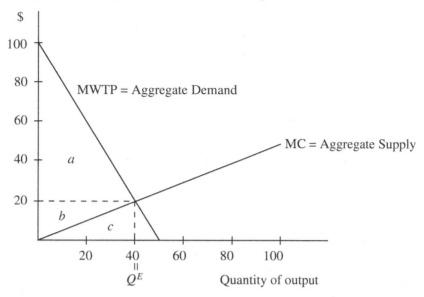

Equating MWTP to MC yields the socially efficient equilibrium. The equilibrium quantity (Q^E) is 40 units with a MWTP of $20 for that amount. The socially efficient equilibrium maximizes the social surplus, areas *a* plus *b*, which is derived from the difference between total WTP and total cost. No other price and quantity combination will yield as large a social surplus and have a price where demand equals supply.

EXAMPLE
How to solve for the socially efficient level of output algebraically

1. To solve for a socially efficient equilibrium, specify equations for MWTP and MC. Let Q^D be the quantity of a good demanded and Q^S the quantity supplied. The equations are assumed to be linear to facilitate calculations. Let

$$\text{MWTP} = 100 - 2Q^D$$
$$\text{MC} = .5\,Q^S$$

2. The equilibrium values are found algebraically by setting MWTP equal to MC and solving first for the equilibrium quantity, where $Q^D = Q^S = Q^E$, where Q^E is the equilibrium quantity.

$$100 - 2Q^E = .5Q^E$$
$$Q^E = 40$$

3. The equilibrium MWTP can be found by substituting Q^E into either the MWTP or MC equations:

$$\text{MWTP} = 100 - 2(40) = \$20$$

There are a number of names for areas *a* plus *b*. This is called the *net social value* or *net benefits* or the *social surplus*.[1] At any other quantity the corresponding value of total willingness to pay minus total

---

1. In Chapter 6, the net social surplus will be linked to the concepts of consumer and producer surplus.

production costs will be less than this area $a + b$. (The analytical problems at the end of this chapter will ask you to prove this statement.)

NUMERICAL COMPUTATION OF THE NET SOCIAL VALUE

1. Compute area a: Area a is a triangle with base equal to 40 and height of 80. Area a equals ½ (40 times 80) = $1,600.[2]

2. Compute area b: Area b is another triangle with base 40 and height 20, for a total value of $400.

3. Add area $(a + b) = \$1,600 + 400 = \$2,000 =$ net social value.

4. There is no need to compute area c because it nets out of the equation:

$$\text{Net social value} = (a + b + c) - (c) = (a + b).$$

Questions to think about (and solve) for this example

1. What would happen to the socially efficient equilibrium and net social value if MWTP $= 200 - 2\,Q^D$? If MC became doubled to MC $= Q^S$?

2. Who gets the social surplus and why is it a surplus?

The models we examine in this book deal with economies at a point in time. While we discuss intertemporal aspects of environmental issues, developing models to explicitly address these effects is beyond the scope of the book. Efficiency in our models is **static efficiency.** That is, it deals with markets and actions at a point in time. **Dynamic efficiency** looks at the allocation of resources over time. While the two concepts both involve equating marginal benefits to marginal costs, dynamic efficiency will be more complex because intertemporal trade-offs involve questions of depletion of environmental capital stocks, irreversibilities, whether or not to discount future values, and so on.[3]

EFFICIENCY AND EQUITY

From the standpoint of society at large, production is at an efficient level when marginal benefits equal marginal production costs; that is, when net benefits are maximized, *no matter to whom those net benefits accrue.* Efficiency doesn't distinguish among people. A dollar of net benefits to one person is considered to be worth a dollar to anybody else.

In the real world, an equilibrium may be efficient but there is no explicit market mechanism by which the winners can compensate the losers. This is why the distribution of income and wealth is a concern to economists. An outcome that benefits very rich people at the expense of poor people would be regarded by most people as inequitable. Which is simply another way of saying that an outcome that is efficient in the above sense need not be equitable in practice.

Equity is tied closely to the distribution of wealth in a society. If this distribution is regarded as essentially fair, then judgments about alternative output levels may justifiably be made using only the efficiency criterion. But if wealth is distributed unfairly, the efficiency criterion by itself may be too narrow. As well, the distribution of income and wealth can have effects on how resources are allocated. Having said this, however, we have to recognize that, in judging economic outcomes, the

---

2. Recall from Chapter 3 that we find the intercept of the MWTP curve by setting $Q^D = 0$ in the MWTP equation.

3. The concept and use of discounting is discussed in Chapter 6.

relative emphasis to be put on efficiency and equity is a matter of controversy. It is controversial in the political arena; it is controversial among economists themselves.

Distributional issues and equity are discussed throughout the book. Chapter 6 develops terminology for describing the distributional impacts of environmental policies. In Chapter 9, economic equity is one of our criteria for evaluating environmental policies.

LO 2

MARKETS

The key question to address in this section is whether a market system—a system where the major economic decisions about how much to produce are made by the more-or-less unhindered interaction of buyers and sellers—gives us results that are socially efficient. Social efficiency produces Q^E units of output. Can we rely entirely on the market to reach this same quantity?

Economists worry about this question because Canada is, by and large, a market-based economy. For all its faults, a market system will normally give us better economic results, overall, than any other system. The market system also contains incentive structures that in many cases can be harnessed toward the objective of improved environmental quality. One of these is the cost-minimizing incentive that stems from the competitive process. Another is the incentive to find ways of producing goods and services more cheaply through different technologies, less expensive inputs, or better ways to organize a company. If we can harness these incentives to help achieve environmental goals, our task both will be easier and will have lower opportunity costs for society than if we tried to jettison the whole system and adopt a different set of institutions.

A market is an institution where buyers and sellers of goods or services or factors of production carry out mutually agreed-upon exchanges. The 'rules' and norms under which markets operate reflect society's values, ethics, regulations, laws, and customs. But in virtually all markets, people are looking for the best terms they can get. Buyers want to pay a low price, while sellers want to receive high prices. What brings all these conflicting objectives into balance is the adjustment of prices on the market. Equilibrium is established where supply is equal to demand, where MWTP = MC of production. At this intersection, the equilibrium price and quantity produced is determined. This is illustrated in Figure 4-2, where Q^M is the equilibrium quantity sold and bought in the market and P^M is the equilibrium price. For the market to work effectively there must be competition among sellers and among buyers. None can be large enough that their own performance affects market prices, or powerful enough that they can control how the market performs. Price must be allowed to adjust freely.

LO 3

LO 4

MARKETS AND SOCIAL EFFICIENCY

Does an unregulated market such as the one represented in Figure 4-2 lead to a socially efficient equilibrium?

This is a fundamental question in economics. Compare Figures 4-1 and 4-2. They look the same, but there is actually a big difference. Figure 4-1 shows a socially efficient rate of output for a particular item. Figure 4-2 shows the rate of output and price that would prevail on a competitive market for that item. Are these two rates of output, Q^M and the Q^E of 40 units, likely to be the same in the real world? The answer is yes if the market demand and supply curves, as pictured in Figure 4-2, are the same as the marginal cost and willingness-to-pay curves, as shown in Figure 4-1. Here is the essence of the problem: When environmental values are concerned, there are likely to be very substantial differences between market values and social values. Market failures cause the divergence. Market failures can affect both the supply and demand sides of the market.

FIGURE 4-2 Determining Equilibrium in a Competitive Market

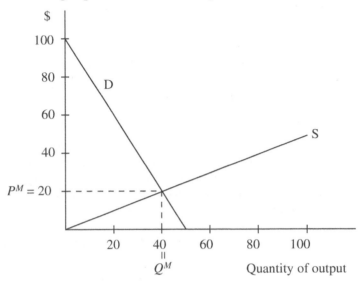

A market equilibrium is defined where demand (D) is equal to supply (S). The equilibrium price of P^M ($20) and equilibrium quantity $Q^M = 40$ are shown. Q^M will be the socially efficient equilibrium output, Q^E, if D is the same as MWTP and S represents social marginal cost. This is unlikely to be the case when environmental problems arise from market failures.

On the supply side, market failures can drive a wedge between normal market supply curves and true or social marginal cost curves. On the demand side, market failures can create a divergence between market demands and social marginal willingness to pay. On the supply side the problem is "external costs," while on the demand side the problem is "external benefits." To reiterate,

> *market failures cause a divergence between market and social values and can prevent a decentralized competitive market from reaching the socially efficient equilibrium.*[4]

We now examine the sources of market failure.

EXTERNAL COSTS

When entrepreneurs in a market economy make decisions about what and how much to produce, they take into account the price of what they will produce and also the cost of items for which they will have to pay: labour, raw materials, machinery, energy, and so on. We call these the **private costs** of the firm; they are the costs that show up in the firm's profit-and-loss statement. Any firm that has the

---

[4.] This chapter examines failures of private markets to achieve a socially efficient equilibrium. Section 5 illustrates that some government policy can also prevent the attainment of social efficiency. This is often called a 'government failure.'

objective of maximizing its profits will try to keep its production costs as low as possible. This is a worthwhile outcome for both the firm and society because inputs always have opportunity costs; they could have been used to produce something else. Furthermore, firms will try to find ways of reducing costs when the relative prices of inputs change.

However, in many production operations there is another type of cost that represents a true cost to society but does not show up in the firm's profit-and-loss statement. These are called **external or social costs and benefits.** They are called "external" because, although they are real costs to some members of society, they will not normally be taken into account by firms when they go about making their decisions about what inputs to use or output levels to produce. Another way of saying this is that there are costs that are external to firms but internal to society as a whole. One of the major types of external cost is the cost inflicted on people through environmental degradation. An example is the easiest way to see this.

EXAMPLE
Paper mill discharges wastes into river
Suppose a paper mill is located somewhere on the upstream reaches of a river that is used for a city's drinking water and supports other beneficial activities. In the course of its operation, it discharges a large amount of wastewater into the river. The wastewater is full of organic matter that arises from the process of converting wood to paper. This waste material gradually is converted to more benign materials by the natural assimilative capacity of the river water; however, before that happens, a number of people downstream are affected by the lower quality of water in the river. The waterborne residuals may reduce the number of fish in the river, affecting downstream fishers. The river may be also less attractive to look at, affecting people who would like to swim in it or sail on it. Worse, when the river water is used downstream as a source of water for a public water-supply system, the degraded water quality means that the city has to engage in more costly treatment processes before the water can be delivered to its residents. All of these downstream costs are real costs associated with producing paper, just as much as the raw materials, labour, energy, and so on used internally by the plant. If there are no regulations that inhibit effluent discharge from the mill's standpoint these downstream costs are external costs. They are costs that are borne by someone other than the people who make decisions about operating the paper mill. Any profit-and-loss statement of the paper mill will contain no reference whatever to these real downstream external costs. The market fails because there is no incentive for producers to include external costs in their decision-making; no way that the market-determined price of the good reflects these externalities in production.

If we are to have rates of output that are socially efficient, decisions about resource use must take into account both types of costs—the private costs of producing paper plus whatever external costs arise from adverse environmental impacts. In terms of full **social cost accounting,**

Social costs = Private costs + External (environmental) costs

This equation is pictured in Figure 4-3. The top panel shows the relationship between the rate of paper production and the occurrence of these downstream external costs. It shows that the marginal external costs increase as paper production increases. The bottom panel shows several things. It shows the demand curve for paper and the marginal private costs of producing paper. The intersection of these occurs at a price of P^M and a quantity of Q^M. This is the price and quantity that would arise on a competitive market where producers pay no attention to external costs. But marginal social costs are in fact higher, as shown, since they contain both the marginal private costs and marginal external costs. Thus, the full socially efficient rate of output is Q^*, and the associated price is P^*.

Compare the two rates of output and the two prices. The market output is too high compared to the socially efficient rate of output. And the market price is too low compared to the socially efficient price. It's not hard to understand the reason for this. In considering just its private costs the firm is essentially using a productive input it is not paying for. The unpaid input is the services of the river, which provide the firm with a cheap way to dispose of its waste products. But while it may be cheap for the firm to do this, it may not be cheap to society; in fact, in this case we have costs being inflicted on downstream users that are being overlooked by the paper mill. So the private market system in this case produces too much paper at too low a price compared to socially efficient results.

Most of the cases of environmental destruction involve external costs of one type or another. Electricity-generating plants burning fossil fuels emit airborne residuals that affect the health of people living downwind. Users of chemicals emit toxic fumes that affect people living in the vicinity. Developers build on land without taking into account the degradation of the visual environment of local inhabitants, and so on. Nor is it only businesses that are responsible for external environmental costs. When individuals drive their automobiles, exhaust gases add to air pollution, and when they dispose of solid waste materials (like old paint cans and solvents), they may affect the quality of the local environment.

FIGURE 4-3 External Costs and Market Outcomes

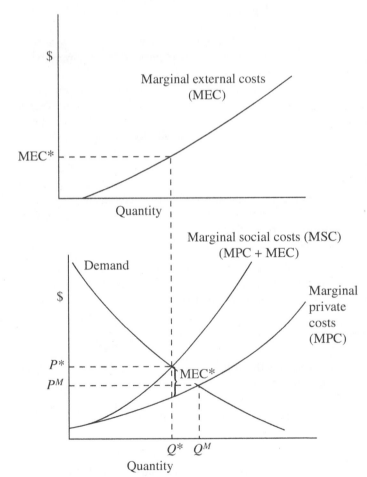

The top panel illustrates a marginal external cost function for a paper mill that discharges untreated wastes into a river. The external costs are the costs borne by people and firms downstream who must purify the water before use. The bottom panel derives the marginal social cost curve, which is the sum of the marginal private cost curve plus external costs for each unit of paper output produced. A socially efficient equilibrium occurs where demand equals marginal social costs. This equilibrium occurs at a lower output (Q^*) and higher price (P^*) than the market equilibrium, where demand is equated to marginal private costs, yielding Q^M and P^M.

At Q^* for example, the marginal external cost is MEC* as shown on the top panel. MEC* is added to the MPC at Q^* as are MECs for all other levels of output, to obtain the MSC curve.

There are many different types of environmental external costs or externalities. Most, but not all, are expressed through physical linkages among parties involved—polluters and those damaged. The simplest is where there are just two parties involved—one polluter and one party suffering damages (the **pollutee**). An upstream pulp mill and a downstream firm that uses the river water in its production operations is an example. There are cases of single polluters and multiple pollutees, such as a power plant that emits suphur dioxide that affects the residents of a community living downwind. Other cases involve multiple polluters but only one damaged party. An example is runoff of nitrates from the use of fertilizers and animal wastes on farms that affects the well water of a single household. And, finally, there are many cases where both polluters and pollutees are several in number; for example, urban air pollution stemming from automobile emissions: each driver is both a producer and a recipient of the externality. The same is true of global phenomena, such as global emissions of greenhouse gases that contribute to climate change. There are some externalities that do not involve physical linkages. Degradation of the scenic environment through land development that does not protect green space in urbanizing areas is an example. And there are some externalities that involve neither physical linkages nor close proximity. People in one part of a country, for example, may feel a loss when those in another region cause damage to an important environmental resource—for example, a unique species of animal or plant, such as the decline in polar bear populations due to the thinning of Arctic ice caused by climate change.

Open-Access Resources

A major cause of market failure is the presence of **open-access resources** (as was defined in Chapter 1). An open-access resource is a resource or facility that is open to uncontrolled access by individuals who find it profitable or useful in some way to use the resource. A classic example from resource economics is an ocean fishery, where anyone willing to buy a boat and take up fishing is free to do so. Other examples are a pasture that is open to anyone to graze their animals, or a forest where anyone may go and cut wood. For the natural environment, the atmosphere is the quintessential open-access resource. Anyone is free to use the atmosphere as a waste depository. The oceans, groundwater, and many surface waters are also open-access.

In these situations we have, in effect, the absence of property rights.[5] No one owns an open-access resource. No one can stop another from using that resource. The resource will be inefficiently used as a result. To illustrate the concept of open access and the inefficiencies created, consider the following examples.

EXAMPLE
Water pollution and treatment costs

Suppose there are four similar firms situated on a lake. The firms use water from the lake in producing their output, and discharge emissions back into the lake. The emissions pollute the lake water, requiring each firm to treat the water before they use it in production. Each firm's treatment costs depend on the ambient quality of the lake, which of course depends on the total emissions of the four firms. Suppose that the cost of intake water treatment is currently $40,000 per year for each firm. A new firm is contemplating starting operations on the lake. If it adds its untreated emissions to those of the current four, it will make ambient water quality worse and drive up the cost of water treatment for each firm to $60,000 per year. When the fifth firm makes its location and production decisions it will take into account its various operating costs, which will include the $60,000 per year of water

(Continued)

---

5. Property rights are discussed in detail in Chapter 10.

treatment costs. But the total social water-related costs of the firm's decisions are higher. There are also external costs inflicted on the other four firms, amounting to $20,000 each of added water treatment costs if the fifth firm locates on the lake. The social marginal costs of water supply when the new firm locates on the lake are $140,000, consisting of the $60,000 in internal costs for the new firm plus $80,000 ($20,000 times 4) for external costs inflicted on firms already on the lake. These are often called *open-access externalities,* because they result from the fact that the firms have uncontrolled access to the lake.

The focus in the example so far has been on the externalities flowing from the fifth firm's decisions, but everything is symmetrical in the sense that we could say exactly the same thing about each one of the other firms. They will make their decisions without regard to the external costs inflicted on other firms. It is this reciprocal nature of these externalities that distinguishes them from the type we talked about before (e.g., the pulp mill upstream inflicting external costs on pollutees downstream). But the effect is the same:

Market supply curves will understate social marginal production costs when there are externalities in production.

If someone owns a pasture, or a forest, he or she will presumably keep out encroachers, or perhaps charge them for use of the resource or otherwise control their rate of access. But when a resource or facility is open to unrestricted access there is no way of ensuring that its rate of use is kept to the level that will maximize its overall value.

EXAMPLE

Road congestion

Road congestion illustrates how unrestricted access leads to inefficiency. A road is not a natural resource, but a person-made facility. But the essence of the uncontrolled-access problem is identical, and it perhaps is easier to understand with this particular example. It uses very simplified assumptions so that we can highlight the basic issues. There is a road connecting two points, call them point A and point B. Table 4-1 shows the average travel time it takes to get from point A to point B along this road, as a function of the number of motorists using the road. For example, if there is just one traveller on the road, it takes 10 minutes to get from A to B (we assume a speed limit that is enforced). Likewise, when there are either two or three motorists on the road the average travel time is still 10 minutes. But when the traffic increases to four travellers, the average travel time increases to 11 minutes. This is because of congestion: cars begin to get in each other's way and average speeds drop. As the number of motorists continues to increase, the congestion increases, thus driving up travel times even more.

TABLE 4-1 Travel Times Related to the Number of Cars on the Road

Number of cars	1	2	3	4	5	6	7	8
Average travel time (in minutes) between A and B	10	10	10	11	12	14	18	24

Now, suppose you are considering using this road to go from A to B, and that there are already five cars using it. Suppose, furthermore, that you have an alternative route that will take you 18 minutes.

(Continued)

We assume you know the state of the traffic and the resulting travel times. Since taking the given road will save you four minutes over the alternative, your individual decision would be to use the road. But from the standpoint of "society," in this case consisting of you plus all the other motorists on the road, this is not efficient. When you enter the highway on which there are already five cars, the added congestion causes an increase in average travel times of two minutes to the people already using the road. Your four-minute individual saving is offset by added travel costs of 10 minutes (five cars times two minutes per car) on the part of the other motorists. This means—if we treat all minutes as equally valuable—a net social loss of six minutes when you decide to use the road.

The problem arises because there is uncontrolled access to the road, and in using it people may inflict external costs on others in the form of added congestion and higher travel times. The same kind of effect holds when a fisher enters a fishery; in catching a portion of the stock, he or she leaves fewer to be caught by other fishers. When one farmer puts animals on an open access pasture, and there are no rules regarding the use of that pasture, he or she reduces the forage available to other herds on that pasture. We can see that this is related to the notion of external costs. The added costs that one user of an open-access resource inflicts on other users of that resource are in fact costs that are external to that user but internal to the whole group of users. When a single individual is making a decision about whether and how much to use an open-access resource, they take into account the costs and benefits that impinge on themselves directly. Some might also altruistically take into account the externalities they inflict on others, but most will not. And the result will be, as it was with the road example, a rate of use that is higher than what is called for on the grounds of social efficiency.

In summary,

when external costs are present, private markets will not normally produce quantities of output that are socially efficient.

Market failure may thus justify public policy to help move the economy toward social efficiency. This may be done sometimes by changing rules, such as property rights rules, so that the market will function efficiently. Other cases may call for more direct public intervention. Chapters 10 through 14 address these issues in more detail. Consider now the demand side of the market and another important source of market failure, that of *external benefits*.

EXTERNAL BENEFITS

An external benefit is a benefit that accrues to somebody who is outside, or external, to the decision about consuming or using the good or resource that causes the externality. When the use of an item leads to an external benefit, the market willingness to pay for that item will understate the social willingness to pay. Consider the following examples.

EXAMPLE

Quiet lawn mowers

Suppose a quiet lawn mower would provide $50 a year of extra benefits to its buyer. This is therefore the maximum incremental amount that person would be willing to pay for this machine above the cost of a noisy mower. But suppose that person's use of the new lawn mower would create $20 of added benefits to her neighbour, because of reduced noise levels in the course of the year. These $20 of

(Continued)

benefits to the neighbour are external benefits for the owner of the lawn mower. The owner makes a purchasing decision on the basis of benefits accruing only to herself. Thus, the marginal willingness to pay for a quieter lawn mower is $50, whereas the social marginal benefit (where "society" in this case includes just the owner and the neighbour) is $70 (the owner's $50 and the neighbour's $20). This is a real problem in many parts of Canada where urban areas are encroaching on agricultural lands and depleting green spaces. The market failure is that there is no effective way to get the public to pay the farmer to protect the ecosystem benefits. Sections 4 and 5 examine policies that may help protect ecosystem benefits.

EXAMPLE
Ecosystem benefits from agricultural land

A farmer has land on the outskirts of an urban area. The farmer cultivates the land and sells his produce to people in the city. Of course, the farmer's main concern is the income he can derive from the operation, and he makes decisions about inputs and outputs according to their effect on that income. But the land kept in agriculture produces several other benefits, including habitat for birds and other small animals and scenic values for passers-by. These benefits, while internal from the standpoint of society, are external from the standpoint of the farmer. They don't appear anywhere in his profit-and-loss position; they are external benefits of his farming decisions. In this case the agricultural value of the land to the farmer understates the social willingness to pay to have the land in agriculture.

When economists discuss the rudiments of supply and demand, we usually use as examples very simple goods that do not have external benefits. Farmers produce and supply so many million apples per year. Individual and market demand curves for apples are easy to comprehend. If we want to know the total number of apples bought, we can simply add up the number bought by each person in the market. Each person's consumption affects no one else. In this case the market demand curve will represent accurately the aggregate marginal willingness to pay of consumers for apples. But in cases involving external benefits, this no longer holds. We can see this by considering a type of good that inherently involves large-scale external benefits—what economists have come to call **public goods.**

LO 5

Public Goods

Consider the provision of national defence services. Once the defence system, with all its hardware and people, is in place, everyone in the country receives the service. Once the services are made available to one person, others cannot be excluded from making use of the same services. This is called **non-exclusion,** and it is one of the distinguishing characteristics of a public good. It is a good that, if made available to one person, automatically becomes available to others.

Another example of a public good is clean air. If the air around a city is free of serious contaminants, anyone in the city can breathe the air without diminishing its availability to all other people within the city. This is the second characteristic of a public good—**non-rivalness.** My consumption of clean air does not diminish your consumption. This is very different from private goods. If I buy and eat an apple, that apple is not available to you. Note carefully that it is not the ownership of the supplying organization that characterizes a public good. Although our two examples require government involvement, a public good is distinguished by the technical nature of the good—non-exclusion and non-rivalness—not by the type of organization making it available. For example, radio signals are free to anyone with a receiver, but most radio stations are privately owned.

Figure 4-4 shows four cases possible when classifying goods by whether they are rival or non-rival and excludable or non-excludable. Examples are provided for each category. Pure private goods, e.g., consumer goods, food, housing, are rival and excludable, pure public goods are non-rival and non-excludable, e.g., national defence, the atmosphere. In between are other cases as shown. Note however that goods could move from one category to another depending on ownership, government policies, and technology. An open access fishery, for example, is non-excludable but rival. Anyone with a boat can fish but my harvest will reduce the total stock of fish in the region and thus make fewer fish available for you to catch. If the fishery becomes managed under private or common property, it then becomes excludable. Those not in the community or covered by the private property rights are not allowed to fish. This characterization of goods can be helpful when thinking about public policies to help reduce pollution as we explore in Section 4.

FIGURE 4-4   **Classifying Goods**

	Excludable	Non-excludable
Rival	Pure private goods Examples: food, housing	Examples: common pool resources (fishing grounds, groundwater), free parking spaces
Non-rival	Can be public or private goods Examples: cable TV, copyrighted media, community services	Pure public goods Examples: national defence, the atmosphere

Environmental quality is essentially a public good. If the quantity of stratospheric ozone is increased, everyone worldwide benefits. Private markets are likely to undersupply public goods, relative to efficient levels as illustrated below. To sum up,

public goods are characterized by non-rivalness and non-exclusion—there is joint consumption of the good and, once provided, everyone can enjoy the good whether they pay for it or not. Environmental quality is a public good.

Aggregate Demand for Public Goods

People's demand for a public good expresses their marginal willingness to pay, just as does their demand for a private good. The difference comes in the way individual demand curves are aggregated across consumers. A detailed example illustrates the complexities public goods introduce for a market economy.

EXAMPLE
Controlling fertilizer runoff into a lake

Consider a small freshwater lake on the shores of which there are two occupied homes. The people living in the houses use the lake for recreational purposes but, unfortunately, the water quality of the lake is contaminated by fertilizer runoff from surrounding farms. The fertilizer is causing algae to grow voraciously in the lake. This lowers the dissolved oxygen content of the lake and many fish species cannot survive. In addition, the lake is becoming undesirable for swimming due to the algae blooms. Dissolved oxygen is the indicator of environmental quality and is measured in parts per million (ppm). It is possible to clean the water by having each household buy a compound that neutralizes the fertilizer and improves dissolved oxygen. The marginal cost of treatment is, however, a rising function,

(Continued)

given by the equation MC treatment $= 5 + 2Q$, where Q is the dissolved oxygen target. Each household is willing to pay for the monthly treatment necessary. Their MWTP functions[6] are given by

$$MWTP^A = 14 - 2Q_A$$
$$MWTP^B = 6 - Q_B$$

Table 4-2 shows each household's marginal willingness to pay for rising levels of water quality and the associated marginal costs. It also shows the total marginal willingness to pay, which is the sum of the individual values. We can aggregate the two households' MWTP by adding vertically their MWTP functions to obtain aggregate MWTP $= 20 - 3Q$ for quantities of water from 0 to 6 units. Note that household B is not willing to pay for a dissolved oxygen level beyond 6 units. Hence the aggregate demand curve reverts to that of household A from 6 to 7 units. At 7 units, demand from both households goes to zero. The aggregate demand curve has a kink in it at 6 units where household B drops out. If there were many households, as would be the case in practice, the aggregate demand curve would have many kinks.

TABLE 4-2   Individual and Aggregate Demand for Increasing Dissolved Oxygen in the Lake

Marginal Willingness to Pay ($/month)

Dissolved oxygen (ppm)	Household A	Household B	Total	Marginal cost of control
0	14	6	20	5
1	12	5	17	7
2	10	4	14	9
3	8	3	11	11
4	6	2	8	13
5	4	1	5	15
6	2	0	2	17
7	0	0	0	19

Note that marginal cost is an increasing function: as the lake becomes cleaner the marginal cost of continued improvement increases. This is also a public-good situation. If either household alone buys the treatment compound, water quality is improved for both households. What is the equilibrium attained? The solution is shown algebraically, graphically, and by examining the table. From Table 4-2, note that marginal cost and aggregate marginal willingness to pay are equal at a water quality of 3 ppm. At levels less than this, aggregate marginal willingness to pay for a cleaner lake exceeds the marginal cost of achieving it; hence, from the standpoint of these two households together, spending more to improve water quality is desirable. But at quality levels higher than 3 ppm, total willingness to pay falls below marginal costs. Thus, 3 ppm is the socially efficient level of water quality in the lake.

This is verified by the algebra. To solve for the socially efficient level of water quality, set the aggregate MWTP function equal to the MC function to obtain

(Continued)

6. Each household's MWTP function is its inverse demand curve for water quality.

$$20 - 3Q = 5 + 2Q$$

$$Q = 3$$

This is depicted graphically in Figure 4-5. The two top panels show the marginal willingness to pay by each of the two households, graphed from the equations above or Table 4-2. When summing individual demand curves for private goods, the individual quantities demanded at each price are added together to get the aggregate quantity demanded. But with a public good, people are, in effect, consuming the same units. Individual demand curves must be aggregated in a different way than for a private good. The principle is this: to aggregate individual demand curves for a public good, each person's MWTP for a given quantity of the good is added.[7]

In Figure 4-5, at a water quality level of 2 ppm, for example, the marginal willingness to pay is, respectively, $10 and $4 per month for households A and B. Total marginal willingness to pay at this level of water quality is $14. The bottom panel of the graph shows the aggregate marginal willingness-to-pay/demand function, the marginal cost function (MC), and the efficient level of water quality, Q^*.

Having identified the efficient level of water quality, the next question is whether a competitive market system—where entrepreneurs are on the alert for new profit opportunities—could get the contaminant in the lake reduced to the socially efficient level. Suppose a private firm attempts to sell its services to the two households. The firm goes to household A and tries to collect an amount equal to that household's true willingness to pay. But household A will presumably realize that once the lake is cleaned up, it's cleaned up for everybody no matter how much they actually contributed. And so household A may have the incentive to underpay, relative to their true willingness to pay, in the hopes that the other household will contribute enough to cover the costs of the cleanup. But, of course, the other may react in the same way. When a public good is involved, each person may have an incentive to *free-ride* on the efforts of others. A **free rider** is a person who pays less for a good than her/his true marginal willingness to pay; a person who underpays, that is, relative to the benefits they receive. The free-rider concept will be observed frequently when addressing environmental problems and the design of policy solutions.

Note as well that we have not solved for an equilibrium "price" for the public good. This is because there is no equilibrium price in the conventional sense. The equilibrium quantity could be substituted back into the aggregate MWTP function to obtain a value of $11, but the market would not clear at that price. A "price" of $11 exceeds household B's MWTP for *any* amount of cleaner water. And household A would want 1.5 units of clean water at a price of $11 per unit, not 3 units. Private markets simply cannot work when a public good of this sort is being supplied. There is no way to charge a uniform price to all consumers that both covers the supplier's marginal costs and equates each consumer's MWTP. And, because of the free-rider problem, private firms would have a very difficult time determining a person's true WTP for a public good.

To recap:

- Environmental quality improvements are essentially public goods.
- A private producer of a public good cannot use the aggregate demand curve to determine a uniform

---

[7.] The aggregation of individual demand curves for a private good can be thought of as a *horizontal summation*—adding up quantities desired at a given price. Aggregation of individual demand curves for a public good is done *vertically*—for a given quantity of the good, each party's willingness to pay as expressed on their demand curve is the value that is added. This is because of the joint consumption of the good, compared to the private good, where consumption is exclusive to the individual.

FIGURE 4-5   Derivation of the Demand for a Public Good and the Socially Efficient Output

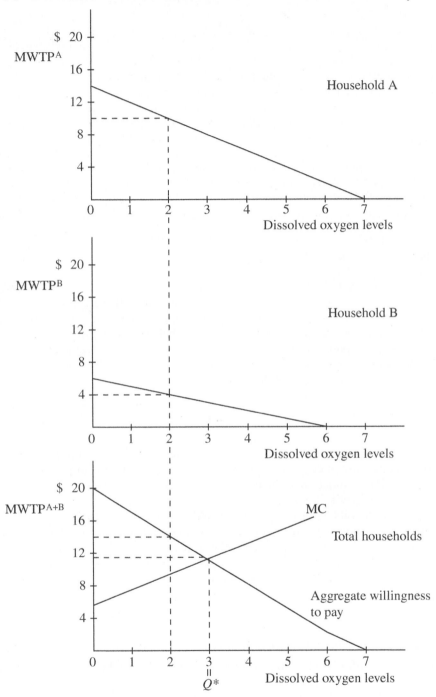

Marginal WTP functions for two households are graphed. Total WTP is the sum of each household's MWTP for a given quantity of dissolved oxygen in their water. At a quantity of 2 ppm, household A is WTP $10 and household B is WTP $4, for a total of $14. Note there is a slight kink in the aggregate demand curve at 6 units of dissolved oxygen. This is where demand comes only from household A. The socially efficient equilibrium is found where aggregate WTP equals MC of improving water quality, $Q^* = 3$ ppm.

price for all consumers. Each consumer must be charged his or her marginal WTP for the good to achieve an equilibrium where demand equals supply.

• But, a private producer cannot extract each individual's marginal WTP for the good due to free-rider problems.

• Therefore, environmental quality improvements/public goods are generally not supplied socially efficiently by decentralized private markets.

Since the market system cannot be relied upon to provide efficient quantities of public goods, we must fall back on some type of non-market institution involving collective action of one type or another. In the lake example, the households may be able to act collectively, perhaps through a homeowners' association, to secure contributions for cleaning up the lake. Of course, the free-rider problem will still exist even for the homeowners' association, but, if there are not too many of them, personal acquaintance and the operation of moral pressure may be strong enough to overcome the problem. When there are many thousands or millions of people, however, as there usually are in most environmental issues, the free-rider problem may be handled effectively only with more direct collective action through a governmental body that has regulatory and taxing power. The goal is not to completely replace market processes in these cases. What we want to do is add sufficient public oversight to the market system that we do finally end up with efficient levels of environmental quality that are equitably distributed. Chapter 5 takes a closer look at these issues.

Summary

Our main goal in this chapter was to apply the market model to situations where environmental quality is an issue. Markets are places where buyers and sellers interact over the quantities and prices of particular goods or services. The intersection of supply and demand curves shows the unique quantity and price that can simultaneously satisfy both buyers and sellers. This is called the efficient level of output, since it was the only output level where marginal willingness to pay is equal to marginal costs of production.

Two main reasons were presented for why, when environmental quality issues are involved, market prices and quantities will not be fully efficient from a social standpoint. The primary reasons for this, on a conceptual level, are the existence of external costs and external benefits. In matters of the environment, external costs are the damages that people experience from environmental impacts that are not taken into account by the firms, public agencies, or consumers whose decisions produce them. A classic case is water pollution from an upstream pulp mill that damages people using the water downstream. Another important case is the external costs that users of an open-access resource inflict upon one another through uncontrolled use of the resource. External benefits are benefits accruing to people other than the direct buyers or recipients of a good. The classic case of an external benefit is public goods. These are goods or services that, when they are made available to one person, automatically become available to others.

Faced with external costs and benefits, public goods, and open-access resources, markets cannot be relied upon to supply efficient levels of environmental quality. Environmental policies are needed to rectify these market failures.

Key Terms

Dynamic efficiency

Economic efficiency

Equity

External or social costs and benefits

Free rider

Market failures

Net social value

Non-exclusion

Non-market values

Non-rivalness

Open-access resources

Pollutee

Private costs

Public goods

Social cost accounting

Socially efficient level of production

Static efficiency

Analytical Problems

1. Let the aggregate inverse demand curve for household pesticide use be: $P = 8 - .08Q$, where A is tonnes of pesticide used by households per month. The marginal private costs (MPC) of pesticides is given by $P = 2 + .04Q$. Pesticide use leads to declines in wild bee populations, and hence its use creates a negative externality. Estimates of the marginal damages from household pesticide use are marginal external costs (MEC) = $0.03Q$. What quantity of pesticide use will the market produce when no one takes into account the negative externality? Derive the solution algebraically and illustrate graphically. What is the socially efficient price and level of pesticide use? What is the net social gain if pesticide use incorporates the externality?

2. Suppose demand for a public park (assume it is a pure public good) for two groups of consumers (A and B) is given by:

   $$Q^A = 10 - P$$

   $$Q^B = 8 - 2P$$

   where Q is the number of hectares each group would like to see incorporated into the park. If the marginal cost to provide the park is a constant $5, what is the socially efficient number of hectares for the park?

3. If the land where the park might be built were private property and the owner of the land could charge admission, what size park would the owner of the land build? Explain why the size of the park under private property will differ from when the park is a public good.

4. Using Table 4-2 and the equations underlying it, prove that a private firm will be unable to supply the public good at a price that clears the market.

5. Consider the example of the two households on the lake. Suppose the lake was cleaned up to the efficient level, and that the total costs of this cleanup are shared equally between the homeowners (stick to integer values here). Will both homeowners be better off? Prove your answer numerically. What problems does this bring up about sharing the costs of public goods?

Discussion Questions

1. What is the relationship between public goods and open-access resources?

2. Some seemingly public goods, such as radio waves, lighthouse services, and even police and sanitation services, can be supplied by private firms. Why is this so? Are there differences between these public goods and environmental services? If so, what are they?

3. Why do we care about attaining social efficiency?

4. Are socially efficient outcomes necessarily equitable? Should they be?

 For more information on the resources available from McGraw-Hill Ryerson, go to www.mheducation.ca/he/solutions.

Chapter 5

The Economics of Environmental Quality

After reading this chapter you will be able to:

LO 1 Distinguish between positive and normative economics.

LO 2 Define the marginal damage function and distinguish among four different shapes and what each means.

LO 3 Distinguish between marginal and total damages and illustrate their derivation graphically.

LO 4 Interpret the meaning of the marginal abatement cost curve and illustrate graphically the distinction between marginal and total costs of abatement.

LO 5 Show graphically how to aggregate marginal abatement cost curves.

LO 6 Explain the equimarginal principle and how it applies to marginal abatement costs.

LO 7 Illustrate graphically the determination of a socially efficient level of pollution and how this equilibrium minimizes net social costs compared to no emission control.

LO 1

Chapter 4 showed that the market system will generally not yield a socially efficient equilibrium when externalities, open-access resources, and public goods exist. Social efficiency is a **normative concept** in economics. It is a statement of what "ought to be." The determination of public policies to deal with environmental problems is another example of normative economics. How much SO_2 in the air, phosphates in lakes, or toxic compounds in the soil should there be and how are these targets reached? **Positive economics** is the study of how events actually occur in the real world, how various outcomes come to pass. The quantity of output that actually occurs on a market and its price are matters of positive economics. Questions such as how much sulphur dioxide (SO_2) actually is produced from a group of power plants and what determines the fuel mix chosen by the power plants are matters of positive economics.

In normative policy analysis, a number of steps are generally taken:

1. Identify the target level of environmental quality to achieve. The target level can be in terms of either an *ambient* or *emissions* level of the pollutant.

2. Determine how to divide that target level among the many polluters that may contribute to the environmental problem.

3. Determine the set of policy instruments to use that will meet the target. Section 4 examines these policy instruments extensively.

4. Address the question of how the benefits and costs of environmental programs are distributed across society and whether this distribution is appropriate. Techniques for computing benefits and costs are covered in Section 3.

This chapter focuses on the first step—determining a target level of environmental quality.

The construction of effective public policy for the environment depends on having "correct" information about both economic and scientific variables. How do pollutants affect environmental quality? How do producers and consumers respond to policy initiatives a regulator could take? In many cases, we know more about how producers and consumers react to different policies than we do about the links between pollutants and environmental quality. While environmental sciences are uncovering more each day about these links, much uncertainty remains. Scientists do not yet fully understand the many diverse effects that specific pollutants (or combinations of pollutants) have on the environment. Debate over the causes of climate change, what exact compounds in pulp mill effluent are responsible for disease and mortality in shell fisheries, whether electric power transmission lines cause cancer—all are examples of scientific uncertainty.

THE TARGET LEVEL OF POLLUTION—A GENERAL MODEL

There is no single public policy that can address all the diverse types of environmental problems. Nonetheless, a very simple model can be used to establish the fundamentals of any policy situation. The model presents a simple trade-off situation that characterizes all pollution-control activities. On the one hand, reducing emissions reduces the damages that people (and the ecosystem) incur from environmental pollution; on the other hand, reducing emissions takes resources that could have been used in some other way, to produce goods and services that people want. For example, the reduction of sulphur dioxide emissions from a coal-fired power plant will reduce air pollution and acid precipitation. Environmental quality will rise, benefiting people and the ecosystem. But to reduce emissions, the power plant will have to install abatement equipment or switch to a fuel input that contains less sulphur (e.g., natural gas). This increases its costs of production. If the plant can pass along these higher costs to consumers, electricity prices will rise. Consumers will then have less to spend on other goods. This trade-off is what is captured in the simple model developed in this chapter.

LO 2

Pollution Damages

"Pollution damages" refers to all of the negative impacts that users of the environment experience as a result of the degradation of that environment.[1] There are many different examples. A factory that discharges its effluent into a river poisons fish stocks. Anglers no longer can eat any fish that they catch. The toxins in the fish may in turn enter the food chain, damaging other species that prey on them—for example, raptors such as hawks and eagles. The city downstream that uses the river for its water supply will incur higher treatment costs to remove the toxins from its drinking water, and so on. Air pollution produces damage through its impacts on human health. Excess deaths from diseases such as lung cancer, chronic bronchitis, and emphysema are related to elevated levels of various pollutants, such as sulphur dioxide, asbestos fibres, and radon emissions. Air pollution can cause damages

---

[1] Refer back to Table 2-1 for a synopsis of the major pollutants in Canada and their probable environmental impacts.

through the degradation of materials (for example, outdoor sculptures in Florence, Italy dating from the Renaissance have had to be put indoors to protect them from air pollution) and the deterioration of the visual environment. Besides damage to human beings, environmental destruction can have important impacts on various elements of the non-human ecosystem. Some of these, such as destruction of genetic information in plant and animal species driven to extinction, will ultimately have important implications for humans. Estimating environmental damages is one of the primary tasks facing environmental scientists and economists; Chapter 7 addresses this problem.

In general, the greater the pollution, the greater the damages it produces. To describe the relationship between pollution and damage, a **damage function** is introduced.

> *A damage function shows the relationship between the quantity of a waste product and the value of its damages.*

There are different types of damage functions:

- **Emission damage functions** show the relationship between the wastes from a particular source or sources and the resulting damages to the environment.
- **Ambient damage functions** show how damages are related to the concentration of a waste product contained in the ambient environment.
- **Marginal damage functions** show the change in damages stemming from a unit change in emissions or ambient concentration.
- **Total damages** are the total amount of damage at each possible emission level.

The marginal damage function is the focus of the general model developed in this chapter.

LO 3

Marginal Damage Functions: Possible Shapes

Examples of marginal damage functions are depicted in Figure 5-1.[2] The top two are marginal damage functions; the horizontal axes measure the quantity of an effluent emitted into the environment during some specified period of time. The exact units (kilograms, tonnes, etc.) used in any particular case dependson the specific pollutant involved. The vertical axes measure environmental damages in dollar terms. In physical terms, environmental damage can include many types of impacts: kilometres of coastline polluted, numbers of people contracting lung disease, numbers of animals wiped out, quantities of water contaminated, and so on. Every case of environmental pollution normally involves multiple types of impacts, the nature of which will depend on the pollutant involved and the time and place where it is emitted. To consider these impacts comprehensively we need to be able to aggregate them into a single dimension. For this purpose we use a monetary scale. It is sometimes easy to express damage in monetary units. For example, it is relatively straightforward to measure the dollars people spend on **defensive expenditures** to protect themselves against pollution (e.g., heavier insulation to protect against noise, more spent on sunscreen and protective clothing with the depletion of

---

[2.] For those with a calculus background, the marginal damage function can be derived from a total damage function. It is simply the first derivative of that function. For example, if total damages are a function such as $TD = .4E_i^2$ then $MD = .8E$. The marginal damage function in this example will be linear with an intercept through the origin indicating that damages begin with the first unit of emissions.

stratospheric ozone, expenditures on bottled water when municipal water supplies are contaminated). But in many situations, measurement of the value of marginal damages is a challenging exercise (as examined more fully in Chapter 7).

FIGURE 5-1 Representative Marginal Damage Functions

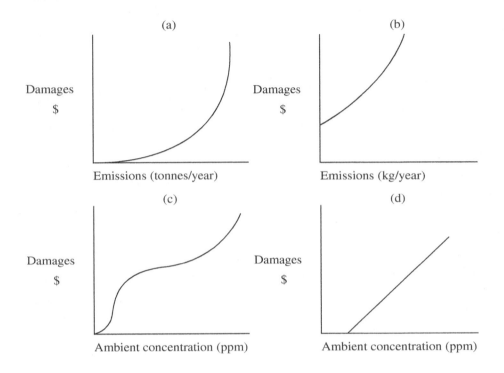

Two types of marginal damage functions are shown for waste emissions and for ambient concentrations of a waste product. Panels (a) and (b) illustrate emissions functions, while (c) and (d) show ambient functions. The marginal damage functions shown illustrate the different slopes that may be possible depending on the type of pollutant and where it is released. Marginal damages need not be a smooth curve. They can have kinks and become vertical at a emission or concentration level where the environmental impacts are catastrophic.

The marginal emission damage function in panel (a) of Figure 5-1 shows marginal damages increasing only modestly at the beginning but more rapidly as emissions increase. Work by environmental scientists and economists seems to suggest that this is a typical shape for a number of pollutants. At low levels of emissions marginal damages may be comparatively small; ambient concentrations are so modest that only the most sensitive people in the population are affected. But when emission levels go higher, damages mount—at still higher levels of emissions, marginal damages become very elevated as environmental impacts become widespread and intense. Panel (a) had the marginal damage function go vertical at a high emission level. This would represent a catastrophic impact on the environment. An example is the prediction of massive climate change if the earth's temperature rises more than 2°C from its current average level.

Panel (b) shows a marginal emission damage function that has the same general shape as panel (a) (i.e., it shows increasing marginal damage), but it begins much higher on the vertical axis and rises more sharply. It might represent a toxic substance that has a deadly effect even at very low levels of emission.

The two bottom relationships in Figure 5-1 are marginal ambient damage functions. While the vertical axes have a monetary index of damages, the horizontal axes have an index of ambient concentration, such as parts per million (ppm). Panel (c) shows a complicated function that increases at low concentrations, then tends to level off until much higher concentrations are reached, after which damages increase rapidly. This might apply, for example, to an air pollutant that causes marked damages among particularly sensitive members of society at relatively low concentrations, and among all people at very high concentrations, while in the middle ranges marginal damages do not increase rapidly. The type of pollutant illustrated in panel (c) could also be represented as a step function where there are discrete jumps in damages, followed by a range where marginal damages are relatively constant. Panel (d) demonstrates an ambient marginal damage function that begins to the right of the origin and then increases linearly with ambient concentration.

Panels (a) and (d) show a characteristic that is in fact quite controversial. The functions have a **threshold**—a value of emissions or ambient concentration below which marginal damages are zero. The pollutant can increase to these threshold levels without causing any increase in damages. As we will see in chapters to come, the assumed existence or non-existence of a threshold in the damage functions for particular pollutants has had important impacts on real-world environmental control policies. There have been long, vigorous arguments about whether the damage functions of certain types of pollutants do or do not have thresholds.

Marginal Damage Functions: Properties and Analysis

The marginal damage function is a key ingredient to normative policy analysis. This section examines its properties. While either ambient or emissions functions could be used, we have chosen emissions relationships because it is easier to design pollution policies when one can identify specific sources of emissions. While Figure 5-1 illustrated non-linear marginal damage functions, linear functions are used for the remainder of the chapter (and in subsequent chapters) to facilitate numerical calculations and the use of simple algebra. Figure 5-2 shows two marginal emission damage functions that show emissions in physical terms per unit time. Two assumptions are made to keep analysis simple:

- This is a single, non-accumulative pollutant that is uniformly distributed.
- No threshold exists; that is, each marginal damage function begins at the origin; impacts on the environment occur with the first unit of emissions.

These assumptions are modified in Sections 4 and 5; while working through this section, think about how the results would change if the pollutant were accumulative or if a threshold did exist.

Marginal damage functions are labelled MD and emissions labelled E. Each can be described by a function:

$$MD_1 = .4E$$

$$MD_2 = .6E$$

Consider first MD_1. A key property is the relationship between marginal and total damages.

The height of the marginal damage curve shows how much total damages change if there is a small change in the quantity of emissions.

FIGURE 5-2 Marginal Damage Functions for a Non-accumulative Pollutant with No Threshold

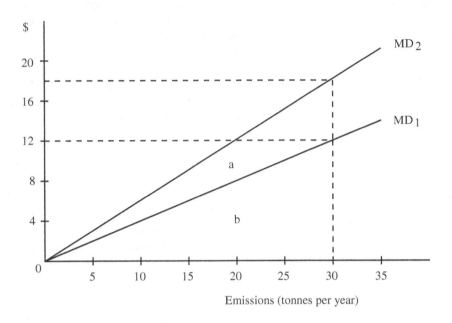

Emissions (tonnes per year)

Two marginal damage functions are shown. Marginal damages for each emissions level are read off the vertical axis. If emissions are 30 tonnes, marginal damages for MD₁ are $12, while for MD₂ they are $18. Total damages are calculated as the area under the MD curves from the origin to the emission level in question. At 30 tonnes, total damages are area $b = \$180$ for MD₁ and areas $(a + b) = \$270$ for MD₂.

When the effluent level is at the point marked $E_1 = 30$, for example, marginal damages, or MD₁, are $12. If emissions were to increase by one tonne, from 30 to 31 tonnes, the damages experienced by people exposed to those emissions would increase by a bit more than $12; by the same token, if emissions decreased by a small amount at 30 tonnes, total damages would be reduced by a bit less than $12. Since the height of the curve, as measured on the y-axis, shows marginal damages, the area under the curve between the point where it is zero and the emissions level in question shows the total damages associated with that level of emissions. In the case of marginal damage function MD₁ and 30 tonnes, total damages are shown by area b, which is a triangle equal to $180 (½ [30 times $12]). At the emission level of 30 tonnes, the marginal damages for MD₂ is $18 and total damages is area $(a + b) = \$270$ (½[18 × 30]). Thus,

total damages for a given level of emissions is the area under the MD curve from 0 to that level.

What factors might account for the difference between MD₁ and MD₂ in Figure 5-2? MD₂ might refer to a situation where there are many people who are affected by a pollutant, such as a large urban area, while MD₁ could be a more sparsely populated rural area; fewer people, smaller damage. Another possibility is that, although they apply to the same group of people, they refer to different time periods. Marginal damage function MD₂ might be the situation when there is a temperature inversion that traps a pollutant over the city and produces relatively high ambient concentrations. MD₁ would be the damage function when normal wind patterns prevail so that most of the emissions are dispersed downwind and out of the area. Thus the same emission levels at two different times could yield substantially different damage levels owing to the workings of the natural environment.

It is now time to develop the other side of the trade-off relationship—the costs of controlling emissions. Two questions to ponder: Why shouldn't the target pollution level be zero emissions? Do costs have to be considered at all?

LO 4

Abatement Costs

The costs of reducing the quantity of residuals being emitted into the environment or of lowering ambient concentrations are called **abatement costs.** Think of a pulp mill located on a river. It produces a large quantity of organic wastes. The cheapest way to get rid of these wastes is simply to pump them into the river. But the mill could reduce these emissions by reducing its output or by using pollution-control technologies or changes in the production process (e.g., non-chlorine bleaching techniques). *Abatement costs* is the catch-all term that describes these costs of abating, or reducing, the quantity of wastes put in the river. It includes all the many ways there are of reducing emissions: reduce output, changes in production technology, input switching, residuals recycling, treatment, abandonment of a site, and so on.

Abatement costs will differ from one type of effluent to another. The costs of reducing emissions of SO_2 from electric power plants will obviously be different from the costs of reducing toxic fumes from chemical plants. Even for sources producing the same type of effluent the costs of abatement are likely to be different because of differences in the technological features of the operation. One source may be relatively new, using modern production technology, while another may be an old one using more highly polluting technology. Refer back to Figure 2-1 that shows ways to reduce the flow of residuals.

Abatement cost functions can be defined algebraically and graphed. The model works with **marginal abatement costs.**[3] The units on the axes are the same as before: quantities of pollutants on the horizontal axis and monetary value on the vertical axis. Marginal emission abatement costs show the added costs of achieving a one-unit decrease in emission level, or alternatively the costs saved if emissions are increased by a unit. On the horizontal axis, marginal abatement cost curves originate at the uncontrolled emission levels (the emission levels prior to undertaking any abatement activities). In general they slope upward to the left, depicting rising marginal abatement costs. In Chapter 3, we showed marginal cost curves sloping upward to the right. The graph for marginal abatement costs goes in the opposite direction because the "quantity" we are producing is a *reduction in emissions*. A key point to remember in all figures used in the general model is that

emissions are read from left to right along the horizontal axis, while pollution abatement is measured from right to left.

[3.] Marginal abatement cost functions are the first derivative of a total abatement cost function.

FIGURE 5-3   Representative Marginal Abatement Cost Curves

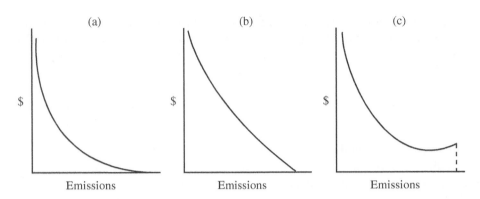

Representative marginal abatement cost curves are shown. In panel (a), costs rise very slowly as emissions are reduced from their initial level then rise rapidly with further reductions in emissions. Panel (b) shows costs that rise relatively uniformly as emissions are reduced. Panel (c) shows marginal costs initially falling as emissions are reduced due to economies of scale in abatement. Marginal costs ultimately must rise as emissions are reduced toward zero.

Figure 5-3 above presents three non-linear marginal abatement cost functions that illustrate the types of relationships one might find in practice. Let MAC be the acronym for marginal abatement costs.

- *Panel (a):* The MAC curve rises very modestly as emissions are first reduced, but then rises rapidly as emissions become relatively small.
- *Panel (b):* The MAC curve rises continuously.
- *Panel (c):* The MAC curve initially declines, then rises again. This might characterize a situation where small reductions can be handled only with technical means that require substantial initial investment. For somewhat larger reductions, the marginal costs may actually decline as it becomes possible to use these techniques more fully. Ultimately, however, marginal abatement costs increase.

Properties of Marginal Abatement Cost Functions

To investigate the properties of a marginal abatement cost consider Figure 5-4, which graphs two MAC curves derived from the following linear functions:

$$MAC_1 = 60 - 4E$$

$$MAC_2 = 75 - 5E$$

From the graph (or setting MAC = 0 for each equation and solving for E), we see that the uncontrolled emissions level for both sources is 15 tonnes per month. From 15 tonnes each MAC slopes upward to the left. This means that marginal costs of abatement rise as more and more emissions are controlled. At 10 tonnes per month of emissions, $MAC_1 = \$20$ while $MAC_2 = \$25$. When emissions are reduced to zero, the marginal cost of the last unit controlled is $60 for polluter 1 and $75 for polluter 2. Thus, the larger the reduction in emissions, the greater the marginal costs of producing further reductions. Note that by drawing these as linear functions with positive intercepts we are saying that the technology exists to reduce emissions to zero at a finite cost. If the MAC curve looks like panel (a) of Figure 5-3, it is technologically impossible to reduce emissions to zero.

It is also possible that the only way a polluter can reduce emissions to zero is to cease the activity that is generating the pollution. This may mean closing a plant or changing the good produced, which will have economic repercussions. If the polluter is one small plant within a large industry consisting of many such plants, the costs of actually closing it down may not be that great. In fact, it may have very little impact on, say, the price to consumers of whatever is being produced (paper in the pulp mill example), though the local impact on jobs and community welfare may be substantial. But if we are talking about the marginal abatement costs for an entire industry—the petrochemical industry in Ontario or Alberta, for example—the "shut-down" option, as a way of achieving zero emissions, would have enormous costs.

FIGURE 5-4   Marginal Abatement Costs for a Pollutant

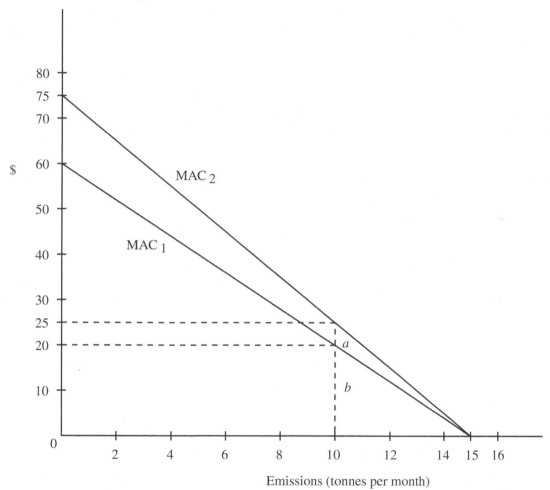

MAC$_1$ and MAC$_2$ illustrate two sources of pollution (or one polluter at two different time periods) that are initially releasing 15 tonnes of pollution per month when no abatement occurs. At 10 tonnes of emissions (that is, abating five units each) MAC$_1$ = \$20 while MAC$_2$ = \$25. Total abatement costs for reducing emissions from 15 to 10 tonnes is area *b* for polluter 1 (\$50 per month) and areas *a* + *b* for polluter 2 (\$62.50 per month). Cost saving for adopting polluter's technology is area *a* (\$12.50 per month).

As with any marginal graph, we can depict not only marginal but also total values. If emissions are currently at 10 tonnes per year, the value on the vertical axis shows the marginal cost of achieving one more unit of emission reduction. The area under the MAC curve, between its origin at 15 tonnes per month and any particular emission level, is equal to the total costs of abating emissions to that level. For MAC_1, the **total abatement cost** of achieving an emission level of 10 tonnes per month is equal to area b = \$50 (the area of the triangle = ½ [5 times \$20]) The total abatement cost for polluter 2 is area $a + b$ = \$62.50 (the area of triangle = ½ [5 times \$25]).

> *The key to calculating total abatement costs (TAC) is to remember to read the graph from right to left.*

What could account for the difference in the slopes of the two MAC curves when they pertain to the same pollutant? Often the reason is differences in **pollution-control technology.** MAC_1 uses a cheaper technology to control its emissions than MAC_2. This could be because they are two different plants and MAC_2 was built many years ago, MAC_1 more recently.[4]

Technological change can therefore result in a lowering of the MAC curve for a given pollutant. We can readily measure the annual cost saving for a plant that adopts a new technology. Suppose again that emissions are reduced from 15 to 10 tonnes per month. Polluter 2 would save area a if it adopts the new technology. We know from before that areas $a + b$ = \$62.50 and area b equals \$50, so the cost saving is \$12.50 per month. This type of analysis will be important when we examine different types of pollution-control policies, because one of the criteria used to evaluate these policies is how much cost-saving incentive they offer to firms to engage in research and development to produce new pollution-control technologies.

LO 5

Aggregate Marginal Abatement Costs

Most environmental policies, especially at provincial or federal levels, are aimed at controlling emissions from groups of pollution sources, not just single polluters. How are the marginal abatement costs of a group of firms (in the same industry or located in the same region) aggregated when their marginal abatement costs differ? The process of aggregation introduces an important concept in the design of effective environmental policy. The least costly way of achieving reductions in emissions for an individual firm is shown by its marginal abatement cost function; for a group of polluting sources, it is the aggregate marginal abatement cost function.

Panels (a) and (b) of Figure 5-5 redraw MAC_1 and MAC_2 from Figure 5-4. Panel (c) is the aggregate marginal abatement cost curve. When we have two (or any other number greater than one) sources with different abatement costs, the aggregate abatement cost will depend on how we allocate the total emissions among the different sources. The principle to follow is

> *to aggregate marginal abatement costs, individual functions must be added horizontally to yield the lowest possible aggregate marginal abatement costs.*

---

[4] The different MAC curves could also be for the same plant, but at different time periods in its existence.

Figure 5-5 provides an example of how to aggregate different marginal abatement costs. The steps are outlined below.

EXAMPLE

How to aggregate MAC curves

1. Select a particular level of marginal abatement cost, for example $40 per month.

2. Find how much each polluter will abate at this cost. At $40, polluter 1 will want to abate to 5 tonnes per month, while polluter 2 will abate to 7 tonnes per month.

3. Add up these emission levels: 5 tonnes + 7 tonnes = 12 tonnes per month.

4. Repeat the process for a different abatement cost level.

5. Graph the aggregate curve as shown on panel (c) of Figure 5-5.

FIGURE 5-5 Aggregation of Marginal Abatement Cost Curves

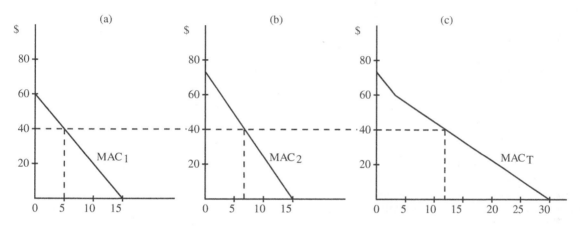

MAC curves are aggregated horizontally by picking a dollar value of marginal abatement costs and adding up each source's emission level at the MAC. For MAC = $40, panel (a) shows that polluter 1 releases 5 tonnes per month (abates 15 − 5 = 10 tonnes), while panel (b) shows that polluter 2 releases 7 tonnes (abates 15 − 7 = 8 tonnes). The aggregate MAC is shown in panel (c), where at a MAC of $40 total emissions are 12 tonnes per month. The aggregate MAC is derived by horizontally adding individual functions for different levels of MACs.

LO 6

THE EQUIMARGINAL PRINCIPLE

We come now to the discussion of a simple but important economic principle, one that we will use repeatedly in the chapters to come. It's called the **equimarginal principle.** The equimarginal principle can be applied at the level of one firm with multiple plants all producing the same good and pollutant or different firms producing the same good and pollutant. We illustrate the principle using two different plants owned by the same firm, but one can readily think about two different firms. For example, we might be examining the emissions of sulphur dioxide from the electricity sector. Electricity is the homogeneous good that can be generated by different techniques, for example, coal-fired or gas-fired generation. The two types of generation could be owned by different companies as would be the case in many parts of the United States or the same company as in many Canadian provinces. The total amount of electricity produced is the sum of the output from each plant. Let us assume that we are examining two gas-fired plants that were built at different times and make use of different technologies. The old one, plant A in Figure 5-6, has older technology; this gives a marginal cost curve that starts relatively low but rises steeply as production increases. The new plant, plant B in Figure 5-6, uses newer technology; it has a higher marginal cost at low output levels, but marginal costs do not rise as steeply as production increases.

FIGURE 5-6   The Equimarginal Principle

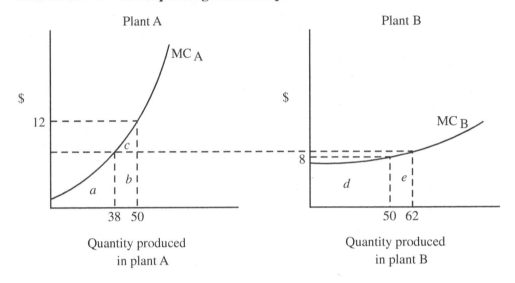

When there are two different plants producing the same good, a firm will minimize its total costs of production by equating the marginal costs of production of the two plants. For example, to produce 100 units at the least total cost when marginal costs are equal, the low-cost plant will produce more (62 units) while the high-cost plant will produce fewer (38 units). This will yield lower total costs than if both plants produced 50 units each.

Consider now a situation where this two-plant firm wants to produce a total output of 100 units. How many units should it produce in each plant in order to produce the 100 units at the *least total cost?* Would it be best to produce 50 units in each plant? This is depicted in Figure 5-6; at an output of 50, plant A has a marginal cost of $12 while plant B has a marginal cost of $8. Total production costs are the sum of total costs at each plant, or $(a + b + c) + (d)$. But here is the important point: We can lower the total cost of our 100 units by reallocating production. Reduce production in plant A by one unit; costs will fall by $12. Then increase the production in plant B by one unit; costs there will rise by $8. The firm is still producing the 100 units, but has saved $12 − $8 = $4. Its total cost, the sum of the costs in the two plants, has gone down.

As long as the marginal costs in the two plants differ from one another, production should be reallocated away from the high-marginal-cost plant and toward the low-marginal-cost plant to get a reduction in total cost. In fact, the total costs of producing the 100 units in the two plants will be at a minimum only when the marginal costs of the two plants are equal—hence, the "equimarginal principle." In the figure, this happens when the output in plant A is 38 units and the output in plant B is 62 units. Total costs in geometric terms are now $a + (d + e)$.

The goal of the equimarginal principle is to minimize the total cost of producing a given quantity of output. This goal is realized when production is distributed in such a way as to equalize the marginal costs between the production sources. More simply put,

> *the equimarginal principle requires that total production be distributed among sources so that their marginal costs of production are equalized.*

Aggregation of MACs invokes the equimarginal principle. To have the minimum aggregate marginal abatement cost curve, the aggregate level of emissions must be distributed among the different sources in such a way that they will all have the same marginal abatement costs. Look again at Figure 5-5. Start at the 12 tonnes/month point on the aggregate curve. Obviously, this 12-tonne total could be distributed between the two sources in any number of ways: 6 tonnes from each source, 10 tonnes from one and 2 tonnes from the other, and so on. But only one allocation will give the lowest aggregate marginal abatement costs; this is the allocation that leads the different sources to the point where they have exactly the same marginal abatement costs. The aggregate MAC has been constructed so that the equimarginal principle is satisfied. In Figure 5-5, at a marginal abatement cost of $40 per tonne, the efficient distribution of emissions between the two polluters is for polluter 1 to emit 5 tonnes (abate 10 tonnes) and for polluter 2 to emit 7 tonnes (abate 8 tonnes).

LO 7

THE SOCIALLY EFFICIENT LEVEL OF EMISSIONS

> *For a particular pollutant being released at a particular place and time, the socially efficient level of emissions is found where the marginal damage function and the marginal abatement cost function are equated.*

We illustrate this equilibrium concept graphically and algebraically.

Graphically: Figure 5-7 shows that the MAC intersects the MD at an emission level of 10 tonnes per month. Marginal abatement costs are equal to marginal damages at this emission level (both equal $20).

Algebraically: E represents the level of emissions. E^* is the socially efficient level of emissions. Assume both the MAC and MD are linear.[5] Let

$$MAC = 60 - 4E$$

$$MD = 2E.$$

Social efficiency requires MAC = MD. Substitute in for MAC and MD.

$$60 - 4E = 2E$$

(Continued)

[5.] The MAC is the same used in the previous section for polluter 1 (MAC_1).

Solve for E^*:

$$E^* = 10 \text{ tonnes per month}$$

Substitute E^* back into either the MAC or MD to determine the "price" (marginal cost, marginal damage) that equates the two curves.

$$60 - 4(10) = \$20.$$

FIGURE 5-7   Determining the Socially Efficient Level of Emissions

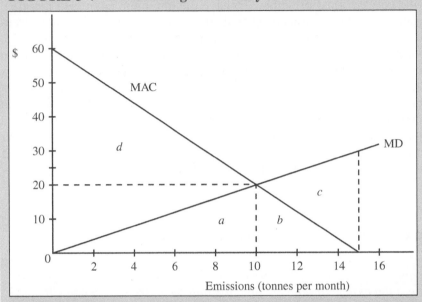

The socially efficient equilibrium is found where the MAC curve intersects the MD curve. This occurs at E^* = 10 tonnes of pollution per month. Area $(a + b + c)$ = total damages at the initial emission level of 15 tonnes per month. At E^*, total damages equal area a for a net gain of areas $(b + c)$. At E^*, total abatement costs equal area b. Therefore, the net social gain is areas $(b + c)$ minus b = area c.

Why is E^* socially efficient? Social efficiency means trading off a marginal increase in pollution damages against a marginal increase in pollution abatement costs. Higher emissions expose society to greater costs stemming from environmental damages. Lower emissions involve society in greater costs in the form of resources devoted to abatement activities. The socially efficient level of effluent is thus the level where these two types of costs exactly offset one another; that is, where marginal abatement costs equal marginal damage costs. Is the socially efficient level always positive? No. If the MD and MAC do not intersect at a positive level of emissions, the socially efficient level will be zero. The slopes and shape of the MAC and MD curves determine the equilibrium.

From an efficiency standpoint, E^* is the best the economy can do; see the proof below.

COMPUTING NET SOCIAL VALUES

E^* is the point where the net social benefits from reducing pollution are maximized relative to starting at the initial emission level of 15 tonnes (social costs from pollution control are minimized). This can be shown using Figure 5-7 and by computing total benefits and costs. The steps are as follows:

(Continued)

1. Suppose no emissions are controlled and are thus 15 tonnes per month.

2. Compute total damages (TD) at 15 tonnes per month.
   Graphically: Total damages are the area under the MD curve from 0 to 15 tonnes. This is shown in Figure 5-6 as area $(a + b + c)$.
   Numerically: TD = \$225 (½ [15 times \$30]).[6]

3. Compute total abatement costs (TACs) at 15 units of output.
   TACs are zero; there is no abatement.

4. Compute net social costs.
   Net social costs are the difference between total damages and total abatement costs, which at 15 tonnes equal \$225.
   Repeat the exercise assuming emissions are now at the socially efficient level of $E^* = 10$ tonnes.

5. Total damages E^* are area a and equal \$100.[7]

6. Total abatement costs are area b and equal \$50.

7. Total social costs are thus \$100 + \$50 = \$150.

8. Compute the difference in the total social costs between the two emission levels.
   \$150 is clearly less than \$225.
   The net saving is area c = \$75 compared to the case with zero pollution control.

Society saves \$75 by reducing emissions from 15 to 10 tonnes. This is the net social benefit of achieving the socially efficient level of emissions compared to no emission control. But how do we know that E^* is the best society can do given the starting point and specific MD and MAC curves? Suppose emissions are reduced to zero. Total damages are then zero. Total abatement costs are areas $(a + b + d)$ = (½ [\$60 times 15]) = \$450, which is considerably larger than \$150. Pick any other emission level and compute the net social cost. It will be higher than that at E^*.

The MAC–MD model is conceptual and allows us to examine a wide variety of cases. In the real world every pollution problem is different. This analysis provides a generalized way of framing the problem that obviously has to be adapted to the specifics of any particular case of environmental pollution. The real world is a dynamic place, and this is especially true of environmental pollution control. The level of emissions that was efficient last year, or last decade, is not necessarily the level that is efficient today, or that is likely to be in the future. Many different factors lie behind the marginal damage and marginal abatement cost functions, and when any of these underlying factors change, the functions themselves will shift and E^* will change.

Social efficiency is a normative concept. E^*, the level that equates marginal abatement costs and marginal damage costs, is presented as a desirable target for public policy. Will the actual economy be at E^*? This is unlikely without some form of government intervention. Unless persuaded to take into account the damages they inflict on society, polluters will have no incentive to incur any abatement costs. They will simply produce at the maximum pollution level. Section 4 examines in detail policies and actions that induce polluters to reduce emissions by whatever means possible to move toward a socially efficient equilibrium.

[6.] The height of the triangle is found by substituting 15 units into the MD function, MD = 2E, the MD at 15 tonnes is \$30.

[7.] Area a = (½ [10 × \$20]) = \$100.

EXAMPLE

Determining the socially efficient level of nitrogen oxides

Are regulations in the United States that govern the emissions of sulphur and nitrogen oxides from electric utilities socially efficient? That was the question asked by three researchers at Resources for the Future.[8] They estimated MAC and MD functions for both pollutants and used that information to calculate socially efficient outcomes. The MD curves cannot be estimated precisely, but appear to be relatively flat over a range of emission levels. The researchers calculated an upper and lower bound MD for each air contaminant. Figures 5-8 and 5-9 illustrate their findings. The socially efficient price

FIGURE 5-8 MAC and MD Curves for Sulphur Dioxide from the U.S. Electricity Sector

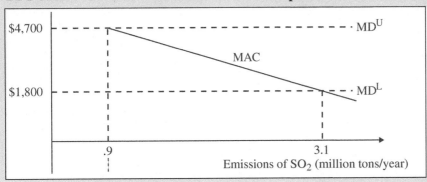

Given estimates of the MD and MAC curves for sulphur dioxide (SO_2) emissions from the U.S. electricity sector, the socially efficient equilibrium lies between .9 and 3.1 million U.S. tons of SO_2 per year. Two estimates of the MD curve are shown: MD^U is an upper bound estimate and MD^L, the lower bound.

Source: *Adapted from Banshaf, S., Burtraw, D., and K. Palmer, "Efficient Emission Fees in the US Electricity Sector,"* Resource and Energy Economics *26 (2004), pp. 317–341.*

FIGURE 5-9 MAC and MD Curves for Nitrogen Oxides from the U.S. Electricity Sector

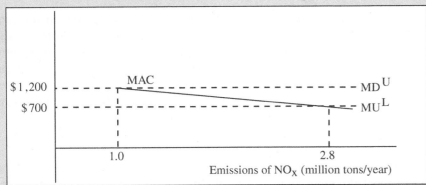

Given estimates of the MD and MAC curves for nitrogen oxides (NO_x) emissions from the U.S. electricity sector, the socially efficient equilibrium lies between 1 and 2.8 million U.S. tons of NO_x per year. Two estimates of the MD curve are shown: MD^U is an upper bound estimate and MD^L, the lower bound.

Source: *Adapted from Banshaf, S., Burtraw, D., and K. Palmer, "Efficient Emission Fees in the US Electricity Sector,"* Resource and Energy Economics *26 (2004), pp. 317–341.*

(Continued)

---

8. See S. Banzhaf, D. Burtraw, and K. Palmer, "Efficient Emission Fees in the U.S. Electricity Sector," Resource and Energy Economics 26 (2004): 317–341. Figures 5-8 and 5-9 are adapted from information in their report.

for sulphur dioxide is between \$4,700 and \$1,800 per U.S. ton, while that for nitrogen oxides is between \$1,200 and \$700 per U.S. ton. Efficient emission levels are then between 0.9 and 3.1 million tons for sulphur dioxide and 1.0 to 2.8 million tons for nitrogen dioxide. The results of this simulation suggest that emission limits contemplated by U.S. regulators and legislators at the time of this study were within the range of the socially efficient equilibrium points; at the higher end for sulphur dioxide and the middle for nitrogen oxides.

ADDENDUM: LINKING THE MAC CURVE TO PROFIT MAXIMIZATION[9]

The simple model in this chapter focuses on the realistic situation in which polluters can invest in abatement technologies that reduce the emissions from their operation. A MAC curve was assumed to exist for polluters. Let's back up for a moment and look more generally at the trade-offs facing polluters to see how the MAC curve can be linked to a firm's profit-maximizing behaviour. Suppose a firm can only reduce emissions by cutting its level of output of the good it produces. This would be the case if there were no abatement technologies or process changes that would reduce emissions per unit output.

Firms operating in a perfectly competitive industry maximize profits where the market price, P, equals their marginal costs of production, MC. Setting P = MC determines the firm's output level, Q. This is shown in the top half of Figure 5-10. But the firm also produces pollution. For simplicity, assume that one unit of output produces one unit of pollution. The bottom half of Figure 5-10 maps output into emissions of pollution (E). When there are no environmental regulations, the polluter is free to dispose of as much pollution as it wishes. What is the maximum amount of emissions? In Figure 5-10 the profit-maximizing firm produces Q_0 units of output, which means that it also produces E_{MAX} units of pollution.

With a rising MC curve, the firm earns profits on all units of output up to Q_0, the marginal unit of output produced where price is just equal to MC. The firm's marginal profits equal (P – MC), and are greatest for the first unit of the good sold at the constant price of P, then fall until P = MC at the competitive equilibrium. These marginal profits are what the firm would give up if it had to reduce its output below Q_0 because it must reduce its emissions. The MAC curve can then be thought of as the forgone profits the firm incurs due to reductions in emissions. The lower panel of Figure 5-10 graphs (P – MC) for all levels of output between 0 and Q_0. The distance $a0$ in the top panel equals $b0$ in the bottom. The MAC function thus has the same shape as the MC curve for the firm's output, but is inverted.

---

[9] The material in this section can be omitted, as it need not be used in subsequent chapters.

FIGURE 5-10 Linking the MAC Curve to Profit Maximization

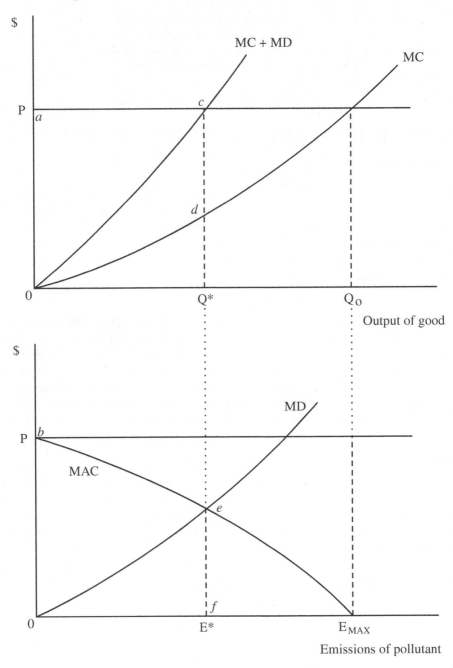

A competitive firm ignoring the damages caused by its emissions of pollution maximizes profit where the price of the good it produces equals its marginal costs of production. For all units of output between 0 and Q_0, the firm earns marginal profits graphed in the lower panel as the downward sloping function. Assuming one unit of output generates one unit of pollution, these marginal profits represent the firm's MAC curve. If it must reduce emissions, the costs it incurs are forgone profits. When the firm is required to incorporate pollution damages as one of its costs of production, the MD curve is added to MC and the firm produces E^* units of pollution.

Suppose now that the firm is required by environmental policy to include the marginal damages due to its pollution as one of its costs of production. The marginal damage curve (MD) from the lower panel represents these costs. The MD curve is thus added to the firm's MC curve. The firm's marginal social costs now equal MC + MD.[10] Given these costs, the firm maximizes profits where P = MC + MD. Output of Q^* produces E^* emissions.[11] A socially efficient equilibrium in the goods market equates market prices of goods to the social costs of production on the margin, where these social costs include marginal costs of production plus marginal damages from production.

The derivation of the MAC curve becomes more complex if the firm also has the option of purchasing abatement technology that would reduce its emissions per unit output. The pollution intensity of its output would decline. Abatement technologies would add to the firm's costs in the form of fixed or variable costs or both. Suppose the abatement technology adds to variable costs. The MC of production would rise, but emissions per unit output would fall. These effects would combine to have the MAC curve shift downward from the one shown in Figure 5-10. That would mean not only is the initial level of emissions lower, but that the efficient level would also be lower.

Summary

This chapter develops a simple model of pollution control. It is based on the notion of a trade-off of environmental damages and pollution abatement costs. The marginal damage function is introduced. It shows the marginal social damages resulting from varying levels of residual emissions or ambient pollutant levels. Marginal abatement cost relationships are then shown, first for an individual pollution source and then for a group of such sources. By bringing together these two types of relationships a socially efficient level of emissions is found. The socially efficient level of pollution is where marginal damages and marginal abatement costs are equal. At this level of emissions, net social costs—the total of abatement costs and damages—are minimized.

A word of caution is appropriate. The model presented in this chapter is very general, and risks giving an overly simplistic impression of pollution problems in the real world. In fact, there are very few actual instances of environmental pollution where we know the marginal damage and marginal abatement functions with certainty. The natural world is too complex, and human and non-human responses are too difficult to identify with complete clarity. Furthermore, polluters come in all types and sizes and economic circumstances and it takes enormous resources to learn even simple things about the costs of pollution abatement in concrete instances. Pollution-control technology is changing rapidly, so what is efficient today will not necessarily be so tomorrow. Nevertheless, the simple model is useful for thinking about the basic problem of pollution control, and it will be useful in our later chapters on the various approaches to environmental policy. Before discussing complicated policy issues, it is appropriate to study the ways economists have tried to measure and make visible marginal abatement costs and marginal damages in specific cases of environmental quality changes.

[10.] This definition of social costs was also covered in Chapter 4: see Figure 4-3. This addendum links the marginal social costs to the MAC–MD diagram.

[11.] Note too that distance *cd* in the top panel is equal to distance *ef* in the bottom panel, both indicating the difference between marginal costs and marginal damages at the socially efficient equilibrium of E^* emissions and Q^* of the good.

Key Terms

Abatement costs	Marginal damage functions
Ambient damage functions	Normative concept
Damage function	Pollution-control technology
Defensive expenditures	Positive economics
Emission damage functions	Threshold
Equimarginal principle	Total abatement cost
Marginal abatement costs	Total damages

Analytical Problems

1. Let $MAC_1 = 100 - 10E$ and $MAC_2 = 50 - 10E$. Graph each function and compute the aggregate MAC curve. Let $MD = 30E$, compute the socially efficient equilibrium. For the equations given above, suppose the government sets the pollution level at four units. What are the net social costs of this policy?

2. Suppose a technological change occurs that reduces the marginal costs of abatement for polluter 1 in the above equation to that of polluter 2. How does this affect the socially efficient level of pollution? Solve numerically and graphically.

3. When pollution regulations are imposed, governments incur enforcement costs that are part of social costs. Assume that enforcement costs are a constant amount, independent of the amount of pollution reduced. How would this change the location of the socially efficient equilibrium? Show graphically and explain.

Discussion Questions

1. Scientists discover that marginal damages rise exponentially with emissions. How would this change the computation of total damages when there is no pollution abatement?

2. How is the equimarginal principle related to the socially efficient level of output?

3. Explain why society wants to minimize net social costs (maximize net social value) when choosing a target level of pollution.

Mc Graw Hill Education connect   For more information on the resources available from McGraw-Hill Ryerson, go to www.mheducation.ca/he/solutions.

Benefit–Cost Analysis

In the last few chapters we have used the concepts of "abatement costs" and "damages" without explaining in any detail how we might measure their magnitudes in particular situations. In the next three chapters, this question is addressed. The focus is on benefit–cost analysis in Chapter 6 as one of the tools economists use to find efficient outcomes and methods available for estimating benefits and costs that can be used to estimate marginal damages and marginal abatement costs relevant to environmental policy decisions in Chapters 7 and 8.

Chapter 6

Framework of Analysis

After reading this chapter you will be able to:

LO 1) Define the basic framework for benefit–cost analysis and how it could be used to assess government projects and regulatory actions.

LO 2) Show graphically that a project which maximizes net social benefits will be equivalent to the socially efficient equilibrium.

LO 3) Explain the role of discounting in benefit–cost analysis and why the social and private discount rates will typically differ.

LO 4) Explain how the equity and the distribution of income enter into benefit–cost analysis.

LO 5) Describe how expected values can reflect uncertainty and how they can be used in benefit–cost analysis.

LO 6) Define cost effectiveness and when it is used instead of benefit–cost analysis.

Policy decisions require information, and, although the availability of good information doesn't automatically mean that decisions also will be good, its *un*availability will almost always contribute to bad decisions. There are a variety of alternative frameworks for generating and presenting information useful to policy-makers, calling for different skills and research procedures. We focus on benefit–cost analysis as one such method of quantifying the theoretical concepts addressed thus far and as a decision tool that governments may use to evaluate policy options and environmental infrastructure investments. A brief discussion of cost effectiveness analysis concludes the chapter.

LO 1)

BENEFIT–COST ANALYSIS

Benefit–cost analysis (BCA) is to the public sector and social valuations what a profit-and-loss analysis is to a private-sector firm. If an automobile company contemplated introducing a new model of car, it would want to get some idea of how its profitability would be affected. The cost side would include all costs of production and distribution of its goods: labour, raw materials, energy, emission-control equipment, transportation, and so on. Revenues are the firm's "benefits" and are calculated as the market price of its goods times the quantity sold. The firm then compares expected revenues with anticipated costs to see if it should introduce the new model. Benefit–cost analysis is an analogous exercise for programs in the public sector. There are two critical differences between social benefit–cost analysis and private investment decisions:

1. Benefit–cost analysis is a tool for helping to make public decisions—what policies and programs to introduce—done from the standpoint of society in general rather than from that of a single profit-making firm.

2. It incorporates social valuation of all inputs and outputs related to the project whether or not they are transacted in private markets.

A major challenge for benefit–cost analysis is how to value non-market costs and benefits. Information about market prices, costs, and profits is very important in this process; it provides useful facts about private valuations. The techniques developed for benefit–cost analysis begin with these private values and compute social values when there is a divergence between the two, as is often the case with environmental issues. Chapters 7 and 8 examine a variety of techniques for social valuation. This chapter looks at how to undertake a benefit–cost study assuming one has already measured the benefits and costs.

Benefit–cost analysis has led two intertwined lives. The first is among its practitioners, economists inside and outside public agencies who have developed the techniques, tried to produce better data, and extended the scope of the analysis. The second is among the politicians and administrators who have set the rules and procedures governing the use of benefit–cost analysis for public decision making. In Canada, benefit–cost analysis has not been officially legislated for use by government agencies at the federal or provincial level. It has been used somewhat randomly, and at times for political self-interest, rather than as a technique for objective decision making. By contrast, in the United States benefit–cost analysis has a much stronger legislative history. It was first mandated for use in conjunction with the United States *Flood Control Act of 1936.* That act specified that federal participation in projects to control flooding on major rivers of the country would be justifiable *"if the benefits to whomever they accrue are in excess of the estimated costs."* Procedures had to be developed to measure these benefits and costs to determine if this criterion was satisfied for any proposed flood-control dam or large levee project. This process has taken many years and, indeed, techniques for measuring non-market benefits and costs are still being developed today.

The status and role of benefit–cost analysis in public natural resource and environmental decision making is still controversial. Some criticisms of the technique include the following:

- Public agencies only use benefit–cost analysis in ways that would help them justify ever-larger budgets.

- Benefit–cost analysis is really an attempt to short-circuit the process of political discussion and decision that should take place around prospective public projects and programs.

- Benefit–cost analysis is a way of curtailing public programs because of the difficulty of measuring benefits relative to costs.

One can find examples to support each of these points. Perhaps because of these problems, benefit–cost analysis is not widely used in Canada by governments. Some programs have been evaluated from a benefit–cost perspective; for example, the examination in the mid-1970s of the proposed Mackenzie Valley natural gas pipeline (which was not built), and resource development projects in British Columbia (such as Northeast Coal, which was undertaken). But, in recent years, little formal analysis has been done by government agencies. Nevertheless, benefit–cost analysis remains an important analytical tool that is used widely throughout the world. And, while full benefit–cost studies may not be done by governments, the measurement of social benefits and costs has become an important ingredient in public-policy decisions.

The Basic Framework

Benefit–cost analysis involves measuring, adding up, and comparing all the benefits and all the costs of a particular public project or program. There are essentially four steps in a benefit–cost analysis:

> 1. *Specify clearly the project or program, including its scale and the perspective of the study.*
>
> 2. *Describe quantitatively the inputs and outputs of the program.*
>
> 3. *Estimate the social costs and benefits of these inputs and outputs.*
>
> 4. *Compare these benefits and costs.*

Each step is covered in general terms and examples follow.

LO2

Scale and Perspective of a BCA Project or Program

Benefit–cost analysis is a tool of public analysis, but there are actually many publics. If you were doing a benefit–cost study for a national agency, the "public" normally would be all the people living in the particular country. But if you were employed by a city or regional planning agency to do a benefit–cost analysis of a local environmental program, you would undoubtedly focus on benefits and costs accruing to people living in those areas. At the other extreme, the rise of global environmental issues requires a worldwide perspective.

Once the perspective is determined, there should be a complete specification of the main elements of the project or program: location, timing, groups involved, connections with other programs, and so on.

There are two primary types of public environmental programs for which benefit–cost analyses are done:

1. *Physical projects* that involve direct public production, such as public waste treatment plants, beach restoration projects, hazardous-waste incinerators, habitat improvement projects, and land purchase for preservation.

2. *Regulatory programs* that are aimed at enforcing environmental laws and regulations, such as pollution-control standards, technological choices, waste disposal practices, and restrictions on land development.

How do analysts determine the scale of the project or which regulatory program to select? There are a number of different approaches to this issue. The key one that links BCA to our theoretical model is the **socially efficient scale**:

> *The socially efficient scale* maximizes the net social benefits *from the project. Net social benefits are maximized where MAC = MD.*

Consider Figure 6-1 (Figure 5-7 from the previous chapter). It shows the standard emission-control model, with marginal damage (MD) and marginal abatement cost (MAC) functions. The figure can be used to prove that the socially efficient scale maximizes net social benefits where the MAC = MD, given the location of the MAC and MD curves when the analysis starts where no pollution is being abated.

FIGURE 6-1 The Socially Efficient Scale of a Public Project

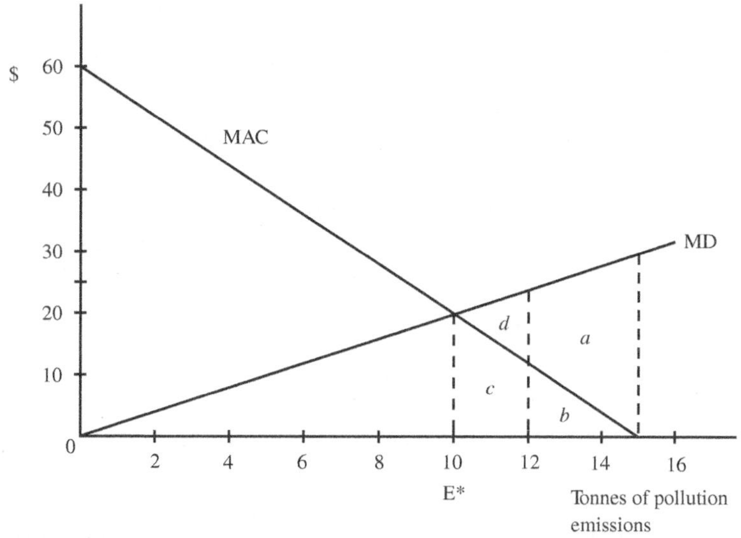

The socially efficient scale of a public project or regulation to reduce emissions is determined where the MAC curve intersects the MD curve. This is at $E^* = 10$ tonnes of emissions per month. The socially efficient scale maximizes the net benefits from the project—areas $a + d$. If the target of the project is to reduce emission to 12 tonnes, the net benefits are only area a. This is not the socially efficient scale.

PROOF

Assume first that no emissions are controlled: $E = 15$. A public program is proposed that would lower emissions to 12 tonnes. At 12 tonnes of emissions, the total benefits of the program are the total damages reduced. This equals areas $(a + b) = \$81$.[1] Total abatement costs are equal to area $b = \$18$.[2] The net benefits of the program are therefore equal to area $a = \$63$.

For an emission reduction program to give maximum net benefits, however, it would have to reduce emissions to $E^* = 10$ tonnes of emissions, the level at which MD = MAC. Net social benefits at 10 tonnes equal $(d + a) = \$75$.[3] The net gain from being at the socially efficient scale of 10 tonnes rather than 12 tonnes of emissions is thus area d, which equals \$12. This may not seem like much, but try multiplying by \$1-million to get a feel for what might be the amounts at stake in practice.

---

[1] The simplest way to compute areas a plus b is to calculate the difference between total damages at the initial emissions level of 15 and total damages at the target of 12 units. This will be the difference between two triangles. At 15 units, MD = \$30 per unit. This can be found graphically or by using the equation for marginal damages: MD = $2E$. Total damages measured from 0 to 15 units are \$225. At 12 units, MD = \$24 per unit emitted. Total damages measured from 0 to 12 units are \$144. The difference is \$81.

[2] At 12 units of emissions, MAC per unit are \$12. This is found graphically or by substituting the 12 units into the marginal abatement cost function: MAC = $60 - 4E$. Area b is then the area of the triangle between 15 and 12 units of abatement.

[3] Again, the simplest way to compute the net social benefits is to calculate the change in total damages (TD) due to the policy and subtract from this the change in total abatement costs (TAC). At $E^* = 10$, the change in TD = area $(a + b + c + d)$, which equals \$125 (TD at 15 emissions are \$225, TD at 10 emissions are \$100). The change in TAC = area $(c + b)$, which equals \$50. The net social benefits are therefore area $(a + d) = \$75$. Be sure you can prove that net social benefits are at a maximum when MD = MAC.

The problem for the benefit–cost analysis of a specific proposal is how do decision-makers know that 10 units of emissions is the socially efficient level? If they can graph or write equations for the MAC and MD curves, computing E^* is straightforward, as Figure 6-1 illustrates. When the MAC and MD curves are not readily identifiable, a procedure called **sensitivity analysis** is undertaken. This means recalculating benefits and costs for programs somewhat larger and somewhat smaller than the target chosen; that is, a program with somewhat more and less restrictive emission reductions to determine which level maximizes net social benefits. Chapter 7 examines ways to quantify the MD curve (or the benefits of reducing environmental contaminants), while Chapter 8 looks more extensively at the cost side of the equation. The key point is that benefit–cost analysis is an attempt to quantify the theoretical relationships that show the benefits of reducing emissions net of the costs of doing so.

Description of the Program's Inputs and Outputs

The next step is to identify the relevant flows of inputs—the costs of the program or project, and the outputs—the benefits. For some projects this is reasonably easy. If we are planning a wastewater treatment facility, the engineering staff will be able to provide a full physical specification of the plant, together with the inputs required to build it and keep it running. The output is also well defined—the flow of treated water per day or year. For other types of programs it is much harder, because both the inputs and outputs are more difficult to quantify—for example, an information program to inform the public of the energy intensity of household appliances or working with industry on pollution prevention programs. A key component of any measurement of inputs and outputs is their time dimension. Most environmentally related projects or programs do not usually last for a single year, but are spread out over potentially long periods of time. The analyst must predict what the values will be for each year that the project or program lasts.

Measurement of Benefits and Costs of the Program

The next step is to put values on input and output flows: to measure costs and benefits. Economists measure benefits and costs in monetary terms. As noted above, this does not mean solely in market-value terms, because in many cases benefits and costs are not directly registered on markets. Nor does it imply that only monetary values count in some fundamental manner. Monetary units provide a single metric into which we can try to translate all of the impacts of a project or program so that benefits and costs can be compared to each other and to other types of public activities. Monetary units are very powerful in decision making: when deciding whether to implement a new environmental tax in the next federal budget the Minister of Finance will want to know the dollar value of all the benefits and costs of the tax compared to other options. As Chapters 7 and 8 will show, it is often difficult to impute monetary values for all environmental impacts of a program. Sometimes the best analysts can do is provide a rough estimate (guess?) of the impacts and illustrate whether the results of the study vary with different estimates of the benefits or cost. The important point is to be very clear about how the estimate is obtained and how confident one is of the estimate.

Comparison of Benefits and Costs

How do we compare benefits and costs? The principles are simple:

- Compute the net benefits (NB) of the project or program.

- If the project lasts more than a year, we must *discount* any future costs and benefits before computing net benefits. The next section shows how discounting is done.

- If there is more than one project that can accomplish the same target or goal, we select the program/project that yields the largest net benefits, subject to any budget constraints the government faces.

Net benefits are the difference between total benefits and total costs. Total benefits are the total damages forgone (the area under the MD curve), and total costs are the total abatement costs incurred (the area under the MAC curve).[4] Maximizing the difference between total benefits and total costs corresponds to the point where the MAC and MD curves intersect.

We illustrate these principles using examples that get increasingly more complex. First we show how to compute the net benefits when there is just one program under consideration and no discounting is needed, then we look at a case where there are different options that accomplish the same target. One must be chosen. Finally, we consider what happens when governments have fixed budgets.

How to Compute Net Benefits

EXAMPLE

Regulatory program to control wastes from pulp mills

The government is contemplating enacting a regulation that requires all pulp and paper mills to reduce their discharges to air and water. These emissions reduce downstream water quality in the river on which they are located and contribute to serious air pollution in the vicinity of the plants. The estimates of costs and benefits are the totals over the life of the program. Costs of the program include private-sector costs of compliance in the form of pollution control costs: $580-million for capital equipment and $560-million for operating costs to control emissions. Public-sector monitoring and enforcement is also required to ensure companies comply with the regulation. These costs total $96-million. Total costs are thus $(580 + 560 + 96) = $1,236. There are three major benefit categories. Downstream recreators (fishers and boaters) benefit from improved water quality: their WTP for these benefits is $1,892-million. Agricultural operators in the vicinity of the plants have a reduction of $382-million in damages to crops and livestock because of reduced airborne emissions. Hence, their benefits are these forgone damages. Finally, there are intangible benefits such as improvement in habitats for many species. Suppose we have no way of measuring these in monetary terms, so just show them as some quantity A. Total benefits are thus $(1,892 + 382 + A) = $2,278 + A.

Total benefits and costs can be compared in several ways. One way is to subtract the total costs from total benefits to get net benefits. This is the numerical counterpart to what Figure 6-1 illustrated graphically: *we are finding the maximum net benefits from the program to attain the socially efficient equilibrium.* Net benefits are $(2,278 + A − 1,236) = $1,042-million plus A. This is the standard method of comparing benefits and costs and the approach we follow in all other cases. Maximizing the net benefits corresponds to the point where the MAC = MD curve in our standard environmental framework.

Another criterion that is sometimes used is the **benefit–cost ratio,** found by taking the ratio of benefits and costs. This shows the benefits the project will produce for each dollar of costs. In this example, the benefit–cost ratio is $(2,278 ÷ 1,236) = 1.8 plus A. There is a major problem with the benefit–cost ratio. The socially efficient program size that we have argued is the appropriate scale of the project is

---

[4.] Remember that abatement costs measure all the costs the polluters incur in reducing their emissions. These include the costs of actual abatement equipment plus loss in profits if output is reduced, diverting workers from producing goods to producing waste management and so on. Total damages measure all the impacts of the emissions on people and the environment. When dealing with people's valuations of damages, the metric is estimates of willingness to pay to reduce emissions.

not the one that gives the maximum benefit–cost ratio. Look back at Figure 6-1. At $E^* = 10$ units, the benefit–cost ratio is equal to $(a + b + c + d) \div (b + c) = \$(63 + 18 + 32 + 12)/\$44 = 2.84$. At 12 units of emissions, the benefit–cost ratio is $(a + b) \div b = \$(63 + 18)/\$18 = 4.5$. The benefit–cost ratio is higher at 12 units because it is dependent on the relative size of the project's total benefits and total costs, not its net benefits. But, as we have argued, it is net benefits that should matter to society, not total values. The benefit–cost ratio may be used to make sure that, at the very least, benefits exceed cost, but beyond this it is a misleading indicator in planning the appropriate scope of public programs.

LO3

Discounting and Choosing among Projects that Achieve the Same Policy Goal

What if there is more than one way to achieve a particular policy goal? What rule do we use to select one of the options? What if each option involves costs and benefits that occur over more than one year? How, then, are net benefits computed? We answer both these questions using another example.

EXAMPLE

Investment in upgrading a municipal sewage treatment plant[5]

Suppose our goal is to improve water quality by investing in better municipal sewage treatment in the community. This is a public project that involves three different levels of treatment, each with a different stream of benefits and costs. The options are:

1. Enhanced tertiary treatment: discharges pure water with no household waste products, viruses, or bacteria;

2. Tertiary treatment: discharges water with no household waste products, but may contain some bacteria and viruses.

3. Secondary treatment: eliminates most household waste products, but may contain some bacteria and viruses.

A normal reaction to the description of these options might be to say, "let's go for the best treatment possible." But is that socially efficient?

Table 6-1 presents the costs and benefits for each option. These differ among the options in both magnitude and over time. Assume the project lasts for six years. In practice, this sort of project would likely extend beyond the six years, but we end it here to make calculations simpler. Year 0 is the time period from when the project starts to the end of the first year. Each project will involve some construction (capital) costs as the plant upgrades must be installed. For the two tertiary projects, there are no benefits until the end of this period (year 1) because the plants are not fully operational until then. The secondary treatment upgrade can be completed more quickly and hence generates some benefits in the initial period (year 0). Year 1 shows some start-up costs for each option, and for the years thereafter the costs shown are operating costs. Note also that the benefits of each type of sewage treatment differ. The benefits of enhanced tertiary treatment rise over time, while those of the other options are constant once the plant begins full operation.

(Continued)

[5.] We have chosen a physical project to illustrate benefit–cost principles. The same principles apply to regulatory programs. One could easily substitute another example, such as three policies to reduce greenhouse gas emissions. Each could have a different benefit and cost stream reflecting different timing, who is affected, and how.

TABLE 6-1   Costs and Benefits for Three Ways to Upgrade a Municipal Sewage Treatment Plant

	Cost ($ million in Year)					
Project	0	1	2	3	4	5
Enhanced tertiary	100	50	20	20	20	20
Tertiary	50	25	15	15	15	15
Secondary	25	15	10	10	10	10
	Benefits ($ million in Year)					
	0	1	2	3	4	5
Enhanced tertiary	0	50	50	70	80	80
Tertiary	0	50	50	50	50	50
Secondary	10	20	20	20	20	20

Our task is first to compute the net benefits. When the costs and benefits differ over time, we must apply **discounting** to add and compare these costs and benefits. Discounting has two facets: first, the mechanics of doing it; then, the reasoning behind the choice of discount rates to be used in specific cases. We take these up in turn.

A cost that will occur 10 years from now does not have the same significance as a cost that occurs today. Suppose, for example, that one has incurred a cost of $1,000 that she must pay today. To do that she must have $1,000 in the bank, or in her pocket, with which to pay the obligation. On the other hand, suppose she has a commitment to pay $1,000 not today, but 10 years from now. If the rate of interest she gets in a bank is 5 percent, and she expects it to stay at that level, she can deposit $613.90 in the bank today and it will compound up to $1,000 in 10 years, exactly when she needs it. The formula for **compounding** this sum is:

$$\$613.91(1 + .05)^{10} = \$1,000$$

We can now turn this around and ask: What is the present value of this $1,000 obligation 10 years from now? Its **present value** (PV) is what we would have to put in the bank today to have exactly what is needed in 10 years, and is found by rearranging the above expression:

$$\text{Present value} = \$1,000/(1 + .05)^{10} = \$613.91$$

The present value is found by discounting the future cost back over the 10-year period at the interest rate, now called the discount rate, of 5 percent. If it were higher—say, 8 percent—the present value would be lower and equal $463.20. The higher the discount rate, the lower the present value of any future cost.

The same goes for a benefit. Suppose you expect someone to give you a gift of $100, but only at the end of six years. This would not have the same value to you today (i.e., the same present value) as $100 given to you today. If the applicable discount rate is 4 percent, the present value of that future gift would be $100/(1 + .04)^6 = $79.03.

[6.] The present value formula for t going to infinity converges to m/r because $[m/(1 + r)^t]$ is a geometric progression with ever-smaller values for the denominator.

The general formula for discounting is:

$$\text{Present value} = m/(1 + r)^t$$

where m is the value in any time period; r is the interest rate used, which is known as the **discount rate;** and t is the number of years involved. The present value for year 0 in our example is $m/(1 + r)^0 = m;$ for year one it is $m/(1 + r)$; for year two: $m/(1 + r)^2$; and so on. If we are considering a project that goes on forever, the PV formula[6] is simply $\text{PV} = m/r$.

EXAMPLE

Application of discounting to the sewage plant options

Our task is to compute net benefits in each time period, then discount these to year 0 so that the stream of net benefits for each project can be calculated. The steps are as follows and values are reported in Table 6-2.

1. *Calculate net benefits.* Net benefits are simply total benefits in each year minus total costs. These are calculated from Table 6-1 and shown on the top half of Table 6-2. In year 0, for example, for tertiary treatment the total costs = $50, total benefits = 0, net benefits = −$50.

2. *Calculate the PV of net benefits for each year.* Take the current value and divide by the appropriate discounting factor: $1/(1 + r)^t$ for $r = 5\%$ and $t = 0, 1, 2, 3, 4, 5$. The results are shown on the bottom half of Table 6-2. For example, in year 3 the PV of NB for the secondary plant = $10/(1.05)^3 = ($10/1.1576) = 8.64.

3. *Sum the present values of net benefits for each year to get the net benefits of each project over its expected duration.* Add up for each treatment option the PV stream from year 0 to year 5. For example, for enhanced tertiary the sum of the PVs = $(−100 + 0 + 27.21 + 43.19 + 49.36 + 47.01) = $66.77 million.[7]

TABLE 6-2   Net Benefits for Three Ways to Upgrade a Municipal Sewage Treatment Plant: Current Values and Present Values

Project	Net Benefits in Current Values ($ million)						
	0	1	2	3	4	5	
Enhanced tertiary	−100	0	30	50	60	60	
Tertiary	−50	25	35	35	35	35	
Secondary	−15	5	10	10	10	10	
	Net Benefits in Present Values ($ million)					$r = 5\%$	
	0	1	2	3	4	5	Sum of PV
Enhanced tertiary	−100	0	27.21	43.19	49.36	47.01	66.77
Tertiary	−50	23.81	31.75	30.23	28.79	27.42	92.00
Secondary	−15	4.76	9.07	8.64	8.23	7.84	23.54

The tertiary plant is clearly the option with the maximum present value of net benefits, and the one to be selected under our benefit–cost decision rule. Note why this project "wins" and the enhanced

(Continued)

[7.] These calculations can readily be done on a spreadsheet.

tertiary project has a lower PV of net benefits. The enhanced tertiary project has very high initial capital costs. These costs are not discounted because they occur in the initial period. The benefits rise over time, but because the large benefits occur later in time (years 4 and 5) their present values are lower than a project that generates smaller current-value benefits in early years. The tertiary project is a case in point. The current values of its benefits are never larger than those of the enhanced tertiary plant ($50-million), but they occur early in time (starting in year 1), so in present-value terms these benefits will add more to the total than the enhanced plant's later benefits. The tertiary plant also has much lower capital and start-up costs than the enhanced plant, again contributing to its higher PV of net benefits. The secondary treatment plant is a clear "loser." While its total costs are relatively low, its benefit stream is too small to dominate the two tertiary plants.

Sensitivity Analysis

An important issue in benefit–cost analysis is how robust these results are to the assumptions the analyst makes. Assumptions may enter in many ways for any project. Consider two key assumptions in this example:

1. The interest rate is 5 percent.
2. The projects last five years after construction is completed.

As noted earlier, sensitivity analysis is generally performed in a BCA study to see if changes in key assumptions affect the ranking of projects. To illustrate how important sensitivity analysis can be, assume that projects last seven years and that the net benefits in current dollars for each additional year are the same as in year 5. Consider only the two tertiary plants. The PV of two more years of net benefits of $60-million for the enhanced plant is $44.78-million for year 6 and $42.64-million for year 7. Adding these to the PV of net benefits for years 0 to 5 yields a sum of $154.19-million. Following the same procedure for the tertiary plant, its PV of net benefits for six years is $26.12-million, and $24.88-million for the seventh year. Its PV of net benefits for seven years is now $143-million. The ranking of the two tertiary plants changes. For a project lasting seven years with the flows of costs and benefits as shown, the enhanced tertiary plant offers the maximum PV of net benefits. This is because it has much higher PV of net benefits in those two years than does the tertiary plant. Will changing the interest rate change the ranking of these projects? We leave that as one of our problems at the end of the chapter. We consider the importance of the interest rate chosen for discounting more fully below.

The Role of Government Budgets and Multiple Programs

Under some circumstances, there may be grounds for sizing programs at less than that which maximizes net benefits. Consider a regional public agency in charge of enforcing air-pollution laws in two medium-sized urban areas. The agency has a fixed and predetermined budget of $1-million to spend. Two possible ways to proceed are to put all the money into one enforcement program in one of the cities or divide it between two programs, one in each city. Suppose the numbers are as follows:

	Costs	Benefits	Net benefits
One-city program	$1,000,000	$2,000,000	$1,000,000
Two-city program			
City A	500,000	1,200,000	700,000
City B	500,000	1,200,000	700,000

In this case, the net benefits of allocating the fixed budget into two half-sized programs exceed the net benefits of putting it into just one. The principle is to

allocate resources so that the net benefits produced by the total budget are maximized.

In the example above, the net benefits from adopting the two-city program are $1.4-million, which clearly exceeds the $1-million from the one-city program for the same total cost.

Choice of the Discount Rate

Discounting is a way of aggregating a series of future net benefits into an estimate of present value. In many projects, the outcome depends greatly on which particular discount rate we use. Using a very low rate would essentially be treating a dollar in one year as very similar in value to a dollar in any other year. A very high rate says that a dollar in the near term is much more valuable to us than one later on. Thus, the higher the discount rate, the more we would be encouraged to put our resources into programs that have relatively high payoffs (i.e., high benefits and/or low costs) in the short run. The lower the discount rate, on the contrary, the more we would be led to select programs that have high net benefits in the more distant future.

There is considerable debate and analytical complexity surrounding the discount rate governments should use to evaluate projects and policies. We provide a brief introduction to this topic. In theory, if there was a single capital market that has no distortions of any kind (e.g., is perfectly competitive, no externalities such as pollution), then the discount rate used in benefit–cost analysis could be the **private rate discount rate** (PDR), that is, one generated by the market. A PDR incorporates savers' **rate of time preference** and the marginal product of the investment that is contemplated. The rate of time preference reflects the view of an individual, firm, or society of the tradeoff between current and future consumption. A person normally will prefer a dollar today to a dollar in 10 years and thus their rate of time preference is positive. People make savings decisions by putting money in bank accounts that pay certain rates of interest. These savings account rates show what interest the banks have to offer to get people to forgo current consumption. We might, therefore, take the average bank savings account rate as reflecting the average person's rate of time preference. But there are other ways of determining people's rates of time preference, and they do not necessarily give the same answer. Many studies have shown that people are remarkably inconsistent when it comes to time preference. They may also have subjective rates that are much higher than current interest rates offered by financial institutions for their savings, so the calculation of a rate of time preference is far from simple. The PDR would also reflect the rate of return an investment in the private sector provides. When investments are made in productive enterprises, people anticipate that the value of future returns will offset today's investment costs; otherwise, these investments would not be made. Private-sector productivity is reflected in the rates of interest banks charge their business borrowers. Competitive markets would equate the marginal rate of time preference to the marginal product of investment to yield the private discount rate.

The real world is not this simple and we have shown in previous chapters that markets generally do not take into account pollution, so discount rates that a person would use in a private decision will typically differ from those governments use to reflect social preferences. Thus, many economists argue that for government decision making, a **social discount rate** (SDR) should be used. The social discount rate (SDR) is based on similar concepts to the PDR except it incorporates a social rate of time preference (SRTP) that reflects the government's cost of borrowing (typically lower than that of the private sector) and some economists argue that it should also include the **social opportunity cost of capital** (SOC). The SOC incorporates the distortions introduced by government taxation and any opportunity costs created when government investment displaces private investment. When resources are used in the public sector for natural resource and environmental programs, they ought to yield, on average, rates of return to society equivalent to what they could have earned in the private sector.

There is considerable debate over how in practice to calculate the SDR with much economic literature devoted to the topic. The references for this chapter provide some examples of this literature. Before delving a bit deeper into the computation of the SDR, it is important to first distinguish between **nominal interest rates** and **real interest rates:**

- Nominal interest rates are what you actually see on the market.

- Real interest rates are nominal rates adjusted for inflation.

Principles for dealing with real and nominal values are

1. If the cost or benefit estimates are expected real costs or benefits—that is, adjusted for expected inflation—use a real interest rate.

2. If the estimates are nominal figures, use a nominal interest rate.

3. If cost and benefit estimates are for a number of years and inflation is expected to occur, then these values should be adjusted for inflation. A standard index to deflate these values should be used. Examples are the gross national expenditure deflator or a selling price index for intermediate goods. The deflated costs and benefits are then discounted by a real discount rate.[8]

EXAMPLE
Real and nominal interest rates

Suppose you deposited $100 in a bank at an interest rate of 8 percent. In 10 years your deposit would have grown to $216. But this is in monetary terms. Suppose that over that 10-year period prices increase 3 percent per year on average. Then the real value of your accumulated deposit would be less; in fact, the real interest rate at which your deposit would accumulate would be only 5 percent (8 percent − 3 percent), so in real terms your deposit would be worth only $161 after the 10 years.[9]

[8.] Most introductory economics texts explain how to deflate nominal values using a price index. Real values are calculated by taking the nominal value and dividing by one plus the rate of inflation. The rate of inflation for, say, the period 1999–2000 can be calculated by taking a price index (e.g., the consumer price index) for 2000 divided by the price index for 1999. The formula is the real value in time $t = $ (nominal value in $t + 1)/(1 + p)$, where p is the rate of inflation between t and $t + 1$.

[9.] These are slight approximations. The deposit would actually be worth $160.64 and the real rate of accumulation would be 4.89 percent.

The social discount rate would then be a combination of the SRTP and the SOC. A typical SRTP would be the after-tax real rate of return on a government bond, for example a Treasury bill. This is the interest rate that savers are willing to 'loan' the government money. If the nominal rate of a Treasury bill is say, 3 percent and the expected rate of inflation is 2 percent, the SRTP would be 1 percent. The SOC could be estimated by a before-tax rate of return for business investment. The SOC will vary with market conditions and the level of risk associated with private investment and is typically higher, sometimes significantly so, than the SRTP. A SOC could thus have a wide range. Suppose the SOC was 8 percent, the SDR would then be 9 percent. However, combining the SRTP with the SOC is highly controversial. Some economists argue that only the SRTP should be used, some even argue for a negligible discount rate when considering very long term projects such as the net benefits to society of reducing greenhouse gas emissions.[10] An approach to the dilemma is to use the SRTP as the lower bound for the SDR and the SOC as an upper bound and undertake sensitivity analysis. Another is to use a weighted average of the two, but the question is then what weights to use. Some government agencies in the United States recommend using a social discount rate that varies with the length of the project; very long term projects have a lower rate than shorter term ones.

With the multiplicity of interest rates the real world offers, and these different arguments for choosing a discount rate, practices could differ among agencies in the public sector. To reduce the potential for a multiplicity of rates being used, governments often specify an official discount rate to be used by all their agencies and ministries. However, there is a difficulty with a fixed rate when economic conditions are changing and interest rates fluctuate. We can conclude that although discounting is widely accepted, the rate controversy is far from being resolved.

Discounting and Future Generations

The logic of a discount rate, even a very small one, is inexorable. A billion dollars, discounted back over a century at 5 percent, has a present value of only slightly over $7.6-million. The present generation, considering the length of its own expected life, may not be interested in programs having very high, but long-run, payoffs like this. The following example (Figure 6-2) illustrates the effects of discounting over a long period of time.

EXAMPLE
The effects of discounting

Discounting is a process that expresses the value to people today of benefits and costs that will occur at some future time. As the time increases between today and the point where these benefits and costs actually occur, their present value diminishes. Figure 6-2, panel (a) shows how much the present value of $100 of net benefits, discounted at 3 percent, diminishes over 100 years. By year 40, $100 is "worth" just over $30 in present-value terms; by year 100, it is just over $5.

The effect the rate of discount has is shown in panel (b). Net benefits of $100 to be received 100 years from now are illustrated for discount rates ranging from 0 to 6 percent. While 6 percent may not seem like a high discount rate, it will lead to a negligible present value of $100 in 100 years.

[10.] See Nicholas Stern, *The Economics of Climate Change,* Great Britain Treasury (2007); and the critique of Stern's choice of discount rate by William Nordhaus, "Critical Assumptions in the Stern Review on Climate Change," *Science* (317), July 13, 2007, available at www.sciencemag.org.

FIGURE 6-2   The Effects of Discounting for 100 Years

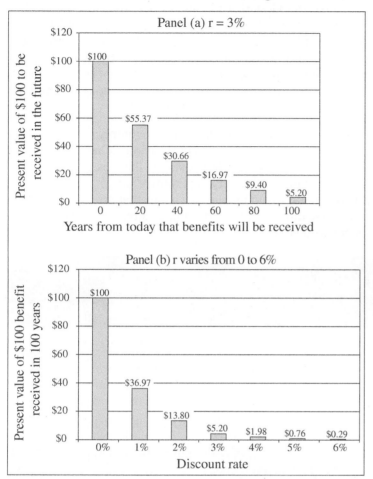

The logic is even more compelling when we break down net benefits into the stream of benefits and costs over time. One of the reasons that environmentalists have looked askance at discounting is that it can have the effect of downgrading future damages that result from today's economic activity. Suppose today's generation is considering a course of action that has certain short-run benefits of $10,000 per year for 50 years, but which, starting 50 years from now, will cost $1-million a year *forever*. This may not be too unlike the choice faced by current generations on discharging accumulative toxic wastes, or on greenhouse gas emissions from fossil fuel combustion. To people alive today the present value of that perpetual stream of future cost discounted at 10 percent is approximately $85,000.[11] These costs may not weigh particularly heavily on decisions made by the current generation. The present value of the benefits ($10,000 a year for 50 years at 10 percent, or $99,148) exceeds the present value of the future costs. From the standpoint of today, therefore, this might look like a good choice, despite the perpetual, and potentially very large, cost burden placed on all future generations.

[11.] The present value of $85,000 is calculated as follows. The present value of a stream of $1-million forever is $1-million divided by the interest rate ($1-million/.1 = $10-million). But we don't incur these costs until 50 years from now. The present value of $10-million incurred in 50 years is $10-million/$(1 + r)^{50}$ = $10-million/117.39 = $85,186.

The problems associated with using positive discount rates for environmental programs with long-run impacts are difficult to resolve. Some people take the view that the appropriate discount rate is zero for long-run environmental projects. And, why should current generations have the 'right' to make decisions that may not incorporate the well-being of future generations. But we have to be very careful here. A great deal of harm has been done to natural and environmental resources by using very low discount rates to evaluate development projects. With low discount rates, it is often possible to justify very disruptive public infrastructure projects, such as hydroelectric dams, because enough distant and uncertain benefits can be accumulated to outweigh the tremendous near-term costs.

Given these uncertainties about discounting when looking at very long-run environmental impacts, we may want to fall back on additional criteria to help us in making current decisions. One of these may be the concept of sustainability discussed in Chapter 1. Sustainability connotes the idea that we should avoid courses of action that reduce the long-run productive capabilities of our natural and environmental resource base. Society may also want to avoid making decisions that are irreversible, or that preclude taking other options in the future. Dealing with long-run impacts remains a very thorny issue, one for which benefit–cost analysis is not well suited.

Does Benefit–Cost Analysis Influence Government Policy?   Case Study

Beginning in the 1970s, the Environmental Protection Agency (EPA) began regulating lead in gasoline with its authority under the *Clean Air Act* to "control or prohibit the manufacture . . . or sale of any fuel additive" if its emission products (1) cause or contribute to "air pollution which may be reasonably anticipated to endanger the public health or welfare," or (2) "will impair to a significant degree the performance of any emission control device or system . . . in general use."[12] Lead had been added to gasoline since the 1920s as a cheap way to boost octane, but by the 1980s, there was widespread concern about the adverse health effects of lead emitted as an air pollutant, especially for children, but also elevated blood pressure in adults. Catalytic converters were installed on new cars beginning in 1975 to reduce other air pollutants. These vehicles required the use of unleaded gasoline, so as the old vehicle stock retires, all gasoline ultimately would be unleaded, but that process could take years. There was the added problem that because leaded gasoline was cheaper than unleaded, some vehicle owners 'misfueled' with leaded gasoline.

By the 1980s, the EPA wanted to accelerate the reductions and contemplate a complete ban on lead in gasoline. A benefit–cost study was undertaken from 1983 to 1985 to examine the net benefits of a

(Continued)

[12.] The authority comes from section 211(c)(1) of the *Clean Air Act*. Information from this case study comes from U.S. EPA (Environmental Protection Agency), *Costs and Benefits of Reducing Lead in Gasoline: Final Regulatory Impact Analysis*, EPA-230-05-85-006 (February 1985), Washington, D.C.: Office of Policy Analysis; U.S. EPA., *Supplementary Preliminary Regulatory Impact Analysis of a Ban on Lead in Gasoline*, Washington, D.C.: Office of Policy, Planning and Evaluation (February 1985); and R.G. Newell and K. Rogers, "The U.S. Experience with the Phasedown of Lead in Gasoline," Washington, D.C.: Resources for the Future, Discussion Paper (2003).

rapid and significant reduction in lead levels in gasoline. The study showed that a very significant reduction had significant positive net benefits and as a result of the findings, the EPA imposed a reduction from 1.1 grams per leaded gallon (gplg) to 0.5 in 1985, and to 0.1 beginning in 1986. Lead was finally banned in gasoline in 1996.

Scientific study of the effects of lead on health was a crucial part of the benefit–cost study. The table below shows the benefits and costs of reducing lead to the stringent level. Higher costs of refining gasoline is the main cost. The health benefits rise as the tighter standards come into effect, then decline as there are fewer adverse impacts with lower lead levels. The net benefits are positive throughout, indicating that at any discount rate, the tighter restrictions on lead are warranted.

Costs and Benefits of a Rapid Phasedown of Lead in Gasoline

Estimated Benefits & Costs	1985	1986	1987	1988	1989	1990	1991	1992
Benefits (millions 1983$)								
Lead effects in children	223	600	547	502	453	414	369	358
Blood pressure in males age 40–59	1,725	5,897	5,675	5,447	5,187	4,966	4,682	4,691
Conventional pollutants	0	222	222	224	226	230	239	248
Vehicle maintenance & fuel economy	137	1,101	1,029	931	922	906	926	913
Costs								
Increasing refining costs	96	608	558	532	504	471	444	441
Net Benefits	1,988	7,213	6,916	6,573	6,284	6,045	5,772	5,770

Source: *U.S. EPA (Environmental Protection Agency), Costs and Benefits of Reducing Lead in Gasoline: Final Regulatory Impact Analysis, EPA-230-05-85-006 (February 1985), data from Table E-2.*

LO 4

Distributional Issues

The relation of total benefits and total costs is a question of economic efficiency. As noted in Chapter 1, decisions about the environment are not just about efficiency, but also about equity—who gets the benefits and who pays the costs. In public-sector programs, the distribution of benefits and costs must be considered along with efficiency issues, which implies that benefit–cost analyses must incorporate studies of how net benefits are distributed among different groups in society. In this section we introduce some of the main concepts of distribution analysis.

Consider the following numbers, which refer to the annual values of a particular program accruing to three different individuals who, we assume, all have the same income. Abatement costs show the costs of the program to each individual; these may be higher prices on some products, more time spent on recycling matters, higher taxes, or other factors. The reduced damages are measures of the value of the improvements in environmental quality accruing to each person.

	Person A	Person B	Person C
Reduced environmental damages ($/year)	60	80	120
Abatement costs ($/year)	40	60	80
Difference	20	20	40

Costs and reduced damages are different for person A and person B, but the difference between them ($20/year) is the same; hence, the difference as a proportion of their income is the same. With respect to these two people, therefore, the program is horizontally equitable; recall from the definitions of equity in Chapter 1, **horizontal equity** treats people in the same circumstances identically. The program is not horizontally equitable for person C, because this individual experiences a net difference of $40/year. Since person C is assumed to have the same income as the other two people, he or she is clearly better off as a result of this program; horizontal equity in this case has not been achieved.

Consider the numbers in Table 6-3. These show the impacts, expressed in monetary values, of three different environmental quality programs on three people with, respectively, a low income, a medium income, and a high income. This enables us to look at **vertical equity**—how the program affects people in different circumstances. Each person benefits from a project from reduced damages and incurs costs in the form of their share of total abatement costs. The "difference" row reflects each person's net benefits: reduced damages minus abatement costs. In parentheses next to each number is shown the percentage that number is of the person's income level. These percentages help illustrate three types of distributional impacts a program can have. These potential impacts are **proportional, regressive, and progressive programs and policies.**

TABLE 6-3 Vertical Equity*

	Person A		Person B		Person C	
Income	5,000		20,000		50,000	
Program 1						
Reduced damages	150	(3.0)	300	(1.5)	600	(1.2)
Abatement costs	100	(2.0)	100	(0.5)	100	(0.2)
Difference	50	(1.0)	200	(1.0)	500	(1.0)
Program 2						
Reduced damages	150	(3.0)	1,400	(7.0)	5,500	(11.0)
Abatement costs	100	(2.0)	800	(4.0)	3,000	(6.0)
Difference	50	(1.0)	600	(3.0)	2,500	(5.0)
Program 3						
Reduced damages	700	(14.0)	2,200	(11.0)	3,000	(6.0)
Abatement costs	300	(6.0)	1,000	(5.0)	1,500	(3.0)
Difference	400	(8.0)	1,200	(6.0)	1,500	(3.0)

* Figures in the table show annual monetary values. Numbers in parentheses show the percentage of income these numbers represent.

1. **Proportional programs and policies.** The program takes the same proportion of income from each income level. In Table 6-3, program 1 is proportional because its net benefits to each person take 1 percent of that person's income.

2. **Regressive programs and policies.** The program provides higher net benefits to high-income people than to low-income people as a proportion of their income. Program 2 is regressive because the high-income person's benefits represent 5 percent of her income while the proportion decreases as the person's income level falls.

3. **Progressive programs and policies.** The program provides net benefits that represent a higher proportion of the lower-income person's income than it does of the rich person's income. Program 3 is progressive because the lowest-income person has the highest net benefits as a share of his income. Net benefits as a share of income fall as income rises.

Thus an environmental program (or any program for that matter) is proportional, progressive, or regressive, according to whether the net effect of that policy has proportionally the same, greater, or less effect on low-income people as on high-income people.

Table 6-3 also illustrates another equity issue—how the benefits and costs are distributed to each income group. For example, although the overall effects of program 2 are regressive, the abatement costs of that program are in fact distributed progressively (i.e., the cost burden is proportionately greater for high-income people). But in this case damage reduction is distributed so regressively that the overall program is regressive. So, also in program 3, although the overall program is progressive abatement costs are distributed regressively.

These definitions of distributional impacts can be misleading. A program that is technically regressive could actually distribute the bulk of its net benefits to poor people. Suppose a policy raised the net income of one rich person by 10 percent, but raised each of the net incomes of 1,000 poor people by 5 percent. This policy is technically regressive, although more than likely the majority of its aggregate net benefits go to poor people.

It is normally very difficult to estimate the distributional impacts of environmental programs, individually or in total. To do so requires very specific data showing impacts by income groups, race, or other factors. In general, environmental and health data are not collected by income and race. Thus, data on environmentally related diseases don't typically allow the comparison of differences across socio-economic and racial groups. Nor is it easy to estimate how program costs are distributed among these groups, because these depend on complex factors related to tax collections, consumption patterns, the availability of alternatives, and so on. Despite the difficulties, however, benefit–cost analyses should try to look as closely as possible at the way in which the aggregates are distributed through the population.

LO 5

Uncertainty

In applications of benefit–cost analysis to natural and environmental resources we are projecting events well off into the future, and when we do this we run squarely into the fact that we have no way of knowing the future with certainty. Uncertainty can arise from many sources. We may not be able to predict the preferences of future consumers, who may feel very differently than we do about matters of environmental quality. For studies of the long-run impacts of climate change, future population growth rates are important, and it is impossible to know these with certainty. Uncertainty may arise from technological change. Technical advancement in pollution-control equipment or in the chemistry of materials recycling could markedly shift future costs of achieving various levels of emission control. Nature itself is a source of uncertainty. Meteorological events can affect the outcomes of pollution-control programs; for example, in some cases we are still uncertain of the exact ways human activities impact natural phenomena.

How should we address the fact that future benefits and costs are uncertain; that is, that future outcomes are "probabilistic"? If we know something about how these future probabilities manifest themselves, we may be able to estimate the "most likely" or "expected" levels of benefits and costs. Consider the problem of predicting the effect of certain policy changes on oil spills. In any given year there may be no tanker accidents, or one, or several; the exact number is not known. But there is enough information to calculate the *risk* that a spill will occur. Economists use the word 'risk' to denote a situation where estimates can be made of the probability that an uncertain event will occur. If no estimate can be made of the likelihood of the event occurring, the event is 'uncertain.' Popular language, however, often mixes up the use of the two terms. Suppose we can estimate the risk of an oil spill. The objective is to calculate the annual number of spills anticipated under different types of oil-spill-control policies. One way of doing this is to estimate the **expected value** of oil spills anticipated in a year's time. Where would we get the information for this? Data may have been collected over a long period of time on past oil spills and could be used to calculate actual long-run averages. If this information isn't available, engineers, scientists, or people familiar with the problem might provide estimates. These estimates can be used to develop a **probability distribution** of the number of oil-tanker accidents, as shown in Table 6-4.

TABLE 6-4   Calculating the Expected Number of "Large" Oil Spills

Number of spills	Probability	Expected value of the number of spills
0	.77	$0 \times .77 = 0$
1	.12	$1 \times .12 = .12$
2	.07	$2 \times .07 = .14$
3	.03	$3 \times .03 = .09$
4	.01	$4 \times .01 = .04$
Over 4	—	—
		Expected value: .39

Table 6-4 presents probabilities of having different numbers of tanker accidents in a year. The numbers are hypothetical. For example, the probability is .77 that there will be no tanker accidents, .12 for one accident, .07 for two accidents, and so on. Expected values are computed as the number of spills times the probably of that event occurring, summed over all possible events. This produces a weighted average of the probably of an event, as shown in Table 6-4. In Table 6-4, the expected number of tanker accidents is .39 per year. One could then go on and estimate the expected quantity of oil that will be spilled and, perhaps, the expected value of damages. Thus, in this case, we are able to proceed by estimating expected values of probabilistic events, in particular the expected values of benefits and costs.

To recap,

an expected value is a weighted average: the number of times the event occurs times its probability of occurrence, summed over all possible events.

This approach is appropriate if we have reliable estimates of the probabilities of future events. But in many cases these may not be available, because we have not had enough experience with similar events to be able to know the future probabilities of different outcomes with much confidence. One approach, made possible by the computer, is to carry out a **scenario analysis.** Suppose we are trying to predict the long-run costs of reducing CO_2 emissions as a step toward lessening the greenhouse effect. These costs depend critically on the future pace of technological developments affecting the energy efficiency of production. We have little experience with predicting technical change over long periods of time, so it is unrealistic to try to estimate the probabilities that technical change will occur at different rates. Instead, we run our analysis several times, each time making a different assumption about the rate at which technical change will occur. Thus, our results might consist of three scenarios, with different results based on whether future technical change is "slow," "moderate," or "fast."

There is, however, another difficulty in using expected values on which to base decisions. Expected values are appropriate when analyzing a relatively large number of recurrent situations; repeated observations reduce the impact of unusual outlying events. In the oil-spill case, the annual number of spills is expected to approach its expected value. But for unique events that will occur only once, we may want to look beyond expected-value decisions. Consider the following numbers:

Program A		Program B	
Net benefits	**Probability**	**Net benefits**	**Probability**
$500,000	.475	$500,000	.99
$300,000	.525	–$10,000,000	.01
Expected value: $395,000		Expected value:	$395,000

These two programs have exactly the same expected value. But suppose we had only a one-time choice between the two. Perhaps it relates to the choice of a nuclear plant versus a conventional power plant to generate electricity. With program A, the net benefits are uncertain, but the outcomes are not extremely different and the probabilities are similar—it's very nearly a 50–50 proposition. Program B, on the other hand, has a very different profile. The probability is very high that the net benefits will be $500,000, but there is a small probability of a disaster (the plant explodes, killing hundreds of people and creating irreversible environmental damage). If we were making decisions strictly on the basis of expected values, we would treat these projects as the same; we could flip a coin to decide which one to choose. If we did this, we would be displaying **risk neutral** behaviour, making decisions strictly on the basis of expected values. On the other hand, if this is a one-shot decision, we might decide that the low probability of a very large loss in the case of project B represents a risk to which we do not wish to expose ourselves. In this case, we might be **risk averse,** preferring project A over project B.

In environmental pollution control, risk aversion may be the best policy in a number of cases. The rise of planetary-scale atmospheric change opens up the possibility of catastrophic human dislocations in the future. The potential scale of these impacts argues for a conservative, risk-averse approach to current decisions. Risk-averse decisions are also called for in the case of species extinction; a series of incremental and seemingly small decisions today may bring about a catastrophic decline in genetic resources in the future, with potentially drastic impacts on human welfare. Global issues are not the only ones where it may be prudent to avoid low risks of outcomes that would have large negative net benefits.

The contamination of an important groundwater aquifer is a possibility faced by many local communities. And in any activity where risk to human life is involved, the average person is likely to be risk averse.

Benefit–Cost Analysis of Reducing Sulphur in Fuels   Case Study

Crude oil can contain considerable amounts of sulphur that persists when oil is refined into gasoline. The sulphur in gasoline contributes to the release of sulphur dioxide, an air contaminant associated with a host of environmental problems including acid precipitation that damages crops, forests, acidifies vulnerable lakes, and kills aquatic life (see Chapter 17). Sulphur dioxide (SO_2) also has significant adverse health impacts especially to people with asthma and other lung diseases. In 1994, the Canadian Council of Ministers of the Environment (CCME) created a task force to examine methods of reducing the sulphur in gasoline and other means of reducing SO_2 such as increasing vehicle efficiency. The task force took a number of years to collect data, and consult experts and stake-holders that would be affected by changes in the regulations. By 1997, sulphur content in gasoline was on average 360 parts per million (ppm) across Canada, with much higher levels in urbanized provinces. Ontario's average was over 530 ppm. The CCME's goal was to phase in over time tighter restrictions to reduce substantially the amount of sulphur in Canadian gasoline.

Regulations came into force in 2002 with an interim requirement limiting sulphur in gasoline to an average level of 150 parts per million, and never to exceed 200 ppm. This was to allow the refining industry to adapt to the regulations. Effective January 1, 2005, the average level was reduced to 30 ppm, and the level at any time not to exceed 80 ppm. That regulation stands today.

Glenn Jenkins, Chun-Yan Kuo, and Aygul Ozbafli used the data generated by the CCME studies to undertake a benefit–cost analysis for the Treasury Board of Canada to determine the level of sulphur reduction in gasoline that generated the maximum present value of net benefits.[13] They calculate the costs and benefits of moving from a 'base case'—the level of sulphur that existed in gasoline in 1997 to six other scenarios of increasing regulatory stringency with sulphur levels from 360 ppm down to 30 ppm. They assumed the new regulation would come into force on January 1, 2001. Costs and benefits are forecast out to 2010.

Two categories of cost are measured: administrative costs of the government and the compliance costs of oil refiners as they adjust their processes to remove sulphur from gasoline. The authors estimate annual administrative costs to be $60,000 per year for each of the scenarios. Seventeen refineries existed in Canada at the time of the study; each with somewhat different characteristics and costs of adjusting their physical plant and processes to meet the regulation. The capital investment needed to meet the targets is assumed to be incurred in 2000, with changes in annual operating cost beginning in 2001. All costs are measured in 1995 prices. Starting with total production of 36 billion litres per year, they assume gasoline output rises by 0.7 percent per year to reflect rising demand. Table 6-5 shows the costs by region for Canada.

(Continued)

---

[13] G. Jenkins, C-Y. Kuo, and A. Ozbafli, "Cost–Benefit Analysis of Reducing Sulphur in Gasoline," manuscript, (December 2009). An earlier version of the paper is available as a Queens' University Economics Department Working Paper No. 1134, "Cost–Benefit Analysis on Regulations to Lower the Level of Sulphur in Gasoline" (March 2007) at: www.econ.queensu.ca/working_papers/papers/qed_wp_1134.pdf.

TABLE 6-5 **Total Investment and Annual Operating Costs by Scenario and by Region (millions of Canadian dollars in 1995 prices)**

Scenario	Costs	Atlantic and Quebec	Ontario	Prairies and British Columbia	Canada
Base Case	Investment cost	79.0	47.0	83.0	209.0
	Annual operating cost	28.5	34.2	11.1	74.0
Alternative Scenarios					
Scenario 1: 360ppm	Investment cost	81.0	96.0	0	177.0
	Annual operating cost	16.6	7.0	0.3	23.9
Scenario 1: 360ppm	Investment cost	144.0	196.0	20.0	360.0
	Annual operating cost	28.5	16.0	16.5	61.0
Scenario 1: 360ppm	Investment cost	226.0	213.0	146.0	585.0
	Annual operating cost	31.7	24.0	7.7	63.4
Scenario 1: 360ppm	Investment cost	243.0	266.0	188.0	697.0
	Annual operating cost	38.4	35.1	15.0	88.5
Scenario 1: 360ppm	Investment cost	282.0	392.0	219.0	893.0
	Annual operating cost	45.3	48.9	22.8	117.0
Scenario 1: 360ppm	Investment cost	532.0	650.0	606.0	1788.0
	Annual operating cost	49.7	47.5	21.9	119.1

Source: *Jenkins, G., Kuo, C–Y., and A. Ozbafli, "Cost–Benefit Analysis of Reducing Sulphur in Gasoline," manuscript, (December 2009). An earlier version of the paper is available as a Queen's University Economics Department Working Paper No. 1134, "Cost–Benefit Analysis on Regulations to Lower the Sulphur in Gasoline" (March 2007).*

Jenkins and co-authors focused on the health benefits of reducing sulphur in gasoline; they did not have the data to incorporate the broader environmental impacts generated by sulphur emissions. Thus, their benefits are likely a lower bound estimate. Estimates of the damages from air pollution (and thus the benefits of reducing air pollution) require information about a chain of effects. The authors take four steps to estimate benefits for each of the scenarios: (1) the change in vehicle emissions caused by changes in the level of sulphur in gasoline; (2) the change in ambient air quality affected by changes in emitted pollutants by vehicles; (3) the impact on human health caused by changes in ambient air quality; and (4) the measurement of the impacts on health in monetary values. Health impacts of pollution are difficult to measure with precision, thus the authors provide low, central, and high values for each relationship between ambient air pollutant concentrations and the health responses. The central estimate is generally in the middle of the range and represents the most likely health effect by experts who study these relationships. Each of the estimates is then given a probability weight to create a probability distribution of expected total health benefits of lowering sulphur emissions. Table 6-6 illustrates the author's estimates of the health benefits.

The value of improved health outcomes is estimated using methods that are explained in Chapter 7. These include how much people would be willing to pay to reduce the risk of an adverse health impact and the value of a statistical life. Data for these estimates comes from a number of studies undertaken in Canada and the United States. Table 6-7 provides the costs and benefits by year. Note that benefits begin in 2001, and after 2007, the costs and benefits are the same each year. The authors assume a real discount rate of 7 percent to compute all the present values.

The distribution of benefits and costs is very revealing and shows clearly the costs are borne by the refiners, while the benefits are received by the public. Table 6-8 illustrates.

(Continued)

TABLE 6-6   Total Reductions of Health Effects for Canada over the 20-Year Period (number of cases)

Note: The number of health effects is a simple summation of cases occurred over the 20-year period.

Health Effects	Alternative Scenarios					
	Scenario 1: 360 ppm	Scenario 2: 250 ppm	Scenario 3: 200 ppm	Scenario 4: 150 ppm	Scenario 5: 100 ppm	Scenario 6: 30 ppm
Premature mortality	829	1,169	1,385	1,591	1,810	2,100
Chronic respiratory disease	3,013	4,184	5,040	5,752	6,555	7,600
Respiratory hospital admissions	533	735	874	1,002	1,126	1,324
Cardiac hospital admissions	423	593	717	814	924	1,076
Emergency room visits	2,694	3,733	4,524	5,153	5,854	6,800
Asthma symptom days	1,307,842	1,814,497	2,185,633	2,500,763	2,840,451	3,300,000
Restricted activity days	634,343	882,402	1,062,847	1,212,450	1,377,466	1,600,000
Acute respiratory symptoms	4,364,822	6,049,747	7,249,041	8,323,223	9,470,413	11,000,000
Child lower respiratory illness	37,798	52,078	63,228	71,131	82,277	93,000

Source: *Jenkins, G., Kuo, C-Y., and A. Ozbafli, "Cost–Benefit Analysis of Reducing Sulphur in Gasoline," manuscript, (December 2009). An earlier version of the paper is available as a Queen's University Economics Department Working Paper No. 1134, "Cost–Benefit Analysis on Regulations to Lower the Sulphur in Gasoline" (March 2007).*

TABLE 6-7   Annual Incremental Benefits and Costs by scenario (& millions, 2000 prices)

	Year 2000	Year 2001	Year 2002	Year 2003	Year 2004	Year 2005	Year 2006	Year 2007	… …	Total NPV	Annualized Value
Scenario 1:											
360 ppm											
Benefits		201.5	205.2	208.9	212.7	216.6	220.5	224.5		2,257.5	—
Costs	192.0	26.1	26.1	26.1	26.1	26.1	26.1	26.1		448.3	—
Net Benefits	(192.0)	175.4	179.1	182.8	186.6	190.5	194.4	198.4		1,809.2	180.63
Scenario 2:											
250 ppm											
Benefits	—	273.8	279.7	285.8	219.9	298.2	304.6	311.2		3,145.4	—
Costs	309.6	66.2	t 66.2	66.2	66.2	66.2	66.2	66.2		1,040.0	—
Net Benifits	(309.6)	207.6	213.5	219.6	225.7	231.0	238.4	244.0		2,104.4	210.10
Scenario 3:											
200 ppm											
Benefits	—	321.1	328.5	336.1	343.8	351.7	359.7	368.0		3,728.0	—
Costs	634.7	71.9	70.2	68.4	68.4	68.4	68.4	68.4		1,311.1	—
Net Benifits	(634.7)	249.2	258.3	267.7	275.4	283.3	291.3	299.6		2,416.9	241.30

(Continued)

TABLE 6-7 (*Continued*)

	Year 2000	Year 2001	Year 2002	Year 2003	Year 2004	Year 2005	Year 2006	Year 2007	... ...	Total NPV	Annualized Value
Scenario 4:											
150 ppm											
Benefits	—	375.2	383.2	391.3	399.5	407.9	416.5	425.3		4,295.5	—
Costs	756.2	107.1	101.9	96.6	96.6	96.6	96.6	96.6		1,719.1	—
Net Benifits	(756.2)	268.1	281.3	294.7	302.9	311.3	319.9	328.7		2,576.4	257.22
Scenario 5:											
100 ppm											
Benefits	—	430.0	438.8	447.8	456.9	466.3	475.8	485.5		4,897.9	—
Costs	968.9	141.1	134.0	127.0	127.0	127.0	127.0	127.0		2,234.8	—
Net Benefits	(968.9)	288.9	304.8	320.8	329.9	339.3	348.8	358.5		2,663.1	265.88
Scenario 6:											
30 ppm											
Benefits	—	484.8	496.1	507.7	519.5	531.5	543.9	556.6		5,641.2	—
Costs	1,939.0	143.2	136.2	129.2	129.2	129.2	129.2	129.2		3,227.1	—
Net Benefits	(1,939.0)	341.6	359.9	378.5	390.3	402.3	414.7	427.4		2,414.1	241.0

Source: *Jenkins, G., Kuo, C-Y., and A. Ozbafli, "Cost–Benefit Analysis of Reducing Sulphur in Gasoline," manuscript, (December 2009). An earlier version of the paper is available as a Queen's University Economics Department Working Paper No. 1134, "Cost–Benefit Analysis on Regulations to Lower the Sulphur in Gasoline" (March 2007).*

TABLE 6-8 **Present Value of Net Benefits by Stakeholder and by Scenario ($ millions, 2000 prices)**

Scenario	Refiners	Refinery Workers	Consumers and Individuals	Governments		Total
				Provincial	Federal	
Scenario 1: 360 ppm	(117.0)	0	2,097.6	5.8	(0.6)	1,985.8
Scenario 2: 250 ppm	(272.9)	0	2,595.9	7.9	(0.6)	2,330.0
Scenario 3: 200 ppm	(339.7)	(4.8)	3,029.9	9.6	(0.6)	2,694.3
Scenario 4: 150 ppm	(444.8)	(14.5)	3,328.4	10.8	(0.6)	2,879.4
Scenario 5: 100 ppm	(578.4)	(19.3)	3,580.5	12.4	(0.6)	2,994.6
Scenario 6: 30 ppm	(826.9)	(19.3)	3,646.6	14.1	(0.6)	2,813.9

Source: *Jenkins, G., Kuo, C–Y., and A. Ozbafli, "Cost–Benefit Analysis of Reducing Sulphur in Gasoline," manuscript, (December 2009). An earlier version of the paper is available as a Queen' University Economics Department Working Paper No. 1134, "Cost–Benefit Analysis on Regulations to Lower the Sulphur in Gasoline" (March 2007).*

Table 6-9 summarizes the net present values of each of the scenarios. All the NPVs are positive, indicating that a reduction from the high levels of sulphur that existed prior to regulation is warranted. The maximum net present value (NPV) occurs with scenario 5, a reduction in average sulphur concentrations to 100 ppm. Notice that there is not much difference between scenarios 4, 5,

(Continued)

and 6. The study could not obtain data on the reduction in damages to the environment. The authors thus caution that these scenarios underestimate total benefits. Sensitivity analysis on key assumptions is also undertaken and finds that lowering emissions to 150 or 30 ppm results in zero probability that the NPV will be negative. The authors recommend that the standard be set at 30 ppm. The government set the regulations for sulphur to be effective January 1, 2005 at an average level of 30 parts per million with a never-to-be-exceeded maximum of 80 ppm. They allowed an interim step from July 2002 to the end of 2004 at 150 ppm with a level never to exceed 200 ppm at any time starting July 1, 2002 until the end of 2004. Refiners moved more quickly to the 30 ppm limit and none of them shut down as a result of the regulation.

TABLE 6-9   **The Net Present Value of Alternative Scenarios to Reduce Sulphur in Gasoline ($ millions, 2000 prices)**

Scenario	Net Present Value @7%
Scenario 1: 360 ppm	1,985.8
Scenario 2: 250 ppm	2,330.3
Scenario 3: 200 ppm	2,694.3
Scenario 4: 150 ppm	2,879.4
Scenario 5: 100 ppm	2,994.6
Scenario 6: 30 ppm	2,813.9

Source: *Jenkins, G., Kuo, C–Y., and A. Ozbafli, "Cost–Benefit Analysis of Reducing Sulphur in Gasoline," manuscript, (December 2009). An earlier version of the paper is available as a Queen's University Economics Department Working Paper No. 1134, "Cost–Benefit Analysis on Regulations to Lower the Sulphur in Gasoline" (March 2007).*

LO 6

COST-EFFECTIVENESS ANALYSIS

Suppose a community determined that its current water supply was contaminated with some chemical, and that it had to switch to some alternative supply. Suppose it had several possibilities: It could drill new wells into an uncontaminated aquifer, it could build a connector to the water-supply system of a neighbouring town, or it could build its own surface reservoir. A cost-effectiveness analysis would estimate the costs of these different alternatives with the aim of showing how they compared in terms of, say, the costs per million gallons of delivered water into the town system. **Cost-effectiveness analysis,** in other words, essentially takes the objective as given, and costs out various alternative ways of attaining that objective. One might think of it as one-half of a benefit–cost analysis, where costs—but not benefits—are estimated in monetary terms. The reason benefits need not be measured is that they are the same—the water supply will be safe; it is the costs of reaching this outcome that differ. Cost effectiveness looks for the lowest cost way of reaching the outcome.

A cost-effective project or policy is the one that achieves a given level of benefits at the lowest cost among all the possible policy/project options.

Table 6-10 shows some of the results of a study done for a remedial action plan to reduce phosphorus (P) concentrations in the Bay of Quinte in Lake Ontario. The study was done for the International Joint Commission, a bilateral organization that studies and makes recommendations to governments for water-related issues along the Canada–U.S. border. Phosphorus comes from leaching of fertilizers into waterways, from sewage treatment plants processing domestic household wastes, and from industrial sources. Excessive amounts of phosphorus lead to algal blooms and eutrophication of water bodies, which depletes oxygen in the water and kills fish and other aquatic life. The secondary sewage treatment plants currently existing in the region cannot remove enough of the phosphorus to prevent eutrophication. The results show the estimated costs of reducing phosphorus concentrations in a region of the bay by 1 microgram per litre (µg/L).

TABLE 6-10   Cost-Effectiveness of Different Options for Reducing Phosphorus Concentration in the Bay of Quinte, Lake Ontario

Strategy	Cost (in $ thousands) per microgram/litre reduction in phosphorus
Tertiary treatment at sewage treatment plants	$1,078
Treatment of wastewater from water treatment plants	98
Reduction in phosphorus inputs from agricultural runoff	2,033
Alum treatment of sediments in lake	2,000
Diversion of 20 square kilometres of Lake Ontario into the upper bay	1,104
Diversion of 35 square kilometres of Lake Ontario into the upper bay	978

Source: *Adapted from Bay of Quinte Remedial Action Plan Committee, "Discussion Paper," September 1989.*

Treatment of wastewater from water treatment plants is by far the most cost-effective alternative. A reduction of 1 µg/L costs $98,000, as compared to a tenfold next higher cost (diversion of Lake Ontario water). Cost-effectiveness analysis is a powerful tool when benefits of a project or policy are identical. It emphasizes the importance of examining alternative options and finding the one that minimizes social costs for a given target.

Table 6-10 can also illustrate that cost coefficients must be interpreted with care. Although the wastewater treatment has the lowest costs per unit of phosphorus reduced, it may not be the best way to reduce phosphorus concentrations in this bay. Perhaps a combination of policies is better. There are a number of additional concerns. Each of the technologies has limits as to the total amount of phosphorus it is capable of reducing; so, depending on what the desired total reduction is, different combinations of these techniques will have to be used. There may be other techniques that could be more cost-effective but were difficult to measure costs for. An example is phosphorus removal from industrial sources. These cost figures also involve quite different mixes of capital to operating costs. Treatment plants are capital-intensive, while the diversions and alum treatment involve high operating costs. This might be an important budgetary concern for governments. Pollution problems may also be multifaceted. One technique (e.g., tertiary treatment plants) may have benefits in addition to phosphorus reduction, while others (dumping alum into the lake, for example) may have some other adverse environmental impacts.

Cost-effectiveness is thus only one step in reaching a decision about environmental policy. A full benefit–cost analysis is clearly superior. However, due to data limitations, especially difficulties in measuring benefits, cost-effectiveness studies may be the only approach possible. It may also make sense to do a cost-effectiveness analysis even before there is a strong public commitment to the objective you are costing out. Once a cost-effectiveness analysis is done, people may be able to tell, at least in relative terms, whether any of the different alternatives would be desirable. They may be able to say something like: "We don't know exactly the level of benefits in monetary terms, but we feel that they are more than the costs of several of the alternatives that have been costed out, so we will go ahead with one or both of them."

Summary

In previous chapters we put the issue of environmental improvement in a trade-off type of format, where there is willingness to pay (benefits) on one side and abatement costs on the other. In this chapter we started to focus on the problem of measuring these benefits and costs. To do this, researchers have to use some underlying analytical framework to account for these benefits and costs. We focused on the primary approach used in resource and environmental economics: benefit–cost analysis. The rest of the chapter was devoted to a discussion of the main conceptual issues involved in benefit–cost analysis. These are

- the basic analytical steps involved,
- determining the appropriate size of a project or program,
- calculating the present value of net benefits,
- issues in discounting of future values,
- distributional issues, and
- uncertainty.

We briefly discussed cost-effectiveness analysis—seeking the lowest-cost alternative among options that all yield the same benefits—and environmental impact analysis. Having discussed the basic structure of benefit–cost analysis, we will turn now to problems of actually measuring the benefits and costs of specific environmental programs.

Key Terms

Benefit–cost ratio
Compounding
Cost-effectiveness analysis
Discount rate
Discounting
Expected value
Horizontal equity
Nominal interest rates
Present value
Private rate discount rate
Probability distribution
Progressive programs and policies

Proportional programs and policies
Rate of time preference
Real interest rates
Regressive programs and policies
Risk averse
Risk neutral
Scenario analysis
Sensitivity analysis
Social discount rate
Social opportunity cost of capital
Vertical equity

Analytical Problems

1. Suppose the government of a municipality is trying to determine how to deal with pesticide contamination of its water supply. It wants to undertake a benefit –cost analysis of two alternative policy options for controlling pesticides:

   • Upgrading its municipal water treatment plant to remove the pesticides, or

   • Banning the use of the offending pesticides in the metropolitan area.

   Assume that either technique reduces the pesticides to a level that does not adversely affect human health. The costs of these control options are as follows:

   • Municipal treatment upgrades: Capital costs = $20-million. The new plant is constructed over the course of the initial year. It starts operating at the end of this year. Once the plant begins operation, it has operating costs of $1-million per year. Once constructed, the plant lasts for five years, then must be replaced with a new plant.

   • Pesticide ban: Annual operating costs due to substitution of non-toxic methods of controlling "pests" = $3.5-million each year.

   Let the discount rate be 5 percent. The municipality's planning horizon is 10 years. Suppose the present value of the benefits of the project are $40-million. Which project should the municipality adopt?

   Assume now that the benefits differ by the type of treatment option chosen. In particular, they remain at a present value of $40-million for the pesticide ban, but there would be additional benefits in the form of less damage to ecosystems from the treatment plant. How high would these benefits have to be each year to make the government indifferent between choosing the treatment plant or the pesticide ban?

2. Using the numbers from Table 6-1 for the three different options to upgrade municipal sewage treatment to illustrate the impact of choosing different interest rates to discount the net benefits, compute the present value of each project if the interest rate is 2.5 percent, then 10 percent, and finally, 20 percent. What would happen to these present values if the benefits from each project did not begin until year 2 instead of year 1? (That is, shift the benefit stream to the right by one year.)

Discussion Questions

1. Are low discount rates "good" or "bad" for the environment? Defend your answer.

2. Distinguish between horizontal and vertical equity. Which is more important a goal for benefit–cost analysis? Defend your answer.

3. Why might governments opt for projects with low risks and low returns?

For more information on the resources available from McGraw-Hill Ryerson, go to www.mheducation.ca/he/solutions.

Chapter 7

Benefit–Cost Analysis: Benefits

After reading this chapter you will be able to:

LO 1 | Distinguish between direct and indirect methods of calculating the WTP for improvements in environmental quality.

LO 2 | Explain the concept of producer surplus and how to calculate it graphically.

LO 3 | Explain the concept of consumer surplus and how to calculate it graphically for a market good and a public good.

LO 4 | Describe four methods of imputing WTP for improvements in environmental quality.

LO 5 | Explain why willingness to accept estimates generally exceed those of WTP.

LO 1

The benefits of a good or service are equal to what people are willing to pay for it, remembering the provisos about the distribution of income and the availability of information. The marginal damage (MD) curve of the MAC–MD model shows society's willingness to pay to reduce emissions of a pollutant and by doing so improve environmental quality.[1] The MD curve is thus analogous to a demand curve for a normal good, but of course is upward-sloping because the good being measured is undesirable and our well-being increases the *less* we have of it. Total benefits are measured as the area under the MD curve from the initial to the target level of pollution, as we have shown in Chapter 5. These are the damages forgone by the reduction in pollution/improvement in environmental quality (EQ). This chapter examines techniques for measuring this WTP to reduce pollution. The challenge is that there are no markets where people buy and sell units of environmental quality, so we can't measure benefits directly the way we can with market goods. Indirect means must often be used. As one environmental economist has put it: "benefit estimation often involves a kind of detective work for piecing together the clues about the values individuals place on [environmental services] as they respond to other economic signals."[2]

[1.] Remember, we are dealing with pollution emissions; the link between reductions in emissions and increases in environmental quality may be complex, as we must also know the effect of emissions on ambient environmental quality. This is especially so with accumulative pollutants. To keep things as simple as possible, we continue to link directly a reduction in emissions to an improvement in environmental quality.

[2.] Myrick Freeman III, "Benefits of Pollution Control in U.S. Environmental Protection Agency, *Critical Review of Estimating Benefits of Air and Water Pollution Control*, Washington, D.C., EPA 600/5-78-014, 1978, pp. II–16.

The measurement of benefits is an activity pursued on many levels. For an analyst working in an environmental agency, it can turn into a plug-in-the-numbers exercise. So many hectares of clam bed destroyed (information provided by a marine biologist) times the going price of clams (provided by a quick trip to the local fish market) equals damages of water pollution in Howe Sound or the Bay of Fundy. In this case the market price of the good clearly reflects people's willingness to pay for it, as was shown in Chapter 3. Market demand curves can be used to determine total benefits (the area under the demand curve) of reducing pollution. This will be equivalent to a reduction in total damages (area under the MD curve). To repeat,

> the loss of one unit of a market good due to pollution can be valued at its price because the market price represents marginal willingness to pay for the good.

At the other extreme, environmental economists deal with all sorts of environmental goods that have no market or market prices to use to measure WTP for pollution reductions/EQ improvements. Methods must be developed to measure WTP and impute the MD curve (or what is equivalent—a demand curve for EQ improvements). Thus,

> valuing the loss of a non-market good due to pollution requires methods of imputing the marginal willingness to pay for damage reduction/EQ improvement because market prices do not exist.

This chapter offers a menu of different techniques for imputing or valuing WTP for reductions in pollution/improvements in EQ. There is no single approach that can be used in all cases; each has challenges in measurement and interpretation.

The techniques can be broken down into two main categories:

- Approaches that can use market prices to reflect WTP. These measure damages in the form of loss of incomes and output, reduced productivity, and expenditures needed to offset environmental damages. Another term often used is a *direct* approach to measurement of WTP.

- Approaches that are based on imputing willingness to pay of individuals as revealed through their behaviour or upon direct questioning. These are used when there is no actual market and hence market prices to reflect environmental values. These techniques are sometimes called *indirect* approaches to measuring WTP.

Table 7-1 lists these methods and gives examples of the types of environmental issues to which they are applied. We begin with economic damage approaches, focusing particularly on health.

ESTIMATION OF ECONOMIC DAMAGES

When environmental degradation occurs, it produces damages; the emissions control model of Chapter 5 is based in part on the relationship between emissions and marginal damages—the MD function. So in a very direct sense the *benefits of improved environmental quality come about because of reduced damages.* To measure a complete emissions damage function, it is necessary to go through the following steps:

1. Measure emissions,
2. Determine the resulting ambient quality,
3. Estimate human exposure,
4. Measure impacts (health, aesthetic, recreation, ecosystem, etc.),
5. Estimate the values of these impacts.

TABLE 7-1 Valuation Methods for Benefit Estimation

Method	Environmental Application
Direct approaches (market prices used)	
1. Changes in productivity	Health effects of pollution
	Pollution impact on agriculture, natural resources
2. Health-care costs	Health effects of pollution
3. Loss of human capital	Health effects of pollution
4. Replacement/restoration of damaged property, businesses	Pollution damage to structures
	Ecosystem damage (e.g., oil spills)
Indirect approaches (willingness to pay imputed)	
1. Preventive/mitigating expenditures	Noise, visual, air, water pollution effects on consumers, industry, ecosystem damage
2. Hedonic estimation	
Property value	Air pollution, toxic waste sites, noise pollution
Wage differentials	Health effects of pollution
3. Surrogate markets	Recreational benefits of improved environmental quality
Travel cost	Environmentally friendly goods as substitutes for pollution-intensive goods (e.g., recycled paper)
"Green goods"	
4. Contingent valuation and choice experiments	Environmental quality—current and future
	All types of pollution

The first three of the steps are largely the work of physical scientists. Models that show the relation between emissions and ambient levels are often called *diffusion models*. Step 4 involves economists to some extent, but also biological scientists and epidemiologists. The linkage of steps 3 and 4 is often called a **dose–response function.** This means estimating the response in terms, for example, of human **mortality** and **morbidity** to varying exposure levels to environmental pollutants. Step 5 is where economics comes strongly into play, in estimating the values associated with different impacts as identified in the previous step. This is generally a major challenge, as we will see in the coming sections.

Direct Estimation of Economic Damages

Health Damages

All forms of pollution can have an adverse impact on human health. For example, air pollution has long been thought to increase mortality and morbidity among people exposed to it, certainly in the episodic releases of toxic pollutants but also from long-run exposure to such pollutants as SO_2 and particulate matter. Diseases such as bronchitis, emphysema, and lung cancer are thought to be traceable in part to polluted air. Estimates of the health costs of air pollution suggest that many billions of dollars are lost each year. Water pollution also produces health damages, primarily through contaminated drinking-water supplies. So the measurement of the human health damages of environmental pollution is a critical task for environmental economists.

Fundamental to this work is the underlying dose–response relationship showing the relationship between human health and exposure to environmental contaminants. Many factors affect human health—lifestyles, diet, genetic factors, age—besides ambient pollution levels. To separate out the effects of pollution, one has to account for all the other factors or else run the risk of attributing to pollution effects that are actually caused by something else. This calls for large amounts of accurate data on health factors as well as the numerous suspected causal factors. Some of this—air or water quality, mortality statistics, and so on—may be available from published sources, but these may be too highly aggregated to give accurate results. Similarly, although published data may give us information on, for example, average air-pollution levels in certain areas of a city, it doesn't give completely accurate exposure data because that depends on how long individuals have lived in that environment. In a mobile society it is hard to develop accurate exposure data for people, since they may have lived in a variety of places throughout their lives. Epidemiologists have developed extensive experience with panel data, information developed through in-depth interviews with people about their lifestyles, consumption habits, locational history, and so on. A number of studies have been done that estimate the reduction in mortality or morbidity due to reductions in pollution. Morbidity measures look at indicators such as days absent from work or days affected by ill health. There is no general consensus on the estimates for the impacts of air or water pollution. One conclusion is that the results one gets are very sensitive to the data used and the way they are handled, which means we are still very uncertain about the exact links between air pollution and human mortality and morbidity rates.

The main work of economists comes after the dose–response research, in putting values on the various health impacts. How should we approach placing a value on a life prematurely shortened or on a debilitating illness suffered as a result of exposure to environmental pollutants? Your first reaction may be that it's a dubious moral exercise to try to attach a monetary value to a human life. Isn't life "priceless"? In a sense it is. If you stop a person in the street and ask her how much her life is worth, you may not get an answer because the question seems to violate a common moral standard. Nevertheless, society as a whole—that is, all of us acting collectively—doesn't behave that way. In fact, through our collective decisions and behaviour, we implicitly assign values to human lives. The clearest place to see this is in traffic control. Each year, thousands of people are killed on the nation's highways. Yet we do not see a massive outpouring of funds to redesign highways, slow traffic, or make substantially safer cars. This is because we are making an implicit trade-off between traffic deaths and other travel-related impacts, especially the benefits of reasonably fast and convenient travel. The same may be said of other risky technologies and practices we see frequently. Thus, it makes sense to examine the values that society actually places on lives and human health in the everyday course of its operation.

For some years it was standard procedure to estimate health damages by looking at such things as

- reductions in worker productivity accompanying deteriorated health and shortened lives that reduces their human capital; and

- increased monetary expenditures on health care.

For example, we might try to measure the value of a human life by looking at the economic contribution that society forgoes when that life is stopped. Over their working lives, people contribute to the production of useful goods and services enjoyed by others in society. When they die, this productivity ceases; thus, we might estimate the cumulative value of production that they would have produced had they lived. Lost productivity would vary among individuals as a function of their age, skills, and employment history, so we might take averages for people in different categories. Disease or disability caused by pollution also reduces one's human capital and, hence, lifetime earnings capacity. For example, children suffering neurological damage from lead (from leaded gasoline, paint) or mercury (contaminated fish, mercury in water) in the environment will not be able to realize the intellectual potential they would have had in a cleaner environment. These approaches are commonly used, but of course only capture the economic contributions a person makes, not their role in their families and community, and non-economic aspects important to society.

Another approach used to measure health damages is medical expenditures. As health is affected by increasing pollution we would expect increased medical expenditures on things like hospitals, doctors, and rehabilitation. Reducing pollution would, therefore, lead to a reduction in medical expenditures, which can be counted as a benefit of the environmental change. Examples of health costs were shown in the case study on lead in gasoline in Chapter 6.

LO 2

Output Losses and Materials Damage

Air pollution can reduce crop yields on exposed farms; it can also reduce the growth rates of commercially valuable timber. Water pollution can adversely affect firms and municipalities that use the water for production purposes or for domestic use. Diminished water quality can also have a negative impact on commercial fishing industries. Soil contamination can have serious impacts on agricultural production. Pollution in the workplace can reduce workers' effectiveness and can often increase the rate at which machinery and buildings deteriorate. In these cases the effects of pollution are felt on the production of goods and services. The damage caused by the pollution comes about because it interferes in some way with these production processes, in effect making it more costly to produce these outputs than it would be in a less polluted world. How we actually measure production-related benefits of reducing pollution depends on circumstances.

EXAMPLE

Increases in agricultural output due to pollution reductions

A small group of agricultural producers in B.C.'s Fraser Valley are affected by airborne emissions coming from an upwind factory. Pollutants from the factory have depressed crop yields, so reducing emissions will cause yields to increase. The crop being produced is sold in a national market, and its price will be unaffected by the output changes in this one region. This situation is depicted in Figure 7-1. In this diagram, S_1 (=MC_1) is the supply curve (marginal costs) for this group of farms before the improved air quality; S_2 (=MC_2) is the supply curve (marginal cost) after the improvement. The demand curve is horizontal at price P_1 because these farmers are price takers in a large competitive market. Before the change, these farmers produce at an output level of q_1, while after the improvement their output increases to q_2.

One way of approximating the benefits of this environmental improvement is to measure the value of increased output produced by this group of farms. The increased output is simply multiplied by the price of the crop. This gives an estimate corresponding to the area ($d + e$) in Figure 7-1.

(Continued)

FIGURE 7-1   Benefits from Reduced Production Costs

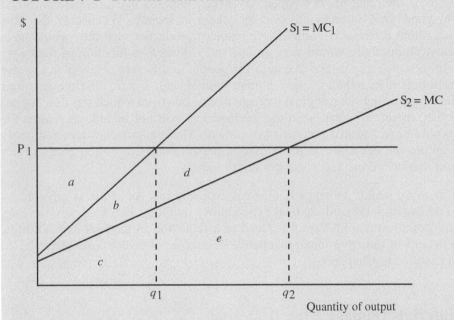

Benefits from reduced production costs due to better environmental quality are shown with a shift of the supply curve from S_1 to S_2. The value of the increase in output from q_1 to q_2 is area d plus e. If farmers also change their input mix, the total benefits can be estimated as the improvement in net income due to the change in environmental quality. This is are $(a + b + d)$ minus area a, which equal area $(b + d)$. This is called the change in producer surplus.

But the value of the increase in output is not consistent with the notion underlying our models that it is the WTP for this environmental quality improvement that matters. The problem with taking just the value of the increased output is that it is not the net benefit to the farmer and hence does not measure WTP. Net benefits are their net incomes.[3] Production costs may also have changed and these must be netted out. When air pollution diminishes, farmers may actually increase their use of certain inputs and farm this land more intensively. How do we account for this possibility?

The full change can be analyzed as follows, using net incomes of the farmers (total value of output minus total production costs).

Computation of net income:

Situation before the change:

Total value of output: $a + b + c$
Total costs: $b + c$
Net income: a

Situation after the change:

Total value of output: $a + b + c + d + e$
Total costs: $c + e$
Net income: $a + b + d$

(Continued)

[3.] In this example net income is also equal to operating profits (total revenues minus variable costs) because there are no fixed costs of production.

Thus, the improvement in net incomes is $(a + b + d) - a$, or an amount equal to area $(b + d)$ in Figure 7-1. The area above the supply curve and below the market price of the good summed over all units produced (i.e., from zero to q_1 or q_2) is called **producer surplus.** Producer surplus represents net income (net benefits) to producers. With a uniform market price and rising marginal costs (as represented by the rising supply curve), producers have net income greater than zero for all units produced up until the last unit (q_1 or q_2), where price is exactly equal to marginal cost in a competitive industry. The improvement in net income from the reduction in production costs is thus the net change in producer surplus from production: at q_1 to q_2 this is area $b + d$. This is the maximum the farmer would be willing to pay to reduce pollution and hence can be seen as her total benefit from reducing pollution damages (area under the MD curve).

To illustrate this case algebraically, let: $S_1 = 5 - .8q_1$ and $S_2 = 4 - .5q_2$. Suppose the market price of the crop is \$10, then we can solve for output levels at different levels of air pollution. With the high pollution levels, setting $P_1 = S_1$, we get: $10 = 6 + .8q_1$ and thus $q_1 = 6.25$ tonnes. When the pollution is reduced, we set $P_1 = S_2$ so $10 = 4 - .5q_2$ and $q_2 = 12$ tonnes. To compute the producer surplus with the high pollution, calculate area a as $\frac{1}{2}[(10 - 5) \times 6.25] = 15.525$. Producer surplus with less pollution is area $a + b + d$ which is the area of the triangle: $\frac{1}{2}[(10 - 4) \times 12] = 36$. The change in producer surplus (area $b + d$) is $(36 - 15.525) = 20.75$, the net gain to the farmers when the level of air pollution declines.

It is often difficult to obtain the data needed to estimate supply curves, but note that information on operating profits may be easier to obtain. However, many studies measure changes in output, rather than changes in producer surplus (net income to producers). A number of studies have been done along these lines.[4] Moskowitz et al.[5] studied the effects of air pollution on alfalfa in the United States. They measured the quantity of production lost because of air pollution and valued this loss at the going price of alfalfa. They found that air pollution was responsible for a loss in 1974 of between \$24-million and \$210-million. The difference between these figures comes about because of uncertainties over the actual pollution dose the alfalfa received in that year. Another study was done by Page et al.[6] to measure crop-related air-pollution losses in a six-state area. They estimated annual losses in the production of soybeans, wheat, and corn and then aggregated these to see what the present value of total losses would be over the period 1976–2000. They came up with an estimate of about \$7-billion. However, these may be underestimates of the annual damages to crops. A recent study done for NASA in the United States, estimated the impact of ozone on soybean crops alone was \$2-billion annually.[7]

[4.] These studies are reviewed in Gardner M. Brown, Jr., and Mark L. Plummer, "Market Measures of User Benefits," in *Acid Deposition: State of Science and Technology*, Report 27, Methods for Valuing Acidic Deposition and Air Pollution Effects (Washington, D.C., U.S. Superintendent of Documents: National Acid Precipitation Assessment Program, 1990) 27–35 to 27–73.

[5.] Paul D. Moskowitz et al., "Oxidant Air Pollution: A Model for Estimating Effects on U.S. Vegetation," *Journal of Air Pollution Control Association* 32(2) (February 1982): 155–160.

[6.] Walter P. Page et al., "Estimation of Economic Losses to the Agricultural Sector from Airborne Residuals in the Ohio River Basin," *Journal of Air Pollution Control Association*, 32(2) (February 1982): 151–154.

[7.] NASA "Satellite Measurements Help Reveal Ozone Damage to Important Crops," May 25, 2009, accessed at: www.nasa.gov/topics/earth/features/soybeans.html , August 31, 2010.

Several Canadian studies have been done on the effects of ground-level ozone on crops.[8] Ozone is seen as the most damaging air pollutant to crops in Canada, impairing the growth and yields of sensitive plants. The value of reduced crop yields per year in southern Ontario ranges from $17-million to $70-million, depending on the year chosen. The reason the range is so large is that the number of severe ozone days varies per year. Lost production in the Fraser Valley of B.C. is estimated at $8.8-million annually.

Air pollutants cause damage to exposed surfaces, metal surfaces of machinery, stone surfaces of buildings and statuary, and painted surfaces of all types of items. The most heavily implicated pollutants are the sulphur compounds, particulate matter, oxidants, and nitrogen oxides. For the most part, the damage is from increased deterioration that must be offset by increased maintenance and earlier replacement. In the case of outdoor sculpture, the damage is to the aesthetic qualities of the objects.

In this case the dose–response relationship shows the extent of deterioration associated with exposure to varying amounts of air pollutants. The basic physical relationships may be investigated in the laboratory, but in application to any particular area one must have data on the various amounts of exposed materials that actually exist in the study region. Then it is possible to estimate the total amount of materials deterioration that would occur in an average year of exposure to the air of the region with its "normal" loading of various pollutants. One must then put a value on this deterioration. Taking a strict damage-function approach, we could estimate the increased cost of maintenance (labour, paint) made necessary by this deterioration.[9]

Problems with Direct Damage Measures

The benefit of using direct damage estimates is that they take advantage of market prices for valuation. The basic problem is that they are almost always seriously incomplete and underestimate total damages. Consider the case of measuring health damages by lost productivity and medical expenditures. They measure the value of marketed goods and services a person might, on average, produce. So the many non-market contributions people make, both inside and outside the home, don't get counted. This method would also assign a zero value to anyone unable to work, or a retiree. There is also the question of whether a person's consumption should be subtracted from his production to measure his actual net contribution. This might seem reasonable, but it leads to awkward conclusions—such as the premature death of a welfare recipient would be a benefit to society. There are numerous monetary, as well as psychic, benefits received by others—friends and relatives, for example—that the productivity measure does not account for. Nor does it account for the pain and suffering of illness. Thus, although the **productivity-study approach** may be useful in some circumstances, it can give misleading results in others because it does not fully reflect willingness to pay in its broadest context.

The same may be said of using medical expenditures to estimate damages from reduced environmental quality. For example, an asthma attack due to urban smog may cost a woman $300 per day for asthma drugs and hospital treatment costs for each severe attack. While $300 per person per high-smog day multiplied by all the asthma sufferers could amount to a lot of damage, it would no doubt be a serious understatement of the true damages of the smog-induced asthma. If the asthma sufferer were asked

---

[8.] These studies are cited in Environment Canada, *Ground-Level Ozone in Canada*, A State of the Environment Fact Sheet, No. 92-1, Catalogue No. EN1-12/92-1E (Ottawa: Ministry of Supply and Services, 1992), 4.

[9.] This approach is taken from R. L. Horst et al., *A Damage Function Assessment of Building Materials: The Impact of Acid Deposition* (Washington, D.C.: U.S. Environmental Protection Agency, 1986). Air Quality Ontario: www.airqualityontario.com

how much she would be willing to pay to avoid the attack or how much she would need to be compensated when she has the attack, the answer is likely to be more than the cost of medical treatment. Similarly, materials damage estimates do not take into account aesthetic losses; crop reductions do not measure damage to species diversity or broad ecosystem values. The key point is that

> *direct measures typically do not fully reflect the person's WTP for EQ improvements.*

LO 3

WILLINGNESS TO PAY

As noted above, a marginal damage function shows the changes in damages suffered by people or other elements of the ecosystem when exposed to pollution or environmental alteration. Damages can occur in many forms, ranging from direct physical damage, such as health impacts, to degradation of the aesthetic quality of the environment (e.g., lowered visibility or psychic damage). In other words, "damages" include all the negative effects of the emissions. Looked at from a different perspective, the marginal damage function for increases in emissions is the same as the demand/willingness-to-pay function for decreases in emissions. If a small increase in emissions causes a person $10 in increased damages, the maximum he would be willing to pay to decrease emissions by that small amount would presumably be $10. We want to focus, therefore, on willingness to pay for environmental improvements.[10]

Change in Consumer Surplus as the Measure of WTP

Our focus in benefit–cost analysis is on net benefits. A key concept economists use is called **consumer surplus.**

> *Consumer surplus measures the net benefit a person derives from consuming a good, what is gained over and above the total expenditure on the good.*

Consumer surplus is illustrated first for a private good where market prices reflect WTP, then for a public good, like environmental quality, where "price" in the form of WTP must be imputed.

Deriving Consumer Surplus for a Private Good

In the case of private goods, consumer surplus is the difference between what a consumer is willing to pay for a particular amount of the good and the market price he or she actually has to pay.[11] Figure 7-2 shows a person's demand for organic apples (and is the same as the demand curve of Figure 3-1). Suppose the market price of apples is $3 per kilogram. Reading off the demand curve, the consumer wishes to buy 4 kg at this price. Now consider the consumer's net benefits for his purchase of 4 kg.

[10.] There are two ways to measure individuals' valuation of environmental damages: their willingness to pay to avoid damage or their willingness to accept (WTA) compensation for damages incurred. Economic theory used to argue that these two measures should be close in size, differing only by the size of income effects. However, empirical studies estimating WTP and WTA and different models of how people value gains versus losses find very significant differences between the two measures, with WTA greatly exceeding WTP. See Knetsch (1994) for a discussion of these issues. We return to this topic later in the chapter.

[11.] Consumer surplus is thus analogous to producer surplus. They show the net benefits of consumption or production, hence the maximum WTP for the change in pollution or EQ.

He would be willing to pay $4.50 for the first kilogram of apples. We can read this off the demand curve in Figure 7-2 or use the inverse demand function from Chapter 3 ($P = 5 - .5Q_D$) to derive that WTP price. This means his net benefit from purchasing the first kilogram is $4.50 minus the $3 per kilogram he has to pay, or $1.50. The second kilogram yields a net benefit of $1 and the third, $.50; the fourth, of course, yields no additional net benefit because price equals the consumer's WTP. Consumer surplus is then calculated as the sum of all these net benefits from zero to the quantity purchased. It is the area under the demand curve above the price of the good from 0 consumption to the 4 kg of apples the person chooses to buy (area *a*). We can readily calculate this area—it is the triangle with base of 4 and height of $2, which equals $4. These are this consumer's net benefits from purchasing 4 kg of apples at a price of $3 per kilogram. The principle is the same whether we are dealing with individual or market demand curves.

FIGURE 7-2   Deriving Consumer Surplus for a Private Good

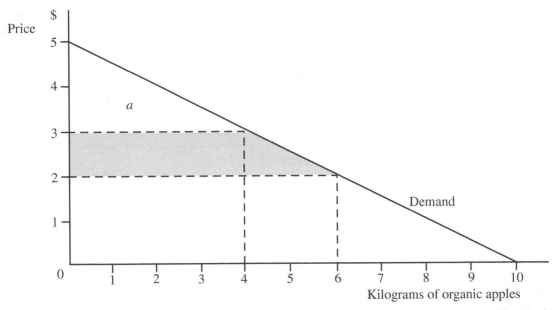

Consumer surplus is the difference between the consumer's WTP for a good as represented by his demand curve and the market price of the good summed over all units of the good purchased. If the market price of apples is $3 per kilogram, the consumer buys 4 kg and his consumer surplus is area *a*, which equals $4. If the market price of apples falls to $2 per kilogram the consumer will buy more apples and get a greater benefit due to the fall in the price. The net gain from the fall in the price is measured by *change in consumer surplus*—the shaded area, which equals the difference in consumer surplus from the equilibrium at a price of $3 per kilogram and 4 kg purchased to that at $2 per kilogram and 6 kg purchased. The net benefit/change in consumer surplus is $5.

To recap,

> *consumer surplus for a private good is measured as the area under the demand curve above the price of the good between zero and the amount of the good consumed.*

How is consumer surplus used to measure WTP? The following example illustrates.

EXAMPLE

Using consumer surplus in benefit–cost analysis

Benefit–cost analysis of public projects and policies involves changes in situations. Consumers may initially be at one equilibrium, then move to another as a result of the policy or project. Their net benefits are then found by looking at the change in consumer surplus with and without the project. For example, suppose the public program is a subsidy to organic apple growers as part of a sustainable agriculture program. The subsidy lowers the equilibrium price of apples from $3 to $2 per kilogram. Look again at Figure 7-2. At $2 per kilogram, the consumer wishes to buy 6 kg. He also has higher net benefits for each kilogram purchased up to 6 kg, because the price per kilogram is $1 cheaper. Total consumer surplus in the new situation is ½($3 times 6) = $9. The change in consumer surplus is thus the difference between total consumer surplus with and without the policy ($9 − $4) = $5. This is shown as the shaded area in Figure 7-2. The change in consumer surplus represents the net benefits accruing to this consumer from the government policy and, hence, his WTP for the policy.

Deriving Consumer Surplus for a Public Good

In the case of a public good, there is no market price for the good but the principle behind consumer surplus is still appropriate. The difference is that the analyst must infer people's WTP rather than use market prices. With a public good, such as environmental quality, what is being offered is a specific quantity of the good. The person is then asked for her WTP for that quantity. Figure 7-3 illustrates: we use exactly the same equation for demand curve as in Figure 7-2 to facilitate comparison, but interpret the quantity axis as some measurable indicator of environmental quality (EQ).

FIGURE 7-3   Deriving Consumer Surplus for a Public Good

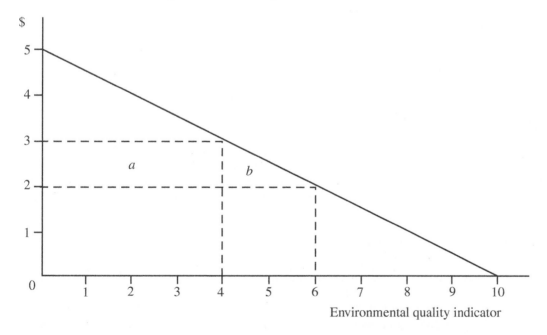

The change in consumer surplus for an improvement in environmental quality from 4 to 6 units is the area under the demand curve between these quantities. This is area (a + b) and equals $5.

Suppose the initial level of EQ is 4 units. The consumer is then asked what she is WTP for 4 units. Her answer (reading off her demand curve): $3. Consider a public project that increases EQ to 6 units. Ask again—what are you WTP for 6 units of EQ? Answer: $2. It then makes intuitive sense to measure the total benefits from the public good as argued in Chapter 3 (see Figure 3-2) as the area under the demand curve between these two quantities, because there is no market price she has to pay. The area under the demand curve between the old and the new quantity represents her WTP for the increase in EQ. The change in consumer surplus can be calculated numerically from Figure 7-3 as the area of the rectangle marked *a* plus the area of the triangle marked *b*. Area $(a + b)$ = $5. This number should be familiar to you. It is exactly the same as the change in consumer surplus measured for the private market (using the same demand curve), and shown by the shaded area in Figure 7-2.

> *The change in consumer surplus resulting from an increase in EQ—a public good can be measured in the same way as the change in consumer surplus for a private good.*

LO 4

METHODS OF IMPUTING WTP FOR IMPROVEMENTS IN ENVIRONMENTAL QUALITY

There are essentially four ways of trying to find out how much people are willing to pay for improvements in environmental quality. All derive measures of changes in consumer surplus associated with the change in environmental quality. These are as listed in Table 7-1:

- Preventive or mitigating expenditures

- Hedonic estimation

- Surrogate markets

- Contingent valuation

Noise pollution can be used as an illustration.

EXAMPLE
How to value reductions in traffic noise

One feature of the modern world is high-speed roadways (highways, expressways, freeways, and turn-pikes), and a major characteristic of these roads is that the traffic on them creates noise. Thus, the people who live nearby suffer damages from this traffic noise. Suppose we would like to estimate the willingness to pay of people living near highways to reduce traffic noise. How might we do this? Three of our four approaches could be used.[12]

Approach 1: Preventive or mitigating expenditures

The homeowners themselves may have made expenditures to reduce the noise levels inside their homes. For example, they may have installed additional insulation in the walls of their homes, put double-thick glass in the windows, or planted shrubs or installed other outside noise barriers to dampen the noise. When people make expenditures like this, they reveal something about their willingness to pay for a quieter environment. In general, then, if we can find cases where market goods are purchased

(Continued)

[12.] It is difficult to see how one could use the surrogate market approach for this example. We illustrate this approach in a later section of this chapter.

in order to affect a consumer's exposure to the ambient environment, we may be able to analyze these purchases and use market prices to infer one component of the value people place on changes in the ambient environment.

Approach 2: Hedonic estimation

The noise in the vicinity of the road may have affected the prices that people have paid for the houses there. If two houses have exactly the same characteristics in all respects but the level of exterior noise, we would expect the one in the noisier environment to be less valuable to prospective buyers than the one in the quieter environment. If the housing market is competitive, the price of the noisier house would be lower than the other one. Thus, by looking at the difference in house prices due to the presence of noise we can estimate the value people place on reduced noise pollution. Any time the price of some good or service varies in accordance with its environmental characteristics, we may be able to analyze these price variations to determine people's willingness to pay for these characteristics.

Approach 3: Contingent valuation

Both of the foregoing techniques are proxies for WTP in the sense that they look for ways of analyzing market data to find out what they imply about the willingness to pay of people for closely associated environmental characteristics. The third way is deceptively direct. We could conduct a survey among homeowners and ask them how much they would be willing to pay for reductions in noise levels around and inside their homes. This direct survey approach has received a lot of attention from environmental economists in recent years, primarily because of its flexibility. Virtually any feature of the natural environment that can be described accurately to people can be studied by this method.

In the remainder of the chapter we illustrate, using more detailed examples, how these techniques have been used to estimate the benefits of improvements in environmental quality, highlighting problems and pitfalls the benefit–cost analyst encounters.

Preventive or Mitigating Expenditures

Air and water pollution can produce a variety of adverse health conditions, ranging from slight chest discomfort or headaches all the way to acute episodes requiring hospital care. People often make **preventive or mitigating expenditures** to try to avoid, or avert, these conditions, and these mitigation costs are an expression of their willingness to pay to avoid them. Consider the following example.

EXAMPLE
Mitigation of asthma attacks from smog by purchasing air purifiers

Urban smog is formed from a combination of air pollutants (sulphur dioxide, particulate matter, nitrogen oxides) during days when temperatures are high, there is little wind to disperse pollutants, or a temperature inversion exists where cold air is trapped in a region by a mass of hot air above it. Certain Canadian cities (e.g., Vancouver, Toronto, Montreal) are more prone to smog because they have high emissions of air pollutants and conditions favourable to the creation of smog. The components of smog (the above pollutants plus the ground-level ozone produced by the interaction of the pollutants with sunshine) contribute to asthma attacks and other respiratory problems.

Suppose you have asthma and want to reduce your exposure to smog. A defensive expenditure would be the purchase of an air purifier. Your costs involve the initial purchase of the purifier (a capital cost) plus the operating costs of running the purifier during high-smog days (electricity, air filters for the purifier). We assume you would not buy the purifier if smog were not a problem in your city.

(Continued)

However, other people (e.g., smokers) might purchase air purifiers for reasons unconnected to urban smog.

The economic analyst could calculate defensive expenditures by looking at market data for air purifiers. The steps the analyst could take are as follows.

1. Collect data on air purifier purchases in two cities—one with a large number of smog days, and one without.

2. Estimate market demand curves from this data.

3. Use the demand curves to calculate the benefits of reducing urban smog by measuring the difference between willingness to pay for air purifiers with and without smog.

We assume the analyst has completed steps 1 and 2. The estimated market demand curves from step 2 are shown in Figure 7-4.[13] Hamilton, Ontario, is in a "smog belt" in eastern Canada with a number of summer days where smog is a problem. Winnipeg, Manitoba, has very few, if any, smog days per year due to its location away from smog-generating activities and a favourable topography and weather (no mountains, lots of wind). The demand curve for air purifiers in Winnipeg lies wholly inside that of Hamilton.

Step 3 requires calculation of the benefits of reducing smog. If Hamilton could reduce smog to the level of Winnipeg, its inhabitants would presumably reduce their air purifying expenditures to a level similar to that of Winnipeg (other things being equal). The WTP to reduce smog to Winnipeg's level is then estimated by *the difference between the two demand curves* in Figure 7-4. This is the difference in *total willingness to pay* for the air purifier. Quantitatively, we simply measure the area under each city's demand curve and subtract Winnipeg's from Hamilton's. Total willingness to pay of people living in Hamilton to remove all smog would be $150,000; total WTP from Winnipeg is $50,000. The difference is $100,000. This represents the WTP of Hamiltonians to have their air quality improve to that of Winnipeg. Now suppose the average price of air purifiers in both cities is $75. WTP should be measured as the change in consumer surplus due to different air quality. This will be the difference between the two demand curves *above the market price of the good,* which is shown as the shaded area in Figure 7-4 and equals $55,468.75.[14] Remember that we use the change in consumer surplus because we need to net out expenditures on the good. If people do not spend money on the good in question, they will spend it on some other good; hence, we measure only the surplus as WTP.

To use the change in consumer surplus as the WTP for improving air quality in a benefit–cost analysis, it would have to be converted into an annual value. This is because the air purifier is a capital asset that yields services over time, but also depreciates. Suppose air purifiers last 10 years and we assume they depreciate evenly over their life. Then the service value (depreciation) each year is one-tenth of the initial value, or $5,547.[15] This amount is then the benefit per year of reducing Hamilton's smog to the level of Winnipeg's and this amount would be discounted in the normal fashion in a benefit–cost analysis.

(Continued)

[13.] It is beyond the scope of this course to explain how to estimate a demand curve. A course in econometrics will cover the regression techniques needed.

[14.] The simplest way to compute the change in consumer surplus is to compute the consumer surplus above the market price of $75 for each city. For Hamilton, consumer surplus is ½($125 times 937.5) = $58,593.75. For Edmonton, consumer surplus is ½($25 times 250) = $3,125. The difference is $55,468.75.

[15.] Other approaches are possible, for example using declining balance depreciation.

FIGURE 7-4   Using Defensive Expenditures to Derive WTP for a Reduction in Smog

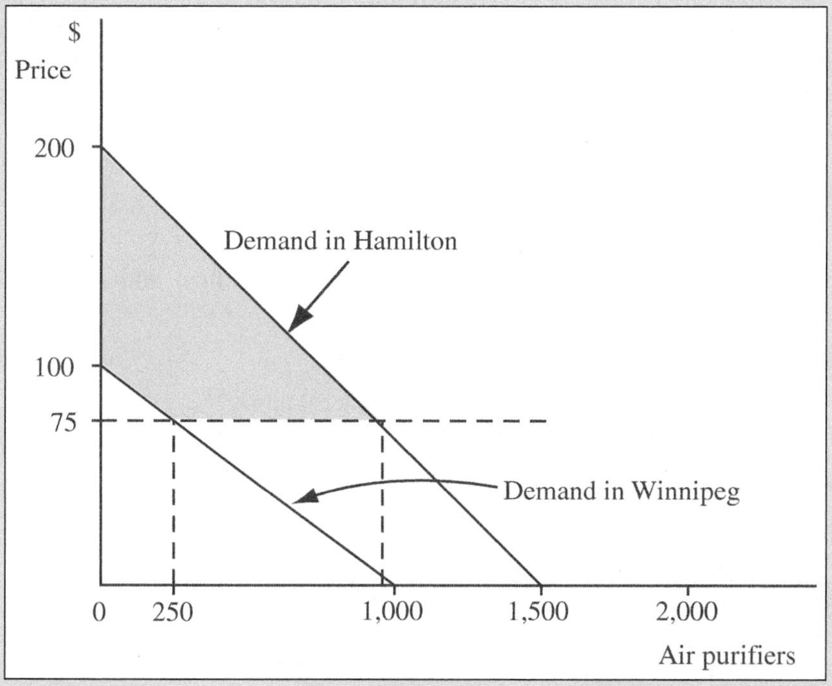

Two demand curves for air purifiers are estimated. Hamilton is a city with many high-smog days; Winnipeg is a city with very few smog days. Hamilton's demand curve lies above that of Winnipeg's because people are engaging in defensive expenditures to mitigate damages from urban smog. The difference in the demand curves shows the willingness to pay of people in Hamilton to protect themselves from smog. Willingness to pay for smog protection is estimated as the shaded area. If smog in Hamilton is reduced to the level of that in Winnipeg, the shaded area would be the benefits of the reduction in smog damage because people in Hamilton would now buy fewer air purifiers.

The example gives you a flavour of the approach taken in using defensive expenditures as a measure of willingness to pay for higher environmental quality or damages incurred from pollution. It is a proxy approach in that we are inferring from people's behaviour how they value environmental quality. There are many practical challenges. The approach cannot be used for all environmental problems because we may be unable to measure defensive expenditures linked to the specific environmental problem, or there are no defensive actions people can take. As the example suggests, it may be difficult to discern whether the expenditure is connected to a specific environmental problem. Do differences in demand curves across cities reflect air pollution or some other characteristic? Finally, defensive expenditures will not capture all the disutility people get from environmental degradation, just the part they can address through defensive actions.

Hedonic Estimation

Hedonic estimation can be used when the price of a market good is related to characteristics it possesses. We can study patterns of price differences to deduce the value people place on one of those characteristics. The characteristic of interest to environmental economists is of course some aspect of environmental quality, such as air quality, noise levels, or proximity to toxic waste sites. The analyst isolates the contribution the environmental variable makes to the total price of the good. This "marginal price" is then a measure of the WTP for an increment in environmental quality. Hedonic estimation has been done extensively for housing markets and has also been applied to wage differentials between industries that have environmental hazards and those that do not. The steps in a hedonic estimation are to

1. define and measure the environmental attribute.
2. specify the hedonic price function.
3. collect data across a region (for housing studies) or industries (wage studies) and/or for each city/industry over time.
4. use multiple regression analysis to value the environmental attribute.
5. derive the demand curve for environmental quality from the statistical study.
6. calculate the change in consumer surplus associated with a change in the level of environmental quality from that demand curve.

Let's turn to an example—housing markets.

EXAMPLE
Using hedonic estimation of housing markets to infer WTP for increases in air quality[16]

Suppose you had two houses that were exactly the same in terms of all their physical characteristics (number of rooms, floor area, age), as well as in locational factors (distance to neighbours, distance to shopping facilities). But assume one house is located in an area of substantial air pollution, while the other is located in an area with relatively clean air. We would expect the market prices of these two houses to differ because of the air-quality difference. This conclusion generalizes to a large housing market involving many properties. The surrounding air quality is essentially a feature of the location of a house—so, as houses are bought and sold in the housing market, air-quality differences would tend to be **capitalized** into the market prices of the houses.[17] Of course, homes differ in many respects, not just in terms of air quality. So we must collect large amounts of data on many properties to use the hedonic approach.

The derivation of a hedonic price function is done using statistical techniques. The analyst typically collects data on a sample of housing units sold over a particular time period. The relationship between

(Continued)

[16.] Hedonic estimation can also be applied to *industrial wage rate studies*. Workers can be exposed to high concentrations of pollutants on the job. Risks are greatest in industries where workers have to handle or are exposed to potentially harmful substances, either through their routine work or when accidents arise. Examples include lung diseases from working in mines and cotton mills and illnesses in agricultural workers who handle pesticides and herbicides. In perfectly functioning markets, wage rates should reflect workers' exposure to pollution. Wage rates should be higher in industries with more risk of injury, morbidity, and mortality from pollution.

[17.] By capitalized we mean that the house price adjusts to reflect the present value of the stream of future air pollution damages year-after-year that homeowners would be exposed to if they were to buy that house.

housing prices and all the possible characteristics that might influence people's willingness to pay for each house is then estimated statistically. These characteristics can include the size of the house, number of bedrooms, bathrooms, age of the home, its location, neighbourhood characteristics such as proximity to schools and parks, and a measurable environmental variable, such as air quality. The analyst graphs what is called a *hedonic price function* for the environmental variable (measured by an air quality index, or AQI), holding all other characteristics constant. Panel (a) in Figure 7-5 illustrates this relationship. The hedonic price function is shown as P(AQI; z), where z is all other characteristics that are held constant. The function is not a straight line to show that for most people, their marginal willingness to pay for a characteristic changes as more of the characteristic is supplied. At low levels of air quality, people's willingness to pay for a small increase in air quality might be quite high. But if the level of air quality is already high, a small increase will not yield a large increase in willingness to pay. If one then measures the slope of this hedonic price function for different levels of air quality she obtains the hedonic demand function for air quality, which depicts the marginal willingness to pay for each increment in air quality, again remembering that all other characteristics of the house and its location are held constant.

FIGURE 7-5 Derivation of a Hedonic Demand Curve for Air Quality

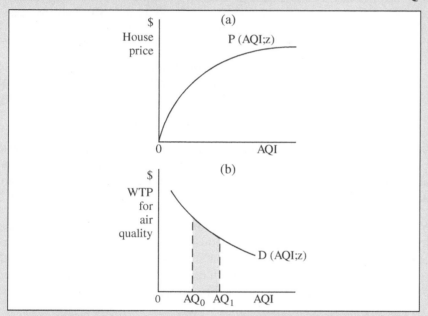

Panel (a) shows a hedonic price function. This is the relationship between the price of the house and one of its characteristics; here, an air quality index (AQI), holding other characteristics (z) constant. The functional form of the hedonic price function indicates that marginal willingness to pay for air quality declines as the AQI increases. Panel (b) illustrates the hedonic demand function, D(AQI;z), derived from the hedonic price equation. It is the slope of the hedonic price function, which flattens as the AQI increases, yielding the downward-sloping demand curve. The area under the demand curve between AQ_0 and AQ_1 is the WTP for an increase in air quality over that interval.

Panel (b) of Figure 7-5 illustrates a hedonic demand function, D(AQI;z). AQI is still on the horizontal axis, but the vertical axis now measures willingness to pay for air quality (AQ). The hedonic demand function is the slope of the hedonic price function, and it shows the marginal WTP for each unit of air

(Continued)

quality.[18] Because marginal WTP is decreasing, the demand function is downward-sloping. Once we have the hedonic demand function, we can compute the benefits of improving air quality. For a change in air quality from AQ_0 to AQ_1, the area under the hedonic demand curve between these two levels (the shaded area in Figure 7-5) shows the total benefits from that air quality improvement, using the technique for valuing the change in consumer surplus for a public good.

The change in consumer surplus is expressed in terms of the total price of the house. House purchasers are buying an asset that yields services over time, as was the case with the example of the air purifier. The researcher has to convert the price of the house into an annual flow of imputed rental values, so that an annual measure of the benefits of increased EQ can be calculated. A simple way to do this is to assume the house will last forever (i.e., ignore depreciation and maintenance costs). For example, suppose a house sells for $200,000. The hedonic study finds that for each 1-percent decrease in air pollution, there is a 2.5-percent increase in the selling price of the house. Thus, a house in an area with 1 percent less pollution than a neighbouring area will sell for an additional $5,000. This is the WTP measure. The $5,000 has to be converted to an annual value, which can be done using discounting. Assuming the house lasts forever, the analyst can use the PV formula for an infinitely lived benefit, $PV = m/r$. The analyst knows that $5,000 is the PV of the equation, and if she knows r, she simply solves for the annual benefit m, where $m = \$5,000$ times r. If r is 5 percent, then $m = \$250$. Therefore, a 1-percent decrease in air pollution will lead to a $250 annual benefit.

Hedonic pricing is feasible and most meaningful when property markets are active—there are a lot of sales, so these markets are competitive. It also requires potential house buyers to perceive the levels of environmental quality (either by sight, smell, or other means) in each neighbourhood they are thinking of living in. As with all techniques, there are some complications and challenges. Housing markets, and hence prices, may be distorted by too few sales (or housing bubbles where there is much speculation). The hedonic technique requires a large amount of data as well as advanced econometric skills to deal with statistical problems that can arise. A common problem is that the environmental variable may not be easily measured. Finally, individuals' perceptions of environmental quality are subjective and may not translate into property valuation.

Despite these challenges many studies have been done, especially in the United States. These studies calculate WTP in terms of *elasticities*, the percentage change in house prices for a 1-percent change in ambient air pollution. Numerous types of air pollutants have been studied, with similar results found. For example, for sulphur dioxide pollution, a 1-percent decrease in ambient concentration is associated with a change in house prices of between .06 and .12 percent. For particulate matter the elasticities range from .05 to .22.

Surrogate Markets—Travel-Cost Approach[19]

One of the first approaches that environmental economists used to estimate the demand for environmental amenities is a method of **surrogate markets** that takes travel costs as a proxy for price. Although we don't observe people buying units of environmental quality directly, we do observe them travelling to enjoy, for example, recreation experiences in national and provincial parks, swimming and fishing experiences in lakes and streams, wildlife viewing, and so on. Travel is costly; it takes time as well as out-of-pocket travel expenses. These travel costs can be viewed as a proxy for the price

---

[18.] The hedonic demand function for air quality is the derivative of the hedonic price function with respect to the air-quality index.

[19.] We look only at travel costs as an example of surrogate markets in this chapter. See Chapter 10 for a discussion of green goods.

that people must pay to experience the environmental amenity. The **travel-cost approach** can be used to derive a demand function for these amenities.

By getting travel-cost data for a large number of people, we can build up estimates of the aggregate willingness to pay for particular environmental amenities. Of course, we must get information on more than just their travel costs. Families will differ in terms of many factors, not just in terms of their travel costs to this park. They will have different income levels, they will differ in terms of the presence of alternative parks and other recreational experiences available to them, and so on. So, surveys have to collect large amounts of data on many visitors to be able statistically to sort out all these various influences on park visitation rates.

We can use this approach to estimate the benefits of improving the quality of the environment at the visitation site; for example, by improving the water quality at a recreation lake so that fishing is better or more wildlife abound. To do this we must collect information not only on the travel costs of recreators to a single recreation site, but also on the travel costs to many different sites with differing natural characteristics. From this, the analyst can derive a demand curve and use it to compute WTP for improvements in environmental quality by measuring changes in consumer surplus.

The steps in a travel-cost approach are as follows:

1. Sample visitors to various natural sites (parks, recreation, or wilderness areas) where the sites differ in terms of a measurable environmental quality variable. Visitors should be asked about

   • where their trip started from (what city, country)

   • number of visitors per travelling unit

   • travel mode (car, airplane, bus)

   • total travel time to site and at site

   • frequency of visits, duration of journey

   • socio-economic characteristics

   • direct travel expenses (transport costs, food, lodging)

   • motives for trip, tastes for recreation/sightseeing

2. Use regression techniques to estimate a demand curve for travel to each site. The demand curve shows the total number of visits as the quantity variable, with travel costs to the site as the price variable.

3. Compare the demand curves to see the impact of higher environmental quality at the site. Compute the change in consumer surplus between the sites.

EXAMPLE
Seaweed contamination of lakes in Ontario

Consider a hypothetical application. Suppose a travel-cost study has been done on two lakes in Ontario: Ahmic Lake and Eagle Lake. Ahmic Lake has been plagued with excessive plant growth due to the introduction of some non-native species by boaters who have transported exotic seaweeds from

(Continued)

the United States on their motors and boat hulls.[20] The seaweed produces a thick mat on the surface of parts of Ahmic Lake, killing native plants and fish. Boating, fishing, and swimming have become less desirable because of the seaweed. Eagle Lake is very close to Ahmic Lake, but because of boating restrictions does not have the exotic seaweed. The province wants to estimate people's WTP for an improvement in Ahmic Lake's water quality. It undertakes travel cost surveys at both lakes; the resulting demand curves are shown in Figure 7-6. The demand curve for Eagle Lake lies above that for Ahmic Lake. If these lakes are really very similar except for the difference in water quality, the analyst can interpret the difference in consumer surplus (as shown by the shaded area) between the two lakes as the visitors' WTP for better water quality. There is no entry fee (price of admission) to these lakes, so no need to compute change in consumer surplus above any price. (Question: How would the computation change if an entry fee existed?) The change in consumer surplus is an annual value because the travel-cost estimation was done for number of trips per year. The consumer surplus estimate can then be used in a benefit–cost study (discounted for future years) of any government program designed to eliminate the offending seaweed.

FIGURE 7-6   A Travel-Cost Estimation of the Benefits of Reducing Seaweed Contamination

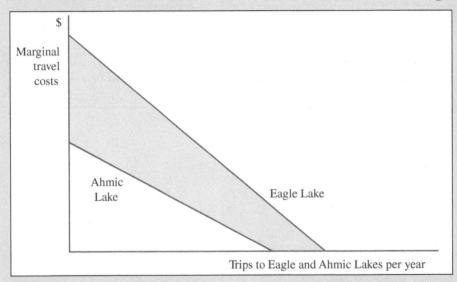

Demand curves are derived from travel cost surveys done at Eagle and Ahmic Lakes. Eagle Lake has higher water quality than Ahmic Lake because it is not infested with seaweed. The value people place on higher water quality is the difference in their consumer surplus between the two lakes, shown as the shaded area. There are no entry fees for either lake.

Critique of the Travel-Cost Method

The travel-cost method is best used when alternative sites have very similar characteristics (except for environmental quality indicators) and where many repeat trips are made each year. There are a number of difficulties encountered in the travel-cost approach. These include the following.

---

[20] This is a real problem for many inland waterways in the United States and may indeed spread to Canada by boaters who fail to clean their boats. Ahmic Lake and Eagle Lake are real lakes north of Toronto, but Ahmic Lake does not yet have this seaweed problem. One of the offending seaweeds, hydrilla, originally came from India and Korea and was introduced into the United States as an aquarium plant. In Florida, 70 percent of the state's freshwater drainages are infested with hydrilla, causing the state to spend $14.5-million per year on pesticides and mechanical harvesting of the pest (*Environment*, Vol. 42, No. 4, May 2000, p. 4).

- *Multi-purpose visits:* The site may not be the final destination; for example, the purpose of visits may be job- or family-related, with a side trip for recreation. The analyst will have to separate out the costs associated with the recreation site—often a difficult task.

- *Utility/disutility from travelling:* Travel to the site may be an enjoyable part of the trip or very unpleasant. This means that travel cost estimates will not be a good proxy for willingness to pay. One way to address this is to ask people to indicate on their survey their subjective assessment of their trip to the site.

- *Sampling biases in surveys:* The biggest problem with the technique is that it samples only users of the site. This may over-estimate or underestimate willingness to pay for environmental quality improvements. An overestimate may occur if those not in the sample have no demand for the site whether environmental quality is high or low. If this is the case, they will not be willing to incur any travel costs. An underestimate may occur if people put a value on a site whether or not they visit it. You may get utility from knowing that Ahmic Lake is weed-free even if you don't intend to visit it. The idea that elimination of the exotic seaweed will lead to greater biodiversity and watershed protection may have value to people. In developing countries, natural areas can provide many goods and services to local inhabitants (fuel wood, game, food, and medicinal plants). These people may not be counted as travellers to the site, so their benefits are not counted.

Measuring the change in environmental quality is difficult. What one typically wants to measure is the value of changes in environmental quality at a site. The travel-cost approach only proxies willingness to pay for a given level of environmental quality at another site. Given these difficulties, travel costs are of limited general use in benefit–cost analyses.

Contingent Valuation Methods

The direct approach to estimating willingness to pay is called the **contingent valuation method** (CVM). CVM is based on the simple idea that if you would like to know the willingness to pay of people for some characteristic of their environment, you can simply ask them. The word "simply" is a little extreme because it turns out not to be so simple, even though the basic idea seems straightforward. The method is called "contingent" valuation because it tries to get people to say how they would act if they were placed in certain hypothetical situations. If the good in question were a market good, the analyst can observe people's actions in the marketplace. But when there are no well-defined markets for something, like an environmental quality characteristic, we can only ask them to tell us how they would choose *if* they were placed in certain situations; that is, *if* they were faced with a market for these characteristics.

When people buy rice, we assume that they do so because they expect to eat it; the value of rice to people lies in its active or **use value.** This reasoning extends also to environmental assets, but in this case there may be more. When people voluntarily donate money for the preservation of unique environmental assets that they may never see except for in photographs, it is an example of a passive or **non-use value.** Other examples of non-use values are the desire to preserve the option of directly experiencing an environmental asset in the future, e.g. they plan to visit a wildlife reserve in Africa, or to ensure that future generations will be able to visit or enjoy the existence of the reserve. Finally, people may simply feel it is their obligation to be good stewards of the natural environment; to maintain environmental health for the continued use of all living organisms. A major benefit of contingent valuation studies is that they are able to explore both use and non-use values people might hold for an environmental attribute.

Contingent value studies have been done to date for a long list of environmental factors: air quality, the value of view-related amenities, the recreational quality of beaches, preservation of wildlife species, congestion in wilderness areas, hunting and fishing experiences, toxic waste disposal, preservation of wild rivers, willingness to avoid ill health due to pollutants, and others.[21] CVM has spread into non-environmental areas such as the value of programs for reducing the risks of heart attacks, the value of supermarket price information, and the value of a seniors' companion program. Over time, the method has been developed and refined to give what we think are reasonably reliable measures of the benefits of a variety of public goods, especially environmental quality.

The steps in a CVM analysis are the following:

1. Identification and description of the environmental quality characteristic to be evaluated.

2. Identification of respondents to be approached, including sampling procedures used to select respondents.

3. Design and application of a survey questionnaire through personal, phone, or mail interviews (in recent years, focus groups have often been used).

4. Analysis of results and aggregation of individual responses to estimate values for the group affected by the environmental change. This may involve simple tabulation or econometric analysis.

5. Use of WTP estimates in benefit–cost analysis. Because the WTP measures will be estimates of the change in consumer surplus, they can be directly inserted as net benefits into a benefit–cost study.

A more complex CVM method is to perform what are called *choice experiments*. A choice experiment puts people into a laboratory-like setting and provides multiple characteristics or attributes of environmental goods and services and assigns prices to each characteristic. For example, a natural area can have more habitat protection, investment in nature trails, and wildlife enhancement. Each will come at a specific price, the respondent is given a budget and chooses the combination of attributes that she likes the best. The researcher can vary the prices of the attributes to see how they influence choice. From these experiments, marginal WTP calculations can be made, but require complex statistical methods.

We can best appreciate the nature of CVM analysis by looking more closely at the questionnaire design phase.

The Contingent Valuation Questionnaire

The CVM questionnaire is designed to get people to think about and reveal their maximum willingness to pay for some feature of the environment. It has three essential components:

- a clear statement of exactly what the environmental feature or amenity is that people are being asked to evaluate.

- a set of questions that will describe the respondent in economically relevant ways, for example income, residential location, age, and use of related goods.

- a question, or set of questions, designed to elicit willingness-to-pay responses from the respondent.

The central purpose of the questionnaire is to elicit from respondents their estimate of what the environmental feature is worth to them. In economic terms this means getting them to reveal the maximum amount they would be willing to pay rather than go without the amenity in question. If they

---

[21.] There are many examples of contingent valuation in the economics literature. See the references for this chapter at the end of the book for a sample of the many different ways CVM has been used.

are answering truthfully, the number they reveal should be what they perceive as their net benefits from the amenity. A number of techniques have been used to get at this response. The most obvious is to ask people outright to provide the number with no prompting or probing on the part of the interviewer. Other approaches include using a bidding game, where the interviewer starts with a bid at a low level and progressively increases the value until the user indicates that the limit has been reached. Alternatively, the interviewer could start with a high figure and lower it to find where the respondent's threshold value is located. Another method is to give the respondents printed response cards with a range of values, then ask the respondents to check off their maximum willingness to pay. A hypothetical example will illustrate a CVM questionnaire and how its results can be used.

EXAMPLE
Willingness to pay for reducing urban air pollution

The Greater Vancouver Region is attempting to reduce air pollution in the region.[22] There are a number of possible policies that could be used to accomplish this objective, including encouraging people to take public transit rather than use their personal vehicles, levying fees on motor vehicles by vehicle type or weight, increasing gasoline taxes, putting tolls on roads and bridges, taxing parking facilities in the downtown core of the city, and so on.

The analyst wants to examine people's WTP between two options: a tax on vehicles based on vehicle weight, and putting a toll on all of Vancouver's bridges. The analyst designs the questionnaire shown later in this chapter.

The analyst surveys 2,000 people and gets the following results. The mean WTP for a vehicle levy is $5 per 100 kg. Passenger vehicles (cars and light trucks) range from 1,500 to 2,500 kilograms in weight. The analyst examines the ownership of vehicles in British Columbia by type, obtains their weights from the manufacturer, and computes the aggregate WTP per year for the vehicle levy. It is $15-million.

The mean WTP for bridge tolls is $1. The analyst obtains traffic survey data from the TransLink engineering department and calculates that there average 100,000 trips across greater Vancouver bridges each day (weekdays have more trips than weekends). Revenue will thus be $100,000 per day or $36.5-million per year.

The analyst reports that the people surveyed are much more willing to pay for bridge tolls than vehicle levies. These numbers can then be used to help design effective policies for the region.

Using Contingent Valuation Methods to Measure WTP to Protect Endangered Species

Canada's *Species at Risk Act* (SARA) allows for consideration of the costs and benefits of measures to help a threatened or endangered species to recover. A paper by Boxell, Adamowicz, Olar, West, and Cantin (2012)[23] uses a combination of contingent valuation and choice experiment to estimate the benefits of improving the survival likelihood of populations of three species of marine mammals in the St. Lawrence Estuary. There are a variety of marine mammals that are residents or visitors to the estuary, some of whom have a SARA status as endangered, threatened, or at risk. See www.ec.gc.ca/alef-ewe/default.asp?lang=en&n=ED2FFC37-1 for information about Canada's SARA

[22.] This is a real issue where a number of studies have been done, some using contingent valuation techniques. The example is hypothetical, but presents some potentially realistic numbers.

[23.] Boxall, P. et al., "Analysis of the Economic Benefits Associated with the Recovery of Threatened Marine Mammal Species in the Canadian St. Lawrence Estuary," *Marine Policy* 36 (2012): 189–197.

and definitions of the categories of risk to species. The focus of the study was on three species: blue and beluga whales and a harbour seal. The resident beluga whale population is deemed threatened and transient blue whales, endangered. Populations of the Eastern harbour seal officially are not considered at risk, but those resident in the estuary are felt to be threatened due to their decreasing population and threats from human activities. Other species of whales, seals, dolphin, and porpoise are visitors to the estuary.

Canada's Department of Fisheries and Oceans (DFO) requested an economic analysis of options to protect marine mammals to assist their decision making and assess whether to establish a marine protected area (MPA). The authors of this study assessed three different MPA options using stated preference approaches to assess both active and passive use values. The study framed the options as a choice between the status quo (no specific program to help improve the species) and six program options that presented combinations of levels of protection in the form of restrictions on shipping and a MPA of varying size. Each program presents costs to a household in the form of an annual increase in their level of income taxation and a rise in the prices of goods that were shipped through the St. Lawrence. The program attributes were chosen after consultation with scientists and the survey pre-tested in focus groups and a trial group.

Table 7-2 below illustrates the program options and Table 7-3 illustrates the choice set for one of the six programs proposed versus the status quo. The respondents were told to "vote" in the form of a referendum for the program they most preferred. Each received a cost within the range tested in the focus groups and assigned randomly.

TABLE 7-2:   Marine Mammal Study: Current Situation (Status Quo) and Six Hypothetical Programs

Program	Species status			Size of marine protected area	Shipping and whale watching industry regulations
	Beluga whales	**Harbor seals**[b]	**Blue whales**		
Current situation	Threatened	Threatened	Endangered	MPA not present	Current
A	Threatened	Recovery to special concern	Endangered	Small	Minor increase
B	Recovery to special concern	Threatened	Endangered	Small	Minor increase
C	Recovery to special concern	Recovery to special concern	Endangered	Small	Minor increase
D	Recovery to not at risk	Threatened	Endangered	Small	Major increase
E	Recovery to not at risk	Recovery to not at risk	Endangered	Small	Major increase
F	Recovery to not at risk	Recovery to not at risk	Recovery to threatened	Large	Major increase

[a] Note that for each program, a price attribute was described as an increase in the household's annual taxes. This cost was randomly assigned to each respondent and held one of the following five values: $5, $15, $50, $100, and $350.

[b] The status of the harbor seal used in this study was not an official species at Risk Act designation but one provided to us from marine scientists based on the low number of individual seals resident in the Estuary.

Source: *Boxall, P. et al., "Analysis of the Economic Benefits Associated with the Recovery of Threatened Marine Mammal Species in the Canadian St. Lawrence Estuary," Marine Policy 36 (2012): 189-197, Table 1, p. 191.*

TABLE 7-3: Example of the Status Quo versus Program A

	CURRENT situation Expected levels in 50 years	**PROPOSED program** Expected levels in 50 years
St. Lawrence Belugas	**THREATENED** 1,000 Belugas	**THREATENED** 1,000 Belugas
St. Lawrence Harbour Seals (*No official status yet. Hypothetical status based on the low number of individuals.)	**THREATENED*** 1,000 Harbour Seals	**SPECIAL CONCERN*** At least 2,500 harbour seals
Atlantic Blue Whales	ENDANGERED 250 Blue Whales	ENDANGERED 250 Blue Whales
MPA size	**NO MPA**	**SMALL MPA**
Regulations on Shipping and WHALE WATCHING	**CURRENT REGULATIONS**	**Additional** minor restrictions focused on **harbour seals** that <u>might:</u> • Reduce jobs • Reduce tourism revenues • Increase the cost of goods <u>shipped in the St. Lawrence seaway</u>
ADDITIONAL annual <u>cost</u> to <u>your household</u> in: • Federal Income Taxes • Increased Prices for Goods	$0	**Each respondent randomly received one of the following prices:** **$5, $15, $50, $100, $350**

Source: *Boxall, P. et al., "Analysis of the Economic Benefits Associated with the Recovery of Threatened Marine Mammal Species in the Canadian St. Lawrence Estuary," Marine Policy 36 (2012): 189-197, Table 2, p. 192.*

Because Quebecers are likely to be more familiar with the issue given the location of the St. Lawrence Estuary, 767 respondents were drawn from Quebec and 1,606 from the rest of Canada. The authors used statistical methods to estimate the willingness to pay and found the highest valued program was the one offering the most potential recovery of the three species, the least protective garnered the lowest values. Respondents' marginal WTP also declined, which means that people were willing to pay a lot for an initial level of recovery of the three species (e.g., from endangered to threatened), but less incrementally for getting them all the way to "not at risk." This suggests willingness to pay follows a pattern similar to other goods whether market or not. The WTP values ranged from $77.37 per household per year for program A to $$229.17 for program F. Extrapolating to all households in Canada, the estimates range from $962 million per year to $2.8 billion. Canadians are indeed WTP considerable amounts to increase the likelihood that iconic marine mammals will be less at risk. The study illustrates the usefulness of contingent valuation methods in a benefit–cost analysis of programs that help species at risk recover. Canadian legislation requires the development of such programs.

Critique of Contingent Valuation Methods

The major strength of CVM is flexibility. CVM can be designed for just about any situation and is thus applicable to a wide range of environmental amenities, not just those that can somehow be measured in conjunction with some marketable good. Virtually anything that can be made comprehensible to respondents can be studied with this technique. It is used worldwide to value environmental benefits.

The major weaknesses of CVM are outlined in the bullet list below.

- *Hypothetical character.* When people buy a marketed good, they actually have to hand over the cash to the seller or they won't get the good. It's a real situation, and if the wrong choices are made people suffer real consequences. But in a CVM questionnaire the same real-world implications are not present. People face a hypothetical situation to which they may give hypothetical responses not governed by the discipline of a real marketplace. In thinking about this, two questions arise. First, will people know enough about their real preferences to be able to give valid responses? Second, even if they know their preferences, will they have incentives to misrepresent them to the investigator?

  Everyone develops experience buying some things, but not others, on the market. In 17th-century New England, people were used to buying and selling pews in the church. In some countries, getting a building or parking permit from public officials requires monetary bribes. In contemporary society there are going prices for cantaloupes and cars. When people face market prices for a good or service over a period of time, they have time to learn about their values, adjust their purchases, and settle on a willingness to pay that accurately represents their preferences. But when asked to place a monetary value on something that does not normally carry a price, it may be much more difficult to state one's true willingness to pay. What would you be willing to pay for 10 more beautiful sunsets per year? If you are not used to paying for environmental goods—and we are not—you may have no idea what sort of price you'd put on that good.

- *Incentives to misstate true willingness to pay.* Environmental quality characteristics are public goods, as we saw in Chapter 4. People can be expected to understate their preferences for these kinds of goods when they expect that their answers will be used to establish payment schedules for the goods. But in CVM studies, there is no threat that responses could be used, for example, to set taxes to pay for the item being evaluated. So, perhaps, this source of bias is unlikely. The opposite bias may be more likely: people may be led to give an inflated estimate of their willingness to pay—hoping, perhaps, that others will do the same thing, realizing that their share of the cost of making the item available will, in any case, be very small.

- *Practical problems.* These involve possible biases the analyst can introduce into the survey (e.g., choice of payment vehicle, range of WTP options, setting the scenario, etc.), small sample sizes, self-selection problems in surveying (only those who really "care" about the environment will answer), and more. Economists are now using other techniques to help validate CVM studies. For example, they examine situations where people reveal their preferences through behaviour (e.g., purchasing fishing licences). This is called a *stated preference approach.*

While there are many critics of CVM, it continues to be a widely used and adaptable tool for benefit estimation.

CVM QUESTIONNAIRE
Setting the Scenario

The Greater Vancouver Region has a serious air-pollution problem. Every year, there are at least 15 days on which air-quality standards fall below the national guidelines set for smog. For at least 50 days per year smog is present, although within the national guidelines. Smog contributes to breathing difficulties in susceptible people, is especially injurious to young children and the elderly, contributes to lower crop yields in the Fraser Valley, and damages materials, especially plastic and rubber

(Continued)

products. Scientists do not know the minimum amount of smog that is safe for all people. TransLink (the transportation authority for the Greater Vancouver Region) is considering a number of policies to help reduce the number of smog days. We would appreciate your assistance in answering a few questions about two of the policies.

Policy 1: Vehicle Levy Based on Vehicle Weight

The proposal is to levy an annual tax based on the weight of the vehicle. Vehicle weight is a proxy for tonnes of air pollutants discharged into the atmosphere. On average, heavier vehicles produce more pollution than lighter vehicles. The tax will be per 100 kilograms of vehicle weight. The objectives of this policy are to induce people to purchase lighter and more fuel-efficient cars and to make those who contribute the most to air pollution pay their fair share.

Policy 2: Tolls on All Bridges in the Greater Vancouver Region

The proposal is to introduce electronic tolling of all bridges. The toll will be paid only on the inbound trip to Vancouver. Most commuter traffic to the city must go over a bridge. The toll will induce people to carpool, take public transit, and change their residence to be closer to their jobs.

Questions for the Respondent

1. Vehicle tax

Which amount would you be willing to pay each year for each 100 kg of vehicle weight (put an X beside the number you feel best represents your preferences).

$ 0	_____
$ 5	_____
$10	_____
$20	_____
$30	_____
$50	_____
Over $50	_____

2. Bridge tolls

Would you be willing to pay $_____* in a bridge toll per trip to cross any bridge in Greater Vancouver?

  Yes   No(circle one)

* The analyst will pick a number of different values to be inserted into the blank. Respondents will get different numbers. These values will cover what the analyst thinks is a reasonable range of options.

LO 5

CONCLUDING COMMENTS ON METHODS OF VALUING ENVIRONMENTAL BENEFITS

Willingness to Pay vs. Willingness to Accept

We have used throughout the text the notion of willingness to pay as a measure of the net benefits of improving environmental quality, and hence measuring the change in total damages (the area under the MD curve). Willingness to pay, besides reflecting a person's tastes and preferences, also reflects one's income level. Another way of approaching the problem of valuing environmental improvements is to ask people how much they would be willing to accept to give up some environmental amenity. To value better air quality we could ask either how much people would be willing to pay for a small improvement or how much they would have to receive to compensate them for a small reduction in air quality. Suppose public authorities are contemplating locating a hazardous waste incinerator in a particular community. As a measure of the potential damages suffered by the community, we could take the amount of money required to get the community willingly to accept the incinerator (rather than, in other words, the amount they would be willing to pay to keep it out).

Clearly, **willingness to accept (WTA)** is not constrained by one's income, as is willingness to pay. So it may be no surprise that when people are asked willingness-to-accept questions, their answers are usually higher than their willingness-to-pay responses for the same item. To some extent it may depend on what they are asked. For a small change we would expect the two measures to be close. Consider a single cantaloupe. If a person is willing to pay $1.49 for one more cantaloupe, that amount is also probably close to what it would take to compensate for his or her loss of a single cantaloupe. But even in cases involving small changes, researchers have found that willingness to accept exceeds willingness to pay. In surveys and experimental work, people are found to compare gains and losses relative to a reference point. They value losses from this reference point much more than gains. The minimum compensation demanded is typically several times larger than the maximum amount they are willing to pay.[24] Canadian students participated in a number of experiments measuring willingness to pay versus compensation demanded. The commodities exchanged were chocolate bars and coffee mugs. These are not goods for which we would expect people to have strong divergences between willingness to pay and willingness to accept, but they do!

For large changes (what are called "non-marginal" changes) the divergences may be even more substantial. If we are talking, for example, of large changes in air pollution in a neighbourhood or the loss of a natural area, one's welfare will change substantially and the two measures will be quite different.

Economists have taken several approaches to resolving this problem. One is to look closely at the questionnaire and the way questions are asked of respondents. Experience has shown that responses will differ according to how questions are phrased, so one possibility is that the differences between willingness to pay and willingness to accept are traceable primarily to the way questions are being framed. The other approach is to use the approach that best fits the real-world problem in question. If

---

[24.] See the work done by Jack Knetsch and others; for example, "Environmental Policy Implications of Disparities between Willingness to Pay and Compensation Demanded Measures of Values," *Journal of Environmental Economics and Management* 18 (1990): 227–237, and the references in that article.

environmental quality is being degraded, willingness to accept is likely a better measure. If people a being asked to indicate how much investment in improving environmental quality they wish, the willingness to pay can be used. In general, it is good practice to estimate both measures to provide a range of estimates.

Summary

Benefit measurement is a major focus of study within environmental economics. New techniques are being developed to uncover values that previously were hidden from view. These values are useful not only in benefit–cost analysis; they also find their way into damage awards in court cases and legal settlements. Public environmental agencies have devoted considerable time and effort to generating benefits estimates to justify their policy rulings. We list and describe in detail the main techniques environmental economists use to measure the benefits of improving environmental quality/reducing the damages from pollution. We covered direct damage techniques for health impacts, production losses, and materials damages and found they are often not a good representation of WTP. The indirect techniques that are based on people's willingness to pay for environmental quality include defensive expenditures, hedonic techniques, the surrogate market approach of travel-cost studies, and, finally, contingent valuation methods. These too have difficulties, because many are proxies for underlying WTP (or willingness to accept) or have to present hypothetical scenarios to elicit WTP. Examples of each technique illustrate how it can be used in benefit–cost analysis. Critiques of the techniques indicate that no method is "perfect," but many environmental economists feel strongly that efforts to measure benefits are worthwhile. If these are not done, only the cost side of benefit–cost analysis remains, making it very difficult to assess the tradeoffs among projects or policies that generate quite different benefits.

Key Terms

Capitalized	Preventive or mitigating expenditures
Consumer surplus	Producer surplus
Contingent valuation method	Productivity-study approach
Dose–response function	Surrogate markets
Hedonic estimation	Travel-cost approach
Morbidity	Use value
Mortality	Willingness to accept (WTA)
Non-use value	

Analytical Problems

1. Compute the change in consumer surplus using Figure 7-2 if the demand curve shifts to $P = 10 - Q$.

2. The federal government introduces new pollution regulations that reduce the pollution threatening lobster stocks on the East Coast. Let $MC = 5Q$ represent the costs of harvest for a lobster harvester before the policy. The regulation reduces harvesting costs by 50 percent. What are the net benefits to the lobster harvester from the regulation? How would you show this on an MD curve?

3. Suppose the people of Winnipeg buy no air purifiers. Can data on defensive expenditure in Hamilton still provide information about a Hamiltonian's WTP for cleaner air? Explain and illustrate graphically.

4. Suppose the researchers estimated demand curves from the CVM questionnaire illustrated in the chapter. Show graphically and explain how these demand curves would measure WTP for improving air quality for each of the scenarios.

Discussion Questions

1. Why don't total expenditures on a good represent the net benefits from purchasing that good? Why are increases in output due to lower levels of pollution likely to be an overestimate of benefits?

2. List and give examples of three problems with using defensive expenditures as a proxy for willingness to pay. How would you address each of these problems in a benefit–cost study?

3. How would you use wage-rate differences among cities to measure the value of reducing health risks from pollution?

4. Would the travel-cost approach be a good technique to use in valuing a policy to increase wildlife corridors in the national parks in Canada's Rocky Mountains? Defend your answer.

5. Critique the contingent valuation example in the chapter. What sort of biases might the analyst have introduced? Is the scenario too hypothetical? Would respondents have any incentive to misrepresent their preferences?

6. Would you like to take a contingent valuation survey that hundreds of other Canadians have taken?

 For more information on the resources available from McGraw-Hill Ryerson, go to www.mheducation.ca/he/solutions.

Chapter **8**

Benefit–Cost Analysis: Costs

After reading this chapter you will be able to:

LO 1 ⟩ Explain how the concept of opportunity cost can apply to environmental regulations.

LO 2 ⟩ Define the with-without principle and how it applies to benefit–cost analysis.

LO 3 ⟩ Distinguish between the private and social costs of a project and provide an example.

LO 4 ⟩ Explain how to measure the social costs of a regulation when industry output adjusts.

LO 5 ⟩ Define what is meant by the incidence of a policy and provide an illustration graphically of how the share paid by consumers versus producers is determined.

The cost side of benefit–cost analysis is the subject of this chapter. The importance of accurate cost measurement has often been underestimated. It is a full half of the analysis, the results of which can as easily be affected by, for example, overestimating costs as by underestimating benefits. Opposition to environmental policies frequently centres on their estimated costs, which means that those doing benefit–cost analyses of these programs are well advised to get the cost estimates right. In this chapter we will first take up some general considerations about costs, then look at some specific issues and examples of cost estimation.

THE COST PERSPECTIVE: GENERAL ISSUES

Cost analysis can be done on many levels. At its simplest, it focuses on the costs to a single community or firm of an environmental program, or of a single environmental project like a wastewater treatment plant, incinerator, or beach restoration project. The reason for calling these the simplest is that they usually proceed by costing out a definite engineering specification that has clear boundaries, and for which the "rest of the world" can rightly be assumed to be constant.

At the next level we have costs to an industry, or perhaps to a region, of meeting environmental regulations or of adopting certain technologies. Here we can no longer rely on simple engineering assumptions; we must do things like predict with reasonable accuracy how groups of polluting firms will respond to changes in laws on emissions or how they will respond to changes in recycling regulations. Problems will arise because not all firms will be alike—some are small, some large, some old, some new, and so on—and each of them will usually have many possible ways to react to regulations, involving many types of costs.

At a still higher level, our concern may be with the costs to an entire economy of achieving stated environmental goals. Estimating costs at the national level calls for an entirely different approach. Here everything is connected to everything else; when pollution-control regulations are imposed, adjustments will reverberate throughout the economy. As will be examined in detail in Sections 4 and 5, the form of regulations can have a big impact on the costs of achieving the target. In the following pages we will deal with cost estimation at these different levels.

LO 1

OPPORTUNITY COSTS

In economics the most fundamental concept of costs is **opportunity cost.** The opportunity cost of using resources in a certain way is the highest-valued alternative use to which those resources might have been put and which society has to forgo when the resources are used in the specified fashion. Note the word "society." Costs are incurred by all types of firms, agencies, industries, and groups. Each has its own perspective, which will focus on those costs that impinge directly on them, but the concept of **social opportunity cost** includes all costs, no matter to whom they accrue.

The curve we are trying to estimate is of course the marginal abatement cost curve (MAC). This is the curve that policy-makers should use to design socially efficient (or cost-effective) policies. It is important to reiterate that the MAC curve reflects the social costs of reducing pollution. Each point on the curve represents the marginal cost to the polluter of reducing its emissions by one unit. The area under the curve represents the total costs of reducing pollution by whatever amount is specified and will represent forgone output, higher capital and operating costs, and costs of changing input mixes— in short, all of the real resource costs for reducing pollution. These are the social costs. While we generally think of polluters as being firms producing a good or service, remember that consumers can also be polluters. The principles are the same: real resource costs consumers incur to reduce the pollution they emit are a component of total abatement costs.

Sometimes items that a private group might consider a cost (for example, a tax) is not a cost from the standpoint of society. And, items that decision-makers do not consider costs really do have social costs. Suppose a community is contemplating building a bicycle path to relieve congestion and air pollution downtown. Its primary concern is what the town will have to pay to build the path. Suppose it will take $1-million to build it, but 50 percent of this will come from the provincial or federal government. From the town's perspective the cost of the bike path will be a half million dollars, but from the standpoint of society the full opportunity costs of the path are $1-million.

When most people think of cost they usually think of money expenditure. Often the monetary cost of something is a good measure of its opportunity costs, but frequently it is not. Suppose the bike path is going to be put on an old railroad right-of-way that has absolutely no alternative use, and suppose the town must pay the railroad $100,000 for this right-of-way. This money is definitely an expenditure the town must make, but it is not truly a part of the social opportunity costs of building the path, because society gives up nothing in devoting the old right-of-way to the new use.

Environmental Costs

It may seem paradoxical to think that environmental protection programs might have environmental costs, but this is in fact the case. Most of our specific emissions-reduction programs are media-based; that is, they are aimed at reducing emissions into one particular environmental medium like air or water. So when emissions into one medium are reduced, they may increase into another. Reducing untreated domestic waste outflow into rivers or coastal oceans leaves quantities of solid waste that must then be disposed of—perhaps through land spreading or incineration. Reducing airborne SO_2

emissions from power plants by stack-gas scrubbing also leaves a highly concentrated sludge that must be disposed of in some way. Incinerating domestic solid waste creates airborne emissions and waste heat.

Media switches are not the only source of environmental impacts stemming from environmental improvement programs. There can be direct effects; for example, sediment runoff from construction sites for new treatment plants or sewer lines. There can also be unforeseen impacts when firms or consumers adjust to new programs. Gasoline producers reduced the amounts of lead in their product, but, since consumers still insisted on high-powered performance, they added other compounds that ended up creating health and adverse environmental impacts. With the beginning of community programs to charge consumers for solid-waste disposal, some have been faced with substantial increases in "midnight dumping"; that is, illegal dumping along the sides of roads or in remote areas. These are examples of **unintended consequences** from projects or policies—impacts that need to be costed because they produce adverse environmental consequences.

Some of the potential environmental impacts from these public projects or programs can be mitigated: steps can be taken to reduce or avoid them. More enforcement resources can help control illegal dumping, extra steps can be taken to reduce construction-site impacts, special techniques may be available to reduce incinerator residuals, waste heat can be converted to electricity (and then the value of the electricity sold becomes an additional benefit), and so on. These mitigation costs must be included as part of the total costs of any project or program. Beyond this, any remaining environmental costs must be set against the overall reduction in environmental damages to which the program is primarily aimed.

No-Cost Improvements in Environmental Quality

Sometimes environmental improvements can be obtained at zero *social* cost, except the political cost of making the required changes in public laws or regulations; these are known as **no-cost improvements.** In virtually any type of political system, some laws and administrative practices are instituted primarily to benefit certain groups within society for political reasons, rather than to move toward economically efficient resource use or achieve deserving income redistributions. These regulations, besides transferring income to the favoured groups, often have negative environmental effects. Of course, changing these regulations may entail substantial private costs to the individuals affected. This may require some form of compensation for losses. Compensation for the introduction of environmental regulation or changes in other regulation is a topical and controversial issue.

Consider some examples of zero-social-cost changes. During the 1970s, the federal government introduced a two-price system for pricing oil and natural gas. The policy was designed to help Canadian energy consumers cope with the rapid increase in energy prices that occurred in the 1970s. Domestic prices for oil and natural gas were held below world prices. Energy consumers in Canada received a subsidy and no doubt were better off than they would have been had they faced the higher world prices. However, these subsidies slowed the Canadian economy's adjustment to a world with higher energy prices. Canadians continued to consume more energy per capita than in any other developed nation, and today remain among the most energy-intensive consumers in the world. Higher levels of energy consumption created more environmental problems than would have been the case had energy prices risen more quickly. These environmental effects range from significant Canadian ones such as increased air pollution and degradation of lands and water due to energy production, to global impacts created by greenhouse gas emissions. After the two-price system was abolished in the early 1980s, Canadian energy consumption per capita declined until the late 1980s. Final energy consumption per capita for residential and agricultural sectors declined by almost 6 percent from the period 1975–79 to 1980–84. The removal of the subsidy thus contributed to a reduction in adverse environmental impacts for a time after the policy changed.

There are many other examples like this. Agricultural subsidies in many developed countries have provided the incentive to develop intensive, chemical-based production methods, which has resulted both in increased agricultural output and in the nonpoint source water and air pollution to which these methods lead. Subsidies for land tillage have also led to the drainage and destruction of wetlands. Wetlands provide a large number of environmental benefits such as water purification and wildlife habitat. Subsidies to ethanol production from corn had many unintended consequences including greater land conversion to corn production with attendant environmental impacts to food shortages due to diversion of corn to fuel production. Reducing agricultural subsidies would increase national income and reduce the environmental impacts, though of course many farmers would be worse off.

Enforcement Costs

Environmental regulations are not self-enforcing. Resources must be devoted to monitoring the behaviour of firms, agencies, and individuals subject to the regulations, and to sanctioning violators. Public environmental facilities, such as wastewater treatment plants and incinerators, must be monitored to be sure they are being operated correctly.

There is an important application of the opportunity cost concept in the enforcement phenomenon. Many environmental laws are enforced by agencies whose budgets are not strictly tailored to the enforcement responsibilities they are given. Thus, budgets can be stable, or even declining, at the same time that new environmental laws are passed. Enforcing the new laws may require shifting agency resources away from the enforcement of other laws. In this case the opportunity costs of new enforcement must include the lower levels of compliance in areas that now are subject to less enforcement, diversion of government funds from other programs such as health care and education, or increases in taxes to pay for higher levels of environmental enforcement.

LO 2

The With-Without Principle

There is an important principle that has to be kept in mind in this work. In doing a benefit–cost analysis of how individuals and firms will respond to new laws, we want to use the **with-without approach** and not the **before-after approach.** We want to estimate the differences in costs that polluters would have with the new law, *compared to what their costs would have been in the absence of the law.* This is not the same as the difference between their new costs and what their costs used to be before the law. Consider the following illustrative numbers, applying to a manufacturing firm for which a pollution-control regulation has been proposed:

Estimated production costs:	
Before the regulation:	$100
In the future without the regulation:	$120
In the future with the regulation:	$150

It would be a mistake to conclude that the added costs of the pollution-control regulation will be $50 (future costs with the regulation minus costs before the law). This is an application of the before-after principle and does not accurately reflect the true costs of the law. This is so because in the absence of any new law, production costs are expected to increase (for example, because of increased fuel costs, unrelated to environmental regulations). Thus, the true cost of the regulation is found by applying the with-without principle. Here these costs are $30 (costs in the future with the regulation minus future costs without the regulation). Of course this makes the whole job of cost estimation harder because we want to know not historical costs of a firm or an industry but what its future costs would be if it were to continue operating without the new environmental laws.

LO 3

COSTS OF SINGLE FACILITIES

Perhaps the easiest type of cost analysis to visualize is that for a single, engineered project of some type. There are many types of environmental quality programs that involve publicly supported construction of physical facilities (although the analysis would be the same whatever the ownership), such as public wastewater treatment plants, of which hundreds of millions of dollars worth have been built over the last few decades. Other examples include flood-control projects, solid-waste handling facilities, hazardous-waste incinerators, beach restoration projects, public parks, wildlife refuges, and the like.

Facility-type projects such as these are individualized and substantially unique, though of course they have objectives and use technology that is similar to that used for many other projects. To estimate their costs, primary reliance is placed on engineering and technical specifications developed largely through experience with similar types of facilities.

EXAMPLE

Projected costs of a wastewater treatment plant

Consider the simple example shown in Table 8-1. It gives the estimated costs of a new wastewater treatment plant for a small community. The plant is expected to use standard technology, as specified in the engineering plans for the treatment plant, collector lines, and other essential parts of the system. It will be built by a private firm but owned and operated by the town.

There are three types of construction costs: the treatment plant proper, conveyances, and sludge-disposal works. The latter refers to disposal of the solid waste produced at the plant. The waste materials extracted from the wastewater stream don't just disappear; these heavily treated substances must be disposed of in some fashion. There are various ways of doing this (composting, land spreading, incineration). In the case of land spreading, the costs involve buying a large area of land on which the sludge will be spread and allowed to decompose and mix with the soil. The assumed life of the plant is 40 years. Some portions of the plant—for example, certain pieces of equipment—will wear out and have to be replaced during this period. The costs of this are listed under "replacement costs." Additionally, certain parts of the plant and conveyance system are expected to have a salvage value at the end of the 40 years; these are shown in the last column. Note that allowances have been made for engineering work and construction contingencies. An estimate has also been included of the initial costs of some environmental mitigation activities.

Annual costs are divided into operation and maintenance (O&M) of the treatment plant, O&M of the pumping station, sludge disposal operation, and environmental costs. The latter includes certain

(Continued)

TABLE 8-1 Projected Costs of a Small Wastewater Treatment Plant ($ millions)

	Construction Cost			
	Initial cost	**Life (years)**	**Replacement costs**	**Salvage value**
Treatment plant				
Mechanical	11.0	20	1.25	—
Structural	13.0	40	—	5.4
Engineering (15%)	3.6	—	—	—
Contingencies (10%)	2.4	—	—	—
Total	30.0	60	1.25	5.4
Conveyances				
Pumping station	2.4	15	2.4	1.6
Metering station	.4	40	—	.1
Piping	10.3	40	—	4.8
Engineering (15%)	2.0	—	—	—
Contingencies (10%)	1.3	—	—	—
Total	16.4	95	2.4	6.5
Sludge-disposal works (land spreading)				
Site work	2.5	40	—	—
Piping	2.3	40	—	1.0
Land purchase	3.5	40	—	—
Other	1.5	40	—	—
Total	9.8	—	—	1.0
Mitigation of construction-related environmental costs	.2	40	—	—

Annual Costs			
Operation and maintenance (O&M)		Environmental costs	
Pumping station	.21	Mitigation costs	.08
Treatment plant		Unmitigated environmental cost	.46
Labour	.60		
Electric power	.45		
Parts and supplies	.13		
Chemicals	.06		
Other	.07		
Sludge disposal	.04		
Total	1.56		

Present Values		
Cost item	**Total**	**Present value (@8%)**
Construction	56.45	56.6
Replacement	3.7	1.1
Salvage values	−1.3	−3.2
Annual O&M	1.6	18.6
Annual Environmental	.45	6.4
Total		79.4

Note: Values in Table 8-1 have been adjusted to reflect realistic current costs.

Source: *Adapted from Table 2-46 of US EPA Environmental Impact Statement, Wastewater Treatment Facilities at Geneva Lake Area, Walworth County, Wisconsin, Washington, D.C., June 1984.*

(Continued)

mitigation costs together with some remaining, or unmitigated, environmental costs. The latter might refer, for example, to odour problems at the plant and on the sludge disposal lands. These are, in fact, environmental damages, which might be estimated, for example, with contingent valuation techniques.

The last section of Table 8-1 includes the present values of the costs, evaluated with a discount rate of 8 percent. Replacement costs are discounted to the present from the year in which they are expected to be required. Salvage values are discounted back from the end of the project's life, in this case 40 years. These appear with negative signs because they act to lower the total cost of the project. The present value of annual environmental costs is also included.

With the exception of unmitigated environmental costs, these items are all expenditure figures, and only close inspection can tell if they represent true social opportunity costs. Suppose, for example, that in the construction phase a number of local unemployed people are hired. Although the construction costs include their wages, their opportunity costs might be negligible because society had to give up nothing (but the value of their leisure time) when they went to work on the plant. It might be that the land on which the plant is to be placed is town land that is to be donated. In this case there will be no specific cost entry for land, but there will be an opportunity cost related to the value the land could have had in its next best use. Suppose that the construction firm, because it is working on a public project, is able to get subsidized loans from local banks (i.e., borrow money at lower than market rates). Then the true opportunity costs of construction will be higher than the monetary costs indicated. There are no specific rules for making these adjustments; only knowledge of the specific situations can reveal when it is important enough to make them and where sufficient data are available to do the job. The key is to focus on measuring social costs after all adjustments have occurred in response to the policy or program, not private costs.

COSTS OF A LOCAL REGULATION

Environmental regulations are frequently enacted at the local level and affect local firms. In fact, in the political economy of pollution control, it is often the fear of these local impacts that deters communities from enacting the regulations. Fears of lost payrolls and the secondary losses to other firms less spending on local goods and services loom large at the local level; from a national perspective the opportunity costs are less severe.

EXAMPLE
Integrated pest management for an orchard

Suppose in a particular small town there is a large apple orchard that provides substantial local employment. Suppose further that the orchard managers currently use relatively large applications of chemicals to control apple pests and diseases, and that the chemical runoff from this activity threatens local water supplies. Assume that the community enacts an ordinance requiring the orchard to practise integrated pest management (IPM), a lower level of chemical use coupled with other means to compensate for this reduction. Assume further, for purposes of illustration, that the IPM practices increase the costs of raising apples in this orchard.[1] What are the costs of this regulation?

If the orchard raises and sells the same number of apples it previously did, the true social opportunity costs of the regulation are the increased production costs. If local consumers are willing to pay somewhat higher prices for locally grown apples, some of this cost gets passed on to these consumers.

(Continued)

---

[1] Various authorities and scientific studies suggest that some IPM practices can actually lower costs relative to chemical-intensive growing techniques.

(Question: Is the loss of consumer surplus a social cost of the project?) But suppose competitive conditions make it impossible for the orchard to sell its apples for any higher price than obtained before. In this case the higher production costs must be reflected in lower incomes of either the apple orchard owners themselves, or perhaps orchard workers if they will accept lower wages.

But suppose the orchard was just breaking even in that its economic profits were zero before the local IPM ordinance, and that the statute leads to such cost increases that production is substantially curtailed; in fact, assume for purposes of argument that the orchard goes out of business. It is socially efficient for them to do so because their social marginal costs (private marginal costs of production plus marginal damages from chemical use) exceed the marginal value of their output (given a constant price). Clearly there will be local costs: lost payrolls of orchard workers, lost income to the local orchard owners, lost income to local merchants because their markets shrink. But these lost incomes are not likely to be social opportunity costs in their entirety, unless the workers become permanently unemployed. Assuming they transfer to other job opportunities (this requires obviously that the economy is able to provide alternative employment), their new incomes will offset, at least partly, the lost incomes they had been earning previously. There may be certain valid opportunity costs in the form of adjustment costs, as workers and owners have to move to new places of employment.

What about the value of the apples no longer produced in this orchard? If we assume that there are many other orchards in neighbouring towns and other regions to take up the slack with essentially no cost increases, then this lost production is offset by their production. Consumer prices are stable, and the social opportunity costs of this marginal rearrangement of apple production are basically nil. Of course, if the orchards in the other regions are still using pollution-intensive techniques, the social costs of environmental degradation remain.

To summarize, when we are dealing with a single local ordinance affecting one firm and the economy is at or near full employment, ensuing resource adjustments ensure that social opportunity costs are small, limited to the costs of actually carrying out the adjustments. From the standpoint of the affected community, of course, costs will seem high, because of lost local incomes brought about by the increased apple production costs.[2]

COSTS OF REGULATING AN INDUSTRY

The conclusions in the previous example do not follow when we impose an environmental regulation on an entire industry. Higher production costs for the industry are true social opportunity costs, because they require added resources that could have been used elsewhere. But when we deal with whole industries, we can't make the assumption, like we did with the single apple orchard, that its production could easily be picked up by the others.

Consider first the standard approach to estimating increased industry production costs, which is to measure the added expenditures that an industry would have to make to come into compliance with an environmental regulation. Cost estimation in this case requires the analyst to predict how polluters will respond to environmental regulations, and then to estimate the costs of this response. If the regulation

---

[2.] It is often difficult for non-economists (and politicians) to grasp the notion that it can be in society's interest for firms to go out of business. If they are unprofitable because an environmental regulation now requires them to incur pollution-control costs that they were getting for free (at society's expense), society will be better off to have the polluter exit the industry.

is very specific, requiring for example that manufacturing firms install a certain piece of pollution-control equipment or that farmers adopt certain cultivation practices to avoid soil runoff, the cost estimation may be fairly straightforward. But if the regulation leaves the polluters considerable latitude in making their response, it may be hard to predict exactly what they will do and, therefore, what their costs will be.

Suppose, for example, a group of pulp mills are required to reduce their emissions by some percentage, and that a public agency wishes to estimate the impact of this on the production costs of the firms in the industry. In effect, the agency wants to estimate the aggregate marginal abatement cost function for this group of firms. To do this with reasonable accuracy, the agency has to know enough about the pulp business to be able to predict how the firms will respond, what treatment techniques they will use, how they might change their internal production processes, and so on. Or suppose we wanted to estimate the costs among farmers of a ban on a certain type of pest-control chemical. We would need to know what alternatives farmers had available to replace this chemical, what impacts this would have on yields, how much additional labour and other inputs they would use, and so on. We don't often have all this information in the detail we would like. The example below illustrates the kinds of data that are available.

EXAMPLE

Canadian pulp and paper regulation

The Canadian pulp and paper industry has undergone major changes because of environmental regulation. An important industry to many regions of the country, more stringent regulation has been imposed at the federal and provincial levels. As well, the industry has felt the impact of recycling legislation in the United States (and proposed for Canada) that requires particular percentages of recycled fibre in newsprint and other paper products.

Regulations require pulp and paper companies to modify their capital stock and operating procedures, incurring expenditures that could be quite large. Statistics Canada has examined the cost to the industry of complying with the 1992 federal regulations.[3] The study looks at how the age of the mill affects potential expenditures; whether compliance costs vary with type of treatment facility, by region, capacity, profitability, and other characteristics of firms in the industry. As is true of most studies of regulatory impacts, there were too many firms in the industry to do a technical study of each one. A common way of addressing this problem is to estimate costs for the "average" or "representative" or "model" plant, one that corresponds to typical operating conditions in the industry but not to any particular plant. But in this case, as in most cases, the size and technical heterogeneity of plants in the industry made it necessary to specify a number of representative plants, each of which corresponded to one portion of the firms in the industry. Abatement costs are shown in Table 8-2 for six different plant sizes, where "size" is given by the capacity in tonnes of output per day from the plants in each group. The first row shows the number of plants in each size class. Note that the majority of plants are in the 300 to 620 tonnes per day category, with the second highest number in the largest category (more than 1,000 tonnes per day).

The first section in the table shows investment costs needed to install the new equipment that will allow the firms to reduce their emissions flows. These are the "upfront" investment costs of new

(Continued)

3. See Craig Gaston, "Pulp and Paper Industry Compliance Costs" in Statistics Canada, National Accounts and Environment Division, *Environmental Perspectives 1993, Studies and Statistics*, Catalogue No. 11-528E, March 1993.

TABLE 8-2   Estimated Costs of Compliance with 1992 Federal Pulp and Paper Regulations (2010 dollars)

	Capacity of Plants (tonnes per day)					
	Under 200	200–300	300–600	600–800	800–1,000	Over 1,000
Number of plants in size class	4	8	34	9	14	17
Average BOD (kg per tonne)	13.8	21.1	32.3	43.4	33.9	24
Average investment costs ($ millions)	8.6	11	29.2	54.2	39.9	53.2
Annual costs ($ millions)						
Capital costs*	0.4	0.6	1.5	2.8	1.9	2.6
Depreciation†	0.8	1.1	2.9	5.4	4.2	5.3
Operating costs	1.1	1.4	2.6	4.3	3.2	4.9
Total	2.3	3.1	7	12.5	9.3	12.8

Notes:

*10% of average investment costs. Annual Investment each year of the project is equal to original investment minus depreciation. Average investment is the mean of these annual investments. Since depreciation is 10-year straight-line, average investment is actually equal to one-half the original investment.

†Straight-line depreciation—10-year life.

Source: *Adapted from Statistics Canada, Environmental Perspectives: Studies and Statistics, 11-528-XPE1993001, 1993, no. 1. Released March 25, 1993.*

buildings, equipment, and the land to put them on. The second part of the table shows annualized costs. These are operating costs that include conventional items like energy, labour, and materials, and also the annualized investment costs. In the waste treatment plant example above, we aggregated discounted annual operating costs and added these to initial investment costs to get the present value of total costs. The other way of adding initial investment costs and annual operating costs is to "annualize" the investment costs; that is, spread them out over the years of life that the investments are assumed to have. This is done in Table 8-2. Annualized investment costs consist of two parts: the *opportunity costs of the capital,* and *depreciation.* The former is the forgone return that one could earn if the investment were made in some other industry. Depreciation is the cost associated with the progressive using up of the equipment and buildings over their useful life.

Total annual costs are shown in Table 8-3 for each of the representative plants. If we wanted to have an estimate of the total costs of meeting the emission standard for the entire industry, we could calculate a weighted total.

Thus, the anticipated total annual cost of the pulp and paper industry to meet the emission-reduction standards is $740.1-million (in 2010 dollars). We reiterate that these costs do not capture all the social opportunity costs of the regulation that should be included in the MAC curve estimation. The example illustrates the type of cost data that are typically available. For example, the data have no estimate of the public enforcement resources that are required if we expect to get large-scale compliance by the regulated firms. Table 8-2 contains nothing about these costs (and other non-measured social costs), but in a full social benefit–cost analysis, they would obviously have to be included. Unfortunately, no follow up study has been done to see how costs have changed over time.

(Continued)

TABLE 8-3   Total Annual Costs of Compliance

Size of Firm (Tonnes/day capacity)	Annual Costs ($ millions)	Number of Firms	Total Costs ($ millions)
Under 200	2.4	4	9.6
200–300	3.6	8	28.8
300–600	7.1	34	241.4
600–800	12.5	9	112.5
800–1,000	9.3	14	130.2
More than 1,000	12.8	17	217.6
Total costs			740.1

Source: *Statistics Canada, Environmental Protection Expenditures in the Business Sector, 2006, Catalogue No. 16F0006X, available on the Statistics Canada website: www.statcan.gc.ca.*

Statistics Canada reports that for paper manufacturing in 2006, total pollution abatement and control expenditures were $21.3-million and $9.5-million was spent on waste management and sewerage services.[4]

Sources of Cost Data

Where does one get the cost data necessary to construct representative firms as shown in the example? Data can be generated through cost surveys of existing firms. In effect, questionnaires are sent out to these firms, asking them to supply information on number of employees, processes used, costs of energy and materials, and so on. With a sufficiently detailed questionnaire and a reasonably high response rate by firms, researchers can get a good idea of basic cost conditions in the industry and how they might be affected by environmental regulations.

One problem with cost surveys is that they are usually better at getting information on past cost data than on future costs under new regulations. Firms can probably report past cost data with more reliability than they can estimate future costs of meeting environmental constraints. Historical data may not be a good guide to the future, especially since environmental regulations almost by definition confront firms with novel situations. In these cases it is common to supplement survey data with technical engineering data that can be better adapted to costing out the new techniques and procedures that firms may adopt.

The "representative firm" approach, while dictated by the large number of firms in an industry, has its own problems, especially when those firms are substantially heterogeneous among themselves. In following this procedure all researchers run into the problem of whether costs of the real plants in the industry, each of which is to some degree unique, can be accurately represented by a composite cost estimate. Government agencies have to be particularly careful if regulations will be based on these

---

[4.] Statistics Canada, *Environmental Protection Expenditures in the Business Sector, 2006*, Catalogue No. 16F0006X, available on the Statistics Canada website: www.statcan.gc.ca.

estimates. They do not want to incur legal and/or political problems that could arise if individual firms argue that their own unique cost situations are misrepresented by the figures for the "representative" firm. This has been a problem in the United States.[5]

Misrepresentation of Costs

Surveys are also problematic because they rely on accurate responses. If firms know that the results of the survey are to be used in developing an environmental control program, there is clearly a question whether these firms will supply accurate data. By overstating the costs of reaching certain reductions in emissions, firms may hope to convince agencies to adopt weaker regulations than they would if the agencies had an accurate idea of costs. Or they may substantially understate their current emissions, which would lead administrators to think that they are higher up on their MAC curve, facing higher marginal abatement costs than they really do. An overestimate of the costs of achieving particular emission standards (given an upward-sloping marginal abatement cost curve) may lead regulators to impose less stringent regulations. The issue of misrepresentation will come up numerous times when we examine the incentives surrounding different types of environmental policies.

Actual vs. Minimum Pollution-Control Costs

The costs shown in Table 8-2 show the estimated costs of the pulp and paper industry meeting the federal environmental standards imposed by law. There is an important question of whether these costs are the *least costs* necessary to achieve the emission reductions sought in the law. This is an important point because, as we saw in Chapter 5, the efficient level of emissions or ambient quality is defined by the trade-off of emission abatement costs and environmental damages. If abatement costs used to define the efficient level are higher than they need to be, the point so defined will not be the "true" efficient outcome.

When there is a single facility involved, we must rely on engineering judgment to ensure that the technical proposal represents the least costly way of achieving the objectives. When what is involved is an entire industry, both technical and economic factors come into play. We saw earlier that in order for the overall costs of a given emission reduction to be achieved at minimum cost, the equimarginal principle has to be fulfilled. Environmental regulations can work against this by dictating that different sources adopt essentially the same levels of emission reductions or install the same general types of pollution-control technology. As we will see in later chapters, many environmental laws are based on administratively specified operating decisions that firms are required to make. These decisions may not lead, or allow, firms to achieve emission abatement at least cost.

There is no easy way out of this dilemma. If one is called on to do a benefit–cost analysis of a particular environmental regulation, one presumably is committed to evaluating the regulation as given. But in cases like this it would no doubt be good policy for the analyst to point out that there may be less costly ways of achieving the benefits.

[5.] Unfortunately there are very few estimates of actual MAC curves for a particular pollutant and its sources. The problem, as the pulp and paper example illustrates, is the lack of data on all the social costs incurred by the polluters and affected parties. Companies are very reluctant to give their confidential data to environmental economists for a number of reasons, not the least of which is that this information may become public and put the company at a competitive disadvantage. As with benefit estimation, this means that economists must often impute costs, rather than measure them directly. Examples are given of MAC estimates for controlling greenhouse gases in Chapter 20.

LO 4

The Effect of Output Adjustments on Costs

The increase in abatement expenditures may not be an accurate measure of opportunity costs when an entire industry is involved. This is because market adjustments are likely to alter the role and performance of the industry in the wider economy. For example, when the costs of a competitive industry increase, the price of its output increases, normally causing a reduction in quantity demanded. This is pictured in Figure 8-1, which shows supply and demand curves for two industries. For convenience the supply curves have been drawn horizontally, representing constant marginal production—costs that do not vary with output. Remember that what we want to measure is the social costs of the policy.

EXAMPLE
Computing the social costs of an environmental policy in two industries

Consider the first panel (a) in Figure 8-1. The initial supply function is assumed to be the same in both industries with marginal costs, $C_1 = 30$. Industry A faces an inverse demand curve given by: $P = 90 - 1.5Q^A$. The initial quantity produced is $Q_1 = 40$.[6] The pollution-control law causes production costs to rise, represented by a shift upward in supply from curve C_1 to C_2, where $C_2 = 45$. Suppose we calculate the increased cost of producing the initial rate of output. This would be an amount equal to the area $(a + b + c) = \$600$ for industry A. In panel (b), the industry's inverse demand curve is $P = 60 - .5Q^B$. When faced with the same regulation, its comparable cost increase is $(d + e + f) = \$900$. But this approach to measuring costs focuses on private costs and will overstate the social costs, because when costs and prices go up, quantity demanded and output will decline. What we want to measure is the changes in producer plus consumer surplus after the change in output.

How much output declines is a matter of the steepness of the demand curve. In panel (a), output declines only from 40 to 30 units. But in panel (b), with the flatter demand curve, output will decline from 60 to 30 units, a much larger amount.

The correct measure of the cost to society is $(a + b) = \$525$ in panel (a) and $(d + e) = \$675$ in panel (b). Why is this? These areas represent the change in producer plus consumer surplus. In this example there is no producer surplus because the marginal cost curves are horizontal. Producers are no worse off after the policy because prices rise to cover their marginal costs of production. The lost output $(Q_2 - Q_1)$ is not a social cost because the resources freed up in these industries will go to work elsewhere in the economy to produce goods and services. Areas $(a + b)$ and $(d + e)$ are the loss in consumer surplus due to the policy. Consumer surplus falls because the price of the good rises. This makes consumers worse off and is a social cost[7].

---

[6]. The equilibrium can be found graphically or algebraically by setting supply (C_1) = demand. $50 = 90 - 1.5Q$, so $Q = 40$. When the cost curve shifts, we find the new equilibrium in the same fashion, setting C_2 = demand.

[7]. But recall that this is only half of the picture. These figures measure only the costs of the policy, not the benefits in the form of higher environmental quality. We'd have to use one of the techniques discussed in Chapter 7 to measure these environmental benefits to get the net benefits for consumers.

Figure 8-1   Computing Social Costs in Industries Subject to Pollution Control Regulation

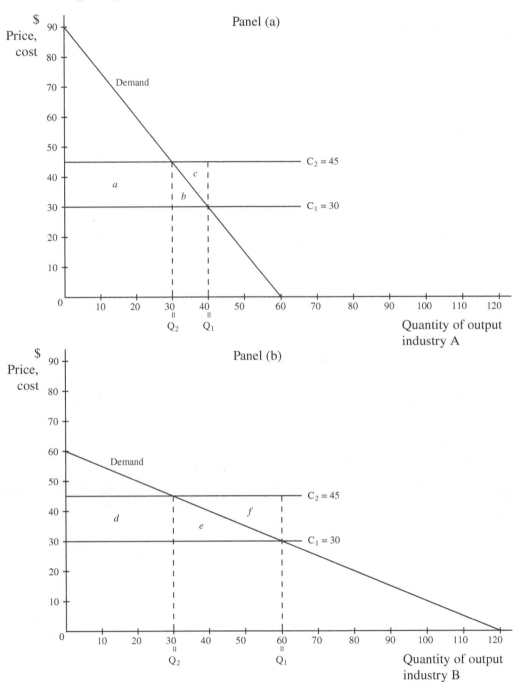

The adjustment of two industries to the introduction of an environmental regulation that raises each industry's costs from C_1 to C_2 is shown. If output did not adjust in response to the regulation, increased costs are shown by areas $(a + b + c)$ in the panel (a) and $(d + e + f)$ in panel (b). But, output falls because demand must equal the new supply curve, C_2. Output falls more in industry B because its demand curve is flatter than that of industry A. Costs to society are $(a + b)$ in panel (a) and $(d + e)$ in panel (b). These represent the loss in consumer surplus due to the policy.

LO 5

The Incidence of Cost Changes

The example above illustrates that social costs of an environmental policy may be borne by someone other than polluter. The term **incidence** means who actually ends up paying the costs. Firms in the affected industries bear these costs in the beginning, but the final burden depends on how the cost increase is passed forward to consumers or backward to workers and shareholders. This, in turn, depends on demand and supply curves. Note that in both panels (a) and (b) the market prices of the goods increased by the amount of the cost increase. But the response is quite different. In panel (a) consumers continue buying close to what they did before; little adjustment is called for in terms of output shrinkage in the industry. Thus, workers and shareholders in this industry will be less affected, in relative terms.

In panel (b) the same price increase leads to a large drop in output, from 60 to 30 units. The demand curve indicates that consumers have good substitutes to which they can switch when the price of this output goes up; in effect, they can escape the full burden of the price increase. On the other hand, the industry adjustment is large. Resources, particularly workers, will have to flow out of the industry and try to find employment elsewhere. If they can, the costs may be only temporary adjustment costs; if not, the costs will be much longer run.

Figure 8-2 illustrates how to derive the incidence of a policy in the general case where supply and demand are neither perfectly elastic nor inelastic. Suppose the policy introduces a tax on producers at level, t. The producers' marginal cost curve, MC shifts up to MC′ where MC′ = MC + t. Output falls from Q to Q' and price rises from P to P'. What is the incidence of the tax? The rise in the price to consumers is from P to P', but the level of the tax is the distance $P''P'$. Hence consumers only see part of the tax in the form of higher prices. Producers receive the new market price, P', for their goods, but

Figure 8-2   Computing the Incidence of a Tax

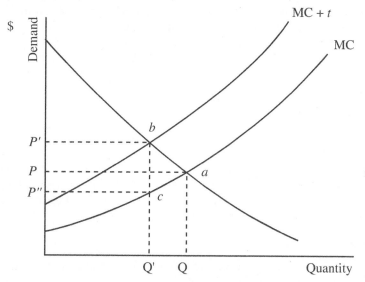

The incidence of a tax equal distance bc per unit, shifts the MC curve to MC + t. Output falls from Q to Q', and price rises from P to P'. The incidence falls on both producers and consumers, with producer surplus loss equal to area $aPP''c$ shown in Figure 8-2 and consumer surplus loss equal to area $abP'P$.

still have to pay the full amount of the tax, so their net price is P'' per unit sold. Consumer surplus loss is thus the area $abP'P$ and producer surplus loss is area $aPP''c$ shown in Figure 8-2. The size of these areas will depend on the elasticities of the supply and demand curves.

Long-Run Adjustments

In the foregoing example, cost estimation required that we predict the effect of emission-control regulations on a group of existing firms, most of which were expected to continue operating in the future. But environmental regulations could have long-run effects on the very structure of an industry; that is, on the number and size of firms. In this case, long-run prediction requires that we be able to predict these "structural" changes with some accuracy. Some examples help illustrate the potential effects of regulation on industry structure. These examples suggest that industries will not remain static in their structure as a result of environmental regulation. The very nature of the industry may also change. Regulation may eliminate the production of certain products and stimulate others. We see that to analyze the impact of environmental policy we will want to study the economics of the industry, or potential industry, that will develop in response to the regulations.

EXAMPLE 1
Effects of pollution regulation on industrial structure

One study looks at the effect of pollution intensity on industrial structure.[8] Pollution intensity of an industry is measured by the ratio of pollution abatement and control expenditures to value added in the industry. The variables examined were changes in the number of plants, the average size of the plant, and other measures of industrial structure. The sample consisted of industries that were pollution-intensive compared to industries with less pollution per unit output. The study found that pollution-intensive industries grew faster over the period 1958 to 1972 than did industries with lower pollution expenditures. However, the pollution-intensive industries had a decrease in the number of plants operating. This means that average output per plant must have risen; that is, plant size had risen. These are the types of changes one might expect with regulation. Another study looked at just one industry—pulp and paper mills in the United States—to see if pollution abatement requirements increased the minimum efficient scale in the industry.[9] If an industry has a large minimum efficient scale of operation, it may make it difficult for new plants to enter. The industry will thus be less competitive than one with a lower minimum efficient scale. While there were some statistical difficulties with the study, it was found that the minimum efficient scale did increase as the stringency of the pollution regulation rose.

EXAMPLE 2
Technological change and environmental regulation

When firms are subject to emission reduction requirements, they have an incentive to engage in research and development (R&D) to find better emissions abatement technology. There is some evidence that this may draw resources away from output-increasing R&D efforts, thereby affecting the firm's ability to reduce costs in the long run. There is also evidence, however, that environmental

(Continued)

[8.] See B. P. Pashigian, "The Effect of Environmental Regulation on Optimal Plant Size and Factor Shares," *Journal of Law and Economics* 27 (1984): 1–28.

[9.] See R. W. Pittman, "Issues in Pollution Control: Interplant Cost Differences and Economies of Scale," *Land Economics* 57 (1981): 1–17.

regulations have led to unanticipated, marketable products or processes stemming from their research. Some studies have even shown that after investing in pollution-control R&D some firms have reduced their long-run production costs. In cases such as this the short-run cost increases arising from pollution-control regulation are not accurate estimates of the long-run opportunity costs of these regulations.

Critical to the success of any effort to innovate in pollution-control technology is the economic health of the "envirotech" industry. This is the industry consisting of firms producing goods and services that are used by other firms to reduce their emissions and environmental impacts. It also contains firms that are engaged in environmental cleanup, such as the cleanup of past hazardous waste dump sites. A strong envirotech industry is one that produces a brisk supply of new pollution control technology and practices. The growth of this industry over time will have a lot to do with how fast marginal abatement costs come down in the future.

The total supply of environmental goods and services in Canada in 2008 was $4.1-billion, of which just under $2.3-billion was for goods and the balance for environmental services. Canada also exported approximately $1-billion worth of environmental goods and services in that year, most of these to the United States.[10]

COSTS AT THE NATIONAL LEVEL

The most aggregative level for which cost studies are normally pursued is the level of the national economy. The usual question of interest is the extent of the macroeconomic cost burden of the environmental regulations a country imposes, or might be planning to impose, in a given period of time. Sometimes interest centres on the totality of the regulations put in place. Sometimes the focus is on specific regulations that will nevertheless impact broadly on a national economy, such as a program for reducing CO_2 emissions.

Considered as a single aggregate, an economy at any point in time has available to it a certain number of inputs—labour, capital, equipment, energy, materials, and so on—that it converts to marketed output. Suppose the firms in the economy are subject to a variety of environmental regulations requiring them, or inducing them, to devote a portion of the total inputs to reductions in emissions. Marketed output must go down (assuming full employment) because of the input diversion. By how much will it drop? There are two answers to this, one applicable to the short run and the other to the long run.

In the *short run,* marketed output must drop because a portion of total resources is devoted to pollution control rather than to the production of marketed output. But if we simply add up the pollution-control expenditures made by all the industries subject to environmental controls, we may not get an accurate picture of how these controls are affecting the national economy. Expenditures for plant, equipment, labour, and other inputs for reducing emissions can affect other economic sectors not directly covered by environmental regulations, and macroeconomic interactions of this type need to be accounted for to get the complete picture. An industry subject to environmental controls and trying to lower its emissions puts increasing demand on the pollution-control industry, which expands output and puts increasing demands on other sectors—for example, the construction sector, which responds by increasing output.

---

10. Statistics Canada (2010) *The Daily*, www.statcan.gc.ca/daily-quotidien/100628/dq100628b-eng.htm, June 10, 2010, accessed August 21, 2010.

Another economy-wide adjustment is through prices. Increased pollution-control expenditures lead to increased prices for some items, which leads to reductions in quantity demanded, which leads to lower outputs in these sectors and thus to lower production costs. Total employment will also be affected by pollution-control expenditures. On the one hand, diverting production to pollution control will lower employment needs in the sector producing marketed output. On the other, it will increase employment in the pollution-control industry. So the net result cannot be predicted in the absence of relatively sophisticated macroeconomic modelling.

In the *long run,* more complicated macroeconomic interactions are at work. Long-run economic change—growth or decline—is a matter of the accumulation of capital: human capital and inanimate capital. It also depends on technical change, getting larger amounts of output from a given quantity of inputs. So an important question is how environmental laws will affect the accumulation of capital and the rate of technical innovation. Diverting inputs from conventional sectors to pollution-control activities lowers the rate of capital accumulation in those conventional sectors. This can be expected to reduce the rate of growth of productivity (output per unit of input) in the production of conventional output and thus slow overall growth rates. The impacts on the rate of technical innovation in the economy are perhaps more ambiguous, as mentioned above. If attempts to innovate in pollution control reduce the efforts to do so in market production, the impact on future growth could be negative. But some people think that efforts to reduce emissions can have a positive impact on the overall rate of technical innovation, which would have a positive impact. Needless to say, the last word on the matter has not yet been spoken.

The standard way to proceed in working out these relationships is through macroeconomic modelling. Mathematical models are constructed using the various macroeconomic variables of interest, such as total output, perhaps broken down into several economic subsectors: employment, capital investment, prices, pollution-control costs, and so on. The model is then run using historical data, which show how various underlying factors have contributed to the overall rate of growth in the economy. Then the model is rerun under the assumption that the pollution-control expenditures were in fact not made. This process comes out with new results in terms of aggregate output growth, employment, and so on, which can be compared with the first run. The differences are attributed to the pollution-control expenditures. In the end though, the macro models are still measuring the same sort of social costs that are illustrated by simpler models.

Summary

In this chapter we examine some of the ways that costs are estimated in benefit–cost studies. We began with a discussion of the fundamental concept of social opportunity costs, differentiating this from the notion of cost as expenditure and from private costs. We then looked at cost estimation as it applied to different levels of economic activity. The first was a cost analysis of a single facility, as represented by the estimated costs of a wastewater treatment facility. We then considered the costs of an environmental regulation undertaken by a single community, distinguishing between costs to the community and opportunity costs to the whole society.

We then shifted focus to cost estimation for an entire industry. We put special attention on the difference between short-run and long-run costs and the problem of achieving minimum costs. We finally expanded our perspective to the national economy as a whole, where cost means the loss in value of marketed output resulting from environmental regulations.

Key Terms

Before-after approach

Incidence

No-cost improvements

Opportunity cost

Social opportunity cost

Unintended consequences

With-without approach

Analytical Problems

1. A wastewater treatment plant is built for a city, thereby improving the water quality in a nearby river. The city has two sites it is considering for the plant. The first is a site (site A) that has been owned by the city for five years. The city initially paid $100,000 for the site. The current market value of the site is $200,000. Site B is land the city would have to purchase for $150,000. Which site should they choose?

2. In the model shown in Figure 8-1, compute the loss of producer and consumer surplus from the regulation if the supply curves (marginal costs) are upward-sloping. Let MC = .5Q. Graphically illustrate the effect of the regulation and illustrate the change in consumer and producer surplus on the graph. What would happen if MC = 10 + .5Q?

3. Review again the example of the orchard and the introduction of an integrated pest management program. Illustrate the various scenarios described using a graphical model; that is, show what happens to producer and consumer surplus, prices, costs, and so on (in qualitative terms). Is it in society's interest to have the orchard shut down completely?

Discussion Questions

1. In the local apple orchard problem, suppose the cessation of production by the orchard led to much more land being put on the local market, producing a drop in local land prices. Is this reduction in the value of land in the community a part of the social opportunity cost of the IPM regulation? Support your answer with a graphical analysis.

2. An economic analyst for an environmental agency has to take two hours off work to attend a public hearing on the siting of a new toxic waste dump. The analyst is paid $20 per hour. If she is not paid for the two hours, what is the social opportunity cost of her attendance at the meeting? If she is paid for the two hours off work, what is the social opportunity cost?

3. An environmental regulation results in the closing down of many firms in an industry, leaving just two or three dominant firms. How might this affect the long-run costs of the regulation?

4. Why are changes in a polluting firm's accounting profits not likely to be a good estimate of the social opportunity costs of an environmental policy?

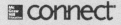

For more information on the resources available from McGraw-Hill Ryerson, go to www.mheducation.ca/he/solutions.

Environmental Policy Analysis

Public-policy problems arise when there is a discrepancy between the actual level of environmental quality and society's preferred level. How can this state of affairs be changed? Something has to be done to change the incentives people face on both the production and consumption sides of the system. The available public policy approaches for doing this are decentralized policies: liability laws, property rights, market responses–green goods, moral suasion; command-and-control policies: standards; and incentive-based policies: taxes and subsidies, transferable discharge permits. Chapters 10 through 14 examine each of these policy approaches in detail. To help identify the policy best suited to any particular environmental problem, Chapter 9 presents different criteria for evaluating policy options.

Chapter 9

Criteria for Evaluating Environmental Policies

After reading this chapter you will be able to:

LO 1 ⎞ Explain why a cost-effective policy minimizes total abatement costs.

LO 2 ⎞ Explain the criteria in addition to efficiency that can be used to assess environmental policies.

There are many different types of environmental policies. No single policy is appropriate for all the many environmental problems the world faces. In evaluating the effectiveness and appropriateness of a policy for addressing a given problem in environmental pollution control, it is important to have clearly in mind a set of policy evaluation criteria. There are many possible criteria that decision makers use to assess environmental policies. We focus on ones where economic analysis can help compare the relative merits of different policies. In addition to the list below, decision makers would also assess the public's support for a policy and other political factors. The criteria to be used in later chapters to discuss specific environmental policies are the following:

- Ability to achieve efficient and cost-effective reductions in pollution

- Fairness

- Incentives for innovation

- Enforceability

- Extent to which policies agree with certain moral precepts

LO 1 ⎞

EFFICIENCY, COST-EFFECTIVENESS, INFORMATION DEMANDS, AND FLEXIBILITY

An efficient policy is one that moves us to, or near, the point where marginal abatement costs and marginal damages are equal. To discover where this point is we must know both costs and damages. Chapter 5 showed how to derive the socially efficient equilibrium in theory, while Chapters 7 and 8 illustrated ways to estimate abatement costs and environmental damages (or damages foregone) in practice.

One way of thinking about environmental policies is along a continuum from centralized to decentralized. A centralized policy requires that some administrative agency be responsible for determining what is to be done. To achieve efficiency in a centralized policy the regulatory agency in charge would have to know the relevant marginal abatement cost and marginal damage functions, then take steps to move the situation to a point where they are equal.

A decentralized policy gets results from the interaction of many individual decision makers, each of whom is essentially making his or her own assessment of the situation. In a decentralized approach, the interactions of individuals themselves serve to reveal the relevant information about marginal abatement costs and marginal damages and to adjust the situation toward the point where they are equal.

When it is difficult or impossible to measure damages produced by environmental degradation, the socially efficient level of emissions (or environmental quality) cannot be determined with certainty. In this case, decision makers may look for the policies that achieve any chosen target at the lowest possible cost, or produce the biggest emission reduction or environmental quality gain for a given level of abatement costs. This notion of cost-effectiveness may then be the primary policy criterion. A policy is cost-effective if it produces the maximum environmental improvement possible for the resources being expended or, equivalently, it achieves a given amount of environmental improvement at the least possible cost. For a policy to be efficient it must be cost-effective, but not necessarily vice versa. A policy might be cost-effective even if it were aimed at the wrong target. Suppose we decided to clean up the St. Lawrence River, regardless of what the benefits are. We would still be interested in finding policies that did the job cost-effectively, at the lowest cost or provides the biggest gains.

The capability of a policy to achieve cost-effective emission reductions, besides yielding the maximum improvement for the resources spent, is also important for another reason. If programs are not cost-effective, the policy-makers and administrators will be making decisions using an aggregate abatement cost function that is higher than it needs to be, leading them to set less restrictive targets in terms of desired amounts of emission reductions. This is shown in Figure 9-1, for a case of SO_2 emissions. With a cost-*in*effective policy the perceived marginal abatement cost is the higher one, labelled MAC_1, whereas with a cost-effective approach marginal abatement costs would be MAC_2.[1] Suppose regulators choose a target level of SO_2 emissions of 100,000 tonnes. They will think that total abatement costs are \$4.5-million, because they perceive abatement costs to be MAC_1.[2]

If a cost-effective program were undertaken and MAC_2 achieved, total abatement costs at 100,000 tonnes would be only \$2.5-million. Alternatively, the regulator could choose a higher level of emission reduction at the same total abatement costs as under MAC_1. In either situation, society is much better off with a cost-effective policy.

To summarize, cost effectiveness

- is a key policy criterion when regulators cannot measure the MD curve;

- minimizes the total costs of reaching a given target level of environmental quality;

- allows society to achieve higher target levels of environmental quality than inefficient policies because of cost savings.

---

[1] MAC_1 could be higher than MAC_2 for a number of different reasons, as will be discussed in detail in upcoming chapters in this section. The key point here is that when policies are inefficient, costs of controlling emissions are higher than they would be under a cost-effective regime.

[2] Recall that total abatement costs are the area under the MAC curve from the initial emission level (in this case 200,000 tonnes) to the target level of emissions (100,000 tonnes).

FIGURE 9-1   **A Cost-Effective Policy Minimizes Total Abatement Costs for a Given Pollution Target**

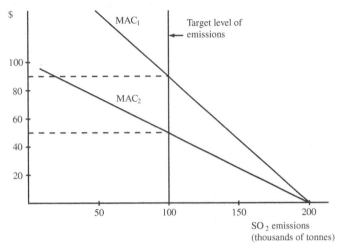

A cost-ineffective policy is shown by MAC_1. If the target level of emissions is 100,000 tonnes of SO_2, total abatement costs at the target will equal \$4.5-million. If a cost-effective policy is used, total abatement costs will be \$2.5-million at the target. This allows regulators to either have lower costs of abatement for a given target or to contemplate more pollution abatement for the same total costs.

Efficiency and cost-effectiveness are important because, although preserving environmental resources is critically important, it is only one of the many desirable things that people seek. Advocates are usually convinced that their objectives are automatically worth the cost, but success depends on persuading large numbers of other people that environmental policies are efficiently designed. Thus, the resources devoted to environmental quality improvement ought to be spent in ways that will have the greatest impact. This is especially important in less developed economies, where people have fewer resources to put in environmental programs and can ill afford policies that are not cost-effective and efficient. Cost-effectiveness also becomes an important issue in industrialized countries during times of recession or economic stagnation.

Policies that can be readily adapted to new information about damages, technological innovation, changing economic or social conditions are flexible. If a policy requires lengthy administrative, legislative, or judicial processes, the risk is that it will not be efficient or cost effective. We will also examine whether some policies require more information to implement than others. If information demands are high, policy delay may occur.

LO 2

FAIRNESS

Fairness, or equity, is another important criterion for evaluating environmental policy (or any policy, for that matter) as we've noted in previous chapters. Equity is not only a matter of morality, it is also a concern for policy effectiveness, because policies may not be supported as enthusiastically in the political arena if they are thought to be inequitable. Having said this, however, we have to recognize that there is no agreement on how much weight we should put on the two objectives: efficiency and equity. Refer back to Chapter 6 and Table 6-3 for an illustration of ways to incorporate distribution impacts into a decision.

It is an open question how much emphasis should be put on the distributional impacts of environmental policy compared to their other characteristics. On one side is the argument that environmental degradation is so pervasive that society should focus primarily on policies that are the most efficient—that give us the most impact for the resources spent. On the other is the position that society should avoid policies, even efficient ones, which have a strongly regressive impact. Whatever one feels about these distributional impacts—and it does depend on personal values to a great extent—we need to keep in mind that distributional considerations should have some weight in the selection of environmental policies.

Equity considerations also loom large in the making of international environmental policy. Countries at different stages of development have different views on how the burdens of international pollution-control programs should be distributed. These views are driven by considerations of what seems fair in the light of the wide economic disparities around the globe.

INCENTIVES FOR INNOVATION

In studying environmental policy much of the focus normally is cast on the performance of public officials, since they appear to be the source of that policy. But it is private parties—firms and consumers whose decisions actually determine the range and extent of environmental impacts[3]—and the incentives facing these private parties that determine how and where these impacts will be reduced. Thus, a critically important criterion that must be used to evaluate any environmental policy is whether that policy provides a strong incentive for individuals and groups to find new, innovative ways of reducing their impacts on the ambient environment; that is, does it stimulate technological progress in this area? Does the policy place all the initiative and burden on public agencies, or does it provide incentives for private parties to devote their energies and creativities to finding new ways of reducing environmental impacts?

It is easy to miss the importance of this sometimes when we concentrate on the abatement cost and damage functions in our standard analysis. These show the efficient level of emissions according to the current functions, but over the longer run it is important to try to shift these functions downward. Lowering the MAC will make it cheaper to secure reductions in emissions because this will justify higher levels of environmental quality, as was illustrated earlier in this chapter. Technological change shifts the marginal abatement cost function downward. So do education and training, which allow people to work and solve problems more efficiently. Ultimately we want to know whether—and how much—a particular environmental policy contains incentives for polluters to seek better ways of reducing pollution. The greater these incentives the better the policy, at least by this one criterion.

ENFORCEABILITY

Imposing regulations and ensuring that they are met requires the resources of people, time, and institutions. There perhaps is a natural tendency among people to think that enacting a law automatically leads to the rectification of the problem to which it is addressed. It is unlikely that polluters will more or less automatically comply with whatever laws are enacted, even in countries that have relatively strong legal traditions and institutions. Policies have to be enforced through the monitoring of emissions or technologies used, negotiations with polluters about timetables for compliance, and the legal system used to address violations of a law. Unfortunately, there will always be people whose interests lie in not having environmental policies enforced. All of these actions are the administrative costs that must be incurred with any policy.

[3.] It is also the case that many serious cases of environmental destruction have been caused by public agencies.

The reason for pursuing this is that policies differ in terms of how easy it is to enforce them. Some may require sophisticated technical measures to get reasonable enforcement; others may be enforceable at much lower cost. There is no sense in attempting a dazzling new policy approach if it is essentially impossible, or very costly, to enforce. We may be better off settling for a less-perfect policy that is more easily enforceable. There are two main steps in enforcement: monitoring and sanctioning. *Monitoring* refers to measuring the performance of polluters in comparison to whatever requirements are set out in the relevant law. *Sanctioning* refers to the task of bringing to justice those whom monitoring has shown to be in violation of the law. The objective of enforcement is to get people to comply with an applicable law. Thus, some amount of monitoring is normally essential; the only policy for which this does not hold is that of moral suasion. Monitoring polluting behaviour is far more complicated than, say, keeping track of the temperature. Nature doesn't really care, and so it won't willfully try to outwit and confound the monitoring process. But polluters who are intelligent human beings and who may stand to lose money if environmental laws are vigorously enforced can usually find many ways of frustrating the monitoring process. And the more sophisticated and complicated that process, the easier it may be for polluters to find ways of evading it.

The other main part of enforcement is sanctioning polluters who are in violation of the law. This may sound like a simple step: if violators are found, simply take them to court and levy the penalties specified in the relevant law. But things are much more complicated than this. Court cases take time and energy and resources. With many laws and many more violators, the burden on the legal system of trying to bring all violators to justice may be overwhelming. Violators are also reluctant participants; they may devote many resources to fighting the sanctions, turning the procedure into long, drawn-out, costly court battles. In many cases the data underlying the sanctions will be imperfect, leading to challenges and costly conflicts. To create a demonstration effect it may be desirable for authorities to sanction only a few of the most egregious violations, but this opens up the problem of trying to determine just which violators to single out. It is perhaps no wonder that in the real world many violators, especially first-time violators, are not sanctioned with the full penalties allowed by the law. Very often authorities try to achieve voluntary compliance and encourage violators to remedy the situation without penalty.

There is a paradox built into the sanctioning process. One might think that the greater the potential sanctions—higher fines, long jail terms for violators, and so on—the more the law would deter violators. But on the other hand, the higher the penalties the more reluctant courts may be to apply them. The threat to close down violators, or even to levy stiff financial penalties, can in turn threaten the economic livelihoods of large numbers of people. Courts are usually reluctant to throw a large number of people out of work or put corporate executives into jail, and so may opt for less drastic penalties than allowed by the law. A trade-off exists between the size of the penalty and the probability that it will be imposed. So the sanctioning process can become much more complicated than the simple model implies.

We have very little information in Canada about these administrative costs. The size of the budgets for environmental ministries at the federal and provincial level are known, but how do we tell what proportion of the costs of the legal system represent environmental compliance costs? We have some sketchy data on enforcement activities—the number of investigations, warnings, prosecutions, convictions and so on—but it isn't clear what these data tell us about compliance. The data indicate that enforcement activity is occurring, but also that very few prosecutions and convictions have resulted. Does this mean that compliance with the regulation is high or that violations aren't being detected? Or does it simply mean that compliance is obtained through methods other than legal enforcement activities? In Canada, negotiation between polluters and government agencies is a common method of obtaining compliance. Another widespread practice is for agencies to require self-reporting of emissions by firms, with the public authorities carrying out periodic audits of these records and perhaps also periodic testing of emissions.

Enforcement costs are an important segment of environmental quality programs. Public agencies virtually everywhere face budget constraints, but also responsibilities that are large and continually growing. Thus, the costs of enforcement, though perhaps not as large as overall compliance costs in most cases, are critical to the success of environmental quality programs and ought to be treated explicitly in evaluating the overall social costs of these programs.

MORAL CONSIDERATIONS

Moral considerations extend beyond the equity and distributional issues discussed above. The innate feelings that people have about what is right and wrong undoubtedly affect the way they look at different environmental policies. These have to be weighed in the balance along with the more technical criteria we have discussed above.

Take, for example, the question of choosing between effluent taxes and effluent subsidies. Both are economic-incentive-type policies, and both might reduce pollution per source by the same amount. From the standpoint of effectiveness, one might argue that subsidies would be better. Polluters might very well respond more quickly and with greater willingness to a subsidy program than to one that is likely to cost them a lot of money. Strictly from the standpoint of getting the environment cleaned up as soon as possible, subsidies might be the most effective. But this may run counter to the ethical notion that people who are causing a problem ought not to be "rewarded" for stopping, which is how subsidies are sometimes viewed. There is much moral appeal in the notion that the "polluter should pay."

Some people would take this idea further and argue that polluting behaviour is immoral. Therefore, we should adopt policies that make certain types of polluting behaviour illegal. Another idea grounded in morality is that those who cause a problem ought to bear the major burden of alleviating it. We see this, for example, in discussions of global environmental issues. The industrial nations, especially the most economically developed among them, are largely responsible for the atmospheric buildup of CO_2 and the deterioration of the protective ozone layer. Many people take the view that these countries ought to bear the major burden in rectifying the situation.

With these criteria in hand, we are now ready to launch into a study of different types of environmental policies. We begin with several approaches that are on the more decentralized end of the continuum, after which we investigate the use of environmental standards, the approach most frequently resorted to in the past. Finally, we look at what are called economic-incentive-based policies.

Summary

The objective of this chapter is to review a number of criteria that may be useful in evaluating environmental policies. These criteria are

- efficiency, cost-effectiveness, information demands, and flexibility
- fairness
- incentives for innovation
- enforceability
- moral considerations

With these criteria, it is now time to examine different types of environmental policies.

Discussion Questions

1. "Efficiency implies cost-effectiveness, but cost-effectiveness does not imply efficiency." Explain this statement.
2. Should efficiency be sacrificed for equity? Defend your answer.
3. Besides having different impacts on people at different income levels, environmental policies could also have varying impacts in different regions of a country. How might a federal policy, applied uniformly across a country, have different impacts in different regions? If a province opposes a federal policy, should it be allowed to opt out of the policy?
4. Should "political feasibility" be a criterion in designing environmental policies?
5. Prove graphically that a technological change that lowers marginal abatement costs can lead to higher levels of environmental quality.
6. Are there regulatory policies that would lower the MD curve?

For more information on the resources available from McGraw-Hill Ryerson, go to www.mheducation.ca/he/solutions.

Chapter 10

Liability Laws, Property Rights, Moral Suasion, Green Goods

After reading this chapter you will be able to:

LO 1 Explain how liability laws can reduce pollution and lead to a socially efficient equilibrium.

LO 2 Explain and show graphically how private property rights and bargaining between parties can lead to a socially efficient equilibrium and how the gains to each party differ depending on the starting point and who has the property rights.

LO 3 Describe the Coase theorem and why it is important for environmental policy.

LO 4 Describe the factors that inhibit private bargaining from reaching a socially efficient equilibrium.

LO 5 Explain how recycling and green goods can reduce pollution and illustrate graphically the potential impacts.

Liability laws, assignment of property rights, moral suasion, and green goods are examples of decentralized methods of internalizing externalities. **Decentralized techniques** allow the individuals involved in a case of environmental pollution to work it out themselves once a set of clearly defined rules for procedures and rights has been established by regulation and/or through the legal system. Environmental regulatory policies such as taxes, subsidies, and transferable discharge permits are somewhat less decentralized because they involve more government intervention in the form of setting tax rates, subsidy levels, or the number of permits to trade. However, they still allow economic agents to decide for themselves how they wish to respond to the policy—for example, how much to reduce emissions. Environmental standards are a very centralized policy: governments set the emission level and polluters have no options but to meet the standard or face penalties for non-compliance. We start with the techniques that are at the decentralized end of the continuum from decentralized to centralized, then examine policies involving more government involvement in the chapters that follow.

Consider a simple example. Suppose there are several industrial plants around the lake. One is a food-processing plant, and the water of the lake is an important input in its operation. The other is an industrial operation that uses the lake for waste disposal. How can the pollution damage suffered by the first firm be balanced with the abatement costs of the second? A very decentralized approach to finding the efficient level of ambient water quality in the lake is simply to let the two plants work it out between themselves. They might do this either through informal negotiations or through more formal interaction in a court of law. A more centralized approach would involve government involvement—ranging from levying taxes on waste discharge to setting water-quality standards.

Decentralized approaches can have several advantages over other types of public policy:

- The parties involved are the ones producing and suffering the environmental externalities. They therefore have strong incentives to seek solutions to the environmental problem.

- The people involved may be the ones with the best knowledge of damages and abatement costs and therefore best able to find efficient solutions.

Property rights must be defined and distributed before any sort of decentralized process can occur. In the case of the environment, the basic decision that must be made by society through its governments and legal system is who should have the right to environmental quality. As you might expect, it is difficult to define this sort of right. But the basic issue is whether people have the right to a particular level of environmental quality or whether those who discharge wastes can do so freely. We will talk about the rights to the environment as "belonging" to the polluter or the pollutee. Once this decision is made, the next decision is how rights will be protected: through liability laws or property rights. We begin with liability laws because they are familiar to most people.

LO 1

LIABILITY LAWS

Most people have an intuitive notion of **liability** and **compensation.** To be *liable* for some behaviour is to be held responsible for whatever untoward consequences result from that behaviour. *Compensation* requires that those causing the damage compensate those damaged in amounts appropriate to the extent of the injury. Questions of liability and compensation are usually worked out in the courts. The party claiming damage proceeds against the party it believes to be responsible, and judges and juries decide according to whatever provisions of common and statutory law are applicable. The courts will also decide the value of the damages. As we'll see below, this is in contrast to *property rights,* where the value of the damages is determined by the parties themselves.

One approach to environmental issues, therefore, is to rely on liability laws. This would work simply by making polluters liable for the damages they cause. The purpose of the laws is not just to compensate people after they have been injured, though that is important. The real purpose is to get would-be polluters to make careful decisions. Knowing that they will be held liable for environmental damages in effect internalizes what would otherwise be ignored external effects. An example on the next page illustrates the principles involved.

Theoretically, the existence of liability laws appears to address the incentive question—getting people to take into account the environmental damages they may cause—as well as the question of compensating those who are damaged. It also appears to solve the problem of determining just where E^* is along the emission axis. This would be discovered as a result of the interactions between polluters and those damaged in court. Both sides would present evidence and claims that, assuming the court is impartial, would lead to something approaching the efficient level of emissions. To recap,

liability laws can lead to the socially efficient level of pollution because they provide an incentive for polluters to reduce emissions so as to minimize their total costs—total abatement costs plus compensation to pollutees.

EXAMPLE

Chemical effluent damages fishery

A chemical factory discharges waste products into a river. These wastes kill many salmon that are swimming upstream to spawn. While there will no doubt be other ecological damages from the chemical effluent, we focus on those of the fishery. Figure 10-1 presents the MAC–MD model developed in Chapter 5.

FIGURE 10-1 **How Liability for Pollution Damages Can Lead to Social Efficiency**

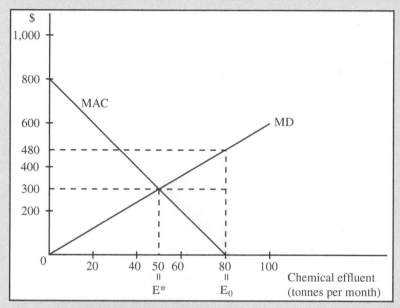

When no liability law exists, a chemical factory will not willingly incur any pollution abatement costs and will discharge 80 tonnes of chemical effluent per month. The salmon fisheries' total damages at this emission level are $19,200 per month. Imposition of liability will provide an incentive for the chemical factory to reduce its emissions. They will minimize their total payments of damage compensation plus total abatement costs if they release effluent at the socially efficient level of 50 tonnes per month.

Let E be tonnes of chemical effluent discharged per month. Then the marginal damage to the fishery (measured in terms of lost salmon stocks) is shown by the MD function. The equation for marginal damages is $MD = 6E$. The chemical factory can reduce its effluent flows by treating its waste products. Its marginal abatement cost (MAC) function is given by $MAC = 800 - 10E$. If emissions are reduced to zero, marginal abatement costs are $800. If no emissions are controlled, MAC will equal zero and the level of emissions will be 80 tonnes per month.

Figure 10-1 illustrates the MD and MAC functions graphically.

How does liability for damages affect pollution levels? Suppose first that there is no liability law that holds polluters responsible for the damages they inflict. The chemical factory will not abate any wastes at all in this case, so pollution levels are where MAC = 0. The chemical factory discharges 80 tonnes per month. Call this amount E_0. At E_0, the salmon fishery is incurring total damages (TD) equal to the total area under the MD curve from 0 to 80 tonnes. Total damages = $19,200 per month.[1] The

(Continued)

---

[1] Total damages are therefore the area of the triangle under the MD curve. One can find marginal damages at 80 tonnes by reading off the graph or by substituting 80 tonnes into the MD function to obtain $480.

government then invokes a liability law that requires polluters to compensate those damaged in an amount equal to the damages caused. The effect of the law is to internalize the environmental damages that were external before the law. They now become costs that polluters will have to pay, and so will want to take into account when deciding on their emission rate. If they do not reduce their discharges, the chemical factory will have to compensate the fishery for its total damages of $19,200 each month.

Will the chemical factory change its emissions levels in response to liability laws? The polluter can reduce its compensation payments by reducing emissions. The factory then incurs abatement costs as shown by its MAC curve as it reduces its emissions. But as long as the marginal abatement costs are less than marginal damages, the chemical factory will have an incentive to move to the left; that is, to reduce its rate of emissions. In theory, a liability system could automatically lead this polluter to a socially efficient level of emissions, $E^* = 50$ tonnes per month.[2] We say "automatically" because it would not require any centralized control authorities to intervene and mandate emission reductions. A system of decentralized courts and liability laws that would permit those damaged by pollution to seek compensation for damages suffered is what is required.

We can prove that reducing effluent to E^* is a better strategy for the chemical factory than not reducing waste discharged and staying at E_0.

Proof that polluters will move from E_0 to E^* when liable for pollution damages.

Steps:

1. Compute the chemical factory's total abatement costs (TAC) at $E^* = 50$ tonnes per month. TAC = the area under the MAC curve working from the right of the figure from E_0 to E^*. This is equal to $\frac{1}{2}[(80 - 50)$ times $\$300] = \$4,500$.

2. Compute total damages to the fishery at E^* (because emissions are greater than zero). Total damages at E^* = the area under the MD curve working from 0 to 50 tonnes. This is equal to $\frac{1}{2}(50$ times $\$300) = \$7,500$.

3. Compute the chemical factory's total payments. Total payments = TAC + compensation to the fishery. This equals $\$4,500 + \$7,500 = \$12,000$ per month.

4. Compare total payments at E^* to those at E_0. At E_0 the factory would have to pay the fishery total compensation of $\$19,200$. This is proof that the factory is much better off at E^* than if it stays at E_0.

Question to ponder: While we've shown that E^* is superior to E_0, is some other emission level even better for the factory than E^*? This is a problem at the end of the chapter.

Liability Laws in Practice

The requirement that polluters be held liable for damages may be part of a country's basic legal code, or it could be provided through special statutory enactments. In common-law countries such as Canada (outside of Quebec), the United States, and the United Kingdom, doctrines of nuisance and liability have been developed through the evolution of court decisions. This law now recognizes the difference between **strict liability,** which holds people responsible for damages regardless of circumstances, and **negligence,** which holds them responsible only if they did not take appropriate steps to avoid damage. A firm disposing of hazardous materials might be held strictly liable for damages done by these

---

[2.] Recall from Chapter 5 that the socially efficient equilibrium is found where the MD intersects the MAC curve. Algebraically, we set MD = $6E$ equal to MAC = $800 - 10E$. Thus, $6E = 100 - 10E$ and $E^* = 50$.

wastes. Thus, any damages that resulted, regardless of how careful the firm had been in disposing of the waste, would require compensation. On the other hand, negligence would hold it responsible only if it failed to take appropriate steps to ensure that the materials did not escape into the surrounding environment.

In civil-law countries and jurisdictions, such as Quebec, liability requirements may be written into the appropriate parts of the code. And in any country environmental laws may specify conditions under which polluters may be held liable for damages. For example, through domestic laws and/or in international agreements many countries have sought to use liability policy to address the problem of maritime oil spills. Several international conventions have been devoted to specifying the liability requirements of companies whose tankers release, accidentally or not, large quantities of oil into the sea. One particularity of oil tanker spills is that it is very difficult to monitor the behaviour of the polluters in this case. It is an episodic emission, so there is no continuous flow to measure, and spill probabilities depend on many practices (navigation, tanker maintenance, etc.) that are difficult for public authorities to monitor continuously. Another recent example where it is difficult to monitor the amount of care companies take to reduce the likelihood of catastrophic events that release pollutions is the explosion of British Petroleum's (BP) well in the Gulf of Mexico in 2010. Millions of litres of oil were released into the ocean before BP was able to stop the flow of oil. While polluter behaviour is extremely difficult to monitor, we nevertheless would like to know that the polluters have undertaken all appropriate steps to reduce the probability of accidents. To provide the incentive for this, the most appropriate response may be to rely on a system of strict liability.

A number of factors work against relying on liability to solve all environmental problems. The critical factors in a liability system are where the **burden of proof** lies and what standards have to be met in order to establish that proof. In Canada, those who believe they may have been injured by pollution must file an action within a specified time period, and then in court must establish a direct causal link between the pollution and the damage. This involves two major steps:

Burden of proof requires injured parties to show

1. *that the polluting material was a direct cause of their damage, and*
2. *that the material did in fact come from the specific defendant that appears in court.*

Both steps are difficult because the standards of proof required by the courts may be more than current science can supply. Consider the first step. Most chemicals, for example, are implicated in increased disease only on a *probabilistic* basis; that is, exposure to the substance involves an increased probability of disease, not certainty. Even though we know that smoking causes lung cancer, for example, this causal link remains probabilistic: an increased number of people will get lung cancer if they smoke, but we can't tell exactly which ones. In parts of rural Ontario, contamination of well water was estimated by some epidemiologists to have contributed to excess cases of leukemia in the areas affected. But under traditional standards of proof, a plaintiff could not conclusively prove that a *specific* cancer was caused by the water contamination. In other words, without being able to show explicitly how the polluting material operated in a particular body to produce cancer, the plaintiff cannot meet the standard of proof historically required in our courts.[3]

[3.] In some cases the law is beginning to change to recognize the special characteristics of pollution-caused damage. For example, statutes of limitation are being changed to count from the time the disease first becomes apparent, in recognition of the fact that many pollution-caused diseases may not show up for many years after exposure. Some courts are also beginning to allow statistical cause-and-effect linkages.

The second step is to show that the material to which one was exposed came from a particular source. This won't be difficult in some cases; the oil on the Alaskan shoreline definitely came from the *Exxon Valdez* wreck, the oil in the Gulf of Mexico came from the BP drilling rig explosion, the sulphur smells in Prince George, B.C. definitely come from the pulp and paper mills, and so on. But in many cases this direct linkage is unknown. In Montreal or Toronto, which specific industrial plant produced the SO_2 molecules that a particular person may have breathed? In cities and towns that take their drinking water from Lake Ontario, which specific companies were responsible for the chemicals that showed up in the water supply? Without being able to trace a polluting substance to specific defendants, those who have been damaged by it may be unable to obtain compensation.

This brings up an additional problem with using the legal system to address environmental problems. If people feel they are harmed, will the courts recognize their claim? This is the legal doctrine of **standing.** A private citizen may bring suit on environmental cases if that person is able to show that he or she is in fact being damaged by the activity in question. Consider some of the following hypothetical situations. People in Victoria pollute the waters of their harbours, but may residents in Edmonton claim that they have been damaged? If fishers in Newfoundland and Labrador exhaust the cod stock to support their families, can people in Winnipeg justifiably claim that they have been damaged? For these hypothetical cases, it would be unlikely that standing would be granted by the courts, because it would be difficult to show that individuals in a distant city were damaged. However, a resident of Victoria who operates a tourist business that has been adversely affected by the presence of sewage in Victoria waters would be more likely to be granted standing.[4] These examples bring up a very important point. A person may feel worse off if fish stocks have been depleted or oceans polluted. They might even be willing to pay some dollar amount to help reduce pollution. But they still have no standing in the courts.

> *The legal doctrine of standing is incompatible with the economist's use of willingness to pay as a measure of value. Values established through legal cases may not fully represent the value people are willing to pay for environmental quality.*

Transaction Costs

All decentralized approaches to pollution control have another impediment that can make it difficult to reach a socially efficient equilibrium—**transactions costs.** In general terms, transactions costs are the costs of reaching and enforcing agreements. The concept was first introduced in economics to apply to the costs that buyers and sellers encounter in making a successful transaction—costs of searching out information, costs of bargaining over terms, and costs of making sure an agreement is actually carried out. But the transactions costs also apply to liability systems where plaintiffs and defendants are competing in a court of law to determine the question of liability and the appropriate amounts of compensation. In this case transactions costs are all the legal costs associated with gathering evidence, presenting a case, challenging opponents, awarding and collecting damages, and so on.

If we are dealing with simple cases, with one party on each side and a reasonably clear case of damage, the liability system may function with a minimum of transactions costs to give something approaching the efficient level of emissions. In the case of the two small factories on a small lake, the two can go to court and argue about the economic values to each of them of using the lake for their purposes. And since these values are comparable, it presumably would not be too difficult for a judge to determine the extent of the damages that one firm is inflicting on the other. But things are very

---

[4.] In practice, few such suits for environmental damages have been initiated in Canada.

different when large numbers of people are involved on one or both sides of an issue. In the case of the *Exxon Valdez* and BP oil spills, for example, probably tens of thousands of people regard themselves as having been directly damaged; hundreds of lawyers represent all the different sides; and numerous environmental groups, government organizations, and business groups are involved.

At the end of a very long series of court battles some compensation will be paid. But the transactions costs will be enormous, and at the end of the process the compensation probably won't accurately reflect real damages. This is no doubt why the major parties tried to settle this case with a lump-sum agreement relatively early in the process, although continuing lawsuits are not ruled out.

To summarize, liability laws and the incentives they create can help lead to efficient pollution levels when

- relatively few people are involved,
- causal linkages are clear, and
- damages are easy to measure.

These conditions may be met in some localized cases of pollution, but for most cases of major environmental externalities they are not.

Liability laws are thus limited when

- there are problems meeting the burden of proof,
- there is difficulty in obtaining standing,
- legal values do not reflect willingness to pay, and
- transaction costs inhibit negotiation and legal action.

LO 2

PROPERTY RIGHTS

The example of a river that was being used by a chemical factory for waste disposal and by a salmon fishery for fish reproduction leads to a more fundamental question: Which one of the two protagonists is really *causing* damage, and which is the one *suffering* damages? This may seem counterintuitive, because you might naturally think that the chemical factory is of course the one causing the damage. But doesn't the presence of the fishery inflict damages on the chemical factory because its presence makes it necessary for the latter to take special efforts to control its emissions?[5] The problem may come about simply because it is not clear who has the initial right to use the services of the lake; that is, who effectively owns the **property rights** to the lake—an ownership right that conveys certain powers. These powers may include the right to exclusive use, to transfer the right to someone else, or to subdivide it into smaller parts. The strongest property right is what we called in Chapter 1 a **private property right.** This gives the holder exclusive rights to do what she or he wishes with the property owned (subject to other laws such as not creating a public nuisance). The property may be a piece of land, a part of a river, an object, a patent, and so on. When someone owns a resource, she has a strong incentive to see to it that it is managed in a way that gives it the maximum value as compared to **open access** where no private property rights exist. To solve the problem of lake pollution, therefore, it is

---

[5.] Assume for purposes of argument that there are no other people using the lake, such as homeowners, recreators, or other firms.

necessary to specify clearly who has the rights of ownership to the lake. Whether or not the specification of ownership rights is also sufficient to solve the problem and reach a socially efficient equilibrium is the topic of this section.

Private-property rights are, of course, the dominant institutional arrangement in most developed economies of the West. Developing countries also are moving in that direction, as are even the ex-socialist countries. So we are familiar with the operation of that institutional system when it comes to person-made assets such as machines, buildings, and consumer goods. Private property in land is also a familiar arrangement. If somebody owns a piece of land, he has an incentive to see to it that the land is managed in ways that maximize its value. If somebody comes along and threatens to dump something onto the land, the owner may call upon the law to prevent it if he wants to. By this diagnosis, the problem of the misuse of many environmental assets comes about because of imperfectly specified property rights in those assets.

Consider again the case of the chemical factory and fishery both using the same river. "Ownership" of the river could be vested in either the chemical factory or the fishery. How does this choice affect the level of pollution in the lake? Would it not lead to zero emissions if owned by the one firm, and uncontrolled emissions if owned by the other? Not so, if the owners and non-owners can negotiate. Of course, this is the very essence of a property-rights system. The owner decides how the asset is to be used and may stop any unauthorized use, but may also negotiate with anybody else who wants access to that asset. We look now at how the assignment of property rights can lead to a socially efficient equilibrium.

The Assignment of Property Rights and Social Efficiency

Questions to ponder: Does it matter who has the property rights to the environmental resource as long as someone has them? Will assignment of rights to either party yield a socially efficient equilibrium? These questions can be answered with graphical help, using the MD and MAC curves from the liability discussion. Figure 10-2 redraws these curves.

Chemical company (the polluter) has the property right to use the river   Case 1

Possession of the property right to pollute means that the chemical company has the right to use the river however it wants. It does not have to pay compensation to the fishery for any pollution damages. From our previous example, we know that the chemical factory will want to avoid any abatement costs and so will release 80 tonnes of chemical effluent per month. Also recall that at this level of emissions, the fishery will incur total damages of $19,200 per month. Is this where matters will remain?

The fishery could offer a payment to the chemical factory to reduce its emissions. Why will it do so? Suppose the fishery says: "We'll pay you $100 per tonne for every tonne of chemical waste you control—that is, do not discharge into the river." What then would happen? The chemical factory would *equate the $100 per tonne payment with its MAC curve* to see where it would break even between abating pollution and thus incurring abatement costs and receiving the payment from the fishery. From Figure 10-2, reading from right to left, we see that the chemical factory would reduce emissions to 70 tonnes per month. We find this point graphically by seeing where $100 intersects the MAC curve or algebraically by setting MAC = $100 and solving the following equation for E:
$$MAC = 800 - 10E.$$

(Continued)

FIGURE 10-2   Assignment of Property Rights Leads to Social Efficiency Regardless of Who Has the Property Rights

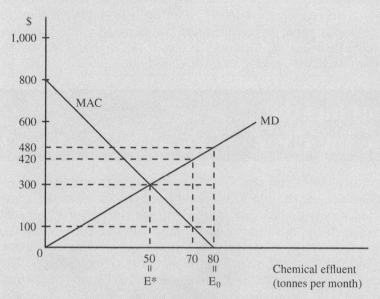

If the chemical factory has the property right to use the river, it will not abate any of its effluent. Eighty tonnes per month is the starting point. To reduce chemical effluent into the river, the fishery will bargain with the chemical plant and offer a payment to the plant. Two payments are shown: $100 and $300 per tonne of effluent reduced. Both parties gain if pollution is abated. The socially efficient equilibrium at 50 tonnes per month can be reached after bargaining. If the fishery has the property rights, the starting point is zero emissions and the socially efficient equilibrium can also be reached from this property-right assignment.

The chemical company is better off at the new equilibrium. At 70 tonnes per month, it pays $500 per month in total abatement costs, but gets a total payment from the fishery of $1,000 per month (the payment of $100 times the 10 tonnes of effluent abated). The net gain to the factory is $500. The fishery is also better off at 70 than at 80 tonnes per month of effluent. It pays $1,000, but total damages have decreased from $19,200 per month (at 80 tonnes) to $14,700 per month (at 70 tonnes). The net change in total damages is a reduction of $4,500. Netting out the $1,000 payment to the chemical factory gives the fishery a net gain of $3,500. Both parties are thus better off. Their total gains are $4,000 (i.e., $3,500 plus $500).

But will the bargaining stop here? The companies could continue to bargain over the marginal unit as long as marginal damages exceeded marginal abatement costs. Starting at 80 tonnes per month, MDs exceed MACs until 50 tonnes per month are reached. This is the socially efficient equilibrium. At 50 tonnes per month, the chemical company receives a payment of $9,000 from the fishery (i.e., 30 tonnes reduced times $300 per tonne) and incurs total abatement costs of $4,500, so its net gain is $4,500 compared to staying at 80 tonnes of effluent per month. The fishery's total damages fall from $19,200 to $7,500, so its net gain is $2,700 (i.e., $11,700 minus $9,000). Total gains are $7,200 (i.e., $4,500 plus $2,700). These total gains are much larger than at emission levels of either 70 or 80 tonnes per month.

Reaching the socially efficient equilibrium thus makes both parties better off than at the starting point, with 80 tonnes of pollution being released per month. But note that the fishery's net gain is higher at 70 tonnes than at 50 tonnes, even though its total damages are much higher at 70 tonnes.

(Continued)

This is because the marginal damage curve is rising. Reducing pollution a bit (10 tonnes) generates a big saving in total damages, while "costing" the fishery relatively little in payments to the chemical factory. Moving to 50 tonnes reduces total damages but also requires a much bigger payment to the chemical factory. The fishery would of course be unambiguously better off at 50 tonnes if it could somehow lower its payment to the chemical plant. If the chemical company gave the fishery a "refund" of at least $800 (the difference between the fishery's net gain at 70 tonnes versus 50 tonnes), the fishery would be willing to move to the socially efficient equilibrium.

The fishery (pollutee) has the property right to use the river   Case 2

If the property right to the river belongs to the fishery the starting point will presumably be clean water; that is, zero emissions from the chemical factory. This would occur if, for example, a law prohibits chemical emissions and the factory is considering locating on the river. If the chemical factory wants to release *any* amount of effluent, it will have to bargain with and compensate the fishery. We now *read Figure 10-2 from left to right* to compute the payment the chemical company must make. Suppose they just happen to offer $300 per tonne of effluent released into the river. The fishery *will equate the $300 per tonne to its MD curve* and tell the chemical factory that it can release 50 tonnes. That is, the fishery will allow emissions as long as the payment at least covers their marginal damages. The $300 payment per tonne exceeds marginal damages up to 50 tonnes, at which point they are equal. Each party will gain from this transaction. The fishery incurs total damages of $7,500, but it receives a payment of $15,000 (i.e., $300 per tonne times 50 tonnes), so its net gain is $7,500. When the fishery has the property right (to zero pollution), the factory would have incurred total abatement costs of $32,000 (the area under its MAC curve from 80 tonnes to 0) if it wanted to locate on the river and engaged in no bargaining. After bargaining to 50 tonnes, its total abatement costs are $4,500. Its net gain is therefore $32,000 minus $4,500 minus the payment of $15,000. Its net gain is $12,500. Gains for both parties are $20,000. The socially efficient equilibrium again makes both parties better off compared to the starting point.

We see that while the same equilibrium output of pollution can be obtained with either party holding the secure property right to the river, the size and distribution of the net gains will likely differ with the holder of the rights in a stronger position to obtain a bigger share of the net benefits. We illustrate this more fully next.

LO 3

This example shows that

> *a socially efficient equilibrium can be reached regardless of the assignment of property rights. If the MAC and MD curves do not change based on who has the property rights, the same socially efficient equilibrium will be reached independent of who holds the rights to pollute.*

The essential ingredients are that the right is clearly defined and supported by law, and bargaining can occur. In fact, this is a famous theorem called the **Coase theorem,** after the economist who invented it.[6]

[6.] Ronald H. Coase, "The Problem of Social Cost," *Journal of Law and Economics*, Vol. 3 (October 1960): 1–44.

While the Coase theorem shows that social efficiency can be obtained, it does not suggest that the gains to each party associated with different property rights need be identical. The equilibrium reached is identical in our example, but the net gains to each party differ depending on who has the rights. This can be easily shown in Figure 10-3, which is identical to Figure 10-2 except that areas are identified with letter labels. The socially efficient level of emissions is 50 tonnes per month regardless of whether we start at zero (fishery has the rights) or 80 tonnes (chemical factory has the rights), but the net gains to the individuals involved differ. Table 10-1 summarizes the gains and payments of each party under the different property-rights assignment.

FIGURE 10-3 Net Social Gains Are a Function of Property Rights

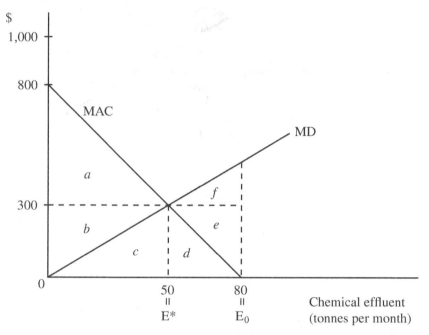

The sum of the net gains to the chemical factory and fishery are shown for the assignment of property rights to each party. If the fishery has the property rights, the sum of the net gains is areas $(a + b)$, where the fishery gets area b and the chemical factory area a. If the chemical factory has the property rights, the sum of net gains is areas $(e + f)$, with e going to the factory and f to the fishery. Areas $(a + b)$ exceed $(e + f)$. This proves that the sum of net gains need not be identical regardless of who has the property right.

When the fishery has the property right to the river, it receives a payment from the chemical factory equal to areas $(b + c)$. Its total damages are area c, so its net gain is area b. The chemical factory makes the payment $(b + c)$, and incurs abatement costs of d. The sum of the net gains to each party is areas $(a + b)$. When the chemical factory has the right to the river, the sum of the net gains is areas $(e + f)$. We see from the graph, and our numbers above prove, that areas $(a + b)$ exceed areas $(e + f)$. Will this always be the case? What does it depend on? The answer is no; it depends upon the shapes of the marginal abatement cost and marginal damage function. Thus "society" may well be better off under one property-right assignment than another, even though either assignment will be socially efficient. To recap,

net social gains are dependent on who has the property rights to environmental resources.

TABLE 10-1 Bargaining under Different Property Rights Assignments

	Fishery	Chemical factory
Property rights belong to the fishery: *Equilibrium at E* compared to 0*		
Total damages @ 0	0	—
Total damages @ E^*	c	—
TAC @ 0	—	$a + b + c + d$
TAC @ E^*	—	d
Total payment to fishery	$+(b + c)$	$-(b + c)$
Net gains	$[(b + c) - c] = b$	$[(a + b + c) - (b + c)] = a$

	Fishery	Chemical factory
Property rights belong to the chemical factory: *Equilibrium at E* compared to E_0*		
Total damages @ E_0	$c + d + e + f$	—
Total damages @ E^*	c	—
TAC @ E_0	—	0
TAC @ E^*	—	d
Total payment to chemical factory	$-(d + e)$	$+(d + e)$
Net gains	$[(d + e + f) - (d + e)] = f$	$[(d + e) - d] = e$

[TAC = total abatement costs]

LO 4

Applicability of Property Rights to Environmental Problems

The wider implication of this example is that by defining private-property rights (not necessarily individual property rights, because private *groups* of people could have these rights), we can establish the conditions under which decentralized bargaining can produce efficient levels of environmental quality. This has some appeal. The good part of it is that the people doing the bargaining may know more about the relative values involved—abatement costs and damages—than anybody else, so there is some hope that the true efficiency point will be arrived at. And, since it would be a decentralized system, some central bureaucratic organization will not be making decisions that are based mostly on political considerations instead of the true economic values involved. Ideas like this have led some people to recommend widespread conversion of natural and environmental resources to private ownership as a means of achieving their efficient use.

How well is this property-rights approach likely to work in practice? As we saw with liability laws, something that looks good in theory may not work well when faced with the complexities of the real world. In order for a property-rights approach to work right—that is, to give us something approaching the socially efficient level of environmental pollution—essentially three main conditions have to be met. These conditions are described in detail below.

Property rights—Conditions for social efficiency:

1. Property rights must be well defined, enforceable, and transferable.

2. There must be a reasonably efficient and competitive system for interested parties to come together and negotiate about how these environmental property rights will be used.

3. There must be a complete set of markets so that private owners may capture all social values associated with the use of an environmental asset.

A property right must be clearly identifiable, known to parties, and enforceable. If firm A cannot keep firm B from doing whatever the latter wishes, a property-rights approach will not work. In other words, owners must be physically and legally able to stop others from encroaching on their property. Owners must be able to sell their property to any would-be buyer. This is especially important in environmental assets. If owners cannot sell the property, this will weaken their incentives to preserve its long-run productivity. Without transferability, owners who deplete the long-run environmental productivity of their resource cannot be punished through the reduced market value of their asset. Many economists have argued that this is a particularly strong problem in developing countries; since ownership rights are often "attenuated" (that is, they do not have all the required characteristics specified above), people do not have strong incentives to see that long-run productivity is maintained.

Problems with Property Rights as a Technique to Internalize Externalities

1. **Transactions costs.** Efficient use of the river in the example depended on negotiations and agreement between the two interested firms. Transaction costs in the form of negotiating costs and costs of enforcement together with the costs of policing the agreement might be modest in this case. But suppose there are dozens of different industries that use the river for a waste depository—and, instead of one fishery, many households and industries use the river for drinking water and recreational purposes. Now the negotiations must take place between dozens of polluting firms on one side and maybe thousands of people on the other side. It is hard to imagine how bargaining could ever occur. The transactions costs would simply be too high.

2. **Open access and free riders.** The level of water quality in the river is a public good for everyone involved. Why should I pay to improve water quality when my neighbour can enjoy the benefits without having to pay a thing? This free-rider problem effectively defeats the chances that a socially efficient equilibrium can be achieved through property rights assignments and bargaining. The more public the environmental good, the less likely that this decentralized technique will work. The most extreme situation is when we contemplate open-access environmental resources (as discussed in Chapters 1 and 4). It is impossible to define private-property rights for open-access resources because they are non-exclusionary. Everyone can have access to them.

3. **Inability of property owners to capture social values.** Even in cases where private-property rights can be assigned, the process must work in such a way that the owner is able to capture the full social value of the resource in its best use. Suppose you own a small island in the Thirty Thousand Islands in Lake Huron. There are two possible uses: Develop a resort hotel or leave the island as wilderness. If you build the hotel, you get a direct flow of monetary wealth because the tourism market is well developed in that part of the world and you can expect customers to find your hotel and pay the going rate for your services. But there is no comparable "market" for

wilderness services.[7] The value of the island as wilderness may well be much higher than its value as a resort, in terms of the actual aggregate willingness to pay of all the people in the country and the world. But there is no good way for them to be able to express that value; there is no ready market like the one in the tourism market where they can in effect bid against the tourists who would visit the island. You might think that a nature conservancy could buy up the island if its value as wilderness really is higher than its value as a resort. But the nature conservancy runs on the basis of voluntary contributions, and islands and other lands are in effect public goods. We saw earlier that when public goods are involved, voluntary contributions to make something available are likely to be a lot less than its true value, because of free-riding behaviour. The upshot is that while you as an owner could certainly expect to reap the full monetary value of the island as a resort, you would not be able to realize its full social value if you held it as a preserve.

This example is actually a local version of a larger problem that has global significance. Much attention has been focused in recent years on biological diversity and the stock of unique genetic material contained in the millions of animal and plant species worldwide. A disproportionately large share of these species is located in developing countries. But these are also countries where development pressures have led to high rates of land clearance and habitat destruction. When landholders in these countries are considering their options, they weigh the value of the land in different uses. Unfortunately, there is no way at present that they can capture the value of the land left as species habitat. No ready economic markets exist where these services can be sold; if they did, landholders could reap private benefits from keeping land undeveloped or using land in ways that are consistent with the preservation of species.

One role for public authorities in this situation might be to create the demand side for such a market. This could be done by offering to pay the landowners an amount equal to the wider ecological value of the land, provided these ecological values were not impaired by the landholders' use of the land. Of course, this would involve enormous difficulties in measuring these ecological values with some degree of accuracy, as well as in finding sources of funds to pay for these services. But without these kinds of market or marketlike institutions, private-property-rights institutions are unable to give society the fully efficient amounts of preservation and environmental quality.

MORAL SUASION

Moral suasion refers to programs of persuasion that appeal to a person's sense of moral values or civic duty, to get him or her to refrain voluntarily from doing things that degrade the environment. The classic case of this is the success of public pressure against littering. While there are fines and penalties for doing these things, anti-littering campaigns were not based on threats of penalties as much as on appealing to people's sense of civic morality.

In the early days of recycling, communities often mounted voluntary efforts, where appeals were made on the basis of civic virtue. In some cases these efforts were successful; in others they fell flat. Today we are moving in the direction of more mandatory recycling programs, though it is true that they still must rely heavily on moral suasion to get high rates of compliance. Other situations clearly exist where appeals to civic morality may be effective public policy. This is especially the case with emissions as in litter, where violators are normally scattered throughout a population in a way that makes it impractical to monitor them and detect violations as they occur.

[7.] The assumption here is that the wilderness will not be accessible for public use. How would the example change if it were?

The good thing about moral suasion is that it may have widespread spillover effects. Whereas an effluent tax on a single type of effluent will have no impact on emissions of other types of waste products, appeals to civic virtue for one problem may produce side effects on other situations. Civic virtue may spread from feeling good when one refrains from littering (when it is very easy to "cheat") to other cases where they clearly could get away with some environmentally damaging activity. People who develop a civic sense about the environment may be less likely to sneak used motor oil or half-filled paint cans into their household waste, or to disable their car's air-pollution equipment to get better gas mileage.

There are problems, however, with relying on moral suasion as a primary policy approach. Not all people are equally responsible from an ethical standpoint. Some people will respond to moral arguments; others will not. The burden of this policy will fall, therefore, on the part of the population that is morally more sensitive; those who respond less to moral arguments will be free-riding on the others, enjoying the benefits of others' moral restraint but escaping their rightful share of the burden. What is especially bad about this is the long-run demonstration value. If those who would be responsive to moral arguments are confronted with the sight of widespread moral free riding, this may in the long run tend to erode the general level of civic and moral responsibility. Thus, appeals to the moral responsiveness of people, although perhaps effective in the short run, could actually have the opposite effect in the long run. This is similar to the cynicism that people often feel when new environmental laws are continually put on the books but never enforced.

While moral virtue is its own reward, it is even better if other people know about it. Moral suasion will be more effective in deterring pollution if information is readily available about emission levels and changes in them. Thus, as a counterpart to campaigns of moral suasion, efforts to measure and publicize emission levels and efforts people take to reduce these emissions are an important adjunct. These factors lie behind the recent attempt by environmental groups in Canada and the United States to develop an anti-pollution code of conduct to which companies could voluntarily subscribe. Canada also has an annual National Pollutant Release Inventory (NPRI) that provides public data on emissions and transportation of approximately 240 toxic compounds from public- and private-sector sources.[8]

It is easy to be cynical about moral suasion as a tool for environmental improvement. In this era of increasing mass society and heightened environmental destruction, tough-minded policy-makers are naturally drawn toward environmental policies that have more teeth in them. This would probably be a mistake. It is perhaps true that we cannot rely very heavily on moral suasion to produce, for example, a significant reduction in air pollution in the Windsor to Montreal corridor, or substantial drops in the use of groundwater-contaminating farm chemicals. But, in our search for new and effective, concrete public policy devices to address specific pollution problems, we perhaps underestimate the contribution of the overall climate of public morality and civic virtue. A strong climate in this sense makes it possible to institute new policies and easier to administer and enforce them. From this we can also deduce the importance of politicians and policy-makers in doing things that replenish this moral climate rather than erode it.

LO 5

MARKET RESPONSES TO ENVIRONMENTAL POLLUTION: GREEN GOODS

Once property rights have been clearly established that limit the amount of pollution emitted or that specify some level of environmental quality, new markets should arise to supply environmental

---

8. The NPRI will be discussed more fully in Chapter 18.

quality. Consumers may be willing to pay for goods that give them the same level of pleasure but involve less environmental damage than ordinary goods either in the production process or in use. If firms can produce such items, a market in so-called "green goods" might arise. In Canada, a number of green goods are currently being sold. They include, for example, household items such as no-phosphate laundry detergent, batteries that do not contain mercury, paper products made from recycled fibre, and appliances such as energy-efficient refrigerators and furnaces. There may also be green inputs into production processes. How do green goods reduce pollution?

Consider Figure 10-4. Panel (a) shows the market for paper products made using virgin fibre. Panel (b) illustrates the market for paper products made using recycled fibres. We assume that recycled fibres result in a less pollution-intensive process than virgin fibres. In each panel two supply curves are shown: S_p is the curve that reflects the marginal private costs of production; S_s the marginal social costs (which are the sum of marginal private costs plus marginal external costs, as we saw in Chapter 4). The pollution intensity of the two types of goods is reflected in the higher marginal social costs for paper produced with virgin fibre. Now let's add some demand curves. Suppose the market is originally supplied only with paper from the pollution-intensive process. Given a demand curve for paper (D_0), an equilibrium price of P_0 is established and quantity Q_0 is produced, as shown in panel (a). Now producers of less pollution-intensive paper enter the market. If consumers feel that recycled paper products are a good substitute for ordinary paper products, there will be some demand for recycled paper goods. If the two goods are substitutes, the demand for pollution-intensive paper will shift to the left with the introduction of the recycled paper. A new equilibrium price will be established where there is less production of ordinary paper (Q_1) and it is sold at a lower price (P_1). There will be some demand for recycled paper. The more consumers wish to substitute recycled for ordinary paper, the greater the leftward shift of the demand curve in panel A. The extent of this shift is dependent upon consumers' tastes, the marginal private costs of production, and so on.

FIGURE 10-4 Marginal Social Costs with Green Goods vs. Pollution-Intensive Goods

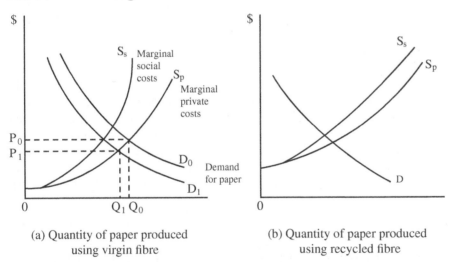

(a) Quantity of paper produced
using virgin fibre

(b) Quantity of paper produced
using recycled fibre

When recycled fibre replaces virgin fibre, the quantity of virgin fibre declines due to a shift in its demand. This moves the economy closer to an equilibrium where demand equals the social marginal costs of production, S_s.

If recycled paper goods capture some of the market, pollution must decrease. This occurs because the marginal abatement cost function shifts down. Why? Think back to our derivation of the aggregate marginal cost of abatement curve (MAC) in Chapter 5. Instead of having one type of production with a lot of pollution per unit output, we now have the output of paper coming from two types of producers: one with much lower emissions per unit output. If total output of paper stays the same, then total pollution must fall. This is shown in Figure 10-5, where MAC_1 is the aggregate MAC with only pollution-intensive suppliers and MAC_2 is the new curve obtained when some of the suppliers have much lower levels of emissions per unit output. We see that maximum pollution levels fall from E_1 to E_2. This means that regardless of where the marginal damage function is located, pollution is lower even without any government policy designed to reach the efficient level of emissions. Note that the MD function does not shift, because the relationship between each unit of emissions and environmental damage does not change.

FIGURE 10-5 How Green Goods Affect the Marginal Abatement Cost Curve

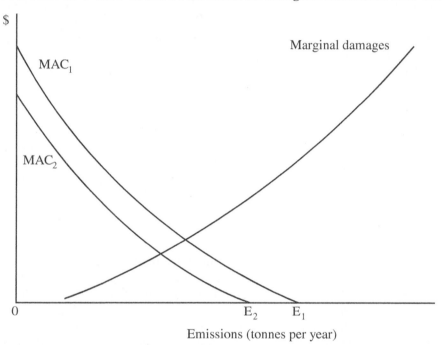

Green goods yield less pollution per unit output than pollution-intensive goods. Use of green goods will shift the MAC curve from MAC_1 to MAC_2. Even without any other environmental policy, this substitution will lower the level of emissions from E_1 to E_2.

EXAMPLE

How recycling can reduce pollution

Suppose the demand for aluminum cans is given by the inverse demand curve: $P = 100 - Q$ and the marginal costs of producing them is a constant \$30 per unit. Let the supply curve (marginal costs) for recycling aluminum cans be given by the inverse function: $P = 10 + Q$. These costs might represent what individuals and recycling companies incur in diverting the cans from the waste stream (recall Figure 2-1). What does the market equilibrium look like with primary production and recycling? Total output of cans is found by setting MC = Demand: $30 = 100 - Q$, thus $Q = 70$. Setting the recycling supply curve equal to the MC of primary production, we find that 20 units will be recycled. How does this help the environment? For every 10 aluminum cans now produced, 5 will be recycled, thus reducing the amount of waste going into landfills and the associated damages. How could recycling be

(Continued)

enhanced? Two ways can be illustrated in this simple framework. If we tax primary production by adding a unit tax of say, $20, its marginal costs rise to $50 and recycling goes from 20 to 40 units. Alternatively, a subsidy of $20 to recycling would shift its marginal cost curve down and would increase recycling to 40 units. We discuss the tradeoffs between taxes and subsidies more fully in Chapter 12.

An economy with a higher proportion of its production and consumption coming from green goods will thus have less pollution than an economy using more pollution-intensive goods. Government policy can of course stimulate the production of green goods. One way to do so is with laws about product labelling. Product labelling laws and regulations can help consumers make informed choices about how "environmentally friendly" the good is. Labels indicating recycled content of the good and energy consumption are examples. Without these regulations, companies have an incentive to "green wash"—to make claims that their products are good for the environment, even if that is not the case. We will talk more about this in Chapter 12. The point here is that even without government intervention, if there is demand for green goods and it is technologically possible to produce them environmental quality will be higher if these goods are produced and consumed.

To recap,

production and consumption of green goods lowers the pollution intensity of an economy's output (shifts the MAC curve down), and leads to higher levels of environmental quality.

Summary

In this chapter, examples of decentralized approaches to environmental quality improvement were examined. The first was to rely on liability rules, which require polluters to compensate those they have damaged. In theory, the threat of liability can lead potential polluters to internalize what would ordinarily be external costs. By weighing relative compensation and abatement costs, polluters would be brought to efficient emission levels. While liability doctrines may work well in simple cases of pollution where few people are involved and cause-and-effect linkages are clear, they are unlikely to work reliably in the large-scale, technically complicated environmental problems of contemporary societies.

Second was reliance on the institution of private-property rights. Looked at from this perspective, environmental externalities are problems only because ownership of environmental assets is often not clearly defined. By establishing clear property rights, owners and others who would like to use environmental assets for various purposes can negotiate agreements that balance the relative costs of different alternatives. Thus, negotiations among parties could theoretically bring about efficient emission rates. But problems of transactions costs, especially related to the public goods/open access aspects of environmental quality, and lack of markets for environmental services work against relying primarily on traditional property-rights institutions in environmental quality issues. In Chapter 13, we will see that some new types of property-rights approaches may hold greater promise.

Third was the idea of moral suasion, which may be useful when it is impossible to measure the emissions stemming from particular sources. The problem of free riding was discussed, as was the problem of public disclosure as a means of encouraging ethical behaviour in environmental matters.

Finally, we discussed the introduction of green goods into an economy by the private sector in response to consumer demands for less pollution-intensive products. The greater the proportion of green goods in an economy's output, the lower the level of emissions and higher the level of environmental quality.

Key Terms

Burden of proof

Coase theorem

Compensation

Decentralized techniques

Liability

Negligence

Open access

Private property rights

Property rights

Standing

Strict liability

Transactions costs

Analytical Problems

1. For the example illustrated in Figure 10-1, prove that the socially efficient equilibrium minimizes the chemical factory's total payments (compensation to the salmon fishery plus total abatement costs) compared to any other emission level.

2. Suppose the MD function in the example of the chemical factory and fishery is MD = 8E. Compute the socially efficient equilibrium and determine whether assigning to the factory or fishery the property rights to the river maximizes the sum of net gains after the parties bargain the socially efficient solution. Explain intuitively why this is different than the example in the chapter.

3. Explain and illustrate graphically how the degree of substitution between green goods and pollution-intensive goods affects the level of environmental quality.

4. Assigning liability for pollution damages and assigning property rights to environmental resources can both lead to a socially efficient equilibrium (assuming no transactions costs). Are the net gains to each party also identical? Prove graphically or algebraically.

Discussion Questions

1. In the case of a pollutant that has an uncertain effect on people, the courts could put the burden of proof either on the people damaged to show that they indeed were injured or on the polluters to show that the pollutant is not harmful. What difference would this make to the working of the liability system?

2. Accidents with trucks carrying hazardous wastes have become fairly common. Suppose the perpetrators of any accident of this type are held liable for a sum equal to the average damages done in all such accidents. Would this lead trucking companies to take the efficient amount of precautions against such accidents?

3. Why might side payments between the parties in a bargaining process be necessary to reach social efficiency? (Side payments are transfers from one party to another after an equilibrium has been reached through bargaining.)

Chapter 11

Standards

After reading this chapter you will be able to:

LO 1 | Define and illustrate graphically the socially efficient equilibrium emission standard and explain its advantages.

LO 2 | Describe and contrast the different types of standards that can be introduced as direct regulation.

LO 3 | Explain the complexities introduced in setting standards when marginal damages differ by region or time of day or other factor.

LO 4 | Describe and illustrate graphically how to achieve a cost-effective equilibrium under a standard when the MAC curves for polluters differ.

LO 5 | Explain the degree of flexibility of different types of standards and their ability to spur investment in new technologies that can lower emission intensity.

LO 6 | Describe the challenges faced in enforcement of standards.

LO 1 |

Standards are a type of **command-and-control (CAC)** technique, also known as *direct regulation*. The CAC approach to public policy is one where, in order to bring about behaviour thought to be socially desirable, political authorities simply mandate the behaviour in law, then use whatever enforcement machinery necessary—courts, police, fines—to get people to obey the law. In the case of environmental policy, the command-and-control approach consists of relying on standards of various types to bring about improvements in environmental quality. In general, a standard is simply a mandated level of performance that is enforced in law. A speed limit is a classic type of standard; it sets maximum rates that drivers may legally travel. An **emission standard** is a maximum rate of emissions that is legally allowed. The spirit of a standard is this: If you want people not to do something, simply pass a law that makes it illegal, then send out the authorities to enforce the law.

Figure 11-1 shows hypothetical marginal abatement costs and marginal damages for emissions (E) of carbon monoxide from a plant that recycles asphalt to reuse in road construction.[1] The units of emissions are kilograms per month. Let the equations for the curves be

$$MD = 10E$$
$$MAC = 600 - 5E$$

---

[1] These plants are called "hot-in-place" asphalt recycling plants and are actually mobile factories. They move along the road site, producing recycled asphalt on the spot. Other pollutants they emit include particulate matter and organic material.

FIGURE 11-1 The Socially Efficient Standard

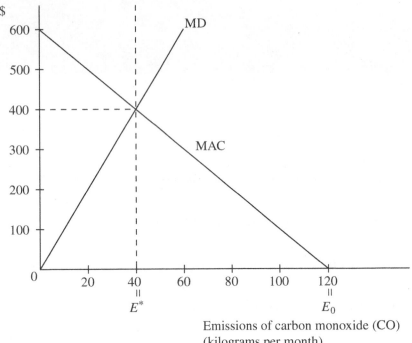

A standard is set where the MD = MAC to determine the socially efficient standard of 40 kilograms of carbon monoxide per month. The standard sets an upper limit on emissions. When the standard is met, the net benefits to society are the difference between total damages at 120 kilograms per month and 40 kilograms per month minus the total abatement costs. Net benefits equal $48,000 per month.

The regulator solves for the socially efficient equilibrium where MD = MAC to obtain the socially efficient pollution level of emissions, E^*. This is the level of emissions that minimizes the sum of abatement plus damage costs and maximizes net social gains. For the equations above, $E^* = 40$ kilograms per month. Before the standard is imposed, the factory releases emissions up to the point where its MAC curve equals 0. Solving the MAC equation above, setting MAC = 0 yields $E_0 = 120$ kilograms per month. To achieve E^* the authorities set an emission standard at 40 kilograms per month. This level becomes a mandated upper limit for the emissions of this factory. If the factory exceeds that level, and is detected doing so, it will be fined or subject to some other penalty. Assuming the factory reduces emissions in accordance with the standard, it would be paying total abatement costs (TAC) equal to the area under its MAC curve from E_0 to E^*. Another name for these total abatement costs is the **compliance costs** of meeting the standard. For this example, compliance costs equal $16,000 when the factory meets the standards. Note that total damages at the socially efficient level are $8,000 per month, compared to $72,000 when there is no control of emissions. The net benefits of the standard are the difference between total damages without the standard ($72,000) and total damages with the standard ($8,000) minus the total abatement costs ($16,000). The net benefits are $48,000 per month.

There are many perceived advantages of using standards to address environmental problems.

Standards

- appear to be simple and direct.

- apparently set clearly specified targets.

- appeal to people's sense of getting environmental pollution reduced immediately.

- are consistent with our ethical sense that pollution is bad and ought to be declared illegal.

- conform to an operation of the legal system, which is to define and stop illegal behaviour.

The standards approach is, however, a lot more complex than it might first appear. In fact, a very practical reason for the popularity of standards is that they may permit far more flexibility in enforcement than might be apparent. What appears to be the directness and unambiguousness of standards becomes a lot more problematic when we look below the surface.

LO 2

TYPES OF STANDARDS

Any action you can think of could be the subject of a standard, but in environmental matters there are three main types of standards: ambient, emission, and technology.

Ambient Standards

Recall from Chapter 2 that ambient environmental quality refers to the qualitative dimensions of the surrounding environment; it could be the ambient quality of the air over a particular city, or the ambient quality of the water in a particular river. An **ambient standard** is a never-exceed level for a pollutant in the ambient environment.

For example, an ambient standard for dissolved oxygen in a particular river may be set at 3 parts per million (ppm), meaning that this is the lowest level of dissolved oxygen that is to be allowed in the river. Ambient standards cannot be enforced directly, of course. What can be enforced are the various emissions that lead to ambient quality levels. To ensure that dissolved oxygen never falls below 3 ppm in the river, we must know how the emissions of the various sources on the river contribute to changes in this measure, then introduce some means of controlling these sources.

Ambient standards are normally expressed in terms of average concentration levels over some period of time. For example, the current national ambient air quality objective for sulphur dioxide (SO_2) has two criteria: a maximum annual average of 23 parts per billion (ppb) and a maximum 24-hour average of 115 ppb.[2] The ambient standard for carbon monoxide from asphalt recycling plants in British Columbia is 500 mg/m^3 for a one-hour average. Refer back to Figure 2-9 to see the different levels of ambient standard for fine particulate matter. The reason for taking averages is to recognize that there are seasonal and daily variations in meteorological conditions, as well as in the emissions that produce variations in ambient quality. Averaging means that short-term ambient quality levels may be worse than the standard, so long as this does not persist for too long and so long as it is balanced by periods when the air quality is better than the standard.

[2.] These are the maximum acceptable concentrations. There are other target levels of concentrations for ambient air quality in Canadian air-quality objectives and standards. We examine these targets in Chapter 17.

Emission Standards

Emission standards are never-exceed levels applied directly to the quantities of emissions coming from pollution sources.

Emission standards can be set on a wide variety of different bases. For example,

1. emission rate (e.g., kilograms per hour),
2. emission concentration (e.g., parts per million of biochemical oxygen demand, or BOD, in wastewater),
3. total quantity of residuals (rate of discharge times concentration times duration),
4. residuals produced per unit of output known as **emissions intensity of pollution** (examples include GHGs per tonne of coal burned, SO_2 emissions per kilowatt hour of electricity produced, grams of CO per tonne of asphalt produced),
5. residuals content per unit of input (e.g., sulphur content of coal used in power generation),
6. percentage removal of pollutant (e.g., 60-percent removal of waste material before discharge).

Continuous emissions streams may be subject to standards on "instantaneous" rates of flow; for example, upper limits on the quantity of residuals flow per minute or on the average residuals flow over some time period.

In the language of regulation, emission standards are a type of **performance standard,** because they refer to end results that polluters who are regulated must achieve. There are many other types of performance standards; for example, workplace standards are set in terms of maximum numbers of accidents or levels of risk to which workers are exposed. A requirement that farmers reduce their use of a particular pesticide below some level is also a performance standard, as is a highway speed limit.

Ambient vs. Emission Standards

There are important distinctions between ambient and emission standards. Setting emission standards at a certain level does not necessarily entail meeting a set of ambient standards. Between emissions and ambient quality stands nature, in particular the meteorological and hydrological phenomena that link the two. The environment usually transports the emissions from point of discharge to other locations, often diluting and dispersing them along the way. Chemical processes that often change the physical character of the pollutant occur in all environmental media. In some cases this may render the emitted substance more benign. Organic wastes put in rivers and streams will normally be subject to natural degradation processes, which will break them down into constituent elements. Thus, the ambient quality of the water at various points downstream depends on the quantity of emissions as well as the hydrology of the river—its rate of flow, temperature, natural reaeration conditions, and so on. Sometimes the environment will convert a certain type of pollutant into something more damaging. Research to link emission levels and ambient quality levels is a major part of environmental science.

The link between emissions and ambient quality can also be vitally affected by human decisions. A classic case is automobiles. As part of the mobile-source air-pollution program, Canada has established emission standards for new cars in terms of emissions per kilometre of operation. But since there is no way of controlling either the number of cars on the roads or the total number of hours each car is driven, the aggregate quantity of pollutants in the air and, thus, ambient air quality is not directly controlled.

Technology Standards

There are numerous standards that don't actually specify some end result, but rather the technologies, techniques, or practices that potential polluters must adopt. We lump these together under the heading of **technology-based standards (TBS).** The requirement that cars be equipped with catalytic converters, or seat belts, is a technology standard. If all electric utilities were required to install stack-gas scrubbers to reduce SO_2 emissions,[3] these would be in effect technology standards, since a particular type of technology is being specified by central authorities. This type of standard also includes what are often called **design standards** or engineering standards. There are also a variety of product standards specifying characteristics that goods must have, and input standards that require potential polluters to use inputs meeting specific conditions. Technology standards often specify that polluters use the *best available technology* (BAT), the *best practicable technology* (BPT), or the *best available technology economically achieveable* (BATEA). Other terms may also be used. BATs are the best possible technology, whether there are any practical applications in use at the time or not. BPTs generally refer to technologies that are known and can be implemented immediately. A BATEA allows some recognition of abatement costs and effect of the technology standard on a firm's profits. Technology-based standards are analyzed and evaluated in more detail in Section 5.

The difference between a performance standard and a technology standard may become blurred at the edges. The basic point of differentiation is that:

- A performance standard, such as an emission standard, sets a constraint on some performance criterion and then allows people to choose the best means of achieving it.

- A technology standard actually dictates certain decisions and techniques to be used, such as particular equipment or operating practices to be used by polluters.

In Canada there are a wide variety of federal and provincial regulations that apply to specific industries. For example, under the *Canadian Environmental Protection Act* (CEPA), there are emission guidelines or regulations for Arctic mineral extraction, asbestos mines and mills, the asphalt paving industry, chloralkali mercury releases, pulp and paper mill effluent, lead, and vinyl chloride, to name a few. Technology standards under CEPA apply to a number of industries including the energy sector, pulp and paper mills, mineral smelters, and many more.

THE ECONOMICS OF STANDARDS

Understanding the way standards work helps us examine the costs of reaching a socially efficient equilibrium using this policy instrument. We can then compare standards to other policy instruments using the criteria developed in Chapter 9. It would seem to be a simple and straightforward thing to achieve better environmental quality by applying standards of various types. But standards turn out to be more complicated than they first appear. In the rest of this chapter we will discuss some of these complications. Section 5 provides many illustrations in Canadian and U.S. environmental policies of the issues identified in this chapter.

[3.] A "scrubber" is a device that treats the exhaust-gas stream so as to remove a substantial proportion of the target substance from that stream. The recovered material must then be disposed of elsewhere.

LO 3

Setting the Level of the Standard in Practice

The first issue is where to set the standard. In the case of the decentralized approaches to pollution control—liability laws and property-rights regimes—there was, at least, the theoretical possibility that the interactions of people involved would lead to efficient outcomes. In theory, setting the level of the standard is even more straightforward. As we have noted many times, the socially efficient standard equates marginal damages to marginal costs. But in practice, standards are often set by examining a narrower set of criteria. Standards emanate from a political/administrative process that may be affected by all kinds of considerations.

You should note that there is, in effect, a certain amount of "balancing" going on when standards are set on the basis of an average over some time period. In this case, short-run periods—when ambient quality is relatively low—are considered acceptable as long as they do not last too long. A judgment is being made, in effect, that it is not necessary to install enough abatement technology to hold ambient quality within the standard under all conceivable natural conditions. In other words, an implicit trade-off is being made between the damages that will result from the temporary deterioration of ambient quality below the standard and the high costs that would be necessary to keep ambient quality within the standard under all conditions.

EXAMPLE

A non-linear marginal damage function

What are some of the approaches that have been taken in practice, and how do they relate to social efficiency? One approach in standard setting has been to try to set ambient or emission standards by reference only to the damage function. A reason for this may be that regulators do not have information about the marginal abatement cost function. The damage function is examined to see if there are significant points where marginal damages change substantially. Figure 11-2 illustrates a different type of marginal damage function than the linear function we have used for analysis. One approach has been to set the standard at a "zero-risk" level; that is, at the level that would protect everyone, no matter how sensitive, from damage. This would imply setting a threshold level, labelled E_T in Figure 11-2. This standard is clearly not socially efficient if the MAC is as shown. Another difficulty is determining whether or not a threshold exists. Recent work by toxicologists and other scientists seems to indicate that there may be no threshold for many environmental pollutants; that, in fact, marginal damage functions are positive right from the origin (the usual way we have drawn the MD curve). If no thresholds exist, a "zero-risk" policy would require that all standards be set at zero. This may be appropriate for some substances—certain highly toxic compounds such as dioxin, for example, where marginal damages are everywhere greater than marginal abatement costs. But for many pollutants, a zero level of emissions would not be socially efficient and would be difficult or impossible to achieve. We might decide, therefore, that we could accept some "reasonably small" damages, in which case we might set it at a place like E_L, the point where the marginal damage function begins to increase very rapidly. Or, if the damage function looks like that in Figure 11-2, where the curve becomes vertical beyond E_{MAX}, a risk-minimizing strategy would be to set E_{MAX} as the "never-exceed" level of emissions. Here again, however, we would be setting the standard without regard to abatement costs. In Figure 11-2, E^* is "close" to E_L and E_{MAX}, but this need not be the case.

(Continued)

FIGURE 11-2   Emissions Standards for Non-linear Marginal Damages

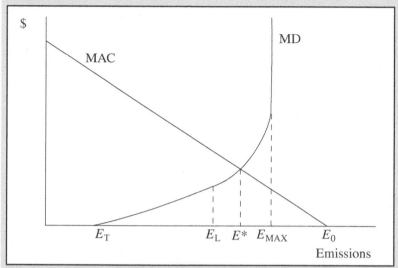

A non-linear marginal damage function illustrates possible levels to set an emission standard when the regulator does not know the exact location of the MAC curve. E_T sets the standard at the minimum threshold at which no damages occur. E_L sets the standard where MD begins to rise rapidly. E_{MAX} is an upper bound on emissions; the point at which the MD curve becomes vertical. None of these are the socially efficient level of E^*.

This example illustrates some key points about standards:

1. Their all-or-nothing quality: either the standard is being met or it isn't.

2. If a standard isn't met, the implication is that it should be, regardless of the cost of doing so.

3. If a standard is being met, the implication is that it is not necessary to do any better, even though the cost of doing so may be quite low.

Uniformity of Standards

A very practical problem in standard setting is whether standards should be applied uniformly to all situations or varied according to circumstances. We can illustrate this using the problem of the spatial uniformity of standards. The ambient air quality standards in the United States, for example, are essentially national. The problem with this is that regions may differ greatly in terms of the factors affecting damage and abatement cost relationships, so that one set of standards, uniformly applied across these local variations, may have serious efficiency implications.

EXAMPLE
Marginal damages that differ among regions
Consider Figure 11-3. It shows two marginal damage functions for carbon monoxide pollution. The first is the MD function from Figure 11-1, which is labelled MD_U because it characterizes an urban area. The second function, labelled MD_R, applies to a rural area.[4] MD_U lies above MD_R because there are many more people living in the urban area, so the same quantity of emissions will affect the health

(Continued)

[4.] The equation for MD_R is $MD_R = 5E$.

of more people there than in the rural region. We assume that marginal abatement costs are the same in the two regions and the same as in Figure 11-1. Since the marginal damages are much higher in the urban than in the rural area, the efficient level of ambient carbon monoxide is much lower in the former than in the latter region; the efficient level is E_R in the rural region and E_U in the urban area. Note that both marginal and total abatement costs will differ at the efficient level of emissions for each region.

FIGURE 11-3 Socially Efficient Standards when Marginal Damages Vary by Region

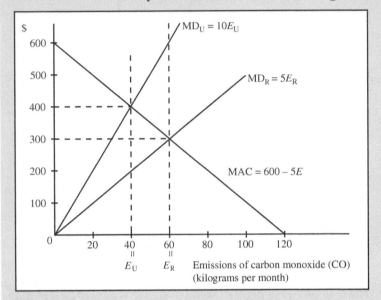

When marginal damages differ by region, standard setting becomes difficult. If marginal damages in urban areas (MD_U) exceed those in rural areas (MD_R), a uniform standard cannot be socially efficient. If set at E_U it over-controls emissions in the rural area; at E_R, emissions in the urban area are under-controlled relative to the socially efficient level where MD = MAC. Individual standards set for each region avoid this problem.

A single, **uniform standard** cannot be efficient simultaneously in the two regions. If it is set at E_U it will be overly stringent for the rural area, and if it is set at E_R it will not be tight enough for the urban region. The only way to avoid this would be to set different standards in the two areas. These can be called **individual standards.** Individual standards create a policy trade-off. Tailoring a policy to heterogeneous situations makes it more efficient in terms of its impacts. But doing so can require much more information to set and enforce the standard. The curves in Figure 11-3 could be used to represent other heterogeneous situations as well as differences in geographical regions. For example, MD_U might represent marginal damages in a particular region under some meteorological conditions, or in one season of the year, while MD_R could represent the marginal damage function for the same area but under different meteorological conditions or at a different time of year. Now a single standard, enforced throughout the year, cannot be efficient at all points in time; if it is efficient at one time, it won't be at the other.

When marginal damages for a particular pollutant differ among sources of the emissions, we will see a dispersion of pollution across sources or regions because the pollutants are not uniformly mixed. This means that regulatory authorities have to monitor ambient environmental quality at different receptor points or monitoring stations within their jurisdiction. A socially efficient equilibrium then requires that the marginal costs of abatement be equal to the marginal damages at each receptor point. This equilibrium can be obtained in theory by imposing standards that reflect the marginal damages of each source at each receptor. Pollution from each source will be translated into ambient concentrations of pollution at each site by using what are called transfer coefficients. A **transfer coefficient** converts emissions from source i into an impact on environmental quality at site j, and is determined by scientific factors such as meteorological relationships and physical/chemical properties of the pollutant. Air-pollution dispersion models have been developed for a number of major urban areas. In practice, as noted above, pollutants that are not uniformly mixed create a much more difficult and costly regulatory environment. We'll return to this problem in Section 5.

To recap,

> *when marginal damages for a pollutant vary by region, time of day, or season, a uniform standard will not be socially efficient. Individual standards that set the MAC equal to each MD are socially efficient.*

LO 4

Standards and the Equimarginal Principle

Having discussed the issue of setting the standard at the efficient level of emissions, we must remember that the efficient level itself is defined by the minimum marginal abatement cost function. Suppose we have a uniformly mixed pollutant released from multiple emissions sources. The equimarginal principle requires that the different sources of emissions must be controlled in such a way that they have the same marginal abatement costs. This means that different sources of a pollutant would normally be controlled to different degrees, depending on the shape of the marginal abatement cost curve at each source. This is a **cost-effective equilibrium**—the total costs of compliance are minimized for a given emissions target. A major problem with standards is that there is almost always an overwhelming tendency for authorities to apply the same standards to all sources. It makes their regulatory lives much simpler, and it gives the impression of being fair to everyone, since all are apparently being treated alike. The key point is that

> *uniform standards will be cost-effective only in the unlikely event that all polluters have the same marginal abatement costs. If MACs for a pollutant differ, individual standards can achieve cost-effectiveness.*

EXAMPLE
Marginal abatement functions that differ between polluters

Consider Figure 11-4, showing the marginal abatement cost relationships for two different sources, each emitting carbon monoxide (the example from previous sections). These polluters are called H and L. Emissions are in kilograms of CO per month. The equations for their MAC functions are:

$$MAC_H = 600 - 5E_H$$

$$MAC_L = 240 - 2E_L$$

(Continued)

FIGURE 11-4   Cost-Effectiveness when Marginal Abatement Cost Curves Differ

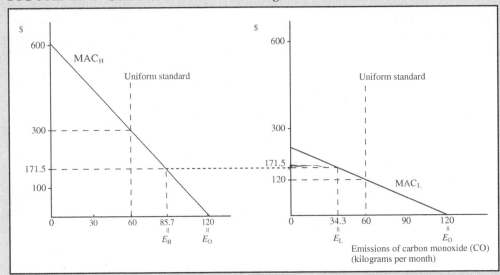

Uniform standards are contrasted with individual standards for two polluters with different MAC curves. A uniform standard set at 60 kilograms/month per polluter violates the equimarginal principle and is, therefore, not cost-effective. At 60 kilograms controlled each, MAC_H greatly exceeds MAC_L. The cost-effective policy is to set individual standards where total emissions equal the target of 120 kilograms, and the MACs of the two polluters are equalized. The individual standards are set at 34.3 kilograms/month for L and 85.7 kilograms/month for H. The cost-effective policy results in lower total costs of abatement to reach the target level of emissions.

Polluter L's abatement costs increase much less rapidly as emissions are reduced than they do for Polluter H. Why the difference? They may be producing different outputs with different technologies. One firm might be older than the other, and older technology may be less flexible, making it more costly to reduce emissions than at the plant with the newer equipment. One plant may be designed to use a different type of raw-material input than the other. This, in fact, mirrors the situation in the real world. Normally one can expect considerable heterogeneity in abatement costs among groups of firms even though they are emitting the same type of residual.

Assume that emissions are currently uncontrolled. Thus, they are 120 kilograms/month at each firm, or a total of 240 kilograms/month. Let us assume now that authorities wish to reduce total emissions to a total of 120 kilograms/month (a 50-percent reduction) by setting emission standards. How should the standards be set? The procedure that may seem most obvious—it certainly has to most environmental regulators—is to apply the same standard to each source; in this case, 60 kilograms/month. This has the superficial appearance of being fair, of treating these sources alike, since each would be reduced in the same proportion from their current levels. Of course, the problem is that the sources are economically *unalike* in that they have significantly different marginal abatement costs. By applying uniform standards to dissimilar sources we violate the equimarginal principle and end up paying far more for a given amount of total emission reduction than we need to pay. Individual standards set where each polluter's MAC equals the MD are cost-effective because they satisfy the equimarginal principle. The proof is as follows:

Proof that a cost-effective policy minimizes total abatement costs

The steps are

1. Compute total abatement costs (TAC) for each polluter under the uniform standard of 60 kilograms/month.

(Continued)

Setting polluter L's MAC to the uniform standards shows that its marginal abatement costs at the standard are $120/kilogram. Doing the same for polluter H yields MAC_H of $300/kilogram.

Total abatement costs are then the area under each polluter's MAC curve from 120 to 60 kilograms. For L, TAC_L = ½(60 times $120) = $3,600. For H, TAC_H = ½(60 times $300) = $9,000. Totalling these abatement costs: $TAC_L + TAC_H$ = $12,600.

2. Compute total abatement costs for each polluter if an individual standard is set that satisfies the equimarginal principle. These are the cost-effective individual standards. This involves some additional calculation.

First, solve for the level of emissions for each polluter that satisfies the equimarginal principle. The easiest method is to use algebra. Two principles are used.

The equimarginal principle requires equality of MACs for the two polluters:

$$MAC_H = MAC_L$$

Substituting in for the MAC equations:

$$600 - 5E_H = 240 - 2E_L \tag{1}$$

Emissions from each polluter must sum to the target level of emissions:

$$E_L + E_H = 120 \text{ kilograms/month} \tag{2}$$

There are thus two equations with two unknowns: E_L and E_H.

Solve the two equations by rewriting the target in terms of one of the emission levels, for example E_L, so equation (2) becomes:

$$E_L = 120 - E_H \tag{2'}$$

Substitute (2') into equation (1):

$$600 - 5E_H = 240 - 2(120 - E_H)$$

Solve for E_H: E_H = 85.7.

Substitute E_H back into either equation (1) or (2) to solve for E_L. E_L = 34.3.

These are each polluter's individual standard.

Substitute E_L and E_H back into each polluter's MAC function to find their MAC at each one's target emission level. We see that $MAC_L = MAC_H$ = approximately $171.5 (there are rounding errors). This calculation proves that the equimarginal principle is satisfied.

Now calculate TACs for each polluter from their initial pollution level of 120 kilograms/month to their individual standard.

$$TAC_L = ½[(120 - 34.3) \text{ times } \$171.5] = \$7,348.78.$$
$$TAC_H = ½[(120 - 85.7) \text{ times } \$171.5] = \$2,941.22.$$

Total abatements costs are $TAC_L + TAC_H$ = $10,290.

3. Compare total TAC under the uniform standard to the cost-effective individual standards:

Uniform standard total TAC = $12,600

Cost-effective individual standards = $10,290.

Proof completed: The cost-effective individual standards achieve the same emission reduction at lower total costs to society.

These results can be interpreted in another way. For the $12,600 compliance cost of the uniform-standards case, we could achieve a larger reduction in total emissions if we cut back in accordance with the equimarginal principle. If polluter L is restricted to 20 emissions of kilograms/month (total cost: $10,000) and polluter H to emissions of 88 kilograms/month (total cost: $2,560), total compliance costs are about the same as the uniform-standards case but with lower total emissions (108 kilograms/month rather than 120 kilograms/month).

In summary, most standards are uniform across emission sources. This practice is almost inherent in the basic philosophy of the standards approach, and this strikes many people as an equitable way to proceed. This section has illustrated a very important point:

When marginal abatement costs vary across sources, the uniform-standards approach will produce less reduction in total emissions for the total compliance costs of the program, or cost more for a given target than would be achieved with a cost-effective approach that satisfies the equimarginal principle.

The greater the differences in marginal abatement costs among sources, the worse will be the performance of the equal-standards approach. We will see in the chapters ahead that this difference can be very large indeed.

Could standards be set in accordance with the equimarginal principle? Unless the applicable law required some sort of equiproportional cutback, the authorities could set different standards for the individual sources. To get an overall reduction to 120 kilograms/month in the example above, they could require polluter L to reduce to 34.3 kilograms/month and polluter H to cut back to 85.7 kilograms/month. The difficult part, however, is that to accomplish this the authorities must know what the marginal abatement costs are for the different sources. We need to stress this strongly. For almost any real-world pollution problem there will normally be multiple sources. Thus,

to set individual standards in accordance with the equimarginal principle, regulators would have to know the marginal abatement cost relationship for each polluting source.

It would take a prodigious effort for any agency to get high-quality information on marginal abatement costs for many different sources, each perhaps producing different outputs using different production technology and methods. The primary source of data would have to be the polluters themselves, and there is no reason to believe they would willingly share this information. In fact, if they realize—as they certainly would—that the information would be used to establish individual source standards, they would have every incentive to provide the administering agency with data showing that their marginal abatement costs rise very steeply with emission reductions. Thus, there are real problems with authorities attempting to establish source-specific emission standards. Nevertheless, a considerable amount of this is done informally, through the interactions of local pollution-control authorities, charged with enforcing common standards, and local sources, each of whom is in somewhat different circumstances. This issue emerges again in the discussion of enforcement.

INCENTIVE EFFECTS OF STANDARDS

As discussed in Chapter 9, one important aspect of evaluating any policy is to look at what sort of incentive effects it has on the polluter. There are short-run and long-run impacts.

In the short run, the question is whether the policy creates incentives for sources to reduce emissions to efficient levels in a cost-effective way. The command-and-control approach based on standards is seriously deficient in this regard. A basic problem is that standards are all-or-nothing: either they are being met or they are not. *If they are being met, there is no incentive to do any better than the standard,* even though the costs of further emission reductions might be quite low. As well, polluters have to meet the standard (or face penalties) even if the costs of complying may be much more than the damages reduced.

Standards also take decision flexibility away from the polluter. This is especially so for technology-based standards, which dictate the procedures that polluters must follow, even though other procedures may be available to achieve the pollution target at lower cost. If control authorities dictate in detail the specific technology and practices that polluters may legally use to reduce emissions, polluters may be motivated to avoid other techniques in order to protect themselves against charges of non-compliance, even if these other approaches may be cheaper. Rather than leave firms free to use their own creativity in devising the technological means to achieve a goal, a technology standard instead places the burden on the public authority to make the correct technology decisions.

In the long run, a desirable quality for a pollution-control policy is to produce strong incentives to search for technical and managerial changes that will make it less costly to achieve a target level of emissions (or reach a lower level of emissions). How well do standards perform according to this criterion?

It is easy to deal with technology-based standards. Here the incentives to find cheaper ways (considering all costs) of reducing emissions are effectively zero. If regulators dictate the specific technology and practices that polluters may legally use to reduce emissions, there are no rewards to finding better approaches. But what are the incentives under emission standards? The following example shows how to measure these graphically.

EXAMPLE
Incentives to invest in new technologies under emission standards
Figure 11-5 shows marginal abatement costs of a firm in two situations. MAC_1 refers to such costs before a given technological improvement. MAC_2 is the marginal abatement cost curve the firm could expect to have after investing resources in R&D to develop better treatment or recycling technology. To be concrete, let

$$MAC_1 = 200 - 5E$$

$$MAC_2 = 160 - 4E$$

$$MD = 5E$$

(Continued)

FIGURE 11-5 Incentives to Invest in New Pollution-Control Technology under a Standard

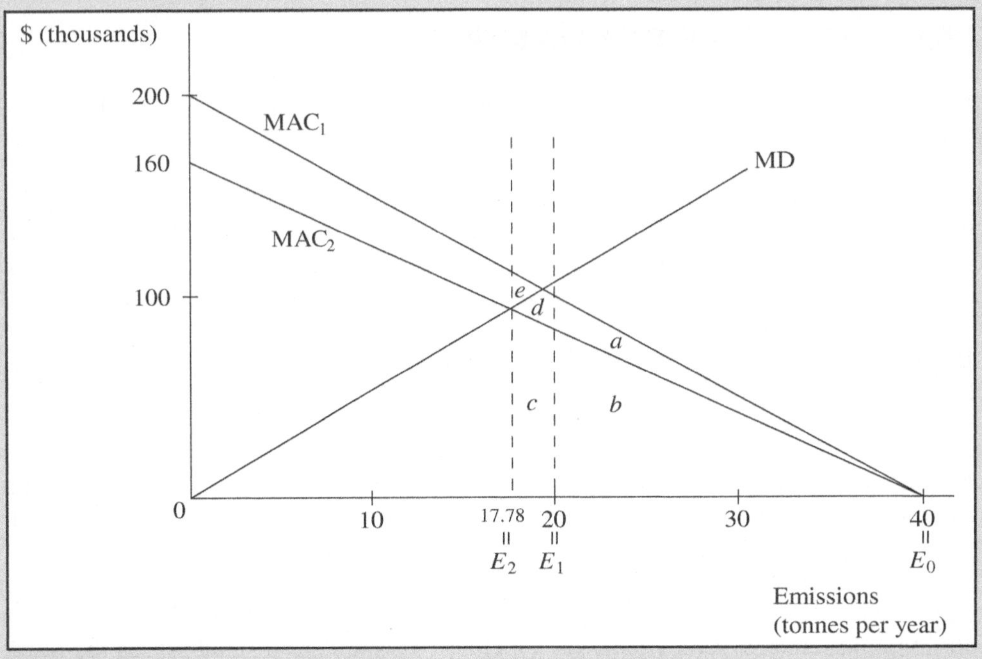

The incentive to adopt cost-saving technologies is area a if the regulator keeps the emission standard at E_1 after the adoption of new technology reduces MAC_1 to MAC_2. If the regulator tightens the standard to E_2, the incentives to adopt the technology are much weaker and equal area $(a - c)$. A technology-forcing standard could be set initially at E_2. This would create cost savings to the polluter equal to areas $(a + d + e)$ if it adopts the new technology.

Without any pollution regulations at all there is absolutely no incentive to spend the money on the R&D. But suppose the firm is now faced with having to meet emission standards of $E_1 = 20$ tonnes/year (the socially efficient equilibrium). With the original marginal abatement costs the total annual cost of compliance for this firm is area $(a + b) = \$1$-million per year (the units on Figure 11-5 are in thousands of dollars). If the R&D program is successful, MAC_1 pivots down to MAC_2 and compliance costs would be area $b = \$800,000$/year. The $\$200,000$ yearly difference (area a) is the amount by which compliance costs would be reduced and represents, in fact, the incentive for engaging in the R&D effort. We will see in the next chapter that this is a weaker effect than is provided by economic-incentive types of programs. Nevertheless, it is an incentive, which is more than we could say for technology standards.

The complete logic of standard setting may do much to undermine the incentive described in the example. Suppose authorities are making every effort to set the standard at something approaching the efficient level of emissions. In Figure 11-5, E_1 is their view of the efficient level before the technical change. But the new technology lowers the marginal abatement cost curve, and we know from Chapter 5 that this will reduce the efficient level of emissions. Suppose the authorities estimate that, given their view of marginal damages, the new technology shifts the efficient emission level to $E_2 = 17.78$ tonnes per year in Figure 11-5—and that they now change the standard to reflect this. Now the firm's compliance cost will be $(b + c) = \$987,457$ per year. The polluter's cost savings is the difference $(a - c) = \$200,000 - \$187,457 = \$12,543$. This cost savings is substantially less than when the standard remained at 20 tonnes per year and may not be sufficient to offset the R&D costs the polluter incurs. Polluters could suppose that because of the way regulators may tighten the standards, they would be worse off with the new technology than with the old methods. The standard-setting procedure in this case undermines the incentive to produce new pollution-control technology.

If emission standards create incentives for technological change, is it not desirable to establish very stringent standards so as to increase that incentive? If, in Figure 11-5, the standard is set at $E_2 = 17.78$ tonnes/year right at the beginning, this would mean cost savings of $(a + d + e)$ with the new technology rather than just a, as it would be with the standard set at E_1. This type of approach goes under the heading of **technology-forcing standards.** The principle of technology forcing is to set standards that are unrealistic with today's technology in the hope that it will motivate the pollution-control industry to invent ways of meeting the standard at reasonable cost. By "unrealistic with today's technology," we mean simply so costly that it would lead to widespread economic hardship. Would a technology-forcing standard improve incentives? We leave this as an exercise.

But stricter standards also create another incentive: the incentive for polluters to seek relief from public authorities through delaying the date when they become applicable. Polluters may take some of the resources that might have gone for pollution-control R&D and devote them instead to influencing political authorities to delay the onset of strict standards. The stricter and more near-term the standards, the more of this activity there is likely to be. Thus, technology forcing is another one of those strategies where the effectiveness of moderate amounts does not imply that more will be even more effective.

To a significant extent, new R&D for pollution control is carried out by a pollution-control industry rather than the polluting industries themselves. Thus, to draw conclusions about the incentives of pollution-control policy for technological change means to predict how these policies will contribute to the growth and productivity of the pollution-control industry. Technology standards are stultifying on these grounds because they substantially drain off the incentives for entrepreneurs in the pollution-control industry to develop new ideas. Emission standards are better in this respect, as we have seen. The evidence for this is the fact that representatives of the pollution-control industry usually take the side politically of stricter environmental standards; in fact, they see the fortunes of their industry tied almost directly to the degree of stringency in the emissions standards set by public authorities.

LO 6

THE ECONOMICS OF ENFORCEMENT

The typical pollution-control law incorporates standards calling for some degree of emissions reduction from current levels, or the adoption of specified pollution-control technologies. When we evaluate these policies based on expected results, we often assume implicitly that the penalties written into the law will be sufficient to produce complete compliance. But this is in fact never the case. Pollution-control laws, like any others, require enforcement, and this takes resources. Since public enforcement agencies always work under limited budgets, it is not a foregone conclusion that enough resources will ever be devoted to enforcement to achieve acceptable levels of compliance. In fact, the notion of "acceptable" is itself subject to debate.

EXAMPLE
The impact of enforcement costs on standards

Like lots of other problems in economics and the allocation of resources, enforcement involves a trade-off, here between the resources used for this activity, which have opportunity costs, and benefits in the form of greater degrees of compliance. This trade-off is shown in Figure 11-6. MD and MAC are the

(Continued)

marginal damage and marginal abatement cost curves, shown as non-linear in this figure because we will not be computing any areas numerically. The curves labelled C_1 and C_2 are curves that combine marginal abatement costs and marginal enforcement costs. Note that these begin at E_1, which is somewhat to the left of the uncontrolled emission rate E_0. When an emission standard is set at E^*, some degree of voluntary compliance may be expected to occur—in this case from E_0 to E_1. But to get emission reductions beyond E_1 requires explicit enforcement resources. Curves C_1 and C_2 correspond to different technologies of enforcement. We have normally thought of E^* as the efficient level of emissions, but when enforcement costs are present this is no longer the case. With relatively high enforcement costs (curve C_1), the socially efficient rate of emissions is E_2. At this point total emission-reduction costs are equal to $(a + b)$ of enforcement costs and $(c + d)$ of abatement costs.

FIGURE 11-6 The Economics of Enforcement

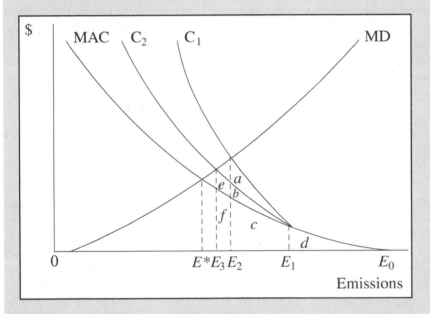

The economics of enforcement are illustrated. Compliance costs, shown by C_1 and C_2, are the sum of the MACs of polluters plus all costs of monitoring and enforcement. The higher the compliance costs, the less stringent the standard. With high compliance costs (C_1), the emission standard is E_2. Total emission costs are $(a + b)$ of enforcement costs plus $(c + d)$ of abatement costs. With lower compliance costs, C_2, the standard can be more stringent at E_3.

The technology of enforcement includes many things: the monitoring of equipment, the expertise of personnel, the operation of the court system, and so on. When changes occur in any of these factors, the effect is to shift the combined cost curve; in Figure 11-6 it shifts to C_2. This leads to a change in the efficient level of emissions to E_3; at this point, total emission-reduction costs would be made up of $(e + b)$ of enforcement costs plus $(f + c + d)$ of abatement costs.

When enforcement costs are included in the analysis, it brings up the question of whether standards should be set, at least in part, with enforcement costs in mind. Stricter standards may involve larger enforcement costs because they require larger operating changes on the part of sources. Less strict standards may be achievable with fewer enforcement resources, for the opposite reason. Public environmental agencies are usually operating with limited budgets. In some cases, greater overall reductions in emissions may be obtained by using less strict standards that can be easily enforced rather than by using stricter standards that involve higher enforcement costs.

However, it needs to be stressed that the "strictness" of the standard is not the only factor affecting enforcement costs. A critical element in enforcement is the size of the sanction written into the laws. Most pollution-control statutes contain provisions on the size of the fine (or jail term) that may be levied against violators, if and when they are caught and found guilty. In many cases, especially when legislation was first introduced, fines have been set too low, lower than the abatement costs required to meet the standards. In these situations firms can actually save money by dragging their feet on compliance. With low sanctions, enforcement may be more difficult and costly than if sanctions are higher. Sources faced with the possibility of having to pay substantially higher fines would presumably have a stronger incentive to come into compliance. In recent years, penalties for failure to comply with Canadian environmental regulations have increased dramatically and there is evidence that the sanctions are providing sufficient incentives to comply with legislation. Keep in mind, however, the paradoxical effect mentioned earlier: If laws attempt to set fines that are extremely high, this could actually dissuade local administrators and courts from pursuing violators vigorously, because of the economic dislocation that would result.

With limited enforcement budgets regulators must often rely on **self-monitoring,** where sources themselves keep the books on emissions flows over time. Self-monitoring is done in many jurisdictions for not only pollution levels but compliance with regulations such as food safety. It is common in Canadian environmental protection. This permits the regulator to visit periodically to audit the records at each source or to make random checks to measure emissions. The rate of auditing and random visits can be varied according to agency budgets. Rates of compliance will certainly be a function of the resources devoted to monitoring, but tolerable levels of compliance may still be attainable with self-monitoring and random visits. Why would a polluter report honestly? The typical reason is a strong incentive to do so provided by the system of fines. Those who fail to report a violation and are detected may face a fine substantially larger than the one incurred for self-reporting a violation. A cynic, or a political realist, might conclude that standards approaches are favoured because of the very fact that, in the real world of tight public-agency budgets, they permit partial or incomplete compliance. The evidence on the degree of compliance under self-monitoring is difficult to ascertain. There are reports that show good results, for example in the chemical industry's Responsible Care program. See Chapter 18 for more details on toxics regulation. In the case of Alberta's system of reporting water pollution, there may be significant under-reporting from oil sands extraction, a topic we address in Chapter 16.

One very common feature of environmental standards is that they are usually set and enforced by different groups of people. Standards are often set by national authorities; enforcement is usually done by local authorities. For example, the air-quality standards established under the *Canadian Environmental Protection Act* are set at the federal level, but much of the enforcement is carried out by provincial agencies. This has a number of important implications. One is that standards can be set without much thought to costs of enforcement; it is more or less assumed that local authorities will find the necessary enforcement resources. Of course, this is often not the case in practice. Another implication is that the standards may end up having a lot more flexibility than might at first appear. Laws written at national levels are specific and apparently applicable everywhere. But at the local level, local pollution-control authorities may be a lot more "flexible" in their enforcement of the standards, due to limited budgets and pressure from local interest groups (the polluters).

Technology standards allow the same flexibility in enforcement. Here we have to distinguish between initial compliance and continued compliance. Initial compliance is the situation where a polluter installs the appropriate equipment to meet the TBS. To monitor initial compliance it is necessary to have inspectors visit the site, check to see that the equipment is installed, and make sure it will operate in accordance with the conditions of the standard. Having ascertained this, the administering agency can then give the firm the necessary operating permit. But this does not ensure that the equipment will continue to be operated in the future in accordance with the terms of the permit. It may deteriorate through normal use, it may not be maintained properly, future operating personnel may not be properly trained, and so on. Without some amount of monitoring, therefore, there is no assurance that the source will continue to be in compliance.

It is important to note in any discussion of enforcement that all policies require monitoring to ensure compliance. As we'll see, policies may differ in terms of the amount and nature of the monitoring required. This is turn affects compliance costs.

Summary

The most popular approach to environmental pollution control historically has been the setting of standards. This has been called the "command-and-control" approach because it consists of public authorities announcing certain limits on polluters, then enforcing these limits with appropriate enforcement institutions. We specified three primary types of standards: ambient, emission, and technology. Initial discussion centred on the level at which standards should be set and the regional uniformity of standards.

A leading problem with standard setting is the question of cost-effectiveness and the equimarginal principle. Many regulations set uniform standards for all sources of a particular pollutant. But pollution control can be cost-effective only when marginal abatement costs are equalized across sources. When marginal abatement costs differ among sources, as they almost always do, uniform standards cannot be cost-effective; individual standards are required.

We examined the incentives standards might have to look for better ways of reducing emissions. Emission standards do create positive incentives for R&D in pollution control, though we will see that these are weaker than those of economic-incentive types of pollution-control policies, the subject of the next two chapters. Technology standards completely undermine these incentives. Finally, we discussed the all-important question of enforcement and the complexities it introduces to pollution control.

Key Terms

Ambient standard	Individual standards
Command-and-control (CAC)	Performance standard
Compliance costs	Self-monitoring
Cost-effective equilibrium	Technology-based standards (TBS)
Design standards	Technology-forcing standards
Emissions intensity of pollution	Transfer coefficient
Emission standard	Uniform standard

Analytical Problems

1. Solve for the two socially efficient equilibria for the two MD functions in Figure 11-3. Suppose the regulatory authority imposes a uniform standard at the emission level mid-way between the two socially efficient emission levels. What are the excess damages from under-control in the urban area and over-control of damages in the rural area?

2. Consider the example of Figure 11-4. Suppose we define as "fair" a cutback in which the two polluters have the same total costs. Would an equi-proportionate reduction be fair in this sense? A reduction meeting the equimarginal principle? Is this a reasonable definition of "fair"?

3. Using Figure 11-5, would area c ever be larger than area a? In other words, can you prove that a technological change that reduces compliance costs (lowers a polluter's MAC) could actually make the polluter worse off than without the technological change? Explain your result.

4. Again using Figure 11-5 and the equations underlying it, show the impact of a technology-forcing standard on a polluter's incentive to invest in R&D to reduce compliance costs.

Discussion Questions

1. List and explain, using graphs to assist your answer, three problems with technology-based standards.

2. What kind of standard would you recommend for a nonpoint pollution source (e.g., runoff of pesticides from agricultural and home use) where emissions per polluter cannot be measured? Explain why.

3. Suppose a regulatory agency has a limited budget for enforcement. Is it better from society's viewpoint to use its limited resources to monitor sources that emit large amounts of pollution and prosecute them vigorously if they violate the standard, or to monitor all polluters? Defend your viewpoint.

4. People have suggested that it would be equitable for all countries to adopt the same emission standards. If, for example, the United States has higher standards than Canada, Canada would be able to produce pollution-intensive goods more cheaply, gaining an advantage in the world marketplace, and also might become a pollution haven (recall the discussion from Chapter 1). From what you have covered in this chapter, do you agree with this suggestion? What are the pros and cons from an economic standpoint?

Chapter 12

Emission Taxes and Subsidies

After reading this chapter you will be able to:

LO 1 Explain and show graphically how a polluter responds to an emission tax set by the government regulator and show how to calculate the polluter's compliance costs.

LO 2 Derive the socially efficient tax rate and illustrate graphically the costs to the polluter, the benefits to society, and the net social benefits.

LO 3 Prove that any tax rate set by the government is cost effective.

LO 4 Explain how an emission tax differs from a uniform standard in terms of social compliance costs and cost effectiveness.

LO 5 Contrast the impact of an emission tax with standards with respect to government revenues, incentives to innovate, enforcement costs, and distributional impacts.

LO 6 Explain how an emission subsidy works and how it differs from an emission tax.

If we want to build a house, we have to buy building materials; nobody is likely to give them to us free. If we want to have architects and carpenters work on the house, we will have to hire them; they won't work for nothing. In other words, in order to use the services of these inputs, we have to pay for them. We are used to doing this, because these goods and services are bought and sold in well-developed markets. The fact that we have to pay for them gives us an incentive to use the inputs as sparingly and efficiently as possible. The economic-incentive approach to environmental policy works in much the same way. Until recently people have been able to use the waste-disposal services of the environment virtually without cost, so there has been little incentive for them to think about the environmental consequences of their actions and to economize on the use of these environmental resources. The incentive approach seeks to change this situation.

There are basically two types of **market-based incentive policies:** (1) taxes and subsidies and (2) transferable emission permits. Both require a regulator to put the program into effect and to monitor outcomes, so they are less decentralized than liability laws or letting parties bargain over emission levels. Regulators set a price for pollution via taxes and subsidies and set quantities of allowed emissions with transferable emission permits. The market determines the price of pollution under the permit approach. Under each policy, polluters make their own decisions about the amount of pollution to emit based on the prices per unit pollution they face. Governments worldwide are increasingly turning to economic incentives, including some examples in Canada.

In the United States and Europe, emission markets have been in place for a number of years; for sulphur dioxide in the U.S. and greenhouse gases in Europe. This chapter examines the economic theory of emission charges and subsidies; Chapter 13 covers the technique of using transferable emission permits. Chapters 17 and 20 look at policies in Canada and other countries in practice.

Economists have long promoted the idea of incorporating incentive-based policies more thoroughly into environmental policies.[1] Incentive-based policies can be more cost effective than standards and provide more stimulus for polluters to seek cost-reducing abatement strategies. But keep in mind something we have said before: *No single type of policy is likely to be the best in all circumstances.* Incentive-based policies are no exception. They have strengths and they have weaknesses. The strengths are sufficiently strong to encourage greater reliance on them in many circumstances. But there are types of environmental problems where they may not be as useful as other approaches, and politically, they may be more challenging to install than standards. Chapter 14 looks in more detail at the tradeoffs among policies and why polluters and regulators may favour one type over another

EMISSION TAXES

The most straightforward incentive-based approach to controlling emissions of a particular residual is to have a public agency offer a financial incentive to change those emissions. This can be done in two ways: by taxing each unit of emissions, or by giving a subsidy for each unit of emissions that the source cuts back.

We deal first with emission taxes, sometimes also called *emission charges*. Emission taxes imply that polluters are able to discharge any amount of the taxed pollutant they wish, but they will be required to pay a tax for every unit (e.g., tonne) discharged. For example, the British Columbia government has imposed a carbon tax in 2008 on over 75 percent of the greenhouse gases emitted in the province as a means of reducing carbon dioxide emissions and ameliorating global warming. B.C.'s goal is to reduce carbon emissions by one-third of their 2007 level by 2020 and to be 80 percent below 2007 levels by 2050. When an emission tax is put into effect, those responsible for emissions must pay for the services of the environment—transportation, dilution, chemical decomposition—just as they must pay for all other inputs or goods they use. Once pollution is "priced" by the tax, those who release it will have an incentive to release less of it; that is, to conserve on their use of environmental services. How do they do this? Any way they wish (within reason). This may sound flippant, but in fact it represents the main advantage of this technique. By leaving polluters free to determine how best to reduce emissions, they can use their own energy and creativity, and their desire to minimize costs, to find the least-cost way of reducing emissions. It could be any combination of pollution abatement, substitution of one good for another, internal process changes, changes in inputs, recycling, or shifts to less-polluting outputs. In the case of B.C.'s carbon tax, people may reduce their dependence on motor vehicles by driving less, taking public transit, car pooling, adding more insulation to their homes to reduce heating costs. Industries may shift from higher carbon-intensive fuels such as petroleum and coal to less carbon-intensive fuels such as natural gas or electricity, which in B.C. is predominately produced by hydro-power and hence, carbon free. More detail on B.C.'s carbon tax is provided below.

The essence of the tax approach is to provide an incentive for the polluters themselves to find the best way to reduce emissions, rather than having a central authority determine how it should be done.

---

[1] An economist who emphasized the role of taxes as a method of internalizing externalities was A.C. Pigou, way back in the 1930s. Environmental taxes are sometimes called *Pigouvian taxes* after him.

LO 1

The Basic Economics of Emission Taxes

The essential mechanics of an emission tax are depicted in Figure 12-1. The numbers refer to a single source of a particular pollutant who has a marginal abatement cost function of $MAC = 200 - 4E$. Assume that the regulator has set the emission tax at $100 per tonne per month. The top panel shows the analysis numerically, while the bottom shows the same information graphically. The second column of the table shows the firm's marginal abatement costs and the third column shows total abatement costs at each emission level. The last two columns show the total monthly tax bill the firm would pay at different emission levels and the **total private cost of compliance.**

FIGURE 12-1 **The Basic Economics of an Emission Tax**

Emissions (tonnes/month)	Marginal abatement cost	Total abatement cost	Total tax bill at tax of $100/tonne	Total polluter's costs ($)
50	0	0	5,000	5,000
45	20	50	4,500	4,550
40	40	200	4,000	4,200
35	60	450	3,500	3,950
30	80	800	3,000	3,800
25	100	1,250	2,500	3,750
20	120	1,800	2,000	3,800
15	140	2,450	1,500	3,950
10	160	3,200	1,000	4,200
5	180	4,050	500	4,550
0	200	5,000	0	5,000

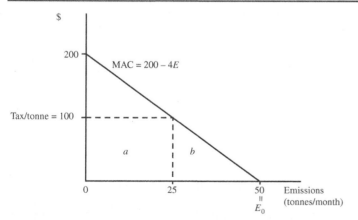

An emissions tax of $100 per tonne of pollutant released per month is levied on a polluter. The table shows marginal and total abatement costs, the polluter's tax bill, and total costs. Total costs are minimized at discharges of 25 tonnes/month. This is shown graphically as the point where the tax rate intersects the polluter's MAC curve. Area a is the tax bill; area b shows the total abatement costs.

Total private cost of compliance of an emission tax is defined as the sum of abatement costs and the tax bill for the polluter.

As we'll see, these are not the same as social costs. The minimum total cost of $3,750 occurs at an emission rate of 25 tonnes/month. The logic behind this can be seen by considering marginal abatement costs. With no regulation, the polluter emits at $E_0 = 50$ tonnes/month and pays a tax bill of $5,000 (i.e., 50 tonnes times $100); if it were to cut emissions to 45 tonnes it would cost $50 in abatement costs, but on the other hand it would save $500 in taxes—clearly a good move. Following this logic, it could improve its bottom line by continuing to reduce emissions as long as the tax rate is above marginal abatement costs. The rule for the firm to follow is this: reduce emissions until marginal abatement costs are equal to the emissions tax rate. This is shown diagrammatically in the bottom part of Figure 12-1. To reiterate,

polluters will minimize their total private costs by reducing emissions until the tax rate equals their marginal abatement cost.

After the polluter has reduced its emissions to 25 tonnes/month, its total (monthly) tax bill will be $2,500. Its monthly abatement costs will be $1,250. Graphically, total abatement costs correspond to the area under the marginal abatement cost function, labelled *b* in the figure. The total tax bill is equal to emissions times tax rate, or the rectangle labelled *a*. Total private cost is thus area (*a* + *b*).

Suppose the polluter is a firm. Why wouldn't the firm simply disregard the tax, continue to pollute the way it has been, and just pass the tax on to consumers in the form of higher prices? If the firm stayed at 50 tonnes of emissions, its total outlay would be $5,000 per month, consisting entirely of tax payment. This is much higher than the $3,750 it can achieve by cutting back to 25 tonnes/month. If a firm operates in a perfectly competitive environment, it survives by maximizing its profits. Emission taxes raise the costs of the firm. Therefore, to maximize profits, the firm must do whatever it can to minimize its total costs inclusive of the emission taxes. The response will depend on several factors. The higher the tax, the greater the reduction, and vice versa. In the example of Figure 12-1, a tax of $50 would have led the source to reduce emissions only to 37.5 tonnes/month, while a tax of $180 would have produced a cutback to 5 tonnes/month. Also, the steeper the marginal abatement cost function, the less will emissions be reduced in response to a tax. We will come back to this below. Recognize, however, that if firms do not operate in perfectly competitive markets, a tax will not work in the way we have shown. Also, firms that sell their products in international markets and compete against others who do not pay environmental taxes may be unable to pass any of the tax along to consumers.

Emission Taxes vs. A Standard

Compare the tax approach with an emission standard. With the tax, the firm's total outlay is $3,750. Suppose that, instead, the authorities had relied on an emission standard to get the firm to reduce emissions to 25 tonnes/month. In that case, the firm's total outlay would be only the $1,250 in abatement costs. Thus, the tax system ends up costing the firm more than the standards approach. With a standard, the firm has the same total abatement costs as in the tax system but it is still essentially getting the services of the environment free, while with a tax system it has to pay for those services.

But while polluting firms would thus prefer standards to emission taxes, there are good reasons, as we shall see, why society would often prefer taxes over standards.

The Socially Efficient Tax

In competitive situations, higher taxes will bring about greater reductions in emissions, but just how high should the tax be set? If we know the marginal abatement cost and marginal damage function, the economist's answer is to set the tax so as to produce the efficient level of emissions, as in Figure 12-2. A marginal damage function, $MD = 4E$, is added to the MAC curve from Figure 12-1. Equating MD to MAC yields the socially efficient tax rate of $100 per tonne. If the regulator knows both functions, the tax per unit pollution is thus readily calculated.

FIGURE 12-2 A Socially Efficient Emission Tax

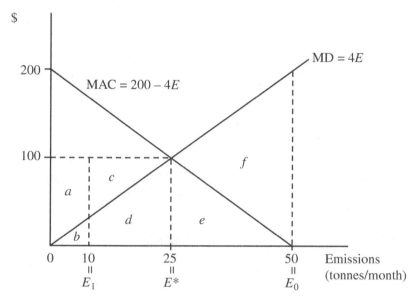

The socially efficient equilibrium is reached with a tax set equal to $100 per tonne. This is the "price" at which MD = MAC. The polluter's private costs of compliance are its total tax bill paid, area ($a + b + c + d$), plus its total abatement costs, area e. Total social costs of compliance are just the TAC. The net benefit of the tax is the total damages forgone, area ($e + f$) net of TAC. This is area f.

What are the compliance costs of the tax policy? We must distinguish between private and social costs. We have already defined private costs of compliance as the polluter's total abatement costs plus its tax bill. In Figure 12-2, private costs are, respectively, area e, which is $1/2[(100 \times 25)] = \$1,250$, plus the tax bill, which is areas ($a + b + c + d$) and totals $3,750. But private costs of compliance do not represent the real resource cost society incurs as a result of levying the emission tax. It is social costs that society is interested in.

> *Social costs of compliance include only the real resources used to meet the environmental target; they do not include the tax bill.*

Taxes are actually **transfer payments,** payments made by the polluters to the public sector and eventually to those in society who are benefited by the resulting public expenditures. The polluter itself may be a recipient of some of these benefits. Transfer payments are therefore not a social cost of the policy. Thus, the social costs of compliance are area *e,* the polluter's total abatement costs.

Society is also interested in the net social benefits from the tax policy.

> *Net social benefits of a policy are defined as the total damages forgone net of the social costs of compliance.*

EXAMPLE
Compute net social benefits for Figure 12-2
The steps are as follows:

1. Compute total damages forgone.

    Total damages forgone is measured by the area under the MD curve from the initial level of emissions to the socially efficient level, E^*.

    This is areas $(e + f) = \$3,750$.

2. Compute total abatement costs.

    TAC = area $e = \$1,250$.

3. Compute net social benefits.

    Net social benefits = total damages forgone minus total abatement costs.

    Net social benefits = areas $(e + f)$ minus area $e = \$2,500$.

Compare the net social benefits of the emission to a standard set at the socially efficient level of emissions, 25 tonnes per month. The net benefits of the standard are identical. Thus a tax and standard, set at the same level, yield identical net benefits to society. What differs is the impact on the polluters.

The reduction of emissions from $E_0 = 50$ to $E^* = 25$ tonnes per month has eliminated damages of $(e + f)$, which are the net gains to victims, given by the difference between areas $(b + d + e + f)$ minus $(b + d) = \$3,750$. Remaining damages are $(b + d)$, an amount less than the firm pays in taxes. This underscores the idea that the emission tax is based on the right to use environmental resources, not on the notion of compensation. But a "flat tax" like this (one tax rate for all emissions) has been criticized because it would often lead to situations where the total tax payments of firms would substantially exceed remaining damages. A way around this is to institute a **two-part emission tax.** We allow some initial quantity of emission to go untaxed, applying the tax only to emissions in excess of this threshold. For example, in Figure 12-2 we might allow the firm $E_1 = 10$ tonnes of emissions free of tax, and apply the tax rate of $100 per tonne to anything over this. In this way the firm would still have the incentive to reduce emissions to E^*, but its total tax payments would be only $(c + d)$. Total abatement costs, and total damages caused by the E^* units of emissions, would still be the same.

How could regulators introduce an emission tax if they do not know the marginal damage function? We know that emissions are connected to ambient quality; in general, the lower the emissions the lower the ambient concentration of the pollutant. So one strategy might be to set a tax and then watch carefully to see what effect this had in terms of improving ambient quality levels. The regulator would have to wait long enough to give firms time to respond to the tax. If ambient quality did not improve as much as desired, increase the tax; if ambient quality improved more than was thought appropriate, lower the tax. This is a successive approximation process of finding the correct long-run emissions tax. It might be a good idea, however, for regulators to give polluters some advance warning of any rate changes. In responding to a tax, polluters might invest in a variety of pollution-control devices and practices, many of which would have relatively high upfront costs. This investment process could be substantially upset if, shortly afterward, the authorities shift to a substantially different tax rate.[2] The setting of the tax could become politicized as a result. While it is better to find the correct tax rate when the policy is introduced, taxes at least allow for the possibility of iterating to the socially efficient tax rate. There is no way to do this with a standard. This issue will be examined in detail in Chapter 14.

LO 3

Emission Taxes and Cost-Effectiveness

Perhaps the strongest case for a policy of emission taxes is to be made on grounds of cost-effectiveness; that is, when controlling multiple sources of emissions in a way that satisfies the equimarginal principle. If we apply the same tax rate to different sources with different marginal abatement cost functions, and each source reduces its emissions until their marginal abatement costs equal the tax, then marginal abatement costs will automatically be equalized across all the sources. To repeat,

> *the imposition of an emission tax will automatically satisfy the equimarginal principle because all polluters will set the tax equal to their MAC curve. MACs will be equalized across all sources.*

This is depicted in Figure 12-3. Assume pollution comes from two sources, plants H and L, and that emissions are uniformly mixed, so that the emissions of the two plants are equally damaging in the downstream, or downwind, impact area. The marginal abatement costs for the two sources are the same as those used in Figure 11-4 of Chapter 11.[3] Now impose a tax of $200 per kilogram on each source, assuming the regulator has computed the MD curve and set the target tax rate accordingly. Plant H will reduce its emissions to 80 kilograms per month, while L will reduce its emissions to 20

[2.] Note, however, that firms and consumers deal daily with prices that can change considerably. A good example is the retail price of gasoline. Adjustments that regulators make to pollution tax rates would probably be far less volatile than prices in many markets.

[3.] Recall from Chapter 11 that differences in the plants' MAC curves can be due to the fact that the firms are using different production technologies. They may be producing different outputs (e.g., a pulp mill and a food-canning firm), or they may be plants in the same industry but using different production techniques (e.g., coal-fired and hydroelectric power plants).

kilograms/month. Their marginal abatement costs have to be identical, because the tax has become the implicit price of pollution and that price is the same for both. The total reduction is 100 kilograms/month, which the effluent tax has automatically distributed between the two firms in accordance with the equimarginal principle. Note very carefully that the emission tax has led plant L to reduce its emissions by more than 83 percent, while plant H has reduced its emissions by only 33 percent. The emissions tax leads to larger proportionate emission reductions from firms with lower marginal abatement costs. Conversely, firms having steeper marginal abatement costs will reduce emissions less, in proportionate terms.

FIGURE 12-3 Emission Taxes Are Cost-Effective

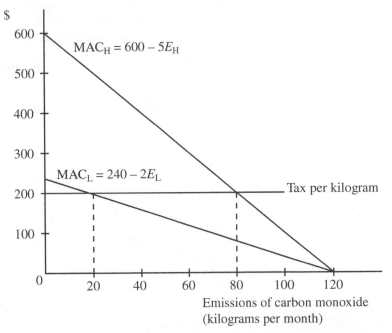

A uniform emissions tax of $200 per kilogram of carbon monoxide released is cost-effective. Both polluters set the tax equal to their MAC curve. H reduces emissions to 80 kilograms; L to 20 kilograms per month.

The higher the tax rate the more will emissions be reduced. In fact, if the tax rate were increased to something over $250/kilogram, L would stop emitting this residual entirely. It would take a much higher tax, $600 per kilogram, to lead H to reduce emissions to zero. A single effluent tax, when applied to several firms, will induce a greater reduction by firms whose marginal abatement costs increase less rapidly with emission reductions than from firms whose marginal abatement costs increase more rapidly. Since the firms are paying the same tax rate, they will have different total abatement costs and different tax bills. Note from Figure 12-3 that H's tax bill ($16,000) is much higher than L's ($4,000).

LO 4

Emission Taxes vs. Standards

How does the tax compare to a uniform standard also set to achieve a total reduction of 100 kilograms per month? The regulator institutes a *proportionate* cutback in emissions from each source; each is allowed to emit no more than 50 kilograms per month. At this point their marginal abatement costs would be different. The table below compares the *social compliance costs* (total abatement costs) under the tax versus the uniform standard.

	Social Compliance Costs ($/month)	
	Uniform Standard (50 kilograms/month each)	**Emission Tax** ($200 per kilogram)
Polluter L	4,900	10,000
Polluter H	12,250	4,000
Total costs	$17,150	$14,000

Note that the totals differ. Total abatement costs under the uniform standard are 22.5 percent larger than those of the emission tax. The simple reason is that the uniform standard violates the equimarginal principle; it requires the same proportionate cutback regardless of the height and shape of a firm's marginal abatement costs. (Question: What are the private compliance costs of a tax versus individual standards for this example?) These are just illustrative numbers. We will see in later chapters that in the real world of pollution control these differences have often been much larger. To summarize,

when MACs differ among polluters, social compliance costs are lower under a tax than a uniform standard meeting the same target level of emissions because the tax is cost-effective and the uniform standard is not.

Another important difference between taxes and standards is that

an emission tax is cost-effective even if the regulator knows nothing about the marginal abatement costs of any of the sources.

This is in clear contrast with the standards approach, where the public agency has to know exactly what these marginal abatement costs are for each firm in order to have a fully cost-effective program—that is, individual standards. In a tax approach, the only requirement is that firms pay the same tax and that they are cost minimizers. After each one has adjusted its emissions in accordance with its marginal abatement costs (which we can expect them to know themselves), they will all be emitting at the appropriate rates to satisfy the equimarginal principle. An emission tax may thus be less informationally demanding than a standard, and very likely less so than individual standards.

LO 5

Emission Taxes, the Double Dividend, and the B.C. Carbon Tax

Taxes have another potential advantage over standards and subsidies—tax revenue is collected. Governments then need to decide what to do with this tax revenue. Their choices are to use it to increase government expenditures or 'recycle' the revenue back to the economy by handing it back to individuals and companies. As long as the recycling does not affect the tax price of pollution, there will still be the same incentives to reduce emissions. Economists have advocated using emission tax revenues to reduce other taxes that provide disincentives to work, save, and invest in the economy;

taxes such as on payrolls, income, and investment. If the pollution tax revenue is used to reduce other taxes, there will be no net gain in the size of government (net of any tax collection costs). By reducing these distortionary taxes, there may be what has become known as the double dividend to society. The first dividend is the reduction in emissions thereby leading to a healthier environment. The second dividend is the increase in consumption, savings, work effort, and investment in the economy due to lower tax rates. While the first dividend is not generally disputed in practice, the second dividend is more controversial.[4] The existence and extent of the second dividend depends on what taxes are reduced and the pre-existing distortions in the economy that affect labour and capital markets and non-competitive industry structures. A careful and complex analysis of data is required and results will differ by jurisdiction.

As noted above, British Columbia introduced a carbon tax and was the first jurisdiction to employ a textbook model of an emission tax with full recycling of the revenue collected. The carbon tax was set initially on July 1, 2008 at $10 per tonne of CO_2e (carbon dioxide equivalent—used to standardize carbon emissions from different fuels). Each July 1 until 2012 the tax rate rises by another $5 per tonne to $30 per tonne, its current level. By law, every dollar collected in carbon tax revenue is returned to the B.C. economy in the form of a reduction in the tax rates on the provincial personal and corporate income taxes, reduce property taxes for business, and provide tax credits for low-income and rural people. In 2012–13 the province raised $1.12-billion and returned $1.38 billion in tax cuts and transfer payments. The forecast for 2013–14 is revenues of $1.21-billion and recycling $1.23-billion. The carbon tax has thus been revenue negative. The province had cut general corporate taxes from 12 percent in 2008 to 10 percent in 2011, but has increased them to 11 percent effective April 1, 2013. This increase is forecast to make the system approximately revenue neutral. See Chapter 20 for more discussion of B.C.'s carbon tax.

Emission Taxes and the Incentives to Innovate

One of the main advantages of emission taxes is that they provide strong incentives for investing in new technologies that have lower marginal abatement costs for controlling emissions. This is shown in Figure 12-4, which shows the two marginal abatement cost curves for a single firm that were represented in Figure 11-5. As before, MAC_1 represents the current condition. It shows the costs the firm would experience in cutting back its emissions with the particular technology it currently uses. MAC_2, on the other hand, refers to abatement costs that the firm would experience after engaging in an R&D program to develop a new method of reducing emissions. What are the incentives for this firm to put money into the R&D program when a tax is levied on its emissions?

Let the tax be $100 per tonne of emissions. The polluter will set that tax rate equal to MAC_1 and reduce emissions to 20 tonnes. At this point its total pollution-related costs will consist of $(a + b)$ worth of abatement costs and a tax bill of $(c + d + e)$. If the polluter can lower its marginal abatement cost curve to MAC_2 through the R&D activities, it would then reduce its emissions to 15 tonnes. At this point it would pay $(b + d)$ in abatement costs and e in taxes. The reduction in total costs has been $\$(a + c)$. If the firm had instead been faced with an emissions standard set at 20 tonnes, its cost savings with the new technology would have been only a, as we saw in Chapter 11. Also, as we saw in Chapter 11, if public authorities make the standard more stringent when the new technology becomes available, the firm's cost saving would be less than if the standard is unchanged.[5]

[4.] See Goulder (1995) and Fullerton and Metcalf (1998) for examples of the debate.

[5.] Review the section in Chapter 11 on incentive effects.

FIGURE 12-4 Incentives to Invest in New Pollution Control Technology under an Emission Tax

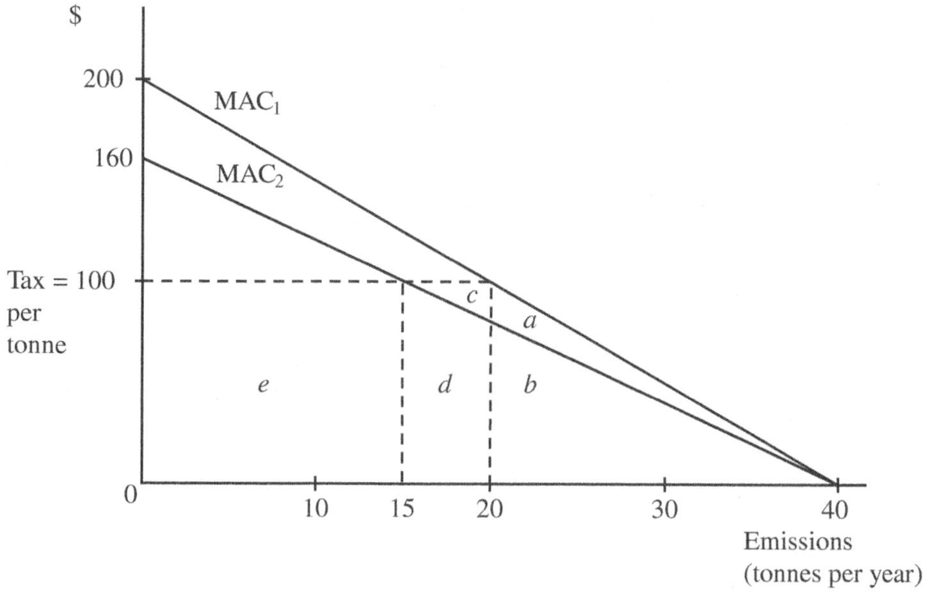

Emission taxes provide a big incentive to invest in R&D to lower marginal abatement costs. The cost saving from using a new technology (MAC_2) is area ($a + c$) under a tax set at $100 per tonne of emission. A standard set at 20 tonnes of emissions yields a cost saving of only area a if the standard remains at 20 tonnes.

There are thus two key differences between incentives to innovate under taxes versus standards.

1. The firm's R&D efforts will lead to a bigger reduction in its pollution-control-related costs (abatement costs plus tax payments) under a policy of emission taxes than under a standards approach.

2. Under the tax system the firm would automatically reduce its emissions as it found ways to shift its marginal abatement cost function downward, whereas under the standard no such automatic process would result.

The difference is that under a tax approach, polluters must pay for emissions as well as for abatement costs, while with standards they need pay only abatement costs. So, their potential cost savings from new pollution-control techniques are much larger under the tax program.

The incentive to innovate induced by pollution policies is often referred to as the **Porter hypothesis**, after economist Michael Porter's 1991 article and elaborated upon with case studies in Porter and van der Linde (1995). The Porter hypothesis can be divided into components. The 'weak' hypothesis is what we have been noting in this and the previous chapter as the impact of the regulation on innovation that lowers a firm's marginal abatement cost curve. The 'strong' version theorizes that the reduction in MAC will lead to higher profits for the firm. An additional aspect of the hypothesis is supported by our theoretical analysis in this section: market-based policies such as emission taxes or transferable emissions permits (covered in the next chapter) will provide a stronger stimulus to innovation than standards. The hypothesis is controversial. Some economists (e.g., see Palmer et al., 1995) argue that the Porter hypothesis is inconsistent with behaviour of profit-maximizing firms who would always look for opportunities to increase their profits. But from standard economics, we know that imperfect information, organizational factors, and market failures can prevent firms from making optimal decisions. There is robust empirical support (see e.g., Ambec et al., 2011 for references to studies) for the weak hypothesis, but evidence for the strong hypothesis is mixed. More recent studies find more support for the strong hypothesis than did those done in earlier years. Part of the reason for the difference may be that impacts of regulation on innovation take time. Evidence for the superiority of market-based policies is also not conclusive. As we'll see in Chapter 17, there is strong evidence that emission markets for sulphur dioxide in the U.S. stimulated more innovation than the technology standards they replaced, but less empirical research exists on the comparison of emission taxes to performance standards due to the paucity of data.

Emission Taxes and Enforcement Costs

Taxes pose a different type of enforcement problem than standards. Any tax system requires accurate information on the item to be taxed. If emissions are to be taxed, they must be measurable at reasonable cost. This means that residuals flowing from a source must be concentrated in a small enough number of identifiable streams that monitoring is possible. This rules out most nonpoint-source emissions, because they are spread thinly over a wide area in a way that makes them impossible to measure. It would normally be impossible to tax the pollutants in agricultural runoff because the diffuse nature of the "emissions" makes them impossible to measure. However, if there is a well-defined relationship between agricultural input use and emissions, an input tax may be easy to impose and enforce. Certain toxic chemical emissions may also be difficult to tax because, in addition to being nonpoint sources, they are often in such small quantities that their flow rates are difficult to measure.

With emission taxes, the taxing authorities would be sending a tax bill to the polluting firms at the end of each month or year, based on their total quantity of emissions during that period. So the agency would require information on cumulative emissions from each source. This process is more involved than just information on rate of discharge, because cumulative discharge is rate times duration. There are several ways of getting this information. Perhaps the most ideal would be to have permanent monitoring equipment that measures emissions continuously over the time period in question. Lacking such technology, one could fall back on periodic checking of the rate of emissions, with an estimate of the duration based on normal business considerations or perhaps self-reporting by firms. Alternatively, engineering studies might be carried out to determine prospective emission quantities under specified conditions of operation, inputs used, and so on.

Are the monitoring requirements of an emissions tax policy more stringent than those for the typical standards program? If the tax is on emissions per day, while a standard is based on annual emissions, the tax policy will have higher enforcement costs. But it is possible that monitoring must be done on exactly the same basis to ensure compliance with the tax or the standard. The frequency of monitoring required will be a function of the environmental characteristics of the pollutants. The frequency of monitoring in practice will often be constrained by government budgets. A question we pose but cannot answer is if frequency of monitoring affects whether polluters are more likely to comply under a standard or a tax. Polluters, of course, have incentives to find ways, legal and otherwise, to get their tax bills reduced or to avoid meeting an emission target under a standard. One way to do this is to influence the monitoring process enough so that reported emissions are smaller. Once they do get their tax bills, recipients will have every incentive to contest them if they appear to be based on uncertain data or have other technical weaknesses. But if they receive a fine for failure to meet a standard, the same incentives apply.

Other Types of Taxes

So far, we have discussed only one type of tax: an effluent or emissions tax. Since it is the emission of residuals that leads directly to environmental pollution, taxes on emissions presumably have the greatest leverage in terms of altering the incentives of polluters. But there are many situations where it is impossible or impractical to levy taxes directly on emissions. In cases where we can't measure and monitor emissions at reasonable cost, taxes, if they are to be used, would obviously have to be applied to something else. A good case of this is the problem of water pollution from fertilizer runoff in agriculture. It is impossible to tax the kilograms of nitrogen in the runoff because it is a nonpoint-source pollutant and thus not directly measurable. The same problem applies to agricultural pesticides. What may be feasible instead is to put taxes on these materials as they are sold to farmers; that is, a tax per tonne of fertilizer or per 100 kilograms of pesticide purchased. This tax exists in some U.S. states. The tax is to reflect the fact that a certain proportion of these materials ends up in nearby streams and lakes. Raising the prices of these items would give farmers the incentive to use them in smaller quantities. The higher price also creates the incentive to use the fertilizer in ways that involve less waste; for example, by reducing the amounts that run off.

EXAMPLE
Taxing trash

Placing a tax on something other than emissions is usually a "second-best" course of action made necessary because direct emissions can't be closely monitored. In cases like this we have to watch out for distortions that can come about as people respond to the tax, distortions that can substantially alleviate the effects of the tax or sometimes make related problems worse. For example, some U.S. communities have tried to tax household trash. One of the techniques is to sell stickers to the residents and require that each bag of trash has a sticker on it. The rate of tax is determined by the price of the stickers, and it is relatively easy to monitor and enforce the system through curbside pickup operations. But the per-bag tax will produce an incentive to pack more into each bag, so the reduction in total quantity of trash may be less than the reduction in the number of bags collected.

EXAMPLE
Taxing emissions from cars

Suppose we tax emissions of nitrogen oxides and hydrocarbons discharged from cars. The tax on any car is determined by the quantity of emissions per kilometre that a car produces, as determined by testing (done either by Environment Canada or the car manufacturers). The objective is to raise the cost of operating heavily polluting cars relative to less polluting ones, thus giving people more incentive to shift to the latter when they make their new-car purchases. The tax is linked to the quantity of residuals emitted during a typical or standardized kilometre travelled. But the factor we really wish to control is the total quantity of residuals emitted. Recall the relationship from Chapter 1:

Total quantity of emissions = Number of vehicles × Average kilometres travelled × Emissions per kilometre

The number of kilometres driven is as important a factor in determining annual emissions as the emissions rate of the car. Although consumers might shift to cars that have lower emission rates, they will have absolutely no incentive to find ways of driving fewer kilometres each year (taking fewer trips, living closer to work, etc.). So, total emissions may go down very little despite the tax on new-car emissions. The point is that this tax is being put on something other than what we want to control, so it will have less "leverage" and produce smaller results than if it had been put directly on total emissions.[6]

[6.] See Robert Crandall, "Policy Watch: Corporate Average Fuel Economy Standards," *Journal of Economic Perspectives* 6 (Spring 1992): 171–180 for an interesting discussion of this same problem arising from technological regulations.

Distributional Impacts of Emission Taxes

There are two primary impacts of effluent taxes on the distribution of income and wealth:

- impacts on prices and output of goods and services affected by the tax

- effects stemming from the expenditures of revenues generated by the tax

Businesses subject to a tax will experience an increase in costs, because of both abatement costs and the tax payments. From the firm's standpoint, these would constitute increases in production cost that, like any cost of production, they would presumably pass on to consumers. Whether and how much they can do this depends on competitive conditions and the conditions of demand. If the tax is applied to a single firm or small group of firms within a competitive industry, it will not be able to push its price up above the industry price, and so will have to absorb the cost increase. In this case, the impacts will be felt entirely by owners of the firm and the people who work there. Many firms fear or pretend to fear being in precisely this situation, and base their public objections to taxes on this outcome. If the tax is applied to an entire industry, then prices will go up and consumers will bear part of the burden. How much prices go up depends on demand conditions. Price increases are often thought of as regressive because, for any given item, an increase in price would affect poor people proportionately more than higher-income people. For something that both poor and well-off people consume, like electricity, this conclusion is straightforward. For price increases in goods consumed disproportionately by more well-to-do people (e.g., airline travel), however, the burden would be mostly on them.

The burden on workers is tied closely to what happens to the rate of output of the affected firms. Here again, the extent of the output effect depends on competitive conditions and the nature of demand for the good. If the emission tax program is applied to a single firm in a competitive industry, or if the demand for the output of an industry is very responsive to price, output adjustments will be relatively large and displaced workers could result. The long-run burden is then a matter of whether good alternative sources of employment are available.

While burdens because of price and output changes may be real, we have to remember that on the other side the tax program is creating substantial benefits in the form of reduced environmental damages. To know how a program affects any particular group we would have to account also for how these benefits are distributed.

If emission tax revenues are recycled back to the community in the form of tax cuts and credits, much of the impact on low-income people can be mitigated. For example, B.C.'s carbon tax cuts the personal income tax rates to the first two tax brackets by 5 percent and provides a tax credit of just over $100 per adult and $30 per child each year to low-income households. For all but the most carbon -intensive families, these tax cuts from the revenue recycling should offset most of the impact of the carbon taxes on energy prices. In Europe, governments return part of their carbon taxes to industry either through tax cuts or to help finance the purchase of pollution-control technology. As long as the payments do not make the marginal emissions tax rate effectively lower, the incentive effects of the tax are not affected. Alternatively, they might be used to pay for other environmental initiatives in places where direct public action is called for. They might even be used to reduce other government debt, with benefits flowing to taxpayers in general.

LO 6

ABATEMENT SUBSIDIES

An emission tax works by placing a price on the environmental asset into which emissions are occurring. Essentially the same incentive effects on the margin would result if, instead of a tax, we instituted a subsidy on emissions. Here, a public authority would pay a polluter a certain amount per tonne of emissions for every tonne the polluter reduced, starting from some benchmark level. The subsidy acts as a reward for reducing emissions. More formally, it acts as an opportunity cost: when a polluter chooses to emit a unit of effluent, they are in effect forgoing the subsidy payment they could have had if they had chosen to withhold that unit of effluent instead. The table in Figure 12-5 shows how this works in principle, using the same numbers used for Figure 12-1. The regulator pays a subsidy for each unit by which the polluter reduces its emissions, starting from a *base level*. We assume the base level is its emissions rate before any policy is imposed: 50 tonnes/month. The polluter receives a subsidy of $100 per tonne for every tonne it cuts back from this base. The fourth column shows its total subsidy revenues, and the last column shows total subsidies minus total abatement costs. This net revenue peaks at 25 tonnes/month, the same emissions level the polluter would choose with the $100 tax. In other words, the incentive is to reduce emissions to the point where the unit price of the subsidy intersects the MAC curve; the equilibrium reached is in theory the same for each polluter as with the emission tax. Figure 12-5 shows the same MAC curve as in Figure 12-1. At a per unit subsidy of $100 per tonne of emission abated, the polluter would set $100 = 200 - 4E$ and thus, reduce its emissions from 50 to 25 tonnes to receive a total subsidy payment of $2,500 (areas $b + c$). Its abatement costs are area b, so netting this out, the polluter's net gain is revenue equal to area c, which is $1,250. Compare this to the results from the emission tax in Figure 12-1. There, the polluter has net costs of $3,750. Thus we see that while a tax and subsidy set at the same rate per unit are equivalent *on the margin*, in that they both reduce emissions from 50 to 25 tonnes, they have very different impacts on the polluter's financial situation. A firm can be making higher profits after the imposition of the subsidy than when it was emitting its maximum amount of pollution. This can have the effect of making this industry more attractive for potential new firms. We have the possibility of having the emissions per firm go down but the number of firms in the industry—and therefore total output and total emissions—go up. This feature is a major drawback of simple subsidies such as illustrated here. Subsidies may raise the total emissions from an industry even though they reduce emissions per firm.

Many of the points we made earlier about emission taxes also apply to emission subsidies. The job of monitoring emissions would be essentially the same. But there would undoubtedly be great difficulties in establishing the original base levels from which reductions are to be measured. Each source would wish to have this base level set as high as possible. Perverse incentives might be present in the planning stages because sources might try to increase their emissions in the hopes of increasing their base. There is, however, an additional problem with subsidies not faced by taxes. To be able to pay subsidies to polluters, governments will have to raise revenue in some way. The extra revenue needed for subsidies could come from more government debt, higher income or sales taxes, and so on. If governments can't raise revenues, they have two other options. They could cut back on expenditures in other programs, or forgo revenues if the subsidy takes the form of a tax write-off (say, for investment in pollution-abatement equipment). In each of these situations, it is likely that undesirable effects on the economy will occur. Given the current difficult fiscal situation in most jurisdictions, subsidies are generally not seen as viable environmental policies except in special circumstances. For illustrations of the challenges with subsidies see Section 5 (Chapters 15–20).

FIGURE 12-5 An Abatement Subsidy

Emissions (tonnes/month)	Marginal abatement cost	Total abatement cost	Total subsidy at $100/tonne	Net payment to polluter (subsidy minus TAC)
50	0	0	$ 0	$ 0
45	20	50	500	450
40	40	200	1,000	800
35	60	450	1,500	1,050
30	80	800	2,000	1,200
25	100	1,250	2,500	1,250
20	120	1,800	3,000	1,200
15	140	2,450	3,500	1,050
10	160	3,200	4,000	800
5	180	4,050	4,500	450
0	200	5,000	5,000	0

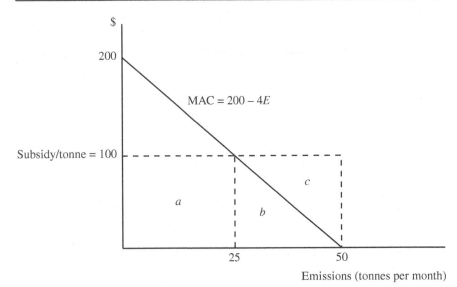

Deposit–Refund Systems

One place where subsidies may be more practical is in deposit–refund systems. A deposit–refund system is essentially the combination of a tax and a subsidy. The tax is the deposit and the subsidy is the refund—a type of penalty and reward program. The purpose of the subsidy is to provide the incentive for people to refrain from disposing of these items in environmentally damaging ways. It is their reward. The funds for paying the subsidy are raised by levying taxes on these items when they are purchased. In this case, the purpose of the tax is not necessarily to get people to reduce the consumption of the item, but to raise money to pay the subsidy. If people choose not to return the item and collect their refund, the tax can be viewed as a disposal charge.

Deposit–refund systems are particularly well-suited to situations where a product is widely dispersed when purchased and used, and where disposal is difficult or impossible for authorities to monitor. In Canada, six provinces have enacted deposit–refund systems for beverage containers, some like B.C. cover all beverages except milk products, and others focus on beer, wine, and soft drinks. The goal of these policies is to reduce litter and to encourage recycling. B.C. also has deposit-refund systems for car batteries, tires, paint, and a growing number of other products. This approach has also been widely used in Europe with what is called 'cradle to grave' recycling. For example, in Sweden and Norway, deposit–refund systems have been instituted for cars. New-car buyers pay a deposit at time of purchase, which will be refunded when and if the car is turned over to an authorized junk dealer. Experience with these systems shows that success depends on more than just the size of the deposit–refund. For example, it is essential that the collection system be designed to be reasonably convenient for consumers. Chapter 19 provides more detail on recycling and waste handling policies in theory and Canadian practices.

Summary

Emission taxes attack the pollution problem at its source, by putting a price on something that has been free and, therefore, overused. The main advantage of emission taxes is their efficiency aspects: If all sources are subject to the same tax, they will adjust their emission rates so that the equimarginal rule is satisfied. Administrators do not have to know the individual source of marginal abatement cost functions for this to happen; it is enough that firms be faced with the tax and then left free to make their own adjustments. A second major advantage of emission taxes is that they produce a strong incentive to innovate and discover cheaper ways of reducing emissions.

The apparent indirect character of emission taxes may tend to work against their acceptance by policy-makers. Standards have the appearance of placing direct control on the thing that is at issue, namely emissions. Emission taxes, on the other hand, place no direct restrictions on emissions but rely on the self-interested behaviour of firms to adjust their own emission rates in response to the tax. This may make some policy-makers uneasy, because firms apparently are still allowed to control their own emission rates. It may seem paradoxical that this "indirect" character of effluent taxes can sometimes provide a stronger inducement to emission reductions than seemingly more direct approaches.

But emission taxes require effective monitoring. They cannot be enforced simply by checking to see if sources have installed certain types of pollution-control equipment. If emission taxes are to have the appropriate incentive effects, they must be based closely on *cumulative emissions*. Thus, point sources where emissions can be effectively measured are the likely candidates for pollution control via emissions taxes.

An advantage of emission taxes is that they provide a source of revenue for public authorities. Many have recommended that tax systems be changed to rely less on taxes that have distorting economic effects and more on emissions taxes. This requires that authorities be able to predict with accuracy the effects of particular emission taxes on rates of emissions.

Emissions subsidies would have the same incentive effect on individual polluters, but they could lead to increases in total emission levels. One place where subsidies have been used effectively is in deposit–refund systems, which are essentially tax and subsidy systems in combination.

Key Terms

Market-based incentive policies

Porter hypothesis

Total private cost of compliance

Transfer payments

Two-part emission tax

Analytical Problems

1. For Figure 12-4 and the equations $MAC_1 = 200 - 5E$ and $MAC_2 = 160 - 4E$, compute the cost savings to the polluter if it adopts the new technology (MAC_2) after the introduction of an emission tax of $100 per tonne. Compute the cost savings under a standard that is set at 20 tonnes. Explain why the tax provides a larger incentive to innovate than does the standard.

2. Suppose a regulator wants to introduce an emission tax on discharges of mercury into waterways. Illustrate the impact of the tax on two industries that discharge mercury: gold mining (as part of its processing), and dentistry (flushing mercury from fillings down the drain). Discuss the following questions: (a) How would the regulator measure mercury discharges from both sources? (b) Would the tax be uniform? (c) What is the likely impact of the tax on the prices of gold and dental services? (You will need to make some specific assumptions here about the nature of demand for these products.) (d) What are some incentives to alter production technologies? (e) What are the distributional impacts of the tax? Use graphs to support your arguments.

3. Using the numbers given in Table 12-1, or knowing that $MAC = 200 - 4E$ for a polluter, illustrate graphically the impact of a subsidy of $100 per tonne on the polluter's emissions. Contrast the subsidy with an emissions tax of the same amount and discuss differences in (a) incentives created, (b) ease of implementation, (c) distributional impacts, and (d) effects on polluting industries.

Discussion Questions

1. Suppose that we institute an emission charge on a particular pollutant, and we use the proceeds of the tax to help subsidize the short-term capital costs by firms in the same industry of installing emission-reduction equipment. Will this approach upset the incentive effects of the emission tax?

2. Suppose the federal government proposes a tax on SO_2 emissions. The tax is to be levied on the sulphur content of the fuel used by utilities and other industries because emissions from these sources are difficult to measure. But in cases where firms have ways of measuring the SO_2 content of exhaust gases, the tax will be levied on the SO_2 content of the gases. Will this system lead to a socially efficient equilibrium? (You will need to make some specific assumptions to answer the question.)

3. Opponents of emission charges argue that polluters will simply pay the taxes and pass the cost on to consumers without reducing emissions. Is this correct? Explain.

For more information on the resources available from McGraw-Hill Ryerson, go to www.mheducation.ca/he/solutions.

Chapter 13

Transferable Emission Permits

After reading this chapter you will be able to:

LO 1 Describe the general principles of a transferable emission permit (TEP) and show graphically how it can achieve a cost-effective equilibrium.

LO 2 Explain the pragmatic issues in setting up a TEP system covering: initial rights allocation, trading rules, non-uniformly mixed pollutants, non-competitive markets, enforcement, and incentives for innovation.

LO 3 Describe the key features of the U.S. sulphur dioxide TEP system and how it achieved target levels of emissions cost effectively.

An effluent tax requires that some central public authority establishes a tax rate, monitors the performance of each polluter, and then collects the tax bills. It is essentially an interaction between polluters and public authorities in which we might expect the same type of adversarial relationship we get in any tax system. In this chapter we will take a look at a policy approach that, while incorporating economic incentives, is designed to work in a more decentralized fashion. Rather than leaving everything to a centralized public agency, it works through the decentralized market interactions of polluters themselves. It's called the system of **transferable emission permits (TEPs)**.

LO 1

GENERAL PRINCIPLES

A transferable emission permit creates a transferable property right to emit a specified amount of pollution.

In a transferable emission permit system a new type of property right is created. This property right consists of a permit to emit pollutants. Each permit (also known as an *allowance*) entitles its holder to emit one unit (kilogram, tonne, or however the permit is calibrated) of the waste material specified in the right. Rights holders would ordinarily have a number of such permits at any point in time. If a discharger owned 100 permits, for example, it would be entitled to emit, during some specified period of time, a maximum of 100 units of the designated type of pollutant. Thus, the total number of permits held by all sources puts an upper limit on the total quantity of emissions. These discharge permits are *transferable;* they can be bought and sold among anybody allowed to participate in the permit market, at whatever price is agreed upon by the participants themselves. Transferability is a key component of the TEP system. If rights are not transferable, the system is effectively the same as the assignment of an individual standard to each polluter. The regulator would then lose many of the key advantages of a TEP system, as we'll see.

A TEP program begins with a centralized decision on the total number of discharge permits to be put into circulation. These permits are then distributed among the sources responsible for the emissions. Some formula must be used to determine how many permits each source will receive; we will come back to this problem below. An economist would advocate using social efficiency (where marginal damages equals marginal abatement costs) as the criterion for determining the total number of permits (tonnes of emissions) chosen. In actual TEP systems, the total number of permits is set at a target level that may be arbitrary because there is limited knowledge about either the MAC or MD curve (or both). We look in more detail at the issue of uncertainty about the location of these curves in Chapter 14. Regardless of where the target level of total emissions is set, if the total number of permits is less than current total emissions, some or all emitters will receive fewer permits than their current emissions.

EXAMPLE
A TEP program to reduce sulphur emissions from electric power plants

Suppose there is a national TEP program to reduce the amount of sulphur emitted by electricity-generating power plants.[1] Current total emissions are 120,000 tonnes of sulphur per year, and policy-makers have decided that this must be reduced to 80,000 tonnes/year. Let's focus on the situation of one of the power plants, which we suppose to be emitting 40,000 tonnes of sulphur currently. Suppose each permit allows the holder to release a maximum of 1,000 tonnes of sulphur annually. This plant is initially given 30 discharge permits. The plant manager now has three choices.

1. Reduce the emissions to the level covered by the number of permits the plant was initially given, or 30,000 tonnes/year.

2. Buy additional permits and emit at higher levels; for example, it might buy an additional 10 permits, giving it a total of 40,000 tonnes. In this case it would not reduce its emissions at all from their initial level.

3. Reduce its emissions below the 30,000 tonnes for which it has permits and then sell the permits it doesn't need. For example, if it reduced its emissions to 20,000 tonnes, 10 permits of its original allocation would not be needed; these could be sold.

It may not be obvious that the buying and selling of permits among polluters (and perhaps others) would lead to the distribution of total emissions among polluters in a way that satisfies the equimarginal principle. Figure 13-1 helps illustrate. Assume there are two polluters whose sulphur emissions are uniformly mixed together (non-uniformly mixed emissions are examined below). Panel (a) shows the MAC function for firm A; panel (b) shows the function for firm B. Emissions (E) are measured in thousands of tonnes. To facilitate computations, the functions for these MAC curves, where units are in thousands of tonnes are:

$$MAC_A = 120 - 3E_A$$

$$MAC_B = 400 - 5E_B$$

Initial emissions of each firm are found by setting MAC = 0 and solving for E^0 (as we have done in preceding chapters). Then:

$$E_A{}^0 = 40,000 \text{ tonnes}$$

(Continued)

---

[1] The example at the end of this chapter examines an actual market in the United States for sulphur dioxide emissions trading.

$E_B{}^0 = 80{,}000$ tonnes,

Total $E = 120{,}000$ tonnes of sulphur emissions annually.

FIGURE 13-1 How Transferable Emission Permits Work

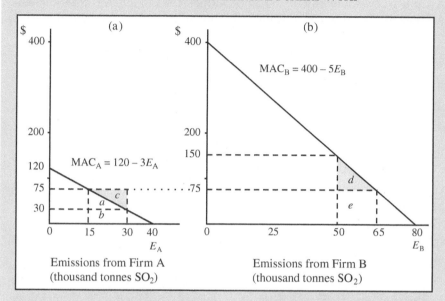

Emissions from Firm A
(thousand tonnes SO_2)

Emissions from Firm B
(thousand tonnes SO_2)

A TEP system is introduced to lower sulphur pollution from an initial level of 120,000 to 80,000 tonnes per year. Polluters are given emission permits in proportion to their initial level of emissions (30 to firm A and 50 to firm B). Polluters will have an incentive to trade permits as long as their MACs differ at each one's emission levels. Polluter A will have an incentive to sell permits to B because it can reduce its emissions at lower marginal cost than can B. The cost-effective equilibrium is reached where the MACs of the two polluters are equal and their total emissions equal the target level. A total of 15 permits are traded. Firm A's net gain is area c; firm B's is area d.

The government regulator has chosen a target level of total emissions to be 80,000 tonnes per year. The regulator creates 80 transferable emission permits, each one of which entitles its possessor to emit 1,000 tonnes/year. This is called an **emissions-based TEP system.** The permits are distributed to the two firms, using some agreed-upon allocation rule. The allocation rule for this example is that each is allocated permits roughly in proportion to its current emission rates.[2] Firm A receives 30 permits and firm B gets 50 permits in the original distribution. The firms cannot release any more than 30,000 tonnes and 50,000 tonnes per year respectively unless they trade. Will permit trading occur?

The basic trading principle is this: A polluter will reduce its emissions and sell its excess permits on the market if the market price is greater than or equal to its MAC at its chosen emission level. A polluter will buy a permit if the price is less than or equal to its MAC of controlling emissions. MAC curves can thus be thought of as a polluter's demand curve for permits (if it is buying) or supply curve (if it is selling).[3] The permit market, if competitive, works like any other market. An equilibrium price and quantity exchanged will be found where supply equals demand.

(Continued)

[2.] We have rounded to avoid having fractions of permits.

[3.] The supply curve for a firm selling permits will be the inverse of its MAC curve.

Which polluters will be the buyers and which the sellers? As long as MAC curves differ, there should be trades and the polluter with the lower MAC will be the seller, the one with the higher MAC the buyer. Note in Figure 13-1 that at the initial allocation of permits, firm A's MACs are substantially lower than firm B's ($30 versus $150). This gives firm A the potential to increase its pollution control, not use some permits, and sell them to firm B, if the receipts from the permit sale compensate for A's additional abatement costs. Firm B will want to buy these permits if their total cost is less than it would have had to pay to control the units of sulphur it can now emit. We now illustrate this numerically.

NUMERICAL EXAMPLE OF HOW THE PERMIT MARKET WORKS
Computing gains to trading

1. Compute A's net gain (cost saving) if it reduces its emissions from 30,000 to 15,000 tonnes per year and sells its excess permits. Polluter A is the potential permit supplier.

   Polluter A's marginal abatement costs at emissions of 15,000 tonnes per year are given by:

   $$MAC_A = 120 - 3 (15) = \$75$$

   The change in its total abatement costs if it reduces emissions from 30,000 to 15,000 tonnes is shown by areas $(a + b)$ in Figure 13-1. Area $a = \frac{1}{2}[(30 - 15) \times (\$75 - 30)] = \$337.50$. Area $b = [(30 - 15) \times \$30] = \$450$. Area $(a + b) = \$787.50$.

   If firm A now sells its 15 surplus permits to firm B for $75 per permit, it will receive areas $(a + b + c) = \$1,125$ in permit revenue.

   Firm A's cost saving is therefore areas $[(a + b + c) - (a + b)] = $ area $c = \$337.50$.

2. Compute polluter B's net gains/cost savings if it buys polluter A's 15 permits and therefore increases its emissions from 50,000 to 65,000 tonnes. Polluter B is the potential permit buyer.

   Polluter B pays A $75 per permit, for a total of $1,125 (area e in Figure 13-1).

   B's TACs fall because B increases its pollution. The reduction in TAC equals areas $(d + e) = \$1,687.50$.

   Firm B's net gain is therefore [areas $(d + e) - $ area $e] = $ area $d = \$562.50$.

   This proves that both firms would be better off after the trade—their combined gains from trading 15 permits are their cost savings compared to their initial permit allocation. Total cost savings equals areas $(c + d) = \$900$.[4]

Gains from trade would continue to exist and permits would continue to be traded until marginal abatement costs are equalized. Note from the example above that at 15 permits traded, both firms have the identical MACs of $75 for the last tonne of sulphur emitted. Total emissions still meet the regulator's target of 80,000 tonnes per year. We can solve for this outcome using the same principles established in Chapter 11, where socially efficient individual standards were determined. Recall that a cost-effective equilibrium (satisfying the equimarginal principle) is where

$$MAC_A = MAC_B \text{ and}$$

$$E_A + E_B = \text{target level of pollution}$$

[4] In an actual trading situation the price will be somewhere between the seller's minimum price and the buyer's maximum price, where the minimum and maximum prices are determined by each party's MAC curve. For example, if the firms were to trade two permits, A's MAC at 28 tonnes of emissions is $36, while B's, at 52 tonnes, is $140. The permit price would lie between these two boundaries.

Using the equations above and the target level of pollution = 80,000 tonnes per year, we obtain E_A = 15 and E_B = 65, with $MAC_A = MAC_B$ = $75 per thousand tonnes.

Note that the TEP system operates like a hybrid between imposing standards and using taxation to reach a target. Because the total number of permits is fixed, there is effectively a standard that cannot be exceeded. But, because the permits are transferable, the market will achieve a uniform price at which polluters' marginal costs of abatement are equal. This is just like a tax, except that the regulator doesn't have to be involved in determining polluters' MAC curves to get just the right tax rate that equates MACs and also meets the target level of emissions. Another key point is that the regulator doesn't even have to know individual polluters' MAC curves—the market does all the work. The trades—permit prices times number of permits traded—reveal each polluter's MAC curve. Of course, in setting a socially efficient emission target, knowledge of the aggregate MAC and MD is still required for a TEP system as well as for all the other regulatory policies we have examined.

How the actual bargaining process takes place will depend on the number of traders, their MACs, and so on. The essential point is that as long as marginal abatement costs are unequal among these sources, they can both become better off by trading permits at some price between these marginal abatement costs. Thus, in the trading of permits and the adjusting of emissions in accordance with their permit holdings, these sources would be led to an outcome that satisfies the equimarginal principle.

When a large number of firms is involved, the TEP system works in the same way, but trading patterns will of course be more complicated. The initial distribution of emission rights will now include many firms, with many potential buyers and sellers. In order for the equimarginal principle eventually to be satisfied in this case, it is obviously necessary that all permit buyers and sellers be trading permits at the same price. What this requires is a single overall market for permits where suppliers and demanders may interact openly and where knowledge of transaction prices is publicly available to all participants. We can then expect that the normal forces of competition would bring about a single price for permits. The permits would in general flow from sources with relatively low marginal abatement costs to those with high marginal abatement costs. Market institutions should develop—and indeed have in the real-world cases of permit trading (see Chapter 20 for examples of GHG markets). In the U.S., there are permit brokers and bankers and emission trading on commodity exchanges, see, for example, the Green Exchange. These markets, if competitive, should work like any other market where the permit price and quantity transacted is determined where the demand for permits equals the supply of permits. The demanders in this market can be new firms that wish to begin operations in the trading area or existing sources that wish to expand their operations and require more permits to cover expected increases in emissions. Supplies of permits would include firms leaving the area or going out of business, and most especially firms who have invested in better abatement techniques and now have excess permits to sell.

Chapter 20 examines emission trading regimes for GHGs. The European carbon market covers emissions of carbon dioxide from many countries in the European Union. While there are a number of practical issues that can inhibit the efficient operation of these markets that we explain below, the concept is popular with decision makers because the system creates property rights that can become quite valuable. Unlike emission tax approaches, which basically make people pay for something they were once getting for free, TEP programs begin by creating and distributing a new type of property right. These property rights will have a market value as long as the total number of permits created is limited. From a political standpoint it is perhaps easier for people to agree on a pollution-control policy that begins by distributing valuable new property rights than by notifying people they will be subject to a new tax. Of course, like any pollution-control policy, TEP programs have their own set of problems that have to be overcome if the programs are going to work effectively. What looks in theory like a neat way of using market forces to achieve efficient pollution reduction must be adapted to the complexities of the real world.

Key points about a TEP policy:

- Like a standard, permits ensure that a target level of pollution is achieved.

- Like a tax, transferable permits that are traded in a competitive market are a cost-effective policy.

- Regulators do not have to know each polluter's MAC curve to find the right "price" that achieves cost-effectiveness. The market does this automatically, because polluters set the permit price equal to their MAC. If the market clears, the permit price equals the MAC of each polluter.

- Once the target level of pollution is set, the market will reveal a polluter's MAC curve.

- Trading occurs if the MACs of polluters are sufficiently different so that some will become sellers of permits and the others, buyers.

- The exchange of permits provides each trader with cost savings compared to their initial permit allocation from the regulator.

LO 2

Issues in Setting up a TEP Market

The Initial Rights Allocation

The success of the TEP approach in controlling pollution depends critically on limiting the number of rights in circulation. Since individual polluters will no doubt want as many as they can get in the first distribution, the very first step of the program is one of potentially great controversy: what formula to use to make the original distribution of emission rights. Almost any rule will appear to have some inequities. Regulators might contemplate distributing them equally among all existing sources of a particular effluent. But this would encounter the problem that firms vary a lot in size. Some pulp mills are larger than others, for example, and the average size of pulp mills in terms of value of output may be different from the average size of, say, soda bottling plants. So giving each polluter the same number of permits may not be fair at all.

Alternatively, a regulator might allocate permits in accordance with the existing emissions of a source. For example, each source might get permits amounting to 50 percent of its current emissions. This may sound equitable but, in fact, it has built-in incentive difficulties. A rule like this does not recognize the fact that some firms may already have worked hard to reduce their emissions. One could easily argue that those firms that have already—out of good conscience or for any other reason—invested in emission reduction should not now be penalized, in effect, by receiving emission permits in proportion to these lower emission levels. This tends to reward firms who have dragged their feet in the past.[5] Incentives could be even more perverse. If polluters believe that permits will soon be allocated on the basis of current emissions, they may have the incentive to *increase* today's emission rate, because this would give them a larger base for the initial allocation of permits.

[5.] This is just another example of the perverse incentives built into any program that asks everybody to cut their consumption by x percent from their current rate. It favours those who have consumed at high rates in the past and hurts those who have consumed less.

Each allocation formula has its problems, and policy-makers must find some workable compromise if the approach is to be widely accepted. Closely related to this issue is the question of whether the rights should be given away or perhaps sold or auctioned. In principle it doesn't matter as long as the permits get distributed fairly widely. Subsequent market transactions will redistribute them in accordance with the relative marginal abatement costs of polluters, whatever the original distribution may have been. What a sale or auction would do, however, is transfer some of the original value of the rights into the hands of the auctioning agency. This might be a good way for public agencies to raise funds that could be used to reduce other fees or taxes (like the double dividend discussed in Chapter 12), but it has to be recognized that a plan like this would create political objections. A hybrid system would be to distribute a certain number of permits free of charge and then auction some number of additional permits, as has been done in sulphur dioxide trading in the United States. Or a small surcharge might be put on permits in the original distribution.

Establishing Trading Rules

For any market to work effectively, clear rules must exist covering who may trade and the trading procedures that must be followed. Furthermore, the rules should not be so burdensome that they make it impossible for market participants to gauge accurately the implications to them of buying or selling at specific prices. This implies a "hands-off" stance by public agencies after the initial distribution of the rights. Working against this is the normal tendency for environmental agencies to want to monitor the market closely and perhaps try to influence its performance. The supervising agency, for example, may want to have final right of approval over all trades, so as to be able to stop any trades it considers undesirable in some way. But this intervention in the permits market is likely to be counterproductive. The problem with this is that it is likely to increase the uncertainty among potential traders, increase the general level of transactions costs in the market, and interfere with the efficient flow of permits. The general rule for the public agency should be this: set simple and clear rules and then allow trading to proceed.

One basic rule that would have to be established is who may participate in the market. Is this to be limited to polluters, or may anyone trade? For example, may environmental advocacy groups buy permits and retire them as a way of reducing total emissions? One's first reaction is to say that such groups ought to be permitted to buy permits, because that is evidence that society's willingness to pay for lower total emission levels exceeds the price of the permits, which should be the same as marginal abatement costs. This conclusion is probably valid if we are dealing with a local or regional environmental group whose membership is roughly coincidental with the trading area, and which has raised money specifically to buy discharge permits in that region. There may, however, be problems if large national advocacy groups were to use their resources to buy permits on a regional market for strategic or political reasons that do not reflect the willingness to pay of the people in the region. There is, however, no evidence that this has happened in any of the operating TEP markets.

Non-uniformly Mixed Emissions

Suppose we are trying to design a TEP program to control total airborne SO_2 emissions in a region where there are numerous different sources—power plants, industrial plants, and so on—scattered rather widely around the area. All the emission points are not equally situated relative to the prevailing wind or to the area of highest population density. Some sources are upwind and others are downwind of the populated area. Assume that they are not all equal in terms of marginal abatement costs, but neither are they equal in terms of the impact of their emissions on ambient SO_2 levels over the populated area. Having distributed discharge permits, we now allow them to be traded. As long as the number of permits in circulation is held constant, total SO_2 emissions are effectively controlled. But if straight trading is allowed, unit for unit, of permits among all sources, the damage caused by that total could change. For example, if a downwind firm sold permits to an upwind firm, the total number of permits would remain the same but there would now be more emissions upwind of the population and, therefore, more damage. This is sometimes called the **hot-spot problem.**

The problem is similar to the one encountered under uniform standards or taxation when pollutants are non-uniformly mixed. If the program were simply to allow trading of permits among all sources on a one-for-one basis, a firm or group of firms whose emissions have a greater impact on ambient quality could accumulate larger numbers of permits and create a hot spot. One way to avoid this problem would be to adjust the trading to take into account the impacts of individual sources. Suppose the emissions from source B were twice as damaging as the emissions of source A simply because of the location of the two sources. Then the administrators of the program might set a rule that if source B is buying permits from source A, it must buy two permits to get one. This is called an **ambient-based TEP system.** When pollutants are non-uniformly mixed, the ambient system is necessary to achieve a cost-efficient equilibrium. However, it is a very complex type of market to operate. With many sources with different marginal damages, authorities would have to determine, for each source, how many permits would have to be purchased from each other source in order for the purchasing source to be credited with one new permit. If there were 5 sources, the regulator has to figure out only 10 trading ratios; if there were 20 different sources, it would have to estimate 190 of these ratios.[6]

A simpler approach would be to use a zoned system. Authorities would designate a series of zones, each grouping sources that were relatively similar in terms of their location and the impact of their emissions on ambient quality. Regulators could then do one of two things: allow trading by firms only with other firms in the same zone, or make adjustments for all trades across zone boundaries using an ambient-based system.

TEPs and Problems of Competition

The question of allowing trading across zone boundaries or, on the contrary, restricting it to within zones has a much wider importance than might first appear. TEP programs work through a trading process, where buyers and sellers interact to transfer title to valuable property rights. Markets work best when there is substantial competition among buyers and among sellers; they work much less well if there are so few buyers or sellers that competitive pressures are weak or absent. In cases where there are few traders, one of them, or perhaps a small group, may be able to exercise control over the market—by colluding on prices, perhaps charging different prices to different people, using the control of discharge permits to gain economic control in their industry, and so on. From the standpoint of fostering competition, therefore, regulators would like to set trading zones as widely as possible, to include large numbers of potential buyers and sellers.

But this may work against the ecological facts. In many cases there may be meteorological or hydrological reasons for limiting the trading area to a relatively narrow geographical area. If we are interested in controlling airborne emissions affecting a particular city, for example, we would probably not want to allow firms located there to trade permits with firms in another city. Or if the concern is controlling emissions into a particular lake or river, we could not allow sources located there to trade permits with sources located on some entirely different body of water. Thus, for environmental reasons regulators may want to have trading areas restricted, while for economic reasons they would

---

[6.] In general, if there were n sources, there would have to be $[n(n-1)]/2$ trading ratios established. It becomes quite obvious that an ambient-based system would be extremely difficult to establish. Regulators then have to look for second-best policies such as zoned systems (or use another policy instrument).

want to have trading areas defined broadly. There is no magic rule to tell us exactly how these two factors should be balanced in all cases. We can only look at specific cases as they come up and weigh the particularities of the environmental features with the subtleties of the competitive conditions in the industries where trading will occur.

TEP Programs and Enforcement

As noted above, TEP programs constrain polluters to keep their emissions at a level no greater than the total number of discharge permits in their possession. Thus, an administering agency would essentially have to keep track of two things: the number of permits in the possession of each source and the quantity of emissions from each source. Since the initial permit distribution will be well known, the agency must have some way of keeping track of permit transactions among market participants. Trades could, in fact, become complicated with multiple buyers and sellers, and with different types of transactions like temporary rentals and long-term leases in addition to permanent transfers. Since permit buyers (or renters) would have a strong incentive to have their purchases revealed to the agency, and since all purchases imply sellers, a system of self-reporting, coupled with modern means of information transfer, may be sufficient to provide reliable information on which sources have the permits.

The administrative agency must be able to monitor polluters to see whether emissions at each source exceed the number of permits it holds. If permits are expressed in terms of total emissions over some period of time, a means has to be available to measure cumulative emissions at each source. This is the same requirement as with any policy. If there were reasonable certainty that emissions were fairly even throughout the year, authorities could get a check on cumulative emissions by making spot-checks of instantaneous rates. For most industrial sources of pollution, however, there are considerable daily, weekly, or seasonal variations in emissions, so more sophisticated monitoring would be required.

One desirable feature of TEP programs is that there may be an incentive for sources to monitor each other, at least informally. When, and if, some sources emit more than they have permits for, they are essentially cheating by not buying sufficient permits to cover all of their emissions. In effect this reduces the demand for permits below what it would otherwise be. And this has the effect of lowering the market price of permits. This clearly works against the interest of any firm holding large numbers of permits, which gives it an incentive to see that other firms don't cheat on emissions.

TEPs and the Incentive for R&D

In Chapters 11 and 12, we showed that emission standards did not create a strong incentive to innovate and find cheaper methods of abating pollution, while emission taxes did. TEP programs are identical to the emissions tax, at least in theory. Consider the firm in Figure 13-2. Suppose that a polluter's marginal abatement cost function is MAC_1. Emission permits that entitle the polluter to release one tonne per year sell for p each. The polluter doesn't expect this price to change. The polluter has adjusted its holdings so that it currently owns E_1 permits. Its emissions are therefore also E_1, and its total abatement costs are $(a + b)$. The incentive to do R&D is to find a less costly way of controlling emissions, so the firm can cut emissions and sell the surplus permits. How much would it be worth to get marginal abatement costs shifted to MAC_2? With MAC_2, the firm would shift to an emissions level of E_2. Its total abatement costs here would be $(b + d)$, but it would be able to sell $(E_1 - E_2)$ permits for a revenue of $p(E_1 - E_2) = (c + d)$.

FIGURE 13-2 TEPs and Technological Change

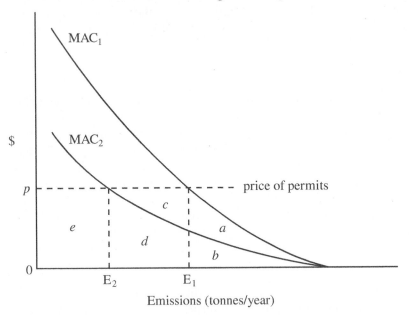

TEPs create a strong incentive to invest in cost-saving technologies to reduce pollution. A polluter who initially holds E_1 permits has a large incentive to engage in R&D to lower its MAC_1 to MAC_2. With MAC_2, the polluter will reduce emissions to E_2. It can then sell its surplus permits at price p and earn area $c + d$ in permit revenues, for a net gain of area c over its additional TAC from moving from E_1 to E_2, and overall net gain of areas $(a + c)$.

The net gain from the R&D is:

$(TAC$ with $MAC_1) - (TAC$ with $MAC_2) + ($Receipts from TEP sales$) =$

$(a + b) - (d + b) + (c + d) = (a + c)$.

Compare this with the savings under an effluent tax (see Chapter 12). It is exactly the same. The market price of the permit has the same incentive as a pollution tax; by not reducing their emissions, firms are forgoing the increased revenues they could have obtained by selling some of their permits.

LO 3

TEPs for Sulphur Dioxide

In the mid-1970s the U.S. Environmental Protection Agency (EPA) began to experiment with limited forms of trading pollution rights. These plans were, and are, meant to be strictly secondary to the primary approach based on technology-based standards (TBSs). The *1990 Clean Air Act Amendments* established an innovative new permit-trading scheme for the control of airborne SO_2 emissions.

The simple outline of the TEP system is as follows. The EPA issues a quantity of emission permits to designated power plants. Each permit will allow the release of 1 ton of sulphur dioxide from that plant; if, for example, operators of a particular plant have 20,000 permits, this plant would be allowed to emit a maximum of 20,000 tons of sulphur per year. The permits may be traded at prices agreed upon between buyer and seller. The purpose of a TEP program like this is to achieve a reduction in total SO_2 emissions at much lower cost than if all plants were required to meet the same proportionate reductions or if all firms were held to the same TBSs. The law calls initially for a reduction of approximately 20 percent from estimated total sulphur emissions of 1980, and a further 20-percent reduction in later years. The program represented a very substantial departure from the command-and-control approaches of the past. Its goal was to achieve targets that reduced emissions substantially below their 1990 levels.

Initial Permit Distribution

The program has two phases. The first ran from 1995 to 2000 and was limited to 110 electric utility plants located in 21 Eastern and Midwestern states. The plants involved were large coal-burning plants that currently emit more than 2.5 pounds of SO_2 per Btu of fuel used. Each of these plants will be allocated a prescribed number of permits (or "allowances," as they are called by the EPA). These allocations were calculated with the following formula:

Number of permits = Average Btus of fuel used (in millions) from 1985–1987 × 2.5 pounds of SO_2 per million Btus

The formula gives more permits to larger plants, as measured by the average quantity of fuel used during the base period 1985–1987. It is not exactly an equiproportionate system, but it moves in that direction by using a common sulphur conversion factor—2.5 pounds of SO_2 per million Btus of fuel—to calculate initial allowances. Two plants burning the same amount of fuel end up with the same permit allocation, even though one of them may have put more effort than the other into reducing SO_2 emissions. But since the plants are all large coal-burning plants, the formula in effect treats them roughly the same.

The initial allocation totalled 5,489,335 permits. About 57 percent of these went to power plants in five states: Ohio, Indiana, Georgia, Pennsylvania, and West Virginia. In a special Phase I allocation, additional permits were given to power plants in Illinois, Ohio, and Indiana.[7] The EPA also held back large quantities of permits. It has a "bonus reserve" of up to 3.5 million permits, which can be used to allow certain states to accommodate growth in their electricity-producing sectors or to provide temporary delays to power plants that wish to install scrubbers[8] to reduce SO_2 emissions. It also may auction off a number of permits, as well as sell a certain number at a fixed (real) price of $1,500 per permit. The EPA will have an additional reserve of permits that it may allocate to utility firms that undertake approved programs in energy conservation or renewable energy development.

Phase II, started in 2000, extended the program to cover power plants throughout the country with capacity of 25 megawatts (MW) or larger. This adds approximately 1,000 power plants burning coal, oil, or natural gas. The formula for allocating permits is much the same as in Phase I except that the SO_2 index is lowered to 1.2 pounds of SO_2 per million Btus of fuel used. Furthermore, Phase II requires an overall cap of 8.95 million permits given out by the EPA. The program has been a resounding success in terms of reductions in emissions. Total U.S. emissions fell more than 50 percent from 11.8 million tons (U.S. short tons) in 1995 to 5.1 million tons in 2010. The price of allowances were somewhat volatile as the participants learned how the market operated, but settled down to a

---

[7] The initial allocation of permits was probably the most controversial issue when the law was being hammered out because it determines how the overall cost burden of SO_2 reduction will be distributed among plants, states, and regions. The extra allocation to the three Midwestern states was simply a way to help get their political support for the program.

[8] A scrubber is a device for treating stack gases; it can remove up to 95 percent of the sulphur in the gas.

level of about $150 to $200 per ton until 2003. In 2003, the EPA announced the Clean Air Interstate Rule (CAIR) that required utilities in the eastern United States to reduce their emissions beginning in 2005, with significant reductions to occur by 2010. The reason for this rule is that emissions in the eastern part of the U.S. have a much larger adverse impact on environmental quality and health than emissions in other parts of the U.S. These are the emissions that flow into Ontario and Quebec as well as New England. The rule called for reductions of 60 to 70 percent below the 2003 levels. The immediate impact was a large spike in the price of allowances, rising to $1,600 per ton in 2005. A legal challenge to the CAIR was launched by some utilities and the state of North Carolina, arguing CAIR violated the Clean Air Act and that the EPA overstepped its authority. The U.S. Court of Appeals agreed and required the EPA to develop new regulations. The allowance market was allowed to operate while the new rules were under development. The price of permits began to fall precipitously as utilities were uncertain about their future demand. In July 2008, the D.C. Circuit Court of Appeals vacated CAIR in its entirety, meaning that the TEP system that allowed unlimited trading across states was no longer valid. The price of allowances fell from $315 to $115 that day. The rulings meant the EPA was tasked with developing new rules. In July 2010, the EPA and the Obama Administration announced new regulations that would significantly limit the use of the market and instead focus on emission reductions mandated at the plant level by state. The proposed rules became finalized as the Cross-State Air Pollution Rule (CSAPR) in July 2011.[9] They were to allow only intrastate trading and some limited trading between two groups of states. The rule was quickly challenged by 27 states and other interveners and the D.C. District Court again ruled that CAIR was to remain until a determination on CSAPR occurred. The message was clear that the TEP system was doomed. The spot price for allowances at the EPA's 2012 auction was 56 *cents* per ton. The case went to the Supreme Court of the United States who ruled in April 2014 to uphold CSAPR, but remanded the case back to the D.C. District Court to address a number of legal issues. In June 2014, the U.S. government filed a motion with that court to lift the stay on CSAPR while they deliberate. It appears that the experiment with a highly successful TEP program may be over due in part to the U.S. political environment. Time will tell if a market can be revived.

Did It Work? Is the Sulphur Dioxide TEP System Cost-Effective?

Before changes in the regulatory environment in 2010, many economists examined the effectiveness of the TEP system for sulphur dioxide in the United States. A key question was: Does the program run smoothly and produce reductions in SO_2 emissions at a substantial cost savings over a CAC-type program? The answer was yes for the following reasons.

1. TEP markets work best if utilities are allowed to use whatever means they find the cheapest (within reason) to reduce SO_2 emissions and then take advantage of this flexibility by buying or selling emission permits. This appears to have happened.

2. Prior to 2010, the EPA did not dictate technology choices made by utilities to reduce their SO_2 emissions. Control over technology will inhibit the market.

3. The move to greater competition in supplying electricity to consumers (though not without many problems in the U.S.) probably aided the efficiency of the market by increasing the number of buyers and sellers.

4. Provisions for banking permits for use in future years allow utilities to hedge against future changes in their emissions due to demand for electricity or if sources expect more stringent

---

[9.] See Schmalansee and Stavins (2012) for an explanation of the complex legal, political, and regulatory environment in the U.S. surrounding the TEP.

government policy in the future (as was the case with the introduction of the CAIR). Banking may inhibit the competitiveness of the market and lead to large price swings. The price volatility may decrease the effectiveness of the market. Banking can change the dynamics of the market in the short term and over time. Permits withheld from the market in a given year by banking may reduce the number of permits traded, thus shifting the supply curve to the left and leading to a higher price. The holder has to reduce emissions accordingly. These permits may be later used by the holder or sold. If sold, there will be a higher supply of permits in that period, leading to lower prices, other things equal.

5. The increasing stringency of the regulations signalled increasing permit scarcity. As prices increase, producers have an incentive to look for cheaper ways of lowering emissions, thus reducing the number of permits they need. They are no longer constrained to use a prescribed TBS. Consider Figure 13-3.

FIGURE 13-3 Incentive to Invest in New Technology Rather Than Trade Permits

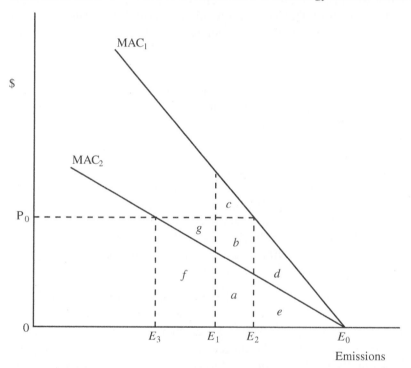

An electric utility may choose to invest in a new technology for controlling emissions rather than engage in permit trades. If MAC_2 represents the new technology, the polluter will save area $(b + c + d)$ compared to staying on its initial MAC_1. This may be a higher return than trading in a permit market. If the utility was initially allocated E_1 permits, it can gain area c by buying $(E_2 - E_1)$ permits at a total cost of area $(a + b)$ and increasing its emissions to E_2. If the amortized cost of the new technology is less than area $(b + d)$ each year, the utility will purchase the technology and not trade in the TEP market.

The utility is initially operating with MAC_1 and given E_1 permits. Suppose the market price of a permit is P_0. At this price, the utility could buy $(E_2 - E_1)$ permits at a total cost of $(a + b)$. It would save in total abatement costs (TAC) area $(a + b + c)$, for a net gain of area c. Alternatively, suppose there is a new technology that reduces its MAC to MAC_2. If it purchases the new technology, the utility can stay at emission level E_1 and save area $(b + c + d)$ in TACs. Alternatively, the utility could control even more of its emissions and sell unused permits. At the permit price of P_0, under the new technology the utility can sell $(E_1 - E_3)$ permits, earning total revenues equal to area $(f + g)$, and incur abatement costs equal to area $(a + e + f)$ for a net gain of areas $(g + b + c + d - e)$. What actually happens depends on the relative cost saving of trading versus buying the new technology under the different scenarios (E_2 versus E_1 or E_3). Apparently, an equilibrium at E_1 with MAC_2 happened during the early years of the TEP system. There were relatively few permits traded but substantial reductions in abatement costs.[10]

A study of the cost-effectiveness of the TEP system in its early years confirms that MAC curves declined considerably since the introduction of the program.[11] This is due to technological changes that allow plants to operate more efficiently. The study estimates that this has lowered MACs by $50 per ton of SO_2 released over the period 1990 to 2000. The second factor is lower coal prices. They are estimated to have decreased MACs by about $200 per ton of SO_2. The graph above is thus representative of the sorts of changes going on and helps explain why in the early years of the TEP program there were fewer trades and at lower prices than expected. However, this is not to say that the TEP program was not effective. Quite the contrary! The TEP policy allowed polluters to find the most cost-effective way of meeting SO_2 standards. They were no longer restricted to a mandatory TBE. Cost savings resulted.

This same study also considered whether or not the TEP system was cost-effective compared to a uniform emission standard and the least-cost solution (a perfectly functioning TEP system or efficient tax). They found that an efficient TEP system would incur total compliance costs of $552-million in 1995 (the first year of operation), compared to $802-million for the uniform standard. The efficient permit price would be $101 per permit. Actual compliance costs for that year were $832-million. In 1996, actual compliance costs were $910-million, compared to $571-million for the efficient market and $777-million for the uniform standard. The actual TEP system was therefore not cost-effective during its first two years, illustrating that an incentive-based system is not necessarily superior to command-and-control policies. The authors caution that this result should not be extended to later years because all new policies have start-up costs (e.g., learning and administrative costs). Over time, they expect greater efficiency. Indeed, studies cited by Schmalansee and Stavins (2012), using data from the later years found cost savings between 15 and 90 percent compared to standards (the amount varying with the type of standard) and strong incentives for innovation.

A study using the MAC estimates from above undertakes a benefit–cost analysis of the TEP program and concludes that the program is an "environmental success."[12] Not only is there 100-percent "environmental compliance," meaning that the emission targets are met, there was over-compliance in Phase I of the program—utilities released less SO_2 than the target level. Costs of the program were one-quarter to one-half of what was originally expected, due in large part to the flexibility given to firms to seek their cost-minimizing actions. The benefits of reducing SO_2, the author argues, far outweigh the costs.

[10] See Dallas Burtraw, "Innovation under the Tradable Sulfur Dioxide Emission Permits Program in the U.S. Electricity Sector, Resources for the Future Discussion Paper 00-38, Washington, D.C., September 2000.

[11] See Curtis Carlson, Dallas Burtraw, Maureen Cropper, and Karen Palmer, "Sulfur Dioxide Control by Electric Utilities: What Are the Gains from Trade?" Resources for the Future Discussion Paper 98-44, Washington, D.C., April 2000. Available online at www.rff.org/disc_papers.

[12] See Dallas Burtraw, "Innovation under the Tradable Sulfur Dioxide Emission Permits Program in the U.S. Electricity Sector, Resources for the Future Discussion Paper 00-38, Washington, D.C., September 2000.

The TEP program represented a considerable innovation in U.S. pollution-control policies. It is the first large-scale example of a system of transferable emission permits tried in the United States; in that sense, it represents a kind of laboratory for environmental economists, who have been talking for many years about the advantages of moving to economic incentive programs to combat pollution.

Summary

Transferable discharge permits are being used more frequently. We examined the U.S. TEP program for SO_2 reduction among electric power producers. A carbon trading system is occurring in a number of countries (see Chapter 20), and voluntarily by some companies. Canada had a type of TEP program for elimination of chlorofluorocarbons (see Chapter 20). There is the expectation that this approach could give us pollution control at a substantially lower cost than the current system of performance and technology-based effluent standards, and also a sense that, politically, they would be more acceptable than emission taxes.

But TEP programs come with their own set of problems. How the TEP market operates is obviously critical to whether this type of policy will work. There are a host of important factors: who gets the permits at the beginning, the strength of their incentives to minimize costs, the degree of competition in the market, the transaction rules set by the administering public agency, the ability to monitor and enforce compliance, and so on.

Both transferable discharge systems and emission tax systems seek to take the burden and responsibility of making technical pollution-control decisions out of the hands of central administrators and put them into the hands of polluters themselves. It is important to stress the following point: Incentive-based policies such as TEPs and taxes are not aimed at putting pollution-control *objectives* themselves into the hands of the polluters. It is not the market that is going to determine the most efficient level of pollution control for society. Rather, the policy instruments are means of enlisting the incentives of the polluters themselves in finding more effective ways of meeting the overall objective of reducing emissions.

Key Terms

Ambient-based TEP system   Hot-spot problem

Emissions-based TEP system   Transferable emission permits (TEPs)

Gains from trade

Analytical Problems

1. Using the MAC curves given in the sulphur-permit example in this chapter, calculate the total costs of each firm before any trading occurs, after the cost-effective trade of 15 permits occurs. Who gains the most from the trade and why?

2. Again, use the MAC equations given in the example. Compute the private versus social costs of a TEP system that initially auctions permits. Contrast this outcome with your solutions to question 1 and explain why any differences occur.

3. Two polluting firms can control emissions of a pollutant by incurring the following marginal abatement costs: $MAC_1 = \$300 - 10E_1$ and $MAC_2 = \$90 - 5E_2$. Assume the *target level of pollution* is 30 units. We do not know if this is the socially efficient level or not.

   (a) Compute the level of emissions per firm that is cost-effective for society.

   (b) Explain how a tradeable emission permit system could be applied to achieve the target level of emissions. Assume the regulator initially assigns 15 permits to each polluter. The government gives these permits to the firms without charge. Solve for the number of permits each firm holds after a permit market operates, the price of the permit, and total private costs of the permit system. How would the private costs to each polluter change if the government initially auctioned the permits to the polluters?

4. Which policy instrument uniform standard provides the largest incentive to invest in R&D to lower MACs: individual standard, emission tax, or TEP? Prove your answer graphically.

Discussion Questions

1. The government has set up a TEP system where it gives away the permits to polluters then lets them trade thereafter. How would this system respond to new firms that enter the industry and have positive levels of pollution? Do you foresee any problems? Explain.

2. What are the pros and cons of letting anybody (e.g., banks, private citizens, environmental groups, government agencies) buy and sell transferable emission permits, in addition to the emission sources themselves?

3. Suggestions have been made to set up a transferable permit system for wildlife preservation and habitat protection. How might this work?

Chapter **14**

Compliance Costs, Uncertainty, and Information

After reading this chapter you will be able to:

LO 1 Compare and contrast graphically and algebraically the social and private compliance costs of standards versus incentive-based policies, incentives to innovate, and informational demands.

LO 2 Explain which policies will minimize social losses when there is uncertainty about the MAC curves.

LO 3 Describe the polluter's incentive to reveal truthful information about its MAC curve under different policies.

The last three chapters have introduced direct regulation and incentive-based policies: standards, taxes and subsidies, and transferable emission permits. This chapter takes the analysis a step further by contrasting the policies in a number of ways. First, using a numerical example and simple algebra similar to that of the previous three chapters, the cost-effective solutions for all the policies are contrasted in terms of their private and social costs of compliance, incentives to invest in new pollution abatement technology, and information requirements to implement the policy. This analysis sets the stage for Section 5, by stimulating you to think about which policy would work best for specific environmental problems. The second section introduces uncertainty about the shape and location of the marginal abatement cost and marginal damage function into the model. **Uncertainty** can prevent the attainment of a socially efficient equilibrium. Another criterion for choosing among policies is introduced—minimizing the social costs of being at an inefficient level of emissions. We conclude with a discussion of the incentives created by each policy to reveal information about the shape of the MAC curve. If the design of a policy can help regulators learn more about polluters' MAC curves, the regulator can set targets that come closer to those that are socially efficient and thus reduce the costs of policy implementation. Knowing whether policies provide incentives for polluters to misreport their MAC or emissions can also help regulators set the policy and enforcement strategy.

LO 1

CONTRASTING POLICY INSTRUMENTS

The Basic Model Revisited: Costs of Compliance

Suppose there are two firms, L and H, with different marginal costs of abatement. As always, emissions are denoted by E_i, where i = L and H. Assume firm L has lower marginal costs of abatement than firm H. Both operate in a perfectly competitive market. There are no distortions in the economy except for pollution from these firms. We also assume that the pollutant in question is uniformly mixed.

$$MAC_L = 900 - 15E_L$$

$$MAC_H = 2000 - 25E_H$$

If there is no regulation against pollution, each firm will incur zero costs of abatement. Emissions from the low-cost firm will equal 60 tonnes, those from the high-cost firm 80 tonnes. These emission levels are found by setting each of these equations equal to zero and solving for E. Total emissions without regulation are thus 140 tonnes. Figure 14-1 illustrates the MACs for each polluter.

FIGURE 14-1 Cost-Effective Emissions

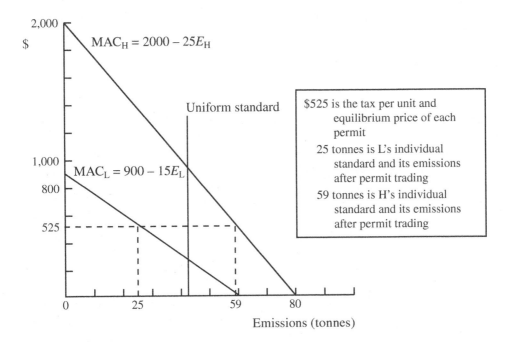

The cost-effective equilibrium for two polluters with different MACs is shown where the MACs are equated. The high-cost polluter (H) reduces emissions from 80 to 59 tonnes, while the low-cost polluter's emissions fall from 60 to 25 tonnes. Both face a marginal MAC = $525. The tax, TEP policies, and individual standards are cost-effective. A uniform standard set at 42 tonnes is not cost-effective because the MACs are not equal at the margin.

Suppose the regulator wants to achieve a 40-percent reduction in emissions. The target level of emissions is therefore 84 tonnes. This target level could represent the socially efficient equilibrium, or be the regulator's best guess at such a point. In the discussion that follows, social efficiency is not crucial to any arguments. Each policy can reach 84 tonnes of emissions. If that target is socially efficient, so is each policy. What will differ among the policies is whether or not they are cost-effective; that is, do they minimize the social costs of obtaining the target level of pollution. We focus on cost-effectiveness in this chapter.

Let's review the two ways to measure costs of compliance with a policy. **Private compliance costs** measure the total costs of abatement incurred by the polluter. This is the polluter's total abatement costs (TAC) plus any taxes paid or transferable emission permits (TEPs) purchased (a cost) or sold (a revenue). The **social compliance costs** are defined as the private compliance costs borne by the polluter net of any redistribution back to polluters of tax or discharge permit revenues collected by the government. These revenues will not influence any decisions on the margin, if they are given back to polluters in lump sums (that is, not dependent on the amount of abatement/emissions).

From society's viewpoint, the social compliance costs are what matters. We calculate private compliance costs because they illustrate quite clearly some political economy features of the policies. When private costs of a policy are high, we can expect a lot of resistance by polluters to the implementation of that policy. The identification of two polluters with different MACs allows us to show that policies can have a different impact on firms operating within the same industry.

A cost-effective equilibrium is found where two conditions are met:

$$E_L + E_H = 84$$

$$MAC_L = MAC_H$$

This ensures that total emissions equal the pollution target and that marginal abatement costs are equal across polluters at the equilibrium level of emissions; that is, the equimarginal principle is satisfied. Solving using the MAC equations above, we find that $E_L = 25$, $E_H = 59$, and $MAC_L = MAC_H = \$525$ at the cost-effective level of emissions for each polluter. Because initial emissions were 60 for L and 80 for H, this means that total abatement is equal to 35 units for L and 21 units for H.

The tax will be set at \$525 per unit of emissions. Individual standards will be set at the cost-effective emissions levels of 25 and 59. We assume that the uniform standard is set at 42 units per polluter; that is, each polluter is required to reach the same emission level regardless of its marginal abatement costs. Two TEP policies are examined. First, we assume that TEPs are given to polluters without charge by the regulator. Suppose the regulator does not know the polluters' initial emission levels. It simply divides total permits by the number of polluters, and issues 42 permits to each polluter. After the initial distribution, polluters can trade the permits. TEPs can also be auctioned. With this policy, the regulator simply offers to sell 84 permits and lets the polluters bid for them. Assume that enough time has passed to allow each policy to reach an equilibrium.

Which of the policies can obtain this cost-effective equilibrium? The only policy that fails to achieve cost-effectiveness is the uniform standard, as noted in Chapter 11. At emission levels of 42 units each, MAC_L is \$270 and $MAC_H = \$950$. This cannot be cost-effective, because the marginal abatement costs of the two firms are not equal at the uniform emission target. An individual standard set at the efficient levels of emissions, a tax set at the efficient price, and both TEP systems are all cost-effective.

Table 14-1 shows the private and social compliance costs for each policy (the other columns are discussed below). As is illustrated, the social costs of compliance are identical for all policies except for the uniform standard. The cost-effective social costs for the two polluters sum to \$14,700.

TABLE 14-1 Compliance Costs, Incentives, and Information Requirements of Pollution Policies

Policy	Private Compliance Costs	Social Compliance Costs	Technological Incentives	Information Required
Uniform standard				
Low-cost polluter	2,430.00	2,430.00	weak	low
High-cost polluter	18,050.00	18,050.00	weak	low
Total costs	20,480.00	20,480.00		
Individual standard				
Low-cost polluter	9,187.50	9,187.50	weak	high
High-cost polluter	5,512.50	5,512.50	weak	high
Total costs	14,700.00	14,700.00		
Uniform tax				
Low-cost polluter	22,312.50	9,187.50	strong	high/medium
High-cost polluter	38,487.50	5,512.50	strong	high/medium
Total costs	58,800.00	14,700.00		
TEPs (given away)				
Low-cost polluter	262.50	9,187.50	weak	low/medium
High-cost polluter	14,437.50	5,512.50	strong	low/medium
Total costs	14,700.00	14,700.00		
TEPs (auctioned)				
Low-cost polluter	22,312.50	9,187.50	strong	low
High-cost polluter	36,487.50	5,512.50	strong	low
Total costs	58,800.00	14,700.00		

The table clearly shows that the uniform standard achieves the emission target at total social costs in excess of all other policies. Next, note the differences in private control costs among the policies and between the two types of firms. The policies can be ranked from lowest to highest private costs for each type of polluter. For the low-cost polluter, the preferred policies in order from lowest to highest cost are (a) TEP that is initially allocated without any charge, (b) the uniform standard, (c) the individual standard, and (d) a tie for the uniform tax and TEP that is auctioned by the government. For the high-cost polluter, the ranking is the individual standard, then the TEP that is not auctioned, followed by the uniform standard, then the tax and auctioned TEP. The standards thus have a different impact depending on whether the polluter is high- or low-cost, but they are clearly lower than the tax or auctioned TEP system. The TEP that is initially allocated without charge is the policy that is either first or second on the list.[1] This may help to explain why there is growing support for the implementation of TEPs among polluters. It is clearly preferred to taxes by all polluters and dominates at least one form of standards for all polluters. The asymmetry of the impact of the standards is also interesting and may help explain support for different policies. The high-cost polluter clearly favours individual standards. If the high-cost polluter also represents the existing firms in the industry, it is obvious that they will oppose any policies that have uniform standards. If new firms can enter the industry *and* have lower MACs, a uniform standard will clearly disadvantage the old firms. Thus, when we see standards in practice, they are frequently one standard for existing firms and a tougher standard for new firms that enter the industry. The table also clearly shows that polluters will resist the implementation of taxes and TEPs that are auctioned because of their high private costs relative to the other policies.

The Technological Incentives column summarizes the information presented in Chapters 11 through 13 about the incentive each policy creates to invest in R&D that may lower MACs. We have shown that all standards provide weaker incentives to invest in R&D than do the other policies. Under individual standards, the lower each firm's costs of abatement the greater the share of total abatement it may have to incur, other things equal. Each polluter even has an incentive to misreport its abatement costs, hoping to convince the regulatory authorities that they are higher than these costs actually are. The regulator interested in cost-effectiveness would then assign the polluter a more lenient standard. In the next section of this chapter, we illustrate graphically the incentives to misreport information under standards versus taxes. For all the other policies, there are strong incentives to invest in abatement equipment, because for each unit of pollution reduced the total private costs of the policy decline. Auctioned TEPs and tax would most likely provide the strongest incentives to seek a lower MAC curve, as the cost savings from reducing one's tax bill or TEP payment is potentially very large.

The Information Required column gives an indication of the amount of information regulators need to determine the target level of emissions. We do not consider information required for enforcement of each policy. Two policies are ranked "low." Uniform standards and auctioned TEPs require the least amount of information. In the case of the uniform standard as defined above (equal distribution of the allowed emissions among the polluters),[2] the regulator does not need to know anything about individual firms. The same is true for TEPs that are auctioned. The regulator simply announces an auction and the market takes care of the rest. Transactions in the permit market will reveal a polluter's MAC curves (as a permit supply or demand curve). The allocated TEPs are rated low to medium. This is because some means of initially distributing the permits must be established. For example, regulators may use each polluter's share of total pollution or, as we have shown, simply divide the permits by the number of polluters (as with the simple uniform standard). We rate the uniform tax at

---

[1.] The ranking of the TEP that is given away without auctioning will be a function of the initial distribution of permits. If, for example, the polluters receive permits in proportion to their initial emissions, L would get 36 and H would get 48. This would change the private control costs to $3,412.50 for L and $11,287.50 for H. This allocation makes the permits the second lowest-cost policy for L. Thus, permits are always preferred to taxes and are always preferred by one of the parties to any form of standard. There will be strong incentives for polluters to lobby for an initial distribution of permits that most favours them.

[2.] The same principle would hold if the uniform standard required each polluter to meet the same percentage reduction in emissions.

medium to high. To compute the cost-effective tax, the regulator has to solve for the cost-effective solution. This means it must know the MACs for all polluters. If there are many polluters, the information costs would be quite high. The reason we've given it a rating of medium is that the regulator may iterate to an efficient tax by setting the tax rate, observing total emissions, then raising or lowering the rate until the target level of emissions is reached. This is illustrated graphically in the next section of this chapter. The individual standard requires a large amount of information. Like the cost-effective tax (that isn't set by iteration), the MACs of all polluters must be known to determine each polluter's individual standard. Unlike the tax, there is no way to iterate to the cost-effective solution. Once the polluters comply with a given standard, the regulator will get no information about their MAC curves.

LO 2

LO 3

UNCERTAINTY AND INFORMATION

Uncertainty about the MD and MAC Curves

We have assumed that regulators know precisely the equations for the MAC and MD curves. This information enables them to determine the socially efficient policy. But, in practice, it is likely that information about these curves will not be known with certainty. Policy options regulators have when there is uncertainty about the MD and MAC curves are examined. The policies considered are a uniform tax, uniform standard, and transferable emission permits.[3] When there is uncertainty about the MAC or MD curve, it is generally impossible to achieve a socially efficient equilibrium. This is called a **second-best situation.** There will typically be some *social loss* associated with the use of any policy. We assume the objective of regulators is to choose the policy that *minimizes the social loss* obtained as a result of the uncertainty. The social loss is defined as the loss of real resources devoted to too much or too little pollution control relative to the socially efficient level. It is measured as the area between the MD and MAC curves from the actual pollution level to the socially efficient pollution level. Of course, regulators do not know the socially efficient level of pollution. The theoretical model developed below allows them under certain circumstances to predict the relative size of social losses without this information. To summarize,

> *a second-best decision rule for regulators when there is uncertainty about the MAC or MD curve is to minimize the social loss associated with the choice of policy. Social loss is the area between the MD and MAC curves from the actual pollution level to the socially efficient level.*

A number of different cases are examined:

[3.] The seminal article that stimulated much of the work on this topic is by Martin Weitzman, "Prices versus Quantities," *Review of Economic Studies* 41 (1974): 477–491.

The regulator is uncertain about the location of the MD curve, MACs are known with certainty

Case 1

Assume that pollution is uniformly mixed and that all polluters have identical MACs. Figure 14-2 illustrates. Two MD curves are shown. MD^E is the curve estimated by regulators; MD^T is the "true" curve that is not observed. The socially efficient equilibrium is at E^*; E' is the level of emissions the regulators have estimated as the intersection of the MD and MAC curves. The regulator would then set the standard or number of permits at E'. The uniform tax would be set at t'. The choice of policy instrument will not affect the size of the social loss in this case. Under a standard or TEP, the total emissions are E'. Under a tax set at t', the total emissions are also E', because the polluter sets t' equal to its true MAC. The social loss is identical for all policies and equal to the shaded area abc.[4] The level of emissions is too low relative to the socially efficient equilibrium. Thus, if there is uncertainty about the MD curve, no policy dominates another in terms of minimizing social losses. The economist cannot help the regulator choose a preferred policy.

FIGURE 14-2 Uncertainty about the MD Curve

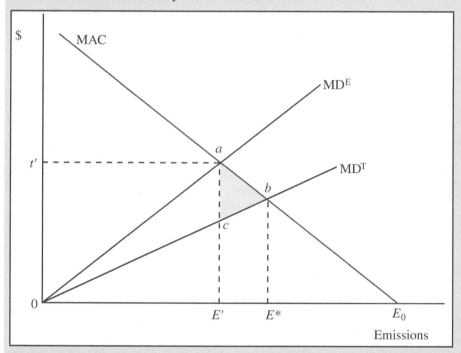

If the regulator is uncertain about the location of the MD curve, both a standard and tax set where the estimated MD function (MDE) intersects the MAC curve yield an identical social loss, indicated by the shaded area.

[4.] The area abc reflects the loss in terms of excess total abatement costs from being at too low a level of emissions. This is area $E'abE^*$ minus the incremental marginal benefits from having more damages controlled than is socially efficient, area $E'cbE^*$.

The regulator is uncertain about the MAC curve, but knows the MD curve with certainty

Case 2

Figure 14-3 illustrates this case. Assume the regulator knows the actual amount of emissions when no policy is in place. Initial emissions are E_0. The regulator is therefore uncertain about the slope of the MAC curve.[5] MAC^T is the true curve; MAC^E the estimated curve. The socially efficient equilibrium is E^* and the estimated equilibrium is E'. The standard or number of TEPs is set at E'; the tax set at t'. The equilibrium under the standard or TEPs is at E', with a social loss equal to the shaded area abc. But now, the use of an emission tax at rate t' will lead to a different equilibrium than under the standard or TEPs. The polluter sets t' equal to its true MAC. Emissions under the tax are E'', which is greater than the socially efficient level of E^*. The social loss under a tax is shaded area adf.

FIGURE 14-3   Uncertainty about the MAC Curve: Steep MD Curve

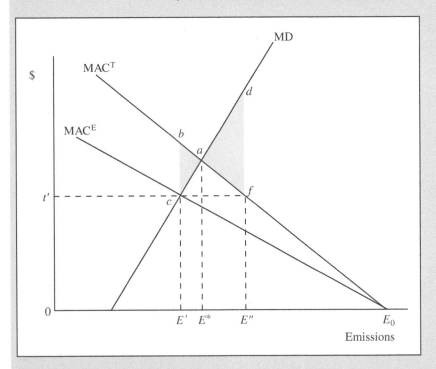

When the regulator is uncertain about the slope of the MAC curve, a tax policy can lead to a different social loss than a standard when both are set by equating the MAC^E to MD. In the case illustrated, the social loss under the tax (area adf) exceeds that of the standard (area abc) because the MD curve is relatively steeper than the MAC curves. A second-best standard set at E' will get the economy closer to the socially efficient level of emissions, E^*.

(Continued)

[5.] It is possible that the regulator knows neither the slope of the MAC nor the initial level of emissions. The basic analysis in this section is the same.

The regulator now has the means to compare policies in terms of which ones lead to the lowest social loss, by examining the relative sizes of area *abc* to area *adf*. But recall that the regulator doesn't know where point E^* is or where MAC^T actually lies. So how can areas *abc* and *adf* be measured? The regulator cannot measure these areas precisely but can determine their relative size if they have some information about the slopes of the MD and MAC curve. In Figure 14-3, the MD curve is relatively steep. Even though the regulator doesn't know the exact slope of the MAC, suppose he or she knows the MD is steeper than the MAC. In this case, area *abc* is less than area *adf*. A uniform standard or TEP will minimize the social losses. The intuition behind this result is that whenever MDs rise considerably as emissions increase, social losses will be larger the farther away actual emissions are from E^*. The equilibrium under a tax is less predictable than with a standard or TEPs. If MAC^E lies below MAC^T, the tax will lead to too high a level of emissions and large social damages. If MAC^E lies above MAC^T, the tax will overcontrol emissions and will lead to large social losses due to too little production of pollution-generating goods. In the extreme case where the MD curve is vertical, it is obvious that the socially efficient policy is a standard or TEP set at E^*.

Figure 14-4 illustrates the case where the MD curve is flat relative to the MAC curves. In this situation, the tax is the policy that minimizes the social losses of failing to be at the socially efficient equilibrium, E^*. Area *adf* is now smaller than area *abc*. Again the intuition is straightforward. If the MD curve were horizontal, the socially efficient policy would be a tax. Uncertainty about the MAC curve wouldn't matter, as the tax rate would be set at the level of MD. Therefore, the flatter the MD curve, the closer a tax will be to the socially efficient equilibrium than a standard or TEP program.

FIGURE 14-4   Uncertainty about the MAC Curve: Flat MD

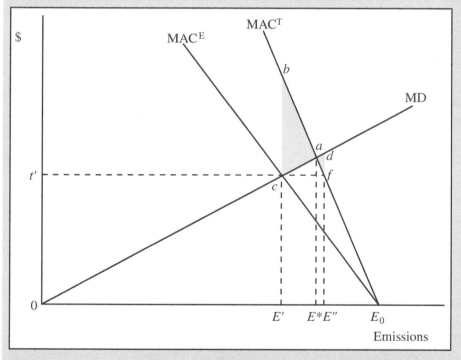

The social loss under a standard set where $MAC^E = MD$ (area *abc*) exceeds the social loss under the tax (area *adf*) because the MAC curves are relatively steeper than the MD curve. A second-best tax will be closer to the socially efficient level of emissions, E^*.

Information Revelation under Taxes, Standards, and TEPs

Earlier chapters have argued that various policy instruments can reveal to the regulator information about the slope of the MAC curve. As well, the policy chosen affects the polluter's **information revelation incentives.** A graphical analysis is used to illustrate both types of information revelation. Assume in all cases that the regulator and all polluters know the MD curve with certainty. Again, a number of different cases are examined.

Information revelation incentives under a standard   Case 3

In Figure 14-5, the regulator has set the emissions standard at E'. First note that the standard reveals no information to the regulator about the polluter's true MAC. If the polluter complies with the standard, actual emissions are what the regulator expected. But standards create incentives for the polluter to reveal false information to the regulator. The polluter knows the socially efficient level of emissions is at E^*, so under the standard set at E' it will be incurring very high marginal abatement costs (shown as MAC' on Figure 14-5) if it complies with the regulation. The polluter wants to minimize its abatement costs, so it has an incentive to tell the government that its MACs are higher than the regulator estimated at MAC^E. But what is to prevent the polluter from telling the regulator that its MACs are even higher than MAC^T? Suppose it tries to convince the regulator that its "true" marginal abatement costs are MAC^R. If a standard is used, the polluter will then have to control far fewer emissions than under the regulator's initial estimate of MAC^E. Under a standard, then, the polluter has an incentive to reveal a MAC that is higher than its true MAC.

FIGURE 14-5   Incentives to Overstate MACs under a Standard

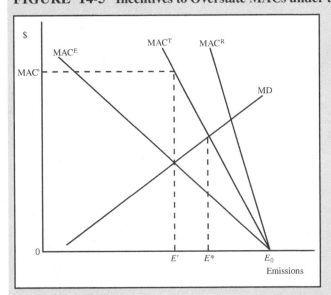

A standard reveals no information to regulators about the location of the MAC curve. Polluters will have an incentive to try to convince the regulator that their MAC curve is MAC^R. This will lead to much less stringent standards than are socially efficient.

Information revelation incentives under a tax

Case 4

Figure 14-6 again presents an estimated MAC that lies below the true MAC. The regulator sets the tax equal to t'. The polluter sets t' equal to its true MAC and releases emissions equal to E'', where E'' exceeds both the socially efficient level of emissions (E^*) and the regulator's anticipated emission levels of E' (which is based on the estimated MAC^E). Note first that the level of emissions provides the regulator with information. Assuming the regulator can monitor emissions, if E'' exceeds E' the regulator knows the tax rate has been set too low. The regulator now has two points on the polluter's true MAC curve, found from E_0 and E'' (MAC equal to zero and to t'). If the MACs are linear, this is all the information needed to go directly to the socially efficient tax of t^*. If the MACs are not linear, and the regulator can adjust tax rates, an iterative process can be followed to reach t^*. The regulator adjusts the tax rate, measures emissions, and then maps out more of the MAC curve.

FIGURE 14-6 Iteration to the Socially Efficient Tax Rate

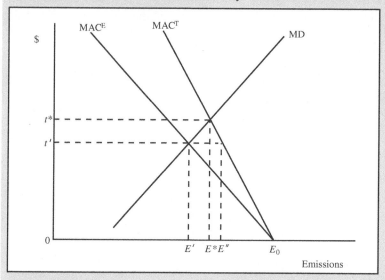

Regulators obtain information from the polluter's response to a tax even if that tax is set at the "wrong" level. Polluters set the incorrect tax of t' equal to their true MAC and release E'' pollution. The regulator expects E' emissions. If E_0 is known, the regulator now has two points on the polluter's true MAC curve, E_0 and E'. The regulator can iterate to the socially efficient tax.

Does the tax provide any incentives for the polluter to reveal true or misleading information to the regulator? This case is more complex than that of the standard. To calculate the incentives for the polluter, the total abatement costs plus the tax bill under different tax rates have to be calculated. The polluter has no incentive to reveal an excessively high MAC, as in the case of MAC^R under the standard. This would result in a very high tax rate and thus tax bill (t' times the level of emissions), and more emissions controlled than if the true MAC curve were revealed.

Does the polluter have an incentive to try to convince the government that its MACs are what the regulator estimated (that is, MAC^E)? The answer here is possibly, yes. Suppose the polluter does not equate the estimated tax of t' to its true MAC, but to the regulator's estimated MAC^E. This is shown in Figure 14-7. The question is whether the polluter is better off by following this strategy rather

(Continued)

than equating t' to MAC^T. At t' and E', the polluter pays a tax bill equal to the area $0t'aE'$. If the polluter sets t' equal to MAC^T, its tax bill is higher and equal to area $0t'bE''$. The difference between the two tax bills is area $abE''E'$, which represents the gain from "pretending" that MAC^E is the true MAC. However at E' emissions, the polluter will incur total abatement costs equal to area $E'E_0c$. If it sets t' equal to its true MAC, total abatement costs equal area $E'E_0b$. The difference between the total abatement costs is area $E'E''bc$, which represents the savings in total abatement costs if the polluter sets t' equal to MAC^T. We can now compare the net costs to the polluter under the two options shown. If it sets the estimated tax equal to its true MAC, the savings in abatement costs exceed the savings in the tax bill if it sets t' equal to MAC^E. Area abc is the net gain by setting t' equal to MAC^T.

Recall that eventually the regulator will iterate to the socially efficient tax rate of t^*. Does it still pay for the polluter to reveal its true MAC, knowing that the tax rate won't stay at t'? Following the same type of analysis, we now compare total abatement costs and tax bills under t' to those with t^*, the socially efficient tax rate. We can no longer predict without knowing the exact slopes of the MAC curves whether or not the polluter will reveal its true MAC. Refer again to Figure 14-7. The net gain to polluters from being at the inefficient tax of t' relative to the efficient tax of t^* is derived as follows. The polluter will calculate the difference between any saving in the tax bill (area $0t^*fE^*$ minus area $0t'aE'$) and the difference in the total abatement costs (area $E'E_0c$ minus E^*E_0f). Whether the polluter reveals its true MAC then depends on the size of area cdf to area $t't^*da$, which in turn depends on the tax rate set by the regulator and the polluter's true MAC. In the case illustrated, the polluter will gain by pretending its MAC is MAC^E.

FIGURE 14-7 Incentives to Reveal the True MAC under a Tax

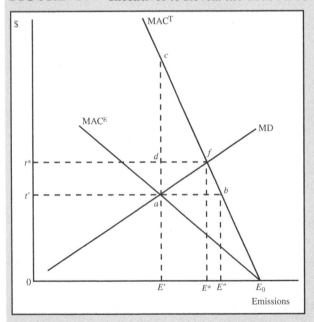

Polluters will set their emissions where $t' = MAC^T$ because it saves them area abc compared to setting $MAC^E = t'$. However, if polluters think that regulators will use their emissions level to calculate true MACs (and thus could raise tax rates), polluters may have an incentive to mislead regulators into thinking that MAC^E is the true MAC curve. If lying lowers the polluter's tax bill by more than it increases its total abatement costs, the polluter will pretend to have MAC^E and emit E' pollution rather than set t' equal to its true MAC curve, MAC^T. This occurs because area $t't^*da$ exceeds area cdf. This need not always be the case.

Information revelation incentives under TEPs   Case 5

To keep the analysis simple, assume that only one MAC represents the entire industry. Figure 14-8 illustrates this case. Suppose the regulator sets the number of permits at E', which is too low a level relative to the socially efficient number. This is analogous to the cases examined above. Assume the regulator attempts to auction the permits. It would expect the permit market to clear at a price equal to P' if the efficient number of permits had been distributed. If there are too few permits, their market-clearing price will be P'', which is above P'.[6] Like the tax, permit prices give information about the true MACs. The regulator could then adjust the number of permits to iterate to the socially efficient equilibrium. Will individual polluters have incentives to reveal false information about their MACs to the regulator for the initial trades and to other polluters for other trades? Analogous to the tax, there is no incentive to reveal a MAC that is higher than the true MAC, for this would simply raise the permit price the polluter would have to pay. If one polluter pretends its MAC is lower than the true one and others don't, the one that revealed false information won't be able to buy sufficient permits in the market to cover its emissions. With our simple analysis, it appears that TEPs, if used in perfectly competitive markets, are likely to reveal information that results over time in the attainment of a socially efficient equilibrium. However, we caution that what is required in a full analysis of TEPs is a game theoretic framework. This is a subject for a more advanced course.

FIGURE 14-8   Information Revealed about MACs under a TEP

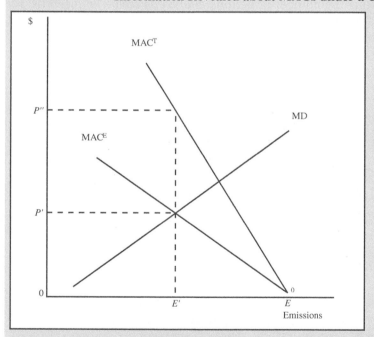

Regulators can examine market prices under a TEP system to estimate true MAC curves. If E' permits are issued, the regulator will expect a market price of P'. When the market clears at price P'', the regulator knows that MAC^T is the true MAC curve for polluters. Market forces also prevent polluters from lying about the true MAC. Lying will either lead them to pay more for permits than necessary or not be able to buy any at the prevailing price.

[6.] If the regulator initially distributes the permits without charge, it will have to monitor subsequent permit prices in the TEP market to obtain information about whether there is an excess supply of or excess demand for permits.

Summary

Regulatory policies are compared using a simple algebraic model of two polluters with different MACs. All policies have the potential to achieve a socially efficient equilibrium, and all are cost-effective except for the uniform standard. Policies differ in terms of the private costs of compliance. These differences help explain polluters' support for or opposition to the implementation of policies. We also discussed the incentives created by each policy to invest in pollution abatement equipment, and the information required by regulators to implement the policy. These criteria can help regulators choose a policy for each particular pollution problem. No single policy is appropriate for all types of pollution.

When uncertainty exists about the MAC and MD curves, regulators may no longer be able to reach a socially efficient level of emissions, but can enact policies that minimize the social losses of having a level of emissions that is too high or too low. If there is uncertainty about the MD curve, all regulatory policies lead to equal social losses and some other criteria must be used to choose among them. If the uncertainty is about the MAC curve, taxes will minimize the social losses when the MD curve is relatively flat compared to the MAC curve and standards or TEPs will minimize social losses when the MD curve is relatively steep.

Incentive-based policies reveal information about the MAC curve of the polluter, while standards do not. Under a tax, a socially efficient policy can be reached by iteration of the tax rate. Under a TEP, social efficiency can be reached by adjusting the number of permits. Standards create an incentive for polluters to reveal a MAC curve that is steeper (higher) than their true marginal abatement costs. Taxes and TEPs do not create this incentive. Taxes may, however, induce polluters to reveal to regulators a MAC that is lower than their true curve. It is unlikely that this will occur with TEPs.

Key Terms

Information revelation incentives   Social compliance costs

Private compliance costs   Uncertainty

Second-best situation

Analytical Problems

1. Suppose you are a government regulator that is trying to design a pollution-control policy for a non-degradable water pollutant such as dioxin. Your objective is to get an immediate reduction in emissions plus provide an incentive to firms to switch to production technologies that yield fewer emissions of these compounds. Which *one* of the following three policies would you recommend, and why? The policies are uniform standard, uniform tax, or individual standard. Support your answer graphically and/or algebraically.

2. Suppose there are two polluters with different MAC curves. Show how the regulator would aggregate these MAC curves and then use them to determine the socially efficient equilibrium level of emissions, E^*. Once E^* is determined, how would the regulator ensure that the sum of emissions from each polluter totals E^*? (Hint: Aggregation should reflect the equimarginal principle.)

3. You are a polluter with a steep MAC curve that is positively sloped and linear. You would prefer to be allowed to freely dump your wastes, but recognize that the government will impose environmental regulation of some sort. Rank, from best to worst, the policies you would like to see imposed, and explain the reasons for your ranking.

4. Suppose the government cannot accurately measure and monitor the pollution emissions from each polluter, but it knows the marginal damages per unit pollution and these are relatively constant. What policy or policies would you recommend that the government implement? Explain why.

5. Assume that the government does not know the location of the polluter's MAC curve. The government plans to impose an emissions tax. Would the polluter have an incentive to reveal its MAC curve to the government? Could an efficient equilibrium be reached? Explain why or why not.

Discussion Questions

1. How do market-based policies differ from command-and-control policies with regard to incentives created by the policy to reveal information about the polluter's MAC curve to the regulator?

2. Why is cost-effectiveness a desirable goal of environmental policy? How is it achieved?

3. Why do pollution taxes have a more uncertain impact on the level of pollution than does a standard?

For more information on the resources available from McGraw-Hill Ryerson, go to www.mheducation.ca/he/solutions.

Environmental Policy in Canada

In the preceding chapters we showed how and why markets fail to achieve social efficiency when externalities associated with the natural environment exist. Chapter 10 looked at the extent to which decentralized policies can work out socially efficient solutions to environmental problems. Chapters 11 through 14 examined the economics of specific government policies designed to achieve social efficiency. In this section, Chapter 15 provides an introduction to some key characteristics of Canadian environmental policy—the Constitution and important features of the parliamentary model of government in a federal system. In the chapters that follow, we examine specific environmental policies that have been used by governments in Canada to deal with *environmental problems*—water and air pollution, toxic substances, solid wastes, and *global problems*— climate change, ozone depletion, and biodiversity, including species at risk. The analytical tools developed in the previous sections are used to evaluate these policies. Canadian policies are contrasted with those in the United States and other countries to get a perspective on where Canada stands relative to other industrialized countries.

Chapter 15

Environmental Policy and Institutions in Canada: An Overview

After reading this chapter you will be able to:

LO 1 Describe the constitutional powers of the federal and provincial governments guiding environmental policy.

LO 2 Explain how federal and provincial authority over the environment can be in conflict.

LO 3 Describe the key features of environmental regulation in Canada's parliamentary democracy.

LO 4 Provide a brief synopsis of federal environmental regulatory history since the 1970s.

It is much more difficult in practice to achieve social efficiency than economic models suggest. There are many reasons for this. Economic efficiency is only one possible objective of environmental policy. Other motivations include equity (ensuring a fair distribution of both the benefits and costs of meeting environmental targets across income groups), regional diversity, and political factors (such as vote seeking on the part of politicians, responses to special groups, ideological beliefs, and so on). Governments are also constrained by constitutional powers, legislation, and the presence or absence of particular institutions. While it is beyond the scope of this text to address all of these factors, this chapter presents the constitutional foundations for developing and implementing environmental policy in Canada, a review of the agencies that make and enforce Canadian environmental policy, and a short summary of the direction of Canadian federal environmental regulation with a guide to where to find more details in the chapters that follow. We start with some general points about Canadian environmental policy to set the stage.

GENERAL POINTS ABOUT CANADIAN ENVIRONMENTAL POLICY

1. Incentive-based policies are much less common than direct regulation also called command-and-control polices.

2. There has been a reluctance to impose specific standards. Most regulation has been in the form of guidelines that suggest a range of pollution targets. Both ambient and emission guidelines and standards are used. Technology-based standards remain in wide use as do intensity guidelines.

(Continued)

3. Environmental legislation in Canada has been based on a co-operative model of negotiation between the government regulator and the polluting party where contracts exist between specific polluters and government.[1]

4. Environmental legislation in Canada has been primarily enabling rather than mandatory. What this means is that officials are authorized to develop regulations. They rarely have the obligation to act. This is quite different from the situation in the United States, where regulations passed by Congress generally require implementation of specific policies.

5. Negotiation and moral suasion have been used to achieve compliance with environmental targets.

6. Jurisdiction over the environment is not always well defined. Conflict among the levels of government and inaction can arise as a result.

LO 1

CONSTITUTIONAL POWERS OVER THE ENVIRONMENT[2]

Federal Powers

Section 91 of the *Constitution Act* (1867) establishes federal powers over ocean and inland fisheries (section 91[12]), navigation and shipping (section 91[10]), and federal lands and waters. Each of these powers has been used by the federal government to enact legislation that has some element of pollution control. For example, under its fisheries powers the *Fisheries Act* was, until recently, one of the strongest and most-used environmental regulations. The federal government enacted under its navigation and shipping powers the *Navigable Waters Protection Act* and the *Arctic Waters Pollution Prevention Act*. The *Northern Inland Waters Act* comes from its powers over federal lands and waters. The federal government also has powers to enter into international agreements and has done so on many occasions in matters that involve environmental concerns. Examples of international agreements regarding the environment are the Montreal Protocol for stratospheric ozone depletion, the Basel Convention on toxic wastes, the Copenhagen Accord for greenhouse gases, and many others. Finally, there is a provision that is increasingly serving as a basis for federal government regulation regarding the environment. This is the preamble to section 91 of the *Constitution Act* that gives the federal government the power to enact legislation in the interests of "Peace, Order, and Good Government." The widely used acronym for this is POGG. The major piece of federal legislation relating to toxic materials, the *Canadian Environmental Protection Act,* was based on POGG power. The federal government also has the power over interprovincial and international trade, and the power to levy taxes and to make expenditures. Its taxation powers have rarely been used to justify environmental policy.

[1.] A memorandum of understanding is a commonly used agreement between governments and the private sector to achieve a particular goal (e.g., reduction of emissions). This allows the government to achieve pollution targets without passing specific regulations. However, it may also thwart achieving these targets. If there is a memorandum of understanding, a company cannot be prosecuted for failure to comply if it has notified the government that it needs more time, for example, to install pollutionabatement equipment or if adverse economic conditions prevent compliance. This has enabled some companies to delay compliance for fairly long periods of time.

[2.] This section of the chapter is based largely on the readings in Robert Boardman, ed., *Canadian Environmental Policy: Ecosystems, Politics, and Process* (Toronto: Oxford University Press, 1992). We will deal with local government powers in Chapter 19.

Provincial Powers

The key to understanding Canadian environmental policy is to recognize that most regulatory powers applicable to the environment lie with the provincial governments.

Most of the provincial powers come from section 92 of the Constitution. Under section 92, the provinces have power over local works (section 92[10]), property and civil rights within the provinces (section 92[13]), matters of a local or private nature (section 92[16]), and authority over provincially owned lands and resources (sections 92[5]; 109). This last authority is extremely significant, as it gives the provinces the right to regulate their natural-resource industries. Development and use of natural resources can often lead to environmental trade-offs and conflicts. As well, the federal government holds relatively little of the public land in the provinces, so whatever policies provincial governments enact will tend to have larger environmental impacts than federal policies related to lands. A 1982 amendment to the *Constitution Act* (section 92A) strengthened the provincial powers over its natural resources. Under 92A, each province has exclusive jurisdiction over the development, conservation, and management of its non-renewable resources, which have been interpreted to include energy resources, forests, and hydroelectric power facilities. Each province has established an environmental regulatory regime that contains provisions for procedures and statutes controlling various sources of pollution and addressing ambient environmental quality.

Overlapping Powers

Having looked at these constitutional powers, it is tempting to generalize by saying that, with the exception of fisheries and navigable waters, the federal government is responsible for federal lands and international aspects of the environment while the provinces are responsible for *intra*provincial environmental quality. Unfortunately, the situation is not this simple. The regulation of specific environmental problems in Canada tends to be done at both the federal and provincial levels. The Constitution does not explicitly prohibit this. For example, provincial water-pollution regulations overlap with federal fisheries regulations. Both have regulations for accidental spills into waterways as well as air-pollution regulations. Pesticide distribution, use, and sale is regulated by the federal government. Provinces have their own pesticide regulations.

Another indeterminate area of constitutional powers concerns *inter*provincial pollution flows. In principle, one would expect that the federal government would have regulatory power when pollution flows across provincial boundaries. This would be analogous to its international and interprovincial powers in other matters. However, federal extrajurisdictional powers can be in conflict with the section 92A powers of the provinces. Interprovincial environmental problems remain an area of potential federal–provincial tension.

Finally, there are even unresolved issues with the federal government's treaty-making powers. While the federal government clearly has the power to negotiate an international treaty, implementing a treaty would be a provincial matter if section 92A and other provincial powers apply. There is the possibility that provinces may refuse to co-operate with the federal government. Individual provinces may also want to make separate arrangements about the conditions of implementation with the federal government, or even act independently for political or other reasons. It is not necessarily a bad thing to have different arrangements with each province because environmental quality and pollution problems can differ widely across the country; policy harmonization across the country is not necessarily required. But, arrangements that differ considerably across the country may lead to unequal and unjust burdens in different provinces, or even thwart the federal government's efforts. If each province enacts its own legislation, this also raises the compliance costs for polluters that deal with myriad regulations.

EXAMPLE

Overlapping powers in regulating oil sands extraction

Extracting and refining Alberta's vast oil deposits is causing growing debate in Canada and on the world stage, centred on the tradeoffs between economic development and environmental sustainability. Removing the heavy bitumen, locked deep within sand deposits in northern Alberta, is an industrial project of unprecedented scale. The oil sands represent the third largest reserve of oil on the planet and 43 percent of the proven global reserves of bitumen oil.[3] The economic benefits from oil sands production provide employment, capital investment, and royalty payments to Albertans and Canadians. Current production stands at 1.9 million barrels per day, and is expected to increase to 5 million barrels per day by 2030.[4] Over the next 25 years, the Conference Board of Canada estimates the oil sands will generate $172 billion in gross wages and salaries and $79 billion in royalty payments to the federal and provincial governments.[5]

Contrary to the economic benefits, however, is the staggering local and global environmental footprint (quite literally, the project is visible from space). From an international perspective, oil sands development is the fastest growing source of greenhouse gas (GHG) emissions in Canada, accounting for roughly 7 percent of national emissions and 0.15 percent of global emissions (2010).[6] Due to the high energy intensities of extracting and producing Alberta bitumen, GHG emissions are 8–37 percent higher compared to producing conventional crude oil (using a full life-cycle analysis).[7]

Total emissions from the oil sands production, according to Environment Canada, increased by 77 percent from 2000–2011 (increasing from 31 to 55 million tonnes of CO_2 equivalent).[8] By 2020, estimates are that emissions will reach 101 million tonnes—roughly the equivalent of Belgium's total emissions in 2009.[9] Barring the development of a viable and effective carbon capture technology, GHGs from oil sands production are predicted to be the main driver of Canada's net increase in national emissions, making it impossible to meet the 17 percent reduction in greenhouse gases from 2005 levels, as mandated by the Copenhagen Accord.

(Continued)

[3.] Kevin Timoney (2012), "Environmental and Health Impacts of Canada's Bitumen Industry: In Search of Answers," *American Chemical Society: Environmental Science and Technology,* pp. 2496–97.

[4.] See: Government of Alberta (2014), "Oil Sands," *Alberta Energy* www.energy.alberta.ca/ourbusiness/oilsands.asp; and Kevin Timoney (2012), "Environmental and Health Impacts of Canada's Bitumen Industry: In Search of Answers," *American Chemical Society: Environmental Science and Technology,* pp. 2496–97.

[5.] Michael Burt, Todd Crawford, and Alan Arcand (2012), "Fuel for Thought: The Economic Benefits of Oil Sands Investment for Canada's Regions," *Conference Board of Canada* www.conferenceboard.ca.

[6.] See: Government of Canada (2013), "Canada's Emission Trends 2013," *Environment Canada* www.ec.gc.ca; and Government of Alberta (2014), "Greenhouse Gases," *Alberta Energy* www.ec.gc.ca www.oilsands.alberta.ca/ghg.html.

[7.] Natural Resources Defense Council (2010), "Setting the Record Straight: Lifecycle Emissions of Tar Sands" http://docs.nrdc.org/energy/files/ene_10110501a.pdf.

[8.] Government of Canada (2013), "Canada's Emission Trends 2013," *Environment Canada* www.ec.gc.ca.

[9.] See: Government of Canada (2013), "Canada's Emission Trends 2013," *Environment Canada* www.ec.gc.ca; and Organization for Economic Co-operation and Development (2014), "Greenhouse Gas Emissions," *OECD Stat Extracts* http://stats.oecd.org/Index.aspx?DataSetCode=AIR_GHG.

At the local level, water contamination and excessive withdrawals, air pollution, and physical damage to fisheries and surrounding habitats are the most pressing issues. While the pace of scientific and peer-reviewed studies lag behind industrial development, studies by Environment Canada (2014) and Kelly et al. (2009), for example, support previous suspicions that toxic tailings ponds are leaking into groundwater and the Athabasca River. Tailings ponds contain heavy metals and other toxic contaminants, and cover an area of 176 square kilometres, leaking as much as 6.5 million litres of toxic effluence per day from a single pond.[10] The cumulative environmental impacts from these leakages are understudied and poorly understood.

In addition to water contamination, the oil sands have disturbed over 715 square kilometres of boreal forest, destroying wetlands, fisheries, and animal habitat. Industry is obligated to provide "financial security equivalent to the cost of reclamation," however, only 0.2 percent of disturbed land from oil sands has been reclaimed and certified by the Alberta Government.[11] Despite government subsidies encouraging new reclamation technologies, the scientific capacity is in its infancy and the regulatory framework for reclaiming disturbed lands to their natural states is lacking.

Compounding these substantive issues is the scattered and overlapping governance framework for environmental management. While the province is responsible for the bulk of regulation, the federal government plays a key role in issues of water and toxic waste management, pipelines, and species at risk. In other cases, such as for aquatic monitoring, reporting effluence levels, and reclamation processes, regulatory power is deferred to industry for self-monitoring. The resulting mishmash of regulatory oversight makes it difficult to fully comprehend the scale and magnitude of environmental impacts. Without a more transparent and coordinated regulatory framework, industry will have poor incentives to invest in environmentally sustainable practices.

All told, the oil sands debate is contentious and often invokes a dichotomy between economic development and environmental sustainability. The debate is muddied by overlapping regulatory jurisdiction, a lack of accessible public information, and fierce attempts by both pro-development and pro-environmental groups to frame the discussion. Through the noise, however, is the unassailable reality that the oil sands lack effective regulatory instruments to ensure sustainable management and a comprehensive assessment of the costs versus benefits of continued development. The environmental degradation to date, massive GHG emissions, and the myriad uncertainties of cumulative impacts, demonstrate the urgency for a more transparent and informed discussion between government, industry, and the public, recognizing the full environmental costs of oil sands development.

The Role of the Courts

The third player in the Canadian regulatory setting for the environment is the legal system. With respect to the Constitution, the role of the courts is to establish principles for interpreting the powers of each level of government through litigation dealing with these powers.[12] The types of rulings the courts must make include determining if only one level of government has the exclusive power (under section 91 or 92) to enact particular legislation. If, for example, the subject matter of a law does not come within section 92 powers, a provincial law is said to be *ultra vires,* which means beyond the province's power. The other type of ruling concerns cases where both levels of government have laws

[10.] Bob Weber (Feb. 20, 2014), "Federal Study Says Oil Sands Toxins are Leaching into Groundwater, Athabasca River," *Globe and Mail* www.theglobeandmail.com/news/national.

[11.] Quoted in: Jennifer Grant, Simon Dyer, and Dan Woynillowicz (2009), "Oil Sand Myths: Clearing the Air," Pemina Institute www.pembina.org/reports/clearing-the-air-report.pdf.

[12.] Chapter 10 discusses the role of the legal system in environmental issues that involve property rights and liability laws (i.e., actions taken by private individuals or companies). These issues will not be discussed again in this chapter.

pertaining to the environment. This is allowed as long as the laws are not in direct conflict. The court's job is to determine whether or not the laws conflict. The term used to describe the situation where both levels of government have laws over the same thing is **concurrency.**

If the laws are in conflict, the federal law has precedence over the provincial law. This is called the doctrine of **paramountcy.** The legal system is driven by cases. Even though there is the potential for conflict between the levels of government, a suit must be launched to generate a legal interpretation of the powers of each government. Very few legal decisions regarding environmental legislation have been rendered. The one exception is in the management of fisheries. However, it is expected that more challenges may emerge if environmental legislation in Canada moves from the level of suggested guidelines to specific standards and/or incentive-based policies. Another component of the legal and environmental regulatory picture is the rights and title of Canada's Aboriginal peoples, also known as our First Nations. Recent court cases have affirmed their right to be meaningfully engaged over the use of the natural resources and environmental impacts on their lands. Many aspects of the constitutional powers over the environment remain unclear. The delegation of the powers between the federal and provincial governments can be ambiguous and has in the past contributed to conflict in the development and implementation of environmental policy. Let's look at some of these problems in more detail.

LO 2

Constitutional Powers in Conflict

Two types of problems that stem from Canada's Constitution and federal system have arisen in environmental policy. These are

- lack of clarity and overlap of jurisdictional responsibilities, and
- conflicting objectives between the federal and provincial governments.

As noted above, the Constitution does not clearly spell out distinct jurisdictional responsibilities for each level of government. Their responsibilities can overlap, causing the potential for uncertainty as to which level of government has the authority to regulate for specific environmental problems and objectives. The overlap may be sustainable, with both levels of government concurrently regulating some sector of the economy. A number of examples are illustrated in the next five chapters. If concurrent regulations are consistent in that they have identical objectives and use similar policy instruments, conflict is less likely. For example, if the government of the province of Nova Scotia and the federal government both require a permit for industries to dump toxic wastes into a waterway, and the allowed amount of wastes is identical, conflict and confusion over the concurrent policies are unlikely. However, if the province issues a permit that allows some waste discharge and the federal government prohibits dumping, obvious problems arise. The example below illustrates one of these conflicts and how it was resolved in the courts.

EXAMPLE
Water resources

The federal government has constitutional powers over water in the area of fisheries, navigation, and shipping. The provinces have the power to manage and conserve natural resources. When there is conflict, legal decisions are basically shaping the conditions for one level of government to have supremacy. Several examples illustrate this point. The Supreme Court of Canada ruled many years ago (in 1929) in *The Water Power Reference* that the federal government may restrict or even prohibit provincial water developments to preserve federal navigation and fisheries rights. Many years later, in

(Continued)

1980, the Supreme Court upheld a federal prosecution against a company that spilled oil into an inlet in British Columbia on the grounds that the federal government had the right to protect fisheries. The company responsible for the spill had argued that the province had the sole authority to regulate pollution under its property and civil-rights power.

Other cases have put conditions on federal powers over water. In a case involving the discharge of logging debris into any waterway, the Supreme Court ruled that a section of the federal *Fisheries Act* was beyond the power of the federal government because logging regulation was a provincial power under the property and civil-rights clause. This ruling might at first be seen as contradictory to the previous ruling. However, the court noted that the federal government had failed to meet certain conditions in this regulation:

1. It did not show that timber debris had a specific deleterious effect on fish.

2. The regulation was too broad. It had no specific limitation on the amount of debris. By implication, then, any amount of debris was deleterious to fish. Clearly, this is unlikely to be the case.

3. The regulation covered all waterways, some of which may not have a fishery.

4. Finally, all aspects of logging operations were covered by the regulation. This is where the conflict with provincial powers emerged.

Other cases have reinforced aspects of this case—for example, overturning convictions under the *Fisheries Act* when the federal government failed to show that discharges went into rivers frequented by fish. So while the courts have interpreted federal water rights as allowing the federal government to impose pollution regulation, certain conditions have to be satisfied to prevent infringement of provincial constitutional rights.

EXAMPLE
Transboundary pollution

The Supreme Court also appears to have given the federal government the power to regulate pollution when the pollution flows outside provincial boundaries even if the federal government has not shown harm to fish or navigation and shipping. The federal right to regulate transboundary pollution was based on the Peace, Order, and Good Government (POGG) power in the Constitution. Ironically, the 1988 case that generated this decision again involved the dumping of logging debris, this time into an ocean cove in British Columbia.[13] The federal policy in question was the *Ocean Dumping Control Act,* which required a permit for discharge into the ocean. The defendant in the case did not have a permit. The key aspect of the ruling was the court's decision that the federal government has regulatory power under POGG to enact regulations when there is "national concern" about pollution. The court ruled that marine pollution was a matter of national concern because marine waters are an indivisible resource, whereas fresh waters are not. If a province failed to control pollution into the marine environment, other provinces or countries could be affected. Thus, the federal government had the authority to enact environmental regulations.[14]

Unfortunately, decisions such as the two cases described above have not completely clarified federal versus provincial powers. The term "national concern" was defined somewhat vaguely. The court noted that a matter of national concern must have a "singleness, distinctiveness, and indivisibility that

---

[13.] The case is *Regina v. Crown Zellerbach Canada.*

[14.] The federal government also has power to intervene with regulation when there is seen to be a national environmental emergency.

clearly distinguishes it from provincial concern."[15] To help decide whether a pollution problem met these criteria, the court added that measurement should be made of any extraprovincial effects that occurred when a province failed to regulate pollution within its own boundaries. There is certainly room for disagreement as to what is a national concern. As well, the court acknowledged in this case that provinces may be granted concurrent jurisdiction to protect local interests.

The proposed Northern Gateway bitumen pipeline illustrates the conflict between national and provincial interests. The pipeline is to ship bitumen from the oil sands to the west coast and then on to markets in Asia. The National Energy Board and federal government approved the project in 2014 (subject to a number of conditions, including resolving environmental impacts). The majority of the pipeline is in British Columbia and the province will benefit from jobs created during construction, but it will also incur the environmental risks. Alberta and the federal government will benefit from the royalty and tax payments. British Columbia has asserted six conditions, including environmental ones that must be met before it will grant approval. If B.C.'s conditions are not met, will the federal government declare this a project of national concern? If so, Northern Gateway's future will undoubtedly be determined in the courts.

Ambiguity and the scope for conflict remain. We may see legal challenges of current and pending legislation once specific regulations and decisions on projects with significant environmental impacts are approved by governments. There is concern that the federal government has been devolving too much authority to provincial governments at a time when these governments have been reducing public expenditures with the result that environmental quality will be threatened. Chapter 16 provides several examples that support these concerns. Time will tell if the federal and provincial governments will co-operate on the setting of national environmental policies. If these conflict with the interests of a province, given past history it is likely that the province would challenge the federal government's right to do so.

LO 3

ENVIRONMENTAL REGULATION IN A PARLIAMENTARY SYSTEM

Overview

Environmental policy in any country is greatly affected by its political system. In this section, the implications for environmental policy of Canada's parliamentary democracy are examined. The Canadian situation is also compared to the policy process in the United States. Key points are as follows.

1. Under a parliamentary system with a majority government, the governing party has a lot of control over the legislative agenda. Our system of government is very good at getting legislation approved that is supported by the party in power. The converse is also true. Federal interest in environmental issues waxes and wanes. Environmental policies and, more importantly, action on these policies by the federal government track quite well the level of environmental concern of the public and the party and the government's overall economic agenda.

[15.] Supreme Court of Canada, 1 S.C.R. 401 (1988), as cited in David VanderZwaag and Linda Duncan,"Canada and Environmental Protection" in Robert Boardman, *Canadian Environmental Policy: Ecosystems, Politics, and Process* (Toronto: Oxford University Press, 1992).

284 Section Five Environmental Policy in Canada

2. There are few, if any, checks and balances in a parliamentary system. There is nothing equivalent to the two different branches of government in the United States, the executive branch (the President) and the legislative branch (Congress). The U.S. Congress may have one or more of its houses controlled by a party different from that of the president. Congress writes and passes laws that need not have the support of the executive branch. In the parliamentary system, this is generally impossible. The executive and legislative branches under a majority government are essentially one. If the federal government wants to drag its feet on dealing with environmental problems, it can. Public pressure plays a very important role, as it does in all democratic political systems, and the government is ultimately accountable at election time. However, a five-year maximum term gives the party in power a lot of time to avoid confronting issues if this is what it wants to do.

3. The parliamentary system can also curtail public debate and scientific inquiry into environmental issues through its control of the federal bureaucracy. In Canada, the party in power basically controls the federal bureaucracy, and the federal bureaucracy controls research and legislative agendas. Environmental research is essential for undertaking regulation. For example, a standard cannot be imposed until there is evidence on what the level of emissions or ambient quality should be. Scientific and economic environmental research is not often a high priority of the federal government. An example is the budget cuts during the early years of the Mulroney government that threatened the monitoring of toxic chemicals in waterfowl. A more recent example is the lack of significant federal action to reduce greenhouse gas emissions and reductions in Environment Canada's budget inhibiting environmental studies. There is no other body independent of federal or provincial governments that can initiate large and potentially expensive studies. By contrast, there are many examples of research on environmental issues done for the U.S. Congress that influence policy. In our federal system, the checks we have are the provinces, First Nations, and the courts. The provinces can have different priorities and public pressures than the federal government. For example, Ontario typically led the country by introducing major environmental initiatives in the 1960s. British Columbia introduced a textbook carbon tax in 2008 (see Chapters 12 and 20) and other policies to reduce GHG emissions. Ontario has introduced incentives to greatly increase the share of renewable resources generating electricity and reducing its dependence on coal-fired generation.

4. With the legislative and executive branches combined, environmental legislation takes on quite a different character in Canada than it does in the United States. The process for setting standards and designing regulations is said to be "far more informal, discretionary and closed than that in the United States."[16] This is true for the provinces as well. Environment Canada typically prepares federal environmental regulations. The ministry has quite a bit of discretion in the scope and formulation of the laws and regulations it proposes to Cabinet.

The situation in the United States is quite different. Congress initiates a bill that *requires* their environmental agency, the Environmental Protection Agency (EPA), to develop regulations within specified time periods, impose those regulations, report back to Congress on progress, and sometimes even to achieve specific targets such as zero discharge by specific dates. In Canada, because Environment Canada designs the legislation without conditions imposed by another political body, it is much less likely to propose a law that binds it to specific timetables, procedures, and so on. In practice, Canadian environmental laws contain less specificity than their U.S. counterparts. They authorize or permit Environment Canada to do something, but do not compel it to act.

[16.] Don Dewees, *Reducing the Burden of Environmental Regulation* (Kingston: School of Policy Studies, Queen's University, Government and Competitiveness Discussion Paper, 1992), 22.

Once a regulation is designed by Environment Canada, its path into application is much less arduous than typically is the case in the United States. In Canada, the only procedural requirement for imposing federal regulations is that they be published in *The Canada Gazette*. Committees of Parliament may review the regulations "gazetted," but typically don't do so until after the regulation is adopted. Environment Canada consults with affected parties, other ministries, and the provinces prior to the adoption of the regulation. Consultation with **stakeholder's groups,** which include public- and private-sector representatives as well as those from non-governmental organizations (NGOs) has varied over time depending on the government. There have been periods of extensive consultation and those with relatively no consultation with environmental communities. A recent example of little consultation is the federal government's omnibus budget bills of 2012. They include not only regulation but also all aspects of environmental policy.

In the United States, the whole system is much more litigious. Federal agencies must publish a notice of proposed regulation in the *Federal Register,* allow interested parties to comment on it, and then publish reasons for the final regulation. The regulations must be supported by what's called "substantial evidence." The courts are the judges of what is substantial. There are many legal challenges to regulations in the United States, and very few in Canada. It is important to note that despite these significant differences in policy making between the two countries, the United States is not more successful than Canada in reducing pollutants or achieving higher levels of environmental quality. In the United States, battles within Congress or between the legislative and executive branches and the large amount of litigation that occurs can impede effective implementation of policies. Our often more co-operative process of setting regulations might lead to higher compliance.

LO 4

A Sketch of the Regulatory Activities of Environment Canada

To understand the regulatory process at the federal level in Canada more fully, we provide a brief history of Environment Canada, Canada's federal environment ministry.[17] Environment Canada (EC) was created in 1971 to bring together a number of different federal agencies that had environmental responsibilities. New responsibilities were also intended for the agency, notably environmental protection through the creation of the Environmental Protection Service, and coordination of federal efforts at preserving environmental quality and/or controlling pollution. There were high hopes at the beginning of the 1970s that Environment Canada would be a world leader in protecting the environment. A number of factors combined to prevent that realization from occurring.

First, Environment Canada has had a number of bureaucratic difficulties. From the period 1971 to 1986, it had 10 different ministers and many reorganizations. At one point, it was under the jurisdiction of the federal fisheries department. It has not been a high-profile ministry. Perhaps some of this was intentional policy on the part of the federal Cabinet: to have in place the institution for environmental policy, but not let it do very much. Evidence for this is in some of Environment Canada's powers and its political influence relative to other federal ministries. For example, EC was limited to duties, powers, and functions—not by law assigned to any other department, branch, or agency of the federal government. This meant that if Agriculture Canada had regulations about water use (that might have significant environmental impacts), EC couldn't also intervene. Secondly, a

---

[17.] This section is based in part on material in M. Paul Brown, "Target or Participant? The Hatching of Environmental Industry Policy" in Robert Boardman, *Canadian Environmental Policy: Ecosystems, Politics, and Process* (Toronto: Oxford University Press, 1992).

number of its initiatives were stopped by budget cuts. EC had designed a program to deal with environmental aspects of federal operations on Indian reserves. This program was terminated in the mid-1970s by budget reductions, and not reinstated until the federal Green Plan in 1990. Further evidence of EC's weak regulatory role comes from a study of the federal bureaucracy done at the end of the Trudeau government. The study identified 82 pieces of federal legislation that had a bearing on the environment. Of these, EC was responsible for 13. The Department of Indian and Northern Affairs had more. Environment Canada was typically thwarted in its efforts because its responsibilities overlapped with other federal agencies and because these agencies had greater political and statutory powers. Upsurges in EC's stature came with the Green Plan in 1990. This has been followed by decline in activity since the mid-1990s with the quiet disappearance of the Green Plan after the election in 1993 and large budget cuts to the ministry. From the late 1990s to mid 2000s, international pressure to take action on climate change and domestic concerns over local air and water pollution led to a partial reinstatement of EC's staff and a major interest in examining economic instruments for environmental objectives. However, government priorities have recently shifted away from environmental issues and EC has again taken a low profile among agencies, with challenges to its staffing levels and ability to engage in significant environmental issues facing Canada.

The federal budgetary process does not favour Environment Canada. The federal budget is allocated among its ministries and agencies by placing each agency into a particular "envelope" based on its principal tasks. Environment was in the "social development" envelope that also included health and welfare, a major recipient of federal funds (some 35 percent of total federal spending in the 1970s to 1980s and even higher in the 1990s). Social development also included statutory transfers to the provinces and to individuals. By the time these two activities received their budgets, there was not much left for Environment Canada. The other significant aspect of placing environment into social development was that it separated it from economic agencies and, more importantly, treated the environment as a social, not an economic, issue. When social policies started to be hit hard in the federal budgets of the 1980s and 1990s, and again after the middle of the decade in 2000, EC declined with them. This separation of economic policy from environmental policy has had a bearing on the type of policies enacted as well. As we'll see in later chapters, there has been virtually *no use of economic incentives* for environmental improvement at the federal level.

The early to mid-1970s saw the delivery of a number of environmental policies, which we examine in the next three chapters. EC had an agreement with the Department of Fisheries and Oceans to allow it to administer the section of the federal *Fisheries Act* that dealt with pollution of fish habitats. Similar agreements with Transport Canada existed for the shipping of hazardous wastes, and with Agriculture Canada for pesticide regulation. But many areas of regulation were essentially left to other agencies. We must not forget as well the powers of the provincial governments over environmental policy. Overall, the period from the mid-1970s to late 1980s is one of missed opportunity to act for the federal government.

By the mid-1980s, public opinion about the environment began to force some changes in federal policy. Public opinion polls started consistently putting environmental concerns at the top of people's lists. Some recognized that environmental protection did not necessarily mean losing one's job. The publication of the Brundtland Commission's *Our Common Future* in 1986 focused attention on the concept of "sustainable development." The Mulroney government found this concept appealing (at least as rhetoric), and moved to create a stronger environmental ministry. The Canadian Council of Resource and Environment Ministers was created in 1986. Its task was to establish a National Task Force on Environment and the Economy. This council was later changed to the Canadian Council of Ministers of the Environment (CCME), a federal–provincial group. When first founded, CCME had an active agenda that led to adoption of a number of accords between the federal and provincial governments. Research programs were initiated and some interesting reports were released. Unfortunately, like so much else in Canadian environmental policy, after a good start the process waned. In recent years, the CCME has been less active, focusing on a few issues where progress has been made (e.g., sulphur in fuels).

The public's environmental awareness also led to the formation of "round tables" on the environment, economy, and sustainable development at both the federal and provincial levels by the end of the 1980s. The round tables involved government, industry, environmental NGOs, and researchers and were quite active in the early 1990s. By the late 1990s, most of the provincial round tables were not very active. The National Round Table on the Environment and Economy (NRTEE) was created by Parliament in 1994 as an independent advisory body whose mandate was to provide advice and recommendations to governments, industry, and the public for promoting sustainable development. When created, the NRTEE reported directly to the prime minister and then later to the Minister of the Environment. Funding for NRTEE was eliminated in the 2012 federal budget and it was shut down by the end of March 2013, leaving no government-funded advisory organization to inform the public and government on important environmental issues. Prior to its demise, NRTEE had produced a number of informative papers on the many topics linking the environment and economy, including the costs and benefits of regulating GHG emissions.

New environmental legislation emerged in the late 1980s with the approval of CEPA by Parliament in 1988. The *Canadian Environmental Assessment Act* also emerged during this period. In January of 1989, the Cabinet Committee on the Environment was created and chaired by the Minister of the Environment. The other departments on this committee included Health and Welfare; Energy, Mines and Resources; Fisheries and Oceans; Transport Canada; Forestry Canada; Consumer and Corporate Affairs; Labour; Agriculture; Science and Technology; and the Atlantic Canada Opportunities Agency. Curiously absent (again) were the "economic" ministries—the Department of Finance and Industry Canada. The mandate of the Cabinet committee was to "manage the government's environmental agenda." The Minister of the Environment was also given a seat on the influential Priorities and Planning Committee and the Operations Committee. A major policy initiative came from Environment Canada during this period—the 1990 "Green Plan."

Canada's Green Plan was a national strategy and action plan for sustainable development. Its goal was "to secure for current and future generations a safe and healthy environment, and a sound and prosperous economy."[18] With an initial budget of $3-billion announced (but never fully delivered), the Green Plan was heralded by the federal government as a major breakthrough in environmental policy; a recognition that the economy and the environment were linked. The Green Plan established seven goals: clean air, water, and land; sustainable use of renewable resources; protection of special spaces and species; preserving the integrity of the North; global environmental security; environmentally responsible decision making; and minimizing the impact of environmental emergencies. While the Green Plan set out an agenda for addressing these goals, it prescribed very few specific regulations. Some of the agenda was simply a consolidation of activities that already existed, but new initiatives were also planned. The Green Plan slowly died over the first few years of the Chrétien government, but did make some contributions to Canadian environmental policies. Some of the initiatives and subsequent outcomes are noted below, along with a notation of the chapters in which the topics are discussed in more detail.

[18.] Government of Canada, *Canada's Green Plan: The Second Year,* Catalogue No. En21-110/1993E (Ottawa: Minister of Supply and Services, 1993), p. 4

1. Many action plans were initiated to help meet the target of clean air, water, and land. Few regulations emanated from these plans. (See Chapters 16, 17, and 18.)

2. Agreements were made with the private sector to reduce pollutants, especially in the area of toxic releases. Environment Canada worked with industry groups to promote **voluntary emissions reductions.** These are reductions done even though there is no regulation requiring it.

3. Bilateral agreements were signed to improve water quality on Canada–U.S. boundary waters (e.g., for Lake Superior). Studies were initiated, but few if any regulations resulted. (See Chapter 16.)

4. Actions authorized under CEPA of 1988 (i.e., before the Green Plan) to control toxic substances were undertaken. Reporting of toxic releases and transfers began in 1994 with publication of the first National Pollutant Release Inventory (NPRI). NPRIs are released to the public annually.

5. More importantly, a new CEPA was passed in 1999. A number of new initiatives coming out of this act are investigated in Chapters 16, 17, and 18. CEPA allows the government to regulate the release of toxic compounds. While some compounds have been banned, there are a large number still under investigation as to the toxicity impact on health and the environment.

6. The Pulp and Paper Regulatory Package (see Chapter 18) came into effect (for most companies) in 1992. The regulations required the industry to change its technologies to prevent the formation of dioxins and furans, to reduce organochlorine levels, and to strictly control other conventional pollutants. This is primarily a technology-based policy designed to reach emission standards, and their production and release has been strictly regulated with the result that emissions have declined considerably.

7. The national smog program was introduced in 1990 with the adoption of a NOx–VOC management plan. The objective was to begin the process of negotiating agreements with the provinces to establish emission targets for these compounds. Most of the policies introduced centre on technology-based standards. Transferable emission permits have been considered, but not implemented. More stringent exhaust emission standards were implemented for new passenger cars and light trucks beginning with 1998 model years and have risen in stringency over time. Increasingly stringent standards for sulphur in fuels and mandated use of ethanol was introduced. A new smog program was introduced in 2001. (See Chapter 17.)

8. The Green Plan established a target of setting aside 12 percent of the country as protected space. Protected spaces include national parks, marine parks, wildlife areas, and migratory-bird sanctuaries. A number of new sites have since been created, as well as programs launched to better conserve existing sites (such as wetlands), but protected areas still only comprise about 10 percent of Canada's lands and waters. Canada passed endangered-species legislation in late 2002 and has signed international agreements covering species protection.

9. Climate-change agreements to limit greenhouse gases were signed at the Rio Earth Summit in 1992 and the Kyoto Protocol in 1997. Canada ratified Kyoto in 2002, but has since withdrawn. Canada did sign the Copenhagen Accord and set new, less demanding targets for GHG reductions. (See Chapter 20.) Most federal GHG policy to date has focused on subsidies for investment in energy efficiency technology, moral suasion, and subsidies for the development of technologies for carbon sequestration (e.g., for carbon capture and storage). No carbon taxes, emission trading, or other pricing policies have been introduced at this time. The current policy stance is that the government will introduce sector-specific standards that focus more on emission intensity than reductions in emission levels. Substantive action on climate change has been at the provincial level as noted in Chapter 1 and is elaborated again in Chapter 20. *The Energy Efficiency Act* came into force on January 1, 1993, and its first regulations came into effect in 1995. The Act provides for making and enforcing regulations that specify minimum energy performance levels for products. Standards

now exist for a number of energy-using products, such as fluorescent lamps and electric motors. More are under study. The federal budget of February 1992 removed an excise tax on ethanol-methanol portions of blended fuels produced from grains and agricultural wastes. This tax change encourages substitution of ethanol-methanol for fossil fuels that are more carbon dioxide and monoxide intensive. Subsidies of up to $2 billion for biofuel production (most going to ethanol) were part of the 2007 federal budget. In the fall of 2010, the government passed regulations requiring oil refineries to include 5 percent ethanol in gasoline, and 2 percent in diesel and heating oil by the end of 2010. These regulations had been in the works for a number of years. See Chapter 20 for more details on climate change and Canadian energy use.

10. An acceleration of the phase-out of ozone-depleting substances agreed to in the Montreal Protocol of 1987 was announced by CCME in 1992. Completion of the phase-out has occurred. (See Chapter 20.)

11. Two reports on the State of the Environment for Canada were produced, in 1992 and 1996, but since then there are sporadic releases of information on the state of our environment in the form of environmental indicator bulletins on selected environmental problems such as ozone depletion, water quality, and urban air quality. These are available on Environment Canada's website, but not regularly updated. Budgets for data gathering and reporting are tight and data collection and dissemination are at times under threat due to inadequate resources. Statistics Canada works with Environment Canada and Health Canada to incorporate environmental factors into Canada's System of National Accounts and other forms of environmental reporting. See Statistics Canada's website: www.statcan.gc.ca and their Environment link for its work on Canada's System of Environmental and Resource Accounts, environmental protection data, sustainability indicators, waste production, and more.

12. Legislation was introduced to protect Canada's oceans, coastline, and inland waters from oil and chemical spills; for example, since 2003, all newly constructed large oil tankers operating in Canadian waters must be double hulled and all single-hulled oil tankers are required to be phased out by 2015. (See Chapter 16.)

13. Recent changes have been made to three core pieces of legislation that have environmental components: the *Fisheries Act, Navigable Waters Protection Act*, and the *Canadian Environmental Assessment Act*. These were part of omnibus budget bills introduced in 2012. The stated objectives of the government in making the changes were to improve the efficiency of the regulatory process, reduce regulatory overlap, and enhance the economy. Critics argue many of the changes significantly weaken federal environmental policy, allowing more development of oil and gas projects that have adverse environmental impacts. Key features from Bills C-38 and C-45 are:

- Revisions to *Canadian Environmental Assessment Act* that include:

  ○ A narrower definition of "environmental effects" that must be assessed and definitions of "impact" will exclude non-Aboriginal human health and socio-economic conditions;

  ○ There is no requirement to consider the impact of projects on renewable resources now and into the future;

  ○ Introduction of strict timelines for environmental assessments and a tightening of eligibility for public participation at hearings;

  ○ The Minister and a province affected can agree to scope of study and provinces can request their processes substitute for a federal environmental assessment. This provision increases the potential for inconsistency between assessments conducted across provinces, and adds the risk that proposed projects may fall through the jurisdictional gaps entirely.

○ Exemption from review of small projects, which means no scope to incorporate the cumulative effects on the environment of these projects.

- Revisions to the *Fisheries Act* and *Navigable Waters Protection Act* (which was renamed the *Navigable Waters Act*) include:

○ Only waters that contain commercially viable, recreational, or Aboriginal fisheries are now covered by the *Fisheries Act*. This leaves waters not deemed important to humans open to environmental threats.

○ Under the new *Navigable Waters Act*, only significant surface waters are covered (three oceans, 97 lakes, and 62 rivers). That sums to approximately 1 percent of Canada's surface water. Pipelines crossing these waters are exempt from the act. Provincial governments cannot modify these provisions—under section 91 of the Constitution the federal government has exclusive power over navigable waters.

While these examples show that progress toward improving environmental quality has occurred by the early part of the 21st century, we find ourselves not much further along than at the beginning of the 1990s. There is still a lot of talk about environmental strategies and initiatives, about action plans to do this or that, but there is precious little in the way of real action. As we will see in the upcoming chapters, Canada has few actual regulations that establish standards for pollutants and has made little progress to protect its natural capital. Very little use has been made of economic instruments. Reliance has been on guidelines and voluntary compliance by industries that target pollution intensity more often than absolute levels of emissions. Much has been left to the provinces. Public and political attention to the environment is fickle. When environmental issues retreat to the "back pages" in media coverage, Canadian governments (like most governments) have a tendency to backtrack or postpone proposed environmental policy initiatives. When media and public attention is focused on high profile environmental issues, there is a flurry of activity in the form of public statements and intent to regulate; less frequently followed by concrete policies to address the problems.

Summary

In this chapter, we examine the constitutional basis for environmental regulation by the federal and provincial governments. Each level of government has unique powers that can be applied to the environment. The federal government has the power to legislate over ocean and inland fisheries, navigation and shipping, and federal lands and waters; to negotiate international treaties; and to implement national concerns under the principle of Peace, Order, and Good Government. The provinces have power over local works; property and civil rights within the provinces; matters of a local or private nature; and authority over provincially owned lands and resources. The last right gives each province exclusive jurisdiction over the development, conservation, and management of its non-renewable resources. These powers do not necessarily mean that only one level of government will enact environmental regulations for a particular problem such as air or water pollution. There are many examples of concurrent regulation, which is allowed under the Constitution unless the laws are in direct conflict. If that is the case, the federal government is said to have supremacy and its laws prevail. Concurrent legislation can lead to overlap in regulation and the potential for confusion and high costs of compliance to polluters. In this federal system, there is also the possibility of conflict between the federal and provincial governments over the interpretation of their constitutional powers. A number of court cases have occurred that have helped to define the powers of each level of government with regard to the environment. Sometimes these cases strengthened the federal powers. Other decisions imposed restrictions on federal powers.

The regulatory process in Canada is highly dependent on the interests of the party in power under our parliamentary system. Because the legislative and executive branches of government are not separate when there is majority rule, the party in power controls the legislative policy agenda. Public pressure can influence policy, but there has been little public involvement in the policy process. The history of Environment Canada illustrates many of the difficulties of sustaining environmental initiatives over time. Particularly lacking federally are incentive-based policies that price pollution, for a wide range of environmental problems.

Key Terms

Concurrency
Paramountcy
Stakeholder's groups
Voluntary emissions reductions

Discussion Questions

1. Would you change any of the powers of the federal and/or provincial governments in Canada's Constitution to facilitate the design and implementation of environmental policy?

2. Some people think that incentive-based environmental policies create more federal–provincial conflict than command-and-control policies. Why might this be the case?

3. "Canadian environmental policy is constrained by its political system." Why is this the case and what can be done about it?

4. "Canada's Green Plan was a failure." State whether you agree with this statement and explain why or why not.

 For more information on the resources available from McGraw-Hill Ryerson, go to www.mheducation.ca/he/solutions.

Chapter 16

Water Pollution-Control Policy

After reading this chapter you will be able to:

LO 1 Describe the characteristics of water pollutants and how that affects the type of policy instrument that can be used.

LO 2 Provide a brief sketch of federal water quality policy.

LO 3 Assess the effectiveness of technology-based standards using an example from Canada and the U.S.

LO 4 Explain the challenges in regulating nonpoint-source emissions.

Water is biologically necessary for life on this planet—but, even beyond this, water resources also play a vital and pervasive role in the health and welfare of a modern economy. Water for direct human consumption is a small but critical part of the domestic system, which also includes water used in food preparation, cleaning, and sewage disposal. Water is an essential element in many industrial and commercial production processes, again both as an input and as a medium of waste disposal. Large amounts of water are used by farmers for irrigation, especially in the Prairie provinces. In-stream, non-consumptive uses of water include water-based sports and recreation as well as simply the enjoyment of a scenic vista.

The water resource system itself consists of a vast array of interconnected components, from the grandiose to the tiny. The surface-water system includes the huge main-stem rivers, the Great Lakes, and other large lakes, such as Okanagan Lake in B.C. and Lake Winnipeg in Manitoba, as well as the thousands of small neighbourhood streams and ponds. Add to these the innumerable person-made components, from the mill ponds of the first industrial era to the vast reservoirs and canals of today. Wetlands, one of nature's ecosystem rechargers and life supporters, abound. And then there is the vast, but unseen, system of groundwater aquifers, typically exceeding surface waters in terms of sheer quantity of water. Saltwater resources are also of vital importance. Marshes and coastal lowlands are critical for fish and wildlife resources; beaches and scenic coasts are important recreational resources; coastal waters provide transportation and pleasure boating services; and saltwater fisheries are a major source of food.

Data on water quality are difficult to summarize as they are collected for specific water bodies at monitoring stations and by intermittent sampling. There is no overall indicator of water quality in Canada. Chapter 2 provided an example of the type of data available. Provincial environment ministries are the place to start to look for data on water quality in a given region, watershed, or body of water.[1]

This chapter provides examples of federal and provincial water pollution-control policies. The objective is to examine the main elements of these policies with the economic concepts that have been developed in preceding chapters. While the primary focus is on Canadian policies, comparison with those in the United States illustrates contrasts and similarities. Experiments in the United States using economic incentives to help achieve improvements in water quality are also highlighted.

LO 1

TYPES OF WATER POLLUTANTS

One way to categorize waterborne pollutants is by their chemical and physical nature.[2]

- Organic wastes: degradable wastes such as domestic sewage and residuals from pulp mills and food-processing plants; chemicals such as pesticides, detergents, and solvents; oil.

- Inorganic substances: chemicals such as toxic metals, salts, and acids; plant nutrients such as nitrate and phosphorous compounds.

- Non-material pollutants: radioactivity, heat.

- Infectious agents: bacteria, viruses.

Waterborne emissions include all the different types of discharges discussed in Chapter 2. **Point-source pollutants** include outfalls from industry and domestic wastewater treatment plants. **Nonpoint-source pollutants** include agricultural runoff of pesticides and fertilizers and the chemicals and oils that are flushed off urban streets by periodic rains. Many sources, especially point sources, have **continuous emissions,** related to the rate of operation of the industrial plant or the domestic sewer system. There are also many **episodic emissions,** such as accidental releases of toxic materials, oil tanker accidents, or occasional planned releases of industrial pollutants.

Chapter 2 also differentiated between **accumulative pollutants** and **non-accumulative pollutants.** In water pollution control it is more common to speak of **persistent pollutants** and **degradable pollutants.** Degradable waterborne pollutants undergo a variety of biological, chemical, and physical processes that change their characteristics after emission. Especially important are the oxygen-using chemical processes that rely on the oxygen contained in receiving waters to degrade the wastes.[3] The reason for focusing on oxygen requirements is that oxygen plays a critical role in water quality. High

---

[1.] For example, British Columbia's Ministry of Water, Land, and Air Protection has a number of reports on water quality in the province. See www.env.gov.bc.ca/wat/wq/. Environment Canada provides some water-quality indicators at www.ec.gc.ca/indicateurs-indicators/default.asp?lang=en&n=68DE8F72-1.

[2.] G. Tyler Miller, Jr. *Resource Conservation and Management* (Belmont, California: Wadsworth Publishing Company, 1990), 201.

[3.] Degradable wastes also include a variety of infectious bacterial agents, parasites, and other microorganisms that can cause acute gastroenteritis, kidney damage, typhoid, cholera, dysentery, and other nasty diseases. Waste heat is also a degradable pollutant; it comes mostly from large-scale industrial processes that use water for cooling purposes.

levels of **dissolved oxygen (DO)** are usually associated with high-quality water, water that will support high-quality recreational uses and aquatic life and that can be used in domestic water-supply systems.

Since DO is used up in the degradation process, one way of measuring the quantity of waste emitted is through **biochemical oxygen demand (BOD),** the amount of oxygen required to decompose the organic material under specified conditions of temperature and time.[4] A substantial proportion of the BOD load introduced into the water resources of the country comes from municipal waste treatment plants. Much of this consists of wastewater from treated domestic waste, which contains a variety of degradable organic compounds. Industrial sources also contribute large amounts of BOD, some stemming from the sanitary facilities within the plants, but more importantly from the great variety of water-using steps in the production processes, such as cleaning, product formation, waste removal, and product transport.

When a BOD load is put into a river or body of water, it produces a temporary reduction in the DO level of that water, as the oxygen is used up to degrade the waste. But over time, through natural aeration processes, the DO content of the water will normally recover. The DO "profile" would thus look like Figure 16-1 (where the time of discharge or point of discharge is marked x). This figure could represent the average DO level at various distances downstream from the point at which a BOD load is introduced, or the DO level at various times after a BOD load has been introduced into a lake. This is called a DO "sag," and illustrates the degradation process by which the water body is assimilating the BOD load. The important thing to see is that the DO reduction is reversible. It is also non-accumulative—if the BOD source were stopped, the DO sag would shortly disappear.

FIGURE 16-1 Dissolved Oxygen Profile in Water After a BOD Load Has Been Introduced

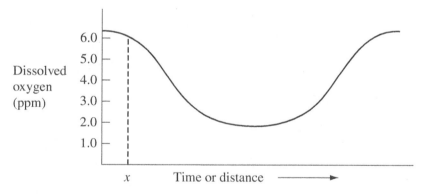

A time path of dissolved oxygen in water is shown after a one-time emission of a non-accumulative pollutant such as organic waste has been introduced at time x. The time path illustrates the assimilative capacity of water—DO first declines, then rises over time as the pollutant is neutralized.

Early water-pollution-control efforts were centred on conventional pollutants like BOD, suspended solids, and so on, for which there are common water quality measures such as DO, turbidity, acidity, and coliform count. Attempts to reduce these pollutants were primarily through greater use of sewage

---

[4.] For example, 10 pounds of BOD10 is a quantity of material requiring 10 pounds of oxygen in order to be completely converted to its constituent elements over a period of 10 days and at a temperature of 20 degrees Celsius.

treatment plants throughout the country and guidelines for discharges of these conventional pollutants into waterways. However, it became increasingly clear over the 1970s and 1980s that *toxic* pollutants had the potential to become a serious problem for the health of water ecosystems as well as of people making use of them. Toxics include heavy metals such as mercury, pesticides, polychlorinated biphenyls (PCBs), dioxins, and other industrial chemicals. Toxicity is often a matter of concentration; substances that are toxic at high concentrations may not be at low concentrations. This implies that the diluting ability of water is a valuable quality in addition to its capacity to transform degradable substances.

Persistent water pollutants are those that remain for a long period of time, either because they are non-degradable or because the rate of degradation is very slow. This category includes thousands of inorganic and organic chemicals of various descriptions, the wastes of a modern, chemical-based economy. Industrial wastes contain many such persistent pollutants. Wastes from mining operations can contain various metals as well as acid-mine drainage. Agriculture is the source of a variety of pesticides, fertilizers, and soil runoff. The concept of "persistent" does not mean permanent in a technical sense; many chemicals, oils, and solvents do break down, but only over a long period of time. In the process they pose a persistent threat. Radioactive waste is physically degradable over very long periods, but measured in terms of a human scale it is essentially a persistent pollutant. Some viruses may also be in this category. Table 16-1 provides an illustration of the types of persistent contaminants found in the Great Lakes.

TABLE 16-1 Critical Pollutants in the Great Lakes

Substance	Description
PCBs (209 related chemicals)	Insulating fluid in transformers, hydraulic fluid, lubricant; major disposal problems
DDT and its breakdown products including DDE, chlordane	Insecticides (now banned in Canada and United States)
Aldrin and dieldrin	Insecticides
Toxaphene (hundreds of related chemicals)	Insecticide (now banned in Canada and United States)
2,3,7,8-TCDD (tetrachlorodibenzo-p-dioxin)	Waste by-product of combustion and some industrial processes using chlorine
2,3,7,8-TCDF (tetrachlorodibenzofuran)	Waste by-product of combustion and some industrial processes using chlorine
Mirex	Pesticide, industrial fire retardant; no longer used
Mercury	Formerly used in paints, electrical equipment, and pulp and paper production; released during coal combustion
Benzo(a)pyrene, representative of polycyclic aromatic hydrocarbons (PAHs)	By-product of incomplete combustion
Hexachlorobenzene (HCB)	Pesticide
Alkylated lead	Gasoline additive (banned in 1988)
Tritium	By-product of nuclear reactors

Sources: *"Critical Pollutants in the Great Lakes," The State of Canada's Environment 1996, Chapter 6, Cat. No. EN 21-54/1996E, www.ec.gc.ca, Environment Canada. Reproduced with the permission of the Minister of Public Works and Government Services, 2010.*

EXAMPLE
Trichloroethylene (TCE) in groundwater

The book *A Civil Action* by Jonathan Harr[5] (turned into a movie of the same name) tells the true story of the health impacts of a persistent water pollutant. A cluster of families in Woburn, Massachusetts discovered that many of them were ill with similar conditions (headaches, insomnia, acute tiredness, diseased organs), and that a number of their children had leukemia (16 of whom ultimately died from the disease). The probable cause of these conditions was TCE, a highly volatile liquid compound that is used to degrease metal. TCE was found in the drinking water of the community. Two companies had allegedly been dumping TCE on the ground for a number of years. The TCE percolated into the groundwater and found its way to two of the municipality's wells. The families sued the two companies, and the book details the court battle—which did not end well for the families.[6] The U.S. Environmental Protection Agency (EPA) later took action against the companies and also lowered the maximum allowable limit for TCE in drinking water.

Is TCE a health threat in Canada? At least one town in Ontario thinks so. TCE has been found in the drinking water in Beckwith Township, a community 60 kilometres southwest of Ottawa.[7] The TCE has apparently come from an abandoned municipal dump and contaminates the town's drinking water obtained from a well. TCE may have been present in the drinking water for 20 to 30 years. While TCE is listed as a toxic substance on Canada's Priority Substances List and is monitored under CEPA (see Chapters 15 and 18), the federal standard for TCE is 0.03 milligrams per litre. The U.S. Drinking Water Regulations specify *zero* TCE in drinking water.

This case illustrates a number of points for public policy. First, this is not an isolated incident. All provinces have similar examples. Second, there can be a long lag between discharge of a pollutant and its discovery in water supplies. This knowledge gap makes it very difficult to regulate effectively with any policy instrument. Third, what is a safe level of a compound in our drinking water? Fourth, linking pollutants to sources (those responsible) can also be problematic. This makes it hard to assign liability and prove damages. Market-based policies, such as taxes, are not good policy candidates when the target level of pollution must not be exceeded. Figure 16-2 illustrates that a regulatory approach, either a ban on a compound or explicit limit on emissions, is warranted when the marginal damage curve shows very adverse impacts at a particular emission level. Recall Chapter 14; if there is uncertainty about the location of the MD curve, a ban might be the optimal policy. Figure 16-2 illustrates two MD curves. If the regulator is certain that MD_1 reflects damages, then a standard set at E_1 is an appropriate policy. If however, it isn't known what the 'safe minimum level' of emissions is, for example, marginal damages could be MD_2, then a complete ban on the release of the compound is warranted.

Other policy questions to consider: Could transferable discharge permits (TDPs) be assigned in some way? Perhaps for some toxic compounds where "safe" levels of discharge can be identified? Maybe the best short-run policy is for people to protect themselves by buying household water purification equipment. Do you drink bottled water because of fears related to your water's safety, or treat the tap water in your home? These are issues to think about while examining Canadian water policy.

(Continued)

---

[5] J. Harr, *A Civil Action* (New York: Vintage Books, 1996).

[6] We won't give away all the plot details, and suggest you read the book!

[7] See M. MacKinnon, "Ontario Town Fears Tap-Water Tragedy," *The Globe and Mail,* October 12, 2000, p. A7.

FIGURE 16-2 **Imposition of Standards for the Release of Toxic Compounds**

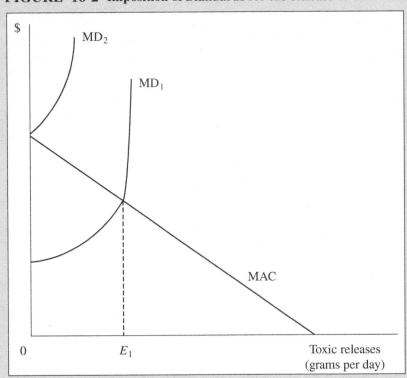

A standard is set at E_1 at the point where the MD curve becomes very steep. If the location of the MD curve is not known with certainty, a complete ban on releases of the compound may be warranted because the MD curve could be as shown by MD_2.

LO 2

CANADIAN FEDERAL POLICIES

The federal government has never played a major role in water-pollution regulation due to constitutional constraints. Its key role has been to

- introduce national standards for some compounds.
- address international and interjurisdictional water-pollution problems.
- establish national guidelines for water quality.

National Standards

The federal *Fisheries Act of 1868* was Canada's first legislation that laid a foundation for environmental regulations. A clause that banned the discharge of substances deleterious to fish has been the basis of much federal water-pollution legislation, beginning with the 1971 amendments to the Act. As noted in Chapter 15, amendments to the Act in 2012 have limited its application to surface water with commercial, recreational, or First Nations' use. The discharge into any waterways of a small number of substances has been banned or limited. These include zero discharges of dioxins and furans from pulp and paper mills (see Chapter 18) and emissions from chloralkali plants, which release mercury as a by-product of their production of chlorine and caustic soda. Other regulations exist for processors of meat and poultry products, metal mining operations, and petroleum refining.

The *Fisheries Act* can thus impose a standard set at zero discharges of substances deemed deleterious/toxic. This standard is socially efficient if the marginal damage function lies above the marginal abatement cost function for all possible levels of emissions as was shown in Figure 16-2 with the MD_2 curve. Note that the MAC shown in Figure 16-2 has a positive intercept. This means that it is technically feasible to prevent the discharge of any emissions. This may not be the case in practice.

Interjurisdictional Water Pollution Policies

Federal legislation that addresses interjurisdictional water-quality issues within Canada is the *Canada Water Act,* approved in 1970. The Act had two parts. Part 1 provided funds to assist municipalities in the construction of sewage treatment plants, and to undertake research on water-quality issues. These issues are examined below. Part 2 provided for Water Quality Management Authorities to set up regional water quality boards in co-operation with the provinces, as the federal and provincial governments have shared responsibilities over water quality. These boards were to establish water-quality management plans involving boundary waters (i.e., between provinces). They also had the power to implement these plans, for example by charging fees, monitoring discharges, imposing standards, and so on. A few boards have been established for particular watersheds that cross provincial boundaries, but there is little evidence of the use of economic instruments.

The boards appear to have been doomed by the terms of the Act. The federal government could act only when water quality had deteriorated to the point of "urgent national concern." Note here the use of the term *national concern* to elicit the federal government's POGG power. Even then, the federal government could intervene only *with the permission of the provinces*. From the provincial point of view, the Act threatened their jurisdiction over environmental problems. The federal government would have the right to unilaterally address water quality issues for that region if, after signing an agreement with a province, the two governments could not agree on what standards to impose. The provinces thus felt more threatened if they agreed to joint management than if they did not. Provinces have thus set up their own regional water-quality boards, often associated with a major river; for example, the St. Lawrence River Plan and the Fraser River Action Plan. One board now exists that combines the levels of government. A master agreement for the Mackenzie River Basin came into effect in 1998 with the objective of sustainable management of the water resources. The federal government, British Columbia, Alberta, Saskatchewan, Yukon, and Northwest Territories are the signatories.

Part 2 of the Act was used to enact the Phosphorus Concentration Regulations. This has been a successful program improving water quality in the Great Lakes. High phosphorus concentrations in the Great Lakes were a major concern in the 1960s and early 1970s. As discussed in Chapter 6, phosphorus contributes to eutrophication of lakes. Lake Erie, by the late 1960s, was choked with algae. This eutrophication was destroying fish populations and commercial fishing operations, and generally creating a very odorous lake unappealing for any uses. Phosphorus control in Canada was coordinated with that in the United States through the International Joint Commission, a binational agency that does research on boundary waters, helps resolve border disputes, and, when asked by the governments, investigates and provides policy advice on air- and water-quality issues.[8] Canadian federal regulations were introduced to limit phosphorus concentrations. Subsidies for sewage treatment plants also helped improve water quality. Lake Erie and the other Great Lakes' water quality improved considerably in a relatively short amount of time.

[8.] The IJC was established in 1909 as part of the Boundary Water Treaty between Canada and the United States signed in that year. It has six members, three each appointed by the federal governments of the two countries. Its website is www.ijc.org . The IJC operates a Great Lakes Water Quality Board. Information about it is available at their website.

Water Quality Guidelines and Groundwater Protection

Canadians obtain their drinking water from surface water and groundwater.[9] The quality of groundwater resources has been increasingly threatened by nonpoint sources such as agricultural runoff, industrial waste, and landfill leakage. The provinces and federal government through CCME have established guidelines for Canada's drinking water. These are not binding on any government. Provinces can adopt these or impose their own guidelines or standards. The guidelines were established in 1968 (*Guidelines for Canadian Drinking Water*). Guidelines as of 2014 are illustrated in Table 16-2 for some of the substances covered and compares them to water quality *standards* in the United States.[10] This is not the full list for either country. Note that Canada's guidelines exceed U.S. standards only for barium, fluoride, and mercury (inorganic).

TABLE 16-2   Examples of Water Quality Guidelines in Canada and Standards in the United States

Substance	Canadian Guideline (mg/litre)	United States Standard (mg/litre)
Antimony	0.006	0.006
Arsenic	0.010	0
Atrazine + metabolites	0.005	0.003
Barium	1	2
Benzene	0.005	0
Benzo(a)pyrene	0.00001	0
Cadmium	0.005	0.005
Carbon tetrachloride	0.002	0
Cyanide	0.2	0.2
Fluoride	1.5	4
Lead	0.01	0
Mercury	0.001	0.002
Nitrates	45	10
Tetrachloroethylene	0.03	0
Trichloroethylene (TCE)	0.005	0
E. coli	0	0

Sources: *Canadian Guidelines available at, http://www.hc-sc.gc.ca./ewh-semt/pubs/water-eau/2012-sum_guide-res_recom/index-eng.php#t2, Health Canada. U.S. Guidelines from Environmental Protection Agency, available at: www.epa.gov/safewater/stds.*

Note: * *Indicates an interim guideline.*

---

[9] The proportion of people in Canada consuming groundwater has more than doubled since 1960, from 10 to 26 percent. All of Prince Edward Island, parts of the Prairies, and many rural and some urban municipalities are dependent on groundwater completely or partially. Groundwater is also a source of bottled water. Ironically, consumption of bottled water has increased in recent years because of concerns about the quality of drinking water from surface-water supplies.

[10] Guidelines for Canadian Drinking Water, Federal-Provincial-Territorial Committee on Drinking Water, May 2008, at: www.hc-sc.gc.ca. Health Canada notes that these guidelines are based on an intake of 1.5 litres daily by a 70-kilogram adult. Accommodations for children and pregnant women are made for some compounds.

Nationwide, concern has been expressed with water quality due to deterioration of water treatment infrastructure, contamination of groundwater by toxic compounds, and nonpoint-source contaminants. Examples of how provinces have dealt with these issues appear below. U.S. examples are also provided for contrast and to highlight key points about the types of regulations in place.

LO 3

WATER POLLUTION POLICIES FOR POINT AND NONPOINT SOURCES

Provincial Regulation

Water-quality regulation is primarily a provincial responsibility.

The first environmental legislation[11] was at the provincial rather than the federal level of government, beginning in Ontario. Regulation of water pollution began in Ontario with the creation of the Ontario Water Resources Commission (OWRC) in 1956.[12] Its mandate was to assist municipalities in financing the construction of their sewage and water treatment plants. The OWRC also had the authority to regulate direct discharges of liquid industrial and municipal wastes; that is, those not going through a sewage treatment process. By 1966, most of the other provinces had followed Ontario in setting up an independent commission to regulate water quality, although some used their provincial health departments for this task. OWRC's powers by the end of the 1960s included setting water-quality objectives and working to meet these through the licensing of polluting industries, and by using administrative orders to enforce pollution abatement requirements. The first type of policy implemented was an *emission or discharge standard* imposed in the form of a licence to emit a specific concentration of a compound. By the end of 1971, 497 industries were discharging wastes into Ontario waters under OWRC permits.[13]

Enforcement of the standards was negotiated. Even when charges were laid, they were often withdrawn as soon as the polluter agreed to a plan to reduce their emissions. The OWRC estimated that on average 60 percent of those regulated met the effluent guidelines.

The other provinces followed suit with water-quality objectives for a number of compounds. Many based their guidelines on U.S. standards. All provincial governments set up environment ministries in the 1970s, either as stand-alone agencies or combined with others. When environmental responsibilities were combined with ministries for natural resource management and development the potential for conflict arose between economic and environmental objectives. From the 1970s to the 1990s, all the provinces introduced environmental legislation for water pollution and some form of administrative system to deal with environmental regulations. There are few market-based policies. Rather, the provinces rely on command-and-control policies in the form of emission guidelines and

[11.] The *Fisheries Act* was not originally designed as environmental regulation. As noted above, its first use as a legal support for federal environmental policies came in 1971.

[12.] Pollution-control policy is rife with acronyms. In the text we use acronyms frequently, but have also occasionally included the complete phrase as a reminder. A list of all acronyms appears at the end of the book.

[13.] Doug Macdonald, *The Politics of Pollution* (Toronto: McClelland & Stewart, 1991), 138.

standards and technology-based standards. Each province has some form of environmental regulation over water quality and drinking water. Examples of these policies are given below for point- and nonpoint-source pollutants.

Point-Source Emissions

Technology-based Standards in Ontario: The Municipal and Industrial Strategy for Abatement (MISA)

In the mid-1980s, Ontario initiated a major program to deal with all types of water pollutants: conventional discharges, toxics, metals, and organic chemicals. The goal of MISA was "the virtual elimination of toxic contaminants in municipal and industrial discharges into waterways."[14] The primary regulatory instrument is a technology-based standard. MISA is based on the federal water-pollution policy of the United States that began in the early 1970s. The U.S. has now had more than 25 years of experience with a technologically based standard that was set to eliminate pollutants from all waterways. MISA covers 60 substances released from 200 facilities in nine sectors of the economy.[15] It took Ontario until the mid-1990s to fully implement the policy, and the process was quite expensive. Regulations were to be reviewed every five years, but it appears this has not happened. For example, the Mininstry of Environment declined to undertake a review scheduled for 2010 on the grounds that it was actively pursuing other regulation that would help water quality. The result is that companies are typically complying with targets and standards set 20 years ago. Many companies control far more than the standards require, but if the standards are set too low to protect health and the environment, then over-control relative to MISA may be inadequate. The Environmental Commissioner of Ontario, in commenting on the lack of review, was concerned about toxics in surface waters, particularly the Great Lakes, inadequate regulation of municipal sewage discharges, and the need to recognize in regulation the cumulative effects of multiple dischargers. See the Annual Report of the Commissioner for 2007–08 available at www.ecoissues.ca.

MISA entails a significant departure from the type of regulation undertaken previously. The major change is in the regulatory instrument used. Emission and ambient standards are supplanted by limits on maximum allowable concentrations per day that are based on the technology available for pollution control from each type of source. The term used in MISA is "best available technology economically achievable" (BATEA). The intent was to base the standard on technologies for pollution control that take into account economic conditions in each industry. It is unlikely that BATEA will be socially efficient when a standard is based on what is technically feasible, rather than marginal benefits and damages. It is also unclear in practice what role economic achievability plays in establishing the standard. Economic achievability could include the same factors that are measured by the MAC curve. It may also incorporate more politically motivated factors, such as the number of jobs lost in the industry at different levels of environmental control. Without some link to MAC and MD, one cannot tell whether elimination of contaminants is socially efficient, even if it is technically feasible.

[14.] Ontario Ministry of Environment, *Municipal-Industrial Strategy for Abatement (MISA)* (Toronto: Ministry of Environment), 7.

[15.] See information on the Ministry of the Environment's website: www.ene.gov.on.ca/envision/water/misa/index.htm.

BATEAs for MISA were developed as follows:

1. Each plant in the nine industrial sectors covered monitored its effluent for 12 months to measure a wide range of contaminants.

2. Regulations were based on the data gathered and estimates of BATEA.

3. Joint technical committees consisting of government (federal, provincial, and municipal) and industry representatives reviewed the proposed regulations and made recommendations about specific standards that are BATEA.

4. Proposed standards were reviewed by a MISA advisory committee that contained industry and government people plus representatives of public interest groups. The draft regulations were released to the public for comment.

5. Enforcement activities were to be introduced to ensure that compliance occurs.

6. Over time, the standards will be tightened as technological changes permit greater control of emissions.

BATEAs have now been developed for each of the industries covered under the policy. One study has estimated MACs for the facilities regulated under MISA.[16] It found that for a number of the regulated sources MACs were far lower than expected at the initiation of the program. This was due in part to the economic downturn of the early 1990s that reduced production and hence emission levels and to lower costs for the technologies than expected. MISA is no longer a high-profile regulation in Ontario, due to political and budgetary factors.

A technology-based standard (TBS) such as MISA raises many important issues and questions. These include determining

- a definition of "virtual elimination";
- rules for monitoring and interpreting the data obtained;
- which chemicals should be monitored and regulated;
- how to verify industry data;
- how to define BATEA;
- how to translate BATEA into an effluent limit;
- what to do for water bodies of very different initial water quality;
- what constitutes compliance with the regulation;
- when the regulations are to be reviewed and revised and what new compounds should be added to the initial list.

No overall assessment of MISA is available to provide analysis of these issues.[17] A key question is this: Have these reductions been obtained at the lowest costs to society? Examination of the economics of TBS will help illustrate some of the problems with a program such as MISA and some potential solutions.

[16.] J. Donnan (2000).

[17.] For a critique of the MISA regulations see Alaine MacDonald and Anastasia Lintner of Ecojustice, "Summary of Concerns: Municipal-Industrial Strategy for Abatement (MISA) Regulations," January 2010, accessed at: www.ecojustice.ca/publications/submissions/EBR%20AfR%20MISA%20Regulation%20Summary%20of%20Concerns.pdf, on October 8, 2010.

The Economics of Technology-based Effluent Standards

How to Set the Standard

A technology-based effluent standard—or, simply, a technology-based standard (TBS)—is an effluent standard set at the level of emissions that a source would produce if it were employing a particular type of abatement technology. It would require enormous effort to establish effluent standards for each and every individual source. In Ontario, the standard was set under the MISA process. Suppose, for example, the regulator is concerned about vegetable-processing plants. This is a process that uses a large amount of water for cleaning and processing purposes; thus, the wastewater may contain large amounts of suspended solids and BOD. Table 16-3 shows hypothetical costs and emissions performance of five different technology options for plants in this industry. These are not costs and emissions for any particular plant; they are anticipated costs and emissions for a "representative" plant of each type. Each technological option refers to a particular collection of treatment equipment, operating procedures, and fuels that the plants might adopt. After having developed these estimates the Ontario Ministry of the Environment, must now choose a particular level of emissions for the standard.

TABLE 16-3   Estimated Total Costs and Emissions from Vegetable-Processing Plants Using Alternative Emission Abatement Technology

	No control	Technological option				
		A	B	C	D	E
Emissions (kg/kkg of raw product processed)						
BOD*	5.8	3.6	2.2	1.05	.23	0.0
TSS†	10.2	5.7	2.5	1.02	.30	0.0
Total cost ($ mill/year)	0.0	8.0	14.4	23.40	36.50	78.8

* Biochemical oxygen demand.
† Total suspended solids.

Lower levels of emissions can be obtained with greater costs; in fact, emissions into water bodies could be reduced to zero at a very high cost. To pick one set of emission levels for the standard requires the use of some sort of criteria. It is typical in setting the regulations that the first emission level set is an interim one, followed by a stricter standard. Initially, standards would be based on the "best practicable technology" (BPT) currently available to the firms. This would be followed in later years by standards based on "best available technology" (BAT).

The determination of BPT or BAT is open to interpretation, since the notions of "practicable" and "available" are certainly not precise. "Practicable" apparently refers to technology that is reasonably well known and readily available without excessive costs. Suppose the regulator decides that technology C, with an estimated cost of $23.4-million per year, represents the best practicable technology for this type of processing industry. Then it would set emission standards at 1.05 kg/kkg for BOD and 1.02 kg/kkg for total suspended solids. All vegetable-processing plants would then be subject to this emission standard. Then it has to determine the best available technology. BAT would appear to imply a more stringent standard than BPT, since all technologies that are available are included whether or not they are practicable. But MISA also specifies that BAT has to be "economically achievable"; that is, BATEA. On this basis, technology E in Table 16-3 might be regarded as the BATEA for vegetable-processing plants. On the other hand, some (especially those in the industry) might argue that technology doesn't realistically exist, that it is too costly to be considered "available" in any economic sense, in which case D is the BATEA.

Setting technology-based effluent standards for an industry is obviously a time-consuming business. It requires large amounts of economic analysis and hinges on an agency judgment about what "available" and "practicable" mean when applied to pollution-control technology, a judgment that can be politically controversial.

Efficiency and Cost-Effectiveness of TBSs

For a TBS policy to be socially efficient, the standard must be set where MAC = MD for a given pollutant and its source. The technology-based effluent standards are designed, however, to be applied on a provincial basis. The same standards for, say, leather-processing plants will be applied to all leather plants in the province, whether they are located on a river just upstream from a large urban area or on a river in some remote part of the province. It is unlikely that MDs are identical across the province or the country, and even more unlikely that MACs are identical for all pollution sources because the imposition of a specific technology may affect firms' abatement costs quite differently depending on their size, product mix, and other factors. A totally technology-based approach to pollution control thus cannot in practice be either cost effective or socially efficient.

Cost-effectiveness examines whether we are getting the maximum effect, in terms of reduced emissions, for the money spent.

> *A policy will be cost-effective if it is designed so that when sources are in compliance they will have the same marginal abatement costs.*

There is nothing in the logic of the TBS process that moves water-pollution sources in the direction of meeting the equimarginal condition. Figure 16-3 illustrates that a TBS will not be cost-effective when the emitters have different MAC curves. The technology standard will lead to different MAC curves, illustrated by MAC_L and MAC_H to represent firms that face different conditions in introducing the technology. With an overall standard set at $\hat{E}$, Firm L will reduce its emissions from $E°_L$ to $\hat{E}$, Firm H from $E°_H$ to $\hat{E}$. At $\hat{E}$, MAC_H exceeds MAC_L, thus violating the equimarginal principle.

> *A TBS will be cost-effective only if all individual plants in each category have exactly the same marginal abatement costs.*

There are thousands of individual industrial water-pollution sources, so some of the subcategories must contain very large numbers of sources. There can be little doubt that the sources in most subcategories are heterogeneous in terms of the production technology they are using, so we would expect them to be heterogeneous in terms of their marginal emission abatement costs. Applying the same emission standards to each firm cannot be cost-effective.

The cost *in*effectiveness of equal treatment-type programs like TBSs has been examined directly in a series of river basin studies in the U.S. carried out by teams of economists and environmental scientists. These use large-scale models of individual river basins, incorporating the different estimated marginal abatement costs of various sources of pollution, together with the main hydrological features of the basins' water resources. They compare the costs of water pollution-control programs in which all sources were treated alike to those where sources are controlled in accordance with relative marginal abatement costs.

FIGURE 16-3 A Uniform Technology-Based Standard when MACs Differ

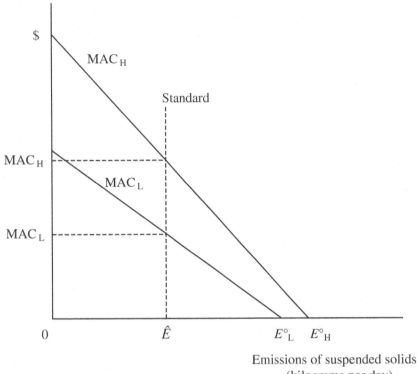

Emissions of suspended solids
(kilograms per day)

Technology-based standards are not cost effective when marginal abatement costs (MACs) differ because the equimarginal principle is violated. Abatement costs are not equalized across emitters.

EXAMPLE OF COST-INEFFECTIVENESS OF TBS
A case study of the Delaware River

While done many years ago, this very well known study is still relevant today as it clearly illustrates how cost-ineffective TBSs are. The lower Delaware River runs through the heavily industrialized sections around Philadelphia and southwestern New Jersey, then opens out into the broad and shallow Delaware Bay. Wastewater emissions contribute to serious water-quality problems in the estuary, both in the traditional measures of dissolved oxygen (DO) and in other types of organic and inorganic wastes. Investigators used a water-quality model that predicted the effects of changing waste loads in any part of the estuary on water quality elsewhere in the estuary. Superimposed on this was a mathematical model showing the relationship of abatement costs at any of the large effluent outfalls on the estuary to emission levels at those outfalls. By operating these models together researchers could estimate the costs of meeting water-quality goals by controlling emissions at each of the various sources.

The main results are summarized in Table 16-4. These show the abatement costs of reducing BOD emissions from sources on the Delaware estuary so as to achieve given target levels of DO in the

(Continued)

waters of the estuary.[18] The exact levels of costs are not as important as the comparison of different types of policy approaches. The table shows two alternative target levels, one at 2 parts per million (ppm) and a higher one at 3–4 ppm of DO. To meet the lower DO target with a uniform treatment approach (reducing emissions at each source in the same proportion) would have cost $5-million per year. The costs of an equal treatment program attaining DO levels of 3–4 ppm would have cost an estimated $20-million annually. Thus MAC curves are an increasing function of emissions controlled.

TABLE 16-4   Summary of Results of the Delaware Estuary Water Quality Control Study

DO objective	Uniform treatment program	Least-cost program	Effluent charge program	
			Single	Zoned
	Million Dollars per year			
2 ppm	5.0	1.6	2.4	2.4
3–4 ppm	20.0	7.0	12.0	8.6

Source: *Allen V. Kneese and Blair T. Bower*, Managing Water Quality: Economics, Technology, Institutions *(Baltimore, MD.: Johns Hopkins Press for Resources for the Future, 1968), 162.*

The same DO targets could be reached at much lower cost by reducing emissions in a cost-effective way. The costs of a program designed to meet the targets with a set of emission controls satisfying the equimarginal principle were $1.6-million for 2 ppm and $7.0-million for 3–4 ppm DO. Note that these costs are roughly one-third of the costs of the uniform treatment program.[19]

To impose a least-cost approach by specifying allowable emissions at each source would, of course, require an administering agency to have an enormous amount of knowledge about marginal abatement costs at each of the sources. Alternatively, authorities could achieve cost-effective emission reductions by imposing an effluent tax on emissions.

Researchers investigated several approaches to emission taxes in the Delaware study. One was a single emissions tax (in this case a single tax on BOD emissions) levied on all sources throughout the estuary. The annual costs of this single tax approach were estimated at $2.4-million for the 2 ppm target and $12.0-million for the target of 3–4 ppm. Why aren't the costs of the single emissions tax as low as the least-cost program? The simple answer is that the MD curve varies with the location of the polluting sources. The polluters have different transfer coefficients with respect to the various points where water quality was measured. Recall from Chapter 12 that when the MD curves differ, a single emissions tax will not be socially efficient (although it is cost-effective). A unique effluent tax would have to be levied on each source, taking into account both its marginal abatement costs *and* its location relative to other sources. Of course, this would be a totally unrealistic administrative burden, given the hundreds of different BOD sources on the Delaware estuary. There is a trade-off, in other words, between lower control costs on one side and administrative complexity on the other.

(Continued)

---

18. Administrative and enforcement costs are not included in the table.

19. Similar results have been obtained in other studies; for example, for the Willamette River: Kenneth D. Kerri, "An Economic Approach to Water Quality Control," *Journal of the Water Pollution Control Federation* 38(12) (December 1966): 1883–1897; the Miami River in Ohio: M. W. Anderson, "Regional Water Quality Management in the Miami Basin" (Ph.D. thesis, Carnegie Mellon University); and the Merrimack Valley of Massachusetts: Alvin S. Goodman and William Dobbins, "Mathematical Model for Water Pollution Control Studies," *Journal of the Sanitary Engineering Division, Proceedings ASCE* 92[SA6], (December 1966): 1–9.

As discussed in Chapter 12, one answer to this is to institute a zoned emission tax. Here the sources are grouped into zones, and all sources in the same zone are charged the same tax, while sources in different zones are taxed at different rates. In the Delaware estuary study, the zoned emission charge has the same annual costs as a single tax approach for the lower DO target, but is substantially less costly for the higher DO target of 3–4 ppm. What this shows in effect is that the larger the improvement we want to achieve in water quality the greater the difference it makes to have a cost-effective program. For targets involving small changes in water quality, a TBS may not be a bad approximation to a fully cost-effective and socially efficient policy. But for targets involving large changes, the TBS will be very cost-ineffective.

TBSs and Technological Improvements

Chapter 12 showed that emission standards lead to weaker incentives to innovate in pollution control than economic-incentive-type policies.[20] In the case of TBSs, incentives are made even weaker by linking the emission standards to particular control technologies. When polluters are faced with this type of technology-linked standard, compliance tends to become a matter of adopting the technology the authorities have used to set the standard. Since permanent emissions monitoring is quite costly, administering authorities can check compliance by making periodic inspections to ascertain whether sources are using approved emissions-control technology. In order to minimize the risk of being penalized for non-compliance, polluters have the incentive to adopt the particular technology that the government used to establish the standard. The result is that although the TBSs are nominally just emission standards, they end up tending to dictate the particular effluent control technologies chosen by firms. This substantially undermines any incentives to search for other, cheaper ways to meet the standards.

There is another dimension to these incentive effects. *It is vitally important in designing a pollution-control program to place the control on the right element in the total input–production–emission process.* This goes for any program, whether it uses standards or an incentive approach. The technology-based standards in water pollution control are normally expressed in terms of quantity of emissions per unit of raw material input used in production. But the real pollution-control issue is the total quantity of emissions during a given time period. The connection between these two factors can be shown as follows:

$$Total\ emissions = output \times [input/output] \times [emissions/input]$$

TBSs apply only to the last expression in this equation. Another way for a firm to reduce its total emissions, however, is to reduce its use of inputs per unit of output; for example, by installing more efficient production equipment or better operating procedures. Still another way of reducing total emissions is to reduce total output, the first term in the expression above. For example, electric power companies can reduce total emissions by promoting energy conservation among their customers. The basic problem, as we can see from the formula, is that the incentive has to be put on the right thing. In this case, expressing the standard in terms simply of total emissions would at least provide incentives to make improvements in all the factors of the equation, not just the last one.

---

[20]. Also recall that a TBS can lead to high costs of compliance when a polluter must switch its existing pollution control technology to the one designated in the regulation. Moreover, if the regulator wants to make the policy more stringent over time, it must require how the pollution abatement equipment has to be upgraded or modified to meet increasing standards. This, too, can lead to very high costs of meeting an environmental target.

Municipal Sewage and Water Treatment

Municipalities are responsible for the construction and operation of sewage and water treatment facilities. Gradually over the 1970s and 1980s the proportion of municipal wastewater that is untreated fell from more than 50 percent to less than 20 percent. However, Canada may well be entering a "crisis" stage in water and sewage treatment. Many wastewater treatment plants need replacement and upgrading of treatment capabilities (which is why this was an example in the benefit–cost chapters). These are typically very capital-intensive operations, and continue to represent a large percentage of total (all levels) government environmental expenditures. The federal and provincial governments used to contribute financially to construction of these plants; the federal government under the *Canada Water Act of 1970*, the provinces in block grants to the municipalities. The federal government no longer provides grants to municipalities and many provincial governments have sharply curtailed their funding of treatment plants. As a result, Canadian municipalities may operate equipment that is inadequate for its job. This can endanger health and affect ecosystems, as an example below illustrates. Municipalities are looking for new ways to fund treatment plants and to reduce the pressures on the system by reducing water use. Economic incentives might provide some help.

Many municipalities continue to charge flat rates for water consumption and sewage services. In 2004 (most recent year of data) Canada as a whole had approximately 63 percent of its municipal population on water meters. When people are charged per unit of water consumed, total water consumption is substantially less than that for people who pay flat rates independent of water use. For population centres with more than 20,000 people, those with meters consumed approximately 250 litres of water per capita per day. Those without meters consumed around 400 litres per capita per day—over 60 percent more![21] Another study of Canadian water use, found metered homes used 34 percent less water than those without meters.[22] Unit pricing alone won't solve the financial difficulties of providing for sewage and water treatment, but it is a step in the right direction.

LO 4

Nonpoint-Source Emissions

Nonpoint-source (NPS) emissions account for a substantial amount of the water pollution in Canada. As noted in Section 1, BOD, suspended solids, phosphorus, and nitrogen come from nonpoint sources. Similarly, nonpoint sources contribute large amounts of toxic pollutants to water resources. Major nonpoint sources are agricultural runoff, urban street runoff, and activities related to land clearance and building construction. Canadian policy is predominantly at the provincial level except when nonpoint sources cross provincial or national boundaries, as was the case with phosphorus regulations examined above. This reflects the recognition that a uniform national program cannot address such diverse sources with significant differences in MACs and MDs across each country.

The fact that NPS emissions are diffuse and not concentrated into specific outfalls has made them very difficult to control. NPS pollutants are also normally very weather-related, which makes the runoff patterns more difficult to monitor. Traditional approaches like emission standards are problematic because it is difficult to measure emissions accurately. Emissions taxes would run into the same

---

[21.] Environment Canada, *The Urban Environment: Water Supply,* State of the Environment Reporting, Environmental Indicator Bulletin No. 93-8 (1993), 4.

[22.] Ken Sharrett, "The Influence of Water Meters on Residential Use in Canada," June 2001, accessed at www.sharratt-watermanagement.ca/pdfs/Sharratt-Influence_Meters.pdf, on October 8, 2010.

problem. Taxes could be applied to those activities or materials that lead to the emissions, rather than the emissions themselves. For example, taxes might be put on fertilizer used by farmers, or on lawn chemicals used by suburban dwellers. The objective in this case is to induce a reduction in the use of materials that may ultimately end up in rivers, lakes, or groundwater aquifers.

TBSs that specify technologies or practices that must be followed are commonly used in Canada. Standards that rule out agricultural cultivation on steep, easily eroded land, standards specifying the design of urban storm sewers, and standards requiring home builders to take certain steps to control construction-site runoff are types of design standards. Regulations also prohibit the discharge of oil by motor vehicle repair shops into sewers. This is an example of a practice that is regulated. While TBSs may be seen as one of the only options in the case of NPS emissions, one should keep in mind all difficulties inherent in their use that were examined above. Difficulties of control explain why NPS pollution has not been addressed as vigorously in the past as point-source emissions, despite their importance.

In many areas of each country point sources and nonpoint sources exist in close proximity, essentially contributing to the same water-quality problems. The equimarginal principle would require the control of point and nonpoint sources to be balanced so that the marginal emission reduction costs are the same in the two cases. Historically, however, point sources have been controlled much more vigorously than nonpoint sources. What this means is that there may be many regions of the country where shifting more of the burden onto nonpoint sources would be an effective way of lowering the costs of water-quality improvements. One way of doing this is the trading of emission reduction credits between point sources and nonpoint sources as is illustrated in the example of Ontario's South Nation River watershed.

EXAMPLE

Phosphorus offsets in the South Nation River watershed, Ontario[23]

The South Nation River watershed lies between the Ottawa and St. Lawrence Rivers in eastern Ontario. It covers 3,900 square kilometres with a population of 125,000 people. The principal economic activity is agriculture, particularly dairy farms. Excessive levels of phosphorus from point and nonpoint sources have exceeded by up to five times the Ontario water quality objectives. Point sources are primarily wastewater treatment by municipalities and nonpoint sources from agriculture. In response, South Nation Conservation (SNC), a watershed organization, initiated a pilot program in 2000 that instituted an offset program, enabled by Ontario government legislation to allow emission trading. Any new or expanding operator of a wastewater lagoon (the point source) can discharge its effluent into the watershed at peak flows as long as they purchase a credit that allows the SNC to offset an equivalent amount of phosphorus from a NPS. The program isn't a market with direct exchange between sellers and buyers of credits, as it operates through the SNC as a 'broker' and assessor of offset projects. SNC uses the funds from the credit to pay farmers and others to engage in activities that reduce NPS phosphorus. Examples include barnyard run-off control, manure storage, and restricting livestock from waterways. The program is deemed a success. From 2000 to 2009, payments of over $700,000 were made for 269 projects, leading to a reduction of almost 12,000 kilograms of phosphorus reaching the watershed. Estimates are that municipalities have saved up to $5,000 per kilogram of phosphorus removed by using the credits instead of upgrading treatment plants.

[23.] Information for this example is taken from Environment Canada, O'Grady, D., "Sociopolitical Conditions for Successful Water Quality Trading in the South Nation River Watershed, Ontario, Canada," *Journal of the American Water Resources Association* 47(1): 39–51, (2011) and McNeil, R., "Water Quality Trading in Ontario," Environment Probe, accessed July 23, 2014 at: http://probeinternational.org/library/wp-content/uploads/2013/05/Water-Quality-Trading-final.pdf.

Canadian provinces are responding to the increased awareness of the environmental damages from nonpoint sources and public pressure to ensure safety of drinking water resulting from recent cases of water contamination. Ontario announced plans in June 2001 to bring in regulations governing runoff of manure and other farm fertilizers. The regulations planned are TBSs that cover agricultural practices, focusing particularly on storage of waste and the use of manure on fields.[24] The regulations will be phased in over a five-year period. The proposed regulation follows one of the most publicized Canadian cases of drinking water contamination—bacterial contamination in Walkerton, Ontario. The case illustrates a number of points including the importance of having effective policies to deal with nonpoint sources as well as ensuring compliance with drinking-water standards and establishing policies to transmit important public-health information.

Case Study: E. Coli Contamination in Walkerton, Ontario[25]

In mid-May of 2000, people in the small town of Walkerton, Ontario starting falling ill. This wasn't just a few sick people: close to half of the town's 5,000 residents had acute gastroenteritis, with varying degrees of bloody diarrhea. Seven people died.[26] The culprit was the *Escherichia coli* bacteria (E. coli for short) number 0157:H7, one of the most dangerous forms of the bacteria, which had contaminated the town's drinking water. The E. coli apparently came from a nonpoint source—runoff of manure from a dairy herd during a time of heavy rainfall, which flowed into the town's well. The contamination was detected in a sample sent for monitoring prior to the townspeople falling sick, but the local official in charge of the town's water supply did not warn the public or take sufficient action to control the contamination. The town's chlorination equipment had failed and nothing was done to repair it. The private lab that did the monitoring notified the Walkerton water authority—not the Ontario Ministry of the Environment regulators, who are charged with overseeing water quality for the province, or the chief medical officer for the region.

Provincial regulation requires that the lab report contamination to the environment ministry, but does not require notification of the chief medical officer. It was the medical officer for the region who raised the first public alert after he received a report from an alarmed physician treating one of the sick children that she suspected E. coli. The medical officer obtained a water sample and sent it in for testing. When the results came back positive for E. coli 0157:H7, he called the provincial ministry. A "boil water" advisory was issued one week after the first cases emerged and one day before the first death.

The *Canadian Drinking Water Guidelines* discussed above specify zero E. coli in Canadian drinking water. The province of Ontario requires every municipality to regularly monitor its water quality. So what went wrong in Walkerton?

---

24. See R. Brennan, "Ontario Farm Runoff Bill Won't Take Effect for Years," *Toronto Star,* June 14, 2001, p. A8. Other provinces, for example British Columbia, already have similar policies in place.

25. Two good sources for details on Walkerton from which the facts of this case have been taken are the *Toronto Star's* website: http://king.thestar.com/editorial/walkerton and the official website for the Walkerton inquiry: www.walkertoninquiry.com.

26. Ontario's chief coroner attributed seven deaths to the E. coli. However, a total of 21 people from the town died during the outbreak and, while E. coli may not have been the direct cause, it may have been a contributor.

Several public inquiries followed the Walkerton incident. Blame has been put on the local and provincial governments and the individual in charge of the water supply in Walkerton. Issues highlighted include

- inadequate provincial regulation to help protect drinking-water supplies. For example, prior to Walkerton, Ontario's government did not have an effective policy to help protect water supplies from farm runoff.
- failure of the municipality to ensure compliance with water-quality guidelines and to ensure public safety.
- downsizing budgets for water quality infrastructure, monitoring, and enforcement.
- Ontario's privatization of water-quality monitoring without ensuring that checks and balances were in place to ensure transmittal of information about hazardous contamination.
- inadequate training and education of municipal water officials.
- no checks to see that municipal officials are complying with regulations.
- inadequate budgets to ensure local water treatment plants are operating properly and are maintained, with old or malfunctioning equipment replaced.

Many believe that Walkerton was a disaster waiting to happen. E. coli had been a problem in the system for at least four years, yet the public was never informed by municipal authorities. The operator of the water treatment plant had no formal training for his position, and it is alleged that he did not think chlorination was essential (he didn't like the taste). False samples were sent in for testing. He failed to inform either the province or the medical officer of health about the contamination. The town of Walkerton had also declined to let the Ontario Clean Water Agency, the provincial Crown corporation, come in and operate their system. This agency operates more than 400 facilities for 200 municipalities in the province. Walkerton also failed to authorize increased spending on its antiquated water treatment system, citing too few municipal funds. Municipal water fees collected each year did not even cover the operating costs of the system, let alone provide for capital replacement. The town tried unsuccessfully to get provincial assistance for upgrading its water system.

The Ontario government failed to implement a policy to protect groundwater sources of drinking water, as repeatedly requested by its own environmental commissioner (who was fired in 1999) and strongly suggested by the federal government. During the "Common Sense Revolution" under Premier Mike Harris, the environment ministry's budget was severely cut, the province's three testing labs were closed, and municipalities had to turn to private labs for tests. There was no requirement that these labs have any sort of accreditation for the tests they performed. While in the case of Walkerton, the lab test performed did correctly indicate the presence of the toxic E. coli, this does not mean that an error could not occur in some other instance due to substandard procedures of an uncertified laboratory. The labs were required to inform the environment ministry of cases of contamination, but no enforcement of this regulation occurred. Labs were not required to report to health officials. The government eliminated grants to municipalities for replacing or upgrading their water (and sewage) treatment plants in 1996. It reintroduced a small grant pool of $200-million in 1997. Its own environment ministry had estimated in 1992 that $19-billion was needed over the next decade to replace and upgrade water and sewage systems province-wide.

In August 2000, Ontario issued new drinking water regulations. The regulations cover such items as minimum treatment levels, sampling, reporting, public information, corrective actions, and notices to medical officers of health. In September 2000, the Ontario environment minister announced the formation of a pollution SWAT team to apprehend and charge those who violate provincial regulations with the "toughest fines and largest jail terms in Canada."[27] Many observers believe that the timing of these announcements is not a coincidence, but rather tacit acknowledgement by the Ontario government that it did not meet its regulatory role to help ensure safe drinking water in the province. Some of the policies announced may be somewhat hasty and not consistent with sound economic principles. For example, are the pollution SWAT team, high fines, and jail terms the most cost-effective policies to promote compliance with regulations, or would other incentive-based policies be better?

What lessons can we draw from this case? Walkerton may have been an extreme situation that may never be repeated again, but there are many other parts of Canada with water-quality concerns. For example, a number of municipalities in British Columbia and many areas in Newfoundland are under continual "boil water" advisories due to microbial contamination. Collingwood, Ontario had its water supply contaminated by a parasite, Cryptosporidium, for a number of weeks. North Battleford, Saskatchewan had an E. coli outbreak in its water supply in 2001. Contamination of groundwater plagues parts of the Maritime and Prairie provinces. The case also illustrates the complexity of command-and-control regulation required to ensure drinking-water safety and the importance of monitoring and enforcing for any environmental policy, whether command-and-control or incentive-based.

Questions to ponder:

- Are water-quality guidelines enough?
- What sort of regulatory policies should be adopted now?
- Would any policies using economic incentives be appropriate?

Summary

Canadian environmental regulation is a complex mix of federal and provincial policies that rely primarily on command-and-control instruments in the form of guidelines and objectives. There are few specific standards. Co-operation among the levels of government and between government and industry is sought. Public involvement has been minimal until recently. Most water-pollution policies are at the provincial level. The federal government has introduced national standards for some compounds, addressed some interjurisdictional water pollution problems, and established national guidelines for water quality. Water quality is a problem in parts of Canada and new policy initiatives are needed both federally and provincially to address the problems.

Technology-based standards are examined in detail, as they are the most commonly used policy in Canada. While TBSs are appealing as "technological fixes," they have a number of drawbacks. They are likely to give far less pollution control for the money spent than alternative approaches, because they normally violate the equimarginal principle. They provide fewer incentives than other policies to find better and cheaper ways of controlling waterborne emissions.

[27.] See the Ministry's announcement of these new initiatives at www.ocwa.com/frpub.htm or www.ene.gov.on.ca.

Key Terms

Accumulative pollutants

Biochemical oxygen demand (BOD)

Continuous emissions

Degradable pollutants

Dissolved oxygen (DO)

Episodic emissions

Non-accumulative pollutants

Nonpoint-source pollutants

Persistent pollutants

Point-source pollutants

Analytical Problems

1. Controlling the pollutants from the production of bleached paper is about five times costlier than controlling the pollutants from unbleached paper. Illustrate this situation graphically using our standard MAC/MD model. What policy instrument would you use for these water pollutants coming from paper production and why? Specify the criteria you have used to pick the policy.

2. The federal government imposed regulations limiting phosphate emissions to the Great Lakes. Could they have used a tax on phosphates instead? Could the tax have led to an equivalent improvement in water quality at lower total costs to society? Discuss and consider the pros and cons of using a tax in this case.

3. For the Delaware estuary example, illustrate graphically the different pollution policy options presented in Table 16-4. Show which are socially efficient, cost effective, and explain why. Which policy would you recommend adopting and why?

Discussion Questions

1. Most technology-based emission standards have focused on "end-of-pipe" treatment technology. What is the reason for this, and what has been the likely impact?

2. Water pollution has been dealt with primarily by the provinces. Would you advocate a larger role for the federal government? If so, what types of policies would you recommend? If not, how do you think water-quality objectives for our major interprovincial waterways, such as the St. Lawrence River, should be achieved?

3. To date, there have been few Canadian policies dealing with water-pollution problems stemming from nonpoint-source emissions. Why is this the case? How might the different types of pollution-control policies be employed in the case of nonpoint-source emissions?

 For more information on the resources available from McGraw-Hill Ryerson, go to www.mheducation.ca/he/solutions.

Chapter 17

Air Pollution-Control Policy

After reading this chapter you will be able to:

LO 1) Provide a brief overview of Canada's air pollution control policies.

LO 2) Explain the policy issues that arise from Canada's regulation of air contaminants.

LO 3) Describe measures that could be taken to reduce emissions from motor vehicles.

LO 4) Describe the basic components of the Canada–United States policies to reduce acid rain.

Earth would be unable to sustain life as we know it without its atmosphere. The surface air (the troposphere) normally contains about 78 percent nitrogen, 21 percent oxygen, small amounts of other gases, varying amounts of water vapour, and many other compounds put there through acts of nature and human activities. The upper layers of the earth's atmosphere (the stratosphere) contain only about 5 percent of the planet's air, but have a critical role to play in making the planet habitable. Trace gases in the stratosphere, particularly ozone, filter out about 99 percent of incoming ultraviolet radiation, acting like a giant sun block without which we would be exposed to damaging levels of radiation. Other trace gases in the stratosphere provide greenhouse services: they trap some of the infrared radiation that is reflected back from the earth's surface, warming it and making it more hospitable to living organisms. Both of these vital phenomena can be disrupted by human activity.

Human disruptions of the atmosphere are not new; instances of local smoke pollution have occurred for centuries. But in the last few decades the severity of air-pollution problems has grown more acute, owing to the sheer scale of airborne residuals released and the nature of some of the emitted substances. There are thousands of potential air pollutants—for example, oxides of carbon, nitrogen and sulphur, volatile organic compounds, suspended particulate matter, photochemical oxidants, radioactivity, heat, and noise. These pollutants cause a diverse set of damages. Prolonged exposure to airborne substances can lead to lung cancer, bronchitis, emphysema, and asthma; accidental releases can have acute impacts. Air pollution damages plants—agricultural crops and forests. Air pollution can lead to severe damage of exposed materials, such as the surface erosion and discoloration of stone and concrete work and the corrosion of metals. Stratospheric ozone depletion and enhanced global warming have significant implications for the sustainability of humans and the earth's ecosystem. Not all air pollution is outdoors; in fact, indoor air pollution is a critical problem in many homes, factories, mines, and farms.

Many airborne pollutants are emitted on a continuous basis. The sulphur dioxide (SO_2) emissions from coal-fired electric power plants, for example, are continuously produced as long as the plants are in operation. For individual motor vehicles, emissions start and stop with their operation, although for an entire urban area auto and truck emissions vary continuously throughout the days and seasons. Air quality in Beijing, for example, is particularly bad in winter when coal burning for heat and electricity releases large amounts of particulate matter. Episodic, especially accidental, emissions have been the cause of severe air-pollution incidents, for example the Bhopal disaster in India and other industrial releases of toxic materials into the air. The links between emissions and ambient air-quality levels can be complicated because of the complexities of meteorological phenomena. The best-known example of this is the creation of local weather conditions that trap air pollutants, sometimes for extended periods of time. These are called *temperature inversions*. The major air pollutants Canadians are exposed to are summarized below.[1]

THE "BIG FIVE" CRITERIA AIR CONTAMINANTS

- *Nitrogen oxides (NO_x).* A brownish, highly reactive gas present in urban atmospheres. Primary sources are transportation and stationary fossil fuel combustion (e.g., power plants). They are an ingredient of smog. Environmental impacts include lung irritation; nitrogen oxides contribute to lung diseases and lower resistance to respiratory infections.

- *Sulphur oxides (SO_x).* Primarily from stationary sources from combustion of fossil fuels (e.g., oil refineries, fossil-fuel-fired electricity generators), steel mills, pulp and paper mills, non-ferrous smelters. Sulphur dioxide is a pungent gas that irritates people's upper respiratory tract. Those particularly affected are children, the elderly, and people with chronic lung diseases such as asthma. It is also the key compound responsible for acid precipitation, a problem in eastern Canada.

- *Particulate matter (PM).* Particulates come in a number of measured sizes (e.g., PM–2.5, and PM–10 are 2.5 and 10 microns, respectively) and include dust, dirt, soot, smoke, and liquid droplets. PM–2.5 is thought to be particularly damaging to the lungs because the particulates are so small that our bodies cannot filter them out. They accumulate in the lungs and contribute to lung and heart disease. They also damage the body's immune system and are carcinogens. Sources of PM are emissions from motor vehicles, point sources from various industrial processes, power plants, fires, and natural sources of dust.

- *Carbon monoxide (CO).* Carbon monoxide is released from incomplete combustion of a fossil fuel. The primary source in urban areas is motor vehicles. This colourless and odourless gas replaces hemoglobin in our bloodstream and reduces the delivery of oxygen to the tissues and organs. At high enough concentrations in the blood, it is fatal. CO poisoning is associated with faulty gas appliances in the home and poorly maintained exhaust systems in cars and trucks. Its concentration in the atmosphere is clearly far from lethal, but in urban areas it can be at levels sufficient to cause headaches, tiredness and irritation, and impaired visual perception, manual dexterity, learning ability, and performance of complex tasks.

- *Volatile organic compounds (VOCs).* VOCs include gases such as propane and benzene. They come from stationary and point sources. The stationary sources are the production and use of paints (oil-based) and solvents, refineries, dry cleaners, gas stations, and a natural source—forests. Motor vehicles are mobile sources of VOCs. VOCs are another contributor to smog. Some, such as benzene, are carcinogenic.

AMBIENT AIR QUALITY IN CANADA

Recall from Chapter 2, Figure 2-8 shows declining ambient comcentration of sulphur dioxide over time, while Figure 2-9 illustrates little change in concentrations of particulate matter. Figure 17-1

---

[1] Environmental policies covering emissions of greenhouse gases and CFCs are discussed in Chapter 20. Review Table 2-1, which summarizes sources and probable impacts of pollutants.

provides data on ambient concentrations of volatile organic compounds over time and Figure 17-2 the same for ozone—a component of smog. These figures reinforce the message that ambient air quality in Canada does not show a consistent pattern of improvement across all the air contaminants. The data give rise to a number of questions and issues.

FIGURE 17-1 Volatile Organic Compound Concentrations, Canada, 1997 to 2011

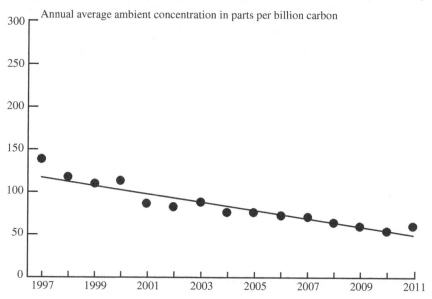

Source: © *Her Majesty The Queen in Right of Canada, Environment Canada, 2014. Reproduced with the permission of the Minister of Public Works and Government Services Canada.*

FIGURE 17-2 Ozone Concentrations, Canada, 1997 to 2011

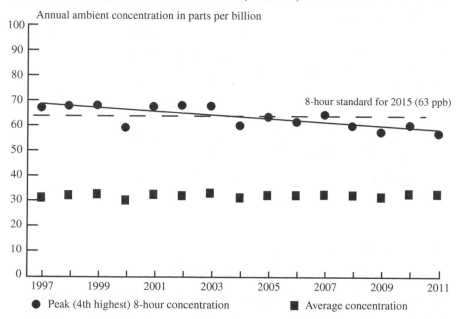

Source: © *Her Majesty The Queen in Right of Canada, Environment Canada, 2014. Reproduced with the permission of the Minister of Public Works and Government Services Canada.*

1. To what extent are the regulations (discussed below) responsible for the improvement? This is a difficult question that economists wrestle with. To analyze the impact of regulations, the analyst typically needs a statistical model to help sort out the various factors that may influence emissions and ambient levels of a pollutant. A question one wants to ask is what would ambient air quality be if the regulations had not been in place.

2. Are the policies cost-effective? Studies have been done in the United States comparing the country's air-quality standards to cost-effective policy alternatives. They find that total compliance costs could be much lower with alternative policies, especially incentive-based policies that price the pollutants. While research is needed in Canada to examine this question, the U.S. results suggest that introducing more incentive-based policies may help reach environmental targets at lower costs to society.

3. Are the guidelines themselves sufficient to safeguard the health of Canadians and our ecosystems? Scientific and economic studies to help determine the marginal damages and marginal costs of abatement for air pollutants are necessary to answer this question.

4. Why have Canadian governments been so reluctant to use incentive-based instruments? There are many reasons; some were covered in Section 4. But conditions can change, and economic analysis of environmental problems and policy options is one tool that can assist governments in choosing among the available policy instruments.

LO 1

AIR POLLUTION-CONTROL POLICIES IN CANADA: A BRIEF SKETCH

Ambient air-quality targets have been set for the criteria pollutants. To achieve a target level of ambient air quality, emission targets for point and nonpoint sources must also be set. Air-pollution policy has followed a path similar to that for water pollution—national targets for the criteria air contaminants have been established as guidelines known as objectives, not binding standards. The first air-pollution legislation was at the provincial level; the federal government entered in the late 1960s and 1970s. The federal government works in conjunction with the provinces to set guidelines. However, a key difference from water quality regulation is that the ministers of environment for all provinces except Quebec (who sets its own targets) have been moving since 2000 to create air quality standards instead of non-binding objectives. The Canadian Council of Ministers of the Environment (CCME) leads this initiative. The path to the present situation federally began with the enactment of the *Clean Air Act* (CAA) in 1971 and now covered under the *Canadian Environment Protection Act* (CEPA). This act serves as the backbone for ambient air quality guidelines and standards along with emissions of toxic compounds. The CAA gave the federal government authority to:

- conduct a national program of air-pollution surveillance;

- establish air-quality objectives (i.e., targets);

- establish regulations including standards at the source; and

- establish guidelines, which were recommended limits on pollutants.

Under the CAA, the federal government adopted national ambient air quality objectives (NAAQOs) for the criteria pollutants defined above. A federal–provincial advisory committee on air quality developed the objectives. While there is no publicly available information on how the objectives were set, they are closely related to those in the United States as well as to the World Health Organization's guidelines and thus primarily reflect impacts on human health. The provinces can adopt these NAAQOs as objectives or enforceable standards if they wish. Most have chosen to adopt them as guidelines; some have more stringent targets. While the government, under the CAA and CEPA, has the authority to set regulations for air emissions to help achieve the NAAQOs, few have been introduced.

The CCME agreed in October 2012 to implement a broad policy for managing air quality in Canada under what is called the Air Quality Management System (AQMS). The objective was to protect human health and the environment with continuous improvement in air quality. Figure 17-3 shows how the CCME translates the broad objectives of the AQMS into a set of actions that are currently underway. Note that the system is comprehensive, covering industrial and transportation sources of air contaminants. The role of the CCME is to design the system of Canada-wide Standards (CWS) and then turn monitoring, enforcement, and reporting over to the provinces and territories. The plan is to have 'State of Air' reports commencing in 2016 that will provide air quality data and information.

FIGURE 17-3 Canada's Air Quality Management System

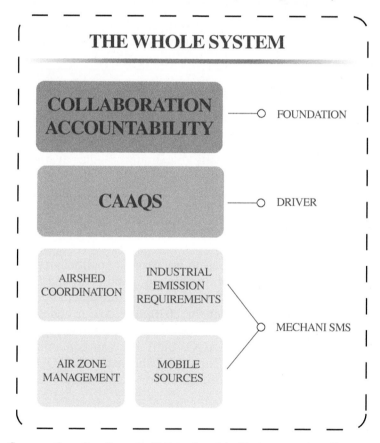

Source: *Canadian Council of Ministries of the Environment, http://www.ccme.ca.*

Canada-wide Standards are intergovernmental agreements that have the following goals:

1. Numeric limits for pollutants,
2. A timetable for attainment, and
3. A framework for monitoring progress and reporting to the public.

The first standards for ground-level ozone and $PM_{2.5}$ came into effect in 2010. These were interim standards while research continued on setting long-term standards. The CCME then announced the standards replacing the CWS that would commence in 2015 and 2020. These were gazetted in May 2013 and called the Canadian Ambient Air Quality Standards (CAAQS) and shown in Table 17-1, along with description of the averaging metric. The CWS standard for $PM_{2.5}$ is $30\mu g/m^3$ over a 24-hour average, and that for ozone is 65 ppb over an 8-hour average. These standards are in effect until 2015.

TABLE 17-1 Canadian Ambient Air Quality Standards (CAAQS) for Fine Particulate Matter (PM$_{2.5}$) and Ozone

Pollutant	Averaging time	Standards (numerical values)		Metric
		2015	**2020**	
PM$_{2.6}$	24-hour (calendar day)	28 µg/m³	27 µg/m³	The 3-year average of the annual 98th percentile of the daily 24-hour average concentrations.
PM$_{2.6}$	annual (calendar year)	10.0 µg/m³	8.8 µg/m³	The 3-year average of the annual average concentrations.
Ozone	8-hour	63 ppb	62 ppb	The 3-year average of the annual 4th-highest daily maximum 8-hour average concentrations.

Note: The 2020 standards will be reviewed in 2015.

Source: *Canadian Council of Ministries of the Environment, http://www.ccme.ca.*

The intent of the standards is to have CCME also set aspirational goals to improve air quality in regions where concentrations are above the standards, prevent degradation in areas in attainment, and try to achieve lower concentrations over time when practicable. Figure 17-4 shows these threshold targets in a colour coded chart for 2015. New targets will presumably be set for 2020. The colour codes will replace the definitions established under the NAAQOs for maximum desirable, maximum acceptable, and maximum tolerable levels. These continue to apply to the NAAQOs until those air contaminants are covered by new standards to replace the air quality objectives. Table 17-2 shows the NAAQOs for sulphur dioxide, carbon monoxide, and nitrogen dioxide with definitions for each category below the table.

Note that both the CAAQS and NAAQOs are ambient standards. To be effective they then need to be translated into targets for **emissions** of the air contaminants. This is to be accomplished through the mechanisms listed in Figure 17-3 and entail creation of six regional airsheds across Canada that are managed jointly with the provinces and territories, guidelines and regulations for industrial emissions and mobile sources. We discuss the activities connected to mobile sources below. For industrial emissions, the CCME in partnership with the provinces and stakeholders are to establish Base-Level

FIGURE 17-4   Air Management Threshold Values and Actions

Management Level	Management Action	Proposed Air Management Threshold Values					
		Ozone (ppb)		PM$_{2.5}$ Annual (µg/m³)		PM$_{2.5}$ 24h (µg/m³)	
		2015	2020	2015	2020	2015	2020
RED	Action for Achieving Air Zone CAAQS						
Threshold		63 ppb	62 ppb	10.0 µg/m³	8.0 µg/m³	28 µg/m³	27 µg/m³
ORANGE	Actions for Preventing CAAQS Exceedance						
Threshold		56 ppb		6.4 µg/m³		19 µg/m³	
YELLOW	Actions for Preventing AQ Deterioration						
Threshold		50 ppb		4.0 µg/m³		10 µg/m³	
GREEN	Actions for Keeping Clean Areas Clean						

Source: *Canadian Council of Ministries of the Environment, http://www.ccme.ca.*

Table 17-2   Canada's National Ambient Air Quality Objectives (NAAQOs)

Pollutant	Averaging Time	Maximum desirable concentration	Maximum acceptable concentration	Maximum tolerable concentration
Sulphur dioxide	Annual	11 ppb	23 ppb	---
	24-hour	57 ppb	115 ppb	306 ppb
	1-hour	172 ppb	344 ppb	--
Carbon monoxide	8-hour	5 ppm	13 ppm	17 ppm
	1-hour	13 ppb	31 ppb	--
Nitrogen dioxide	Annual	32 ppb	52 ppb	--
	24-hour	--	106 ppb	160 ppb
	1-hour	--	213 ppb	532 ppb

Source: *"Canada's National Ambient Air Quality Objectives (NAAQOs)," www.hc-sc.gc.ca/ewh-semt/air/out-ext/ reg-eng.php#4, Health Canada. Reproduced with the permission of the Minister of Public Works and Government Services, 2010.*

Definitions:

Maximum desirable level is the long-term goal for air quality to protect the population and ecosystems. It provides a basis for preventing degradation of air quality in relatively unpolluted parts of the country.

Maximum acceptable level is the next lower level of air quality. It is seen as the level of air quality needed to provide adequate protection against adverse effects of air pollutants on human health and comfort, soil, water, vegetation, animals, materials, and visibility. At or near the maximum acceptable level, susceptible populations (children, the elderly, and those with chronic lung and cardiovascular disease) may incur adverse impacts. This is the target against which Environment Canada typically reports ambient air quality.

Maximum tolerable level represents the lowest boundary before immediate action is required to protect the health of the general population.

Industrial Emission Requirements (BLIERS). These are defined as quantitative or qualitative emission requirements for new and existing major industrial sectors and also will cover some equipment types. The requirements will be set looking at the experience in other jurisdictions inside and outside Canada for areas that have attained their air quality objectives and will consult with affected sectors. The focus is on sulphur dioxide, nitrogen oxides, volatile organic compounds, and particulate matter. Targeted sectors include: alumina and aluminum, base metal smelting, cement, chemicals and fertilizers, electricity generation, iron ore pellets, iron, steel, ilmenite, oil sands, petroleum refining, natural gas transmission pipelines, potash, pulp and paper, and upstream oil and gas. The CCME estimates that the health and environmental benefits of the requirements will be 15 to 34 times greater than their costs.[2]

What progress has been made to achieve the ambient air quality objectives and standards? Refer back to Figure 2-9, which illustrates that for PM the 24-hour standard for 2015 was met in all years from 2000 to 2011, the most recent year available. Ambient levels would even meet the orange-level target in two of the years, but there is a way to go to attain the yellow threshold (referred to in Figure 17-4). The annual standard set for 2015 has been met in all previous years, suggesting that a more stringent target might be appropriate to consider. A different story emerges for ground-level ozone. Figure 17-2 provides the data for 1997 to 2011 graphed against the 2015 CAAQS. The standard would have been exceeded in many of the years, but the good news is that the ambient levels appear to be declining for the 8-hour daily maximum. However, Figure 17-2 also shows little change in average concentrations, suggesting the need for more aggressive policies to reduce emissions that contribute to ground-level ozone (nitrogen oxides and volatile organic compounds, as noted in Table 2-1).

In addition to the ambient air quality policies, there are guidelines and standards for emissions of certain toxic air pollutants, with plans to expand to more. Under CEPA, emission guidelines were created for the cement industry, coke ovens, asphalt paving, mining in the Arctic, types of incinerators, the wood pulp industry, and thermal power generators. In each case, there is a distinction between old and new plants. The guidelines are less stringent for old plants, that is, those already in existence at the time the guidelines were introduced. In some cases, the old plants are required to meet the guideline, but are given a longer time in which to do so than the new plants. There are federal standards for lead from secondary smelters, asbestos from mining and milling, mercury from chloralkali plants, and vinyl chloride from vinyl chloride and polyvinyl chloride manufacturing. Note the overlap between this list and that of the federal water-pollution standards. In the case of these

---

[2] CCME, "Air Quality Management System, Update on Progress" Webinar June 19, 2014, www.ccme.ca/assets/pdf/aqms_update_webinar_june_19_2014.pdf, accessed July 24, 2014.

standards, old and new plants are treated symmetrically. This might be because some of these compounds, such as mercury, are quite toxic. Under the CWS and AQMS the provinces have ratified an agreement covering benzene, and mercury from incineration and metal smelting. Under its CWS for mercury from coal-fired electric power plants, CCME reports that emissions have fallen from 2695 kilograms in 2003 (their base year) to just under 826 kilograms in 2012.[3] The goal was a 60 percent capture rate; the level came close at 56 percent. CCME approved in principle targets for dioxins and furans from waste incineration and pulp and paper boilers. Other sources of toxic air contaminants are under investigation for future standards. The federal government also regulates sulphur content in transport fuels. For gasoline, the limit was 150 parts per million (ppm) from 2002 through 2004, then fell to 30 ppm on January 1, 2005 (but never to exceed 80 ppm). That level remains in effect today. Sulphur in diesel fuel was regulated beginning in 1998 with a limit of 500 ppm. The limit became 15 ppm starting June 1, 2006.

Provincial Air Quality Policy

The first specific air-pollution standards were established in 1963 in Ontario, under its *Air Pollution Control Act*. Maximum concentrations for 13 substances at the **point of impingement** were established for stationary sources of pollution. This is defined as the point where pollutants from a factory stack or other discharge point first encountered the ground, a building, or other object. Point of impingement is therefore an ambient standard that is applied to all pollution sources. No source can release emissions that result in a concentration exceeding the standard at each point of impingement. By 1974, the list of regulated substances reached 100. The key difference between air-pollution and water-pollution regulations in Ontario is that the former apply to any source. Recall that water-pollution discharge guidelines have been in the form of negotiated licences between the government and specific polluters. Air-pollution regulation covers emissions from all sources. Since 1983, the province has been revising its regulations. It is moving from point of impingement standards based on scientific and health studies to BATEA standards, analogous to those planned under MISA. Draft regulations were released in 1990.

Ontario, Newfoundland and Labrador, and Manitoba are the only provinces that use or have used point of impingement concentrations for their air-quality regulations. Saskatchewan sets ambient standards that specify maximum concentration levels for pollutants such as particulates, oxidants, and nitrogen dioxide. If there are multiple sources of a pollutant, the aggregate discharge from all sources must not exceed the ambient standards. These standards are thus analogous to point-of-impingement regulations. British Columbia and Nova Scotia have air-quality objectives. Alberta, Quebec, and New Brunswick have imposed regulations. These objectives and regulations are based primarily on the NAAQOs. Alberta, for example, sets emission limits for visible emissions, particulates, lead from secondary smelters, and vinyl chloride. There are guidelines for the fertilizer industry, asphalt plants, and ammonia storage. The guidelines and standards are based on BPT—best practicable technology.

Ontario broke with the mould of using predominately guidelines and standards when it introduced a form of tradable emission permit system for nitrogen oxides and sulphur dioxide in 2001. The regulation covered electricity generation, iron and steel, cement, petroleum refining, pulp and paper, glass, and carbon black industries to reduce their emissions in stages. The province set an overall cap and allocated allowances (without charge) to the sectors. Non-capped sectors could sell offsets (called

---

3. Canadian Council of Ministers of the Environment, "Canada Wide Standards for Mercury Emissions from Coal-fired Electric Power Generation Plants, 2012 Progress Report," PN 1518, CCME: 2014.

earned reduction credits) to the covered sectors, thus providing the potential for purchases beyond the cap. Between 1999 and 2008, Ontario reduced its nitrogen oxide emissions by 32 percent, and between 2000 and 2009, its sulphur dioxide emisisons by 54 percent.[4] No estimate could be found of the share of the decline in emissions due to the TEP. An additional policy level over that period was Ontario's phasing out of electricity generated by coal-fired power plants. Economic activity in general is also a factor. Nonetheless, a TEP system likely aided in the emission reductions.

Air Pollution Policy Issues Challenging Policy Makers

Before continuing the discussion of Canadian air-pollution policy, we will consider some issues that challenge policy-makers.

LO 2

POLICY ISSUE #1

How do we protect areas that have higher air quality than the maximum acceptable level (the nondegradation dilemma)?

The three levels of NAAQOs and CAAQS take into account the existing level of pollution in a region. The maximum desirable level is supposed to guard against having a region's air quality degrade to the maximum acceptable level. All regulators face the problem of how to prevent degradation of areas with air quality better than the national standards. This is the **non-degradation** dilemma. The concern that areas with air quality already better than a national ambient standard could compete unfairly for new industrial development. New firms might be attracted to these areas by the promise of less strict emissions controls than firms would face in areas where air quality was already worse than the standards. In 1977, amendments to the U.S. *Clean Air Act* differentiated PSD areas (PSD stands for "prevention of serious deterioration"), and **non-attainment** areas. Non-attainment areas have lower air quality than required by the NAAQOs. Stricter technology-based effluent standards would apply to PSD regions, where air quality was already better than the standard, than to non-attainment regions.

The PSD policies can give existing firms a significant competitive advantage compared to a new entrant to an industry. The new entrant is likely to face significantly higher MACs because it has to meet a tougher standard than existing firms in its industry. If new entry does not occur, this can make consumer prices higher than they otherwise would be. Secondly, is it really cost-effective to have a PSD (non-degradation) policy? A cost-effective policy has the MACs of all polluters equal on the margin. A non-degradation policy could, in principle, be chosen so as to have the MACs equal, acting like an individual standard. But, as shown in Chapter 11, it would take a tremendous amount of information for governments to choose the "correct" individual standards. Market-based policies such as emission markets and taxes might be alternative policy choices.

POLICY ISSUE #2

Should old plants be treated differently than new plants?

Federal standards in the U.S. are often less stringent for older plants than for new plants in any location. For example, the U.S. regulates emissions from stationary sources of air pollution with technology-based standards (TBS) that can differ between existing and new sources. New sources, or

(Continued)

[4.] See Ontario, Ministry of Environment, "Emission Trading Fact Sheet," available at: www.moe.

existing sources that are modified in some major way, are usually held to stricter standards than existing, established sources. This is called a **new-source bias.** The case for holding new sources to stricter standards than those applied to existing sources is usually made on the basis of cost; it normally costs more to retrofit existing plants with pollution-control equipment than to incorporate the equipment into new plants when they are being built. In effect, the argument is that the marginal abatement costs of existing plants are normally higher than those of new plants, so cost-effectiveness justifies more restrictive emission standards for the former than for the latter.

To a large extent, this is probably an economic argument being used to justify a course of action that is politically expedient. It is easier to put stricter limits on new sources than on existing ones because, by definition, the former will have less political clout than the latter. And existing firms may not be so opposed to applying stricter controls that make it relatively costly for new competitors to get into business.

From an administrative standpoint a new-source bias is also easy to understand. In any given year there are many times more existing sources than there are new or modified sources, so more administrative resources may be concentrated on the latter. A focus on new sources also implies a gradualist approach, since it means that stricter standards will gradually spread through the various industries as old capital is replaced with new.[5]

However, there may be problems associated with this policy principle. A new-source bias creates incentives to hold on to existing plants because they will be subject to less strict environmental standards than new or modernized plants. In trying to ease the transition to lower pollution levels through a new-source bias, governments may inadvertently slow up the rate of adoption of new pollution-abatement technologies. If so, this can mean that MAC curves will shift down more slowly than would be the case without the more restrictive standards for new sources. Not only does this increase total costs of meeting a given target, it also impedes reaching targets with lower levels of emissions/higher environmental quality. Old, more costly technologies will have a MAC curve that intersects the MD at a higher emission level than could be the case with new technologies. This no doubt is an important reason why so many urban regions of the United States continue to suffer from substantial air-pollution problems many years after the beginning of the federal program.

POLICY ISSUE #3
Uniformity of standards

The NAAQOs and CAAQS are examples of a uniform target. This creates a policy problem. From the theory chapters, we know that unless marginal damage and marginal abatement costs happen to be the same in all regions, uniform national standards will not be efficient. They will be overly stringent where marginal damages are relatively low and/or marginal abatement costs relatively high; or not stringent enough where marginal damages are relatively high and/or marginal abatement costs are relatively low. Thus, standards cannot in general be efficient unless they are established with an eye toward both marginal benefits and marginal control costs. Standards that take into account differences in MACs and MDs across regions may be cost-efficient. They will, however, be much more complex to define and administer. Again, governments might do better by considering market-based policies such as TEPs and taxes.

---

[5] In the United States, the states have the primary responsibility to set TBSs. Because of this, there was some fear among federal policy-makers that economic competition among them would motivate some to set less-restrictive standards to attract business. Thus, the EPA is empowered to set a floor level for standards applying to new or modified stationary sources. These are called new-source performance standards (NSPSs).

POLICY ISSUE #4
Inefficiency of command-and-control (CAC) policies

Environmental economists have estimated the excess costs of the command-and-control (CAC) approach to air pollution control inherent in technology-based standards. The analyses involve complex models that incorporate economic factors, such as control costs at each source, with emission and meteorological factors that show how ambient air quality is affected by various patterns of emissions. The models are used to simulate a least-cost approach to achieve a given environmental target and compare that to TBSs under CAC policies. A multitude of studies done in the United States find that CAC programs cost more than market-based approaches to achieve a specific level of improvement in air quality. Ratios of CAC costs to a least-cost program range from 1.07 to 22.0. The problem with not being cost-effective is not just that society is paying much more than is necessary to get the improvements in air quality, though this is certainly a serious shortcoming. The real problem is that the actual control programs are so much more costly than they need be. This creates an aggregate marginal abatement cost function that is much higher than it need be, and means that society is probably settling for smaller improvements in ambient quality than might be achieved if control programs were fully cost-effective.

In summary, some key points about the direction of Canadian policy governing criteria air contaminants can be gleaned from the discussion above:

- Virtually all of Canada's air-pollution policies use direct regulation in the form of guidelines and standards. This is contrasted with the use of TEPs and transferable emission trading in the United States to address sulphur dioxide emissions as we saw in Chapter 13, and as Policy Issue #4 indicated, these policies may not be cost effective.

- Provinces can design their own policy instruments to reach the targets. This may make sense in the context of air pollutants. There are pros and cons of provincial control over policy instruments. A pro is flexibility in adapting the policy instrument to the particular needs of the region—its sources of emissions, geography, and so on. A con is that a polluting company that operates in more than one province could face 10 different sorts of policies that govern its operations.

- Canadian governments could use a number of incentive-based policies to meet their targets. These could include taxes on the pollution content of fuels that in combustion produce the criteria pollutants, or an increase in existing federal and provincial excise taxes on fuels. Governments might use the concept of **environmental tax shifting** to help the public and corporations accept any new taxes that might be introduced. Tax shifting involves the introduction of an environmental tax that corrects an economic distortion and the recycling of the tax revenue received back to the economy in the form of lower taxes on income, savings, investment, and so on. The important point is that the environmental taxes introduce a price for pollution, while the tax shifting ensures that the overall tax burden for society does not rise. Alternatively, a transferable emission permit might be introduced for various pollutants. Or, the governments could continue to follow their path of using standards for things such as the sulphur content of fuels. Think about which of these policies is likely to best achieve the targets in a cost-effective way.

LO 3

MOTOR VEHICLE EMISSIONS

The federal government regulates emissions from new motor vehicles under the *Motor Vehicle Safety Act,* which is now administered by Environment Canada under CEPA.[6] These are called the corporate average fuel standards (CAF).[7] As we saw in Chapter 1, there are specific standards for nitrogen oxides, hydrocarbons, and carbon monoxide. One question you may have had in Chapter 1 is, Why does the regulation cover only new vehicles? This stems from the federal government's constitutional powers regarding trade and commerce. As we saw in Chapter 15, the federal government can regulate only interprovincial or international trade and commerce. Therefore, once a car leaves the assembly line, the provinces are responsible for any air-pollution regulations that apply.

Most provinces have not regulated emissions of vehicles once in use. From 1992 to the end of 2014, British Columbia had mandatory testing of all light-duty vehicles in Greater Vancouver that were more than a few years old under its AirCare program. Vehicles not meeting emission standards had to be repaired or would not be granted a licence to operate. Those whose vehicles failed the test and wanted to scrap them could get a voucher toward the purchase of a fuel-efficient vehicle or transit pass. Why end the program? As owners replaced their older vehicles with newer, more fuel efficient ones that contained increasingly sophisticated pollution control devices, the number of vehicles who failed the test declined, thus decreasing the rationale for mandatory testing. AirCare will be replaced by a provincial program of spot checks of vehicles, particularly trucks. Other provinces have had testing programs, for example, Ontario's Drive Clean mandatory program implemented in 1999 first for the Greater Toronto area then the province. Mandatory testing may seem like a good way to ensure that vehicles are maintained properly and thus minimize their emissions. But are they cost effective? Some points will illustrate that they may not be. Mandatory testing can be an expensive method of ensuring people maintain their vehicles if only a small proportion of the total number of vehicles tested actually exceed the emission standards. The program could then be scaled down so only older vehicles or specific models (with maintenance problems) are tested. Annual testing also does not ensure compliance with standards every day. Remote sensing could also be used to detect high-pollution vehicles, and other forms of monetary incentives such as expanded buy-back programs for old vehicles (or higher fuel taxes) might be more cost-effective.

As suggested in Chapter 1, there is a fundamental problem with all the regulations currently in place. They are based on the emissions per kilometre travelled; there is no control for the *total* number of kilometres driven. Pollution may therefore initially decrease as emissions per car fall, but if there is an increase in the number of cars driven each year, and/or an increase in the number of kilometres driven, emissions may start rising again. In the U.S., for example, NO_x emissions have stayed relatively constant despite fuel efficiency standards, due to an increase in the number of vehicles on the road and total miles/kilometres driven.[8] Recall the formula given in Chapter 1:

[6.] Transport Canada administered these policies until the early 1990s.

[7.] The Canadian standards are harmonized with those in the United States. The North American automobile industry is so integrated across the countries that it would be very costly for producers to meet different standards in different countries, provinces, or states.

[8.] See Environmental Protection Agency, National Air Pollutant Emission Trends, for data on emission levels at www.epa.gov/ttnchie1/trends/ (accessed October 10, 2010), and the U.S. Energy Information Administration, Annual Energy Reviews, available at www.eia.doe.gov/aer/ (accessed October 10, 2010) for data on motor vehicle mileage and fuel consumption.

Total quantity of emissions = Number of vehicles × Average kilometres travelled × Emissions per kilometre

In devising a cost-effective way of reducing the total quantity of emissions, one would want to balance the three factors on the right side of this equation according to the equimarginal principle. In fact, the federal motor vehicle emission standards focus only on the last of these factors. Air pollution continues to be a serious problem in many regions because the first two factors in the equation have continued to grow. There has also been a shift in consumer taste to more pollution-intensive sport-utility vehicles (SUVs), light duty trucks, and minivans. As these vehicles replace smaller cars, emissions rise because these vehicles release more emissions per kilometre. The average fuel consumption of passenger cars in Canada fell from approximately 12.8 litres per 100 kilometres in 1977 to 7.4 litres per 100 km in 2003. However, if one includes light-duty trucks, fuel efficiency of all vehicles has not increased as much because the light-duty trucks make up a larger share of the market today than they did in the late 1970s and their fuel efficiency in 2003 was approximately 10.6 litres per 100 km. Estimates by Natural Resources Canada for 2005 show the average over all passenger vehicles ranges from 9.9 litres per 100 kilometres in Nova Scotia to 11.9 in Saskatchewan.[9] Another problem is with the maintenance of motor vehicles. As a car ages and accumulates kilometres, emissions can increase unless the equipment is properly maintained. Policies that increase the costs of new cars (such as the CAF standards) increase the average age of vehicles on the road, thus increasing the likelihood of improper maintenance.[10]

Vehicle emission policies in Canada and the United States rely on technological fixes to solve a massive air-pollution problem. The CAF standards of Canada are largely invisible to the public and may give the illusion that the technology will solve urban air-pollution problems. Without incentives to reduce kilometres travelled or the total number of vehicles, total emissions may not fall and society may be paying more than is necessary to reach targets.

What about other technologies to power motor vehicles? Electric cars generate no criteria pollutants, but where does the electricity come from to recharge the vehicles? If it is generated by power plants burning fossil fuels, we will simply shift the source of emissions but not their presence in the atmosphere. Hybrid vehicles are becoming more cost competitive, and changes in vehicle and engine construction are further reducing fuel consumption. Technologies such as fuel cells may become viable for mass production and fall in price. These other technologies also have no impact on the number of vehicles, so urban congestion would remain a significant problem.

This argues for more direct incentive-based approaches to mobile-source emissions. One approach that has been suggested is to levy a significantly higher tax on motor-vehicle fuels. BC's carbon tax is an example. With these fuels being more expensive, motorists would have the incentive to think more about their driving habits, organize their driving more coherently, reduce total kilometres travelled, shift to more fuel-efficient vehicles, use mass transit to a greater extent, and so on. The effects of the higher fuel price would filter throughout the transportation system and lead people to shift their behaviour in places where the marginal costs of doing so are lowest, much as they have done when fuel prices rise substantially. Another suggestion is to place a tax directly on vehicle emissions. As part of each province's annual vehicle licensing, the total kilometres that a vehicle had been driven

---

[9.] See http://oee.nrcan.gc.ca/Publications/statistics/cvs05/chapter2.cfm?attr = 0m, accessed October 10, 2010 for the Canadian Vehicle Survey. The 2005 data was released in 2009. The Canadian Vehicle Survey has been terminated and search for current data on average fuel efficiency in Canada was unsuccessful.

[10.] New vehicles have pollution-control devices that require little or no maintenance over most of the vehicle's life.

could be recorded. This total could be multiplied by the emissions per kilometre, also measured at the time of licensing, to yield an estimate of total emissions in the preceding year. A tax could then be levied on these emissions. Unlike a fuel tax, which would have no direct incentive for drivers to worry about emissions, a tax on emissions would create an incentive to look at all the ways of lowering them, including reducing total kilometres driven, driving low-polluting vehicles, and so on. One attractive aspect of this approach is that the tax could be varied among regions to match the severity of regional air-quality problems.[11]

How well would these policies work? Could we predict the total quantity of emissions? Economists can use information on **elasticities** to predict changes in a target variable. Table 17-3 presents elasticity estimates that might be helpful in choosing a policy to reduce vehicle emissions. Suppose for example that we want to see how demand for new cars that are "gas guzzlers" will decrease if we introduce a new tax on them. The elasticity estimate says that for, say, a 10-percent increase in the price of the car, the quantity demanded will fall by 6 to 8.7 percent. How about a rise in fuel taxes? Here, a 10-percent increase in the tax will lead to a 1.8- to 10-percent fall in fuel consumed. Why such a big gap? The difference no doubt reflects the short-run versus long-run price elasticity of demand. With sufficient time, consumers can more readily change their behaviour in response to the price change. These sorts of elasticity estimates are key to undertaking benefit–cost studies of alternative policy instruments. What is clear to economists is that innovative approaches that go beyond technology standards will be required to meet air-pollution problems from mobile sources.

TABLE 17-3 **Elasticity Estimates for Policy Options to Reduce Air Pollution Emissions from Motor Vehicles**

Elasticity of	Estimate Range	Elasticity Type
Fuel consumption with respect to fuel price	−0.18 to −1.0	Own price
Vehicle travel with respect to fuel price	−0.1 to −0.26	Cross price
Vehicle trips with respect to parking fees	−0.05 to −0.30	Cross price
New vehicle purchases with respect to new vehicle price	−0.6 to −0.8	Own price

Source: *"Options to Reduce Light Duty Vehicle Emissions in British Columbia" (Discussion Paper), Victoria, BC: Ministry of Finance and Corporate Relations (2000). Copyright © Province of British Columbia. All rights reserved. Reprinted with permission of the Province of British Columbia, www.ipp.gov.bc.ca.*

An example of an innovative policy used in Canada was the tax on leaded fuel. The federal government regulates the lead content in gasoline. By the 1970s airborne lead was recognized as a serious health threat, especially to children. In 1976, the lead content in gasoline was limited to 0.77 grams per litre. In 1990, this was reduced to 0.26 grams per litre. That limit, combined with federal taxation of gasoline, effectively eliminated lead as a fuel additive for automobiles. Some lead is still used in fuel for farm equipment, trucks, and fishing boats. The innovative part of the federal government's policy with respect to lead in gasoline was that it used an excise tax to speed the switching by motorists to unleaded fuel. When unleaded gasoline first appeared on the market, it was

---

[11.] There is, however, a concern that this sort of tax would provide an incentive for people to tamper with their car's odometer requiring methods of ensuring this does not occur.

more expensive than leaded. Motorists whose vehicles were supposed to burn unleaded fuel had an incentive to "misfuel" by buying leaded fuel instead. Many did. In 1989, the federal government announced an additional excise tax on leaded gasoline of 1 cent per litre. Six provinces followed suit by increasing their own taxes on leaded gas. The tax differential between leaded and unleaded gasoline ranged from 1.5 to 3 cents per litre. Not only did misfuelling disappear, but most motorists switched to the now-cheaper unleaded gasoline. By 1992, leaded gasoline had disappeared from the retail market.[12]

LO 4

ACID RAIN: A TRANSBOUNDARY POLLUTION PROBLEM

Sulphur dioxide is a transboundary pollutant in North America. The most serious problems occur in the eastern parts of Canada and the United States. In these regions, sulphur dioxide is responsible for the acidic precipitation that lowers the pH of susceptible lakes, damages forests and buildings, and may also contribute to health problems of susceptible individuals. The flow of sulphur dioxide both ways across the Canada–U.S. border has been the source of a political struggle between the two countries. There are barriers to an efficient solution to this cross-border pollution problem. Many levels of government are involved. The distribution of benefits and costs of reducing sulphur dioxide emissions are unequal across and within the jurisdictions. Scientific information about damages took time to be established, and was debated by the various interest groups.

In Canada, the major sources of sulphur emissions are metal smelting companies in Sudbury, Ontario and until their closure is complete, coal-fired electric power plants operated by Ontario Hydro (now Hydro One). While the Ontario government began regulating the metal companies in the early 1900s,[13] it wasn't until the 1970s that acid rain became a topical issue in Canada. The major contributor to sulphur dioxide emissions in Ontario was from Inco, Ltd., the major producer of nickel in the world. The area around Inco's smelter in Sudbury was largely barren due to sulphur dioxide emissions. The Ontario provincial government responded by requiring Inco to lengthen the height of the stack on its smelter. This regulation reflected thinking at the time that "the solution to pollution was dilution." The "super stack," as it was called, did result in fairly rapid improvement in Sudbury's air quality. Scientists then began discovering that lakes in the Canadian Shield downwind of the superstack were becoming acidified and fish stocks were threatened. These lakes were susceptible because they lacked buffering capacity. The Great Lakes, for example, are not susceptible to acidification because their bedrock is mostly limestone, a highly alkaline mineral that neutralizes the sulphuric acid created by the sulphur dioxide emissions.

Canada saw acid rain as a bilateral issue because it "imports" substantial quantities of sulphur dioxide from the United States. The coal-fired power plants in the midwestern states, primarily along the Ohio Valley, have been the major sources of these transboundary flows of pollution. Until the 1990 amendments to the U.S. *Clean Air Act* (discussed below), Canada took the position that the United States was not "doing its share" in regulatory actions to protect the environment from acid rain. Even

---

[12.] In the U.S., a lead-trading system was used for refineries in their transition from leaded to unleaded gasolines. It should also be noted that eliminating lead as an additive to gasoline may reduce one environmental problem while creating others. Benzene, toluene, and xylenes are added to motor vehicle fuels to help engine performance. Each of these are known carcinogens and also increase emissions of VOCs.

[13.] See Don Dewees, "The Efficiency of the Common Law: Sulphur Dioxide Emissions in Sudbury," *University of Toronto Law Journal* 42 (1992): 1–22, for a discussion of the early legal actions regarding metal mining and smelting and air pollution.

though this was a bilateral problem, U.S. "exports" of sulphur dioxide to Canada exceed Canadian exports to the U.S. Canada's position was that the ambient air quality standards in the U.S. weren't strong enough.[14] One reason for this was that certain states were not implementing the national standards—specifically, those in the U.S. midwest that were heavily dependent on coal as the feedstock for their electricity-generating power plants. Another problem was the very slow phase-in of technology standards for existing plants. By the early 1980s, it was clear that strong actions from the U.S. were unlikely. This position reflected in part the fact that Canada would benefit more than the U.S. from sulphur dioxide controls, while the U.S. would bear the largest proportion of control costs.[15] The official view of the U.S. federal administration at the time was that not enough was known about the problem and additional scientific research was needed before more stringent regulations would be passed.[16]

In Ontario, acid rain was a major issue. Many environmental groups took part under the umbrella of an organization called the Canadian Coalition on Acid Rain (CCAR). The CCAR began a massive lobbying effort in Canada and the U.S. that ultimately succeeded in accomplishing the regulatory targets it had established. Its efforts were supported by the federal and Ontario governments, who were happy to keep attention focused on the United States as the main culprit. Canada became increasingly frustrated with the lack of action in the United States and began taking unilateral action while continuing scientific studies to document damages. Ontario imposed increasingly strict emission limits on Inco and Ontario Hydro. In 1982, the federal government announced a federal–provincial agreement (for all provinces east of Saskatchewan) to cut sulphur dioxide emissions by 50 percent of the 1980 levels by 1990. This plan was to be contingent on the U.S. following suit. The U.S. federal government rejected the plan and nothing was done until 1985, when Canada adopted the plan unilaterally. As part of the plan, the federal government was to contribute $150-million to assist the mining industry in complying. Provincial subsidies were also forthcoming. The government in Ontario also extended its acid rain commitments to include all major sources of SO_2, and brought in regulations that would reduce emissions by 67 percent of their 1980 levels by 1994. The other eastern provinces implemented regulations over the next few years.

In December 2000, Canada signed the Ozone Annex, an agreement with the United States to reduce transboundary smog. The overall target is to reduce NO_x by 44 percent in the transboundary region by 2010. The Annex commits Canada to

- reduce emissions of NO_x in Ontario and Quebec. An annual cap of 39 kilotonnes of NO_x (as NO_2) is to be reached by 2007 for central and southern Ontario, while a cap of 5 kilotonnes is set for Quebec. The federal government has allocated funds to help the fossil-fuel electricity generators meet these targets.

- improve air pollution monitoring.

- ensure that Canadian fuels and vehicle emissions are in line with U.S. standards. As noted in Chapter 1, Canadian vehicle emission guidelines now align with those in the U.S.

[14.] Note in Table 17-2 that the U.S. ambient air quality standards for sulphur dioxide remain more lenient than Canada's ambient guidelines.

[15.] And certain regions of the U.S. would bear some of the highest costs, namely the high-sulphur coal-producing region of Appalachia (e.g., states of Kentucky and West Virginia). These regional inequities and the political fallout were a factor the U.S. had to contend with.

[16.] This argument is used frequently by regulators in Canada as well as the United States. Canada has many examples of inaction on environmental policies because it is necessary to further study a problem. See the discussion on greenhouse gases in Chapter 20.

These commitments suggest that Canada will continue to rely on command-and-control policies to reach environmental targets. While the policies will help reach environmental targets, a key policy question is whether they are the most cost-effective policies that could be used.

The Canadian program has succeeded in significantly reducing emissions and meeting the targets. CCME reports every two years on the progress toward goals as part of the Canada-Wide Acid Rain Strategy for Post-2000. SO_2 emissions fell by 63 percent overall from 1985 to 2010, while NO_X fell by about 17 percent. Figure 17-5 illustrates the major reduction in SO_2, with somewhat less success for

FIGURE 17-5 **National Trends in Sulphur Dioxide and Nitrogen Oxide Emissions in Canada, 1985 to 2010***

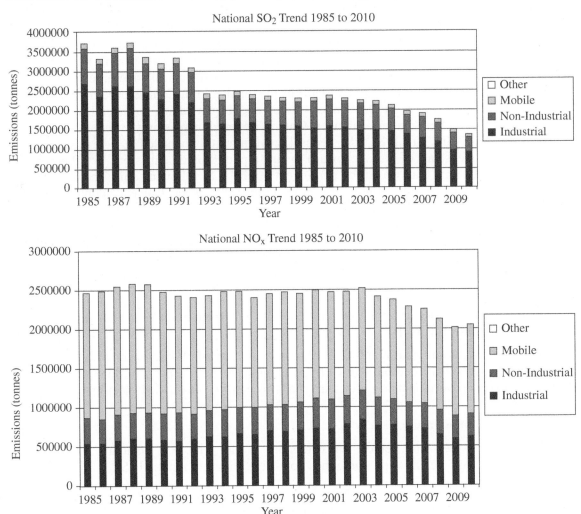

* "Other" includes incineration (e.g., industrial, commercial, municipal, crematorium) and miscellaneous sources (e.g., printing, surface coatings, general solvent use, dry cleaning, structural fires). "Other" excludes open sources (e.g., agriculture, prescribed burning, construction operations, dust from roads, mine tailings) and natural sources (e.g., forest fires). Due to the relatively small contribution made by "Other" sources, they are barely visible on the bar graphs.

Source: *Canadian Council of Ministers of the Environment "2010–2011 Progress Report on the Canada-Wide Acid Rain Strategy for Post-2000," PN 1490, Canadian Council of Ministers of the Environment, 2013.*

NO_X from 1985 to 2010. Some lakes are beginning to recover, but not as quickly as scientists had hoped. Studies are underway to see if further reductions in SO_2 emissions are needed. The Canada-Wide Acid Rain Strategy for Post-2000 calls for

- new emissions targets in eastern Canada,
- pursuing emissions reduction commitments from the United States,
- ensuring the adequacy of acid rain science and monitoring, and
- minimizing growth in areas that currently have low emissions levels (a non-degradation objective).

A very significant policy change that has dramatically reduced SO_2 emissions in the U.S. occurred with the passage of the *1990 Clean Air Act Amendments*.[17] This is the Act that established a TEP market in the U.S. for sulphur dioxide, which was covered in Chapter 13.

Summary

Air-pollution control in Canada, like water-pollution control, is primarily a provincial responsibility. However, due to the transboundary nature of many air pollutants, the federal government has played a larger role than in the case of water pollution. The federal government provided a strong advisory role with the creation of the NAAQOs—national ambient air quality objectives for criteria pollutants and CAAQS—ambient air quality standards. Most provinces have chosen to use the federal objectives as the basis for their guidelines and standards.

Policy problems associated with non-degradation and differential standards versus uniform standards were discussed. Canada and the U.S. still rely heavily on TBSs for air pollution regulation. Most economic studies of these TBSs in air-pollution control show that for the total amount of money spent on pollution control they achieve only a fraction of the emission reduction that a fully cost-effective program would attain.

Vehicle emissions from new cars are controlled by federal design standards. Provinces have the authority to regulate emissions from mobile sources of air pollution. Little attention has been given to the important problem of reducing total vehicle kilometres in urban areas with seriously degraded air quality. The federal and some provincial governments used an incentive-based policy, an excise tax on leaded gasoline, in combination with a standard to eliminate the use of leaded gasoline in Canada.

The bilateral problem of acid rain led to unilateral command-and-control actions by Canada in the 1980s to reduce domestic emissions of sulphur dioxide. The U.S. finally agreed in 1990 to significant reductions in its emissions and introduced an innovative national TEP program that covers more than 1,000 power plants and other sources of SO_2.

[17.] Another factor that contributed to reductions in SO_2 emissions in the U.S. was the substitution of coal from the western United States that had a lower sulphur content for eastern, high-sulphur coal as a fuel in power plants.

Key Terms

Elasticities

Emissions

Environmental tax shifting

Maximum acceptable level

Maximum desirable level

Maximum tolerable level

New-source bias

Non-attainment

Non-degradation

Point of impingement

Discussion Questions

1. The federal regulation of emissions from new automobiles and light trucks means that those vehicles sold in rural regions meet the same emissions standards as vehicles sold in urban areas. Since there are a lot fewer vehicles in rural areas, this means that air quality will be a lot better in rural areas than in the cities. Is this efficient? Is it equitable?

2. What are the advantages and disadvantages of a new-source bias in stationary-source air-pollution control? Consider especially its impacts on the incentives of the operators of existing sources.

3. What are the regulatory problems governments might encounter in trying to reduce a transboundary pollutant? Is any one policy instrument better than another to deal with the intergovernmental issues?

4. Why do you think sulphur levels in diesel fuel are allowed to be much higher than sulphur levels in gasoline? Does this make economic sense?

5. Using the elasticity data from Table 17-3, choose one policy to reduce air pollutants from motor vehicles and show how effective it would be. Use economic arguments to support your answer.

6. Why might buying back older vehicles in "cash for clunkers" programs be a very expensive way to reduce air pollution?

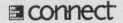

Chapter 18

Policy on Toxic and Hazardous Substances

After reading this chapter you will be able to:

LO 1 Describe the role of the *Canadian Environmental Protection Act* in regulating and reducing the emissions intensity of toxic compounds.

LO 2 Explain the lessons learned about the cost effectiveness of regulating dioxins and furans in Canada's pulp and paper industry.

LO 3 Describe the potential for cost effective policies to mitigate hazardous waste.

LO 4 Explain how B.C.'s waste permit fee system works.

LO 5 Assess Canada's policy framework to address clean up of toxic waste sites.

There is a class of pollutants that have come to be called "toxic" substances and "hazardous" materials. While all pollutants are damaging to some extent, these have been singled out for their special short- or long-run potency. Most are chemicals, constructed organic and inorganic compounds that are now ubiquitous throughout all industrialized economies, and even widespread in developing countries. Today, chemicals and chemical products have permeated every corner of the economy. In product improvements, new materials, food safety, health innovations, and many other dimensions, chemicals have enriched the lives of almost everyone. There is, however, a downside. A large number of these substances may cause human and ecosystem damages, certainly from exposure to concentrated doses, but also from long-run exposure to the trace amounts that show up virtually everywhere in workplaces, consumer products, and the environment.

Rachel Carson's book *Silent Spring* brought public attention to the impact of chemicals on the environment. She documented the ecosystem damage caused by the popular pesticide DDT and was largely responsible for getting it banned in Canada, the United States, and many other countries. Other events have multiplied concern. Health damages to workers exposed to chemicals in the workplace, such as vinyl chloride and certain potent agricultural chemicals, have occurred with disconcerting frequency. In various parts of Canada and the United States, people have found chemicals oozing into their yards and houses that have been built on top of abandoned hazardous-waste-disposal sites. Accidental releases of chemicals have become a growing problem, from the large-scale episodes like those in Milan, Italy, in 1976 and Bhopal, India, in 1984 to innumerable smaller airborne and waterborne accidents. There is rising concern about the damages from long-term exposure to chemical residues in food, clothing, and other consumer products.

The primary concern is the impact of chemicals on human health. The EPA, for example, computes the excess cancer deaths per year in the U.S. from different toxic airborne pollutants. Health damages arise from accidental releases and workplace exposure. Exposure to trace amounts of chemicals in water, air, and soil also affect health, but their impacts are much harder to measure. Toxics in the ecosystem have killed many species and threaten long-term viability of the ecosystem. Accidental waterborne chemical releases have killed fish and other organisms, often with long-term impacts. Agricultural and industrial runoff has substantially damaged ground water and many rivers and estuaries around the world.

In Canada, data on the releases of toxic compounds have been collected since 1994. Table 18-1 provides a snapshot of the 20 compounds that collectively contribute almost 85 percent of the total tonnes of compounds released from Canadian sources to air, water, land, and underground injection in 2012. The total represents the substances on the original National Pollutant Release Inventory of Canada. There was a slight increase in total tonnes released of these pollutants in 2012, compared to 2008, and a 21 percent increase compared to 2000. The main sources of increase over the 12 years are from ammonia released to air and water, nitrates released into waterways, and ethylene glycol (de-icer of aircraft) released on to land. Releases from most of the other toxic compounds were lower in 2012 than in 2008 except for hydrogen fluoride. Hazardous and toxic materials have characteristics that present unique problems for monitoring and control:

1. They are ubiquitous in the modern economy; each year sees the development of new chemicals. This makes it difficult even knowing what substances are being used and in what quantities. It accounts for the fact that much public policy has been directed at simply getting better information about quantities of hazardous and toxic materials at various places in the system.

2. With the thousands of substances in use, each with different chemical and physical properties, it is virtually impossible to be fully informed about the levels of danger that each one poses to humans and other parts of the ecosystem, let alone what possible effects arise from the multitude of compounds when present together in the ecosystem.

3. In many cases the quantities used are relatively small, as are the quantities that end up as emissions. This substantially increases monitoring problems. It also makes it easier for users to carry out surreptitious disposal. It is easy to see the plume of smoke coming out of the stack of an industrial plant; it is harder to track the much smaller quantities of chemicals used in production.

4. The damages caused by exposure to hazardous materials can often take many years, even decades, to show up. And whenever there is a long time gap between cause and effect, there is a tendency to downgrade the overall seriousness of the problem.

In the next few sections government policy on hazardous and toxic substances and some of the major economic issues in the management of these materials are considered. Canada has only recently begun to develop policies. There is, as always, scope for conflict and co-operation. But all levels of government face a situation where thousands of different substances are in use, hundreds more are introduced each year, massive uncertainties exist about the human and non-human effects of most of them, and public concerns flare up and die down in unpredictable ways.

TABLE 18-1 Twenty-five NPRI Core Contaminant Pollutants Released on Site in 2012, by Environmental Medium (tonnes)

Pollutant	2012 Air	2012 Water	2012 Land	2012 Total	2008 Total	2000 Total	% Change 2000–2008	% Change 2008–2012
Ammonia	19,686	46,379	592	66,667	69,709	42,386	64.5	−4.4
Nitrate ion (in solution at pH = 6.0)	26	67,223	52	67,302	62,791	19,745	218.0	7.2
Methanol	12,592	1,474	43	14,123	15,703	21,808	−28.0	−10.1
Hydrochloric acid	5,889	108	0.12	6,006	8,243	16,209	−49.1	−27.1
Sulphuric acid	5,066	153	14	5,243	6,185	10,472	−40.9	−15.2
Hydrogen sulphide	2,036	89	0.06	2,129	3,464	7,735	−55.2	−38.5
Xylene (all isomers)	2,458	11	14	2,517	5,931	6,715	−11.7	−57.6
Toluene	2,404	70	12	2,528	4,517	6,528	−30.8	−44.0
Methyl ethyl ketone	1,277	5.4	0.15	1,291	1,671	5,076	−67.1	−22.7
Carbon disulphide	1,319	0.001	–	1,321	2,827	3,164	−10.7	−53.3
n-Hexane	4,266	6.2	3.2	4,304	5,691	3,563	59.7	−24.4
Zinc (and its compounds)	487	220	387	1,105	1,141	2,692	−57.6	−3.2
Hydrogen fluoride	8,754	0	–	8,755	3,332	3,601	−7.5	163.8
Ethylene	1,451	–	–	1,452	1,242	2,710	−54.2	16.9
Ethylene glycol	47	887	5,113	6,053	5,563	2,564	117.0	8.8
Manganese (and its compounds)	296	1,205	127	1,637	1,765	1,740	1.4	−7.3
Styrene	1,788	–	4.9	1,798	1,924	1,700	13.2	−6.5
Isopropyl alcohol	1,232	–	0.07	1,245	1,365	1,696	−19.5	−8.8
Formaldehyde	1,055	39	–	1,098	1,278	1,803	−29.1	−14.1
Acetaldehyde	714	15	0.01	731	1,044	955	9.3	−30.0
Largest on-site releases	72,817	117,885	6,362	197,305	205,386	162,861	22.4	−3.9
National Total				233,986	232,518	182,930	27.1	
Percent of National Total				84.3	88.3	89.0	−3.9	

Sources: *Adapted from: 2000 NPRI Data by Substance: 2001 National Overview—National Pollutant Release Inventory, Releases, Table 3-1: Twenty-five NPRI Pollutants Released On Site in the Largest Quantities in 2001, by Environmental Medium, page 8, Environment Canada 2003. Reproduced with the permission of the Minister of Public Works and Government Services Canada, 2010.*

2008 NPRI Data by Substance: National Pollutant Release Inventory (NPRI) 2008 Facility Data Summary," Summary by Substance: Part 1A, http://www.ec.gc.ca/inrp-npri/default.asp?lang=en&n=BF14CADF-1, Environment Canada, 2009. Reproduced with the permission of the Minister of Public Works and Government Services Canada, 2010.

2008 National Totals: National Pollutant Release Inventory (NPRI) 2008 Facility Data Summary, Summary of reported on-site releases, disposals and transfers for recycling, Figures 3.1.1.2-1, 3.1.2-1, and 3.1.3-1, www.ec.gc.ca/inrp-npri/default.asp?lang=En&n=F3B474E9-1#3-1, Environment Canada, 2009. Reproduced with the permission of the Minister of Public Works and Government Services Canada, 2010.

2012 Summary Report: Reviewed 2012 NPRI Facility Inventory Reported Data, from Table 5.1, Part A, "Substances listed at the original NPRI threshold," http://www.ec.gc.ca/inip.npri./default.asp?lang=En&n=386BAB5A-1, accessed July 25, 2014.

LO 1

CANADIAN POLICIES TO REDUCE EMISSIONS OF TOXIC SUBSTANCES

Toxic emissions come in a great variety of forms, from small airborne releases of cleaning fluid from dry cleaning establishments to large-scale releases of toxics from substantial industrial plants. Also included are the concentrated accidental releases that have helped in the past to spur public concern about toxics in the environment. Not all toxics are chemicals; some, like heavy metals (mercury, cadmium, etc.), are by-products of various industrial and mining operations. Emissions-control policies at the federal and provincial levels have focused largely on the management of conventional airborne and waterborne pollutants. For air this has meant the criteria air contaminants studied in Chapters 1 and 17—SO_2, CO, O_3, NOx, total suspended particulates, and lead—and for water it has meant BOD, suspended solids, coliform count, and so on examined in Chapter 16. However, it was known during the initial regulatory days that there was a potentially serious class of toxic emissions stemming from industrial production operations, as well as from household sources. But the difficulties with even enumerating all of the possible substances involved, and of knowing what impacts each might have, essentially led to postponing coming to grips with the problem. In addition, the control of conventional pollutants has been effective to some extent in controlling toxics, since they are often closely associated. In recent years more effort has gone into specific toxic emissions reduction programs, but as of now, little has been accomplished compared to efforts in other environmental areas.

The discussion of toxics policies is divided into two topics—policies dealing with the emission of toxic substances and the management of the disposal and storage of toxic substances. The first section focuses on strategies to reduce emissions. The key federal policy is the *Canadian Environmental Protection Act of 1999* (CEPA, 1999).

CEPA, 1999

The *Canadian Environmental Protection Act of 1999* amalgamates, supersedes, and works in conjunction with other federal regulations dealing with toxic substances.[1] Environment Canada and Health Canada jointly administer the act. CEPA, 1999 is to "provide a framework for protecting Canadians from pollution caused by 'toxic' substances."[2] CEPA, 1999 continues the principles established in CEPA, 1988.[3] Namely, it gives the federal government

1. the right to obtain information from manufacturers, processors, and importers of substances Environment Canada considers dangerous;

---

[1] CEPA, 1999 replaces CEPA, 1988, which replaced the *Environmental Contaminants Act of 1975*. Many of the provisions of these earlier acts are carried over to CEPA, 1999. Information about CEPA can be found at the Environment Canada website at www.ec.gc.ca/CEPARegistry/default.cfm.

[2] See Health Canada's information on CEPA, 1999, available at www.hc.gc.ca , under Healthy Living, Assuming and Managing the Health Risks of Existing Substances under the Renewed Canadian Environmental Protection Act, 1999.

[3] The source for this list and other general information about CEPA, 1988 is Environment Canada and Health and Welfare Canada, *Preparing the Second Priority Substances List*, An Invitation to Stakeholders to Comment on the Federal Government Proposals (April 1993): 2–4.

2. the power to conduct research on dangerous substances in co-operation with provincial governments; and

3. the right to prevent discharges of substances authorized jointly by the Minister of the Environment and Minister of Health and Welfare that "pose a significant danger to human health or the environment."

The federal government's regulatory powers under CEPA stem from the Peace, Order, and Good Government clause in the Canadian Constitution. The federal government argued that regulation of toxic compounds is a national concern. The courts have upheld these powers.[4] The federal government can thus establish national standards under CEPA. It does so in consultation with the provinces.

Key Features of CEPA, 1999

The key features of CEPA, 1999 are as follows:

Definition of CEPA Toxic. A substance is toxic if it enters or may enter the environment in a quantity or concentration that:

- Has or may have an immediate or long-term harmful effect on the environment or its biological diversity;
- Constitutes or may constitute a danger to the environment on which life depends; or
- Constitutes or may constitute a danger in Canada to human life or health.

  Health Canada determines what is a danger to human health; Environment Canada addresses ecosystem health.

The Domestic Substances List (DSL). This is a list of approximately 23,000 substances that are already being used in Canada (whether produced domestically or imported). CEPA, 1999 requires that *all* of these be categorized by September 2006 as to whether they are toxic or not and, if so, how toxic (i.e., which pose the greatest threats to health and the environment). Those identified to be "of concern" go to a second stage of assessment.

The Priority Substance Assessment Program and List (PSL). The second stage of assessment actually began as part of previous regulation (CEPA, 1988). The first Priority Substances List was established in 1989 and contained 44 chemicals suspected to be toxic. Twenty-five of these were declared toxic. A new PSL was produced in 1995 containing 25 additional substances that were to be completely assessed by 2000. The current PSL is available at both ministries' websites (www.ec.gc.ca and www.hc.gc.ca). Once a substance is declared toxic, it is placed on what is called Schedule 1 of the act and regulation of it can begin. Regulations can be in the form of guidelines, codes of practice, and standards. Products can be regulated over their entire life cycle (from development to disposal). Note that neither Environment Canada nor Health Canada has the legislative authority to impose taxes on products. Any formal tax instrument would have to come from the Ministry of Finance. Fees for disposal permits are possible (in co-operation with the provinces). The most dangerous substances—those that are toxic, persistent, or bioaccumulative; that result primarily from human activity (i.e., its release is not due solely to natural forces); and that have no "safe threshold" of emissions—will be slated for "virtual elimination."

[4.] The case was *Canada Metal Co. v. The Queen* (1982), 144 D.L.R. (3d) 124 (Man. Q.B.).

Enforcement. Environment Canada has the authority to monitor all sources of toxics to enforce any regulations established. Maximum penalties are up to $1-million per day in fines, imprisonment up to three years, or both. Violators may also have to pay for clean-up costs or forgo profits obtained from polluting activities. One wonders how Environment Canada will be able to establish what profits from polluting activities are.

National Pollutant Release Inventory (NPRI). CEPA, 1999 requires all facilities releasing or transferring a pollutant on the NPRI list (of 268 substances) to report annually their on-site releases and off-site transfers.[5] The NPRI is made public as soon as the data can be compiled.[6]

Assessment of CEPA, 1999

As with all Canadian environmental policy, CEPA, 1999 provides not only some strong opportunities for improving environmental quality and protecting health, but also some significant challenges. These are summarized below.

1. *Federal authority.* CEPA 1999 continues to give the federal government a strong legislative basis for regulation that was established in CEPA, 1988. Toxics could have been deemed an area predominantly for provincial authority, but in CEPA, 1988 the federal government argued that toxic substances were a matter of national and international concern. Federal authority will minimize duplication and overlap, provide for public access to data, and ensure that polluters will face the same level of regulation across the country.

2. *Burden of proof.* All substances on the DSL are already in the environment. The government's powers under CEPA effectively enable it to act on these substances only after it has shown that a danger to health or the environment exists. This means that the burden of proof is on the government to get information about substances and determine their toxicity. Companies are thus allowed to produce the compounds and release them into the environment without proving that they aren't dangerous. If the government then regulates the substance, it may be years after it has been in use. This is like the old expression "shutting the barn door after the horse is out." The policy is thus *reactive,* not *proactive.* The legislation is very different from that of other chemical compounds entering our environment. For example, pharmaceuticals cannot be licensed for human use until extensive tests are done to show that they deal with the problem they are designed for without endangering human health. Food additives undergo a similar process. Even pest-control products have to be registered before being sold (but do not have to verify safety). While testing prior to release for sale is not foolproof, it is more proactive than waiting until the compound is in use. The precautionary principle would argue to reduce the risk of adverse impacts on health and the environment with a policy that required chemical compounds to go through a similar process. The difficulty is that it is too late for the chemicals that are already in the economy and environment, so the proactive policy cannot be applied to existing substances. CEPA, 1999 gives the government authority to be proactive with regard to new substances. If the substance is not on the DSL, industry will have to provide data certifying its safety before the substance can be produced or used. However, the government will still do its own testing of new substances.

3. *Timing and progress to date.* The government's track record on delivering regulation of toxics is thin. Regulations have been adopted for approximately 50 of the compounds. Among those

---

[5.] CEPA, 1988 contained the original legislation for the NPRI.

[6.] The NPRI and information about it is available through Environment Canada's website at www.ec.gc.ca/pdb/npri/npri_home_e.cfm.

compounds were dioxins and furans in pulp mill discharges (discussed below). The task of examining and designing regulations for potentially hundreds of substances is daunting and has meant that the federal government has been unable to meet the deadlines CEPA, 1999 imposes.

4. *Policy instruments.* CEPA, 1999 continues with the Canadian tradition of relying on command-and-control policies. While standards make sense when a substance is to be phased out of existence, it makes much less sense for the potentially hundreds of substances that will continue to be produced and used in Canada. Incentives to reduce the use of these substances are needed, and the strongest incentives come in the form of some sort of pricing of pollution. Unless the federal ministries of finance, environment, and health work together to design incentive-based policies, CEPA, 1999 offers no more or no less than other Canadian environment policies that rely on command-and-control regulation.

5. *The role of public information on polluting activity.* One of the goals of releasing NPRI data to the public is to provide incentives for polluters to voluntarily reduce their emissions even when there is no regulation requiring them to do so. This is called **voluntary compliance.**[7] Why would a polluter ever voluntarily reduce its emissions? The logic is twofold: First, it may make good business sense if consumers are sensitive to environmental data. When consumers read that a company is the largest source of some toxic compound that is producing cancer and damaging ecosystems, its sales may fall. Proving to society that it is an "environmentally sensitive" producer may increase revenues by more than it adds to costs. Second, the company may be avoiding future liability or forestalling the introduction of regulations that can be very costly. If government thinks that emissions are falling over time even without regulation, it is less likely to introduce policies such as technology-based standards or performance standards.[8]

There have been studies of the impact of "right-to-know" legislation in the United States from its version of the NPRI—the Toxic Release Inventory (TRI), after which Canada's system was modelled. The U.S. studies do find evidence that emission levels have fallen since release of TRI data began in the early 1990s. There is some skepticism that some of the decreases may be "phantom"; that is, neither real nor permanent. Reasons include fraudulent reporting by companies, the result of short-term economic downturns and resulting output reductions, changes in monitoring or accounting techniques, and over-reporting of the initial emissions by companies so that it looks like significant reductions have occurred when in fact they have not.

A Canadian study looked at the role the NPRI had on toxic releases over the period 1993–99.[9] Using statistical techniques, the authors found that command-and-control regulation appears to have been a greater stimulus to reductions in toxic emissions than public disclosure. The strongest reductions are associated with industries facing federal regulations such as the *Fisheries Act.* These tend to be large firms in pollution-intensive industries.

---

[7] Canada has other examples of voluntary compliance in the toxics area. The *Accelerated Reduction/Elimination of Toxics* (ARET) program set a target of 90-percent reduction in toxic emissions by 2000. Companies have reported progress in reaching this goal. The Canadian Chemical Producers' Association set up a "Responsible Care" program in 1990. Part of the program includes a hazardous-waste management code to deal with handling and disposal of wastes and waste disposal sites.

[8] For a critical assessment of voluntary compliance that is largely negative, see the special issue on "Voluntary Initiatives" in *Alternatives Journal* 24(2) (Spring 1998): 8–25.

[9] See Kathryn Harrison and Werner Antweiler, "Incentives for Pollution Abatement: Regulation, Regulatory Threats, and Non-Governmental Pressures" *Journal of Policy Analysis and Management* 22(3) (2003): 361–382.

The Toxic Intensity of Canadian Industry

Data from the NPRI allow us to examine the **toxic intensity of pollution** of Canadian industry. Table 18-2 presents data on aggregate emissions from Canadian industries as a proportion of the value of industry shipments from manufacturing activity. Emissions in tonnes of each of the toxic compounds released into the environment by firms in these industrial sectors are aggregated then divided by the value added in that industry.[10] This gives a ranking of each industry's **emissions intensity.** In addition, a toxicity index is used to weight releases of all the compounds released from each industry to obtain an estimate of their potential impact on the environment, not just the aggregate tonnes of emissions of all sorts released.[11] A source that emits large quantities of a not-very-toxic substance may have far less deleterious effects on health and the environment than one emitting a small amount of a highly toxic material. Table 18-2 shows that the most toxic-intensive industries are chemicals, mining, rubber, plastics, and fossil fuels, while the least toxic-intensive are food, beverage, machinery, and electrical and electronic. This sort of data can be very helpful in designing regulatory policies. How? Governments can focus attention on the most toxic compounds coming from the most pollution-intensive sectors. This will yield the greatest return in the form of lowering emissions that have the biggest adverse impact on health and the environment.

Figure 18-1 illustrates the time trend in toxic releases by type of media to which they are released (air, surface water, land).[12] The top half shows aggregate emissions unweighted by toxicity. We see that the largest decline is in discharges to surface water. There have been increases in discharges to air, land, and underground injection since 1993. An implication of this trend is that polluters may be simply reallocating their wastes to another medium—away from water and on to soils in response to differences in the stringency of regulations. Table 18-1 and data from the NPRI shows that this trend has changed. Releases to air declined 24 percent from 2001 to 2008, while those to water rose by 125 percent, and to land increased 24 percent. Shifting releases from one medium to another is a likely response to command-and-control regulation that is media-based. An incentive-based policy, for example waste discharge taxes that reflect marginal damages to the different media, would reduce these incentives.

The bottom half of Figure 18-1 presents the toxicity weighted releases. The aggregate levels have risen somewhat over time (up for air and land, down for water and underground injection ignoring 1993 for that medium). This suggests that polluters could be shifting from high-volume but low-toxicity emissions to low-emission–high-toxicity releases. Why might they do this? The NIPR has received substantial publicity, but the data released are not weighted by toxicity (methods for weighting are somewhat controversial). Polluters may think that if they reduce the volume of emissions, this will help convince the public that environmental progress is being made. The NPRI is valuable in that it provides the data for analysis of the emissions and pollution intensity of Canadian industry. However, the data suggest that public disclosure is not a substitute for environmental regulation.

[10.] See N. Olewiler and K. Dawson (1998) *Analysis of National Pollutant Release Inventory Data on Toxic Emissions by Industry*, Working Paper 97–16, prepared for the Technical Committee on Business Taxation for more details of the derivation and interpretation of emissions and toxic intensity numbers. Also see *Report of the Technical Committee on Business Taxation*, Chapter 9. This report can be requested from the Department of Finance Canada through the following site: www.fin.gc.ca/toc/1998/brie_-eng.asp.

[11.] The toxicity index is for data from 1994 rather than 1997. It would still be representative for 1997 unless the types of compounds released by each industry changed considerably over the three years. This was not likely.

[12.] The data for this figure and some of the policy conclusions come from Harrison and Antweiler (2003), cited above.

TABLE 18-2 Emissions and Toxic Intensity of Canadian Manufacturing Industries, 1997

SIC	Industry	Emissions/$ Output[a]	Toxic Intensity[b]
37	Chemicals	2,345	756
29	Primary metal	1,507	422
15	Rubber	268	305
16	Plastics	1,090	232
36	Refined petroleum & coal	1,027	227
35	Non-metallic mineral	294	157
26	Furniture & fixture	355	51
32	Transportation equipment	153	43
30	Fabricated metal	208	42
28	Printing & publishing	190	39
19	Textile products	365	39
27	Paper & allied products	1,798	33
39	Other-manufacturing	189	31
18	Primary textiles	47	23
17	Leather	163	19
25	Wood	155	17
33	Electrical & electronic	12	9
31	Machinery	17	3
10	Food	31	>0.5
Average		556	

Notes:

(a) Emissions output are the releases of toxic compounds by each industry in pounds divided by the value of industry shipments in millions of Canadian dollars.

(b) Toxic intensity values are based on the compounds released by industry in 1994.

Sources: *Canadian emissions data are from Environment Canada, National Pollutant Release Inventory (NPRI), "Twenty-five NPRI Pollutants Released On Site in the Largest Quantities in 2001," Table 3-1 at www.ec.gc.ca. Reproduced with the permission of the Minister of Public Works and Government Services, 2010.*

Canadian Output was value of shipments and other revenue, adapted from Statistics Canada, Manufacturing Industries of Canada, National and Provincial Areas, 31-203-XPB1996000 1996. Released October 2, 1998.

Toxic intensity data are from "Technical Committee on Business Taxation," Table 9.2, p. 9.9, 1998. Department of Finance Canada. Reproduced with the permission of the Minister of Public Works and Government Services, 2011.

FIGURE 18-1 Annual Releases and Releases Adjusted for Toxicity, 1993–1999

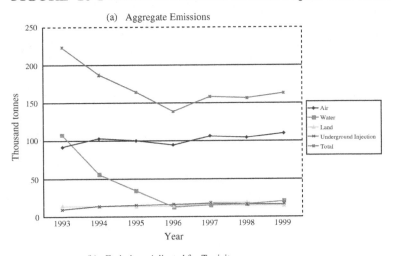

(a) Aggregate Emissions

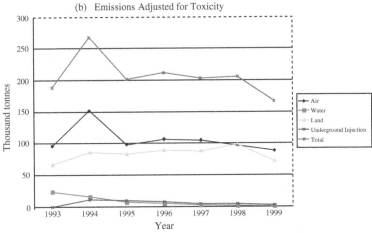

(b) Emissions Adjusted for Toxicity

On-site releases of toxic substances as reported by companies on the NPRI are shown for the period 1993 to 1999. Panel (a) presents emissions unweighted by their toxicity. The decline in emissions to water is large, while releases to the other media increase somewhat. Overall releases decline. Panel (b) weights these releases by an index of their toxicity. While releases to water continue to show a decline over the time period, aggregate emissions now rise due to increases in releases to land and air.

Source: *Kathryn Harrison and Werner Antweiler: "Incentives for Pollution Abatement: Regulation, Regulatory Threats, and Non-Governmental Pressures" (Working Paper, 2002).*

An example of how a pollution-intensive industry—pulp and paper—has been regulated is examined below.

LO 2

EXAMPLE
The regulation of toxic compounds from Canada's pulp and paper industry

Much has been written about the regulation of toxic compounds coming from pulp mills. Some governments and environmental organizations offer studies that show that the chlorinated organic compounds in mill effluent are very dangerous compounds that should be banned. The forest industry

(Continued)

counters with research that says the other studies are inconclusive; that the chlorine bleaching in their pulping process isn't necessarily the guilty technology, and that they are already spending large amounts of money to control their wastes.

Historical Background on Regulation

Federal pulp and paper regulation began under the *Fisheries Act* in the early 1970s with standards that divided the pollutants in the mill effluent into three categories: total suspended solids (TSS), biochemical oxygen demand (BOD), and acute toxicity.[13] TSS and BOD pollutants have been discussed in Chapter 16. The concern here is with toxicity, defined in the regulations as the unknown mix of chemicals lethal to fish and other organisms in the immediate vicinity of the effluent outfall. The federal regulations were in the form of standards based on best practicable technology. The federal government had to be careful not to impinge on provincial powers, so it tried to "sell" the standards to the provinces as minimal national standards that would ensure that no one region of the country would become a haven for polluters. As well, existing mills were exempted from the standards, thus reducing the burden for provinces where pulp mills were a significant contributor to local economies. Once again, the ability to control emissions and political factors were criteria used for regulation, not a balancing of the marginal benefits and costs of control.[14] Throughout this early process the industry remained the source of information on what was practicable technology. It was said that government regulators at the time had no way of checking the industry's information. The toxic regulations were in the form of discharges per unit of output produced. There were no absolute limits on total **loadings** to the environment; that is, how the emissions affected toxic concentrations in soils, water, or air. The test of acute toxicity was pass/fail, based on fish mortality.

Once the regulations were promulgated, implementation was difficult because the pulp and paper industry argued that it could not afford to invest in pollution-abatement processes that did not contribute to output in some way. This continued to be a problem into the 1980s.[15] The standards were enforceable by the provinces. Compliance with the regulations was sought through individual negotiation with each company; prosecution was not used until later years. Over the period 1969 to 1982, a large number of mills were not meeting the toxicity requirements even though the industry received considerable financial assistance from the federal government.[16]

Between 1979 and 1985, the industry received a total of $544-million from the federal government and the provinces of Ontario, Quebec, New Brunswick, Nova Scotia, and Newfoundland under the Pulp and Paper Modernization Program. This program was designed to assist the industry in improving its capital stock to be more competitive with pulp and paper producers in other countries. Of the

(Continued)

[13.] Information for this section comes from Doug Macdonald, *The Politics of Pollution* (Toronto: McClelland & Stewart, 1991), 225–240.

[14.] Think about whether exemption of old mills is good policy from the viewpoint of economics (e.g., do they have different MAC curves and hence merit different standards?).

[15.] See William F. Sinclair, *Controlling Pollution from Canadian Pulp and Paper Manufacturers: A Federal Perspective* (Environment Canada, 1990), for a very detailed examination of the industry's spending on capital improvements to expand production capacity versus expenditures for pollution abatement.

[16.] Between 1971 and 1979, this amounted to $10.6-million under accelerated capital cost (depreciation) allowances in the federal corporate income tax. Another $3-million was given to the industry in the form of direct support for installing pollution-abatement equipment in a program begun in 1975.

industry's total spending on capital improvements over this period, 18 percent was spent on pollution-abatement equipment. It is thus somewhat difficult to accept the industry's repeated insistence that it was unable to comply with pollution regulations due to its fierce competitive environment. Significant gains were made in BOD and TSS reductions. This happened in part because of greater technical efficiency in using its wood inputs.

Public pressure against the industry intensified in the late 1980s, when Greenpeace stepped up its campaign to eliminate emissions of chlorine compounds associated with dioxin and other chlorinated organic compounds. A flurry of research was done on dioxin concentrations and their likely impact on ecosystems and human health. An expert committee investigating pulp effluent in Ontario reported in 1988 that the health threat of dioxins and furans was overstated. The real problem was that 97 percent of the chemicals in the waste products had never been analyzed or even identified. The committee recommended that steps be taken to reduce the total quantity of organochlorine emissions. This illustrates an important point with the regulation of any compound when it is released with a number of other contaminants: focusing on a few such compounds may not result in an improvement in the ecosystem and human health if *all* the compounds responsible for adverse effects are not controlled. Environmental policy is then seen as a useless expense. The Ontario committee's recommendation is rarely taken into account in environmental regulation. The committee also found that the cost of pollution control was not prohibitive given the industry's financial situation.

Continued pressure from the public, environmental groups, and a report by Environment Canada on the pulp and paper industry led to an announcement in 1989 of new dioxin and furan regulation under CEPA (1988).[17] Later that year, British Columbia, Ontario, Quebec, and Alberta announced they would be bringing in regulations within several years. In 1990, Environment Canada announced that organochlorine discharges would be added to the regulations and that the *Fisheries Act* would be amended to make these standards or guidelines applicable to all plants, regardless of when built. Environment Canada said the discharge requirements would be met though provincial regulation and enforcement where equivalency of standards for the two levels of government was met. If there were no equivalency, Environment Canada would enforce the requirements.

Current Regulations

The current federal regulation of the effluent from pulp mills is based on the 1971 amendments to the *Fisheries Act* and as updated in CEPA (1988 and 1999).[18] It is as follows:

1. Two substances are banned from pulp and paper effluent—dioxins and furans. These compounds are bioaccumulative. They cause reproductive failure in fish-eating birds, contaminate shellfish and other inshore fisheries, and have a number of adverse health effects on laboratory animals. Scientific uncertainty exists about their impact on human health, but they have been declared toxic under CEPA and there is an emission *standard of zero discharges* from pulp and paper mills that use a chlorine bleaching process. These were to be eliminated by 1994; actual elimination took a few more years.

2. Under the *Fisheries Act,* limits for toxic discharges, BOD, and TSS are set and apply to all mills.

3. Other regulations for organochlorine discharges will be developed.

(Continued)

---

[17] This Environment Canada report was known as the Sinclair Report, after its author, William Sinclair, cited above.

[18] Provinces may impose regulations that are more stringent than the federal ones.

Impact of the Regulations: Compliance Costs

In the early 1990s, the industry estimated that compliance with the regulations would cost $5-billion (in 1989 dollars or $7-billion in 2010 dollars).[19] Statistics Canada estimated the total capital costs of compliance at $2.2-billion ($3.1), with a lot of variation in costs across mills of different sizes and vintages. The costs per mill could vary from more than $100,000 to $100-million ($139,000 to $139-million).[20] Average annual investment from 1978 to 1989 by mills in the study done by Statistics Canada was $16.8-million per mill ($23.4). The average capital cost of compliance per mill (for those not already in compliance) is estimated at $25.7-million ($35.7) over the life of the equipment. These costs can thus be thought of as consuming about 1.5 years of what would be ordinary investment. This can also be converted into an annualized cost over the life of the capital asset. Statistics Canada estimates the average annualized cost per mill at $4.4-million ($6.1), which represents just under 8 percent of their average annual surplus. Annual surplus is defined as the value of shipments minus the cost of energy, materials, and labour. Surplus therefore includes head-office overhead, some purchased services, depreciation, and profit. The differences in the industry's and government's estimates of compliance costs illustrate some familiar themes and lessons learned:

1. There is always uncertainty about the costs of complying with a new policy.

2. Initial compliance cost estimates (of MACs) are generally much higher than they turn out to be in practice.

3. MACs tend to fall over time *if* polluters are not regulated by a technology-based standard.[21]

4. The ban has led to a change in technologies used for bleaching pulp. New plants use non-chlorine processing that produces no dioxin or furans. Technological changes induced by regulation have lowered compliance costs over time.

5. Remember that compliance costs (the MAC curves) are only one-half of a full estimate of the net benefits of a policy. Damages forgone (the MD curve) should also be calculated.

Environmental Impact of the Regulations

Canada's total emissions of dioxins and furans declined from 450 grams (measured in toxic equivalents) in 1988 to 42 grams in 2008 and to 11 grams in 2012. These banned substances have been eliminated from the effluent of pulp and paper mills. In this sense, the policy is a success. But the real question that must be answered is this: Does the elimination of these toxics improve measured environmental quality? The answer is not clear, because these compounds bioaccumulate. Their impact on ecosystems and species took time to be recognized and understood; their elimination from the waste stream does not mean that they are no longer present in the ecosystem. There will continue to be impacts as long as the *stock* of these compounds still is present in plants and animals. A key feature of toxics is that many decompose or dissipate very slowly. Government policy therefore also needs to consider waste management—intercepting toxics before they enter the waste stream and remediation (cleanup) of toxic sites. Dioxins and furans from pulp effluent are too dispersed in the environment to be "cleaned up," but other toxics can be. We turn now to issues of waste management.

[19] Costs adjusted for inflation up to the year 2010 are shown in parentheses following each dollar amount in this section.

[20] Craig Gaston, "Pulp and Paper Industry Compliance Costs" in Statistics Canada, *Environmental Perspectives*, 1993, Catalogue No. 11-528E Occasional (Ottawa: Statistics Canada, March 1993), 20. This is the source for all the numbers reported in this section.

[21] Recall from Chapter 13 what happened in the U.S. sulphur dioxide TEP system: MACs fell considerably over time because polluters were not constrained to use a particular technology to meet emission targets.

LO 3

ECONOMIC ISSUES IN HAZARDOUS WASTE MANAGEMENT

What are Hazardous Wastes?

Not all toxic compounds on the DSL will be so damaging to health and the environment that they will ultimately have to be banned. How can a government manage its wastes that are hazardous but not Schedule 1 CEPA toxics? Each year millions of tonnes of hazardous waste are produced in Canada. Hazardous waste consists of a diverse set of materials. In liquid form there are waste oils, solvents, and liquids containing metals, acids, and so on. There are hazardous wastes in solid form (metals dust, polyvinyls, and polyethylene materials). There are many materials between liquid and solid, called sludges (sulphur sludge, heavy metal, solvent and cyanide sludges, and dye and paint sludges). Then there are a variety of mixed substances such as pesticides, explosives, lab wastes, and the like.

Hazardous-waste generation is not spread evenly over the country. As expected, areas where the most manufacturing and resource processing occurs will produce the most waste. The industrialized provinces, Ontario and Quebec, contribute to the largest percentage of Canada's hazardous waste. Hazardous wastes can be disposed of in injection wells—that is, deep wells driven into underground geologic formations (salt caverns and aquifers). From an industry standpoint this method is relatively cheap and flexible. However, a substantial proportion of these wastes are no doubt discharged in wastewater, either directly into a stream or river or into a municipal waste treatment plant. Surface impoundment and landfill disposal, into both hazardous waste (lined) landfills and unlined landfills, accounted for most of the remaining hazardous waste. Disposal of hazardous wastes through chemical treatment is probably a relatively small proportion of the total. Most hazardous waste is probably disposed of on-site; that is, at the site of the industrial plant where it was manufactured and/or used.

The two major pathways leading to damage are through accidental releases and through releases stemming from improper handling, either at the site of use or at waste-disposal facilities. A Quebec study found, for example, that approximately one-third of the hazardous wastes sent off-site for processing or disposal could not be accounted for. Wastes are obviously not being controlled properly either through mismanagement or deliberate avoidance. Accidents have led to severe and obvious damages, to humans and to other parts of the ecosystem. It has been less easy to document the damages coming from long-run exposure to small amounts of hazardous wastes. Ecosystems in the vicinity of industrial-waste dumps are sometimes visibly affected. Human health effects have been harder to show, particularly when what is at issue is long-run exposure to small quantities of hazardous materials. Much more epidemiological and laboratory work remains to be done.

In this section, two regulatory issues are examined:

- the disposal of toxic wastes
- the cleanup of toxic waste sites

Canada is only beginning to address the problems associated with toxic waste disposal and storage. Federal jurisdiction over hazardous waste disposal and management is limited to interprovincial and international flows. Provincial and municipal governments regulate the disposal of hazardous wastes. The federal government has called for better harmonization of definitions of waste, tests, and criteria for classification of hazards from waste products across the country. There is concern that Canada is importing an increasing amount of hazardous waste from other countries because of a perception that our standards of waste management are less stringent than those in the United States.

The early policies on hazardous waste were aimed at managing the flow of hazardous emissions coming from firms to reduce potential impacts, especially on human health. In this respect it mirrored the approach taken in conventional pollutants. But hazardous emissions are more difficult to manage. Smaller quantities make them much more difficult to monitor, even though in many cases small quantities can be quite damaging. This has led policy-makers to think about attacking the problems by "moving back up the line"; that is, by trying to reduce the amounts of material that are in need of disposal. This can be done in two ways: (1) by recycling residuals back into the production process, and (2) by shifting technologies and operations so that the amount of residuals actually generated by firms is reduced. These methods can be called **waste reduction.**[22]

Waste Reduction

The thought behind waste reduction is that by changing production processes and adopting new technologies and operating procedures firms can substantially reduce the quantities of hazardous waste they produce per unit of final product. For example, a firm might find a new way to operate a materials cleaning process to get the same effect but with less cleaning solvent. Or a firm might shift from using a process requiring a toxic material to one involving a non-toxic substance. Or an end product might be redesigned in a way that permits its fabrication using smaller quantities of hazardous materials. These are industrial counterparts to our discussion on "green" consumer goods in Chapter 10.

Waste reduction is obviously very complicated and firm-specific. This means it is essentially impossible to achieve efficient controls by having a regulatory agency dictate particular technology choices for firms using toxic substances. The technical aspects of production processes and the situation of each firm are too heterogeneous for this approach. Instead, more effective means need to be found that will give firms themselves strong incentives to reduce toxic emissions in cost-effective ways. What are some options?

Potential Cost-Effective Policies to Reduce Waste

1. *Changes in hazardous-waste disposal laws.* If waste disposal is made more difficult and costly, firms will be motivated to search for better ways of reducing the quantities of waste requiring disposal. A major flaw in this approach, however, is that the vast majority of hazardous waste is not subject to disposal regulations because it never leaves the premises of the firms where it is used. A second problem is that it will encourage illegal discharges of wastes.

2. *Liability and compensation laws.* Requiring polluters to compensate those harmed induces firms to take the external costs into account in making their decisions (review Chapter 10). Polluters will either modify their actions to minimize the risk of damage (i.e., they "self-insure"), or insurance markets may develop. Polluters will pay an insurance premium that reflects the probability of damage and costs if damage occurs. As illustrated in Chapter 10, a major problem is whether enough is known about risks to be able to develop an efficient insurance market and compensation system. Although there are thousands of chemicals in use, very little hard information exists on exactly how much damage they may cause to humans; most of the dose–response information comes from laboratory studies, not human data. This lack of information also impedes the use of all regulatory instruments.

---

[22] Some people prefer to distinguish between "waste reduction" and "recycling" as separate processes, but in our discussion we will lump them together.

3. *Incentive-based mechanisms.* A tax on hazardous emissions could be very difficult to implement. In principle, the federal government could use the NPRI data to levy a tax on emissions. However, two problems emerge. First, the NPRI data are self-reported by each source of emissions. There is little (if any) monitoring of emissions by government regulators at present. The incentive to under-report emissions is strong when a tax is levied. The costs of monitoring could be quite high. Second, if monitoring occurs, emission taxes increase the incentive to illegally dump one's toxics. However, a waste tax may be highly feasible for undifferentiated wastes in a bulk form, levied at a discharge site. Canadian municipalities often have differentiated fees for waste disposal based on the nature of the waste. Another possibility is to levy a tax on the inputs used to manufacture chemicals, since these would be fewer in number and easier to measure than the chemicals themselves. Still another possibility might be to institute deposit–refund systems for chemicals. Firms would pay a deposit along with the purchase price when the chemicals were bought. They could recover that deposit, or a portion of it, by documenting a reduction of emissions—that is, of the recovery of the chemical from the normal waste stream.

4. *Public release of pollution data.* As discussed above, the release of NPRI data may create incentives for voluntary reduction of waste flow even in the absence of regulation on emissions.

This list shows that governments have a number of potential incentive-based options when it comes to waste management. They need not rely solely on command-and-control regulation. What have Canadian governments been doing to reduce waste?

LO 4

CANADIAN POLICIES ON THE MANAGEMENT OF HAZARDOUS WASTE

Federal Waste-Disposal Policies

Federal policies are now covered by CEPA, 1999. They pertain to ocean dumping, transportation of dangerous goods, and radioactive wastes. The policies are basically command-and-control regulations that cover things such as providing lists of items that can be disposed (for ocean wastes and radioactive materials) and specifying requirements for equipment, procedures, training personnel, emergency preparations for accidents and spills, and documentation of waste shipments. Generators of hazardous waste are responsible for its proper handling at all stages. Canada is the tenth country to sign an international treaty on pollution prevention,[23] and is working toward creation of a "National Action List" that establishes maximum levels of discharge for interprovincial and international shipments of hazardous wastes. Fees are set for waste-disposal permits, but they have no environmental incentive effects. They are meant to cover a share of administrative costs (about one-half since 1993).

Provincial Waste-Disposal Policies: B.C.'s Waste-Disposal Permits and Fees

Each province regulates how hazardous wastes are stored and specifies security measures, fire protection, labelling, container design, and other aspects that relate to environmental safety. Provinces may require all waste dischargers to have a permit that specifies the quantities allowed and where

---

[23.] This is the 1996 Protocol to the Land Convention of 1972.

disposal can occur. A fee may or may not be levied. British Columbia's *Environmental Management Act of 2004* illustrates this type of policy. The *Environmental Management Act* establishes strict liability against the discharge of wastes into the environment without a permit. The B.C. Ministry of Environment issues and manages the permit system. Each permit specifies the maximum quantity of pollutants allowed for discharge. There may also be other specific provisions connected to individual permits.[24]

In designing these permits, the government had to set maximum discharge levels. These are called "pollution-control objectives," and they have been set for five industrial groups: chemicals and petroleum; mining, smelting, and related activities; forest products; food processing and miscellaneous agriculture; and municipal waste. A permit is needed for each environmental medium into which wastes are discharged (air, water, land), and there is also a permit for special waste storage. The provincial government monitors discharges and enforces the scheme.

Fees for the permits were introduced in 1987 under the original legislation called the *Waste Management Act (1982)*. The system in place until September 1992 for industrial sources based fees on industry production levels rather than wastes discharged from individual sources. The industrial fees covered only a small proportion of the government's costs of administering the system, not any measure of the economic and environmental costs of waste disposal. Fees that are not only low but also unconnected to actual discharges provide no incentive to reduce (or recycle) wastes. The old fee system was also based on increasing block charges. This meant that average fees per unit volume fall as volume increases. This fee structure likewise provides no incentive on the margin to reduce wastes.

In 1992, a new system was introduced that moved the province much closer to effluent taxes, and the *Environmental Management Act* continued that system. There is now a two-part fee. The first is a flat-rate annual fee that is like a licensing charge of $100 per medium for authorized discharges into air, water, for refuse, and storage. The second part is a variable fee based on discharges authorized by the ministry times a unit fee per tonne discharged. Fees are set for each waste product. Tables 18-3 and 18-4 list the fees that came into effect April 1, 2006, for contaminants released into air and water. Fees are now based on the government's assessment of the risks of the contaminant to the environment, as well as the administrative costs of the program. They will be adjusted as information about environmental impacts improves. For some industries, there was a substantial increase in fees. Revenues from the permits are being placed in a special fund, the Sustainable Environment Fund, rather than deposited into general revenues. The fund is to be used to address environmental problems and develop environmental protection projects.

One problem not yet addressed by the fee structure is that the permits are based on the volume of discharges, not loadings (concentration, time, volume) to the environment. Under a volume-based system, dischargers have an incentive to increase the concentration of the waste material per unit volume. Higher concentrations of wastes generally lead to more environmental problems. Of course, if loadings became the unit for the permit, monitoring of discharges would become essential to ensure compliance. This could raise the costs of the program substantially. Despite these concerns, the B.C.

[24.] The permit can also require the permit-holder to repair, improve, or construct new works; post security; monitor the method of landing, treating, transporting, discharging, and storing wastes; conduct studies and report information; use specified procedures in waste handling; or recycle certain wastes to recover certain resources (e.g. energy). See Ministry of Environment, Environmental Protection Division, "Waste Discharge Regulation Implementation Guide," available at: www.env.gov.bc.ca/epd/main/pdf/WDR_implement_guide.pdf, accessed October 12, 2010.

waste-permit fees represent a substantial movement by a Canadian government toward an incentive-based system where the fees are essentially a tax on releases.

TABLE 18-3 Contaminant Fees for Air Emission Permits in B.C., Effective April 1, 2006

Contaminant	Fee per tonne discharged
Ammonia	16.78
Asbestos*	16.78/unit
Carbon monoxide	0.45
Chlorine and chlorine oxides	11.29
Fluorides	673.60
Hydrocarbons	16.78
Hydrogen chloride	11.29
Metals	673.60
Nitrogen oxides	11.29
Phenols	16.78
Sulphur and sulphur oxides	13.07
Total particulate	16.78
TRS	561.33
VOCs	16.78
Other contaminants not otherwise specified	16.78

Notes: * Units of asbestos are equivalent to 5 cubic metres of air emissions per minute at a concentration of 2 fibres per cubic centimetre.

Source: *BC Ministry of Environment, Table 2. Copyright © Province of British Columbia. All rights reserved. Reprinted with permission of the Province of British Columbia, www.env.gov.bc.ca/epd/main/pdf/WDR_implement_guide.pdf.*

LO 5

The Cleanup of Toxic Waste Sites

Canadian governments have been coming to terms with the management of toxic waste sites slowly. There have been various cleanups of waste sites, but these tend to be on an ad hoc basis. There are no identified sources of revenue to fund these very expensive activities, few procedures to establish priorities for which sites to clean up, and no legislation governing these activies. Determining where and how to dispose of ongoing toxic waste being generated is also an extremely contentious and unresolved issue in Canada.

Existing toxic waste sites are located primarily in or near urban areas. They are the result of past industrial activity, such as coal gasification in the 19th century. Many of these sites are known as "orphans" because liability cannot be established, the responsible firm(s) no longer exists, or the liable firm(s) is unwilling or unable to pay for remediation. Site remediation is required by municipal laws before a piece of land can be used for redevelopment. Many sites in major cities across Canada have had to be cleaned before new residential and commercial development could occur. One reason why federal and provincial action on waste sites has been minimal could be because these sites have been construed as "local" problems. Federal policies apply only to federal and some Aboriginal lands.

TABLE 18-4 Contaminant Fees for Effluent Permits in B.C., Effective April 1, 2006

Contaminant	Fee per tonne discharged
Ammonia	102.91
AOX	273.24
Arsenic	273.24
BOD	20.64
Chlorine	273.24
Cyanide	273.24
Fluoride	102.91
Metals	273.24
Nitrogen and nitrates	41.13
Oil and grease	68.61
Other petroleum products	68.61
Other solids	13.66
Phenols	273.24
Phosphorus and phosphates	102.91
Sulphates	4.01
Sulphides	273.24
Surfactants	68.61
Suspended solids	13.66
Other contaminants not otherwise specified	13.66

Source: *BC Ministry of Environment, Environmental Protection Division, Waste Discharge Regulation Implementation Guide, Table 3. Copyright © Province of British Columbia. All rights reserved. Reprinted with permission of the Province of British Columbia, www.bclaws.ca/Recon/document/ID/freeside/37_299_92.*

The identification of toxic sites in Canada began in the 1980s, stimulated by the revelations at the Love Canal—a location in New York State where homes were constructed on a reclaimed toxic waste site. The toxicity of the land was so high that the homes were deemed unfit for habitation and their occupants relocated. The Atlantic and western provinces and the territories joined the federal government in attempting to locate problem sites. Ontario and Quebec carried out their own surveys. The federal government was not involved because Environment Canada did not have the budget or personnel to work with the provinces. By 1990, 10,000 sites had been identified—of these, 719 were classified "Priority 1," which essentially meant that they represented a high risk to health and the environment and should be immediately assessed. The Canadian Council of Ministers of the Environment (CCME) studied these sites, with guidelines and criteria for identifying sites at risk, but the priorities were not made public.

Current estimates are that over 22,000 sites exist across Canada, and that may be a significant underestimate of the true number. Jurisdiction is shared between federal and provincial governments, with the federal government responsible for sites on federal property or sites with contractual/legislative obligation and the provinces covering sites on Crown land. The federal government considers contaminated sites a national issue and sets overarching regulation, while the provinces are responsible for regulations/standards for remediation, liability, and administrative processes. In 2005, the federal government began implementing the Federal Contaminated Sites Action Plan with the goal to "Reduce environmental and human health risks from known federal contaminated sites and [to reduce] associated federal financial liabilities."[25]

While federal authority to regulate comes from the *Canadian Environmental Protection Act,* there is no federal legislation that specifically covers contaminated sites. The federal approach is based in policy outlined by the Treasury Board, rather than in legislation. They establish four principles:

(a) Known and suspected sites be assessed and have the most appropriate and cost-effective cleanup methods applied;

(b) Costs of contamination management should be recovered where possible;

(c) Priority is given to sites posing the highest ecological and human health risks;

(d) Management and remediation efforts are guided by standards endorsed by the CCME.

The Federal Contaminated Sites Action Plan has three phases. The first phase (2006–2011) focused on the identification and assessment of sites, with remediation commencing on a number of sites. The second phase (2011–2016) is to remediate the highest-priority sites while reducing liability. The third phase (2016–2020) is under development to determine the long-term strategy. The federal government had committed $4.9-billion up to 2014 for federal sites, and faces an estimated $4.3-billion in liability. Liability is growing as costs of remediation increase and new sites are discovered. Of the 22,000 identified sites across Canada, about 7,400 have been closed because remediation has been completed or little to none was required; 7,000 have not yet reached the initial testing step. The number of sites across Canada has nearly tripled since 2005, indicating that liability is growing.

An auditor general's report in 2012[26] offered the following critiques of the federal plan, many of which remain. These were as follows: The full extent of financial liabilities is not known for the majority of the identified sites. Approximately 2,000 of the 14,500 active sites had developed or were developing site-specific remediation plans, which is when there is a reasonable estimate of costs. No apparent strategy was in place to determine costs for sites not yet assessed. The development of a strategy for measuring performance was just underway at the time of the report but no comprehensive annual report for all contaminated sites is available to the public or Parliament, making it difficult to assess plans versus outcomes. Finally, there is no uniform site-closure policy. The current policy of funding assessment and remediation would thus seem wanting. What policy changes could be introduced?

Canada could contemplate a policy similar to that of the United States with its *Comprehensive*

---

[25] Information for the current federal policies comes from Government of Canada (n.d.), *Federal Contaminated Sites Portal,* retrieved March 21, 2014, from www.federalcontaminatedsites.gc.ca and Environment Canada (2012), *Update on The Federal Contaminated Sites Action Plan (FCSAP),* retrieved March 21, 2014, from www.rpicibic.ca/documents/RPIC_FCS2012/FCSAP_1.pdf.

[26] Office of the Auditor General of Canada (2012), *Chapter 3—Federal Contaminated Sites and Their Impacts,* Retrieved March 21, 2014, from www.oag-bvg.gc.ca/internet/English/parl_cesd_201205_03_e_36775.html.

Environmental Response, Compensation and Liability Act of 1980 (CERCLA).[27] CERCLA has four main features:

1. A financial fund, derived first, from a tax on chemical and petroleum feedstocks used by industry and from private parties held to be responsible for past dumping, then broadened to an environmental tax on all corporations of 0.12 percent of their taxable income over $2-million. The fund, known as the Superfund, was to be used to carry out site investigations and cleanups of orphan sites. The principle of the fund was that the polluter should pay for the damages created, in essence, putting liability for damages on the polluter (refer back to Chapter 10). The U.S. Treasury Department's authority to collect Superfund taxes expired in 1995 and was not reauthorized by Congress. Funding now comes from appropriations from Congress and fines levied against polluters.

2. A method for selecting sites for cleanup and deciding who would pay. Estimates are that the parties responsible for the toxic sites paid for about 70 percent of the cleanup costs.

3. Authority for the EPA to clean up sites or identify private parties to do so.

4. A liability provision for cleanup costs and environmental damages arising from spilled or released toxic materials.

The Superfund process is long and complex, characterized by complex issues surrounding liability, leading to costly litigation, and no guarantee of speedy remediation. The stronger regulatory power in the U.S. compared to Canada thus is not a guarantee of success. The Treasury Department's authority to collect these taxes expired and was not reauthorized by Congress in 1995. The funding for remediation now comes from Congressional appropriations and fines levied against polluters.

One further set of actions regarding remediation of damaged areas involves the International Joint Commission (IJC). As noted in Chapter 16, the IJC is a binational organization set up to deal with Canada–U.S. border issues. It has identified 43 sites around the Great Lakes that require decontamination and ongoing efforts to reduce further discharges. Twelve of these sites have been in Canada, 26 in the U.S., and five shared. The IJC facilitates coordination among all of the involved governments, the public, and industry to accomplish what are called Remedial Action Plans (RAPs), established by these groups. Statistics Canada estimated that the total cost of implementing all the RAPs could range between $100-billion and $500-billion for Canada and the U.S. combined. These costs include not just remediation of sites but also, for example, construction and upgrading of sewage treatment plants to prevent further damage to health and the ecosystem. The RAP process reported some success when measured against benchmarks in the late 1960s to 1970s. For example, through the initiatives of all levels of government coordinated by its RAP, Hamilton Harbour in Ontario has seen a marked improvement in water quality and improvement in habitat for fish and other species. As of 2010, four sites (three in Canada and one in the U.S.) have been delisted because their remediation goals established by their RAP have been achieved. However, there are still many challenges. Once of the biggest is the lack of funding for remedial measures identified by the RAPs and for data-collection and scientific studies. The IJC, in reviewing Hamilton's RAP, found some disturbing trends in the past decade. Monitoring of concentrations of some key toxins including cyanide ended in the 1993. It is therefore impossible to tell if progress has been made since then. The IJC also noted an increase in concentrations of nitrogen (from ammonia), phosphorus, and suspended solids since the late 1980s. This suggests a U-shaped time trend. These are partly due to inadequate wastewater treatment—again, a victim of insufficient funding and inadequate pricing of wastewater services.

---

[27] For more information see: Superfund. (2013). United States Environmental Protection Agency. Retrieved from www.epa.gov/superfund/about.htm.

Summary

The coming of the chemical society has led to new sources of environmental damage and opened up new requirements for managing toxic and hazardous materials. Canadian policy is only beginning to come to terms with the problems of toxic materials. Federal regulation of toxic compounds involves the identification and regulation of dangerous contaminants once they have entered the ecosystem. While thousands of potentially dangerous compounds are in everyday use, very few have been banned or strictly regulated. The cornerstone of federal policy is CEPA, 1999 and the commitment to study the toxicity of substances on the Domestic Substances List and design appropriate regulations. But this task is enormous and the built-in bias toward using command-and-control regulation for all hazardous substances, whether they should be banned or not, may lead to an unwieldy system with high compliance costs. The collection and publication of toxic releases in the NPRI is an important component of our regulatory policies, but it is not a replacement for other regulation. Attention has to be paid to the toxicity of substances, not just aggregate emissions unweighted by toxicity.

Waste management in Canada is primarily a provincial responsibility, except for the interprovincial and international waste flows. Some provinces use permits to regulate disposal. These permits do not yet have fees attached that reflect the external costs of disposal. There is scope for incentive-based policies to complement CAC regulation and provide continuous incentives to reduce wastes.

Canada lags in its management of hazardous-waste sites, lacking explicit and funded programs to deal with the cleanup of existing sites.

Key Terms

Emissions intensity of pollution

Loadings

Toxic intensity

Voluntary compliance

Waste reduction

Discussion Questions

1. Handlers of hazardous wastes—that is, firms that accept hazardous materials and transport them for disposal—sometimes dispose of the materials illegally or in unapproved landfills. How might a deposit–refund system be designed to provide incentives to dispose of hazardous materials in approved ways?

2. What are the advantages and disadvantages of using a limited liability approach to cleaning up hazardous waste sites; that is, an approach whereby firms that dumped material in a site are held liable only for their own wastes?

3. The cost of cleaning up toxic waste sites is thought to be enormous. At present there is no dedicated funding for this task. How might Canadian governments finance remediation while simultaneously providing incentives to reduce waste generation?

4. What type of fee structure would you recommend for provincial disposal permits?

5. It has frequently been suggested that taxes be placed on toxic materials at point of production; these would be easier to administer (as compared to taxes in intermediate-use stages) and would discourage overall use of the chemicals taxed. What are the efficiency implications of this approach?

6. What toxic substances are released in your city? What has happened to their emissions over time? Consult the NPRI (www.ec.gc.ca/npri). Choose two substances and see what types of industries produce them and what their potential damages might be. The Environment Canada and NPRI websites have a number of good links that might be helpful to you.

7. The House of Commons Environment Committee has recommended the phasing out and ultimate ban on using lawn chemicals and other pesticides for "cosmetic" purposes on household lawns and gardens. Evaluate this policy proposal. Consider its likely cost effectiveness, administrative costs, compliance issues, and social efficiency.

Chapter 19

Local Environmental Issues: Recycling, Solid Waste Management, and Land Use

After reading this chapter you will be able to:

LO 1) Explain how materials use can be reduced and contrast that with reductions in materials intensity.

LO 2) Explain and illustrate graphically efficient versus inefficient recycling of household waste.

LO 3) Explain and illustrate graphically efficient versus inefficient pricing and production of goods.

LO 4) Describe ways policy actions can increase the reuse ratio.

LO 5) Explain the major issues municipalities face in waste disposal.

LO 6) Describe policies that governments can use to incorporate ecological attributes into land use decision making.

In Canada, local governments are responsible for many important activities that improve environmental quality, in particular waste management and sewage treatment. Total expenditures on solid waste management by local government increased from approximately $1.5-billion in 2002 to $2.6-billion in 2008.[1] Figure 19-1 shows where these dollars went in 2008. Federal and provincial governments have decreased their funding of waste management, primarily due to reductions in funding for water and wastewater treatment. Municipal governments have found themselves faced with the need to replace and upgrade much of their environmental infrastructure with limited budgets. Municipalities are increasingly interested in using economic instruments such as user charges to help in this plight. However, they remain at an early stage in this process. This chapter examines the issues of solid waste disposal and the potential to reduce it through economic incentives involving recycling, reducing, reusing, and more efficient pricing of waste services. Land-use issues and how to protect natural capital are briefly considered.

---

[1] The source for the data for 2002 and 2008 is Statistics Canada, *Human Activity and the Environment, Waste Disposal, 2012—Updated*. Catalogue no. 16-201-X, September 2012, www.statcan.gc.ca/reference/copyright-droit-auteur-eng.htm, accessed July 25, 2014. This is the most recent data available as of July 2014.

Figure 19-1   Current Expenditures by Local Government on Waste Management by Activity, 2008

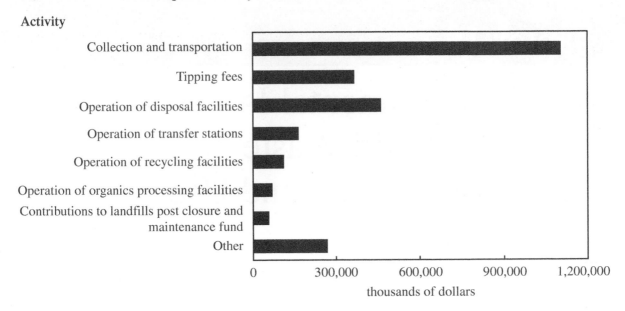

Source: *Data from Statistics Canada, CANSIM table 153-0045 as reproduced in Statistics Canada, Human Activity and the Environment, Waste Disposal, 2012—Updated. Catalogue no. 16-201-X, September 2012, www.statcan.gc.ca/reference/copyright-droit-auteur-eng.htm, accessed July 25, 2014, Chart 3.1, p. 17.*

LO 1

MUNICIPAL SOLID WASTE

The disposal of solid wastes has emerged as a leading problem in many cities and towns across the country, especially in localities with large populations and/or constrained landfill space. The problem is of less immediate concern in areas with the opposite characteristics. Landfilling, for a long time the preferred disposal method for urban solid waste, has come up against a scarcity of sites willing to take wastes in many parts of the country. Some localities have had to ship their solid wastes long distances for disposal, while others are moving into incineration, which have additional emission issues, including the production of dioxins and polyaromatic hydrocarbons (PAHs) from the combustion of plastics. The public policy problem would simply be one of governments trying to minimize the costs of providing a public service, except for the presence of two externalities:

- Producers pay for input costs for their products, but not for the ultimate waste disposal done by the consumers of the products. Consumers typically do not pay for the unit costs of disposal, but rather pay a flat charge through their property taxes. This is a market failure.

- Neither producers (who do pay the unit costs for their own waste disposal) nor consumers pay for the environmental damages released from waste disposal sites (landfills, incinerators, etc.). These environmental costs include possible groundwater contamination from landfill leachate (a potent chemical mix of "landfill juice") and air pollutants including carbon dioxide (from landfills and incinerators), and the release of tonnes of methane—a greenhouse gas that is 23 times more potent than carbon dioxide. There are also social costs from illegal dumping of wastes and littering.

Thus, the rationale for minimizing the waste stems from both the shortage of land and the environmental externalities created.

Policy issues and options to reduce waste flows and address the externalities from solid waste disposal are the key topics of the next sections.

The Nature of the Problem

The municipal solid waste (MSW) stream is actually a trickle at the end of a long and very large flow of materials used in the Canadian economy. Household waste is composed of a very diverse set of materials—everything from lawn clippings to mouldy bread to household chemicals to used refrigerators to construction and demolition debris. The solid waste problem is not equally acute everywhere.

Technical Options for Reducing MSW

Define the following terms:

TM is total materials used, by a firm or industry or economy, in a period of time;

VM is virgin materials used; and

RM is recycled materials used.

Then the following identity must hold for any time period:

$$TM = VM + RM$$

Recall from Chapter 2 that all materials inputs taken into an economic system must eventually end up back in the environment in some fashion. The form may change, as when solid materials are burned to yield energy and waste products. The time span can differ; some materials do not lend themselves to reuse and so are discarded almost immediately, while others can be recycled, perhaps many times. But recycling can never be perfect, because of conversion losses, wastage in consumption, and so on. This means we should focus on the quantity of virgin materials used. Rearranging the above expression gives

VM = TM − RM, or

VM = TM $(1 - r)$

where r is the rate of reuse, or RM/TM. There are essentially two ways to reduce the use of virgin materials: reduce the overall quantity of materials (TM), and/or increase the reuse rate, r; in other words, waste reduction and recycling.

Total materials use can be reduced in two ways:

1. By reducing the rate of economic activity, or
2. By reducing the materials intensity of that activity. By "materials intensity" we mean the quantity of materials used per unit of production or consumption.

Materials intensity can be lowered by:

1. Rearranging the composition of output and consumption away from products that use relatively large amounts of materials and toward those that use less; for example, a shift away from tangible goods toward services, or by

2. Decreasing the materials intensity of particular products; for example, reducing the amount of packaging material in consumer electronics or food products.

Recycling means reaching into the waste stream to extract materials that may be reused. Some may be reused directly, as when consumers reuse old boxes. But most require some reprocessing. Of course, the separation, transportation, and reprocessing technologies that are available critically affect the costs of recycled materials, and thus their ability to displace virgin materials. Recycling also has another cost—any pollution released in processing recycled items (for example, air pollution and sludge from recycling aluminum cans). The economics of recycling are now examined in more detail.

LO 2

LO 3

LO 4

THE ECONOMICS OF RECYCLING

In the recycling process two types of exchanges are of interest: that of material from producers to consumers; and that of recycled material from consumers to producers. In the first flow, producers are the suppliers of material and consumers are the demanders. With recycling their positions are reversed. How much material can be recycled depends on decisions made by both producers and consumers. Producers determine the component parts of a product; do these parts contain materials that lend themselves to recycling? For example, do they use paper packaging instead of non-recyclable plastic blister packs? The decisions of consumers will also affect the extent of recycling—how easy is it for them to recycle products?

Solid waste is a problem because of defects in the pricing systems that govern these transactions. Most Canadian municipalities do not charge households a fee per unit waste discarded. There are volume restrictions (bag limits) that have implicit weight limits, but there is no financial incentive to reduce one's garbage below the volume limit, as nothing is gained but moral satisfaction. Thus, there is no incentive for consumers to be very concerned about the amounts of solid waste they discard, nor is there any reason for them to be concerned about the amount of "excess" materials or the form of packaging, that accompany their purchases.

Figure 19-2 illustrates inefficient versus efficient disposal of household waste. Demand for goods is shown by curve D. Implicit in the price of the goods people buy is a subsidy when they are not paying the full social cost of waste disposal. Consumption of goods is too high at Q_0 and the price too low at P_0 to have social efficiency. Now suppose a fee per bag of trash disposed is introduced. The consumers' demand curve shifts down, reflecting the fee. Because goods now include a waste disposal charge, the quantity of goods demanded declines and therefore so does waste produced. Consumers pay P_C, which is the market price P_1 plus the fee per bag. Of course, in practice the situation will be more complicated than this simple diagram illustrates. Goods will have different amounts of waste associated with them. A reallocation of spending away from waste-intensive toward less waste-intensive goods in response to the efficient pricing of waste disposal is one expected result. More recycling of wastes should also occur when disposal is efficiently priced.

Figure 19-2 Waste Disposal Fees and Household Consumption

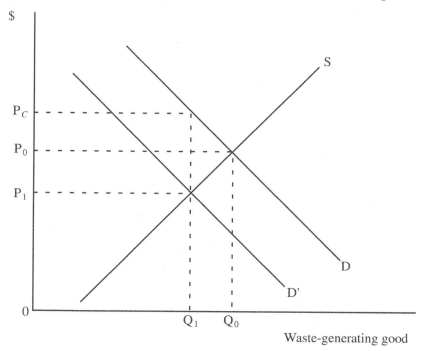

Waste-generating good

Socially inefficient consumption of waste-producing goods (all goods!) occurs when people are not paying the full social cost of waste disposal on demand curve D. Because of the implicit subsidy, consumption at Q_0 is too high, and the price at P_0 is too low to be socially efficient. A waste-disposal charge will shift demand to D', reducing consumption to Q_1, with consumers paying a price of P_C.

Producers also have to make decisions about waste disposal and recycling. When environmental costs of input use and waste disposal are not reflected in the prices paid by producers, producers will use a higher proportion of virgin materials in production rather than recycled inputs because firms typically do not pay for any environmental costs of harvesting virgin materials. This makes the prices of virgin materials too low from the standpoint of social efficiency and output of goods too high. Recycled inputs may thus typically cost more than virgin inputs. There are also environmental costs associated with processing recycled materials. Concentration of large scale recycling plants in a few regions of the country means higher transportation costs with associated emissions of air pollutants. A social cost accounting of the relative impact of using virgin versus recycled inputs would help determine the least environmentally damaging impact.

Figure 19-3 shows the effect on producers of having their costs of production fully reflect environmental costs. Full social-cost pricing of inputs will shift producers' supply curves from S to S'. Quantity produced will fall, prices will rise. If the social-cost pricing were accomplished by imposing a tax on production (equal to $P_1 - P_S$), consumers would pay P_1 and producers would receive P_S per unit sold. With less output produced, input use will decline as well. Figures 19-2 and 19-3 can be combined to see the effect in the goods markets of efficient pricing of waste generation. Figure 19-4 illustrates a possible result. All that is known for certain is that efficient waste pricing will reduce the quantity of goods produced and consumed, holding constant the waste generation per good. Because the demand curve shifts down and the supply curve shifts up, we cannot predict what will happen to market prices. However, it is clear that consumers will pay more for their garbage relative to the case without efficient pricing (P_C exceeds P_0), and producers will receive less per unit good sold (P_0 exceeds P_S). In the next two sections the producer and consumer sides of solid waste generation and recycling are examined using a more complicated model.

Figure 19-3   **Efficient Input Pricing and Production**

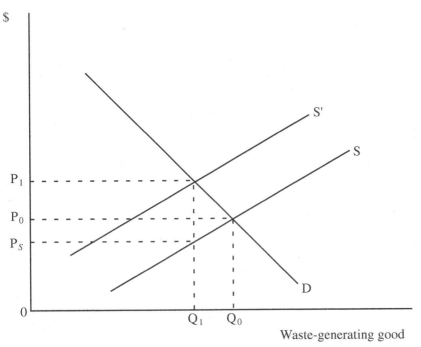

Full social-cost pricing of inputs will shift producers' supply curve from S to S'. The quantity of waste-generating good produced falls from Q_0 to Q_1, and prices rise from P_0 to P_1. If the social-cost pricing were imposed with a tax on production, the net price per unit received by producers is P_S.

Producer Use of Recycled Material

Figure 19-5 is an analysis of the producer side. The demand curve shown applies to a firm or industry; it shows the quantity demanded of a particular type of material in a given period, for example a year. There are two sources of this material, virgin and recycled. Assume that this firm or industry is small relative to the total use of this material; thus, it can obtain virgin material feedstocks in whatever quantity it wishes at a constant price. This price is marked p_v, and is shown as a horizontal line intersecting the demand curve at a quantity level q_0. But this material may also be obtained from recycled sources. The procurement cost picture is now more complicated. Reaching into the waste stream for recycled materials involves a number of special costs—of collection, separation, transportation, reprocessing, cleaning, and so on. Assume that these costs increase with the amount of recycled material used. The supply curve of recycled material to this firm or industry is therefore an increasing function, like S_1 or S_2. These two supply curves refer to situations with different recycling technology. For S_1, costs go up relatively rapidly; S_2 increases much less rapidly. Consider for the moment the recycled-material supply curve labelled S_1. If this is the one faced by this firm or industry, it will end up using q_1 of recycled materials. In other words, the producer will use recycled materials up to the point where its cost is equal to the price of virgin materials. Since the total materials used is q_0, the difference ($q_0 - q_1$) consists of virgin materials.

Figure 19-4   Efficient Consumption and Production with Wastes

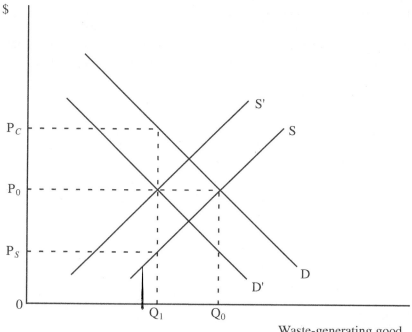

Waste-generating good

A possible equilibrium in the market for a waste-producing good after social-cost pricing of the good occurs will lead to an unambiguous decrease in the quantity sold from Q_0 to Q_1. Consumers pay P_C, producers receive P_S, given the policies to charge them for waste generated. The underlying equilibrium price may stay constant, rise, or fall relative to the initial price depending on the magnitude of the shifts in the supply and demand curves.

The reuse ratio, the proportion of total materials coming from recycled feedstock, is q_1/q_0. If analysis of the socially efficient amount of waste generations leads to the conclusion that the reuse ratio is too low, there are a variety of ways to change the relative price of recycled to virgin materials to provide incentives to producers to change the ratio.

The reuse ratio can be changed in three ways:

- Increase q_1 while holding q_0 constant,

- Decrease q_0 while holding q_1 constant, or

- Change both q_0 and q_1.

Most community efforts at recycling are aimed at the first of these. For example, public curbside sorting and collection programs are ultimately aimed at making the supply of recycled material more abundant and, hence, less costly to producers. In terms of the model of Figure 19-5, these programs have aimed at shifting the recycled supply curve downward; say, from S_1 to S_2. If this is done, recycled materials use increases to q_2 and the recycling rate increases to q_2/q_0.

Another way of increasing the recycling ratio is to reduce the demand for materials in general, while holding constant the use of recycled materials. Diagrammatically, this means shifting the whole materials demand curve back. This might be done, for example, by finding ways of producing output using fewer materials. It also might simply happen as consumers shift away from materials-intensive products to products that are less so. Finally, there is one way of simultaneously reducing total materials used and increasing recycled materials: Increase the price of virgin materials. If on Figure 19-5 the price of virgin materials increases to p_2 through a tax, this will lead both to a move up the recycling supply curve and up the materials demand curve. This means an increase in the quantity of recycled materials and a decrease in the quantity demanded of materials in total. Raising the price on virgin materials with a tax thus has a double effect on the reuse ratio, since it works at both ends of the problem.

Figure 19-5   Use of Recycled Materials in Production

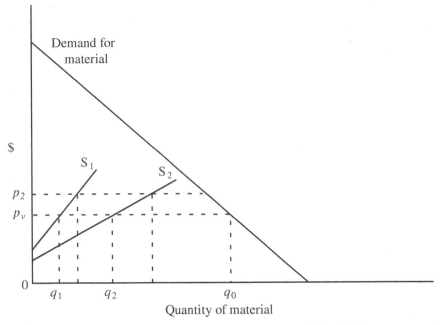

A producer's decision to use recycled materials is modelled. If the producer faces a constant price of p_v for virgin materials and a supply curve for recycled materials of S_1, it will use $(q_0 - q_1)$ of virgin materials and q_1 recycled materials. With a more abundant supply of recycled materials, as shown by supply curve S_2, recycled-material use will increase to q_2.

This simple model can be used to examine recent proposals for recycled-content standards in manufacturing industries. Early enthusiasm for community recycling efforts led to situations in which the amounts of collected material outstripped technical ability to turn it into useful raw material, and, in the absence of demand, large quantities of sorted and collected material actually ended up in landfills. This has generated quite a bit of controversy about the "success" of recycling programs. It may be the case that public policies have subsidized recycling activities more than the level required to achieve social efficiency. Alternatively, it could be that externalities associated with waste generation still haven't been fully internalized because waste disposal fees are too low to achieve social efficiency.

To deal with these problems in the United States, recent policy efforts have turned toward trying to increase the strength of demand for the recycled material. A number of states have thought to try this by introducing minimum content standards for materials-using production processes. Minimum content standards require that all materials-using products manufactured or sold within a given state contain some specified percentage of recycled material. Some Canadian jurisdictions are also contemplating standards such as these.

The *cost-ineffectiveness of uniform standards* in the face of heterogeneous MAC curves has been discussed throughout the text. In the case of uniform content standards for materials the same principle applies, but here the important factor is heterogeneity across manufacturing firms in terms of the costs of obtaining and using recycled materials. For a truly cost-effective approach to the problem, equality across industries and materials in terms of *marginal recycling costs* is the goal. What this implies is having higher rates of recycled materials used by industries whose recycling costs are relatively low, and lower rates for industries with relatively high recycling costs. One way to achieve this is to apply a tax on virgin materials. As mentioned above, a tax of, say, $p_2 - p_v$ per unit of virgin materials charged to all firms would lead each to increase its recycling ratio in a way that satisfied the equimarginal principle. Another way would be to initiate a tradeable permit system in the recycling market. A regulatory agency or statute would set an overall recycling objective for an industry, expressed in terms of the socially efficient recycling rate. Each individual firm would then have three options from which to choose:

1. Increase its own recycling rate to the industry standard;

2. Increase to a rate higher than the standard, and sell "excess" recycling permits; or

3. Increase to less than the industry standard, buying however many permits are necessary to make up the difference.

In the real world, of course, things are a lot more complicated than they appear in this simple model. For example, one underlying assumption built into Figure 19-5 is that recycled material and virgin material are physically interchangeable. This is hardly ever true in practice. Although newspaper can be produced largely from recycled newspaper, some virgin newsprint is usually necessary to achieve minimum quality levels. The same is true of many recycled metals. It is also true that the recycling market, like any economic market, is very dynamic, whereas the model displayed in Figure 19-5 is essentially static; that is, it is limited to events happening in a single time period. But producers normally look well into the future when making decisions. For example, even though current virgin materials prices are low, producers may nevertheless invest today in recycling and reprocessing works, if they *anticipate* that prices will increase in the future. But the simple model offers insight into basic recycling economics.

Consumer Recycling Decisions

Consumers' choices of how much recycling they are going to do actually begins before they dispose of waste products. What goods do they buy, and in what quantity?[2] These decisions critically affect the total quantity of the solid waste stream and its composition. Figure 19-2, discussed above, illustrated efficient versus inefficient consumption of waste-generating goods. Subsequent recycling decisions determine how much of that waste stream ends up in the landfill.

To examine these choices consider some illustrative benefit and cost numbers pertaining to two goods. Assume there are two similar products, but perhaps with different packaging, like bulk cereal and cereal in boxes, or drinks in plastic and drinks in glass containers. The data are in Table 19-1, and they

---

[2] Consumers may also wish to buy more goods that have recycled components as a way of reducing their demand for virgin inputs. A policy problem with green goods is how to ensure "truth in advertising." What do labels that say, "made from recycled products" actually mean? Requirements to list the percentage of material recycled would provide more information, but even in labelling, greenwashing can still exist. Think of all the food labels that say, "gluten free" when the food naturally would contain no gluten. Or, "made from 30 percent plant material" on a plastic bottle that would be recycled no matter what it is made from.

apply to the situation of a single consumer. Products A and B each sell for the same price, but one (Product B), because of handling convenience, has a higher value to this consumer. Of course, for other consumers the numbers pertaining to "value to consumer" could be different. For this consumer the net value before disposal of these two goods is in favour of product B.

TABLE 19-1　Individual and Community Benefits and Costs in Product Choice and Recycling (numbers are assumed to be in cents)

	Product A	Product B
Purchase price	100	100
Value to consumer	140	160
Net value	40	60
Conventional (landfill) disposal alternative		
Disposal costs		
Private	10	10
Social	10	40
Net benefits		
Private	30	50
Social	20	10
Recycling alternative		
Disposal costs		
Private	10	40
Community transport	(cannot be recycled)	10
Environment damage	10	0
Value of recovered material	0	20
Net benefits		
Private	30	20
Social	20	30

- *Disposal costs.* Suppose the consumer faces disposal costs. Disposal costs are in two parts, private and social. The private costs refer to the consumer's costs of handling and discarding the materials, while the social costs refer to the environmental damages caused by the material when disposed of in the community's landfill. The private disposal costs of the two containers are the same—the time it takes to bag up the trash and set it on the curb is the same no matter which product the consumer is dealing with.[3] But the environmental costs for product B are substantially above those of product A, for example because of the quantity or composition of the packaging material. The consumer maximizes net benefits by looking only at private costs and benefits. The community is assumed to maximize net social benefits. The consumer chooses product B; society would choose product A. This is a classic externality problem.

[3.] The private disposal costs might be a bit lower for the good without the packaging as the consumer will not have to wrestle with bulking materials and try to squeeze them into the trash bin. This complexity is ignored; assume private costs are identical.

- **Recycling.** Now introduce recycling. Assume that product A cannot be recycled for technical reasons, but product B may be recycled, and the costs of doing so rest partly on consumers and partly on the community. There are private costs coming from the need to separate trash and handle the recycled goods in the home. The community also faces a transport cost, but offsetting this is the fact that the recycled material has a market value. (These costs are shown in Table 19-1.) Recompute net benefits. The net benefit of product A stays the same, since it cannot be recycled. The social net benefit of product B is now substantially higher than it was before the recycling program, primarily because of the avoided environmental damage and the market value of the recycled material.

- **The consumer's choice.** The consumer now has three alternatives: (a) Buy product A, disposing of it in the community landfill; (b) buy product B, recycling the associated material; and (c) buy product B, but disposing of it in the landfill. The net benefits to individual and community are tabulated as follows:

	Net Benefits	
Option	Individual	Community
(a) Buy A	30	20
(b) Buy B, recycle	20	30
(c) Buy B, landfill	50	10

The individual's preferred choice is product B without recycling, but the community only wants product B if it is recycled. The fundamental question is—what incentives can be provided to encourage the individual consumer to adopt the recycling alternative?

Recycling Policy Options

1. **Mandatory recycling.** A local regulation makes it illegal not to recycle the material from product B. If enforced, what this does is take away option (c) from the consumer. The next best alternative for the consumer is to buy product A. The important point is that the recycling process starts back at the choice of purchase made by the consumer. The impacts of recycling ordinances on this purchase decision, as well as on recycling decisions themselves, have to be examined. In the present case the mandatory recycling law has the effect of causing the consumer to shift purchasing away from recyclable products to non-recyclable ones, thus substantially undermining the intent of the law.[4]

2. **Disposal charges.** A disposal charge is essentially an emissions tax. A completely efficient set of disposal charges would involve a charge on each item at a level equal to the social costs of disposal. Each unit of product A produces damages of 10¢ per unit, so its tax would be that much. The tax on a non-recycled unit of product B would be 40¢. For a recycled unit of B the tax is a little more complicated. If B is recycled, there is no environmental cost, but there is a community transportation cost of 10¢. But this cost is more than offset by the fact that the item has a 20¢ market value. Thus, the net tax is actually 10¢ − 20¢, or −10¢. The tax is actually a 10¢ subsidy to the consumer. If we levy these taxes on these products at the point of disposal, the net

---

[4.] However, note for this example that purchasing Good A is socially superior to purchasing Good B and *not* recycling it. The law thus has some positive incentive effects in this case. Of course, this need not always be so.

benefits of the various options to the individual consumer would now become: (a) 20¢, (b) 30¢, (c) 10¢, which are the same as the social net benefits of the previous tabulation. Now the consumer will choose (b), the recycling option. In effect, *these taxes have changed the pattern of private net benefits so that they are the same as community net benefits.*

When this is done a consumer will have the incentive to (1) choose the product and (2) make the recycling decision in ways that are efficient from the standpoint of the community. A charge based on the social costs of disposal for each item is not going to be feasible in the real world; it would be unmanageably complex to establish tax rates and administer. What many communities are doing, rather, is establishing a single charge per bag or can of undifferentiated waste and collecting separated and recyclable materials for free. In this case the charge on non-separated trash ought to be some average of the disposal costs of the various items in the waste stream. In our example, the social costs (in terms of environmental damages) of a unit of A are 10¢; a unit of B, if not recycled, 40¢. If the authorities took an intermediate value, setting a charge of 25¢ per container thrown away, the private net benefits of the different alternatives would be (a) 5¢, (b) 30¢, (c) 25¢. So in this case the tax would be sufficient to lead the consumer to buy B and recycle. A tax much lower than this, however, would lead the consumer to buy B and dispose of it in the landfill, owing to the relatively high private costs of recycling.

3. ***A deposit–refund program.*** Suppose a 40¢ deposit were put on item B, reflecting the damages done if it were thrown away rather than recycled. The array of net benefits for the individual would now be (a) 30¢, (b) 20¢, (c) 10¢. The consumer refrains from throwing out the recyclable item, but also shifts back to buying A, the non-recyclable good. This is the same effect as with mandatory recycling. One way around this is to have a deposit on *all* materials, equal to their disposal costs. For product A, the non-recyclable item, this essentially acts as a tax and gives a result similar to the "perfect" tax discussed above.

These results are illustrative, but of course do not represent all possible cases. In practice, private disposal costs will depend on the individual's own subjective valuation of the burdens of handling different types of products. These could differ among consumers and this could obviously lead to differences in response to various solid waste policies. It is also quite true that many people obtain a certain amount of civic satisfaction from engaging in behaviour that is efficient from the community's standpoint. But to get as much benefit as we can from recycling decisions made by consumers, we have to consider the benefits and costs of these decisions through their eyes.

LO 5

Recycling and Waste Disposal Issues in Canada

The present policy picture across Canada is very complicated, as one would expect from the nature of the physical problem, the large number of materials involved, and the thousands of municipalities, small and large, searching for solutions. When solid waste first became an issue, it was regarded primarily as a disposal issue—people were taking to the landfill materials and products that could be recycled. Thus, the initial response of most communities was to think about the recovery and recycling of materials. Recovery and recycling policies can be aimed at both the residential and non-residential sector. Table 19-2 lists some of the measures that are being pursued in various provinces. For the most part, these focus on some facet of recycling. All provinces have one or more packaging-waste-reduction programs, and all except Ontario and Manitoba have deposit–refund systems for beverage containers.

TABLE 19-2   Solid Waste Reduction and Recycling Activities Undertaken in Provinces and Municipalities

Returnable disposal fees: returnable deposits on beverage containers

Taxes on tires, beverage containers, high-energy consuming motor vehicles car batteries

Mandatory bottle deposits

Consumer fees on municipal solid waste

Prohibitions on landfilling certain products, e.g., tires

Voluntary material separation and curbside recycling

Organics collection and large scale composting

Recycled or recyclable labels on products

Technical assistance for recycling programs

Grants and loans to municipalities for recycling programs

Public construction of waste separation and reprocessing plants

Public construction of waste-to-energy plants

Tax credits and exemptions for waste-control investment by private businesses

From 2002 to 2008, solid waste disposal from all sectors in Canada increased by 7 percent from 769 kilograms per capita to 777 kilograms, while solid waste diversion increased from 212 to 254 kilograms per capita.[5] Non-residential waste makes up two-thirds of the total waste disposal, rising 11 percent from 2002 to 2008, while residential waste rose just over one percent. The largest increases in non-residential waste over that period occurred in Alberta (52 percent) and Newfoundland/Labrador (21 percent). Of all the provinces, only Nova Scotia recorded a decline in waste disposal (9 percent) over this period.

Voluntary recycling programs began in many municipalities during the 1980s and have expanded to cover most of the country. Data from a Statistics Canada survey of households finds that 95 percent of households reported in 2007 that they had access to one or more types of recycling. This percentage is up from 74 percent in 1994.[6] Private contractors generally handle collection and preparation for sale of recyclable materials. Figure 19-6 illustrates the breakdown of materials prepared from recycling for 2008. Organics make up the largest percentage of all materials at close to 29 percent.

People generally receive no financial reward for their efforts; recycling has become part of Canadian culture. However, even though per capita amount of waste that has been diverted from landfills or incineration to recycled products has risen, aggregate waste is a function of total production and consumption. More economic instruments to reduce materials use are warranted. The reward to firms is the reduction in their disposal charges (tipping fees) or special waste fees, an example of which we saw in B.C.'s waste fees in Chapter 18.

[5.] The source for the data for 2002 and 2008 is Statistics Canada, *Human Activity and the Environment, Waste Disposal, 2012—Updated.* Catalogue no. 16-201-X, September 2012, www.statcan.gc.ca/reference/copyright-droit-auteur-eng.htm, accessed July 25, 2014. This is the most recent data available as of July 2014.

[6.] Statistics Canada, Environmental Accounts and Statistics, Analytical and Technical Paper Series: Recycling by Canadian Households, 2007, 16-001-MWE2010013, no. 13. Released July 17, 2010.

Figure 19-6   Material Prepared for Recycling, by Weight, 2008

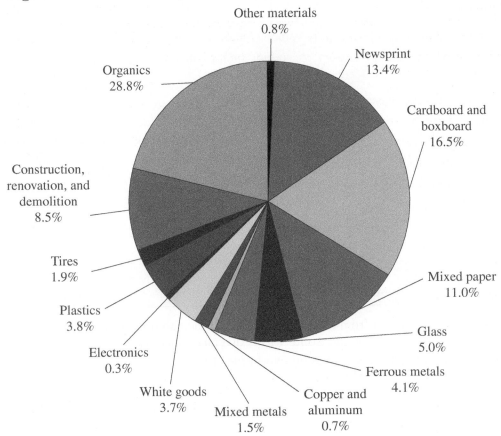

This information covers only those companies and local waste management organizations that reported non-hazardous recyclable material preparation activities and refers only to that material entering the waste stream and does not cover any waste that may be managed on-site by a company or household. Additionally, these data do not include those materials transported by the generator directly to secondary processors, such as, pulp and paper mills while bypassing entirely any firm or local government involved in waste management activities.

Source: *Data from Statistics Canada, CANSIM table 153-0043 as reproduced in Statistics Canada, Human Activity and the Environment, Waste Disposal, 2012—Updated. Catalogue no. 16-201-X, September 2012, www.statcan.gc.ca/reference/ copyright-droit-auteur-eng.htm, accessed July 25, 2014, Chart 3.3, p. 21.*

Many municipalities in Canada have established targets to significantly reduce the amount of waste going into landfills. A number of initiatives, called **diversion policies,** are being used. Many cities have enhanced their residential recycling programs to recycle and recover a greater share of "dry" recyclables (paper products, plastics, textiles, light bulbs) and "wet" garbage (food waste, organic material, soiled paper). Most of the wet garbage is converted to compost. Organics diversion is crucial as it represents over 50 percent of the waste stream by weight. Halifax's "three-stream" system, which began in 1999, has a diversion rate in excess of 60 percent. Metro Vancouver has set a target of an increase in its diversion rate from 55 to 70 percent by 2015. It plans to institute a ban of disposal of compostable organic material to landfills in 2015.[7] The list of municipalities with diversion rates of

---

[7.] See Metro Vancouver, *Integrated Solid Waste and Resource Management Plan.* Retrieved from www.metrovancouver.org/about/publications/Publications/ISWRMP.pdf, accessed July 25, 2014.

over 50 percent has grown over time, leading to substantially less waste going into landfills. A key policy question is the relative costs of disposal versus diversion. Diversion requires new infrastructure in the form of waste processing facilities with associated operating costs (labour, energy) and perhaps more garbage trucks. It also requires a change in behaviour on the part of consumers, who must now spend more time sorting their garbage. Whether these costs are lower than landfill disposal fees will vary by municipality.

Food waste makes up a significant share of total organic waste. Canadians are estimated to waste approximately 40 percent of all the food produced domestically.[8] Most of Canada's food waste comes from households and at the retail level. Figure 19-7 presents the U.S. Environmental Protection Agency's schematic for cost effective ways to reduce food waste. Note that composting is ranked below reduction at the source, the use of the food to nourish people and animals, and industrial uses. This would reduce the flow of organic material for recycling.

Figure 19-7 **Food Recovery Hierarchy**

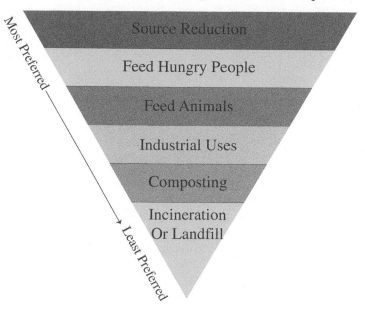

Food Recovery Hierarchy

The food recovery hierarchy shows that composting is a less preferred means of dealing with food that is wasted in the supply chain. Policies directed at reducing the generation of waste, then reusing it in productive ways rank above composting, incineration, and disposal in landfills.

Source: *United States Environmental Protection Agency, Food Recovery Hierarchy Figure, 2014, retrieved from www.epa.gov/ smm/foodrecovery/, accessed April 28, 2014.*

---

8. The estimate comes from M. Gooch, A. Felfel, and N. Marenick, "Food Waste in Canada," George Morris Research Centre and Value Chain Management Conference White Paper. Mississauga, Ontario, November 2010, p. 2. Also see K. Schilt, *Preventing Food Waste: Opportunities for Behaviour Change and the Expansion of Food Recovery and Donation in Metro Vancouver,* Simon Fraser University, School of Public Policy, 2014 for a discussion of food waste policy options.

Other policies to reduce the flow of solid wastes to landfills include "fee for bags," for example, most municipalities in B.C. now restrict weekly trash pickups to two standardsize garbage bags or a bin of particular volume. If a household wants to dispose of more garbage, it must buy stickers (approximate price is $2 to $3 per bag). Potential problems with these programs include non-compliance in the form of illegal dumping. In most urban areas, compliance with these policies does appear to be high (probably because the opportunity for illegal dumping is low). But there is another problem, colourfully called the "Seattle stomp": when the city of Seattle first introduced a fee-for-bags program, the number of bags of garbage fell, but the mass per bag increased by 42 percent.[9]

EXAMPLE

Toronto's garbage woes

Toronto has been engaged in a lively debate over where to send its garbage because of rising costs for disposal to landfills.[10] Costs of collecting garbage from households range from $32 to $169 per tonne over the metropolitan area.[11] Landfill disposal charges range from about $60 per tonne in fees to nearby landfills (e.g., in Keele Valley) to $90 and more for alternative sites (e.g., shipping waste to Michigan or to abandoned mines in Canada). The rising costs of disposal fees create a big incentive to look for ways to reduce waste flows. What sort of policies should Toronto adopt?[12] There are a number of alternatives, including

- increase curbside recycling

- decrease curbside recycling because it is too expensive

- introduce more regulatory programs such as mandatory packaging regulations, mandatory deposit–refund programs

- implement greater use of user fees for waste collection

One study looked at two payment vehicles: user fees and maintaining the standard practice of funding waste collection through property taxes.[13] Studies for the United States and elsewhere repeatedly find that user fees provide a strong incentive to reduce waste. If Toronto continues to use the current system of collection and disposal, a study estimated that it would cost $141 per single-family household per year and 26 percent of the waste stream will be diverted through recycling and composting. An expanded "blue box" recycling program combined with user fees would double diversion rates to 54 percent and lower the cost of collection to $120 per household per year. While these numbers are certainly subject to more scrutiny, they suggest that pricing waste disposal through user fees combined with providing recycling opportunities (for free) might be very cost-effective.

(Continued)

[9.] Thanks to a reviewer for pointing out this term and supplying the information.

[10.] See the City of Toronto's web page on solid waste management for a chronology of the landfill debate and links to other related documents: www.city.toronto.on.ca/involved/#solidwaste.

[11.] The $32 per tonne was for Etobicoke, which had contracted out garbage collection to a private-sector company.

[12.] See Donald N. Dewees and Michael J. Hare, "Economic Analysis of Packaging Waste Reduction," *Canadian Public Policy* XXIV(4) (December 1998): 453–470 for an in-depth discussion of these policy options. This paper is the source of much of the material in this example.

[13.] See Resource Integration Systems, *Preliminary Metro 3Rs Strategy*, Draft report, 1997.

A second study examined curbside recycling costs for rural and urban municipalities in Ontario.[14] The study found that recycling aluminum yields for municipalities net revenues that can be substantial (from $450 to over $2,000 per tonne). In other words, municipalities make money by collecting recyclable aluminum. For rural municipalities, recycling other items leads to a net cost per tonne. Recycling paper, glass, and high-value plastics yields net revenues in urban areas. Overall, recycling yields positive net revenues in urban areas, and negative revenues in rural areas. This study does not consider any of the environmental benefits from reducing total waste flows by recycling. The net return to the municipality is the total costs of collection minus credits for savings in disposal costs and revenue from the sale of recycled materials. The net benefits of recycling will be higher the greater the disposal fees, as the credits for waste diverted will be larger.

What about *mandatory deposit–refund systems* on beverage and other containers? The costs of these programs are generally higher, about 2 cents per container, than for curbside recycling.[15] There are some environmental benefits of reusable containers—less litter and materials use. The question is, then, are these environmental benefits high enough to offset the additional costs of the deposit–refund system relative to curbside recycling?

Another option is to reduce the materials intensity of production. This is also called **source reduction.** Source reduction can be substantial. For example, the weight of packaging materials sent for disposal per litre of soft drinks consumed in Ontario fell from 218 grams in 1972 to 19 grams in 1995.[16] This is a 91-percent reduction, and 88 percent of this was due to source reduction (the rest to recycling). No regulations imposed this reduction: it was done because it was profitable to producers. Dewees and Hare find that source reduction has decreased the quantity of beverage-container waste by more than has recycling (over 55 percent compared to 11 to 30 percent).

What should Toronto do? Think about the options given above (and others) and decide what sort of policy advice you would offer the city of Toronto (or your own municipality, which may be facing similar problems). Remember that any calculations of the costs and benefits of a policy should also take into account the environmental costs of disposal in landfills. And it is *net benefits* that should be computed, not just total costs of abatement.

Quiz: What is the most recycled object in the United States (and probably Canada as well)? If you guess newspapers or aluminum cans, you are wrong! Asphalt pavement is the winner. According to a report in the United States,[17] 80 percent of asphalt removed each year is recycled right back into new pavement, roadbeds, and so on. By contrast, annual recycling of aluminum cans is 60 percent, newsprint is 56 percent, and glass beverage bottles is 31 percent.

[14.] First Consulting Group, "Activity-Based Costing: Implications for Curbside Recycling Systems," Final Report to the Paper and Paperboard Packaging Environmental Council, Toronto, 1995, as cited in Dewees and Hare (1998).

[15.] Dewees and Hare (1998).

[16.] Dewees and Hare (1998).

[17.] "A Surprise Recyclable," *Environment,* 42(6) (July/August 2000): 6.

LO 6

LAND-USE CONTROL POLICIES

Land-use issues, and the public control over land-use decisions, are also matters that historically have been left to the provinces and individual communities in Canada. There are a variety of land-use initiatives—for example, wetlands preservation and management, and the creation of "action plans" for the Fraser River Basin, the St. Lawrence River, and the Atlantic Coast. While these projects involve all levels of government, it is felt by many that land use is primarily a local issue and therefore requires local policy responses.

Land-use policies involve fundamental decisions about how society decides the human and non-human uses of particular pieces of land. Since almost all environmental externalities have a spatial dimension, it might be tempting to think of all pollution as essentially a land-use issue. But while many of the large cases of air and water pollution are indeed spatial, they do not lend themselves to solutions through altered land-use patterns. The acid rain problem is not a land-use problem, for example. Certain local cases of environmental externalities, however, may be more closely related to decisions on land use. Local air-pollution problems are typically related to how cities have grown and developed their transportation network. Is there sprawl with people dependent on their motor vehicles or more compact cities where public transit is available? Noise pollution is a local issue as well.

But many contemporary land-use issues are not pollution-related; rather, they are about the human use of land that substantially reduces or destroys its environmental value. Recall the discussion of natural capital from Chapter 2. Canada's natural capital is threatened by land-use changes that destroy or degrade the goods and services (ecosystem goods and services) it provides. At risk are:

- Wetlands, which provide important environments for plants and animals, water purification, flood and silt control, and are linked into other components of the ground- and surface-water system.

- Coastal lands, where scenic and recreational qualities are important, as well as provision of habitat for many species.

- Critical habitats, such as wildlife corridors, where land-use patterns (e.g., roads, towns, agricultural and forestry practices) affect the health or survival of plant and animal species.

- Scenic and open land, where people may find vistas and experiences that have spiritual significance and recreational value.

To examine the economic logic of public and private land-use decisions, the following example focuses on one particular piece of land. All land parcels are essentially unique and will have varying values in different uses, but illustrative numbers can be used to demonstrate the essence of the problem. Assume the parcel is currently a natural area, with all environmental values intact. A single individual owns the land. Suppose there are three mutually exclusive options for the parcel:

(a) Develop without public restraints

(b) Preserve in its current state

(c) Develop with certain restrictions set by the local environmental agency

The illustrative numbers in Table 19-3 show the returns and costs of these different courses of action. When land-use decisions of this type are made, there is actually a stream of returns and costs off into the future, so the numbers in Table 19-3 in effect represent the *present* values of these streams of returns and costs.

TABLE 19-3 Returns and Costs of Various Land-Use Options

	Land Use		
	Develop (a)	Preserve (b)	Develop with restrictions (c)
Returns			
Private	100	—	90
Public	—	50	—
Total	100	50	90
Costs			
Private	80	20	80
Public	50	—	10
Total	130	20	90
Net return			
Private	20	–20	10
Public	–30	30	0

First, consider options (a) and (b). If the owner were to develop the land, he or she would realize a gross return of 100 and have construction costs of 80. But developing the land would have serious environmental costs, namely, the destruction of its ecological value, which is set at a value of 50. Assume that this lost ecological value is a loss to society but the individual does not care about ecological values. Could private bargaining lead to a socially efficient outcome? Perhaps the landowner and those people interested in ecological values could attempt to bargain over the use of the land if transactions costs are low and no other market imperfections exist. The party with the highest value for the land will bid the most for it, and a socially efficient use results. However, for many land-use decisions, transactions costs will be very high and this private bargaining approach to land use will not work. For example, those interested in ecological values may be dispersed across the country and not aware of each other's existence. It is hard to imagine that information about all such land-use decisions will be available to the ecologically concerned public. If private transactions are impossible, the owner of the land will be unable to realize the ecological value of the land. The owner's decisions about using the land will be predicated on its private development value. The private net return is 20, while the full social return of developing the land is –30. In the absence of any public land-use policy, the land would presumably be developed, even though it represents a net loss to society.

It is instructive to look at it from the reverse perspective, the returns and costs of option (b): preservation. In this case private returns are nil, but public returns from the preserved ecological values of the land are 50. The cost in this case is the forgone net return from developing the land, or 20. Thus, the net social returns from preservation are 50 − 20 = 30. Market failure prevents the attainment of this socially efficient equilibrium.

Policy Options to Incorporate Ecological Values into Land Use

Prohibition of Specific Land Uses

Outright prohibition of certain land uses that are thought to have low or negative social returns, even though they may have positive private returns, is a commonly used policy. This is done through the exercise of the *police power,* which is a power that communities have of prohibiting private activities that are detrimental to the wider public. The most common technique is zoning, in which communities rule out certain types of land uses where they would be destructive to the surrounding land values; for example, factories in residential areas. Environmental restrictions on development also come under this heading, since these contribute to the health and welfare of the community. Thus, a police power approach to the problem would be simply to develop a zoning law or environmental preservation law that rules out option (a).

A major problem with a police power approach like this is that, although it may legally prohibit certain land uses, like option (a), it does not change any of the numbers in the table, so it does not change any of the underlying incentives of the situation. An owner whose land has been subject to a development restriction by public authorities has much to gain by getting the authorities to relax the restraint. In fact, it would make sense for the landowner in Table 19-3 to spend some portion of the expected net returns to try to get the authorities to reverse their decision.

Development Controls

Instead of outright prohibition, the police power may be used to place conditions on development. For example, a developer might be required to leave a certain amount of open space, to avoid certain ecologically sensitive areas, or to install a public sewer system. The landowner is allowed to develop, but certain constraints are placed on this process, which have the effect of avoiding some of the ecological costs. Since the restrictions lower the developed value, the private net return is now only $90 - 80 = 10$. The social net return is now $90 - 90 = 0$, because all but 10 of the ecological costs have been avoided by the development restrictions.

Economic Incentives

The federal government provides an incentive for landowners to incorporate ecological values into their decisions through the tax system. In 1996, the federal *Income Tax Act* established ecological gifts as a new type of charitable donation. This is a modest beginning; the total amount of land donated as an ecological gift is quite small. Governments could also stop subsidizing agricultural practices that destroy ecological values (e.g., conversion of wetlands to crops). Removal of a subsidy will, however, bring with it demands for compensation. Alternatively, governments could provide positive incentives by offering landowners tax credits for conservation activities, or offer to purchase what is known as a conservation easement that dictates the uses on some or all of one's land. Some countries (Australia and the United States) have introduced markets for the ecosystem goods and services that require no net loss in natural capital in the region. These are but a few of the potential innovative incentive-based policies.

The "Taking" Issue

One of the most contested issues in using local land-use controls for environmental protection purposes is the "taking" problem.[18] In Canada, an individual's property rights are protected in the Constitution, but governments can appropriate one's land under certain conditions. Generally, the government has to show that the appropriation or **taking** is reasonable, clearly enhances public welfare, and is not arbitrary or discriminatory. The problem is in knowing when these conditions are met. In the example of Table 19-3, a local restriction that ruled out option (a) but permitted option (c)

[18.] A good discussion of the policy issues associated with the taking issue in Canada is R. Schwindt and S. Globerman, "Takings of Private Rights to Public Natural Resources: A Policy Analysis," *Canadian Public Policy* XXII(3) (September 1996): 205–224.

would lower the net private return from 20 to 10, thus lowering the private value of the land by that amount. Is this a valid taking? A major difficulty with cases like the one the table illustrates is that, although private revenues and costs of land-use restrictions are usually known with accuracy, the same cannot be said about environmental values. In the example of Table 19-3 a precise value was given for the environmental attributes, but usually this is not the case. There is a need to try to balance known private values with unknown public environmental values. From the standpoint of public health, there may be little difficulty barring development in sensitive wetlands, on the grounds that these are linked into the hydrological systems on which many people depend for water supply.

But when public health is not so directly involved, things can be much less clear. Suppose that there is a particular piece of land in a community that is privately owned and that over time the people of the community have come to value the scenic qualities of this land. Clearly the land has environmental (scenic) value, but should the town pass a regulation saying that the landowner must preserve the land and cannot develop it? In doing this, the town is essentially putting the entire burden of preserving scenic values on the private landowner.

One way around the taking issue is *compensation to the landowner*. A straightforward way of doing this is for a public agency or a private environmental group to purchase the land in question outright. In the case of Table 19-3, a purchase price of 20 would just compensate the landowner for the lost development opportunities. The land is then taken out of the private market and its environmental values are preserved. If this sort of market transaction is possible, then no further regulation may be needed. These transactions may require that the community or some private group have substantial financial resources. The Nature Conservancy, for example, is a private group, funded largely through contributions, that preserves sensitive land by outright purchase. Ducks Unlimited, an organization of hunters, helps governments buy wetlands to protect waterfowl habitat. It may be difficult, however, to get people to contribute to land purchases because of free-rider problems, inefficient capital markets (will banks loan an individual money to preserve ecological values if that person doesn't have title to the land?), and other types of market imperfections. Thus, takings with compensation may be necessary to reach the socially efficient land-use. Governments, too, face budget constraints, so compromises might be necessary. For example, governments may purchase certain partial rights in the land, not the land in its entirety. In the case of Table 19-3, for example, the community might buy from the landowner just the right to undertake option (a), but not the right to pursue option (c). The value of this one right would be 10, the difference in net returns between the two options. This purchase of just the development right would preserve some, though not all, of the land's environmental values. Social efficiency may be difficult to obtain.

In Canada, compensation for a taking is not established in the Constitution. Compensation is thus becoming an increasingly important public policy issue because of the growing public pressures for preservation of environmentally important regions of the country. While many of the areas in question are Crown lands, the rights to extract resources from these lands had frequently already been granted to private individuals or corporations by provincial governments. This is where much of the conflict lies. As yet, there is virtually no official policy established by any level of government.[19]

[19.] The taking issue is also an important component of Canadian deliberations on endangered species legislation.

Summary

Local governments deal with important aspects of environmental quality—providing clean drinking water, sewage treatment, solid waste management, and protection of their natural capital on lands in the region. Community efforts at recycling are a major part of the effort to address solid waste issues. We saw how recycling decisions depend on incentives faced by consumers in their buying and disposal decisions and producers facing the relative prices of recycled materials versus virgin inputs. Municipalities in Canada have greatly increased recycling programs over the past two decades, with most Canadians having access to recycling programs and participating in these programs. The most significant increase in recent years had come from organics recycling initiatives by municipalities.

Key Terms

Diversion policies

Source reduction

Taking

Analytical Problems

1. Suppose the demand for a product is $P = 100 - 1/2Q$ and the supply of virgin inputs is 20 units. The marginal cost curve for recycled inputs is $r = Q/4$. Compute the socially efficient output level, the use of recycled inputs, and the efficient recycling ratio. Recompute all these under the following changes (take them one at a time) and compare them to the original case.

    (a) Demand falls to $80 - 1/2Q$;

    (b) The MC curve for recycling inputs becomes $r = Q/6$;

    (c) The supply curve for virgin inputs increases to 30.

2. Another way of increasing the use of recycled material by industry is to subsidize its purchase of materials taken from the waste stream. How would you analyze this in terms of Figure 19-5?

3. Many communities have been successful in collecting recyclable material, but have been unable to find buyers for the recovered materials. Analyze this situation graphically using the model of recycling covered in this chapter.

Discussion Questions

1. If the reuse ratio is lower than is socially efficient, what economic incentives could be used to encourage the recovery and recycling of a substantially larger proportion of the solid waste stream?

2. Suppose there is a wetlands that can be used for ecological values or drained and houses built on it. How could the socially efficient use of the wetlands be reached?

3. Many communities are instituting a "pay as you throw" system for solid waste. Discuss the equity implications of this type of system.

4. In trying to incorporate ecological values into land-use decisions, what sort of economic incentives might be used?

Chapter 20

Global Environmental Problems

After reading this chapter you will be able to:

LO 1 Describe desirable design features of GHG pricing policies.

LO 2 Explain how design principles apply to examples of emission trading.

LO 3 Describe the features of Canadian GHG policies and how they use carbon pricing.

LO 4 Explain how international agreement was reached to eliminate CFCs and how price incentives helped achieve the goal.

LO 5 Explain why it is important to conserve biodiversity.

People all around the world are struggling to come to grips with local environmental problems and improve their immediate surroundings. But over the last few decades, the outlook has been broadened because of the recognition that many environmental issues are global in nature. For all of history, one of the ways humans have reacted to local environmental destruction is migration. But at the planetary level this option is not available. There is no escape if we degrade our natural environment to make the planet less habitable.

Political and economic reality makes it extremely difficult for the world's nations to act collectively. Nations are still accumulating scientific data that help us understand the factors giving rise to global changes. While there are growing efforts to develop international institutions and perspectives that will make concerted action possible, the world is far from agreement on how to combat the potential changes scientists warn of.

In this chapter the focus is on global environmental problems and Canada's policy initiatives to address these problems. The topics covered are: climate change, depletion of stratospheric ozone, and international treaties such as measures to protect the oceans, endangered species, and biological diversity. We provide an overview of the global policy framework in each case, then Canada's policy responses.

LO 1

GLOBAL CLIMATE CHANGE

Chapter 1 illustrated how human releases (anthropogenic sources) of greenhouse gases (GHGs) are contributing to massive changes in the globe's climate and briefly noted what sort of policy actions are possible. This chapter briefly examines international actions to address the challenge of reducing GHG emissions and explores the policies that Canadian governments—the provinces and federal government—have implemented.

GLOBAL GREENHOUSE GAS PRICING POLICIES

Under the UN Framework Agreement on Climate Change (UNFCC) the Conference of the Parties (COP) is a meeting every other year of the world's nations where agreements are proposed to address climate change by setting targets to reduce GHGs, and support adaptation initiatives and carbon sequestration (e.g., by preventing deforestation). The most recognized COP was that held in Kyoto, Japan in 1997 that produced the Kyoto Protocol. Canada was one of the early signatories and it was ratified by Parliament in 2002. The Protocol is not binding on any country—there is no way to enforce these targets. Each signatory to the Kyoto Protocol set its own target and policies for reductions in GHGs to be met by 2008 to 2012, known as the first commitment period. Subsequent commitments were to be made for future time periods. As of 2014, the Kyoto Protocol covers 12 percent of the world's emissions. Canada withdrew in 2011, abrogating its commitment to reduce its emissions by 6 percent from their 1990 level no later than 2012. While many western European countries have introduced specific policies to mitigate GHGs, as we discuss below, the majority of the world's countries, including Canada, have made little progress toward meeting their Kyoto targets. The Copenhagen Accord in 2009 is the most substantive of recent meetings and sets five conditions.

1. Annex I countries (e.g., the European Union, U.S., Canada, Japan) will commit to **emission reduction targets** by January 31, 2010.

2. Non-Annex I countries (e.g., China, India, Brazil, the African countries) will implement mitigation strategies and report on their emission levels every two years to the Conference of Parties.

3. Establish a "Green Climate Fund" to help support mitigation, adaptation, technology development and transfer, as well as help reduce deforestation and forest degradation for non-Annex I countries. The target was to raise $30-billion from the wealthier nations over the period 2010 to 2012 and by 2020, $100-billion per year.

4. Signatories are to implement policies to stabilize GHG emissions so as to keep global temperatures from rising more than 2°C as soon as practicable given their level of development.

5. Develop mechanisms to provide incentives to reduce deforestation and forest degradation.

Rounds of meetings subsequent to Copenhagen have worked on details and other sub-agreements and expectations are for more substantial actions in future meetings.

A Sample of GHG Policies Worldwide That Use Carbon Pricing

If the world community is serious about keeping global temperature from rising more than 2 degrees, then significant reductions in emissions will be required, and quickly. As Chapter 1 indicated (see Figure 1-1), the rise in global emissions accelerated from 1.3 percent annually from 1970 to 2000, to 2.2 percent annually post-2000. Economists are generally united in advocating some form of pricing mechanism to help achieve emission reduction targets. The reasons are what we have discussed in previous chapters—pricing in the form of taxes, transferable discharge permits, and crediting (offset) mechanisms are more likely to be cost effective, and provide stronger incentives for emission reductions than direct regulation. This is not to say that direct regulation and technological changes are not needed or desirable to help reduce GHG emissions, but a world carbon price would accelerate international progress to moderating and ultimately reducing its emissions. By 2014, approximately 40 countries worldwide were using some form of carbon pricing, covering between 12 and 17.5 percent of world emissions.[1] Figure 20-1 illustrates the distribution of carbon pricing worldwide and the form it takes.

[1.] The source for this data and information in this section comes from The World Bank, *State and Trends of Carbon Pricing, 2014*. Washington, D.C.: The World Bank, 2014. Accessed at: www-wds.worldbank.org/external/default/WDSContentServer/WDSP/IB/2014/05/27/ 000456286_20140527095323/Rendered/PDF/882840AR0Carbo040 Box385232B00OUO090.pdf on July 28, 2014.

FIGURE 20-1 Carbon Pricing Instruments Contemplated or In Use

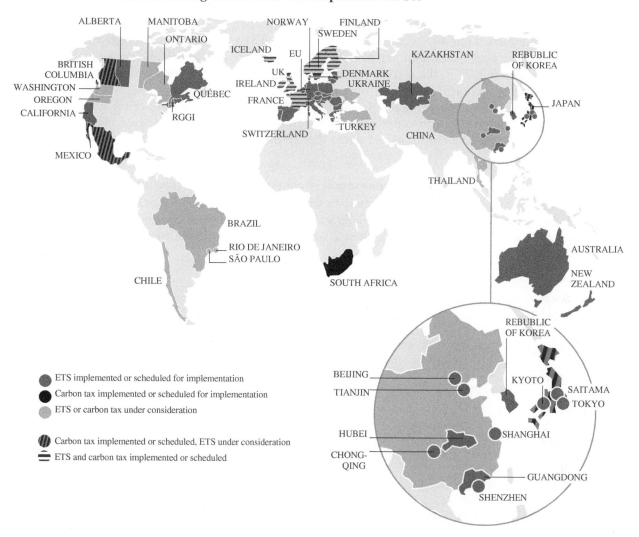

Carbon pricing has spread to many parts of the world, now including China, the world's second largest emitter of GHGs after the United States.

Note: ETS stands for an emission trading system—what we have called TEP (tradable emission permits).

Source: *The World Bank, State and Trends of Carbon Pricing, 2014. Washington, D.C.: The World Bank, 2014, Figure 11, page 50. Accessed at: www-wds.worldbank.org/external/default/WDSContentServer/WDSP/IB/2014/05/27/000456286 _2014 0527095323/Rendered/PDF/882840AR0Carbo040Box 385232B00OUO090.pdf on July 28, 2014.*

Some regions, such as Europe, introduced carbon pricing mechanisms a number of years ago. Others, such as China, have begun recently to use pricing to help reduce emissions in addition to direct regulation. Canada and the United States, among the developed nations, are notable for the absence of a country-wide pricing policy. The action is at the sub-national level. At the federal level, Canada has been largely a passive player in the world's efforts to limit emissions of GHGs. Over the past 25 years, successive Canadian governments have failed to deliver meaningful policy to reduce Canada's GHGs, with emissions rising from 591 million tonnes CO_2e in 1990 to 702 million tonnes in 2011. There are no federal carbon pricing policies; our Canadian examples will be examples of provincial carbon pricing.

The two principle carbon pricing mechanisms are taxes and TEPs. They both set a price on carbon. To review, a carbon tax establishes a known price per unit emission with emission levels determined by the covered sources. In a TEP, the market sets the carbon price and emission levels set by the overall cap. If the TEPs are auctioned, both will raise revenue which provide governments with options to reduce other taxes or use the revenues to support investments in carbon-reducing activities (e.g., public transit, new renewable technologies). While there has been much debate over which system is best to implement, most economists would agree that getting the design details right is the first order of priority.

Ian Parry, a notable environmental economist and fiscal policy expert for the International Monetary Fund, summarizes important design characteristics in the box below.[2] We turn next to principles of emission trading followed by examples of TEPs and carbon taxes in the European Union, Canada, and the United States to augment our theoretical coverage of these policies in previous chapters and illustrate design features and impacts.

From the perspective of economic efficiency, desirable design features for carbon pricing schemes include:

*– **Comprehensive coverage of emissions,** which can be achieved through implementing pricing in proportion to carbon content on the supply of petroleum products, coal, and natural gas. Alternatively, for some sectors (e.g., electricity) charges can be levied at the point of fuel combustion, though administration may be more involved (and small-scale emitters are often excluded).*

*– **A uniform price applied to all emissions,** which is appropriate as the damage per ton of emissions is the same, regardless of which fuel they come from or who is using the fuel.*

*– **Stable and predictable emissions prices,** which promote cost-effectiveness through equating incremental abatement costs at different points in time and help to establish the longer-term signals needed to promote clean technology investments. Provisions to prevent prices declining are also needed to improve compatibility with other mitigation measures (e.g., incentives for renewables).*

*– **Emissions prices aligned with environmental damages or climate stabilization goals.** Estimates of future climate change damages suggest CO_2 should be priced in the order of $35 per ton, though damage assessments are highly contentious. Alternatively, for example, a global CO_2 price starting at about $30 per ton (in current dollars) in 2020 and rising at around 5% a year would be roughly in line with ultimately containing mean projected warming to 2.5°C at least cost.*

(Continued)

---

[2]. In 2008, over 250 Canadian economists signed a letter calling for carbon pricing and an end to misleading rhetoric about the differences between carbon taxes and TEPs that permeated the 2008 federal election. Parry's design features capture many of the same points the Canadian economists raised.

- *Maximizing the fiscal dividend,* which means raising revenues and using the revenues productively, particularly lowering the burden of broader taxes that distort the economy or funding socially desirable (climate-related or other) spending. Failure to exploit the fiscal dividend can undermine the case for carbon pricing over regulatory approaches on cost-effectiveness grounds.

- *Carefully targeted compensation schemes for vulnerable households and firms.* Excessive compensation has a high cost in terms of diverting funds from the public budget. With regard to trade-exposed firms, international price floor agreements (analogous to those applied to value added and excise taxes in the EU) provide some protection against losses in competitiveness while allowing individual countries the flexibility to price emissions more aggressively (e.g., due to fiscal and ancillary environmental benefits or green preferences).

Source: *Ian Parry, International Monetary Fund, Fiscal Policy to Mitigate Climate Change: A Guide for Policymakers (Washington D.C., 2012).*

LO 2

Emissions Trading Principles and Application

Review Chapter 13 so that you are familiar with the principles and concepts behind a TEP system. Some of the practical issues of implementing and operating a TEP system are discussed below, followed by a discussion of the **European Union's Emission Trading System (ETS)** and the Western Climate Initiative (WCI) of U.S. states and Canadian provinces.

How Will Permits be Allocated?

Recall how an emissions trading system works. Figure 20-2 illustrates in the context of supply and demand curves for a source covered by the system. As examined in Chapter 13, permits can be either auctioned or distributed without charge. Figure 20-2 shows how the two methods of allocation would affect producers and consumers of GHG-related goods. With no GHG policy, the initial equilibrium is at Q_0 output with a price of P_0. Assuming that the introduction of a TEP system on producers of GHG goods does reduce the amount of emissions of GHGs (e.g., the permits issued whether auctioned or not are less than current emissions), the supply curve will shift from S to S', reflecting costs of abating emissions.[3] Output falls to Q_1 and price increases to P_1. The magnitude of these changes will depend on how elastic are the supply and demand curves. If the permits are auctioned, the producer will incur permit plus abatement costs equal to area P_1BCP_2. Its producer surplus will fall by P_0ACP_2. Consumer surplus will decline by area P_0ABP_1. If the government recycles the revenues from the initial permit auction back to the economy in the form of reductions in, say, income-tax rates, some of the loss in consumer and producer surplus would be offset. But, because these losses also reflect real resource costs in the form of total abatement costs, there will be a net loss in consumer and producer surplus. This is the cost of the policy. The benefits are, of course, the potential improvement in environmental quality resulting from a reduction in GHGs. If a proportion of the permits are given to the producer without charge, its loss of producer surplus will diminish. For example, if the government gives the producer permits sufficient to produce Q_2 units of output, it will receive an effective lumpsum transfer of area P^1EFP^2.

[3.] This reflects a movement up the MAC curve in the MAC–MD framework from, for example, no abatement to some positive level of pollution abatement to comply with the number of permits issued.

FIGURE 20-2 The Impact of an Emissions Trading System on Output and Price of a GHG-Intensive Good

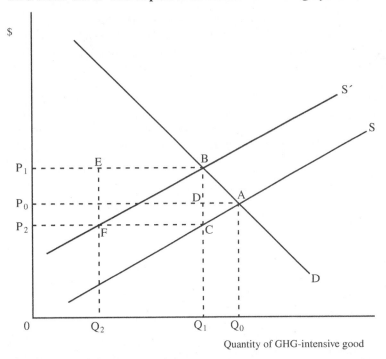

Quantity of GHG-intensive good

The introduction of a TEP system increases the costs of producing a GHG-intensive good, as producers must either cut production or incur abatement costs to reduce GHG emissions. The supply curve shifts from S to S' as a result. Output will fall to Q_1 and price will rise to P_1. The magnitude of these shifts is dependent on the elasticities of each curve. If the permits are auctioned, the producer will pay P_1BCQ_1 for permits and abatement costs. Producer surplus will fall by P_0ACP_2, consumer surplus by P_0ABP_1. If some permits are given to the producer without charge (e.g., enough to produce Q_2 units of output), producers will get a scarcity rent transfer of P_1EFP_2. This transfer will not affect the equilibrium price of the good, simply the net change in producer surplus.

The simple economics of the TEP system show that

1. *the TEP system will affect product prices and quantities produced of GHG-intensive goods.*

2. *producers and consumers will "share" in the burden of the system. There will be a loss of producer and consumer surplus, ignoring any of the benefits of GHG reductions.*

3. *if permits are given away instead of auctioned, the loss of producer surplus can be greatly reduced (producers who are low-cost abaters of GHGs will gain the most, as was shown in Chapter 14). Consumer surplus losses are unaffected.*

4. *if permits are auctioned, governments could recycle the revenue in the form of tax cuts to offset some losses.*

Design Issues: What Exactly Will Be Traded?

In Chapter 13, we simply referred to TEPs as emission permits. The holder of the permit is entitled to emit x units of pollution. In practice, a TEP system can be designed not only for emissions, but also for other actions polluters take to reduce emissions. While the vocabulary is not uniform, the following are the types of TEP schemes under discussion around the world.

- *Credit trading.* Credits are given to polluters from documenting a reduction in emissions. This is also called a **baseline-and-credit system.** The credits can be sold to others to use for compliance with regulations. Credit trading has already occurred in Canada on a voluntary basis. A key issue is how to verify that the reductions represent actual decreases in emissions from what previously existed. Monitoring of emissions is crucial to this (and all systems). The ultimate use of credits will depend on how government determines the allowed level of emissions of each source, (i.e., what is the baseline).[4] A related issue is whether any credit will be given for the creation of carbon sinks.

- *Substance trading.* This approach allows for the trading of permits denominated in units of the polluting substance. In the case of GHGs, this could be the carbon content of fuels, the nitrogen content of fertilizers, and so on. In a TEP system of emission trading, there will be an overall limit or cap on the total quantity of the substance consumed domestically, which means a limit on the sum of production plus imports minus exports. The system works on GHGs indirectly, through the reduction in demand by consumers in response to price increases of GHG-intensive products (as was illustrated in Figure 20-2).

- *Emission-rights trading.* This system limits aggregate emissions of a GHG from specific sources at the point of release into the atmosphere. Sources emitting the GHG would have an annual cap on emissions, and permits can be traded among the sources. This is also called a **cap-and-trade system**—the system proposed by the Western Climate Initiative and operating in the eastern United States in the Regional Greenhouse Gas Initiative (RGGI).

No one system is likely to be perfect. Each has pluses and minuses depending on the GHG and its source. No one policy can effectively deal with as complex an environmental problem as climate change. No one is suggesting, for example, that a TEP system directly cover GHGs released from household energy use (home heating, transportation). Other policies would have to apply to this sector.

Implementation Issues

Cap-and-trade markets are complex; care must be taken to ensure the market will operate effectively, efficiently, and equitably. The process of designing the specific aspects of the policy include: how many emissions are covered, what share of allowances are auctioned versus distributed to emitters (some form of grandfathering), whether to introduce safety valves and other means of reducing **price volatility** in the market, and how to handle offsets—the market for activities that sequester carbon. The following are principles that economists studying cap-and-trade systems have developed to help design the system.

- *Cover a broad base of emitters with a cap set at the targeted level of emission reduction.* A broad base helps provide sufficient buyers and sellers to operate competitively, achieve cost efficiencies, and lead to significant reductions in emissions.

- *Auction as high a percentage of allowances as possible to ensure efficiency and obtain revenue needed to address equity issues.* Auctioning, as we saw in Chapter 13, helps maximize the trading volume and hence, makes it more likely an efficient price will be set in the market. Auctioning also avoids establishing complex rules for the free allocation of **carbon allowances** and avoids distributing all the rents that a cap-and-trade system generates to non-government parties. On the other hand, auctioning makes it more difficult politically to introduce a cap-and-trade system.

[4.] The clean development mechanism under the UN is a type of baseline-and-credit system that allows emitters in the developed countries to purchase a credit for emissions reductions in developing countries.

- *Minimize price volatility.* Estimates for a nation-wide cap-and-trade system in the U.S. show that prices may fluctuate initially between $24 and $160 per tonne CO_2e. We saw the large fluctuations in prices in the U.S. sulphur dioxide market in Chapter 17. Large swings in prices make it difficult for covered sources of emissions to plan their efficient responses to the policy. Volatility can be reduced by a number of means. One is to allow banking and borrowing (as described in Chapter 13). Safety valves in the form of price ceilings and floors are another option. If the price floor and ceiling are close together, cap and trade becomes much like a carbon tax, and a carbon tax is a much simpler pricing policy instrument. Another response to volatility is to index the system to economic activity. The Alberta cap-and-trade system (and the proposed, but never implemented federal system) operates with a cap that is tied to emissions intensity, which allows emissions to grow in absolute terms, but the economy becomes relatively less carbon intensive over time. An indexed cap provides covered sources with more flexibility, but reduces the likelihood the policy will be effective in reaching targets.

- *Use offsets with care in their design.* One way to expand the range of options for covered sources and keep costs lower than they might otherwise be is to allow them to purchase verifiable emission reductions known as **carbon offsets** from the uncovered sectors. An offset policy allows reductions in emissions from the uncovered sectors below a set baseline level to be sold into the market. Offsets either allow the same level of emission reduction at lower cost than in a system without them (due to the expansion of ways to reduce emissions; an offset would not be purchased if its price exceeded that of the allowance), or allows the system to achieve greater emissions reduction at the same cost because the offset works like a withdrawal of allowances from the market.

Offsets add considerable complexity to a cap-and-trade system. The main challenge is to be convinced that reductions actually occur that would otherwise not exist. The literature has come up with five criteria that should be satisfied to establish an effective offset system that leads to real emission reductions.

- *Certainty* in the measurement and monitoring of emission reductions or sequestration;
- Verify *additionality:* the emission reductions backing the offset would not have occurred in the absence of the cap-and-trade system;
- The *baseline* level of emissions from the offsetting source is appropriately measured;
- *Leakage* in the form of shifts in emissions outside the market boundaries is minimized; and
- Any *reversals* in the form of subsequent releases of carbon from the offsetting source are themselves offset or covered by allowances.

An oversight agency is necessary to monitor the actions by the entities selling offsets and guard against fraud. The success of a cap-and-trade system with offsets is dependent on the success of the monitoring agency.

Examples of Emission Trading Systems

Figure 20-3 illustrates emission trading systems worldwide, the percentage of emissions covered, and the sources of emissions. Table 20-1 shows how TEPs (allowances) are distributed.

The European Union. Figure 20-3 shows that the European Union's (EU) Emission Trading System (ETS) is currently the largest in the world, covering 40 percent of the EU's emissions and requiring allowances from electric utilities, industrial sources, and airlines. The EU has been successful in

FIGURE 20-3 Emission Trading Systems at the Regional, Sub-National, and National Level

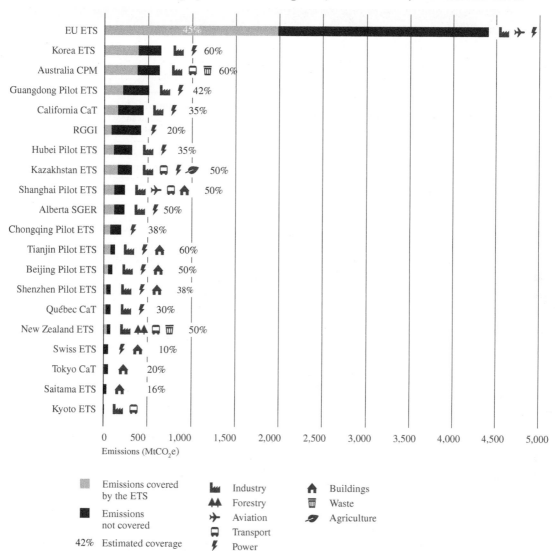

Symbols stand for the sectors covered. Black bars represent emissions. Grey bars indicate how much of the total emissions are covered by the ETS. Some schemes could cover more sectors than shown in the figure due to the way liable entities are defined. The total emissions covered by the Kyoto ETS are not provided as it is a voluntary ETS.

Source: *The World Bank, State and Trends of Carbon Pricing, 2014, Washington, D.C.: The World Bank, 2014, Figure 13, p. 52. Accessed at: www-wds.worldbank.org/external/default/WDSContentServer/WDSP/IB/2014/05/27/000456286_20140527095323/ Rendered/PDF/882840AR0Carbo040Box385232B00OUO090.pdf on July 28, 2014.*

reducing its overall emission levels. In 2012, total emissions from its 28 members were between 17 and 19 percent below their 1990 level, well on their way to a target of 20 percent reduction by 2020.[5] A combination of carbon taxes, direct regulation, incentives for renewable energy, and the ETS have

---

[5.] See European Environment Agency, "Why Did Greenhouse Gas Emissions in the EU Decrease between 1990 and 2012?" Accessed July 28, 2014 at: www.eea.europe.eu/publications/why-are-greenhouse-gases-decreasing. Calculating the progress to Kyoto targets is complex, as is explained in this document.

TABLE 20-1 How Allowances Are Allocated in Emission Trading Systems

Jurisdiction	Free allocation		Purchase allowances		Other mechanisms or comments
	Benchmarking	Grand-fathering	Auction	Fixed	
EU ETS	●	●	●		● Grandfathering for process emissions only (<1% of allowances) Rest is benchmarking
Swiss ETS	●	●	●		● Grandfathering for process emissions only, rest is benchmarking
California CaT	●	●	●	○	● Allowances must be resold at auction
RGGI			●		
Alberta SGER					● Other mechanism: crediting (earning emission allowances after reductions made)
Québec CaT		●	●	○	
KAZ ETS		●			
Australia CPM	●	●		○	
NZ ETS	●	●		○	
Tokyo, Saitama and Kyoto CaT					● Other mechanism: crediting (earning emission allowances after reductions made)
Beijing Pilot ETS	●	●			
Chongqing Pilot ETS	○	○	○	○	○ No information available at this moment
Guangdong Pilot ETS	●	●	●		
Hubei Pilot ETS	●	●	●		
Shanghai Pilot ETS	●	●			
Shenzhen Pilot ETS	●				
Tianjin Pilot ETS	●	●			
Korea ETS	●	●			

The table shows how the allowances are distributed in each ETS.

Source: *The World Bank, State and Trends of Carbon Pricing, 2014, Washington, D.C.: The World Bank, 2014, Figure 14, p. 53. Accessed at: www-wds.worldbank.org/external/default/WDSContentServer/WDSP/IB/2014/05/27/000456286_20140527095323/ Rendered/PDF/882840AR0Carbo040Box385232B00OUO090.pdf on July 28, 2014.*

contributed to the overall decrease in emissions. The ETS is notable as being the first mandatory GHG trading system and has operated in a series of phases. Phase III began in 2013. Its contribution to the decline in emissions is controversial due to design issues that affect the overall performance of the market. These include:

- While trading was EU wide, a cap was set per country. This created complexity in determining compliance and the current system now has an EU-wide cap on the total number of allowances set per sector covered. From 2013 onwards, the cap on emissions from power stations and other fixed installations will be reduced by 1.74 percent every year.[6]

- Aviation has a separate cap.

- Allowances (permits) were allocated to covered entities during the first two trading periods rather than auctioned and many observers argue too many were allocated. Starting in 2013, the system became mixed with 100 percent of the allowances auctioned for electricity production, and a transition for industrial sources from 80 percent freely allocated in 2013 to 30 percent by 2020. One reason given for continuing free allocation is to minimize carbon leakage for those sectors that are energy intensive and trade exposed. As noted above, when allowances are allocated, rules are needed for distribution, raising the complexity of the system compared to auctioning and creating potential for over-allocation.

The recession of 2007–2009 reduced economic activity worldwide. With the allocation system in place in the ETS (an inflexible and pre-determined cap leading to a fixed number of allowances), there was a surplus of allowances and prices have been volatile, plummeting from approximately U.S. \$40 a tonne (€29) before the recession to as low as \$4/tonne (€3) in 2013. The ETS did not have a mechanism to stabilize the market in light of a major and unforeseen macroeconomic event such as the recession. This then led to uncertainty about how the EU would adjust the provisions of the trading system. Member states went back and forth about issues such as 'backloading,' which withholds permits from auction temporarily to decrease the total supply. The ETS members finally agreed to withhold from auction 400 million allowances in 2014, 300 million in 2015, and 200 million in 2016 to help stabilize the market. When and if these allowances will be reintroduced is a design issue that may contribute to continued market instability. Time will tell if the revisions to the ETS design help improve its operation.[7]

The Western Climate Initiative: California and Quebec. The Western Climate Initiative (WCI) was to be a regional cap-and-trade market. Initially, four Canadian provinces (B.C., Manitoba, Ontario, and Quebec) signed on in addition to a number of the western U.S. states, led by California. For political and economic reasons, six of the original signatories in the U.S. have withdrawn from the agreement, and others have put implementation on hold (e.g., B.C., Ontario, Manitoba). The first two jurisdictions to engage in emission trading are California and Quebec. The WCI sets an overall target reduction in greenhouse gas (GHG) emissions of 15 percent below 2005 levels by 2020. California's target is to reduce emissions to their 1990 level by 2020, while Quebec's is a 20 percent reduction from its 1990 level by 2020. It covers large stationary sources emitting 25,000 tonnes of CO_2e or more. These sectors include combustion at industrial and commercial facilities, industrial process emission sources including oil and gas process emissions, and electricity generation. The market will operate in what are called compliance periods that vary in length. GHGs from residential, commercial, and industrial fuel combustion at facilities with emissions below the threshold as well as transportation fuel combustion from gasoline and diesel are to come into the system in the second compliance period

---

[6.] For details on the current state of the ETS, see European Commission, "The EU Emissions Trading System (EU ETS)," European Commission, 2013. Accessed July 28, 2014 at http://ec.europa.eu/clima/publications/docs/factsheet_ets_en.pdf.

[7.] For additional information about the performance of the ETS, see European Union, "The ETS in Perspective," accessed August 1, 2014 at www.c2es.org/docUploads/EU-ETS-In-Perspective-Report.pdf.

in 2015, but individual units will not hold allowances as this would be impractical. Allowances will be distributed to entities upstream of these points of discharge where the fuels enter into commerce. The coverage is thus quite comprehensive and by 2015, expects to cover 87 percent of total California emissions and 77 percent of total emissions in Quebec. Key design features of the WCI include:[8]

- Auctioning. The WCI mandates a minimum of 10 percent of allowances must be auctioned in the initial compliance period; rising to 25 percent by 2020.

- Measures to minimize price volatility. The WCI will allow banking but not borrowing.

- Offsets. The WCI omits fugitive emissions from agriculture and forestry due to the complexity and high cost of monitoring these sources, but allows offsets from these sectors.

Performance of the WCI in its initial year was largely as expected. California prices for the 2013–2014 vintage allowances ranged between $10 and $18 (U.S.) per allowance (per tonne CO_2e), with volumes ranging from approximately 12 to 23 million tonnes throughout the year. In Quebec, average trading volume was 1 million tonnes up to February 2014, at prices ranging from $7 to $10 (Canadian). The two markets are to be integrated in 2014. Whether other jurisdictions will join the WCI remains to be seen.

Regional Greenhouse Gas Initiative. This TEP system covers emissions from power plants in nine Northeast and Mid-Atlantic states of the U.S. The program reduced its overall cap by 45 percent in 2014 to 91 million short tons of CO_2 and it will decline 2.5 percent each year from 2015 to 2020. Prices have fluctuated around a narrow range of $2 to $4 (U.S.) per ton since operations began in 2008.

Alberta's Specified Gas Emitters Regulation. We end with Alberta as an example of a hybrid system that will segue to our discussion of carbon taxes. The Alberta system is not a standard cap-and-trade system, but rather a baseline-and-credit system where the regulator establishes a baseline level of emissions for each covered source and emitters that reduce emissions beyond the baseline can earn **credits**, which can be traded at market rates among other emitters. The baseline is a requirement for covered emitters to reduce their GHG **emissions intensity of pollution** 12 percent compared to its level in 2003–2005. Sources that emit more than 0.1 million tonnes CO_2e per year are covered. In aggregate this means approximately 50 percent of Alberta's total emissions are covered by the regulation. Emitters can meet their reduction obligation in three ways in addition to abating emissions:

- Deliver credits to the Alberta government earned by reducing their emissions more than 12 percent. The credits can be banked for future use or sold to other facilities.

- Deliver offset credits for projects created by the Alberta government.

- Pay into a Climate Change and Emission Management fund at a set price of $15 per tonne for emissions above the 12 percent target. The funds are used by the Alberta government to invest in projects that help reduce GHG emissions. As of 2013, close to $400-million was collected in the fund.

Thus, this system differs from the TEP examples above in a number of ways. It is based on emissions intensity rather than the level of emissions. There is no overall cap on emissions due to the presence of the tax option and the credits. Progress to date appears to show that Alberta has reduced its emissions by approximately 40 million tonnes since 2007. The program expired in September 2014 and substantive changes may be forthcoming. We turn now to a look at other carbon pricing policies in Canada.

[8.] See Purdon, Houle, and Lachapelle (2014) for a comprehensive examination of the WCI in California and Quebec.

LO 3

Canadian Policy to Reduce GHG Emissions

Canadian federal policy is based largely on direct regulation and subsidies to encourage substitution away from carbon-intensive fuels. There is no federal carbon tax or TEP system. The main features of federal policy are:

- subsidies to renewable energy, ethanol;
- technological incentives to find ways to sequester carbon dioxide (e.g., carbon capture and storage);
- moral suasion to induce people to reduce their emissions;
- voluntary agreements with industry to reduces their GHG emissions;
- incentives to increase **energy efficiency** (e.g., increase vehicle fuel efficiency);
- direct regulations to be introduced for emitting sectors.

Why economists are leery of mandated fuel content rules. Canada's Bill C-33 requires gasoline sold in Canada to contain 5 percent renewable fuel content as of 2010. On the surface, this policy sounds like it will help reduce GHG emissions, but it is possible emissions could rise. One has to look at the life cycle of production of the renewable fuels to estimate net impact on GHGs. Ethanol production requires plant matter. In Canada much of this has come from corn, an energy-intensive crop that uses considerable amounts of fertilizer. The production of the fertilizer requires energy that typically comes from fossil fuels. The corn then has to be refined into ethanol. At least one ethanol refinery in Canada burned coal to process its ethanol. Coal is one of the highest producers of GHGs per unit of energy (Gigajoule). The U.S. EPA estimates that ethanol produced from corn using coal as an energy source will increase GHGs by 13 to 34 percent (depending on the time horizon and discountrate used). By comparison, biodiesel produced from waste grease reduces GHGs by 80 percent. Thus, regulations that specify fuel content, but don't look at life cycle GHGs, may be counterproductive.

See EPA "Lifecycle Analysis of Greenhouse Gas Emissions from Renewable Fuels," EPA 420-F-09-024, May 2009, at www.epa.gov/oms/renewablefuels/420f09024.htm, accessed October 15, 2010.

Our focus is on carbon pricing policies of the Canadian provinces. Table 20-2 shows provincial emission levels over time as well as their 2020 emission reduction targets. Canadian provinces had adopted their own versions of many of the federal policies—energy efficiency incentives, subsidies to promote the use of renewable energy sources to generate electricity, consumer information on how to reduce GHG emissions, subsidies for technology, etc., but starting in 2007, a number of provinces began to take more substantive action to use pricing to aid in reaching the targets most had set for the year 2020. Each province has set explicit target reductions in their GHG emissions from a base year to a target year. Canadian provinces and the country as a whole face many challenges. Note that two provinces—Ontario and Quebec—have reduced their emissions below their 1990 level. The marginal abatement cost at province's 2020 targets ranges from a low of $134 in Alberta to a high of $266 in B.C. The range is due in part to the carbon intensity of electricity generation. Because Alberta and Saskatchewan use coal as their major feedstock, the substitution of lower-carbon fuels could provide them with significant GHG reductions. GHG reductions in other provinces will have to come from other sources due to their use of zero-carbon hydroelectricity. The bottom line is that no single policy instrument, even carbon pricing in the form of a tax or cap-and-trade system will allow the provinces to reach their targets cost effectively. There is no uniform carbon price across the country that will allow each province to meet its target. Provinces thus need to employ a suite of policies to reduce GHG emissions as well as provide incentives to invest in new technologies to reduce emissions and/or sequester carbon.

TABLE 20-2   Provincial GHG Targets, Emissions, and Marginal Abatement Costs

Province	1990 GHG Emissions Mt CO_2e (million tonnes)	2012 GHG Emissions Mt	Emission Reduction Target for 2020	Estimated Marginal Abatement Costs to Reach Target
British Columbia	49	60	33% below 2007 level (22 Mt)	$266/tonne CO_2e
Alberta	170	249	50 Mt below business as usual	$159
Saskatchewan	44	75	20% below individual baselines	$134
Manitoba	19	21	6% below 1990 level	$226
Ontario	177	167	15% below 1990 level	$257
Quebec	84	78	20% below 1990 level	$219
Canada	591	699	17% below 2005 level	

Sources: *Emissions data: Greenhouse Gas Emissions Tables. Accessed November 3, 2014 at www.ec.gc.ca/indicateurs-indicators/default.asp?=BFB1B398#ghg4.*

Emissions targets: Provincial Web pages.

Marginal abatement costs: Nic Rivers, "Federal and Provincial Climate Change Policy: Repeating Past Mistakes?" in Tom Courchene and John Allen (eds.) Carbon Pricing and Environmental Federalism, in the series, Canada, The State of the Federation, 2009. Montreal: Queen's-McGill Press, 2010.

Consider the following identity that expands on the one presented in Chapter 1.

$$GHG = [(GHG/Energy) \bullet (Energy/Output) \bullet (output)]$$

An energy efficiency policy only addresses the ratio of energy to output. Subsidies to renewable energy affect the GHG/Energy ratio. An emission standard covers [(GHG/Energy) • (Energy/Output)]. It is only carbon pricing that covers all three terms on the right-hand side. This is one important reason why economists feel carbon pricing is a necessary part of any climate change policy package. Table 20-3 illustrates the type of carbon pricing policies implemented at the provincial level.

TABLE 20-3 Provincial Carbon Pricing Policies

Province	Carbon Pricing Policy	Date Enacted or Expected Implementation	Approximate Percent of GHGs Covered
British Columbia	Carbon tax at $30 per tonne CO_2e by	2008	77%
	Western Climate Initiative (WCI) signatory	Legislation 2008, implementation on hold	50% initially rising to 80% over time
Alberta	Intensity-based cap and trade with a ceiling at $15/tonne; paid into a technology fund energy industry can access	2007	55%
Saskatchewan	None	—	—
Manitoba	WCI signatory	Implementation date tbd	50% rising to 80%
Ontario	WCI signatory	Implementation date tbd	50% rising to 80%
Quebec	Carbon tax at $3/tonne CO_2e	2007	70%
	WCI signatory	Implemented in 2013	50% rising to 80%
New Brunswick, Nova Scotia, Prince Edward Island, Newfoundland & Labrador	None	—	—

Source: *Adapted and updated from Nic Rivers, "Federal and Provincial Climate Change Policy: Repeating Past Mistakes?" in Tom Courchene and John Allen (eds.), Carbon Pricing and Environmental Federalism, in the series, Canada, The State of the Federation, 2009 (Montreal: Queen's-McGill Press, 2010).*

Carbon Taxes in Canada

British Columbia's carbon tax was noted in Chapter 17. It is a broad-based tax that covers all GHG sources from combustion in the province. Emissions not covered are predominately 'fugitive emissions' not easily measured that need to be covered by regulations, methane from agriculture and landfills, and non-combustion industrial sources. The majority of B.C.'s emissions emanate from transportation. This is because unlike some other parts of Canada (e.g., Alberta, Saskatchewan, Ontario and some of the Maritime provinces), a very small share of GHG emissions comes from the combustion of fossil fuels to generate electricity. B.C., like Manitoba and Quebec, rely predominately on hydroelectricity. By applying to all motive fuels, the carbon tax in B.C. thus covers these significant sources of GHGs. When the legislation for the carbon tax was introduced, the government announced the tax rates through to 2012. Starting at $10 per tonne CO_2e, the tax would rise each year by another $5/tonne. The rate now stands at $30 per tonne, frozen at that level by the provincial government until further notice. As explained in Chapter 12, all the revenues from the carbon taxes collected flow back to households and industry in the form of cuts to personal and corporate income tax rates, tax credits for low income and rural households, and some property tax relief for industry. In fact, the tax has been 'revenue negative' as noted in Chapter 12.

B.C.'s carbon tax led to heated political debate when first introduced, and the rhetoric from opposing parties and individuals tried to paint the carbon tax as unfair, a 'gas tax,' and conveniently ignored its broad base and return of tax revenues to the province. The "axe the tax" movement was prevalent in the 2009 provincial election, but did not lead to a change in government. Since that time, opposition has mostly abated. B.C.'s carbon tax was hailed worldwide as a textbook tax on pollution, just as put forth in Chapter 12. While it is still early to gauge its success in reducing GHG emissions, early indications are that it is having an impact.[9] Table 20-4 compares B.C.'s GHG performance to the rest of Canada. We see that there is a significant difference in per capita reductions with B.C.'s falling 10 percent over the period from the time the tax was implemented to 2011. Critics had argued that the 2007 to 2009 recession was the primary factor contributing to reductions in GHG emissions, but there are two reasons why that argument may not apply. First, as Table 20-4 shows, BC's emissions continued to fall after 2009, while those in the rest of Canada rose in 2011. Second, B.C.'s per capita GDP fell by less than the rest of Canada over the period 2008 to 2011 (−0.15 percent compared to −0.23 percent) and its GDP growth in 2010 and 2011 grew marginally more than that of the rest of Canada. Sales of all major petroleum fuels fell in B.C., while gasoline and diesel sales rose in the rest of Canada.

TABLE 20-4   Reductions in GHG Emissions, B.C. and Canada, 2008 to 2011

	2008	2009	2010	2011	Total 2008–2011
B.C.	−1.5%	−6.7%	−1.1%	−2.4%	−10.0%
Rest of Canada	−3.6%	−3.9%	−0.9%	+3.9%	−1.1%

Note: GHG emissions data are from Environment Canada, National Inventory Report; population data from Statistics Canada, as cited in Elgie and McClay (2013). Excludes aviation and fugitive emissions and those from electricity and heat generation.

Figure 20-4 shows B.C.'s progression to its target of a 33 percent reduction in GHG emissions by 2020. B.C. will face challenges if planned development of its natural gas deposits occurs. Whether carbon tax rates will rise above $30 per tonne is something to watch.

Is there room in Canada to introduce more carbon pricing and raise the prices we see in B.C.'s carbon tax, Alberta's Specified Gas Emitters Regulation, and Quebec's cap-and-trade TEP system? A recent study by Lachapelle (2010) compares Canada to other OECD countries, and also reports rates of **implicit carbon taxes** in Canada over time.[10] The tax rates are shown per tonne of CO_2 to ensure a common metric and values are converted to Canadian dollars (adjusting for exchange rates).

Table 20-5 shows the large range in implicit carbon tax rates for Canada, the U.S., and a selection of European countries.

TABLE 20-5   Implicit Carbon Tax Rates Across OECD Countries, 2008 (in Canadian $/tonne CO2)

Fossil Fuel	Canada	United States	Germany	United Kingdom	Norway
Gasoline	$146	$62	$590	$560	$625
Diesel	99	56	273	368	275
Light fuel oil	34	17	108	93	229
Heavy fuel oil	17	9	13	50	72
Steam coal	0	0	0	3	34
Natural gas (industrial use)	0	0	17	5	N/A

Source: *Data from International Energy Association as compiled by Erick Lachapelle, "The Hidden Factor in Climate Policy: Tracking Implicit Carbon Taxes in the OECD and Implications for Canadian Policy Makers" (2010) (Ottawa: Sustainable Prosperity), www.sustainableprosperity.ca.*

---

[9] For more in-depth discussion of the impact of B.C.'s carbon tax see: Elgie and McClay (2013), Rivers and Schaufele (2013), and www.sustainableprosperity.ca.

[10] Erick Lachapelle. "The Hidden Factor in Climate Policy: Tracking Implicit Carbon Taxes in the OECD and Implications for Canadian Policy Makers" (2010) (Ottawa: Sustainable Prosperity), www.sustainableprosperity.ca.

FIGURE 20-4 Progression to GHG Targets in British Columbia

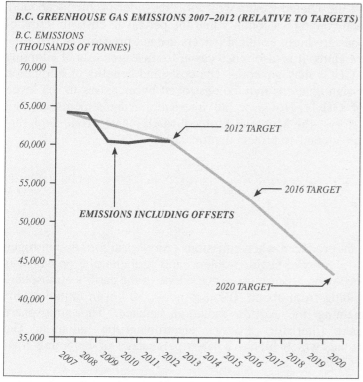

B.C. GREENHOUSE GAS EMISSIONS 2007–2012 (RELATIVE TO TARGETS)

Source: *"B.C. Greenhouse Gas Emissions 2007–2012 (Relative to Targets)" found on page 4 of Province of British Columbia publication Climate Action in British Columbia—2014 Progress Report at http://www.env.gov.bc.ca/cas/pdfs/2014-Progress-to-Targets.pdf. Copyright © Province of British Columbia. All rights reserved. Reproduced with permission of the Province of British Columbia.*

Two points are immediately clear:

1. Canada, while having implicit carbon tax rates that are above those of the United States, has rates significantly below those in Europe.

2. Implicit carbon taxes are inversely related to the carbon intensity of the fuel. The lowest rates in all countries are on the most carbon intensive fuel—steam coal.

Canadian governments thus have 'fiscal room' to raise these taxes to keep pace with inflation. Raising these tax rates would provide stronger incentives to reduce GHG emissions.

WHY DO INTERNATIONAL ENVIRONMENTAL AGREEMENTS WORK OR NOT?

Climate Change: Countries meet every other year as part of the UN Framework Agreement on Climate Change (UNFCC) process to discuss setting targets to reduce GHG emissions and policies to help achieve these targets. There was hope that the meeting in Copenhagen in 2009 would result in an international accord with specific targets set for major emitters, but the meeting ended with a weak statement that promised to provide more funds to developing countries for climate adaptation, but no meaningful agreement on targets or policies. However, even if a country signs an agreement to cut their GHG emissions, there is no method by which it can be forced to meet its targets. Some of the world's largest sources of GHGs, notably China, India, and the United States, continue to emit large quantities of CO_2. World emissions continue to rise as we saw in Chapter 1. Countries ask why they should reduce their emissions if China and the United States will not. Free-rider problems abound. Fossil fuels are such a pervasive part of each country's economy that the perceived costs in terms of forgone output from reducing GHG emissions are high. Political leaders are not prepared to make the current sacrifices to achieve uncertain future gains. It is also much easier to measure costs of adopting a policy than the benefits the reduction of GHGs may generate. The costs and benefits of mitigation are also very unequally distributed. Small island nations may be destroyed by increases in sea level, yet they contribute negligible amounts of GHGs. However, all international agreements are not doomed to fail. We turn first to a success story—the Montreal Protocol to eliminate ozone-depleting compounds, and then look at examples of agreements to protect natural capital.[11]

LO 4

OZONE DEPLETION

The Environmental Problem

At the surface of the earth ozone is a pollutant produced when emissions of hydrocarbons and nitrogen oxides interact in the presence of sunlight. A variety of health problems and agricultural crop damages have been traced to elevated levels of surface ozone. But most of the ozone in the earth's atmosphere is located in the stratosphere, a zone extending from about 10 km to about 50 km in altitude. This stratospheric ozone is critical in maintaining the earth's radiation balance. The atmosphere surrounding the earth essentially acts as a filter for incoming electromagnetic radiation. The atmospheric gas responsible for this is ozone, which blocks a large percentage of incoming low-wavelength, or ultraviolet, radiation.

Several decades ago scientific evidence began to appear that the ozone content of the atmosphere was showing signs of diminishing. In the late 1970s a large hole appeared in the ozone layer over Antarctica. Significant ozone reduction has now been found throughout the entire stratosphere, including parts of Canada, Australia, New Zealand, and South America. In the 1970s scientists discovered the cause of this phenomenon. It had been known for some time that the chemical content of the atmosphere has been changing at a rapid rate and on a global scale. Atmospheric concentrations of carbon dioxide, nitrous oxide, and various chlorinated gases were increasing at rates of 0.2 percent to 5.0 percent per year.[12] Ozone disappearance was linked to the accumulation of chlorine in the stratosphere. The source of the chlorine turned out to be a variety of manufactured chemicals that, released at ground level, slowly migrated up to higher altitudes. The culprits are substances called halocarbons. The primary halocarbons are called chlorofluorocarbons (CFCs) and halons.

[11.] Another international treaty that addresses environmental issues is the North American Free Trade Agreement (NAFTA) signed by Canada, the United States, and Mexico in 1993. NAFTA contains a 'side agreement' that addresses the impacts of trade on the environment. The objective of this agreement was to monitor the impacts of trade liberalization on the environment in the three countries to ensure that pollution did not rise as a result of greater volumes of trade or by creating incentives for industries to move to regions where environmental regulations were less strict. An agency, the Commission for Environmental Cooperation (CEC), was created to address these concerns, help prevent trade and environment conflicts, and promote enforcement of international environmental law. The CEC provides environmental information on the three countries and produces reports in a number of areas including biodiversity conservation, the impact of the economy on the environment, the effects of toxic chemicals on health and the environment, and enforcement of environmental regulations. Their web page is: www.cec.org.

[12.] Robert T. Watson, "Atmospheric Ozone," in James G. Titus (ed.), *Effects of Changes in Stratospheric Ozone and Global Climate,* Volume 1, Overview (Washington, D.C.: U.S. Environmental Protection Agency, 1986), 69.

CFCs were developed in the 1930s as a replacement for the refrigerants in use at the time. CFCs are extremely stable, non-toxic, and inert relative to the electrical and mechanical machinery in which they are used. Thus their use spread quickly as refrigerants and also as propellants for aerosols (hairsprays, deodorants, insecticides), industrial agents for making polyurethane and polystyrene foams, and industrial cleaning agents and solvents. Halons are widely used as fire suppressors. When these substances were introduced attention was exclusively on their benefits; there was no evidence that they could have long-run impacts on the atmosphere. After surface release, they drift up through the troposphere into the stratosphere, where they begin a long process of ozone destruction.

It was thought that ozone depletion might confine itself to small parts of the stratosphere, in which case damages from the increasing surface flux of ultraviolet radiation would be limited. But strong evidence has appeared that damages are likely to be much more widespread. Scientists generally believe that each 1 percent drop in stratospheric ozone will produce a 2 to 3 percent increase in ultraviolet radiation at the earth's surface.[13] On this basis, radiation increases over this century are expected to be at least 3–4 percent at the tropics and 10–12 percent at the higher latitudes. Two main sources of damage from ozone depletion are health impacts and agricultural crop losses. Health damages are related to the increased incidence of skin cancers (including melanomas, the most dangerous form of skin cancer) and eye disease such as cataracts in both humans and animals. Increased UVB radiation can also be expected to increase food production costs because of the physical damages it produces in growing plants. Damages are also expected in other parts of the earth's physical ecosystem, such as phytoplankton, a vital organism in the food chain in oceans.

Policy Responses: The Montreal Protocol

The seriousness of the ozone-depletion problem led to some vigorous policy responses. Initially several countries took unilateral actions. In 1978, Canada, the United States, Sweden, Norway, and Denmark banned CFCs in aerosol cans, but not as a refrigerant. In the 1980s the continued scientific evidence of ozone depletion led to international action. Under the auspices of the United Nations, in 1987, 24 nations signed the *Montreal Protocol on Substances That Deplete the Ozone Layer*. It committed the high CFC-using signatories to phasing down CFCs and halons to 50 percent of their 1986 levels, to be achieved by 1998. Signatory countries then using low levels of CFCs were given a 10-year grace period: starting in 1999 they were to cut back to 1995–1997 levels.

Soon after the Montreal agreement it became clear that this reduction was not enough for two reasons: continuing research showed that the problem was getting worse, and some large CFC-producing countries had not signed the original agreement. In 1990 the Montreal Protocol countries agreed to phase out the production of CFCs completely by the year 2000, to add carbon tetrachloride and methyl chloroform to the list, and to introduce a longer-run schedule for phasing out HCFCs. It also instituted a fund, created from contributions of developed countries, to be used to help finance CFC-reducing technological changes in developing countries. Additional countries signed the agreement in subsequent years. In the 1991 meeting, China finally agreed to sign the protocol, leaving only India as the major CFC-using nation still outside the agreement. In 1992, phase-out of ozone-depleting compounds was accelerated once again. It was believed that substitution of hydrochlorofluorocarbons (HCFCs) for CFCs would result in limiting equivalent CFC use to 5 percent of its 1989 level. HCFCs were then supposed to be phased out by 2030. Another ozone-depleting substance, methyl bromide, used as a pesticide and soil fumigant, was to be frozen at 1991 production levels by the year 1995. The

---

[13.] Alphonse Forziati, "The Chlorofluorocarbon Problem," in John H. Cumberland, James R. Hibbs, and Irving Hoch (eds.), *The Economics of Managing Chlorofluorocarbons* (Washington, D.C.: Resources for the Future, 1982), 54.

following factors help explain why the Montreal Protocol was a successful international treaty, while efforts to reach international agreement on how much to reduce GHGs have stalled.

> *Factors helping to make the Montreal Protocol a successful international treaty:*
>
> 1. *The link between the pollutants released and environmental damages was clearly established by the science.*
> 2. *Political leaders accepted the scientific evidence.*
> 3. *There were relatively few compounds responsible for ozone depletion. The CFC-producing industry comprises a few large chemical companies. So international policy has been driven not only by scientific results, but also by international competition in this industry. Large multinational firms such as DuPont have been leaders in developing substitutes for CFCs, and they, therefore, have led the charge for a CFC phase-out.*[14]
> 4. *The treaty contained a compensation method for developing countries that allowed them to sign the agreement. Without the compensation fund, developing countries would have been much less likely to participate because the costs of phasing out the ozone-depleting compounds would put a bigger burden on their economies than those of the wealthier nations.*[15]

Have the targets of the Montreal Protocol been met? For the developed countries, the answer is yes. Canada and the United States have eliminated the production and importation of CFCs, and are phasing out other ozone-depleting compounds. Each country enforces its own cutbacks as it sees fit. One of the side effects of the ban was, however, a black market (especially in CFCs used as refrigerants) that operates out of some developing countries that have a longer time period to comply with the treaty. This undermines the protocol, allowing illegal CFC sales to continue in countries that have already banned production and consumption. There are no direct enforcement steps that may be undertaken by international authorities, in this or in any other agreement. International embarrassment is not enough of a deterrent to stop these practices. And, while great progress has been made on reducing the flow of new CFCs to the stratosphere, ozone depletion is only slowly diminishing due to the large stocks of ozone-depleting compounds still in the atmosphere. Scientists estimate it will take almost to mid-century before the process is completely reversed.

Policies Used by Canada and the United States to Phase Out CFCs

In economic terms, we have a problem here that is similar to the phasing out of leaded gasoline. The objective is reasonably clear and widely shared; the basic problem is how to bring it about in different countries. In advanced economies the main focus has been put on developing substitute chemicals that will perform the same tasks as CFCs—as refrigerants, cleaning agents, and so on—but that have little or no ozone-depleting impact. What essentially drove the rate of CFC phase-out in advanced economies was the cost of developing these substitutes, together with the costs of changeover from the old to the new chemicals. Some substances may be simply "drop-in" substitutes, while others will require getting rid of old capital equipment (refrigerators, air conditioners) and installing new equipment.

[14.] DuPont was very supportive of the Montreal Protocol because it had already developed substitutes for CFCs and was therefore in a position to capture a large share of the new market for these compounds.

[15.] The fund for developing countries is an example of the Coase theorem at work (refer back to Chapter 10). The parties bargained to a solution that internalizes the externality and compensates those made worse off.

Canada

To meet timetables agreed upon under the Montreal Protocol, each country adopted policies for production, imports, and exports of the targeted substances. In Canada, manufacture of CFCs ceased early in 1993. Consumption was banned in 1995. Environment Canada has used a type of *quota system* to phase out the chemicals. The quota limited total supply (production and importation) of CFCs and halons to their 1986 levels, beginning in 1989.[16] There were no restrictions on the supply of *specific* CFCs or halons: the quota was in terms of **ozone-depleting potential (ODP)**,[17] which allowed for flexibility in meeting the target. For example, a company can increase its production of a CFC compound with a low ODP as long as it cuts production of another CFC compound enough that the total ODP is not exceeded. Although the quota was not marketable, it is possible that private agreements were struck among the Canadian producers to redistribute production of the different CFC compounds in a cost-effective way. Total costs of the phase-out were likely lower than they would have been if producers had to meet specific quotas for each chemical. As well, the market system would work with regard to consumption. Given the quota on ODP, one would have expected to see price variability among the types of CFCs in response to production costs, degree of substitutability in use, and so on. The key point is that efficiency is enhanced by putting the quota on ODP rather than on each compound. However, as pointed out below, producers of CFCs could still have earned high profits due to the restriction in aggregate supply.

The United States

In the United States, the approach has been for the U.S. Environmental Protection Agency to allocate *transferable production quotas* among the five domestic CFC producers. Each of these firms is required to reduce its CFC production in stages to meet the mandated phase-out schedule. A major problem with setting production ceilings in this way is that it can lead to unwarranted increases in profits for current manufacturers of CFCs. In effect it gives firms in the industry, which may have been operating as rivals, a way of acting like monopolists.

Figure 20-5 illustrates the potential impact of the production ceiling using a simple market model. It shows a typical downward-sloping demand curve for CFCs, together with a flat marginal cost curve. In a competitive market, production would be at q_1 and a price that equals marginal production costs. But if public authorities limit production to q_2, the price increases to p_2, which is substantially above production costs. Area a is then the potential excess profits earned in the industry because of the output restrictions.

There was widespread feeling in the United States that at least some of these excess profits should accrue to the public. Several means were discussed. One was to auction off CFC production rights to the various chemical-producing companies. The bidding process, if it worked well, would transfer some portion of the excess profits to the public. The other approach, which was finally adopted, was to *tax the production of CFCs.*

[16.] Information on the Canadian CFC policy is taken from Douglas A. Smith, "The Implementation of Canadian Policies to Protect the Ozone Layer," in G. Bruce Doern, *Getting It Green* (Toronto: C. D. Howe Institute), 1990.

[17.] The ozone-depletion potential (ODP) of a compound is defined as the estimated ozone depletion of a unit mass of the compound divided by the ozone depletion of a unit mass of CFC-11.

FIGURE 20-5 Government-Imposed Production Limitations Lead to Monopoly Profits

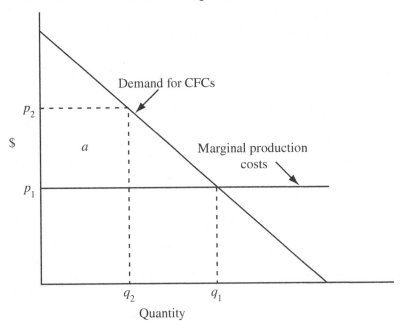

A production ceiling of q_2 in an industry leads to a price, p_2, which is above the competitive price of p_1. Area a represents the excess profits earned in the industry due to the production ceiling.

In theory, a tax equal to $(p_2 - p_1)$ would transfer all of the excess profits to the public. It could then be used for any number of purposes, perhaps put into general revenues or used specifically to help the CFC conversion process. The system adopted establishes a base tax rate, then sets different taxes on the various ozone-depleting chemicals according to the expression:

$$\text{Tax rate} = \text{Base rate} \times \text{Ozone-depleting potential}$$

Canada did not experiment with any taxes on ozone-depleting chemicals. One of the difficulties seen with using a tax in Canada is that we import products containing ozone-depleting chemicals. The U.S. deals with this problem by levying a tax on the amount of these chemicals in the products. Canadian officials were unwilling to implement this complex tax. To deal with the problem of these compounds still in use in refrigerators, air conditioners, and other products, all provinces began implementing CFC recycling and recovery initiatives in 1993. The most common approach has been to use regulations on the disposal of products containing ozone-depleting compounds rather than any economic incentive-based strategies.

The Montreal Protocol also contains a type of pollution-trading arrangement that could reduce the overall cost of meeting its targets. This is the trading of emission-reduction credits among countries. Thus, if a country fails to meet its required production cutback because of the needs of "industrial rationalization," it is supposed to offset the excess emissions by getting comparable reductions in other countries.

LO 5

BIOLOGICAL DIVERSITY AND PROTECTING NATURAL CAPITAL

A global problem of perhaps great importance to the survival of life on earth is the worldwide destruction of natural capital, and, in particular, reduction in diversity among the elements of the biological system. Biological diversity refers to several levels: diversity in the stock of genetic material, species diversity, or diversity among ecosystems. But the long-run health of the whole system requires that there be diversity among its parts. Biological uniformity produces inflexibility and weakened ability to respond to new circumstances; diversity gives a system the means to adapt to change.

The human population cannot maintain itself without cultivating certain species of animals and plants. But the continued vigour of this relationship actually also depends on the stock of wild species. About 25 percent of the prescription drugs in the developed societies are derived from plants.[18] Diseases are not static; they evolve in response to efforts made to eradicate them. Thus, wild species of plants constitute a vital source of raw material needed for future medicines. Wild species are also critical for agriculture. Through traditional plant and animal breeding, and even more through modern methods of biotechnology, genetic material and the qualities they entail may be transferred from wild species into cultivated ones. In 1979, a species of wild maize resistant to an important crop virus was discovered in a remote corner of Mexico. When transferred to species of domestic corn, this characteristic substantially enhanced the agricultural value of that crop.

The stock of species at any particular time is a result of two processes: the random mutations that create new species of organisms and the forces that determine rates of extinction among existing species. Scientists currently estimate the number of extant species at between 5 and 10 million, of which about 1.4 million have been described. When a species goes extinct, we lose forever whatever valuable qualities that organism may have had. The normal, long-run rate of species extinction has been estimated at about 9 percent per million years, or 0.000009 percent per year.[19] Thus, this is the normal rate at which the information contained in the species stock vanishes. At several times in the geological past, the rate of extinctions has been very much higher. One of these times was the period, millions of years ago, during which the dinosaurs died off. Another is today. But while the earlier period was the result of natural causes, today's rapid destruction of the stock of species is due primarily to the actions of human beings.

Some species go extinct because they are over-exploited. But the vast majority are under pressure because of habitat destruction. This comes primarily from commercial pressures to exploit other features of the land—logging the trees for timber or wood, converting the land to agricultural uses, clearing the land for urban expansion, and so on. This has been a particular problem in many developing countries, which contain a disproportionately large share of the world's wild species, but which are also under great pressure to pursue modern economic development. Developed countries have already undergone massive changes in habitats and have seen extinction of species and reductions in biological diversity.

[18.] U.S. Office of Technology Assessment, *Technologies to Sustain Tropical Forest Resources and Biological Diversity* (Washington, D.C., May 1992), 60.

[19.] Edward O. Wilson (ed.), *Biodiversity* (Washington, D.C.: National Academy Press, 1986).

The information contained in the global stock of genetic capital has consistently been undervalued. This is partly because we do not know what is there or what portions of it may turn out to be important in the future. It is also because, almost by definition, it is impossible to know the value of the genes in a species that has gone extinct: How can society value something it never realized it had? But primarily the undervaluation of the stock of wild germ plasm is a function of the institutional structures governing the management of wild species. Whereas the market values of conventional products ensure that their production will be pursued with vigour, there are normally no comparable market values for the information contained in the wild gene pool.

Canada's efforts with regard to biological diversity are varied, but involve little in the way of specific regulation. The federal government passed endangered species legislation in 2002. Canada monitors certain at-risk species, particularly migratory birds. The federal government contributes to the Endangered Species Recovery Fund, which involves the World Wildlife Fund Canada, the Natural Sciences and Engineering Research Council, and Environment Canada. The fund's objective is to support universities and the private sector in undertaking projects that benefit endangered species and their habitat. Canada is also a signatory of the U.N. Convention on Biological Diversity and CITES—the Convention on International Trade in Endangered Species. There are a number of other international conventions devoted to the protection of species and prevention of pollution in oceans, as well as protection of specific species (e.g., whales) from harvest. The federal government has set aside land as protected space, and is investigating the creation of more wildlife corridors to permit migration of species. Some provincial governments have been active in setting aside land in parks. However, only 10 percent of Canada's vast lands are in protected areas. Many natural areas, especially those close to urban development are highly threatened.

The effective maintenance of **biological diversity** (or biodiversity) depends on the maintenance of habitats in amounts big enough that species may preserve themselves in complex biological equilibria. This involves first identifying valuable habitats and then protecting them from development pressures that are incompatible with preserving the resident species. Canada has a network of reserved lands that have been preserved in the public domain in national and provincial parks, wilderness areas, wildlife refuges, and the like. However, the world's primary areas of genetic and species abundance and diversity are in developing countries in Central and South America, Africa, and Southeast Asia.[20]

Efforts have been made in some of these countries, sometimes vigorously and sometimes not, to protect areas of high biological value by putting them into some sort of protected status—sanctuaries, reserves, parks, and so on. But here the situation is usually much more complicated by high-population pressures. People who are struggling to get enough resources to achieve some degree of economic security may feel that something called "biological diversity" is not particularly relevant. Land reservation for species preservation is essentially a zoning approach, and it suffers the same fundamental flaw of that policy: it does not reshape the underlying incentives that are leading to population pressure on the habitats.

One suggestion that has been made to change this is to create a more complete system of property rights over genetic resources. At the present time, property rights are recognized for special breeder stock, genetically engineered organisms, and newly developed medicines. This provides a strong incentive for research on new drugs and the development of improved crops. But this incentive does not extend backward to the protection of wild gene plasm, especially in developing countries. Some have suggested clarifying property rights in wild species, then letting countries themselves exercise

---

20. The countries especially recognized for biological diversity are Mexico, Colombia, Brazil, Zaire, Madagascar, and Indonesia.

these property rights in world markets for genetic information.[21] By being allowed to sell the rights to parts of the genetic stock, countries would have a way of realizing the values inherent in these stocks and so would be motivated to devote more effort and resources to their protection. Countries would also have stronger incentives to inventory and describe species that are still unknown.

Despite these efforts, habitat destruction and species loss continue to occur. There is still much more to do both nationally and internationally. This chapter just alerts the reader to this topic, vital to the earth's survival. Ultimately, each one of us will have to decide what sort of world we want to live in. If it is one with diverse and healthy ecosystems, environmental consequences of economic decisions will need to be assessed. This text has provided an introduction to the role that environmental economics and economists can play in a quest for better environmental quality.

Summary

The world is now faced with a number of global environmental problems, especially those dealing with the disruption of the global atmosphere. These are public externalities in the purest form. Burning fossil fuels has increased the CO_2 content of the atmosphere and may affect the earth's radiation balance and lead to an increase in mean global temperatures and other climate changes. Major climate change would affect all aspects of life and economic activity on the planet—aquatic and terrestrial life, agriculture and forestry, water supplies and levels, and much more. A rise in the sea level will have profound impacts on coastal communities. Reduction in CO_2 emissions will require cutting back on the use of fossil fuels and other GHG-generating activities. All countries are dependent to a greater or lesser extent on fossil fuels to power their economies. Cost-effective policies such as carbon taxes and tradeable permits could be used to improve energy efficiency and to provide incentives to switch to fuels that emit less CO_2. International consensus on reducing GHG emissions is now largely form without substance. The record of Canada's federal government has been abysmal—while there are a number of programs supporting the reduction of GHG emissions, there are no explicit price incentives to help spur substitution away from carbon-intensive fuels and activities at the federal level. A number of Canadian provinces are taking more definitive steps including the introduction of carbon taxes and an emissions trading.

Depletion of the earth's protective ozone layer has been a result of the widespread use of chlorofluorocarbons for refrigerants, solvents, and other uses. The increased ultraviolet radiation this will produce at the earth's surface is expected to increase skin cancers and eye cataracts, and have a substantial impact on agricultural production. Chemical companies have had success in developing substitutes for CFCs. This greatly facilitated the signing of the Montreal Protocol, an international agreement among most of the nations of the world that has led to the phase-out of the production and consumption of CFCs.

The destruction of biological diversity is an insidious global problem because often people don't recognize how serious the impacts are on the planet until the species and ecosystems are gone. Dealing with this problem will require greater efforts and incentives to preserve habitat and promote economic activities compatible with species preservation.

---

21. See the discussion in Roger A. Sedjo, "Property Rights for Plants," *Resources* 97 (Fall 1989): 1–4.

Key Terms

Baseline-and-credit system

Biological diversity

Cap-and-trade system

Carbon allowances

Carbon offsets

Credits

Emissions intensity of pollution

Emission reduction targets

Energy efficiency

European Union's Emission Trading
    System (ETS)

Implicit carbon taxes

Ozone-depleting potential (ODP)

Price volatility

Analytical Problem

1. Using Figure 20-2, analyze the impact of a TEP system. Assume (1) that demand for the GHG-intensive good is perfectly inelastic, then (2) that supply is perfectly elastic. How then would the TDP system affect consumer and producer surplus, market prices, and output?

Discussion Questions

1. What are the potential costs and benefits of introducing a carbon tax in Canada? List these and explain.

2. Contrast mitigation with adaptation as means of addressing GHG emissions and accumulation in the atmosphere.

3. Should Canada adopt a carbon tax or TEP system for GHGs if no other countries do so? Take a position and defend it using economic arguments.

4. Why are TEP systems receiving more attention and interest than carbon taxes as instruments to help reduce GHGs?

5. Rather than placing a tax on fuels or the carbon content of fuels, taxes might be put on fuel-using items, such as gas-guzzling cars, less efficient appliances, or houses with poor insulation. Which type of tax would be more efficient?

6. Look at the data in Table 20-2. What factors do you think might explain why Canadian GHG emissions declined for some provinces and not others? Provide economic arguments.

Glossary

Abatement costs   The costs of reducing the quantity of residuals that are emitted into the environment or of lowering ambient concentrations of the residual.

Ability to pay   How much an individual can pay for something is determined by one's income level.

Accumulative pollutants   Pollutants that build up in the environment over time because they do not degrade or only do so very slowly. May also be called stock pollutants. Metals such as arsenic or mercury are an example.

Adaptation   Actions taken to adjust to, offset, or reduce the adverse impacts of climate change (or other major environmental changes).

Aggregate demand   The total demand for a particular good or service. It is derived from horizontal summation of the demand curves of all those who buy the good—the amount they want to buy at a given price. Aggregate demand for a public good is the vertical summation of the demand curves of the people consuming that good—the amount they are willing to pay for a given quantity.

Aggregate supply   The total supply of a particular good or service in a region by its producers. It is the horizontal summation of the individual supply curves of all the firms producing the good.

Ambient-based TEP system   A TEP system that could be used when pollutants are non-uniformly mixed. Permits cannot necessarily be traded one-for-one within a jurisdiction but must be based on the transfer coefficient for each source of the pollution.

Ambient damage functions   The relationship between the concentration of a waste product contained in a particular environmental medium (air, water) and measured at a particular location and the resulting damages to the environment.

Ambient standard   A never-exceed limit on the amount of a pollutant that can be present in the ambient environment. These are typically expressed in terms of average concentration levels over a specific interval of time (e.g., per hour, per day).

Ambient environmental quality   Ambient refers to the surrounding environment. Ambient quality is the quantity of pollutants in a particular region (e.g., the concentration of $SO2$ in the air over a city).

Anthropogenic   Something that is created by human activity; for example, anthropogenic releases of greenhouse gases caused by burning fossil fuels.

Assimilative capacity   The ability of the natural environment to render pollutants benign or less toxic.

Baseline-and-credit system   In a transferable emission market, credits may be given to polluters who document that they have a permanent reduction in their emissions of a pollutant. The credits can be used for compliance with regulations or sold to others.

Before-after approach   An examination of a policy change from the viewpoint of the new costs (and benefits) compared to the costs and benefits without the policy. This is not the appropriate way to undertake benefit-cost analysis.

Benefits   How much better off someone is by having something. They are conferred on an individual by giving him or her something they value in the sense of being willing to pay for that item.

Benefit–cost ratio   The ratio of total benefits of a project or policy to its total costs. This is a flawed criterion for ranking projects or policies because it is dependent upon the relative size of the project's benefits and costs, not its net benefits. Decisions based on these ratios may result in choosing a project that does not provide society with the maximum net benefits.

Biochemical oxygen demand (BOD)   The amount of oxygen required to decompose organic material under specified conditions of temperature and time.

Biological diversity   Biodiversity, for short, is the variability of living species and the ecological systems they are part of. These include genetic material, plants, and animals and the diversity within and between species as well as ecosystems.

Burden of proof   The conditions that injured parties have to satisfy to bring a legal case against parties responsible for a specific environmental problem that has harmed them. These include proof that the polluting material was a direct cause of the damage and that the material did in fact come from a specific defendant.

Cap-and-trade system   A transferable emission permit that limits aggregate emissions from a source of a pollutant at the point of release. Permits can be traded among sources.

Capitalized   An event or policy is capitalized into the value of asset by adjusting the present value of that asset by the stream of costs or benefits that the policy or event

409

gives rise to. For example, a reduction in air pollution in an urban area should raise the price of a house because each year there are lower damages from air pollution to the property and its owners.

Carbon allowances   The right to emit a unit of carbon (generally denominated as one tonne) that can be traded in carbon markets.

Carbon offsets   A reduction in a unit of carbon emissions (e.g., one tonne) from a specified baseline level of emissions by an entity. Offsets must be verifiable and additional to business as usual to be valid for trade in carbon markets.

Carbon sinks   Ecosystems that absorb carbon dioxide. Examples are wetlands, forests, and the oceans.

Coase theorem   A theorem that shows when a socially efficient equilibrium can be reached by parties bargaining over compensation and actions, independent of which party has the property rights to pollute (or a clean environment).

Command-and-control (CAC)   A public policy designed to reach a socially efficient equilibrium where political authorities mandate behaviour in law, then use enforcement techniques (courts, police, fines) to get people to obey the law. Emission standards are an example of a command-and-control pollution policy that sets the maximum allowed level of emissions.

Common property rights   The rights a group of individuals collectively has to exclusive use of a natural resource. An example is a pasture or fishery that is managed by a distinct community.

Community indifference curve (CIC)   The choice society makes on alternative bundles of goods available in the economy. Each indifference curve represents a constant level of utility for combinations of commodity bundles. One of these bundles may be environmental quality.

Compensation   Those held liable for damages created by their actions pay those damaged in amounts appropriate to the extent of the injury.

Compliance costs   Total abatement costs required to be in accordance with an environmental policy such as a standard.

Composition of output   The mix of goods and services produced and sold in an economy. In environmental economics, the focus is on the amount and nature of residuals released by a good or service. Changing the mix of output can then change the total quantity of residuals produced.

Compounding   Taking the dollar value of an asset today and multiplying it by the interest rate that sum could earn if invested for each year the asset is held. The formula for compounding is $X(1 + r)^t$, where X is the asset value, r is the rate of interest used for compounding, and t is the number of years in question.

Concurrency   A situation where more than one level of government has laws applying to the same activity or thing.

Consumer surplus   The net benefit a person derives from consuming a good; the difference between what the consumer is willing to pay and the price of the good. The surplus for a private good is measured as the area under the demand curve above the price of the good between zero and the amount of the good consumed. The change in surplus due to a change in environmental quality can be measured as the area under the demand curve between the old and new levels of environmental quality.

Contingent valuation method   Inferring a person's willingness to pay for an improvement in environmental quality by presenting that person with a hypothetical scenario that asks the person to state their willingness to pay (or willingness to accept compensation). This is also called the "stated preference" approach.

Continuous emissions   Release of a pollutant that continues at a relatively constant rate over time.

Cost-effective equilibrium   An equilibrium in which different sources of a pollutant are controlled so that the marginal abatement costs of the sources are equal for each polluter's last unit of pollution not released into the environment. This minimizes the total compliance costs of reaching a target level of emissions. It satisfies the equimarginal principle.

Cost-effectiveness analysis   An analysis that takes a policy target as given then examines the total costs of different alternatives that reach the target. A policy is cost effective if it achieves the target at the lowest possible costs to society (i.e., it satisfies the equimarginal principle).

Credits   A reduction in the emissions of a pollutant that can be certified by a trusted agency and then sold in an emissions market. An example is a carbon credit earned for each tonne of GHG emissions an entity permanently abates.

Damages   The negative impacts produced by pollution. These include health effects, loss of output, ecosystem degradation and destruction, species extinctions, and other environmental impacts.

Damage function   The relationship between emissions of a pollutant and their impact on ecosystems and economy (e.g., agricultural output, fisheries), human health, and materials. They are typically positively sloped, rising at either a constant or increasing rate.

Decentralized techniques Actions taken by individuals affected by pollution to work out themselves how best to deal with the pollution. These require a clear set of rights and laws established by regulation and the legal system. Examples include liability laws, assignment of property rights, moral suasion, and the development of markets for environmentally friendly (green) goods.

Decouple To grow the economy without increasing negative impacts on the environment. Relative decoupling reduces adverse environmental impacts per unit GDP (but environmental damages can still increase). Absolute decoupling means that environmental quality does not decline as output of the economy rises.

Defensive expenditures The amount of money people are willing to pay to protect themselves against pollution damages. Examples are expenditures on sunscreen, noise proofing, bottled water, and air purifiers.

Degradable pollutants A non-accumulative pollutant that is broken down into less toxic components by the natural environment.

Demand curves Show the quantity of a good or service that an individual or group of individuals wishes to purchase and consume at any particular price.

Design standards Technology-based standards that require polluters to use a specified technology to control emissions of a pollutant. These can also be called engineering standards.

Discount rate The interest rate used in compounding or computing the present value of an asset or liability (benefit or cost).

Discounting Taking the present value of a stream of benefits and costs that occur over time periods greater than one year.

Dissolved oxygen (DO) The amount of oxygen present in a body of water.

Diversion policies Government policies that create incentives to reduce the amount of waste going into landfills. Recycling is an example.

Dose–response function Estimating the human exposure from a pollutant (or other pathogen) and measuring its impacts on health (and/or the ecosystem).

Dynamic efficiency Examines the allocation of resources over time (i.e., seeing if marginal benefits equal marginal costs at each point in time, over a long time horizon). It allows one to examine questions of intertemporal trade-offs such as depletion of natural and environmental resources.

Ecological economics The study and modelling of the linkages between economic and ecological systems.

Economic efficiency Occurs when the economy's resources are allocated to their best uses; an equilibrium is reached in which the marginal benefits of an activity equal the marginal costs (e.g., supply equals demand, or marginal benefits equal marginal damages).

Efficiency Achieving the maximum output per unit input or for a given level of output, minimizing the costs of attaining it.

Effluent The residuals (pollutants) entering the environment either directly or after treatment with abatement technologies. Some environmental texts use the term effluent to describe only water pollutants.

Elasticities The percentage change in a dependent variable of interest (quantity demanded or supplied) that results from a percentage change in an independent variable (price, income). For example, the price elasticity of demand is the percentage change in the quantity demanded of a particular good due to a one-percent change in the price of the good. Demand for the good is said to be inelastic if the elasticity is less than one, elastic if greater than one, and unitary elasticity if equal to one.

Emissions The residuals (pollutants) entering the environment either directly or after treatment with abatement technologies. Some environmental texts use the term emissions to describe only air pollutants.

Emissions-based TEP system A transferable emission system that allows the holder of the permit to discharge specific amount of pollution per unit time. Permits can be traded on a one-for-one basis anywhere in the jurisdiction.

Emissions intensity of pollution The emissions of a toxic compound from a firm or industry that release the compound expressed per unit of output, or value added, or employment from that firm or industry.

Emission damage functions The relationship between the wastes coming from a particular source or sources of pollution and the resulting damages to the environment.

Emission reduction targets Targets set by a government authority to reduce emissions of a pollutant by a specific time period. Examples are Canadian GHG targets: a reduction in emissions of X percent from year A levels by year B.

Emission standard A never-exceed level for quantities of emissions coming from a pollution source.

Energy efficiency The amount of energy used per dollar of output.

Environmental economics The study of the impact of the economic system on the natural environment and policies to improve environmental quality.

Environmental medium Components of the natural world—land, water, air.

Environmental quality A broad term to describe the state of the natural environment. This includes the notion of ambient quality plus visual and aesthetic quality of the environment.

Environmental tax shifting The recycling of tax revenues received from environmental taxes back to the public in the form of a reduction in distortionary taxes (e.g., lower taxes on income and investment).

Environmentally friendly good Good that releases relatively small amounts of residuals and thus has a less deleterious impact on environmental quality than a good that is more pollution intensive.

Episodic emissions Releases of a pollutant that may be intermittent or accidental.

Equimarginal principle A fundamental concept in economics used to show how to minimize the total cost of producing a given quantity of output. If production is organized among different producing sources so that their marginal costs of production are equalized for the last unit produced by each source, the equimarginal principle is satisfied. This will be a cost-effective outcome.

Equity Concern about how a public policy or other economic decision affects people with different levels of income or other distinguishing characteristic (e.g., geographic location, household size): examining who gets the benefits and who pays the costs.

European Union's Emission Trading System (ETS) A cap-and-trade market for the exchange of carbon allowances involving the member countries of the European Union. It has been the largest multinational carbon market operating.

Expected value A weighted average of the number of times an event occurs times its probability of occurrence, summed over all possible events. More generally, a measure of the central tendency of the distribution of a random variable (i.e., a mean).

Externalities/external effects An externality (or external effect) exists when markets fail to incorporate the social costs or benefits a person's or firm's actions have on others. Externalities arise because of open access to environmental resources and the characteristic of joint consumption.

External or social costs and benefits An external cost in the case of the environment is the damage resulting from environmental impacts that are not taken into account by the firms, public agencies, or consumers whose decisions produce them. An example is waste products coming from a firm located on a river that damage downstream users of the water. External benefits are the benefits accruing to people other than the direct buyers or recipients of a good. The classic example is a public good (such as air quality). Once it is made available to one person, all people in the community automatically receive the same level.

Free rider A person who pays less for a good than her/his true marginal willingness to pay; that is, someone who "underpays" relative to the benefits they receive. This occurs most often with public goods that are jointly consumed by people once provided.

Gains from trade The net benefits received by each party in an exchange of goods, services, or property rights such as transferable emission permits.

Hedonic estimation An empirical technique that decomposes the prices of a market good into a number of different characteristics of the good. This allows one to estimate the demand for a specific characteristics (holding other characteristics constant). An example of a characteristic is an environmental quality indicator, such as air quality, that affects the value of one's property.

Horizontal equity Ensuring that people with the same income levels (or other identifiable characteristic they all share) are treated equivalently by a policy.

Hot spot problem When non-uniformly mixed pollutants accumulate in a particular part of a jurisdiction causing a high concentration of pollution/low level of environmental quality at that site.

Implicit carbon taxes The interpretation of an existing tax on fossil fuels, for example, a tax on gasoline, in terms of its carbon dioxide emissions. The implicit tax is based on the carbon content of the fuel.

Incentive Something that attracts or repels people and leads them to modify their behaviour in some way. An economic incentive is something in the economic world that leads people to channel their efforts at economic production and consumption in certain directions.

Incidence The determination of who actually ultimately pays the costs (or receives the benefits) associated with a particular policy. The entity that initially bears the costs may pass them to others; for example, a tax levied on a firm may be borne by both the firm (and its workers and shareholders) and consumers of the goods produced by the firm.

Individual standards Performance or design standards that are set so that at the amount of emissions controlled per source, the marginal abatement costs of each polluter are equal.

Information revelation incentives Use of a policy instrument to induce a person or firm to reveal information about the shape and location of a curve of interest to the regulator. For example, a pollution tax can reveal information about the shape of a polluter's marginal abatement cost curve.

Intertemporal "Over time." An analysis that considers the impact of decisions taken today on outcomes in the future.

Inverse demand curve Expressing the demand curve for a good in terms of the price people are willing to pay as function of the quantity (rather than quantity demanded as a function of a good's price).

Liability To be liable for some behaviour is to be held responsible financially for whatever consequences result from that behaviour. Those held liable for damages created by their actions pay those damaged in amounts appropriate to the extent of the injury.

Loadings The concentration of a toxic compound in an environmental medium.

Marginal abatement costs The incremental cost of reducing emissions (or ambient concentrations) of a pollutant by one unit. This is also the first derivative of a total abatement cost function.

Marginal benefits The incremental benefits (in dollar terms) of increasing some good or service by one unit. They are also the derivative of a total benefit function.

Marginal costs The incremental costs (in dollar terms) of increasing the output of a good or service by one unit. They are also the derivative of a total cost function.

Marginal damage functions The relationship between a unit change in emissions or the ambient concentration of a pollutant and the change in damages that result.

Marginal willingness to pay A person's willingness to pay for one more unit of a good or service. It can be read off a demand curve as the price the person is willing to pay for a given quantity of the good.

Market-based incentive policies The use of market or market-like forces to encourage polluters to reduce emissions to the target level set by the regulator. These include taxes and other forms of charges or fees, subsidies, and transferable emission permits.

Market failures Occur when there is a divergence between the market value of inputs or outputs and its social value. It prevents a decentralized competitive market from reaching a socially efficient equilibrium. They can arise from externalities, open-access resources, and public goods.

Maximum acceptable level The level of air quality set by the Canadian federal government to provide adequate protection against adverse effects of air pollution on human health and comfort, soil, water, vegetation, animals, materials, and visibility. Populations susceptible to air pollutants may be adversely affected if air quality is at the maximum acceptable level.

Maximum desirable level The long-term goal of the Canadian federal government for air quality, designed to protect the population and ecosystems. It provides a basis for preventing degradation of air quality in relatively unpolluted parts of the country.

Maximum tolerable level The lowest boundary set by the Canadian federal government for air quality before immediate action is required to protect the health of the general population.

Microeconomics The study of economic actions from the viewpoints of the individual who is making decisions about what and how much to consume and the firm that is deciding what and how much to produce. The focus is on individual decision makers, rather than the economy in aggregate.

Mitigating expenditures Expenditures people are willing to make to reduce the impact of pollution on them. These may involve installing equipment to reduce pollution, moving to another location with lower levels of pollution, or modifying their activities to reduce exposure to pollution. The amount of money people are willing to pay to protect themselves against pollution damages. Examples are expenditures on sunscreen, noise proofing, bottled water, and air purifiers.

Mitigation Policies and actions designed to reduce emissions and impact of a pollutant.

Morbidity A state of illness or incapacitation.

Mortality Death.

Natural capital Consists of the earth's ecosystems, their renewable and non-renewable resources, environmental resources (atmosphere, water), and land. Ecosystem goods and services flow from natural capital.

Natural resource economics The study of nature in its role as a provider of raw materials—land, minerals, energy, forests, aquatic species—for production and consumption.

Negligence Parties who create environmental damage are held responsible and liable only if they did not take appropriate steps to avoid damage.

Net social value The total benefits from a project or policy minus the total costs where benefits and costs are measured using all associated market and non-market values.

New-source bias Environmental standards or objectives that are set at a more stringent level for new firms or plants wishing to locate in a region than for older plants that are already resident in the region.

No-cost improvements Environmental improvements that result from changes in regulations. These have no social cost, only the political cost of making changes in laws or regulations.

Nominal interest rates   The actual rate of interest being earned on an asset in the market at a point in time.

Non-accumulative pollutants   Pollutants that can be assimilated or buffered by the natural environment and hence do not build up over time. An example is noise. Once emissions of noise are stopped, it no longer acts as a pollutant in the environment.

Non-attainment   Regions in a jurisdiction that have lower air quality than required by the standards or objectives set for the jurisdiction.

Non-degradation   Preventing the level of environmental quality from falling below its current level, where the current level exceeds the standard or air quality objective.

Non-exclusion   The inability to prevent someone from consuming a good or service even if they do not pay for it. This is a characteristic of public goods.

Non-market values   The willingness to pay for an item that does not have a well-defined market and, hence, market-determined price. They have to be imputed by looking at the behaviour of people, using direct questioning, or other proxy methods.

Nonpoint-source pollutants   Pollutants that do not have a well-defined source of discharge. An example is runoff of agricultural wastes or pesticides into rivers or groundwater.

Non-renewable resource   A natural resource that does not have a process of replenishment. Examples are minerals and fossil fuels.

Non-rivalness   When one person's consumption of a good does not diminish the amount available to another person to consume. This is a characteristic of public goods. An example is clean air—one person's consumption of that air does not diminish another's.

Non-use value   The value people assign to a good that they do not and will not consume. An example is willingness to pay to protect a wilderness area or endangered species.

Normative concept   A statement about what "ought to be."

Open access   The lack of property rights; no one has exclusive right to the natural resource and no one can be excluded from using that resource. An example is the atmosphere.

Open-access resources   Resources that can be used by anyone; there is no exclusion. The atmosphere, oceans, groundwater, many surface waters, and even land can be open-access resources.

Opportunity cost   A fundamental concept in economics. The opportunity cost of using resources (land, labour, capital, natural resources) in a particular way is the highest valued alternative use to which those resources might have been put and thus which society forgoes by using the resources in the specified way.

Ozone-depleting potential (ODP)   The estimated depletion of stratospheric ozone of a unit mass of a compound divided by the ozone depletion of a unit mass of CFC-11.

Paramountcy   If more than one level of government has a law covering the same thing, the federal government's law has precedence over the provincial law.

Performance standard   Another name for an emission standard, named so because it refers to end results that regulated polluters must achieve.

Persistent pollutants   Accumulative pollutants released into an environmental medium such as a body of water.

Point of impingement   The point where air pollutants from a source first encounter the ground, a building, or other object. These standards are a type of ambient standard where no source can release emissions that result in a concentration exceeding the standard at each point of impingement.

Point-source pollutants   Pollutants with a well-defined point of discharge into the environment; for example, air pollutants from the stacks of electricity-generating plants or other industries.

Pollutant   A substance, energy form, or action that, when introduced into the natural environment, results in a lowering of the ambient quality level.

Pollutee   A party suffering damages caused by pollution.

Pollution   Derived from Latin words meaning defilement and soiling. It refers to residuals from production and consumption introduced into the environment that degrades air, water, or land quality.

Pollution-control technology   The technology used to reduce the amount of pollution being released into the natural environment. This may involve capital equipment or operating processes.

Pollution-intensive goods   Goods that release relatively large amounts of residuals and have a significant adverse impact on environmental quality.

Pollution prevention   Reducing the residuals from production by adopting technologies and production practices that yield smaller amounts of residuals per unit output produced.

Porter hypothesis   An assertion that a well-designed environmental policy can not only reduce pollution but improve productivity and competitiveness if it results in innovation and efficiency gains that the firm had otherwise not recognized or engaged in.

Positive economics   The study of how events actually occur in the real world. Statements about "what is."

Precautionary principle As applied to the environment, when an action may lead to significant environmental degradation whose effects are not known with certainty, steps should be taken to reduce the likelihood of the damage occurring including prohibiting the action that could create the damage.

Present value The value today of an asset or liability (benefit or cost) that is received or due more than one year into the future. The formula is: Present value = $X/(1 + r)^t$, where X is the value of the asset or liability, r is the rate of interest used to discount that asset's value back to today, and t is the length of time in question.

Preventive or mitigating expenditures The amount of money people are willing to pay to protect themselves against pollution damages. Examples are expenditures on sunscreen, noise proofing, bottled water, and air purifiers.

Price volatility Fluctuations in the price of a good or service due to the interplay of supply and demand.

Private compliance costs The total abatement costs incurred by a polluter in response to a regulatory policy, plus any taxes, fees, or payments for the purchase of transferable emission permits, or net of any subsidies and receipts for the sale of transferable emission permits. For example, the total private cost of compliance for an emission tax is the sum of the polluter's total abatement costs plus its tax bill paid to the government.

Private costs Private costs are the market value of labour, raw materials, machinery, energy, and so on that firms incur in producing goods and services. They are the costs that appear on a profit-and-loss statement of the firm.

Private property rights A right that is exclusive (i.e., "I own this and you do not") and typically transferable (to others). An example of a private property right is one's title to land.

Private rate discount rate The market rate of interest charged at a point in time by banks or other financial institutions.

Probability distribution Identifies all possible outcomes of a random process and the probability associated with each possible outcome.

Producer surplus The net benefits from production to the producer. It is measured as the area between the price of the good per unit and the marginal costs of producing that unit, summed over all the units produced.

Production possibilities frontier (PPF) A graphical depiction of the choice faced by a community between two desirable alternatives. These alternatives may be two different goods. It can be used to illustrate the trade-offs between having more market goods versus higher levels of environmental quality. Because of resource scarcity, the community can have more of one thing only by giving some of the other.

Productivity-study approach A direct measure of the costs of environmental damages based on lost wages and health-care costs. This approach does not tend to fully capture the willingness to pay to avoid these damages.

Progressive programs and policies The program or policy provides net benefits that represent a higher proportion of a lower-income person's income than it does of a high-income person's.

Property rights Rights that give the holder the right to do certain things with a tangible asset. In environmental economics, the asset is typically a type of natural resource—land, water, or the atmosphere. Characteristics of property rights include whether or not they are exclusive, transferable, divisible, and protected by law. Rights are defined as private or common property or open access depending on which of these characteristics they have.

Proportional programs and policies Provide the same percentage of net benefits to people regardless of their income level. For example, a program that yields net benefits equal to 1 percent of a person's income.

Public goods Characterized by non-exclusion and non-rivalness—there is joint consumption of the good and, once provided, everyone can enjoy the good whether they pay for it or not. Environmental quality is a public good.

Rate of time preference The marginal rate of substitution between receiving a benefit today versus in the future as captured by an interest rate.

Real interest rates The nominal rate (current market rate) of interest adjusted for inflation.

Recycling The process of returning some or all of the production and consumption residuals to be used again in production or consumption.

Regressive programs and policies Provides net benefits that represent higher net benefits to high-income people as a proportion of their income than it does to low-income people.

Renewable resource Resources that can grow over time according to natural processes. Examples include living resources such as fish and timber, and non-living resources such as solar energy and the hydrological cycles. Use of these resources can be sustainable over time.

Residuals Matter that has been left over after something has been produced or consumed.

Residuals intensity of production The quantity of residuals produced per unit of output of goods and services produced in an economy.

Risk averse When facing uncertain returns in the future, there is a preference for return that has the lower risk (is more certain) even if it has a lower expected value than an outcome with higher risk.

Risk neutral Basing decisions entirely on the expected value of an uncertain outcome, indifferent to the level of risk.

Scarcity Not having enough of something relative to one's wants; the limits to what the natural environment can provide.

Scenario analysis When one is highly uncertain about the probability of an event occurring, a range of values for these probabilities are used in calculating expected values and potential outcomes.

Second-best situation When the economy is already operating with some pre-existing distortion and government regulators seek to correct a new distortion (e.g., pollution), taking into account that it cannot achieve the first-best equilibrium, one that is socially efficient.

Self-monitoring Polluters report their level of emissions to the regulator; the regulator does not routinely measure emissions.

Sensitivity analysis Recalculating the benefits and costs of a policy or project using different assumptions about key variables (e.g., discount rates, length of the project, benefit and cost estimates) to allow for uncertainty about the values of these variables or incorrect measurement.

Shadow prices Imputing a price for an input or output that reflects their opportunity costs when markets fail to fully account for these opportunity costs. They measure opportunity costs as if markets operated perfectly, without distortions introduced by externalities and other factors.

Social capital A broad definition of capital that includes everything the economy can invest in—physical capital to produce goods and services, education, infrastructure, and renewable and nonrenewable natural resources including environmental resources.

Social compliance costs Private compliance costs borne by a polluter net of taxes, subsidies, or transferable emission payments to the government (i.e., from government auctions of permits).

Social cost accounting The enumeration of the private costs plus the external (environmental) costs of production.

Social discount rate Reflects society's tradeoff of present benefits for future benefits, in other words, society's rate of time preference.

Social opportunity cost Inclusion of both the monetary costs (e.g., materials, energy) and nonmonetary costs (e.g., the value of one's time spent in the activity in question instead of doing something else) when computing opportunity cost. The non-monetary costs must be converted to dollar values by imputing a price to the activity. This is called shadow pricing. Social opportunity costs are the opportunity costs incurred by society regardless of to whom they accrue.

Social opportunity cost of capital Society's expected rate of return foregone when making one investment compared to alternative investments.

Socially efficient level of pollution The level of pollution where the marginal damages from another unit of pollution released into the environment equal the marginal costs of reducing a unit of pollution (the marginal abatement costs). Social efficiency requires the buyers and sellers of goods and services to take into account the impact of their actions on the environment—it means assigning prices, generally through government policy, to ecosystem goods and services and the waste products (pollutants).

Socially efficient level of production The level of production where all social costs and benefits are incorporated into supply and demand curves and there is equilibrium where supply equals demand. It is also where the marginal abatement costs equal the marginal damages from pollution. Also known as socially efficient scale.

Source (of pollution) The location at which emissions occur, such as a factory, an automobile, or a leaking landfill.

Source reduction To reduce the materials intensity of production so that fewer inputs are used to produce a given level of output. An example is a reduction in packaging material.

Spatially differentiated Emissions of a pollutant have a different impact on ambient environmental quality depending on where they are released. Ambient quality is affected by factors such as geography, weather, and environmental absorptive capacity. Sulphur dioxide from coal burning power plants is an example.

Stakeholder's groups Public, private-sector, and nongovernmental organizations that have an interest in a particular aspect of public policy such as the environment.

Standing Whether the courts will allow a party (the plaintiff) to sue another party (the defendant) for damages. A private citizen may bring suit in an environmental case if that person is able to show that he or she is in fact being damaged by the activity in question.

Static efficiency   Economic efficiency at a point in time that does not take into account intertemporal tradeoffs.

Strict liability   People are held liable for damages they cause regardless of the circumstances surrounding the creation of the damages; that is, how much care they took to prevent the damage.

Surrogate markets   Using a market that does exist as a proxy to measure the willingness to pay for an activity that is not exchanged in a market. An example is using the amount of money people spend to travel to a recreation site as a proxy for their willingness to pay for environmental quality at the site.

Sustainability   A sustainable economy is one in which investment in social capital allows the economy to grow so that people are at least as well off in the future as they are in the present, while ensuring the health of ecological systems.

Taking   The expropriation of property by government when that property is needed for the community, e.g., land taken to create a park.

Technology-based standards (TBS)   A type of standard that dictates polluters use specific techniques (e.g., a particular type of pollution abatement equipment) or follow a specific set of operating procedures and practices.

Technology-forcing standards   Standards set at an emission level that is lower (i.e., more stringent) than the socially efficient level. This is done to provide an incentive for polluters to engage in research and development to invent cheaper ways to meet the standard; that is, to find a technology that yields lower marginal abatement costs.

Threshold   An emissions or ambient concentration level of a pollutant below which marginal damages are zero.

Total abatement cost   The total cost of abating a given level of pollution. They are the area under the marginal abatement cost function between two specified levels of pollution (e.g., the initial level and level after introduction of a regulatory policy).

Total costs   The costs of producing the total amount of output. The cost of producing each unit of the good times the quantity produced summed across all units produced.

Total damages   The total amount of damage from a pollutant at each possible level of emissions. It can be measured as the area under the marginal damage curve from zero to the level of emissions.

Total private costs of compliance   The total abatement costs incurred by a polluting industry in response to a regulatory policy, plus any taxes, fees, or payments for the purchase of transferable emission permits, or net of any subsidies and receipts for the sale of transferable emission permits (if these types of policies are used).

Total willingness to pay   The total amount a person is willing to pay to attain a particular level of consumption rather than go without the good entirely. Total WTP can be measured as the area under the demand curve from zero to the amount to be consumed.

Toxic intensity   A measure of the impact of a toxic compound on the environment. An index of toxicity is used to weight the emissions of each compound released by a firm or industry. The index reflects such factors as whether the compound is a carcinogen, mutagen, its lethal dose, and so on.

Trade-offs   The alternatives individuals, firms, and society face; for example, whether to choose one good or input or another, whether to visit a park or go to a movie.

Transaction costs   The costs required to reach and to enforce an agreement between parties. These include costs of acquiring information, bargaining over the terms of the agreement, and enforcement.

Transferable emission permits (TEPs)   A property right to emit a specific amount of pollution. The right is transferable; that is, it can be sold or given away.

Transfer coefficient   A method of converting emissions of a pollutant from a particular source into an impact on environmental quality at a monitoring station or receptor point. They are dependent upon scientific factors such as meteorological relationships and the physical and chemical properties of the pollutant.

Transfer payments   Payments made by a party to the government that are eventually recycled back to the public in the form of government expenditures. They are not counted as a social cost of an environmental policy.

Travel-cost approach   The use of people's travel costs to a recreation site as a proxy for their willingness to pay to experience the environmental amenities of that site. Using a market that does exist as a proxy to measure the willingness to pay for an activity that is not exchanged in a market.

Two-part emission tax   A tax rate that varies with the level of emissions released into the environment. For example, a relatively low tax rate may be set on emissions up to a specific threshold; thereafter a higher tax rate applies.

Uncertainty   Imprecise knowledge about a parameter, relationship, or event.

Uniformly mixed   Emissions of a pollutant have the identical impact on ambient environmental quality independent of where they are released. Greenhouse gases are an example.

Uniform standard   A single standard set at the same level for all sources of a pollutant.

Unintended consequences   When an action by people or government creates a response that was not anticipated and the consequence is of great concern and could be damaging to the initial intent of the action.

Use value   The value derived from the actual use of a good or service whether or not that good or service is traded in a market.

Vertical equity   Recognizes that people in different circumstances may need to be treated differently. For example, requiring people with more ability to pay (e.g., higher incomes) to pay a higher percentage of their income in taxes than those with lower incomes.

Voluntary compliance   Actions taken by polluters to improve environmental performance in response to non-binding environmental quality targets.

Voluntary emissions reductions   The amount of reduction in emissions taken by polluters even though there are no laws or regulations requiring these reductions.

Waste reduction   Methods of reducing the amount of material that needs to be disposed of in society. Reduction can be accomplished by recycling residuals back into the production process and by shifting technologies and operations so that the amount of residuals discharged is reduced.

Willingness to accept (WTA)   A fundamental concept in economics. The amount of money a person requires in compensation if a good or service that they were previously consuming is taken away from them.

Willingness to pay (WTP)   A fundamental concept in economics. The monetary value to an individual of enjoying the benefits of a particular good or service, rather than go without that good or service.

With-without approach   In benefit–cost analysis, the measurement of the net benefits of a policy or program should compare the differences in the costs and benefits with the policy compared to what the costs and benefits would have been in the absence of the policy. This is not the same as the costs and benefits before and after the policy because time will have passed, bringing with it changes in conditions (e.g., production costs may be rising even if no policy is introduced).

Glossary of Acronyms

AQI	Air quality index
AQMS	Air Quality Management System
BAT	Best available technology
BATEA	Best available technology economically achievable
BCA	Benefit–cost analysis
BOD	Biochemical oxygen demand
BPT	Best practicable technology
CAA	*Clean Air Act* (Canada)
CAAQS	Canadian Ambient Air Quality Standards
CAC	Command-and-control (policy)
CAF	Corporate average fuel (standards)
CAFC	Company average fuel consumption
CCAR	Canadian Coalition on Acid Rain
CCME	Canadian Council of Ministers of the Environment
CEAA	*Canadian Environmental Assessment Act*
CEPA	*Canadian Environmental Protection Act*
CERCLA	*Comprehensive Environmental Response, Compensation, and Liability Act* (U.S.)
CFCs	Chlorofluorocarbons
CIC	Community indifference curve
CO	Carbon monoxide
CO_2	Carbon dioxide
CWS	Canada-wide Standards
CVM	Contingent valuation method
CS	Consumer surplus
DO	Dissolved oxygen
DSL	Domestic Substances List
EARP	Environmental Assessment and Review Process
EC	Environment Canada
EIA	Environmental impact analysis
EKC	Environmental Kuznets curve
EPA	U.S. Environmental Protection Agency
EQ	Environmental quality
ETS	European Union's Emission Trading System
FDI	Foreign direct investment
FEARO	Federal Environmental Assessment and Review Office (Canada)
GDP	Gross domestic product
GHG	Greenhouse gas
IJC	International Joint Commission
MAC	Marginal abatement cost
MC	Marginal costs
MD	Marginal damages
MEC	Marginal external costs
MISA	Municipal-Industrial Strategy for Abatement (Ontario)
MPC	Marginal private costs
MSW	Municipal solid waste
MWTP	Marginal willingness to pay
NAAQOs	National Ambient Air Quality Objectives (Canada)
NB	Net benefits
NGO	Non-governmental organization
NO_2	Nitrogen dioxide (NOx—nitrogen oxides)
NPRI	National Pollutant Release Inventory (Canada)
NPS	Nonpoint source of pollution
NRTEE	National Roundtable on the Environment and Economy
O_3	Ground-level ozone
ODP	Ozone-depleting potential (stratospheric)
OECD	Organization for Economic Co-operation and Development
OWRC	Ontario Water Resources Commission
PM	Particulate matter
POGG	Peace, Order and Good Government (federal power)
PPF	Production possibility frontier
PS	Producer surplus
PSD	Prevention of serious deterioration
PSL	Priority Substances List
PV	Present value
R&D	Research and development
RAP	Remedial Action Plan
RCRA	*Resource Conservation and Recovery Act* (U.S.)
RM	Recycled materials
SO_2	Sulphur dioxide (SOx—sulphur oxides)

SUV	Sport-utility vehicle	**TM**	Total materials
TAC	Total abatement cost	**TSS**	Total suspended solids
TB	Total benefits	**UVB**	Ultra-violet—B (radiation)
TBS	Technology-based standards	**VM**	Virgin materials
TC	Total costs	**VOC**	Volatile organic compound
TCE	Trichloroethylene	**WTA**	Willingness to accept
TEP	Transferable emission permit	**WTP**	Willingness to pay

Selected References

Chapter 1

Arrow, K., B. Bohlin, R. Costanza, P. Dasgupta, C. Folke, C.S. Holling, B.O. Jansson, S. Levin, K.G. Maler, C. Perrings, and D. Pimentel. "Economic Growth, Carrying Capacity, and the Environment," *Science* (April 18, 1995): 520–521.

Barbier, E. "Introduction to the Environmental Kuznets Curve Special Issue." *Environment and Development Economics* (Special Issue: The Environmental Kuznets Curve), Vol. 2(4), (1997): 369–381.

Brundtland, G. H., et al. *Our Common Future.* Oxford, UK: Oxford University Press, 1987.

Carson, R.T., Jeon, Y., and D.R. McCubbin. "The Relationship between Air Pollution Emissions and Income: US Data," *Environment and Development Economics 2* (1997): 433–450.

Costanza, Robert (ed.). *Ecological Economics: The Science and Management of Sustainability.* New York: Columbia University Press, 1991.

Costanza, Robert, John H. Cumberland, Herman Daly, and Robert Goodland. *An Introduction to Ecological Economics,* 2nd ed., CRC Press, 2011.

Daly, H. and J. Farley. *Ecological Economics: Principles and Applications,* 2nd ed. Washington, D.C.: Island Press, 2010.

Fredrikkson, P.G., ed., *Trade, Global Policy, and the Environment.* World Bank Discussion Paper No. 402. World Bank, Washington D.C., 1998.

Grossman, G.M. and A.B. Krueger. "Economic Growth and the Environment," *Quarterly Journal of Economics* 110(2), (1995): 353–377.

Hardin, G. "The Tragedy of the Commons," *Science* 162 (1968): 1243–1248.

Hettige, H., R.E.B. Lucas, and D. Wheeler. "The Toxic Intensity of Industrial Production: Global Patterns, Trends and Trade Policy," *American Economic Review,* 82(2) (1992): 478–481.

Leonard, H.J. *Pollution and the Struggle for the World Product.* Cambridge: Cambridge University Press, 1988.

List, J.A. and C.Y. Co. "The Effects of Environmental Regulation on Foreign Direct Investment," *Journal of Environmental Economics and Management* 40(1) (2000): 1–20.

Low, P. (ed.) *International Trade and the Environment.* World Bank Discussion Paper 159, The World Bank, Washington, D.C., 1992.

Mani, M. and Wheeler, D. "In Search of Pollution Havens? Dirty Industry in the World Economy, 1960 to 1995," *Journal of Environment and Development* 7 (1998): 215–247.

Seldon, T. and Song, D. "Environmental Quality and Development: Is There a Kuznets Curve for Air Pollution Emissions?" *Journal of Environmental Economics and Management* 27 (1994): 147–162.

Shafik, N. "Economic Development and Environmental Quality: An Econometric Analysis," *Oxford Economic Papers* 46 (1994): 757–773.

Tobey, J.A. "The Effects of Domestic Environmental Policies on Patterns of World Trade: An Empirical Test," *Kyklos* 43 (1990): 191–209.

Victor, Peter. *Managing Without Growth: Slower by Design, Not Disaster.* Northampton, MA, Edward Elgar, 2008.

Wheeler, David. "Racing to the Bottom? Foreign Investment and Air Quality in Developing Countries," *World Bank Working Paper.* November 2000. Available at www.worldbank.org/nipr.

World Bank. *World Development Report 1992: Development and the Environment.* Oxford, UK: Oxford University Press, 1992.

Chapter 2

Archibugi, F., and P. Nijkamp. *Economy and Ecology: Towards Sustainable Development.* Dordrect, The Netherlands: Kluwer Academic Press, 1989.

Ayres, Robert U. *Resources, Environment and Economics, Applications of the Materials/Energy Balance Principle.* New York: John Wiley and Sons, 1978.

Baumol, William, and Wallace Oates. *Economics, Environmental Policy and the Quality of Life.* Englewood Cliffs, N.J.: Prentice-Hall, 1979.

Enthoven, Alain C., and A. Myrick Freeman III (eds.). *Pollution, Resources and the Environment.* New York: Norton, 1973.

Environment Canada. *The State of Canada's Environment.* Ottawa: Government of Canada, 1996.

Kneese, Allen V., and Blair T. Bower. *Environmental Quality and Residuals Management.* Baltimore, Md.: Johns Hopkins Press for Resources for the Future, 1979.

Krutilla, John V. "Conservation Reconsidered," *American Economic Review* 57(4) (September 1967): 777–786.

Miller, Alan S. *Gaia Connections: An Introduction to Ecology, Ecoethics, and Economics*. Lanham, Md.: Rowman and Allenheld, 1991.

Organization for Economic Co-operation and Development: *The State of the Environment*. Paris: OECD, 1991.

Pearce, David, Anil Markandya, and Edward B. Barbier. *Blueprint for a Green Economy*. London: Earthscan Publications, 1989.

Statistics Canada. *Human Activity and the Environment*. Ottawa: Minister of Supply and Services, 1994.

Wilson, Edward O. "Biodiversity, Prosperity and Value," in F. Herbert Bormann and Stephen R. Kellert (eds.). *Ecology, Economics, Ethics: The Broken Circle*. New Haven, Conn.: Yale University Press, 1991, 3–25.

World Resources Institute. *World Development Indicators*. Washington D.C.: World Resources Institute, 2000.

Chapter 3

The subjects treated in this chapter (demand, supply, willingness to pay, costs, etc.) are treated in most introductory microeconomic texts. The best way to proceed, in order to get a somewhat deeper explanation of these concepts, or a slightly different perspective, is to consult the appropriate chapters of one of these books. Some of the more popular texts are the following:

Mankiw, N. Gregory et al. *Principles of Microeconomics*. Toronto: Dryden, 1999.

McConnell, Campbell R., Stanley L. Brue, and Thomas P. Barbiero. *Microeconomics*. 8th Canadian ed. Toronto: McGraw-Hill Ryerson Limited, 1999.

Parkin, Michael, and Robin Bade. *Microeconomics: Canada in the Global Environment*. 4th ed. Don Mills, Ontario: Addison-Wesley Publishers Limited, 2000.

Chapter 4

The same comment is relevant here as appeared in the references for the last chapter: consult the appropriate chapters of one of the popular microeconomics texts. To review the material in Chapter 4, look specifically for efficiency and market failures in the face of externalities, public goods, and common-property resources.

Chapter 5

Banzhaf, S., D. Burtraw, and K. Palmer, "Efficient Emission Fees in the U.S. Electricity Sector," *Resource and Energy Economics* 26 (2004): 317–341.

Environmental economics textbooks that cover the topics in this chapter range from very introductory to advanced texts. Some examples are:

Baumol, W.J. and W.E. Oates. *The Theory of Environmental Policy,* 2nd ed., Cambridge: Cambridge University Press, 1988.

Duane Chapman. *Environmental Economics: Theory, Application, and Policy*. Reading, Mass.: Addison-Wesley, 1999.

Hanley, N., Shogren, J.F. and B. White. *Environmental Economics in Theory and Practice*. Macmillan Press Ltd., 1997.

Pearce, David W. and R. Kerry Turner. *Economics of Natural Resources and the Environment*. Baltimore: Johns Hopkins Press, 1990.

Perman, R., Y. Ma, and J. McGilvray. *Natural Resource and Environmental Economics,* 2nd ed. London: Longman, 1999.

Tietenberg, T. *Environmental and Natural Resource Economics*. 5th ed. Reading, Mass.: Addison-Wesley, 2000.

Chapter 6

Boardman, A. et al. *Cost–Benefit Analysis,* 2nd ed. Upper Saddle River, NJ: Prentice Hall, 2001.

Dasgupta, Ajit K., and D. W. Pearce. *Cost–Benefit Analysis: Theory and Practice*. New York: Barnes and Noble, 1972.

Freeman, A. Myrick, III. *Air and Water Pollution Control: A Benefit–Cost Assessment*. New York: John Wiley, 1982.

Government of Canada, Final Report of the Government Working Group on Sulphur in Gasoline and Diesel Fuel—Setting a Level for Sulphur in Gasoline and Diesel (July 14, 1998).

Jenkins, G., C-Y. Kuo, and A. Ozbafli, "Cost–Benefit Analysis of Reducing Sulphur in Gasoline", manuscript, (December 2009). An earlier version of the paper is available as a Queen's University Economics Department Working Paper No. 1134, "Cost–Benefit Analysis on Regulations to Lower the Level of Sulphur in Gasoline" (March 2007), www.econ.queensu.ca/working_papers/papers/qed_wp_1134.

Kilborn, Inc. The Costs of Reducing Sulphur in Canadian Gasoline and Diesel, Phase III (March 1997).

Kneese, Allen, and Blair Bower. *Environmental Quality Analysis*. Baltimore, Md.: Johns Hopkins Press, 1972.

Lave, Lester B. *The Strategy of Social Regulation: Decision Frameworks for Policy*. Washington, D.C.: The Brookings Institution, 1981.

Nordhaus, William. "Critical Assumptions in the Stern Review on Climate Change," *Science* (317), July 13, 2007.

Stern, Nicholas. *The Economics of Climate Change,* Great Britain Treasury, 2007.

Sugden, Robert, and Alan Williams. *The Principles of Practical Benefit–Cost Analysis.* Oxford, England: Oxford University Press, 1978.

Townley, P.G.C. *Principles of Cost–Benefit Analysis in a Canadian Context.* Scarborough: Prentice Hall Canada, 1998.

Chapter 7

Braden, John B., and Charles D. Kolstad (eds.). *Measuring the Demand for Environmental Quality.* Amsterdam: North-Holland, 1991.

Brookshire, D.S. et al. "Valuing Public Goods: A Comparison of Survey and Hedonic Approaches," *American Economic Review* 72 (1982): 165–177.

Brookshire, D.S., L.S. Eubanks, and A. Randall. "Estimating Option Prices and Existence Values for Wildlife Resources," *Land Economics* 59 (1983): 1–15.

Diamond, P.A. and J.A. Hausman. "Contingent Valuation: Is Some Number Better than No Number?" *Journal of Economic Perspectives* 8(4) (1994): 45–65.

Dixon, John A., and Paul B. Sherman. *Economics of Protected Areas, A New Look at Benefits and Costs.* Washington, D.C.: Island Press, 1990.

Freeman, A. Myrick, III. *The Benefits of Environmental Improvement: Theory and Practice.* Baltimore, Md.: Johns Hopkins Press for Resources for the Future, 1979.

Hanemann, W.M. "Valuing the Environment through Contingent Valuation," *Journal of Economic Perspectives* 8(4) (1994): 19–43.

Kahneman, D., J. Knetsch, and R. Thaler. "The Endowment Effect, Loss Aversion, and Status Quo Bias," *Journal of Economic Perspectives* 5 (1991): 193–206.

Kneese, Allen V. *Measuring the Benefits of Clean Air and Water.* Washington, D.C.: Resources for the Future, 1984.

Knetsch, Jack L. "Environmental Policy Implications of Disparities between Willingness to Pay and Compensation Demanded Measures of Values," *Journal of Environmental Economics and Management* 18 (1990): 227–237.

Krutilla, John V., and Anthony C. Fisher. *The Economics of Natural Environments.* Baltimore, Md.: Johns Hopkins Press for Resources for the Future, 1975.

Mitchell, Robert Cameron, and Richard T. Carson. *Using Surveys to Value Public Goods: The Contingent Valuation Method.* Washington, D.C.: Resources for the Future, 1989.

NASA. "Satellite Measurements Help Reveal Ozone Damage to Important Crops," May 25, 2009, www.nasa.gov/topics/earth/features/soybeans.html.

Organization for Economic Cooperation and Development. *Benefits, Estimates and Environmental Decision Making.* Paris: OECD, 1992.

Pearce, David W., and Anil Markandya. *Environmental Policy Benefits: Monetary Valuation.* Paris: Organization for Economic Cooperation and Development, 1989.

Rowe, Robert D., and Lauraine G. Chestnut. *The Value of Visibility: Theory and Application.* Cambridge, Mass.: Abt Books, 1982.

Schelling, Thomas. "The Life You Save May Be Your Own," in Samuel Chase (ed.). *Problems of Public Expenditure Analysis.* Washington, D.C.: Brookings Institution, 1968, 127–158.

Smith, V. Kerry, and William H. Desvouges. *Measuring Water Quality Benefits.* Boston, Mass.: Kluwer-Nijhoff Publishing, 1986.

Chapter 8

Babcock, Lyndon R. "Costs of Pollution Abatement," in George S. Tolley, Philip E. Graves, and Glenn C. Blomquist (eds.). *Environmental Policy, Volume I.* Cambridge, Mass.: Ballinger, 1981, 75–91.

Environmental Protection Agency. *Environmental Investments: The Cost of a Clean Environment.* EPA0230-90-084, Washington, D.C., 1990.

Kneese, Allen V. "Costs of Water Quality Improvement, Transfer Functions and Public Policy," in Henry M. Peskin and Eugene P. Seskin (eds.). *Cost Benefit Analysis and Water Pollution Policy.* Washington, D.C.: The Urban Institute, 1975, 175–206.

Morgenstern, R., W. Pizer, and J. Shih. "Are We Overstating the Economic Costs of Environmental Protection?" Discussion Paper 97-36, Resource of the Future, Washington D.C., 1997.

Palmer, Karen L., and Alan J. Krupnick. "Environmental Costing and Electric Utilities' Planning and Investment," *Resources, 105,* Washington, D.C.: Resources for the Future, Fall 1991.

Statistics Canada, Environmental Protection Expenditures in the Business Sector, 2006, Catalogue No. 16F0006X, www.statcan.gc.ca.

Chapter 9

Bernstein, Janis. "Alternative Approaches to Pollution Control and Waste Management: Regulatory and Economic Instruments," Discussion Paper INU 79. Washington, D.C.: World Bank, Infrastructure and Urban Development Department, May 1991.

Bohm, Peter, and Clifford S. Russell. "Comparative Analysis of Alternative Policy Instruments," in Allen V. Kneese and James L. Sweeney (eds.). *Handbook of Natural Resources and Energy Economics,* Vol. 1. Amsterdam: North-Holland, 1985, 395–460.

Bromley, D.W. "The Ideology of Efficiency: Searching for a Theory of Policy Analysis," *Journal of Environmental Economics and Management* 19 (1990): 86–107.

Dewees, Donald N. "Instrument Choice in Environmental Policy," *Economic Inquiry* 21(1) (January 1983): 53–71.

Environment Canada. *Economic Instruments for Environmental Protection,* Discussion Paper, catalogue no. En21-1199/1992E. Ottawa: Supply and Services, 1992.

Eskeland, Gunnar, and Emanuel Jimenez. *Choosing Among Policy Instruments in Pollution Control: A Review.* World Bank, Country Economics Department, June 20, 1990.

Organization for Economic Cooperation and Development. *Environmental Policies for Cities in the 1990s.* OECD: Paris, 1990.

Organization for Economic Cooperation and Development: *Evaluating Economic Instruments for Environmental Policy.* OECD, Paris, 1997.

Ruff, Larry E. "The Economic Common Sense of Pollution," *The Public Interest,* No. 19 (Spring 1970): 69–85.

Chapter 10

Anderson, Terry L., and Donald R. Leal. *Free Market Environmentalism.* San Francisco: Pacific Research Institute, 1991.

Coase, Ronald H. "The Problem of Social Cost," *Journal of Law and Economics,* Vol. 3 (October 1960): 1–44.

Dales, J. H. *Pollution, Property and Prices.* Toronto: University of Toronto Press, 1968.

Dewees, D. "Is Tort Law the Solution to Environmental Pollution?" *Canadian Public Policy,* Vol. XVIII (4) (December 1992): 425–442.

Hoffman, W. Michael, Robert Frederick, and Edward S. Petry, Jr. (eds.). *The Corporation, Ethics, and the Environment.* New York: Quorum Books, 1990.

Kneese, Allen V., and William D. Schulze. "Ethics and Environmental Economics," in Allen V. Kneese and James L. Sweeney (eds.). *Handbook of Natural Resource and Energy Economics,* Vol. 1. Amsterdam: North-Holland, 1985, 191–220.

Tietenberg, T.H., ed. *Innovation in Environmental Policy.* England: Edward Elgar, 1992.

Chapter 11

Crandall, Robert W. *Controlling Industrial Pollution.* Washington, D.C.: The Brookings Institution, 1983.

Laplante, B. "Environmental Regulation: Performance and Design Standards," in G.B. Doern, ed., *Getting it Green.* Toronto: C.D. Howe Institute, 1990.

Russell, Clifford S. "Monitoring and Enforcement," in Paul Portney (ed.). *Public Policies for Environmental Protection.* Washington, D.C.: Resources for the Future, 1990, 243–274.

Russell, Clifford S., Winston Harrington, and William J. Vaughan. *Enforcing Pollution Control Laws.* Washington, D.C.: Resources for the Future, 1986.

Viscusi, W. Kip. *Risks by Choice: Regulating Health and Safety in the Workplace.* Cambridge, Mass.: Harvard University Press, 1983.

Chapter 12

Ambec, Stefan, Mark A. Cohen, Stewart Elgie, and Paul Lanoie. "Can Environmental Regulation Enhance Innovation and Competitiveness," *Resources for the Future,* January 2011.

Bohm, Peter. *Deposit-Refund Systems: Theory and Application to Environmental, Conservation and Consumer Policy.* Baltimore, Md.: Johns Hopkins Press for Resources for the Future, 1981.

Bosquet, Benoit. "Survey: Environmental Tax Reform: Does It Work? A Survey of the Empirical Evidence," *Ecological Economics,* 34(1) (July 2000): 19–32.

Fullerton, Don, and Gilbert Metcalf. "Environmental Taxes and the Double-Dividend Hypothesis: Did You Really Expect Something for Nothing?" *Chicago-Kent Law Review* 73(1) (1998): 221–256.

Goulder, L.H. (1995) "Environmental Taxes and the 'Double Dividend': A Reader's Guide," *International Tax and Public Finance* 2, 157–184.

Ontario Fair Tax Commission: *Final Report—Environment and Taxation.* Toronto: Environment and Taxation Working Group, 1992.

Organization for Economic Co-operation and Development: *Economic Instruments for Environmental Protection.* Paris: OECD, 1989.

Organization for Economic Co-operation and Development: *Environmental Taxes in OECD Countries,* Paris: OECD, 1995.

Organization for Economic Co-operation and Development: *Subsidies and the Environment: Exploring the Linkages.* Papers from the Workshop on Subsidies, Tax Incentives and Environment: 20–21 November 1995. Paris: OECD, 1996.

Organization for Economic Co-operation and Development: *Taxation and the Environment, Complementary Policies.* Paris: OECD, 1993.

Palmer, Karen, W. Oates, and P. Portney. "Tightening Environmental Standards: The Benefit-Cost or the No-Cost Paradigm?" *The Journal of Economic Perspectives* 9(4) (Autumn 1995): 119–132.

Porter, Michael. "America's Green Strategy," *Scientific American* 264(4): 168.

Porter, Michael and Claas van der Linde. "Toward a New Conception of the Environment-Competitiveness Relationship," *The Journal of Economic Perspectives* 9(4) (Autumn 1995): 97–118.

Schelling, Thomas E. (ed.). *Incentives for Environmental Protection.* Cambridge, Mass.: MIT Press, 1983.

Taylor, A., Jaccard, M. and N. Olewiler. "Environmental Tax Shift: A Discussion Paper for British Columbians," British Columbia: Ministry of Environment, Lands, and Parks, 1999.

Tietenberg, Tom H. "Economic Instruments for Environmental Regulation," *Oxford Review of Economic Policy* 6(1) (Spring 1990): 17–33.

U.S. Environmental Protection Agency. *Economic Incentives, Options for Environmental Protection.* Washington, D.C.: EPA (21P–2001), March 1991.

_____ (1992). *The United States Experience with Economic Incentives to Control Environmental Pollution.* EPA Draft 230-R-92-001. Washington, D.C., March.

Chapter 13

There are many sources for information about transferable emission trading markets. Sustainable Prosperity has an annual publication on environmental markets accessible at: www.sustainableprosperity.ca. The World Bank annually produces a publication called *The State and Trends of Carbon Pricing* accessible on their website: www.worldbank.org. Resources for the Future (www.rff.org) and the OECD (www.oecd.org) have working papers on the topic that cover both the theory and practice.

Hahn, Robert W. "Economic Perspectives for Environmental Problems: How the Patient Followed the Doctor's Orders," *Journal of Economic Perspectives* 3(2) (Spring 1989): 95–114.

_____. *A Primer on Environmental Policy Design.* Chur, Switzerland: Harwood Academic Publishers, 1989.

Hahn, Robert W., and Roger G. Noll. "Designing a Market for Tradeable Emission Permits," in Wesley Magat (ed.). *Reform of Environmental Regulation.* Cambridge, Mass.: Ballinger Publishing Company, 1982, 119–146.

Project 88—Round II Incentives for Action: Designing Market-Based Environmental Strategies. A Public Policy Study sponsored by Senators Timothy E. Wirth and John Heinz, Washington, D.C., May 1991.

Schmalansee, Richard and Robert Stavins. "The SO_2 Allowance Trading System: The Ironic History of a Grand Policy Experiment," NBER Working Paper No. 18306, August 2012.

Tietenberg, Tom H. *Emissions Trading: An Exercise in Reforming Pollution Policy.* Washington, D.C.: Resources for the Future, 1985.

Chapter 14

Adar, Z. and J. M. Griffin. "Uncertainty and the Choice of Pollution Control Instruments," *Journal of Environmental Economics and Management* 3 (1976): 178–188.

Baumol, William J. and Wallace E. Oates. *The Theory of Environmental Policy,* 2nd ed. Cambridge: Cambridge University Press, 1988, Chapters 6–8, 14.

Cropper, Maureen L. and Wallace E. Oates. "Environmental Economics: A Survey," *Journal of Economic Literature* 30 (1992): 675–740.

Pezzey, John. "The Symmetry between Controlling Pollution by Price and Controlling it by Quantity," *The Canadian Journal of Economics* 25 (1992): 983–991.

Watson, W. D. and R. Ridker. "Losses from Effluent Taxes and Quotas Under Uncertainty," *Journal of Environmental Economics and Management* 11 (1984): 310–326.

Weitzman, Martin L. "Prices versus Quantities," *The Review of Economic Studies* 41 (1974): 477–491.

Chapter 15

Boardman, Robert. *Canadian Environmental Policy: Ecosystems, Politics, and Process.* Toronto: Oxford University Press, 1992.

Doern, G.B. *Shades of Green: Gauging Canada's Green Plan.* Toronto: C.D. Howe Institute, 1991.

Doern, G.B. and T. Conway. *The Greening of Canada: Federal Institutions and Decisions,* Toronto: University of Toronto Press, 1994.

Fafard, P.C. and K. Harrison, eds. *Managing the Environmental Union, Intergovernmental Relations and Environmental Policy in Canada,* Kingston: School of Policy Studies, Queen's University, 2000.

Fenge, Terry, and L. Graham Smith. "Reforming the Environmental Assessment and Review Process." *Canadian Public Policy* 12 (1986).

Government of Canada. *Canada's Green Plan.* Ottawa: Supply and Services, 1990.

_____. *Canada's Green Plan: The Second Year.* Catalogue No. En21-110/1993E. Ottawa: Supply and Services, 1993.

Harrison, K. *Passing the Buck: Federalism and Canadian Environmental Policy.* Vancouver: UBC Press, 1996.

Hoberg, G. and K. Harrison. "It's Not Easy Being Green: The Politics of Canada's Green Plan," *Canadian Public Policy* 20 (1994): 119–137.

Hood, G. *Against the Flow: Rafferty-Alameda and the Politics of the Environment.* Saskatoon: Fifth House Publishers, 1994.

Kelly, E.N., J.W. Short, D.W. Schindler, P.V. Hodson, M. Ma, A.K. Kwan, and B.L. Fortin. Oil sands development contributes polycyclic organic compounds to the Athabasca River and its tributaries. *Proceedings of the National Academy of Sciences of the United States of America* 106(52): (2009).

Macdonald, Doug. *The Politics of Pollution.* Toronto: McClelland & Stewart, 1991.

Nemetz, Peter. "Federal Environmental Regulation in Canada," *Natural Resources Journal* 26 (1985): 578–590.

The television show, *The Nature of Things* had a two-hour documentary on the oil sands, originally aired in 2011. This show can be accessed at: www.cbc.ca/natureofthings/episodes/tipping-point.

Chapter 16

Dewees, D. "The Effect of Environmental Regulation: Mercury and Sulphur Dioxide," in M. L. Friedland (ed.). *Securing Compliance: Seven Case Studies.* Toronto: University of Toronto Press, 1990.

Donnan, J. and S. Garibam. "Environmental Protection and Economic Performance of the "Countdown Acid Rain Program in Ontario," mimeo, 2000.

Freeman, A. Myrick, III. "Water Pollution Policy," in Paul R. Portney (ed.). *Public Policies for Environmental Protection.* Washington, D.C.: Resources for the Future, 1990, 97–149.

Government of Ontario. *The Public Review of MISA White Paper and the Ministry of the Environment's Response to It.* Toronto: Ministry of the Environment, 1990.

Kneese, Allen V., and Blair T. Bower. *Managing Water Quality: Economics, Technology, and Institutions.* Baltimore, Md.: Johns Hopkins Press for Resources for the Future, 1968.

Luken, Ralph A. *Efficiency in Environmental Legislation: A Benefit–Cost Analysis of Alternative Approaches.* Boston: Kluwer Academic Publishers, 1990.

Magat, Wesley A., Alan J. Krupnick, and Winston Harrington. *Rules in the Making: A Statistical Analysis of Regulatory Agency Behavior.* Washington, D.C.: Resources for the Future, 1986.

Webb, Kernabham. *Pollution Control in Canada: The Regulatory Approach in the 1980s.* Ottawa: Law Reform Commission of Canada, 1988.

Chapter 17

Crandall, Robert W., Howard K. Gruenspecht, Theodore E. Keeler, and Lester B. Lave. *Regulating the Automobile.* Washington, D.C.: Brookings Institution, 1986.

Crandall, R. "Policy Watch: Corporate Average Fuel Economy Standards," *Journal of Economic Perspectives* 6 (Spring 1992): 171–180.

Dewees, Donald. *Reducing the Burden of Environmental Regulation,* Discussion Paper, Government and Competitiveness Reference. Kingston, Ontario: Queen's University School of Policy Studies, 1992.

Doern, G.B. *Getting it Green: Case Studies in Canadian Environmental Regulation.* Toronto: C.D. Howe Institute, 1990.

Downing, Paul B., and William D. Watson, Jr. "Cost Effective Enforcement of Environmental Standards," *Journal of the Air Pollution Control Association* 25(7) (July 1975): 705–710.

Hahn, Robert W., and Gordon L. Hester. "Where Did All the Markets Go? An Analysis of EPA's Emission Trading Program," *Yale Journal of Regulation* 6(1) (Winter 1989): 109–153.

Harrison, David, Jr. *Who Pays for Clean Air: The Cost and Benefit Distribution of Federal Automobile Emissions Standards.* Cambridge, Mass.: Ballinger, 1975.

House of Commons, Special Committee on Acid Rain. *Report of the Special Committee on Acid Rain,* 2nd Session, 33rd Parliament, Ottawa, September 1988.

Krupnick, Alan J., and Paul R. Portney. "Controlling Urban Air Pollution: A Benefit–Cost Assessment." *Science* 252 (April 26, 1991): 522–528.

Liroff, Richard. *Reforming Air Pollution Regulation.* Washington, D.C.: Conservation Foundation, 1986.

Long Range Transport of Air Pollutants Steering Committee. *Management Plan for Nitrogen Oxides and Volatile Organic Compounds.* Ottawa, March 1990.

National Research Council. *Rethinking the Ozone Problem in Urban and Regional Air Pollution.* Washington, D.C.: National Academy Press, 1991.

Nivola, Pietro S. and Robert W. Crandall. *The Extra Mile: Rethinking Energy Policy for Automotive Transportation.* Washington D.C.: The Brookings Institution, 1995.

Portney, Paul R. "Air Pollution Policy," in Paul R. Portney (ed.). *Public Policies for Environmental Protection.* Washington, D.C.: Resources for the Future, 1990, 27–96.

Tietenberg, Tom H. *Emissions Trading, An Exercise in Reforming Pollution Policy.* Washington, D.C.: Resources for the Future, 1985.

Chapter 18

British Columbia Government. *Revising British Columbia's Waste Discharge Permit Fee System.* A Discussion Paper, Ministry of Environment, Lands and Parks, Environmental Protection Division, 1992.

Dorfman, Robert. "The Lessons of Pesticide Regulation," in Wesley A. Magat (ed.). *Reform of Environmental Regulation.* Cambridge, Mass.: Ballinger, 1982, Chapter 2.

Harris, Christopher, William L. Want, and Morris A. Ward. *Hazardous Waste, Confronting the Challenge.* New York: Quorum Books, 1987.

Harrison, K. and G. Hoberg. *Risk, Science, and Politics: Regulating Toxic Substances in Canada and the United States.* Montreal: McGill-Queen's University Press, 1994.

Hirschhorn, Joel S., and Kirsten U. Oldenburg. *Prosperity Without Pollution: The Prevention Strategy for Industry and Consumers.* New York: Van Nostrand Reinhold, 1991.

Macauley, Molly K., Michael D. Bowes, and Karen L. Palmer. *Using Economic Incentives to Regulate Toxic Substances.* Washington, D.C.: Resources for the Future, 1993.

Mendeloff, John. *The Dilemma of Toxic Substance Regulation.* Cambridge, Mass.: MIT Press, 1988.

Sinclair, William F. "Controlling Effluent Discharges from Canadian Pulp and Paper Manufacturers," *Canadian Public Policy* 17(1) (March 1991): 86–105.

U.S. Environmental Protection Agency. *Waste Minimization—Issues and Options.* Vols. I, II, and III. (EPA/530/SW-86/041, 042, 043), Washington, D.C., 1986.

U.S. Office of Technology Assessment. *Technologies and Strategies for Hazardous Waste Control.* Washington, D.C., 1983.353

Chapter 19

Ackerman, Frank, D. Cavander, J. Stutz, and B. Zukerman (1995), "Preliminary Analysis: The Costs and Benefits of Bottle Bills" (Boston: Tellus Institute), draft report to the U.S. Environmental Protection Agency.

Alexander, Judd H. *In Defense of Garbage.* Westport, Conn.: Prager, 1993.

Dewees, Donald N. and Michael J. Hare. "Economic Analysis of Packaging Waste Reduction," *Canadian Public Policy* 24(4) (December 1998): 453–470.

Fischel, William. *The Economics of Zoning Laws.* Baltimore, Md.: Johns Hopkins Press, 1985.

Jenkins, Robin R. *The Economics of Solid Waste Reduction: The Impact of User Fees.* Vermont: Edward Elgar, 1993.

Ley, Eduardo, Molly K. Macauley, and Stephen W. Salant. "Spatially and Intertemporally Efficient Waste Management: The Costs of Interstate Flow Control," Resources for the Future Discussion Paper 96-23, Washington, D.C.: Resources for the Future, 1996.

Macauley, Molly K. and Margaret A. Walls. "Solid Waste Reduction and Resource Conservation: Assessing the Goals of Government Policy," Resources for the Future Discussion Paper 95–32, Washington D.C.: Resources for the Future, 1995.

Malone, Linda A. *Environmental Regulation of Land Use.* New York: Clark Boardman, 1990.

Menell, Peter. "Beyond the Throwaway Society: An Incentive Approach to Regulating Municipal Solid Waste" *Ecology Law Quarterly* 17 (1990): 655–739.

Miranda, Marie Lynn, Jess W. Everett, Daniel Blume, Barbeau A. Roy, Jr. "Market-Based Incentives and Residential Municipal Solid Waste," *Journal of Policy Analysis and Management* 13(4) (1994): 681–698.

Porter, R.C. "A Social Benefits–Cost Analysis of Mandatory Deposits on Beverage Containers," *Journal of Environmental Economics and Management* 5 (1978): 351–375.

Porter, R.C. "Michigan's Experience with Mandatory Deposits on Beverage Containers," *Land Economics* 59 (1983), 177–194.

U.S. Environmental Protection Agency. *Economic Incentives for Land Use Control.* (EPA-600/5-77-001). Washington, D.C.: EPA, 1977.

———. *Flow Controls and Municipal Solid Waste: Report to Congress.* Washington D.C.: USEPA Office of Solid Waste, 1995.

USGAO, United States General Accounting Office. *Solid Waste: Trade-offs Involved in Beverage Container Deposit Legislation.* Washington: General Accounting Office, GAO/RCED-91-25, 1990.

U.S. Office of Technology Assessment. *Facing America's Trash: What Next for Municipal Solid Waste?* Washington, D.C., 1989.

Chapter 20

Benedick, Richard. *Ozone Diplomacy.* Cambridge, Mass.: Harvard University Press, 1991.

Chandler, William U. (ed.). *Carbon Emission Strategies: Case Studies in International Cooperation.* Washington, D.C.: World Wildlife Fund and the Conservation Foundation, 1990.

Chapman, Duane, and Thomas Drennen. "Equity and Effectiveness of Possible CO_2 Treaty Proposals," *Contemporary Policy Issues* 8 (3) (July 1990): 16–25.

Cline, William R. *Global Warming: Estimating the Economic Benefits of Abatement.* Paris: Organization for Economic Cooperation and Development, 1992.

Courchene, Tom, and John Allen (eds.). "Carbon Pricing and Environmental Federalism." In the series, *Canada, The State of the Federation, 2009.* Montreal: Queen's-McGill Press, 2010.

Cumberland, John H., James R. Hibbs, and Irving Hoch (eds.). *The Economics of Managing Chlorofluorocarbons.* Washington, D.C.: Resources for the Future, 1982.

Dixon, John A., and Paul B. Sherman. *Economics of Protected Areas: A New Look at Benefits and Costs,* Washington, D.C.: Island Press, 1990.

Donaldson, D. M., and G. F. Betteridge. "The Relative Cost Effectiveness of Various Measures to Ameliorate Global Warming." *Energy Policy* 18 (6) (July/August 1990): 563–571.

Dudek, Daniel J., and Alice LeBlanc. "Offsetting New CO_2 Emissions: A Rational First Greenhouse Policy Step." *Contemporary Policy Issues* 8 (3) (July 1990): 29–42.

Elgie, Stewart and Jessica McClay. "Policy Commentary BC's Carbon Tax Shift Is Working Well after Four Years," *Canadian Public Policy* 39 (Supplement 2, August 2013): S1–S10.

Jansen, H. and G. Klaassen. "Economic Impacts of the 1997 EU Energy Tax: Simulations with Three EU-Wide Models," *Environmental and Resource Economics* 15 (2000): 179–197.

Manne, Alan S., and Richard G. Richels. *Buying Greenhouse Insurance, The Economic Cost of CO_2 Emission Limits.* Cambridge, Mass.: MIT Press, 1992.

Marchant, Gary E. "Freezing Carbon Dioxide Emissions: An Offset Policy for Slowing Global Warming," *Environmental Law* 22 (2) (1992): 623–683.

McNeely, Jeffrey. *Economic and Biological Diversity, Developing and Using Economic Incentives to Conserve Biological Resources.* New York: Columbia University Press, 1989.

Nordhaus, William D. "The Costs of Slowing Climate Change: A Survey," *The Energy Journal* 12 (1) (1991): 37–65.

OECD. *Economic Incentives for the Conservation and Sustainable Use of Biological Diversity,* Group on Economic and Environmental Policy Integration, Expert Group on Economic Aspects of Biological Diversity, Paris, 1994.

Purdon, Mark, David Houle, and Erick Lachapelle. "The Political Economy of California and Quebec's Cap-and-Trade Systems," Ottawa: Sustainable Prosperity, 2014.

Rivers, Nicholas, and Brandon Schaufele. "Salience of Carbon Taxes in the Gasoline Market." In: SSRN Scholarly Paper ID 2131468 (2013).

Smith, Douglas A. "The Implementation of Canadian Policies to Protect the Ozone Layer." In G. Bruce Doern, *Getting It Green.* Toronto: C. D. Howe Institute, 1990.

Smith, Douglas A. and Keith Vodden. "Global Environmental Policy: The Case of Ozone Depletion," *Canadian Public Policy* 16 (December 1989): 413–423.

Tietenberg, T. *Combating Global Warming: Possible Rules, Regulations, and Administrative Arrangements for a Global Market in CO_2 Emissions Entitlements.* New York: United Nations, 1994.

Titus, James G. (ed.). *Effects of Changes in Stratospheric Ozone and Global Climate,* Volume 1, Overview. Washington, D.C.: U.S. EPA, 1986.

U.S. Office of Technology Assessment. *Technologies to Sustain Tropical Forest Resources and Biological Diversity.* Washington, D.C., May 1992.

Wilson, Edward O. (ed.). *Biodiversity.* Washington, D.C.: National Academy Press, 1986.